GREGG SHORTHAND

FOR THE ADMINISTRATIVE ASSISTANT

CHARLES E. ZOUBEK

CENTENNIAL
EDITION

Gregg Division / McGraw-Hill Publishing Company

New York Atlanta Dallas St. Louis San Francisco Auckland Bogotá Caracas
Hamburg Lisbon London Madrid Mexico Milan Montreal New Delhi
Paris San Juan São Paulo Singapore Sydney Tokyo Toronto

Sponsoring Editor: Elizabeth Rodenz
Editing Supervisor: Elizabeth Huffman
Design and Art Supervisor: Caryl Valerie Spinka
Production Supervisor: Frank Belantoni
Production Assistant: Mary C. Buchanan

Interior/Cover Designer: Susan Brorein
Cover Photographers: Ken Karp
Karen Leeds/Everett Studio

Library of Congress Cataloging-in-Publication Data

Zoubek, Charles E., date
Gregg shorthand for the administrative assistant / Charles E. Zoubek. — Centennial ed.
p. cm.
ISBN 0-07-073678-2 — ISBN 0-07-073675-8 (pbk.)
1. Shorthand—Gregg. 2. Office management. I. Title.
Z56.2.G7Z695 1990
653′.4270424—dc20 89-12123
CIP

The manuscript for this book was processed electronically.

Gregg Shorthand for the Administrative Assistant, Centennial Edition

1 2 3 4 5 6 7 8 9 0 VNHVNH 8 9 6 5 4 3 2 1 0 9

ISBN 0-07-073678-2 (hardcover)
ISBN 0-07-073675-8 (softcover)

CONTENTS

UNIT VIII
SAMUELS, KEELEY, AND FRANK

UNIT IX
WCAC-TV

UNIT X

KEITH MANUFACTURING COMPANY

TO THE STUDENT

Gregg Shorthand for the Administrative Assistant, Centennial Edition, is tailored to meet your needs in studying advanced shorthand. In most cases, you and the other students using this text will be in your final phase of shorthand study. The text is carefully designed, therefore, to provide you with opportunities to refine both dictation and transcription skills to maximum levels.

Objectives

Gregg Shorthand for the Administrative Assistant, Centennial Edition, has been prepared to achieve the following main objectives:

1. To achieve speed and accuracy in writing shorthand.
2. To acquire an increased vocabulary of shorthand outlines you can write quickly and accurately.
3. To write comfortably new or unfamiliar words and to construct the outlines applying the Gregg Shorthand principles.
4. To transcribe shorthand notes into mailable copy in a variety of formats, using correct spelling, capitalization, and punctuation.

Organization

The first unit, Lessons 1 to 8, reviews rules for capitalization, punctuation, and formatting and provides an exercise, *Skill Teaser,* to apply these rules. Also, in each lesson there are two letters—a brief-form and a theory letter.

Lessons 9 to 80 are divided into nine units consisting of eight lessons each. Each unit provides practice with the vocabulary and documents used for a specific business and industry: insurance company, real estate agency, publishing firm, banking industry, travel agency, retail store, legal firm, television station, and medical office.

Each lesson in the unit provides you with a Speed Dictation Practice and Transcription Practice. There are also goals stating the speed dictation rate and transcription rate that you should strive to achieve.

The first lesson of each unit describes the general activities and responsibilities of the department or division and gives the name and title of the executive or executives who initiate and receive communications. The remaining lessons provide mailable production copy that you must complete within the time allotted.

UNIT I

SKILL development

LESSON 1

SKILL DEVELOPMENT

DICTATION SPEED BUILDING

The shorthand outlines below appear in the speed dictation practice that follows. Practice writing these words using the shorthand outlines. Then, using the key that follows, dictate the words to yourself in preparation for the speed dictation practice.

Dictation Preview

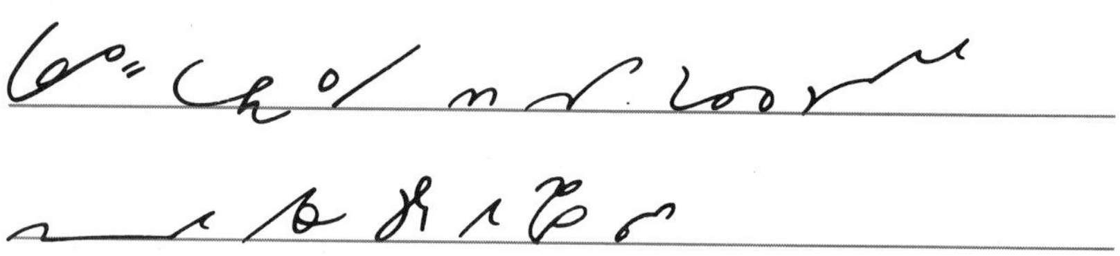

Key: Brady, pleasure, include, world, continue, frequently, standards, comments, desire, satisfaction, it is, we hope that, with your

Speed Dictation Practice

1.1 Goal: 70 wam speed dictation

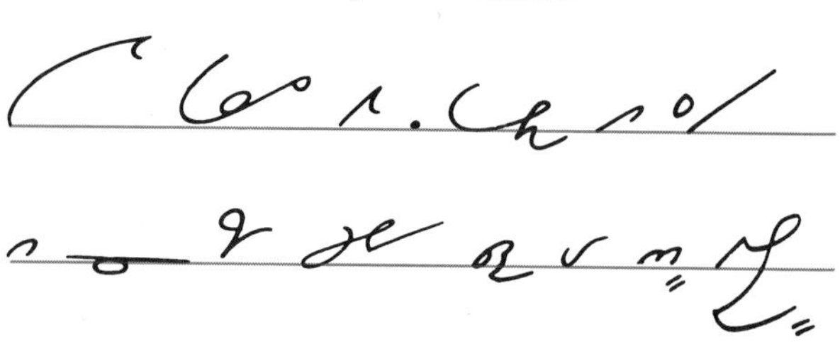

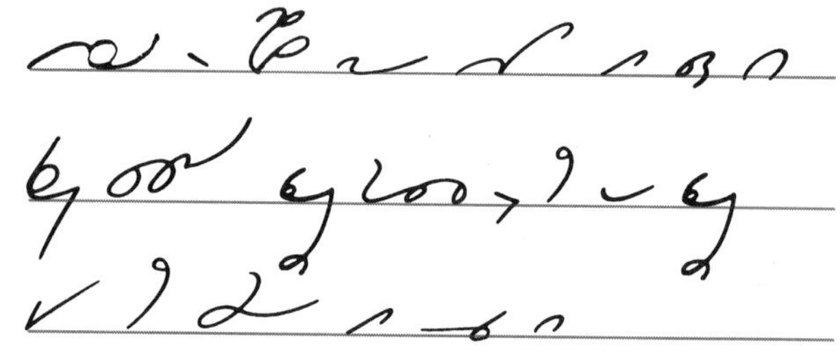

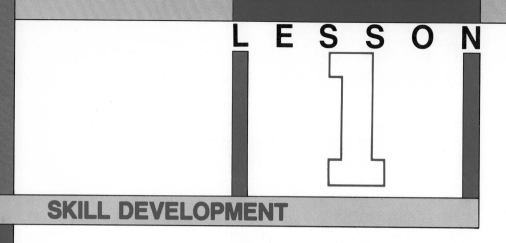

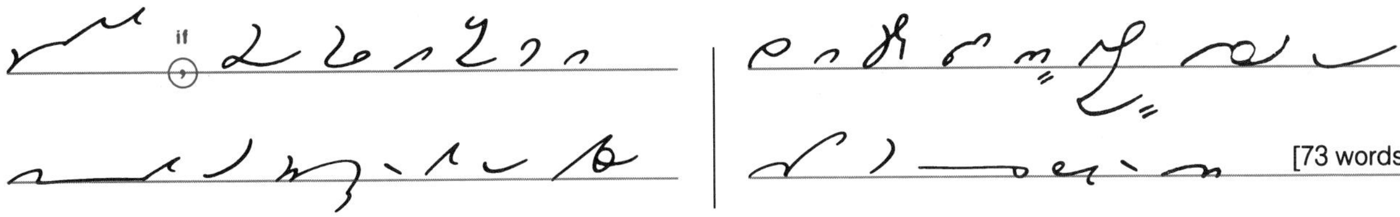

[73 words]

TRANSCRIPTION SKILL DEVELOPMENT

Transcription Practice

Transcribe the following letter for 2 minutes in unarranged format, applying transcription rules and assuring correct spelling. For every word not transcribed and every keyboarding error, deduct one word from the total word count.

1.2 Goal: 25 wam transcription rate

Word Count

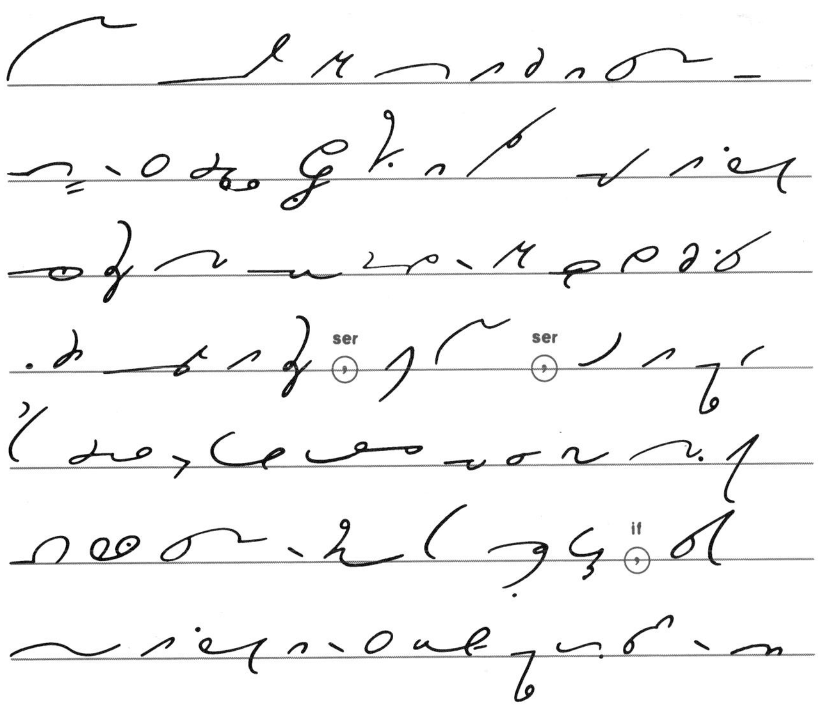

10
25
35
46
58
72
86

Block-Style Letter

Every part of the block-style letter begins at the left margin. The date should begin 15 lines from the top edge. Letters should always be single-spaced with a double space between paragraphs. See the illustration below.

Graham and Associates
482 Market Street Chicago, IL 60607

↓ 15
February 20, 19-- ↓ 5

Parsons and Company, Inc.
316 West Street
Chicago, IL 60607 ↓ 2

Attention: Personnel Director ↓ 2

Dear Sir or Madam ↓ 2

Subject: Sales Position ↓ 2

Recently I wrote to Michael Fairfield about the possibility of his joining your staff as a sales representative. You will recall I mentioned to you that he was going to change positions and that he might be interested in joining your organization as a sales representative in Florida and Georgia.

Today I had a reply from him in which he thanked me for writing him about the position at Parsons and Company but said he had accepted a job with the National Products Company.

From our perspective I am sorry that he obtained a new position so quickly. I know that he would have made a good addition to your staff. ↓ 2

Sincerely yours ↓ 4

John H. Graham
President ↓ 2

ee

Attention Line. When a letter is addressed directly to a company, an attention line may be used to direct the letter to a particular title (name unknown) or to a particular department. Use the guidelines for the attention line at the top of page 5.

1 The attention line should be typed on the second line below the inside address at the left margin. The salutation follows the attention line.
2 The attention line may be typed in capital and small letters or entirely in capital letters.
3 Type a colon after the word *Attention*.
4 The word *Attention* should not be abbreviated.
5 Do not underscore the attention line unless additional emphasis is required.

Attention: Sales Manager

Subject Line. The subject line is used to introduce the topic or message set forth in the letter.

1 The subject line appears between the salutation and the body, with one blank line above and below.
2 The subject line is usually placed at the left margin.
3 The subject line can be typed in capital and small letters or entirely in capital letters.
4 The subject line is not usually underscored but can be underscored for special emphasis.
5 The term *Subject:* or *Re:* usually precedes the actual subject but may be omitted.

Subject: Subscription Renewal

Addressing an Envelope

Return Address. When the envelope contains a printed return address, type the name of the writer above the printed address.

If a printed address does not appear on the envelope, type the return address in the upper left corner, beginning on line 3 about 1/2 inch from the left edge. The return address should list the following information, arranged on separate lines:

1 The name of the writer
2 The name of the company
3 The street address or post office box number

P.O. Box 183

4 City, state, and ZIP Code

Letter Address. When typing a letter address on an envelope, use the following guidelines:

1 Always use single spacing and block each line at the left.
2 Capitalize the first letter of each word except conjunctions, articles, and very short prepositions used within a name or title.
3 Type the city, state, and ZIP Code on the last line.
4 Use the two-letter state abbreviation.
5 Use a large envelope, and start the address on line 14 at 50 for elite type and at 42 for pica type.

Special Notations—Personal and Confidential. A notation such as *Personal* and *Confidential* goes below the return address. It should begin on line 9 or a triple space after the return address. Begin each word with a capital letter, use underscoring, and align at the left with the return address.

Attention Line. If an attention line was used within the letter, it should appear on the envelope. The attention line can be typed exactly like a personal or confidential notation, or it can be typed on the second line of the letter address.

Mailing Notations. If a special mailing notation—such as *Special Delivery* or *Registered*—is used, type the notation in capital letters in the upper right corner of the envelope on line 9 or a triple space below the stamp. Begin backspacing the notation (one space for each letter) 1/2 inch from the right edge of the envelope.

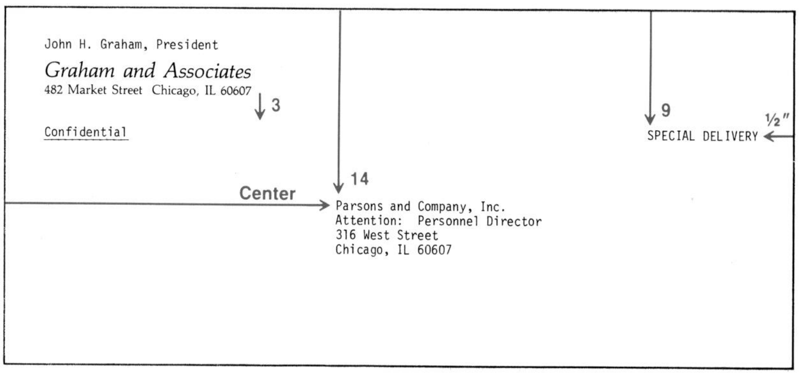

Skill Teaser

The following letter is an example of a block-style letter. On a separate sheet of paper identify the ten transcription errors.

July 16, 19--

Mesa Manufacturing Company
424 Skyline Drive
Tempe, AZ 85281

attention: Personnel Director

Dear Sir or Madam

subject: Reference Letter for Jennifer Jackson

It has been my pleasure to have Jennifer Jackson as my student during her years at Western Comunity College. In all classes she received an A, and I can honestly atest that she is an outstanding student.

As my student in two semesters of shorthand, Jennifer proved that she has the self-discipline to excell in the courses needed by business and industry. She is self-motivated and works very well without supervision.

Equally admireable with Jennifer's scholarship and self-direction is her human relations ability. She has an excellent personnelity that is characterized by friendlyness, concern, good humor, and sincerity.

Jennifer Jackson will be an excellent addition to any organization that is lucky enouf to hire her.

Sincerly

Gregory Manning

urs

Dictation and Transcription Practice

1.3 Brief-Form Letter

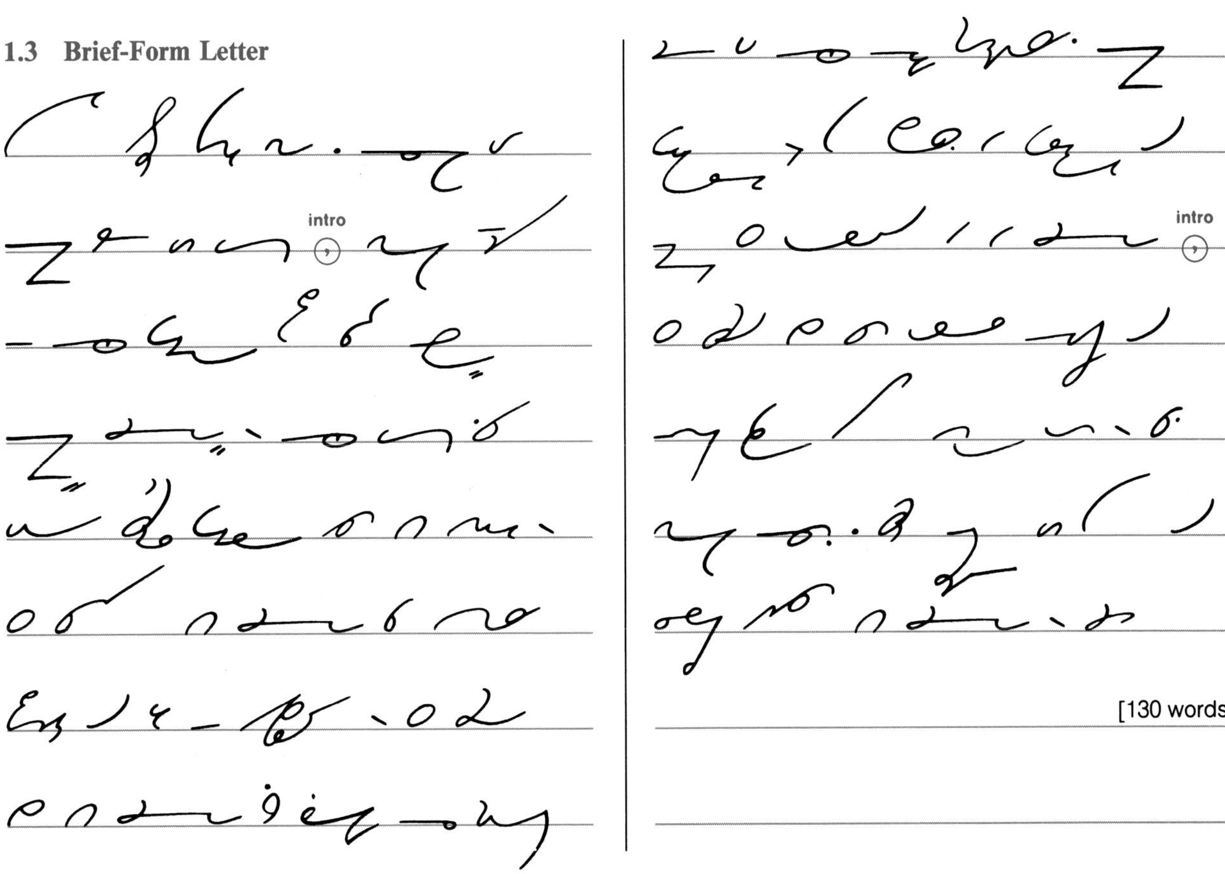

1.4 Theory Letter

[100 words]

LESSON 2

SKILL DEVELOPMENT

DICTATION SPEED BUILDING

The shorthand outlines below appear in the speed dictation practice that follows. Practice writing these words using the shorthand outlines. Then, using the key that follows, dictate the words to yourself in preparation for the speed dictation practice.

Dictation Preview

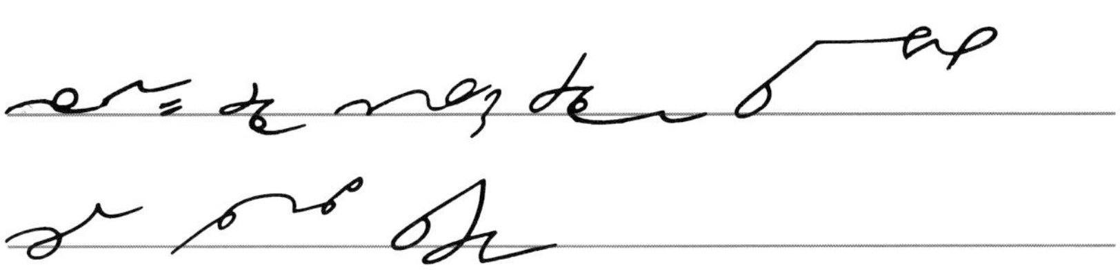

Key: Carter, sincere, congratulations, chancellor, administration, candor, dignity, advancement

Speed Dictation Practice

2.1 Goal: 70 wam speed dictation

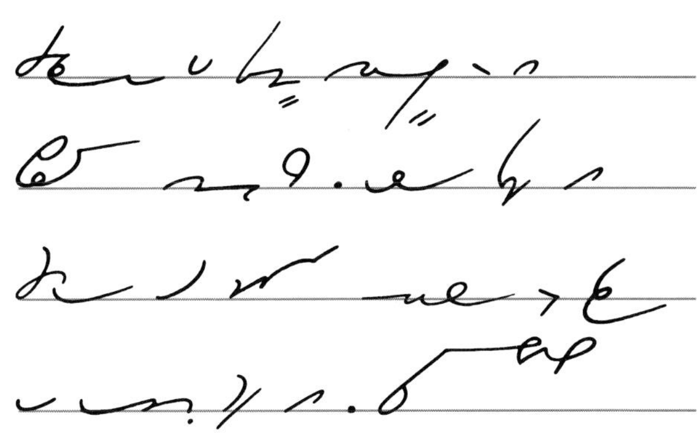

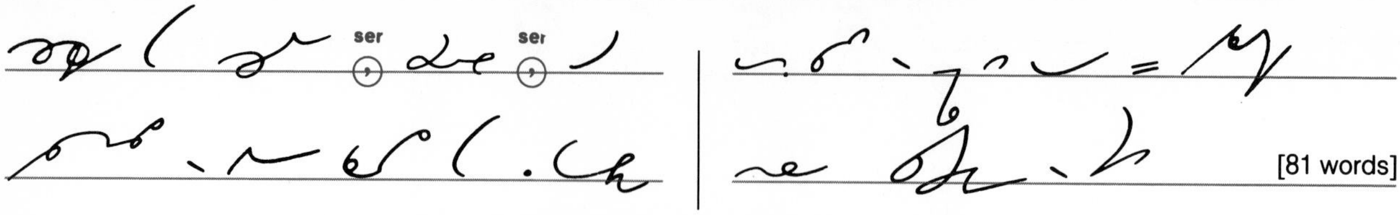

[81 words]

TRANSCRIPTION SKILL DEVELOPMENT

Transcription Practice

Transcribe the following letter for 2 minutes in unarranged format, applying transcription rules and assuring correct spelling. For every word not transcribed and every keyboarding error, deduct one word from the total word count.

2.2 Goal: 25 wam transcription rate

Word Count

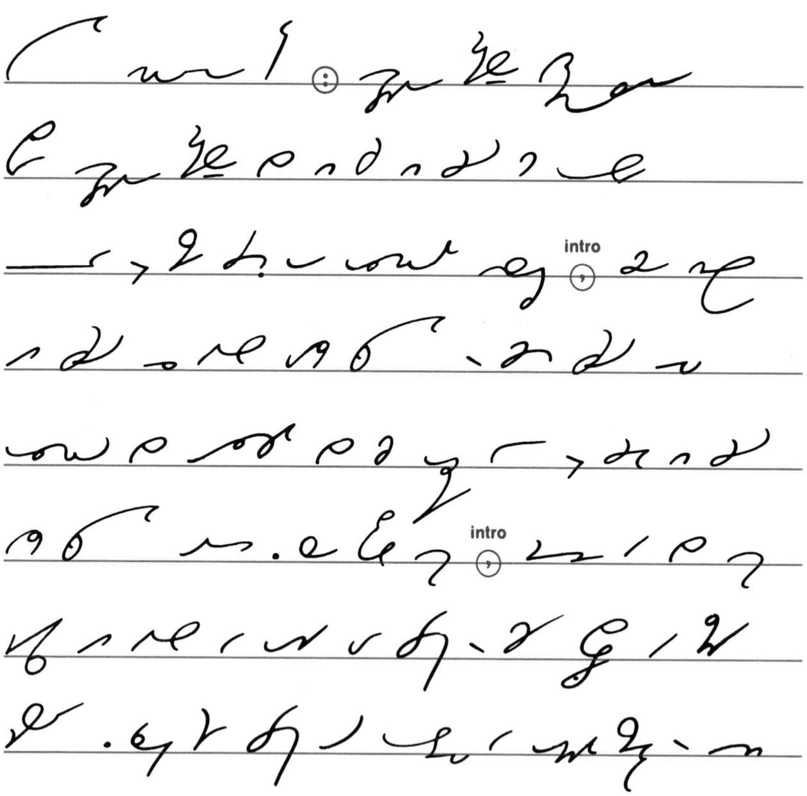

14
25
37
47
59
72
89
106

Series Comma

A series consists of three or more items in sequence. The items may be words, phrases, or clauses, and the last item is preceded by *and*, *or*, or *nor*. A comma is placed before the words *and*, *or*, or *nor* as well as between the other items.

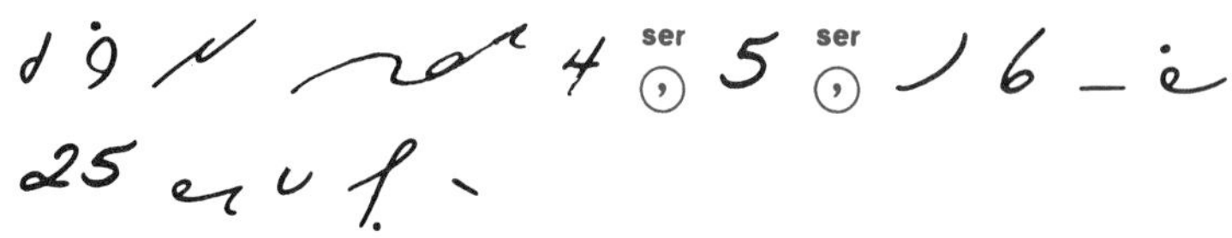

She has taught grades 4, 5, *and* 6 in her 25 years of teaching.

As, *If*, and *When* Clauses

A dependent clause introduced by *as*, *if*, or *when* and followed by a main clause is separated from the main clause with a comma.

As you know, I will be on vacation next week.

Apposition Comma

The appositive is a word or a group of words that provides additional information about a preceding word or phrase. The appositive is indicated by commas.

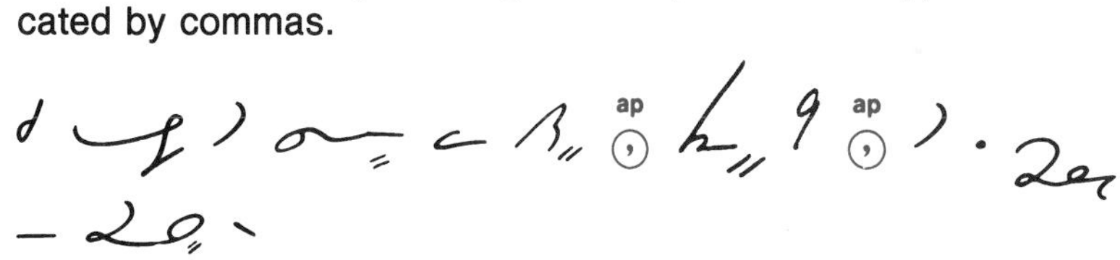

She left for Akron on Tuesday, *June 9*, for a conference in Philadelphia.

Conjunction Comma

Two complete sentences may be joined by a connecting word such as *and*, *but*, *or*, or *nor*. This connecting word is called a *conjunction* and is preceded by a comma.

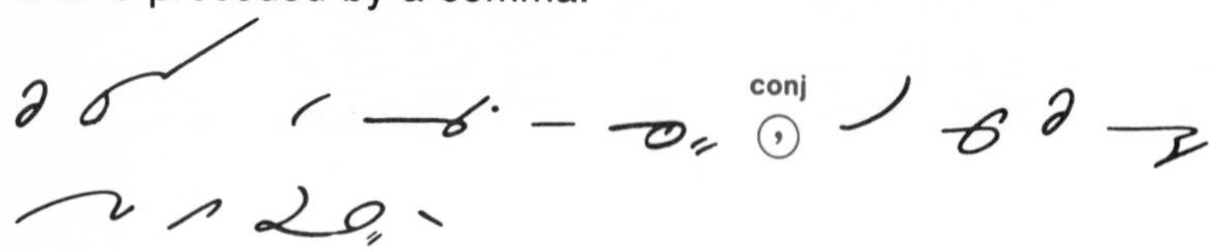

We attended the meeting in New York, *and* now we must go to Philadelphia.

Introductory Comma

Use a comma after introductory words such as *accordingly*, *however*, *therefore*, or a similar word.

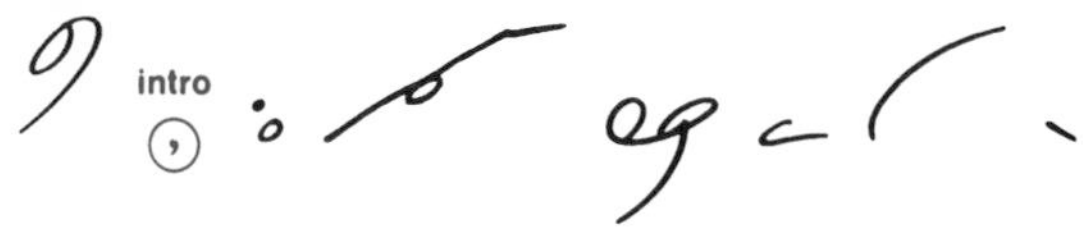

However, he did not arrive on time.

Use a comma after a dependent clause at the beginning of a sentence.

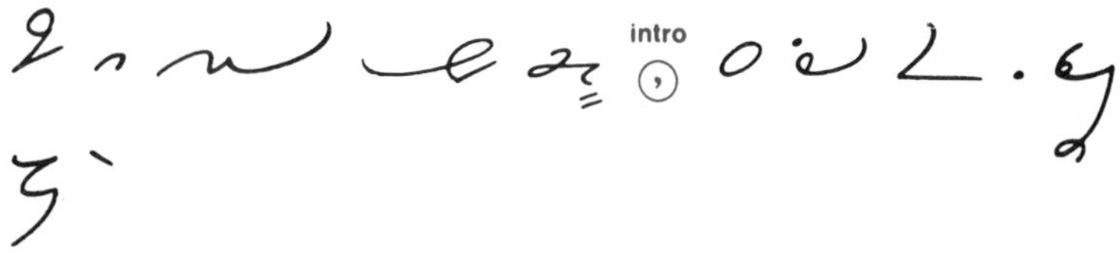

After you called last Wednesday, I heard from a service representative.

Parenthetical Comma

A parenthetical expression is a word or phrase within a sentence that does not contain any factual information but is an expression of emphasis. The word or phrase *can be omitted* without changing the meaning of the sentence. Therefore, it should be set off by commas.

She can, *of course*, take a vacation next month.

Skill Teaser

On a separate sheet of paper identify the six transcription errors and seven punctuation errors in the following letter.

October 11, 19--

Mrs. Helen Kramer
418 First Avenue
Philadelphia PA 19104

Dear Mrs Kramer

As a business executive who is up to date on current business topics you are cordialy invited to attend a breakfast seminar at the Parker Hotel in Philadelphia on Saterday November 3, 19-- at 9:30 am.

The topic to be discussed at the seminar concerns recent tax legislations for existing tax-sheltered annuity contracts. If you currently have a tax-sheltered annuity contract or are considering one come and learn about the legislation that permits greater flexability within your contract.

In order to receive the complimentery breakfast please fill out and return the attached reply card by Tuesday October 23.

Sincerely

Charles Jennings

urs
Enclosure

Dictation and Transcription Practice

2.3 Brief-Form Letter

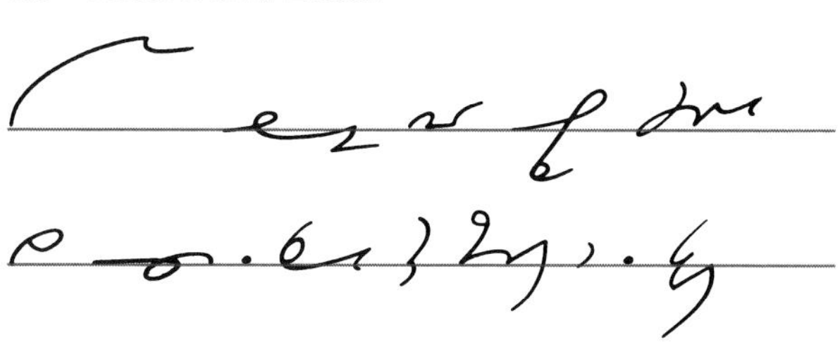

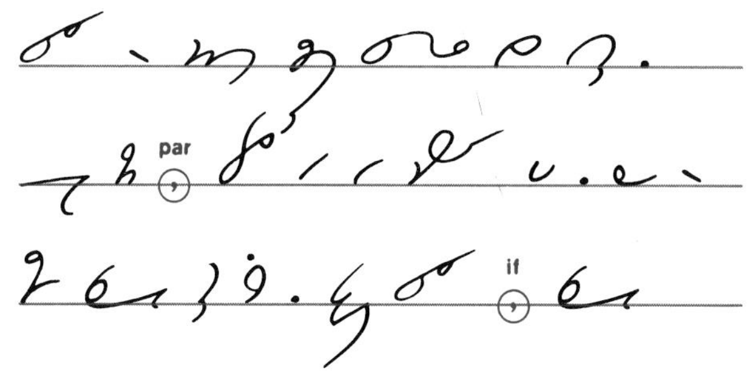

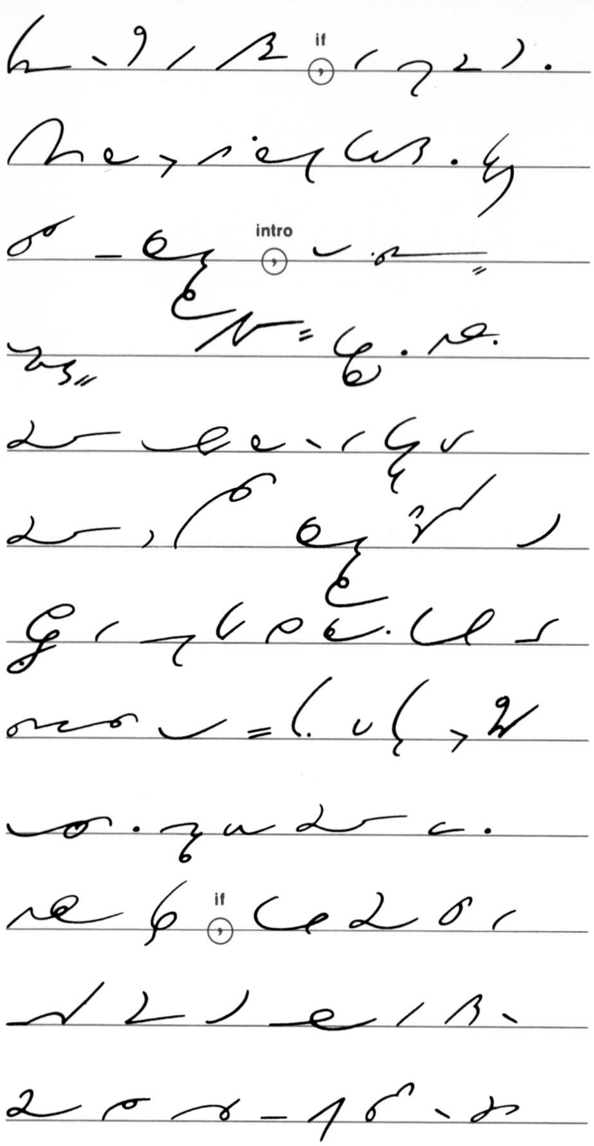

[140 words]

2.4 Theory Letter

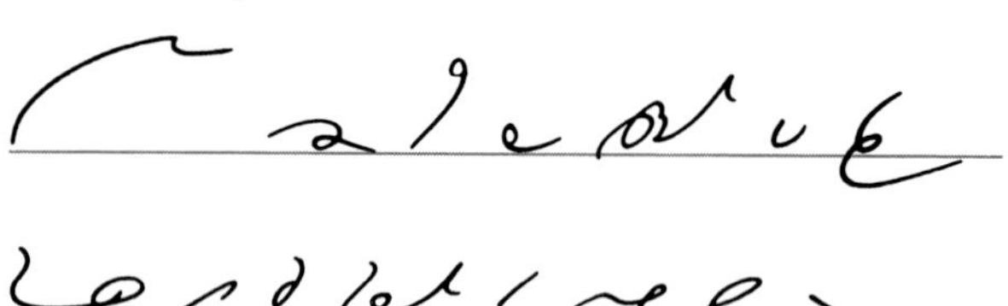

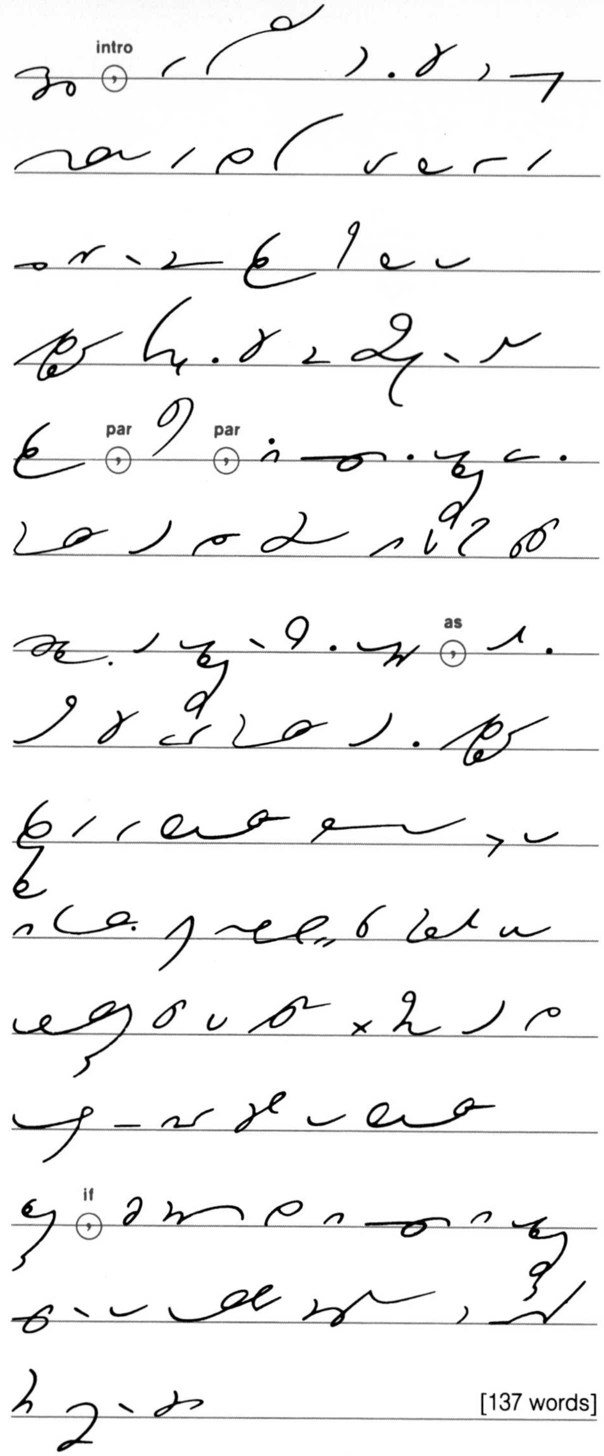

[137 words]

LESSON 3

SKILL DEVELOPMENT

DICTATION SPEED BUILDING

The shorthand outlines below appear in the speed dictation practice that follows. Practice writing these words using the shorthand outlines. Then, using the key that follows, dictate the words to yourself in preparation for the speed dictation practice.

Dictation Preview

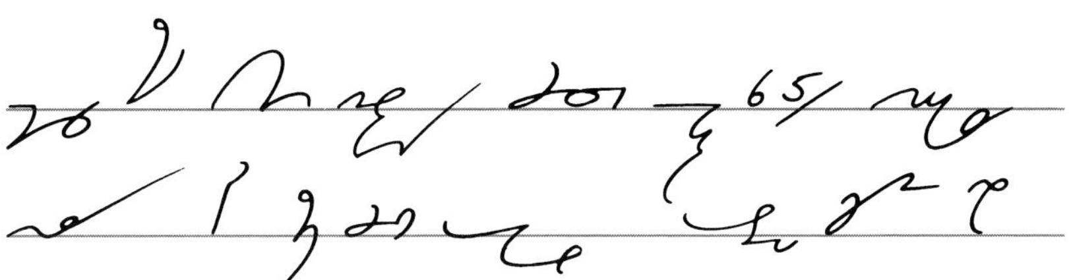

Key: unfortunate, event, difficult, unexpected, financial, impossible, $65, cooperate, credit, such, if you have, send us, will you please, let us know, we do not, we hope

Speed Dictation Practice

3.1 Goal: 70 wam speed dictation

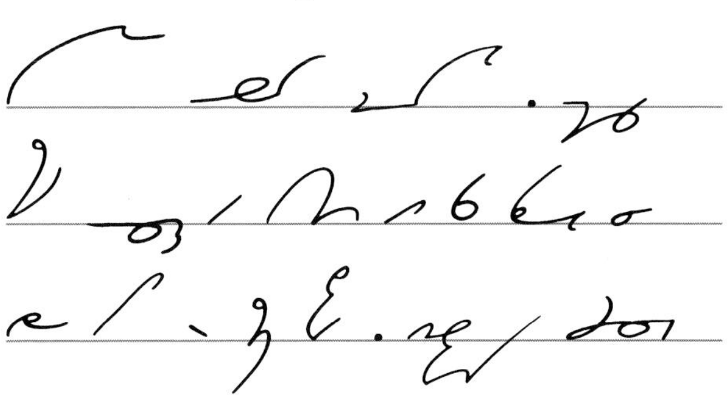

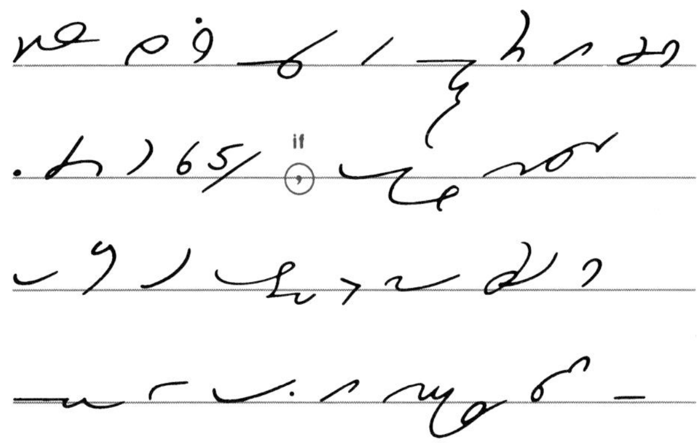

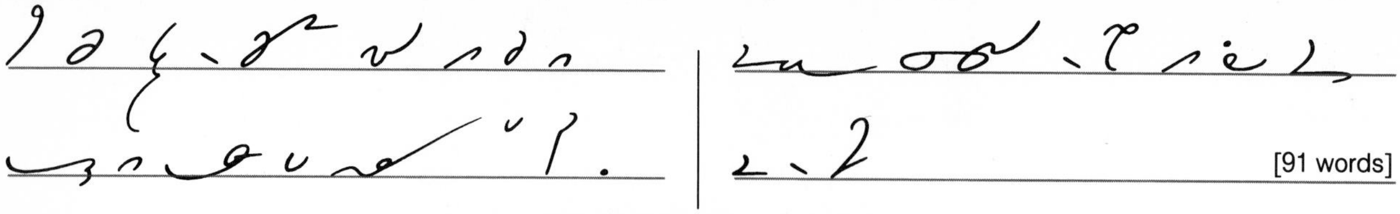

[91 words]

TRANSCRIPTION SKILL DEVELOPMENT

Transcription Practice

Transcribe the following letter for 2 minutes in unarranged format, applying transcription rules and assuring correct spelling. For every word not transcribed and every keyboarding error, deduct one word from the total word count.

3.2 Goal: 25 wam transcription rate

Word Count

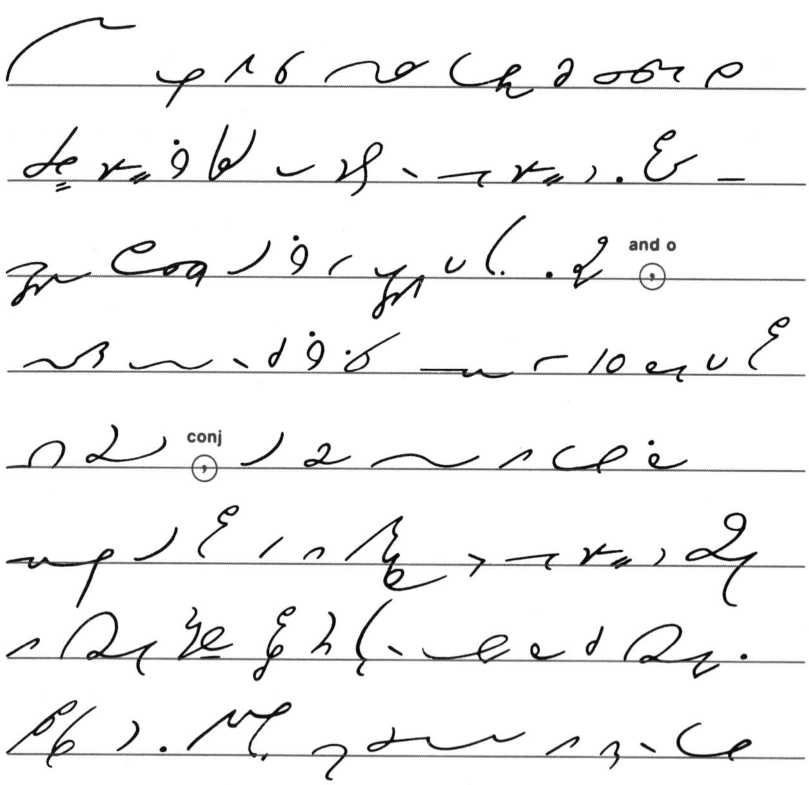

11
23
36
49
58
72
86
99

 117

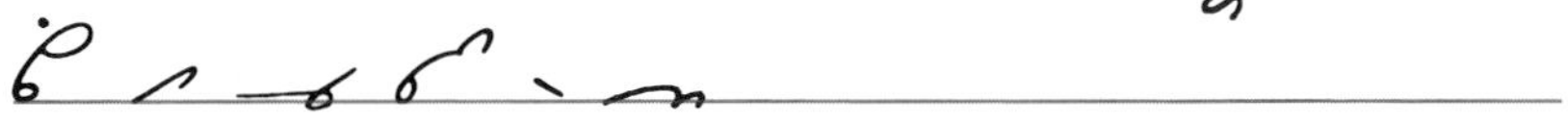 126

Transcription Review

Geographic Expressions

A comma is used to separate the name of a city from the name of a state. A comma is also used to separate the name of a foreign city from the name of a country. Since the state or country is actually an appositive modifying the city, a comma follows the state or country as well.

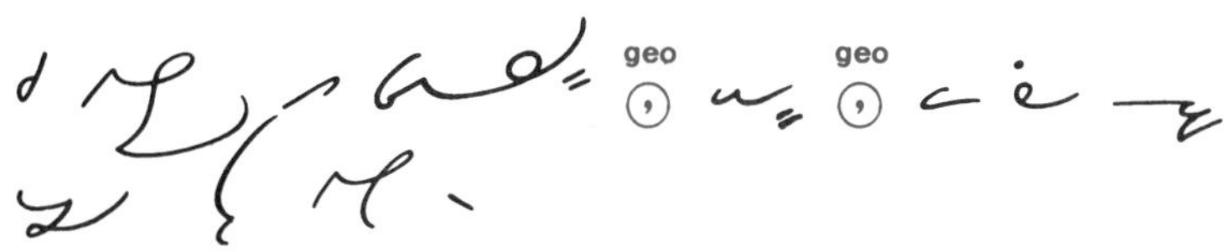

She traveled to Portland, *Oregon*, on her most recent business trip.

And Omitted Comma

When two or more consecutive adjectives modify the same noun and the word *and* has been omitted, the adjectives are separated by commas.

He found that she was a *competent*, *efficient* worker.

You can easily determine whether to insert a comma between two consecutive adjectives by mentally placing *and* between them. If the sentence makes sense with *and* inserted between the adjectives, then the comma is used.

Semicolon in Compound Sentence

Two complete sentences that are closely related may be joined into one sentence without a conjunction to serve as a connecting word. In conversation this results in an abrupt pause. The pause is denoted by a semicolon in writing.

Since there is no conjunction between the two complete sentences, the abbreviation *nc* will be used for *no conjunction*.

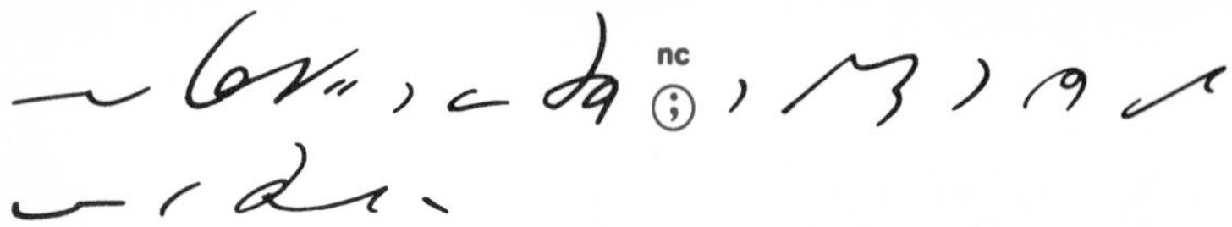

Mr. Bradford is on vacation; his directions for these orders are in the files.

Semicolon in a Series

When one or more of the items in a series already contains a comma, semicolons are used to separate the items in the series.

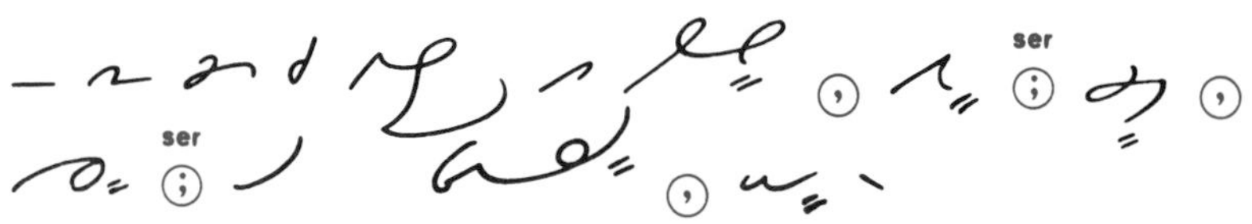

In one week she traveled to Dallas, Texas; San Francisco, California; and Portland, Oregon.

Punctuation at End of Courteous Request

Often a request is phrased in the form of a question so that it will seem less severe. If you expect your reader to respond by acting rather than by giving you a yes-or-no answer, it is a courteous request and, therefore, the sentence ends with a period.

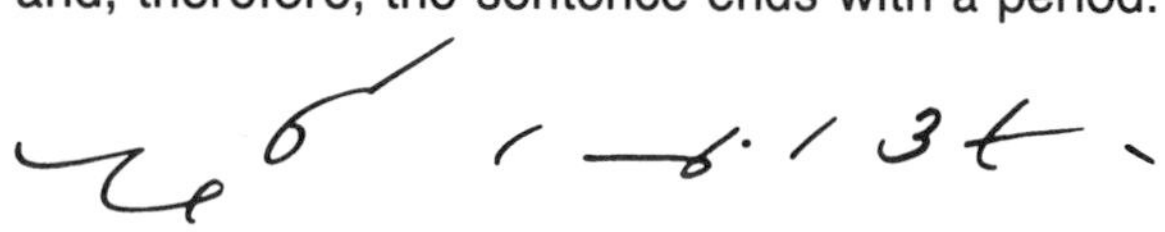

Will you please attend the meeting at 3 p.m.

Skill Teaser

On a separate sheet of paper identify the three transcription errors and six punctuation errors in the following memo.

Date: March 20, 19--
To: John Monroe
From: Roberta Jensen
Subject: San Diego office

No doubt you have heard about the new office that we are opening in San Diego California. In order to improve our service to the computer manufacturers on the west coast we have added Marilyn Fox to the sales staff.

The purpose of the San Diego office is to serve the customers that we already have in that city, and to acquire a larger distribution of our computer chips. We hope that you will feel free to use this office while you are in San Diego. Our office in San Diego will be a welcome affiliation to our offices in Eugene, Oregon, Kansas City, Missouri, and Reno, Nevada. If you have any more questions be sure to get in contact with me.

urs

Dictation and Transcription Practice

3.3 Brief-Form Letter

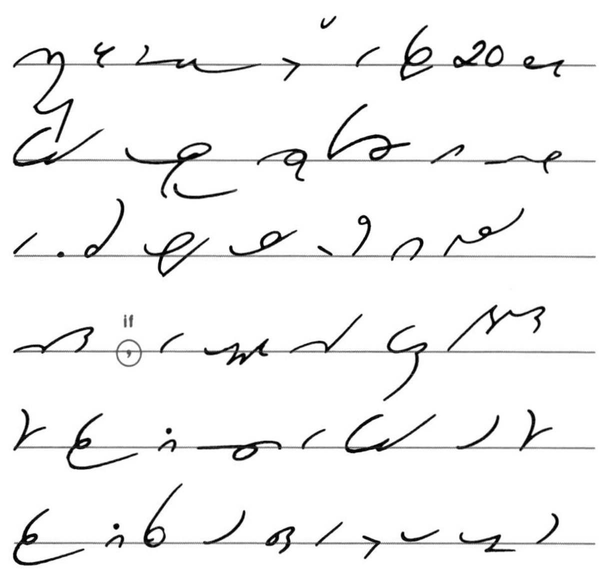

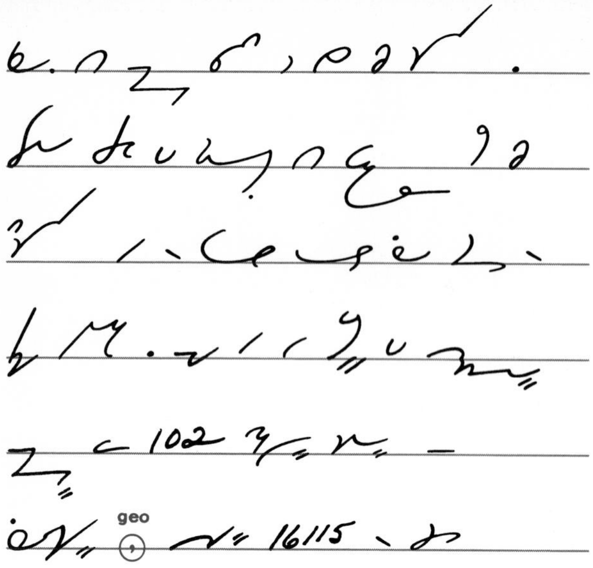

[142 words]

3.4 Theory Letter

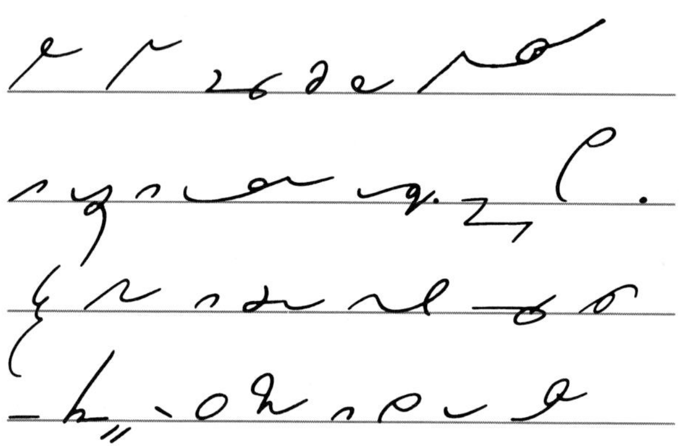

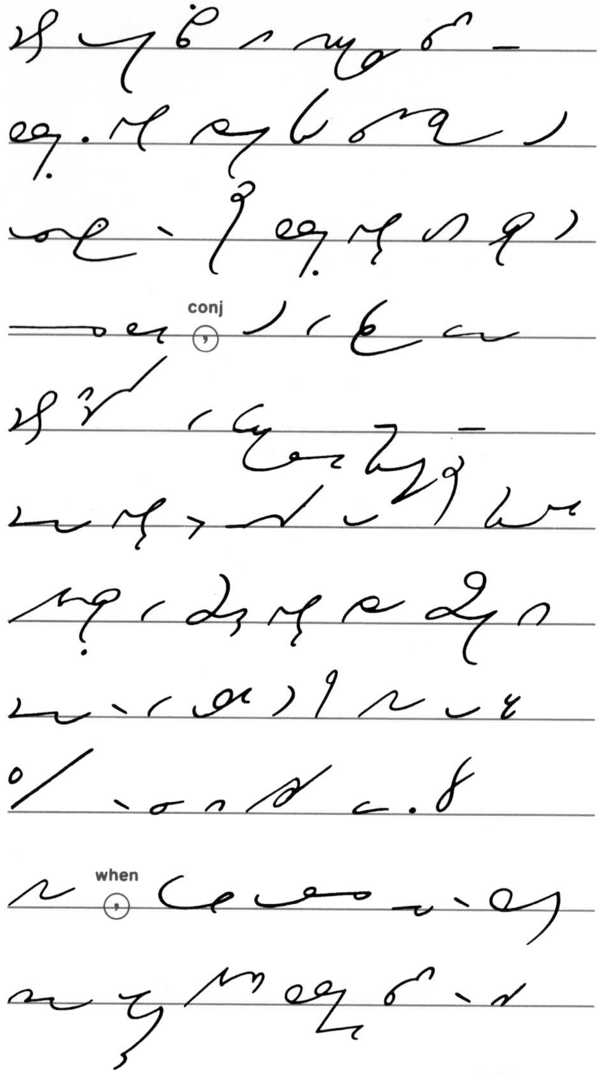

[128 words]

LESSON 4

SKILL DEVELOPMENT

DICTATION SPEED BUILDING

The shorthand outlines below appear in the speed dictation practice that follows. Practice writing these words using the shorthand outlines. Then, using the key that follows, dictate the words to yourself in preparation for the speed dictation practice.

Dictation Preview

Key: Dear Ms. Ortiz, bulletin, establishing, allowance, cents, representatives, inquiry, decided, 15,000, additional

Speed Dictation Practice

4.1 Goal: 70 wam speed dictation

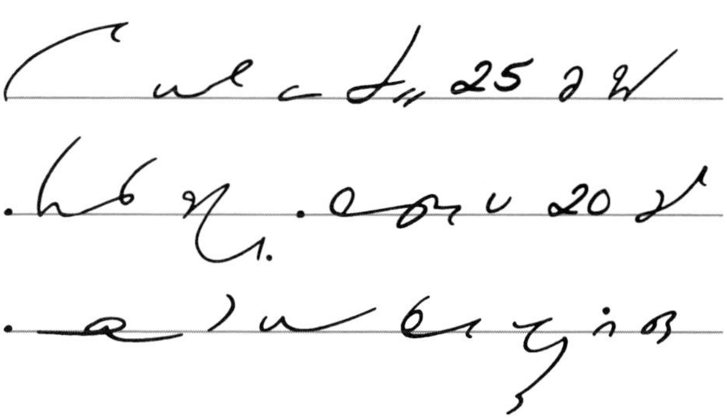

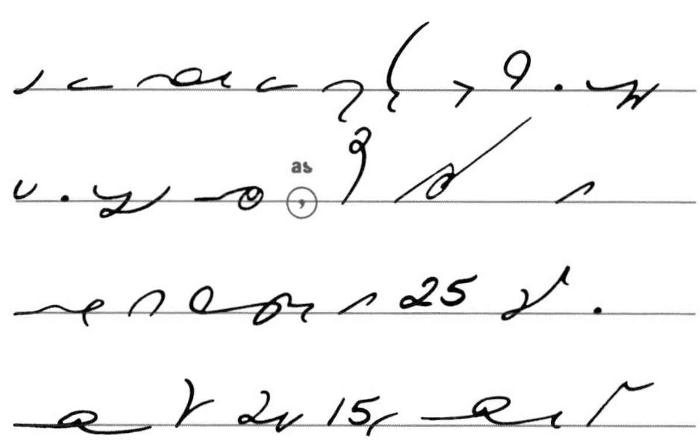

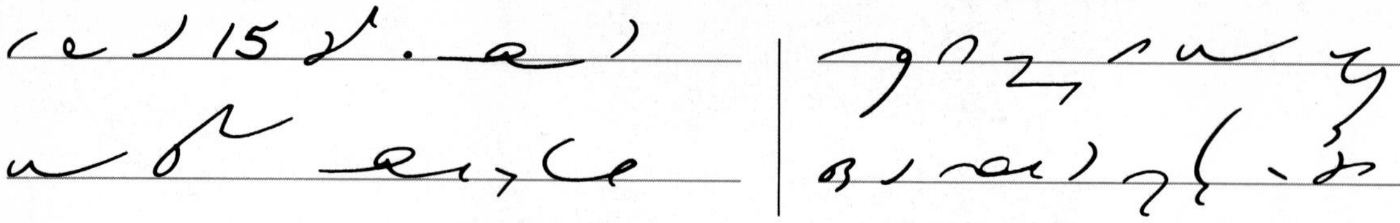

[98 words]

TRANSCRIPTION SKILL DEVELOPMENT

Transcription Practice

Transcribe the following letter for 2 minutes in unarranged format, applying transcription rules and assuring correct spelling. For every word not transcribed and every keyboarding error, deduct one word from the total word count.

4.2 Goal: 25 wam transcription rate

Word Count

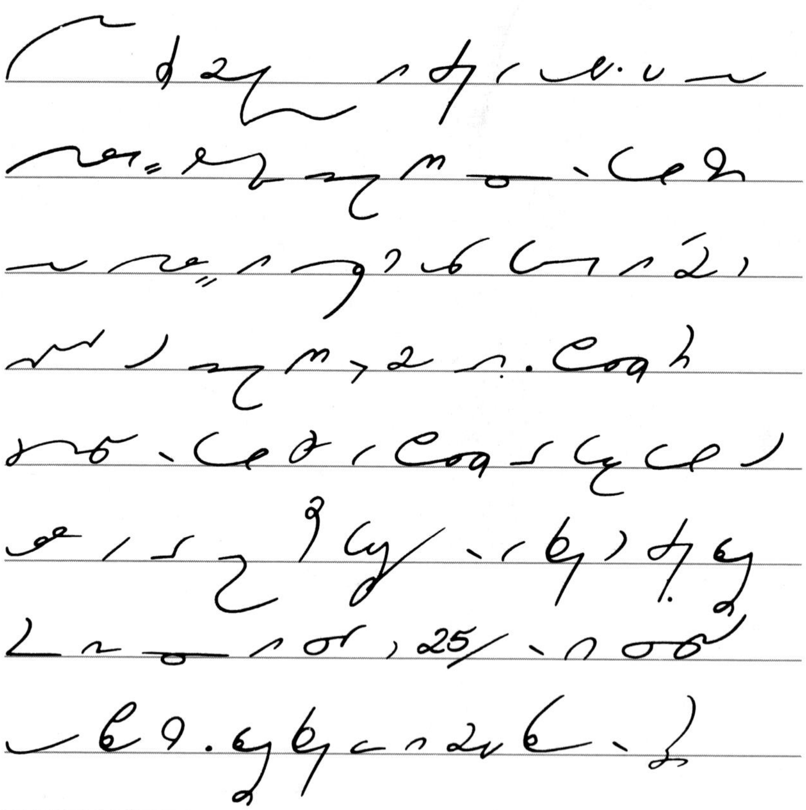

12
22
33
47
60
75
84
98

Interoffice Memo

An interoffice memo is intended to facilitate the exchange of written information within an organization.

It is customary for many organizations to provide printed forms that standardize all the information that should be contained in the heading. However, there are times when a memo will be typed on plain paper. When typing a memo on plain paper, use the following procedure:

1. Type the heading *MEMORANDUM*, centered in all-capital letters, on line 7 from the top.
2. On the third line below the heading *MEMORANDUM*, start typing the guide words *DATE:*, *TO:*, *FROM:*, *SUBJECT:*, and any other items that may be appropriate.
3. Double-space the guide words, and type them in blocked format at the left margin. Use all-capital letters. Type a colon after each guide word.
4. If the word *SUBJECT:* is the longest guide word, you can set a tab ten spaces in from the left margin for proper placement.

It is important to type all the guide words before you begin filling in the information that follows since you want all the entries to be blocked at the left, two spaces after the longest guide word.

Enclosure Notation

If one or more items are to be enclosed with a letter or memo, indicate that fact by typing the word *Enclosure* or *Enclosures* at the left margin on the line below the reference initials.

If the letter states that the material will be sent "under separate cover," the material is not enclosed. Therefore, an enclosure notation is not used, and the material is to be sent in a separate envelope.

Copy Notation

A copy notation alerts the addressee that one or more persons will be sent a copy of the letter. Follow the guidelines below to type a copy notation.

1. Use the initials *cc* to denote the copy notation.
2. Type *cc* at the left margin on the line below the last notation.
3. Type *cc* with or without a colon.
4. If more than one person is to receive a copy, list the names according to the rank of the persons or in alphabetic order.
5. Omit personal titles such as *Mr.*, *Mrs.*, or *Ms.*
6. The *cc* notation appears on the original and all the copies.

Blind Copy Notation

If the addressee is not to know that one or more persons are being sent a copy of the letter, a blind copy notation is used. To type a blind copy notation, follow these guidelines:

1 First remove the original letter and any copies on which the blind copy notation is not to appear.
2 On the remaining copies type the blind copy notation at the left margin on the second line below the last notation.
3 Use the initials *bcc* to denote the blind copy notation.
4 Type *bcc* with or without a colon.
5 If more than one person is to receive copies, list the names according to the rank of the persons or in alphabetic order.
6 Omit personal titles such as *Mr.*, *Mrs.*, or *Ms.*

Skill Teaser

On a separate sheet of paper, identify the four transcription errors and the five punctuation errors in the following memo.

Date: December 10, 19--
To: All Professors
From: Young Executive Club
Subject: positive first impressions

As you are aware of the importance of first impressions on a person's success especially during interviewing you are encouraged to announce the following lecture to all your classes.

The Springbrook College Young Executive Club is sponsoring a lecture and slide show "How to Make a Positive First Impression," on Tuesday January 29 at seven p.m. in the Spruce Room of the Student Center. The cost is $1 per participant. Your entrance ticket is enclosed. Please plan to attend.

urs
Enclosure

bcc: Department Chairpersons

Dictation and Transcription Practice

4.3 Brief-Form Letter

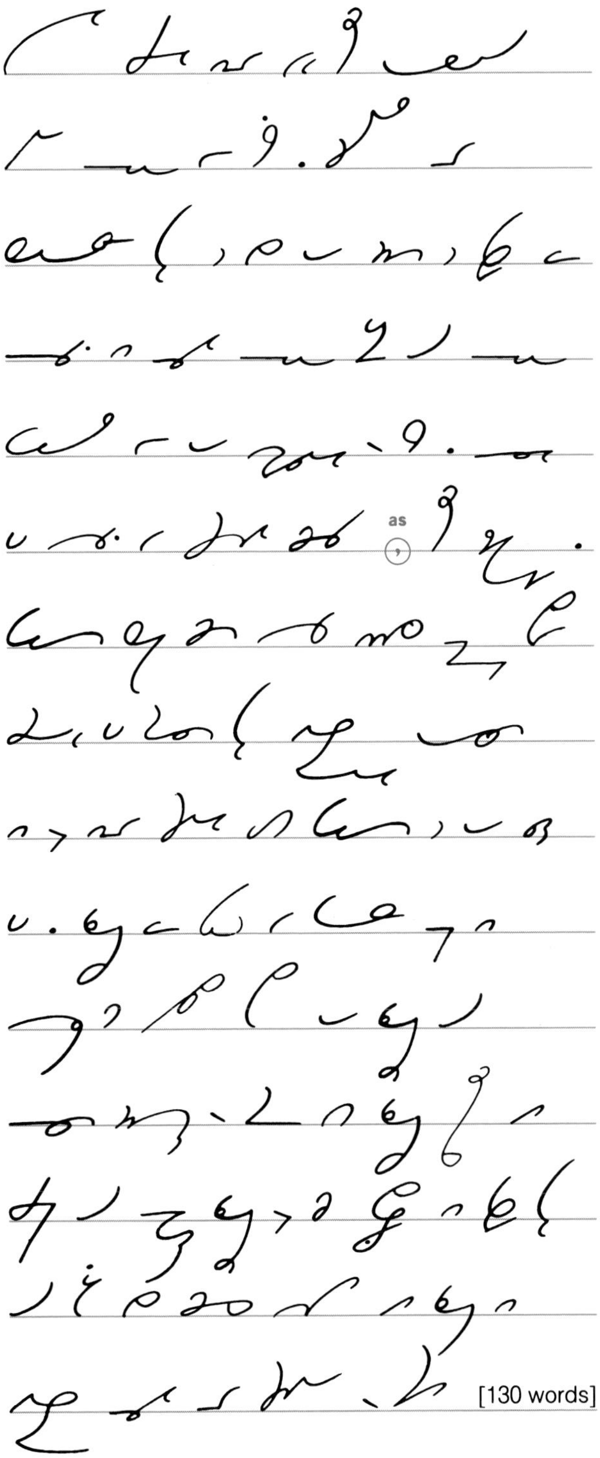

[130 words]

4.4 Theory Letter

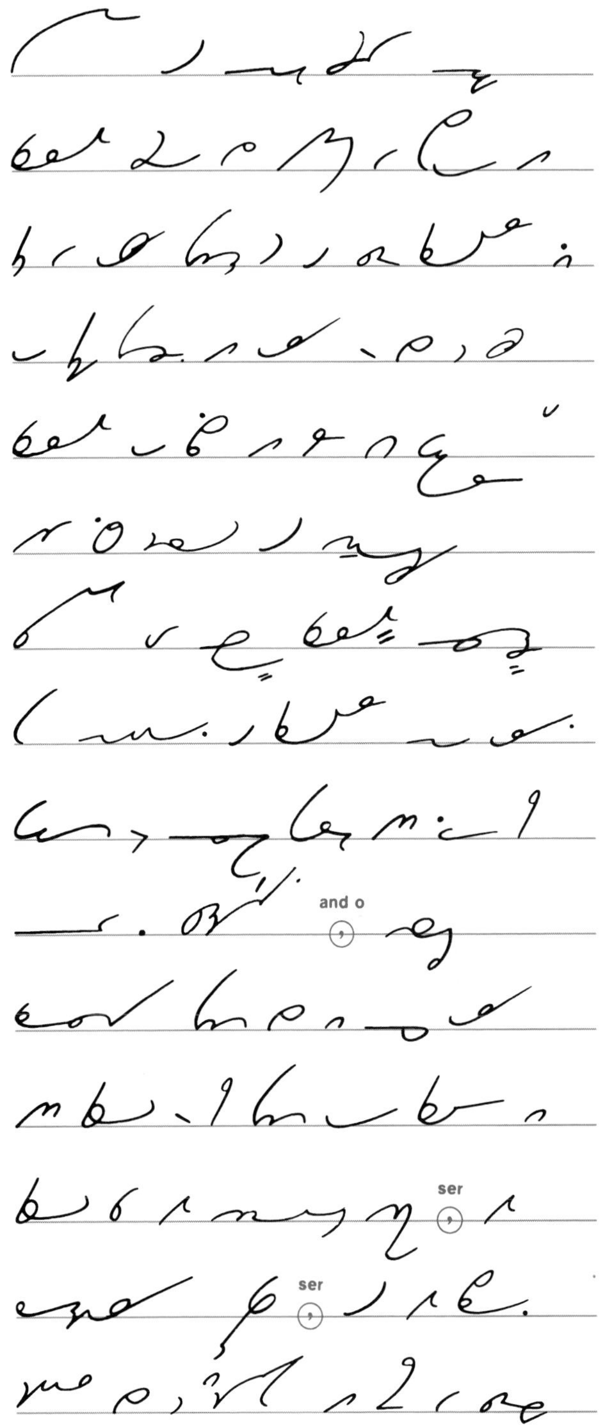

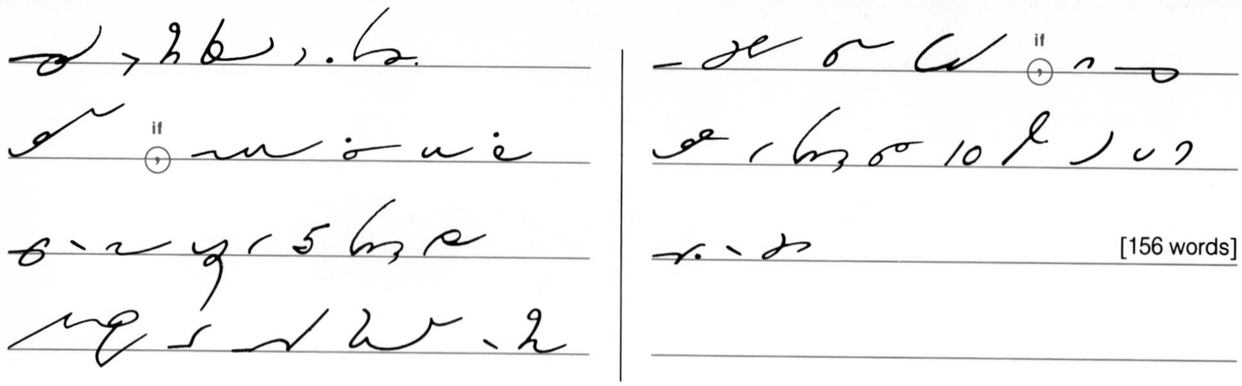
if
if
[156 words]

LESSON 5

SKILL DEVELOPMENT

DICTATION SPEED BUILDING

The shorthand outlines below appear in the speed dictation practice that follows. Practice writing these words using the shorthand outlines. Then, using the key that follows, dictate the words to yourself in preparation for the speed dictation practice.

Dictation Preview

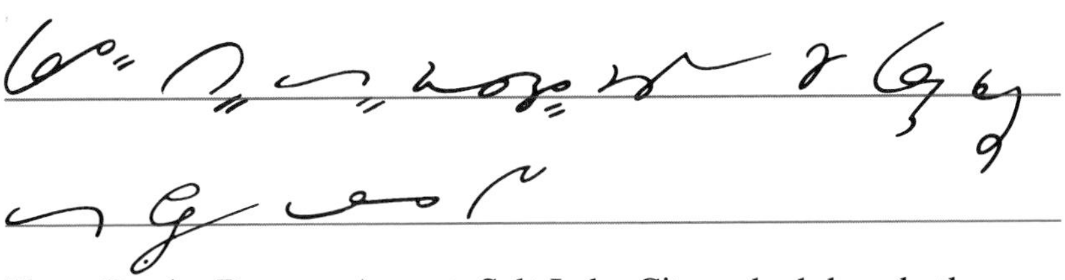

Key: Brady, Denver, August, Salt Lake City, schedule, whether, branches, surveys, organization, appreciated, let me, to know

Speed Dictation Practice

5.1 Goal: 70 wam speed dictation

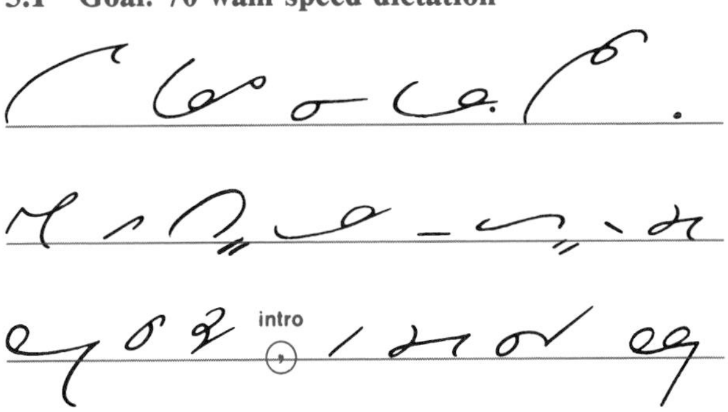

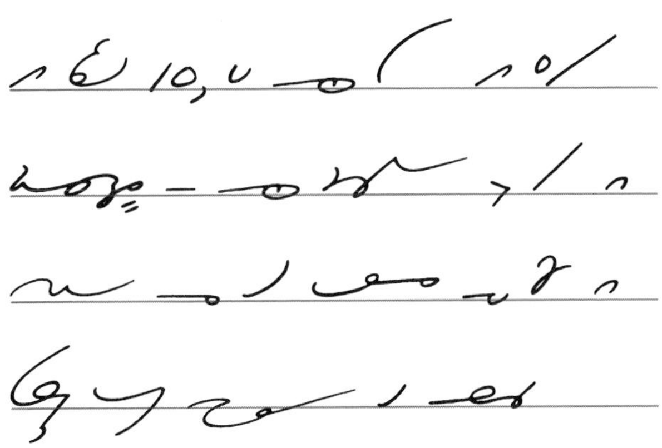

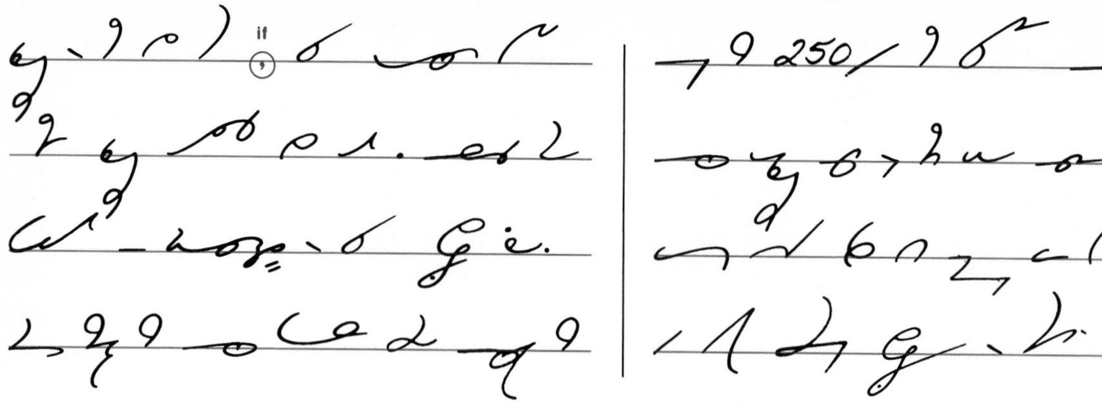

[132 words]

TRANSCRIPTION SKILL DEVELOPMENT

Transcription Practice

Transcribe the following memo for 2 minutes in unarranged format, applying transcription rules and assuring correct spelling. For every keyboarding error, deduct one word from the total word count.

5.2 Goal: 25 wam transcription rate

Word Count

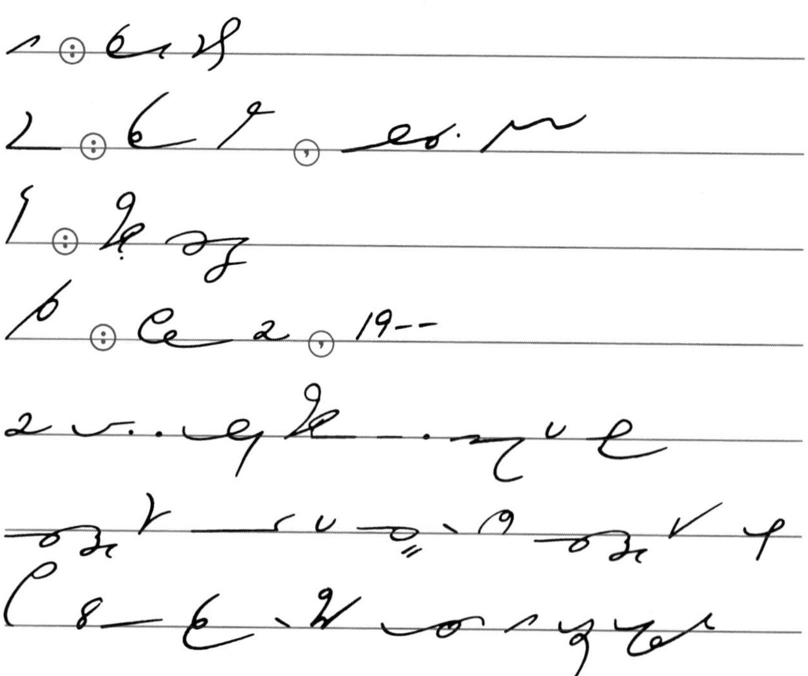

3
10
16
20
32
44
57

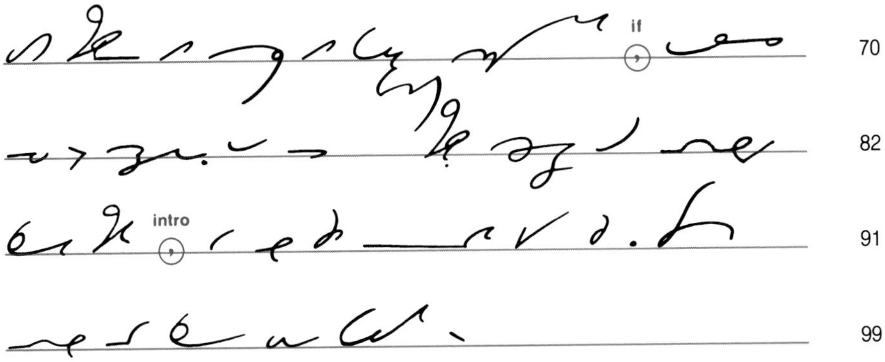

Transcription Review

Transcription of Numbers

The basic number rule specifies that the numbers from one through ten are to be spelled out, while the numbers higher than ten are to be written in figures.

She will have *seven* friends attend her party on Saturday.

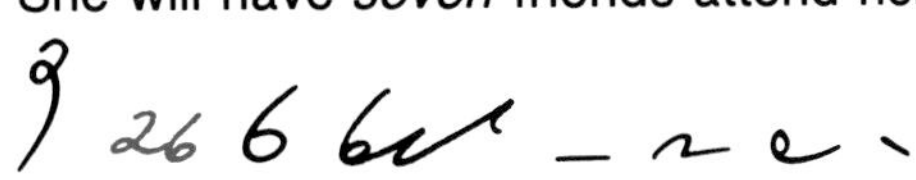

We have *26* pay periods in *one* year.

When transcribing, use a comma and ciphers to express *thousand*.

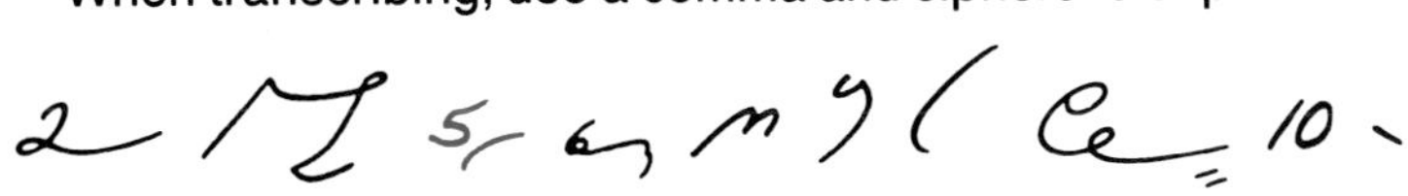

We will deliver *5,000* circulars to your office by April 10.

When transcribing *million* and *billion*, replace the commas and ciphers with the word *million* or *billion*.

Approximately *5 million* people fly to Chicago yearly.

Number as First Word of a Sentence

Spell out a number that begins a sentence, as well as any related numbers that appear in the sentence.

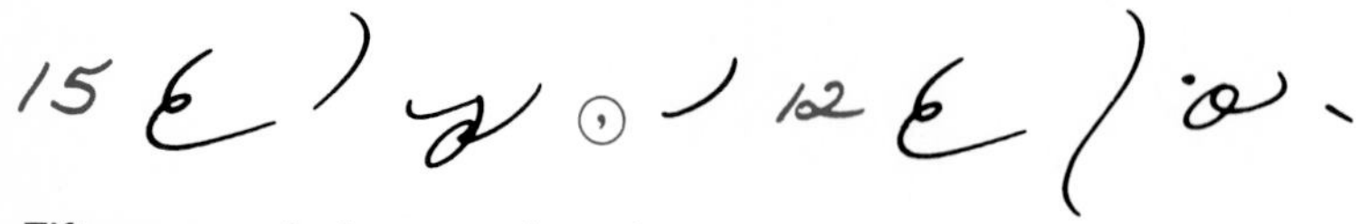

Fifteen people have resigned, and *twelve* people have been hired.

Amounts of Money

Numerals are used to express exact amounts of money. A decimal point and zeros are not used with whole-dollar amounts.

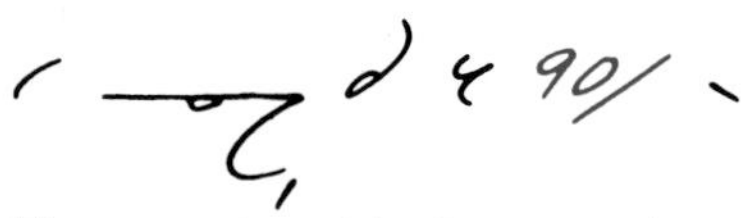

The membership fee was *$90*.

When transcribing, use a comma to express *thousand dollars*.

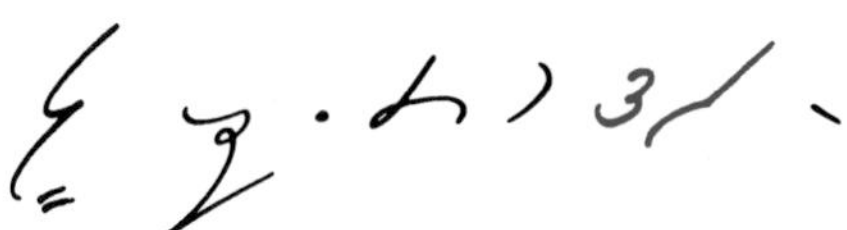

Bob received a check for *$3,000*.

When transcribing *million dollars* or *billion dollars*, replace the commas and ciphers with the word *million* or *billion*.

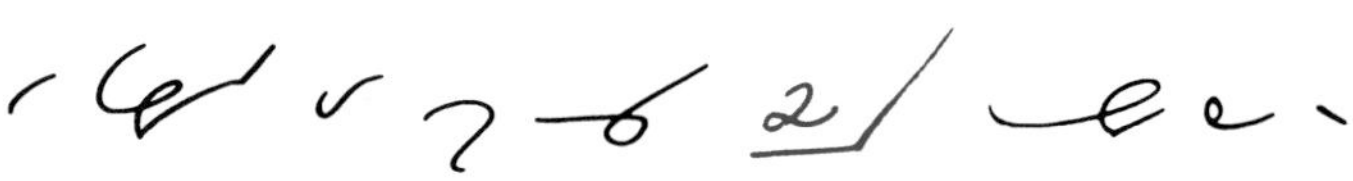

The president of the company made *$2 million* last year.

Percentages

The number preceding the word *percent* is always expressed in figures in sentences, and the word *percent* is spelled out.

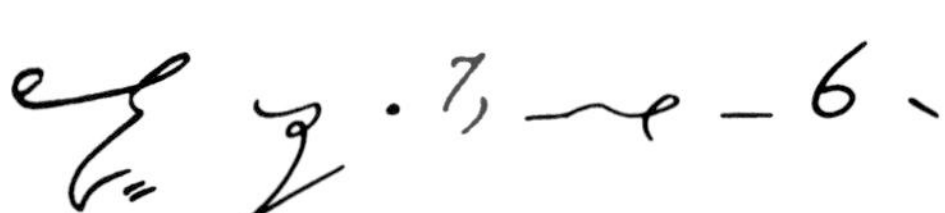

Elizabeth received a *7 percent* increase in pay.

Expressions of Time

Time is expressed in figures when used with *o'clock*, *a.m.*, and *p.m.*

She made a date for *7 p.m.*

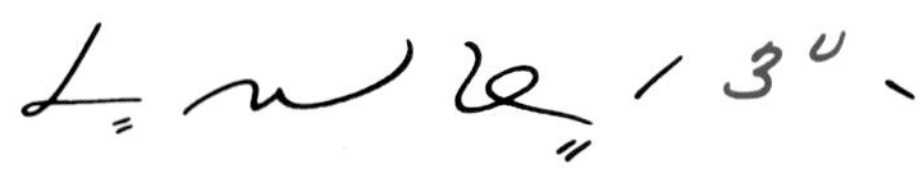

Jim called Frank at *3 o'clock*.

Skill Teaser

On a separate sheet of paper identify the nine transcription errors and four punctuation errors in the following letter.

September 26, 19--

Mrs. Kathleen Friedman
382 Maple Avenue
Greensburg, PA 15601

Dear Mrs Friedman

A regular meeting of the national magazine publishing association will be held at the brown hotel on the evening of Friday October 26. Please plan to attend. Dinner will be served at 6 the business meeting will start at 8. You and your friends are cordially invited.

As an additional feature Louis Jones made an extensive trip to Europe this past summer. He will tell us about his talks with members of the magazine publishing industry in various countries that he visited.

Please fill out the enclosed reservation card and return it to us by October 15. The meeting is sure to be an interesting pleasant event.

Cordially yours

Catherine Jorgansen

urs
Enclosure
cc: NMPA Members

Dictation and Transcription Practice

5.3 Brief-Form Letter

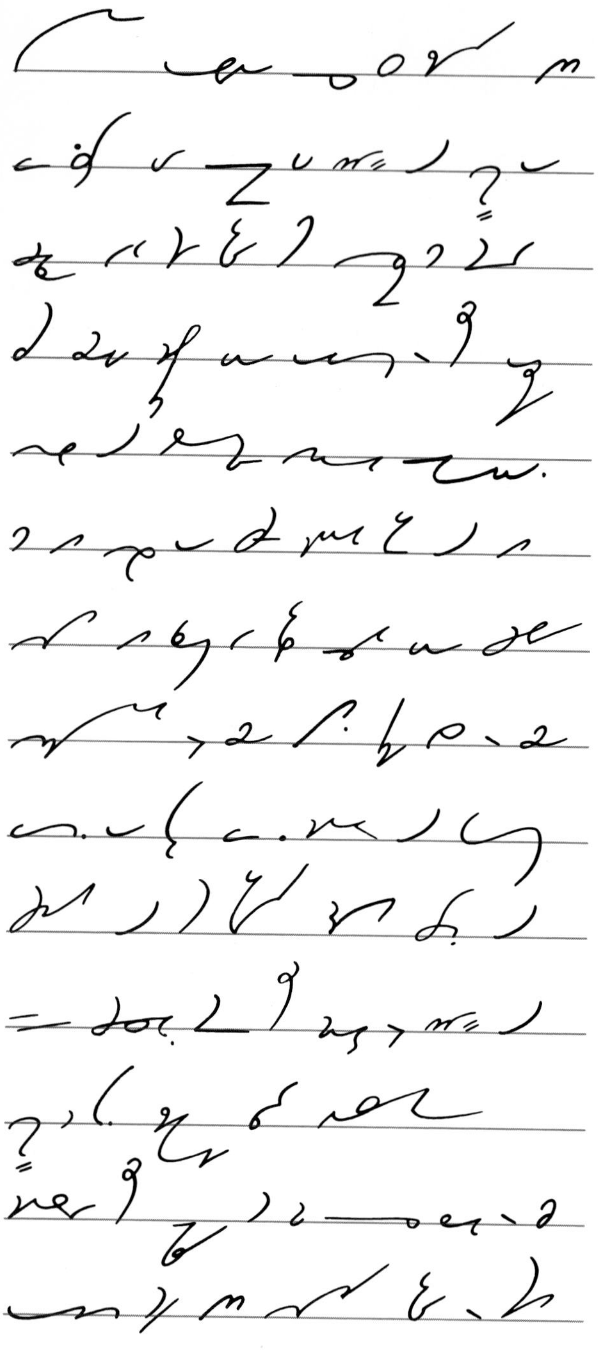

[134 words]

5.4 Theory Letter

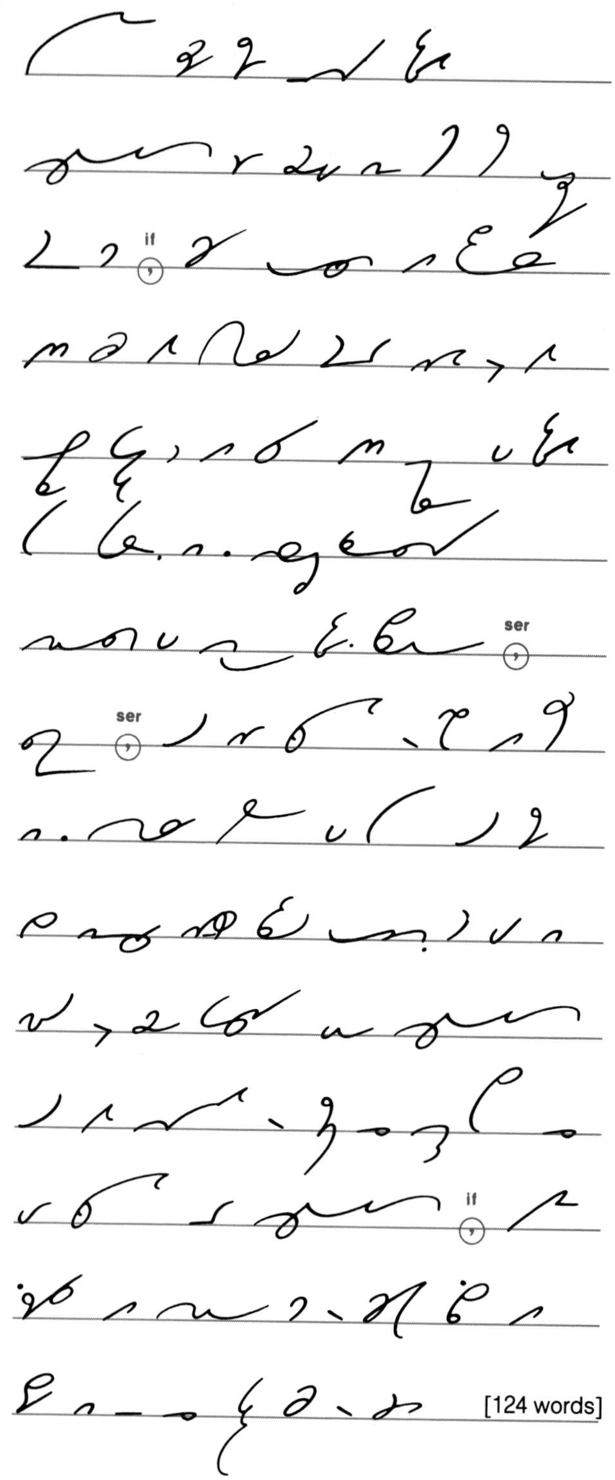

[124 words]

LESSON 6

SKILL DEVELOPMENT

DICTATION SPEED BUILDING

The shorthand outlines below appear in the speed dictation practice that follows. Practice writing these words using the shorthand outlines. Then, using the key that follows, dictate the words to yourself in preparation for the speed dictation practice.

Dictation Preview

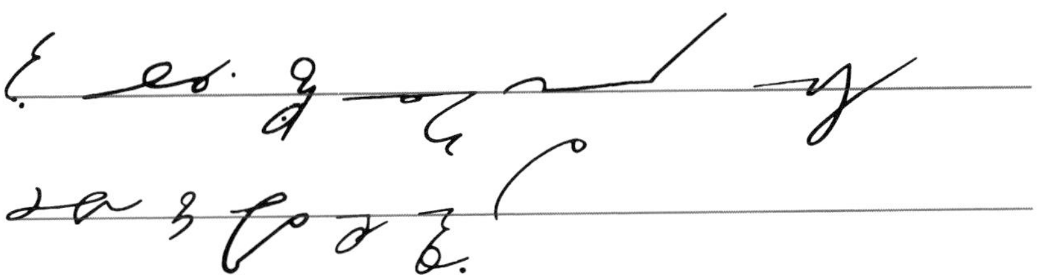

Key: speaking, marketing, association, members, commented, motivated, semester, issues, anybody, insight, inspiring, to me

Speed Dictation Practice

6.1 Goal: 70 wam speed dictation

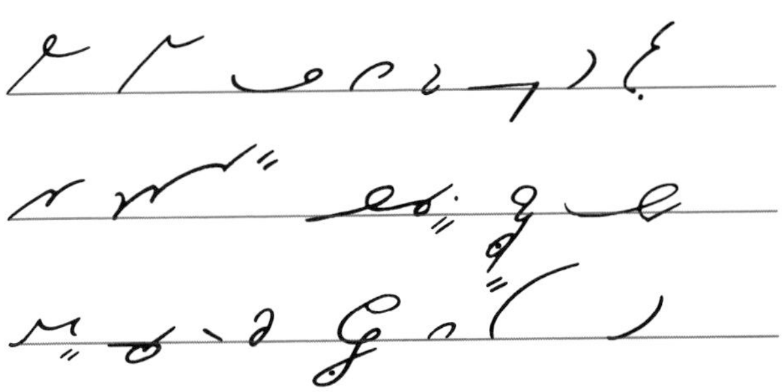

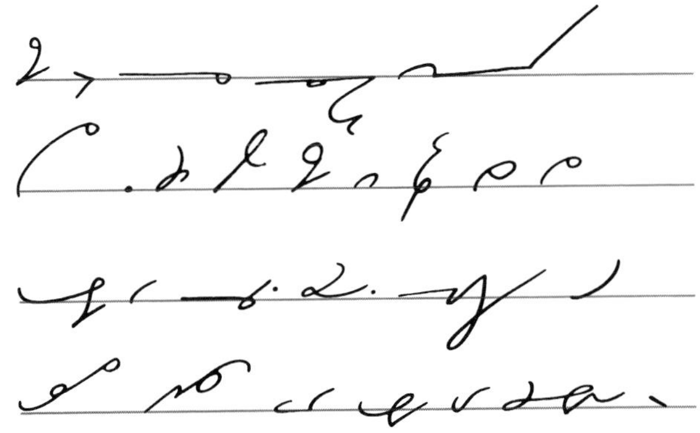

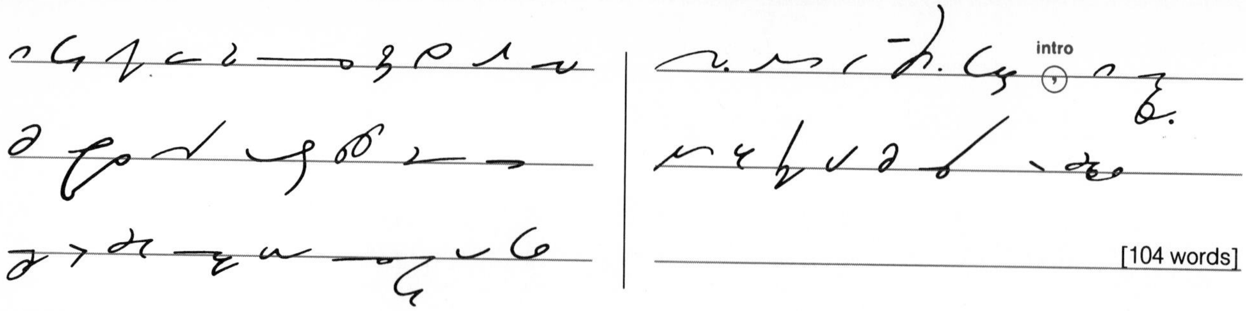

TRANSCRIPTION SKILL DEVELOPMENT

Transcription Practice

Transcribe the following letter for 2 minutes in unarranged format, applying transcription rules and assuring correct spelling. For every word not transcribed and every keyboarding error, deduct one word from the total word count.

6.2 Goal: 25 wam transcription rate

Word Count

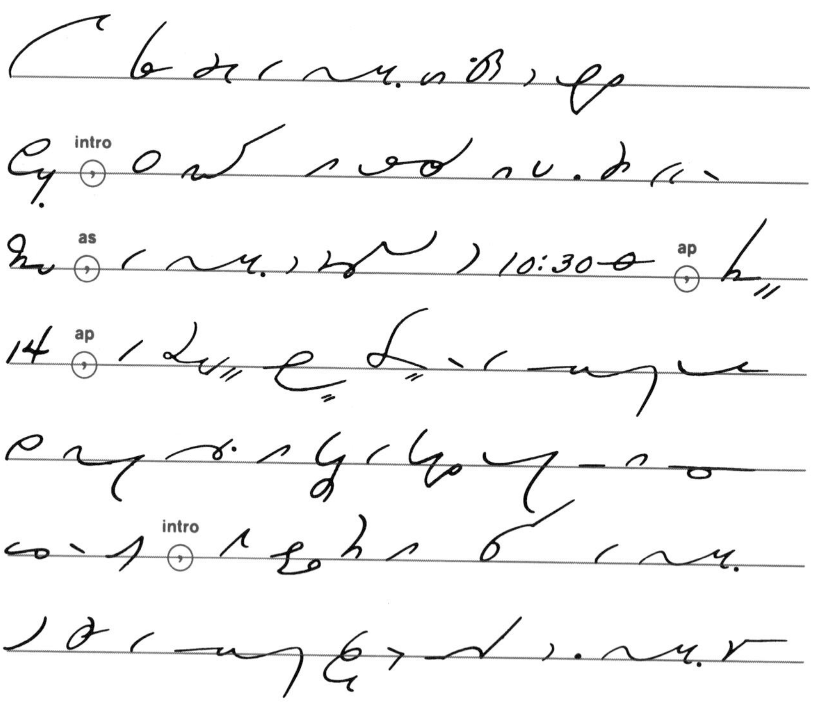

10
21
32
41
55
67
79

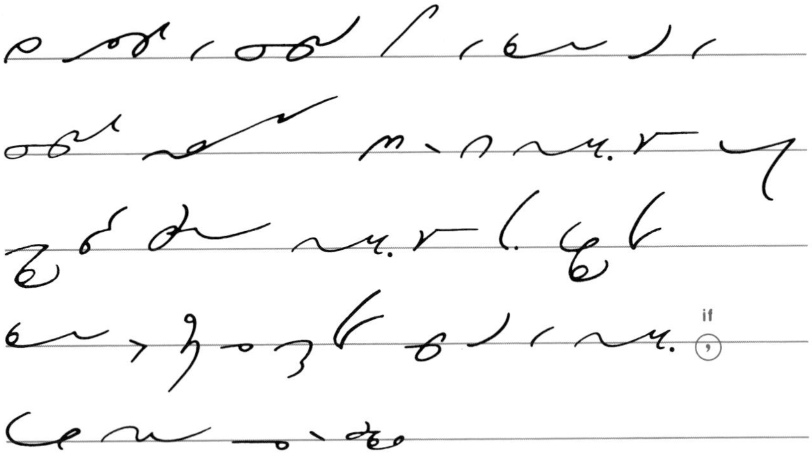

89
100
113
126
131

Transcription Review

Capitalization of Titles

Titles of company officials should not be capitalized when they follow or replace a personal name.

I will meet with Joe Andrews, *president*.

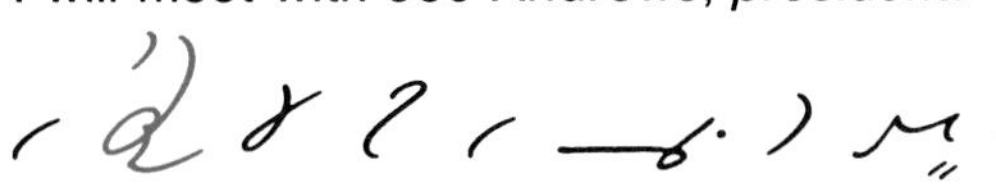

The *supervisor* set up the meeting for Thursday.

Do not capitalize such titles when the personal name that follows is in apposition and is set off by commas.

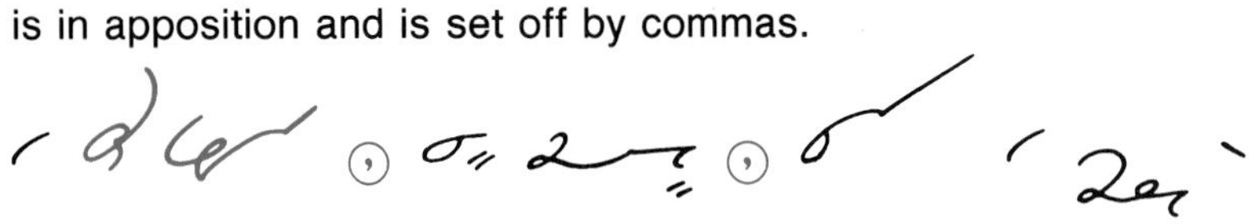

The *vice president*, Anne Williams, attended the conference.

Capitalize all official titles of honor and respect when they replace the titles *Mr.*, *Mrs.*, *Ms.*, and *Dr.*

President Ruth Dillon

Professor Allen Cooper

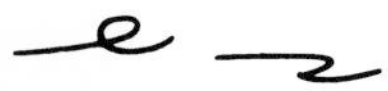

Mayor Moore

Academic Degrees

Academic degrees such as *Ph.D.* and *M.D.* require a period after each element but no internal space. When academic degrees follow a person's name, do not use such titles as *Dr.*, *Mr.*, *Mrs.*, or *Ms.* before the name.

Dr. Steven Bishop
Steven Bishop, Ph.D.
(*Not*: Dr. Steven Bishop, Ph.D.)

Compound Adjectives

A compound adjective is a one-thought modifier and is usually followed by a noun. It consists of two or more words that express a single meaning and is generally hyphenated.

We received the *up-to-date* report.

The compound adjective *up to date* expresses one thought and is followed by the noun *report*. In addition, the words *up to date* cannot be used separately to convey the intended meaning.

The report we received is *up to date*.

In this example, *up to date* is a prepositional phrase instead of a compound adjective. Note that it is not hyphenated.

Skill Teaser

On a separate sheet of paper, identify the five transcription errors and four punctuation errors in the following memo.

Date: April 30, 19--
To: Staff
From: Mary Walters, Ph.D.
Subject: Resignation

As was anounced on Monday April 16, our art director Jerry Walsh has resigned his position in the art department and is leaving the company.

Until someone is named to replace him Sue Knapp has been apointed as acting director of the Art Department, effective immediately. Please give Sue your full support during this transition time.

I am sure you will all join me in wishing Jerry all the best in his future indeavors.

urs

Dictation and Transcription Practice

6.3 Brief-Form Letter

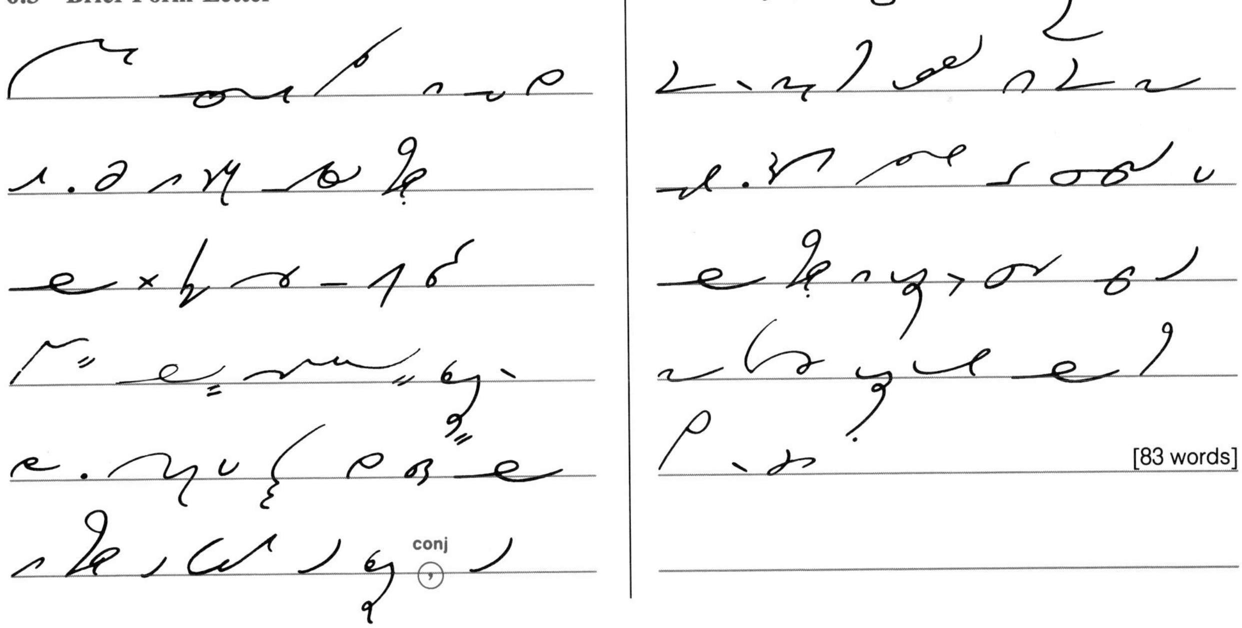

[83 words]

6.4 Theory Letter

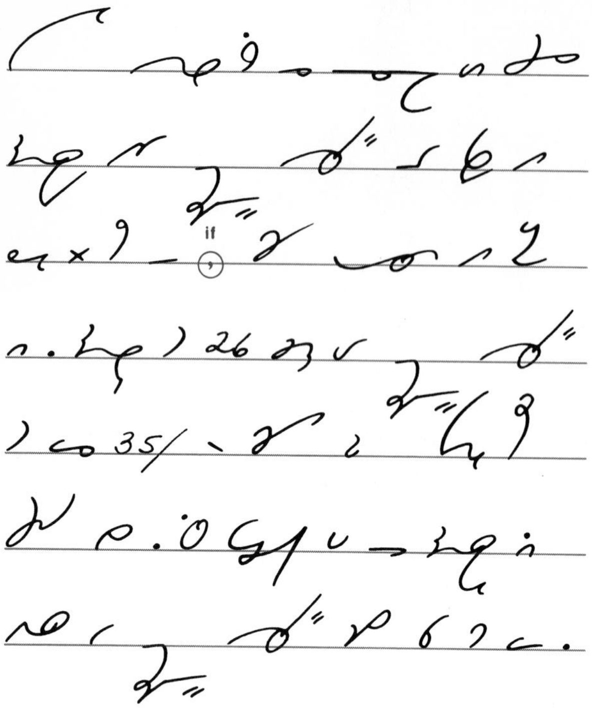

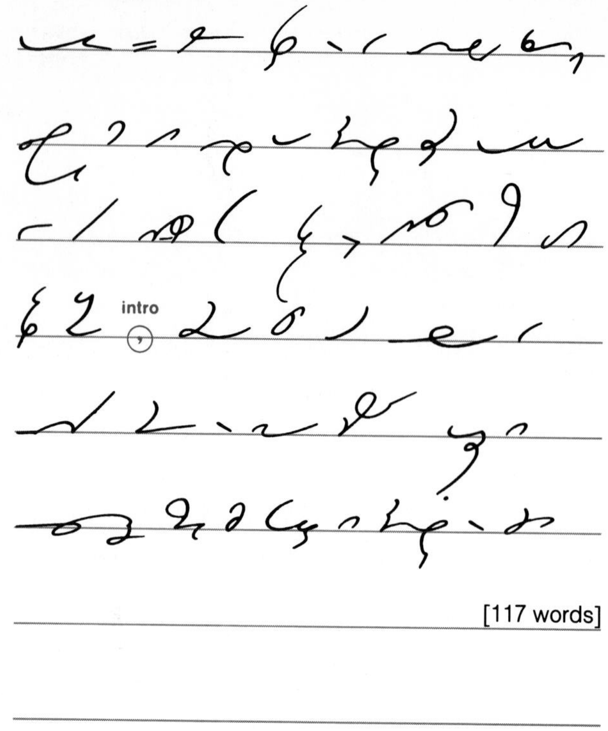

LESSON 7

SKILL DEVELOPMENT

DICTATION SPEED BUILDING

The shorthand outlines below appear in the speed dictation practice that follows. Practice writing these words using the shorthand outlines. Then, using the key that follows, dictate the words to yourself in preparation for the speed dictation practice.

Dictation Preview

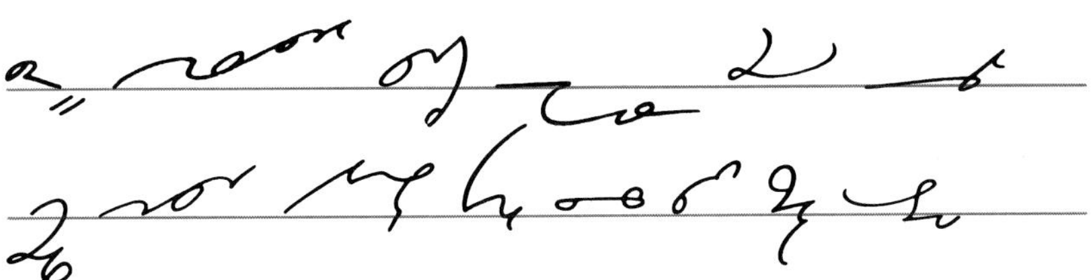

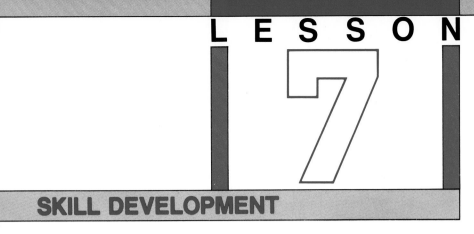

Key: Young, graduates, actively, employment, field, minutes, conversation, contact, description, because, immediately, with you, as soon as possible, let us know

Speed Dictation Practice

7.1 Goal: 70 wam speed dictation

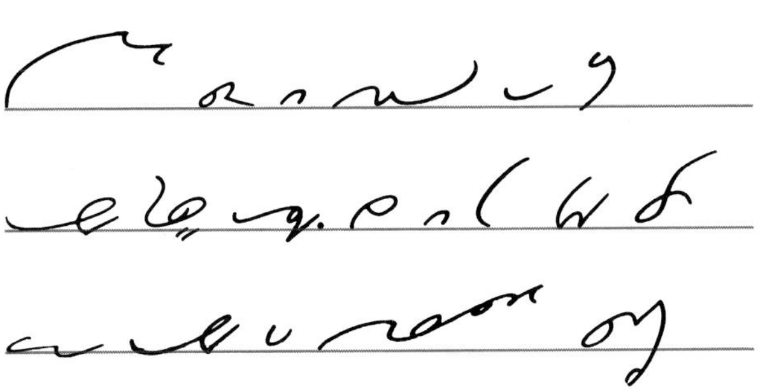

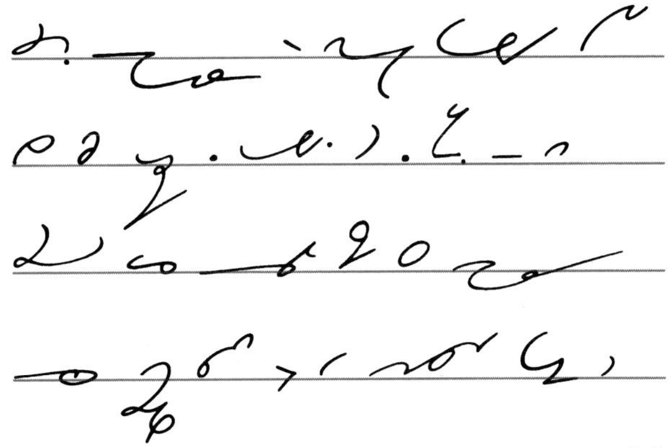

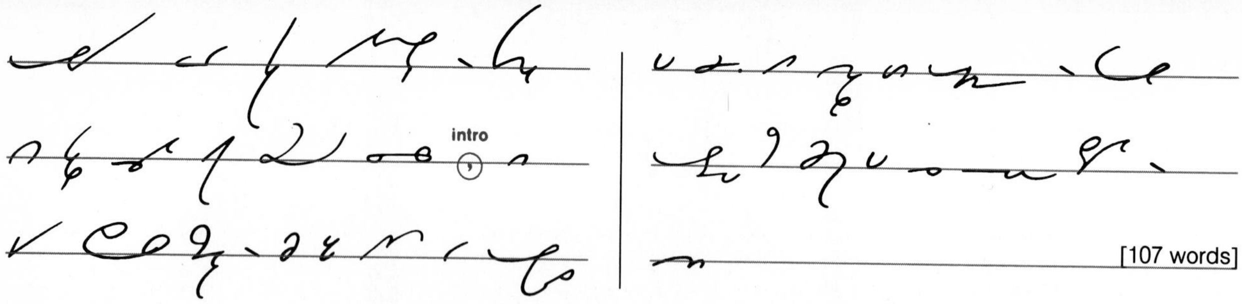

[107 words]

TRANSCRIPTION SKILL DEVELOPMENT

Transcription Practice

Transcribe the following letter for 2 minutes in unarranged format, applying transcription rules and assuring correct spelling. For every word not transcribed and every keyboarding error, deduct one word from the total word count.

7.2 Goal: 25 wam transcription rate

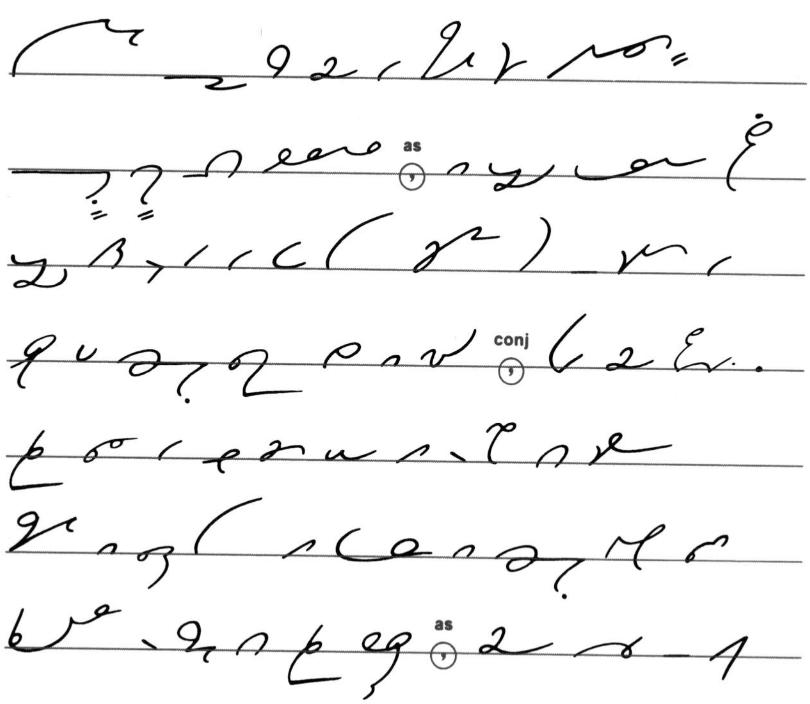

Word Count: 10, 24, 37, 50, 61, 73, 86

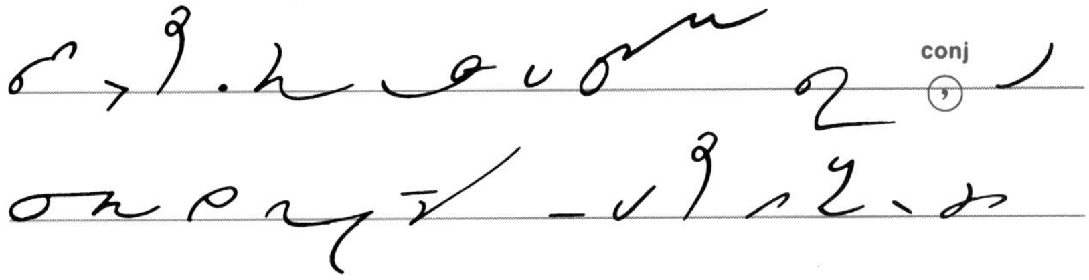

97

113

Transcription Review

Forming Plurals

When transcribing words ending in *s*, there is no clue as to the spelling of these words. Therefore, it is important to apply the following rules when forming plurals:

1 Add *s* to the singular form.

flight	chance	taxi	menu
flights	chances	taxis	menus

2 Add *es* when the singular form ends in *s*, *x*, *ch*, *sh*, or *z*.

lens	tax	sketch	marsh
lenses	taxes	sketches	marshes

3 Change the *y* to *i* and add *es* when a singular noun ends in *y* preceded by a consonant.

liability	commodity
liabilities	commodities

4 Add *s* when a singular noun ends in *y* preceded by a vowel.

boy	guy
boys	guys

5 The plurals of some nouns are in a different form and do not end in *s*.

mouse	goose	child	ox
mice	geese	children	oxen

Compound Nouns

1 When a compound noun is a solid word, pluralize the final element in the compound as if it stood alone.

wineglass	grandchild
wineglasses	grandchildren

2 The plurals of hyphenated or two-word compounds are formed by pluralizing the main element of the compound.

runner-up	letter of credit
runners-up	letters of credit

3 When a hyphenated compound does not contain a noun, simply pluralize the final element.

show-off	has-been
show-offs	has-beens

Skill Teaser

On a separate sheet of paper identify the seven transcription errors and four punctuation errors in the following memo.

Date: January 31, 19--
To: Dr. Charles Burke
From: Maria Sanchez
Subject: Campus Surveys

The university bookstore is earnestly seeking your assistance to help us improve our service to the campus community. Survays will be conducted on campus by three graduate student from February 25 through March 2 19-- concerning the bookstore's present service.

Would you allow one of the students to come to your classroom and conduct the survay? It would take approximately 15 minutes to complete. Please indicate "yes" or "no" on the inclosed card and return it to the bookstore by February 15.

If you answer "yes" you will be contacted to set up a date and time at which the survay can be given. Thank you for your assistance, in this important program.

urs
Enclosure

Dictation and Transcription Practice

7.3 Brief-Form Letter

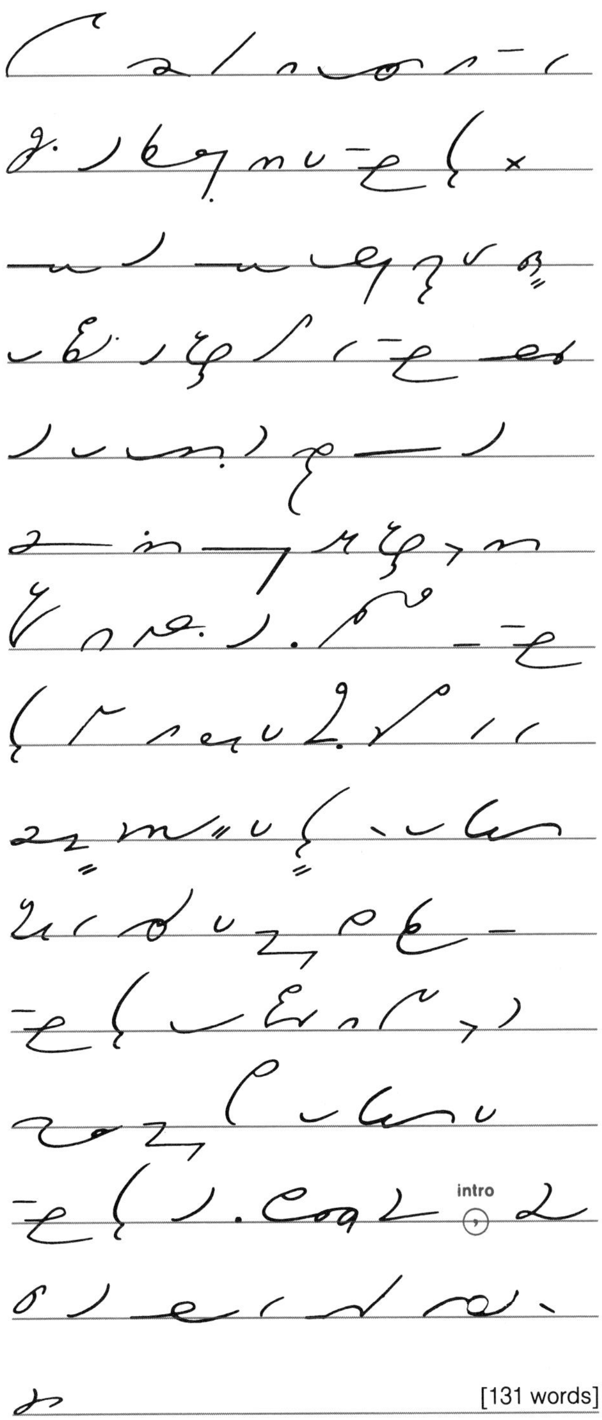

[131 words]

7.4 Theory Letter

[108 words]

LESSON 8

SKILL DEVELOPMENT

DICTATION SPEED BUILDING

The shorthand outlines below appear in the speed dictation practice that follows. Practice writing these words using the shorthand outlines. Then, using the key that follows, dictate the words to yourself in preparation for the speed dictation practice.

Dictation Preview

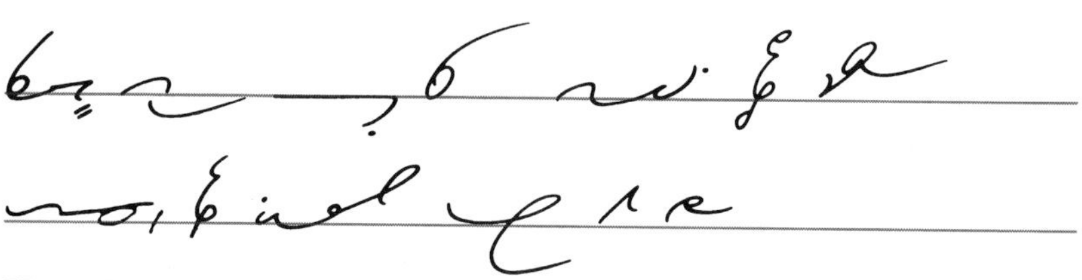

Key: Barnes, quality, manufacturing, item, clothing, especially, style, workmanship, special, holidays, label, it is, they are

Speed Dictation Practice

8.1 Goal: 70 wam speed dictation

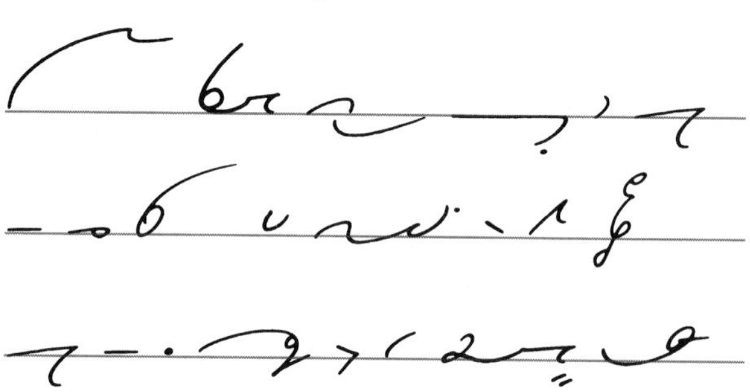

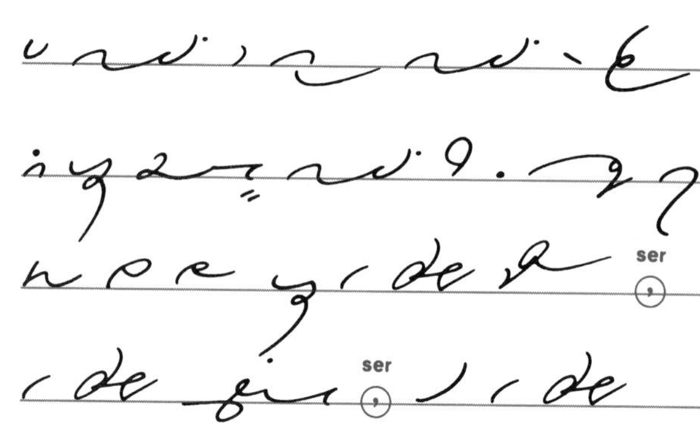

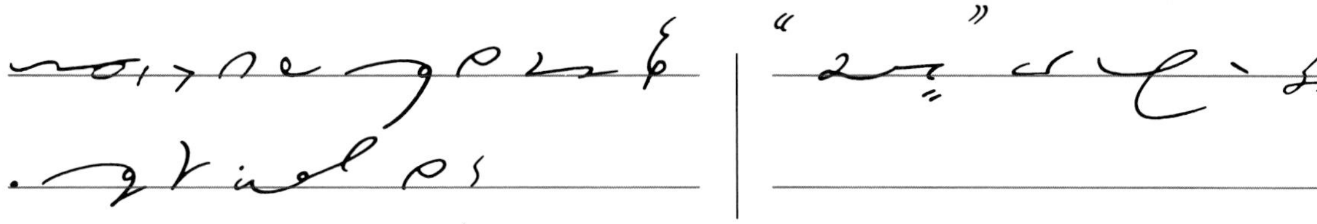

[84 words]

TRANSCRIPTION SKILL DEVELOPMENT

Transcription Practice

Transcribe the following letter for 2 minutes in unarranged format, applying transcription rules and assuring correct spelling. For every word not transcribed and every keyboarding error, deduct one word from the total word count.

8.2 Goal: 25 wam transcription rate

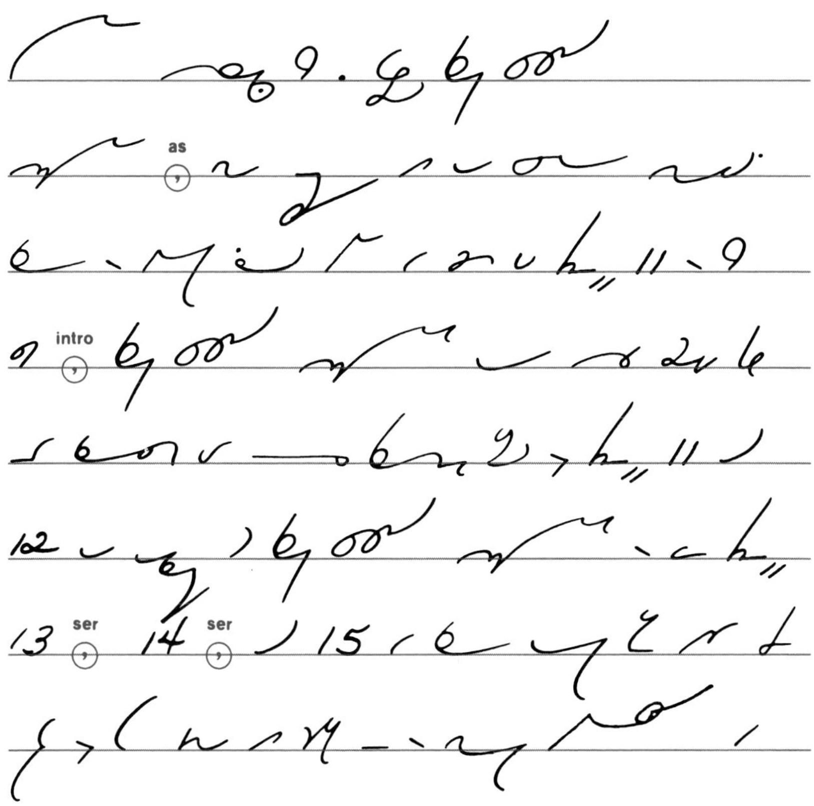

Word Count

9
19
30
41
53
64
74
85

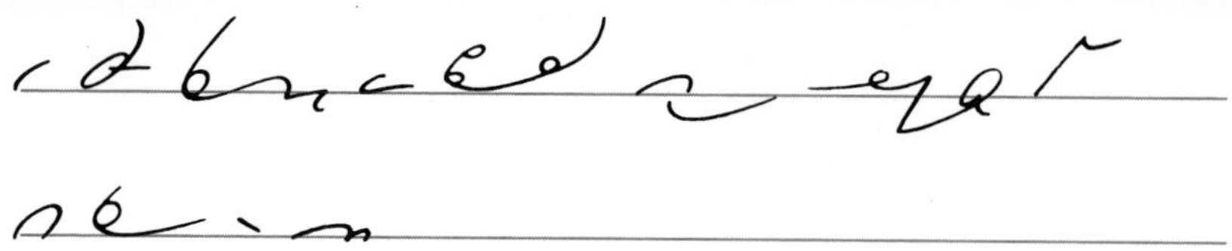

97

102

Transcription Review

Forming Singular Possessives

When transcribing connected matter in shorthand, it is not always readily evident that a word is in the possessive form as opposed to the plural form. Therefore, it is important to transcribe carefully and read for meaning.

A noun ending in the sound of *s* is usually in the possessive form if it is followed immediately by another noun. Try substituting an *of* phrase to determine if the possessive form should be used. If the substitution sounds correct, the possessive form should be used.

Ms. Bright's career (the career of Ms. Bright)	my sister's party (the party of my sister)

When forming singular possessives, apply these rules:

1 Add an *'s* to form the possessive of a singular noun not ending in an *s* sound.

the patient's medicine

2 Add an *'s* to form the possessive of a singular noun that ends in an *s* sound if a new syllable is formed.

your boss's approval

Forming Plural Possessives

When transcribing connected shorthand material:

1 Add only an apostrophe to form the plural possessive of a plural noun that ends in *s*.

the agencies' rules	attorneys' reports

2 Add an *'s* to form the plural possessive of a plural noun that does not end in *s*.

men's clothing

Note: It is important when forming the possessive of a plural noun that you first apply the rule for making the word plural; then apply the rule for forming the plural possessive.

Skill Teaser

On a separate sheet of paper, identify the nine transcription errors and two punctuation errors in the following letter.

June 18, 19--

Ms. Carla Morris
National Products Company
485 Powell Street
San Francisco, CA 94101

Dear Ms. Morris

It is my pleasure to recommend John S Tyler for a manageral position in your company.

Mr. Tylers qualifications are outstanding. He was associated with our firm for 6 years. He was a associate branch manager initially and only 1 year later he was promoted to branch manager of our Boston operation.

Mr. Tyler has done an excellent job hiring, and training people for our organization. I am also sure that he will be a fine addition to your companys management team. Mr. Tylers excellent record makes him extremely well qualified to serve as an executive in any corporation.

Cordially yours

Elizabeth Tarkington

urs
Enclosure

Dictation and Transcription Practice

8.3 Brief-Form Letter

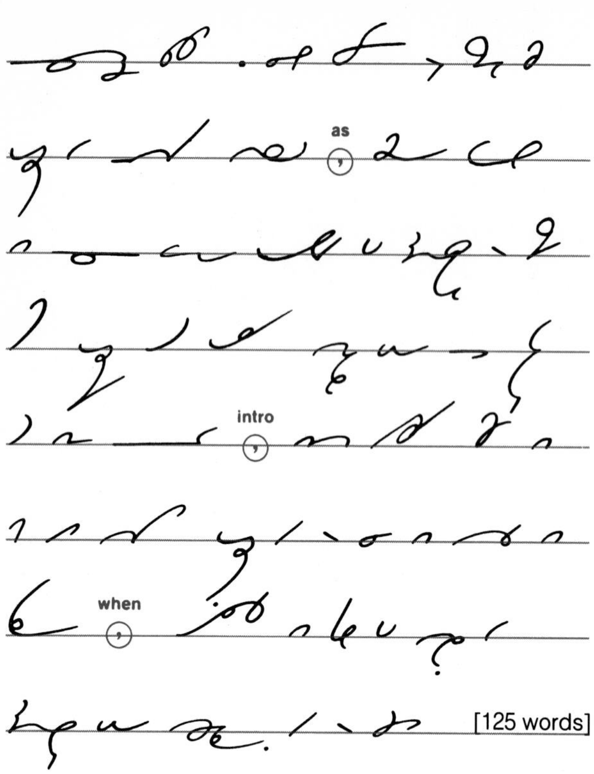

8.4 Theory Letter

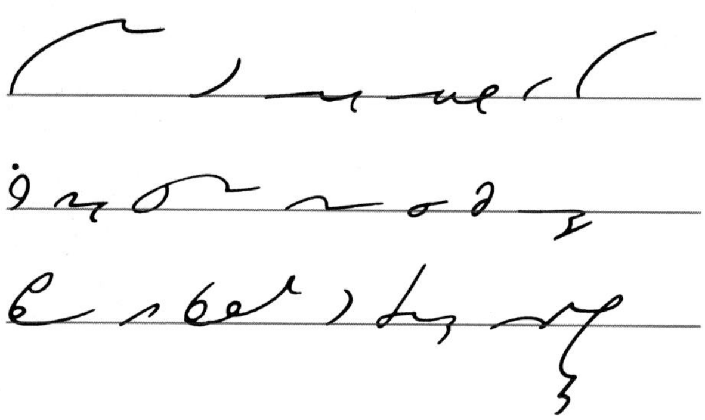

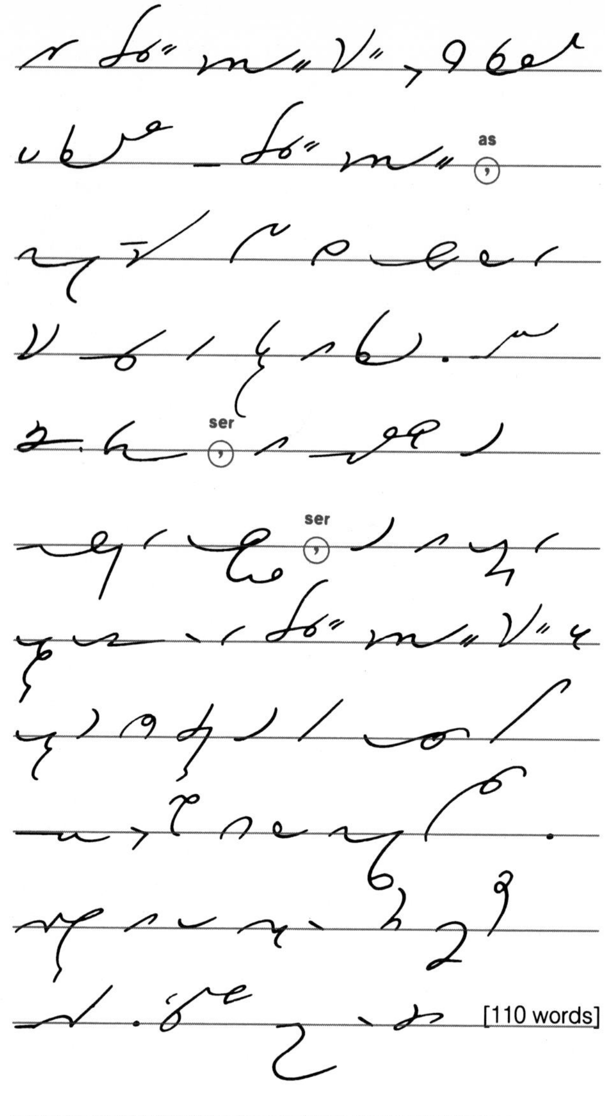

UNIT

II

MIC

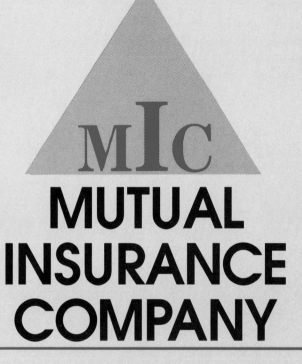

MUTUAL INSURANCE COMPANY

LESSON 9

MUTUAL INSURANCE COMPANY

You are employed as an administrative assistant for the Mutual Insurance Company with an office in Hartford, Connecticut. In your position you work with George Sinclair and Elizabeth Barnes, insurance agents, and Frank Jennings, account manager. See the organization chart below.

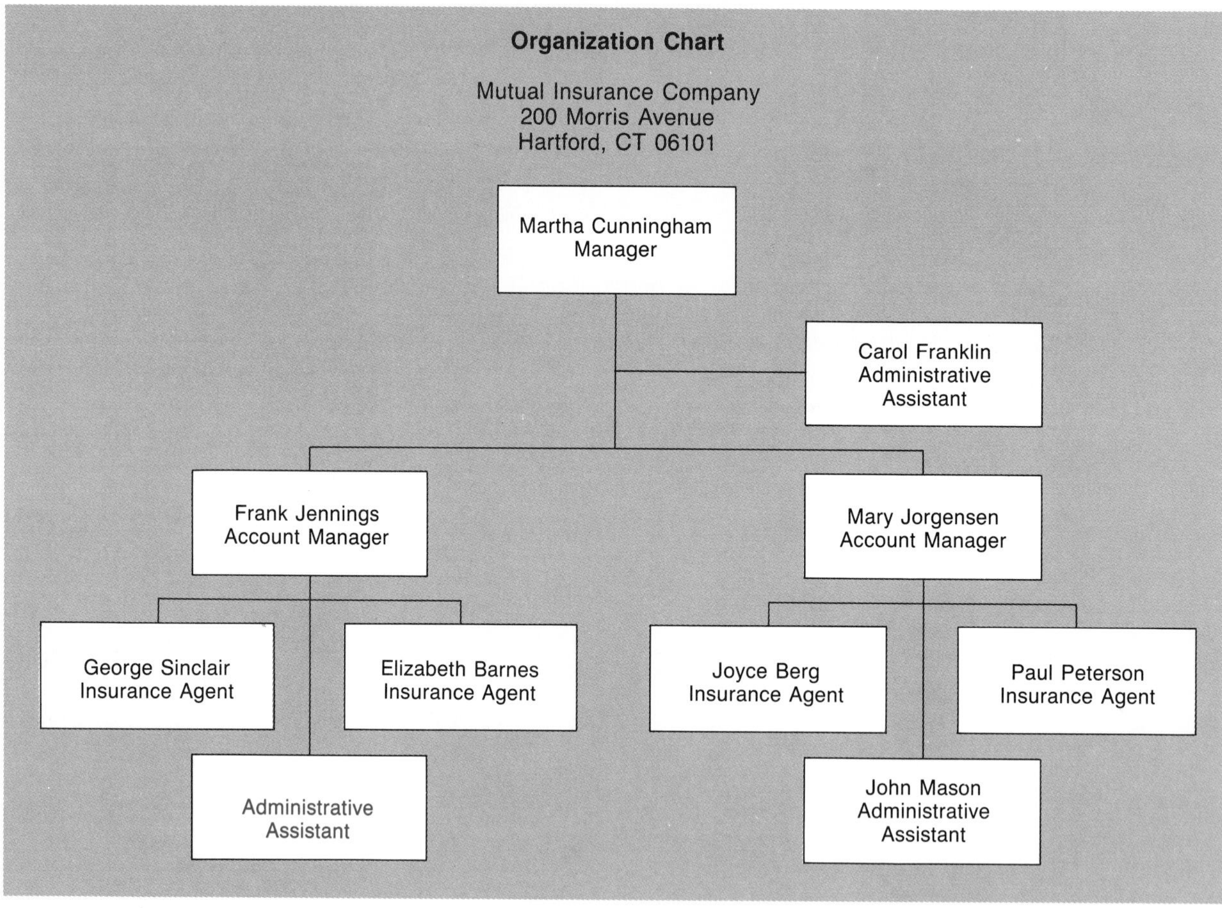

Your responsibilities will include answering the telephone; replying to inquiries about insurance coverage; using spreadsheet software to track types of insurance coverage, payments, beneficiaries, and so on; taking dictation; and typing correspondence. As you work through the materials, you will acquire knowledge about the many facets of the insurance business, as well as develop additional proficiency in dictation speed and increase your transcription speed and accuracy. The mailable production letters in the lessons and the letters the instructor dictates will provide you with the opportunity to type correspondence to be sent to customers.

Below is a copy of your company letterhead. Develop the return address that you will use to type the envelopes for the mailable production letters.

MUTUAL
INSURANCE
COMPANY
MIC
200 Morris Avenue
Hartford, CT 06101
(203) 555-7821

You should also be familiar with a variety of terms used in the insurance industry and their shorthand outlines.

Shorthand Outline	Word	Definition
	insurance premium	Amount paid for insurance coverage.
	expiration date	Date insurance expires.
	disability insurance	Pays an amount of money monthly to the insured if disabled.
	whole life insurance	Pays face value of the policy to the survivors when the insured dies.
	term life insurance	Provides payment if the insured dies within a certain number of years stated in the policy.
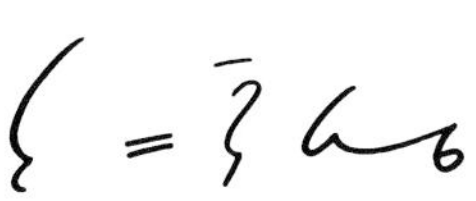	business-interruption policy	Covers temporary loss of income from a variety of insurable causes such as fire, loss of power or fuel, or other occurrences that cause loss of business income.

Policy Numbers

If an identifying noun such as *policy* precedes a figure, the word *number* is usually unnecessary. However, your employer may require its use. Therefore, if the term *number* precedes a figure, express the term *number* as an abbreviation. Use *No.* for singular and *Nos.* for plural.

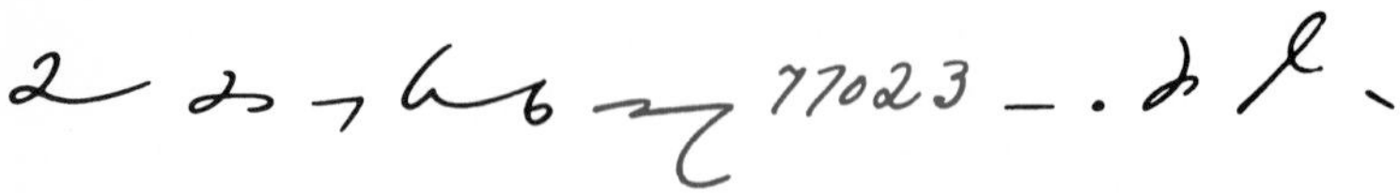

We will send you Insurance Policy *No. 77023* in a few days.

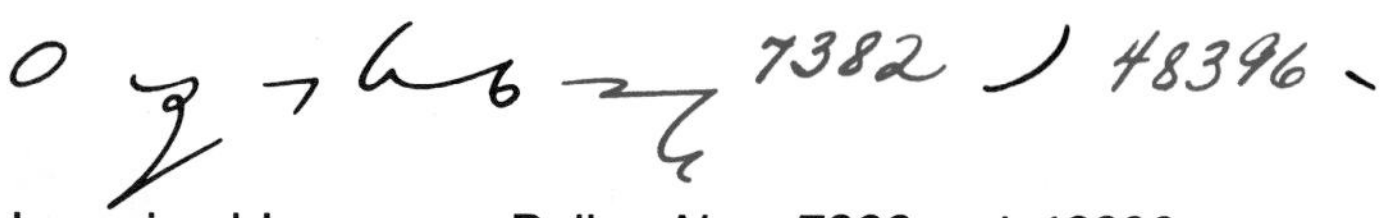

I received Insurance Policy *Nos. 7382* and *48396*.

DICTATION SPEED BUILDING

The shorthand outlines below appear in the speed dictation practice that follows. Practice writing these words using the shorthand outlines. Then, using the key that follows, dictate the words to yourself in preparation for the speed dictation practice.

Dictation Preview

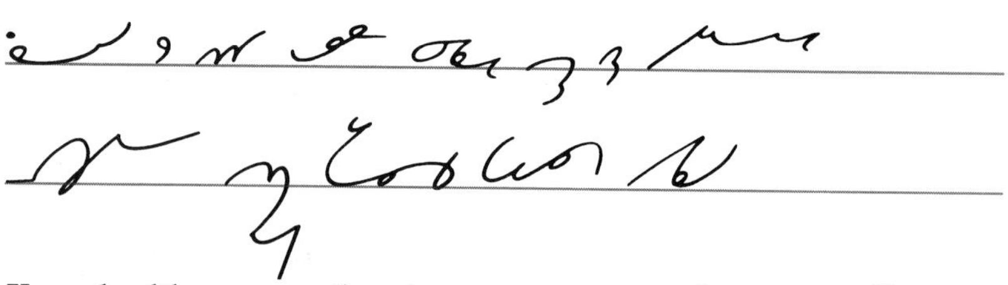

Key: health, yes, worth, return, answers, questions, yourself, dollars, individual, coverage, obligate, protection, depend

Speed Dictation Practice

9.1 Goal: 70 wam speed dictation

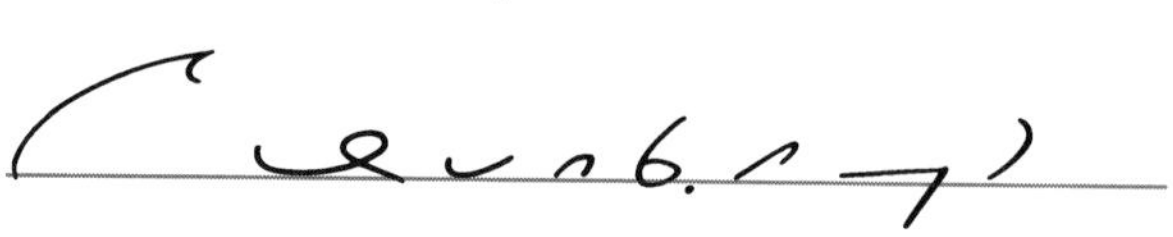

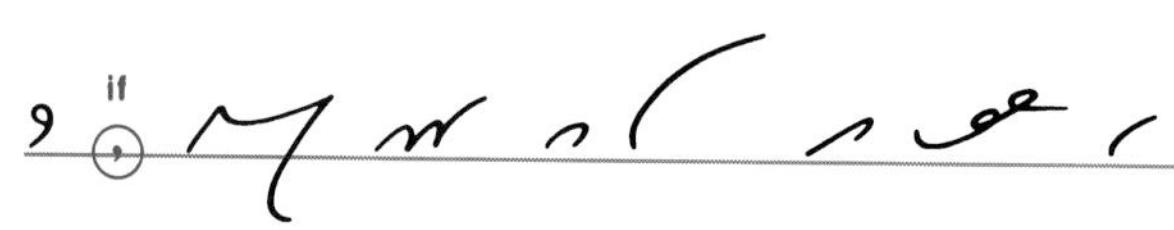

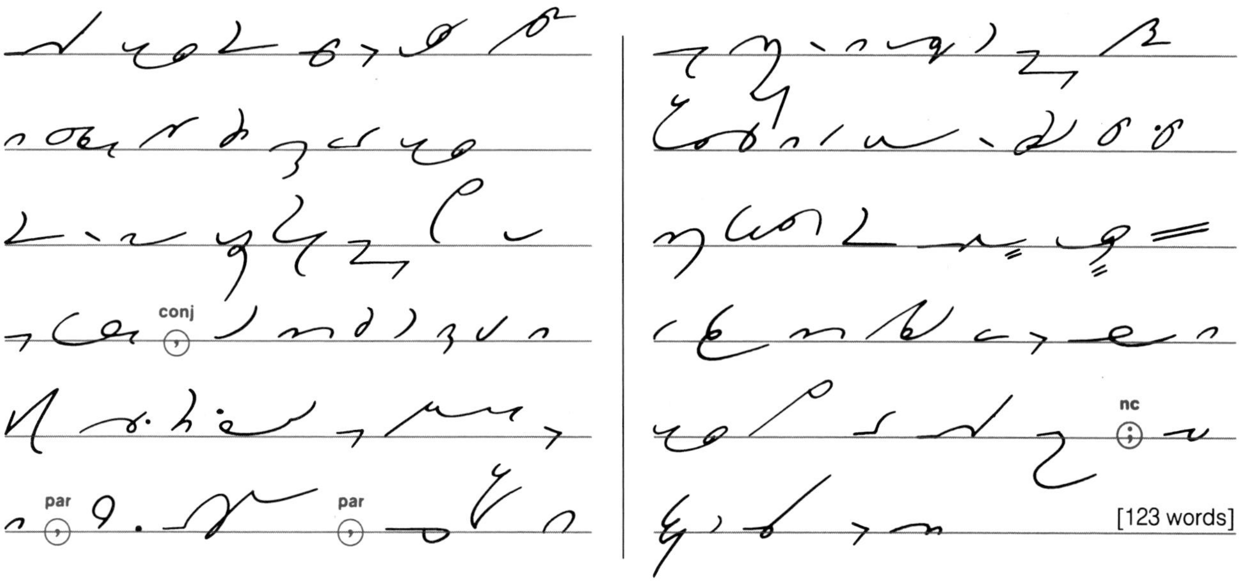

TRANSCRIPTION SKILL DEVELOPMENT

Transcription Warmup

Transcribe the following groups of words for speed and accuracy, applying transcription rules and assuring correct spelling.

9.2

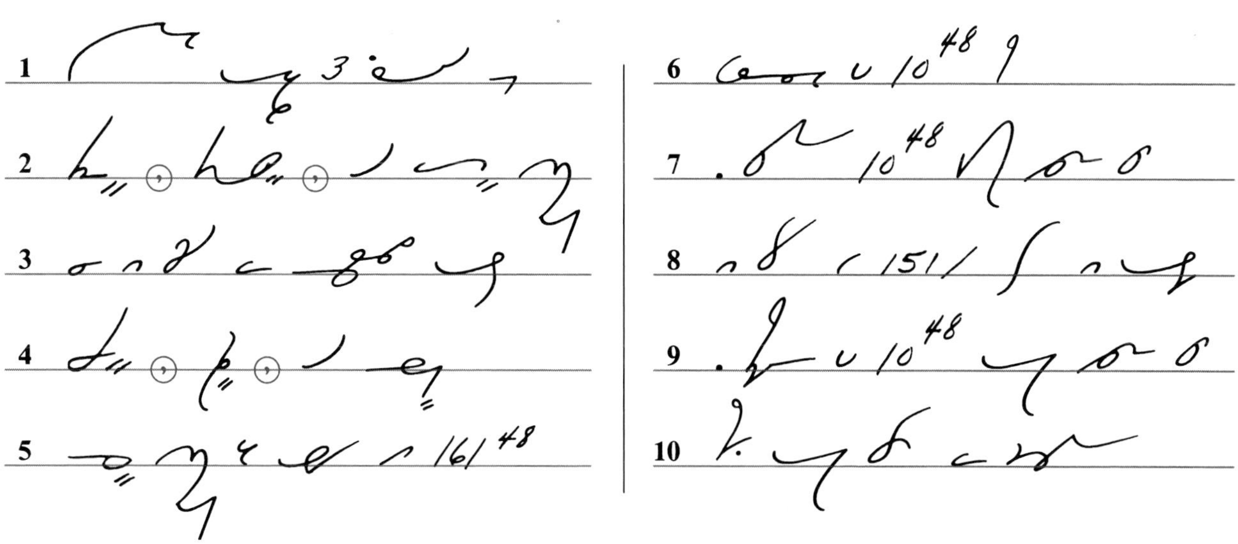

Transcription Practice

Transcribe the following letter for 2 minutes in unarranged format, applying transcription rules and assuring correct spelling. For every word not transcribed and every keyboarding error, deduct one word from the total word count.

9.3 Goal: 25 wam transcription rate

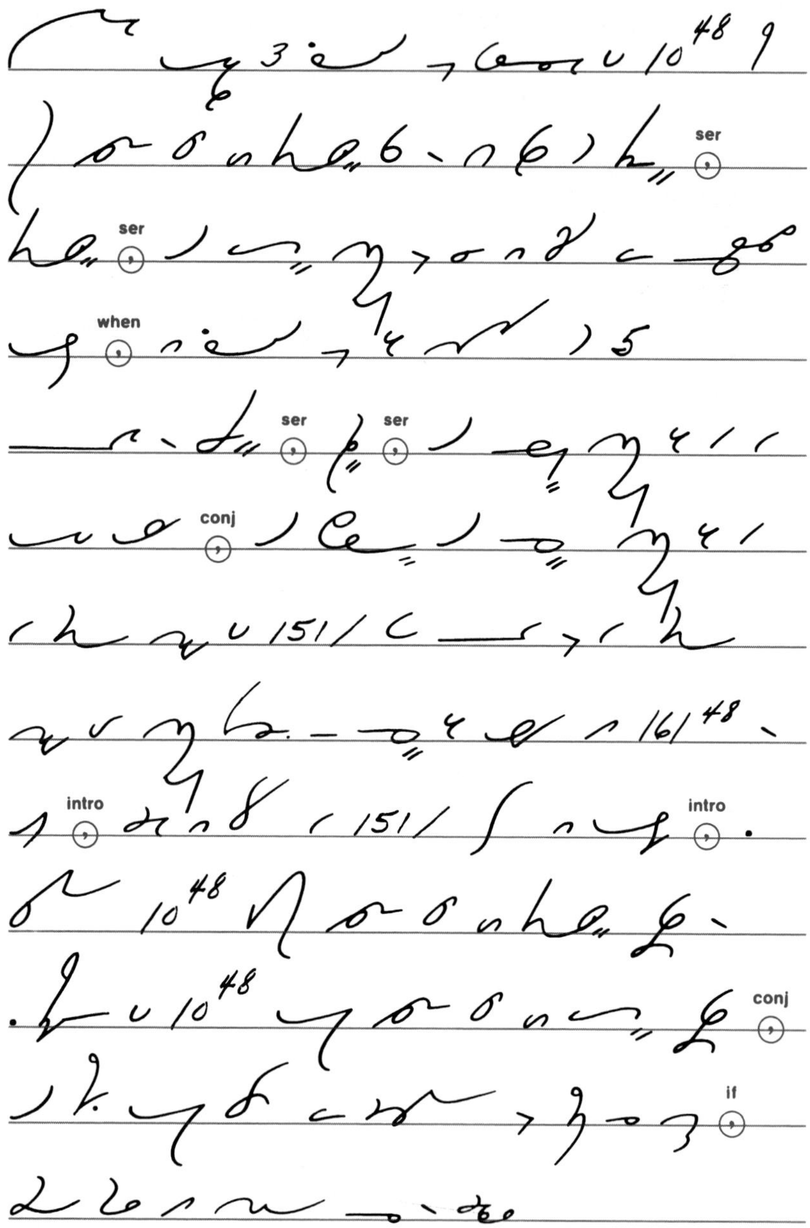

Word Count

12
24
35
45
57
66
75
87
98
113
126
140
146

LESSON 10

MUTUAL INSURANCE COMPANY

DICTATION SPEED BUILDING

The shorthand outlines below appear in the speed dictation practice that follows. Practice writing these words using the shorthand outlines. Then, using the key that follows, dictate the words to yourself in preparation for the speed dictation practice.

Dictation Preview

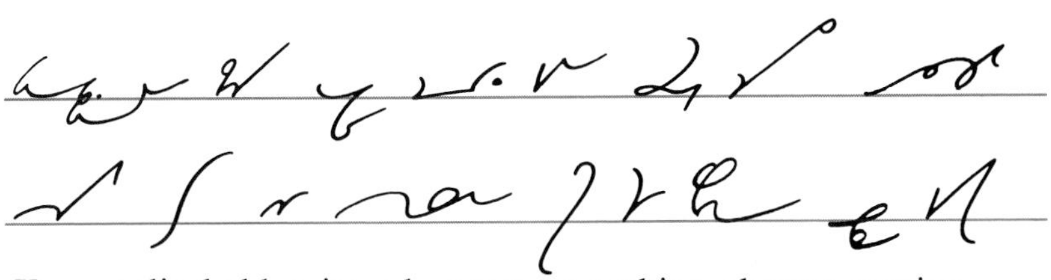

Key: policyholder, issued, report, something, shorter, version, study, indicates, condition, before, other, greater, you have been, for the, I hope you will, next year, should be

Speed Dictation Practice

10.1 Goal: 70 wam speed dictation

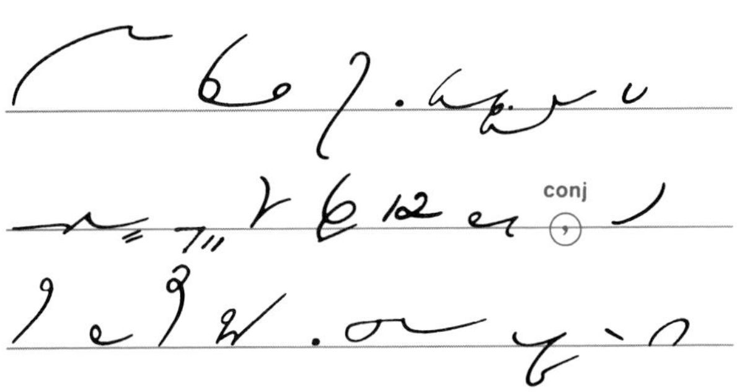

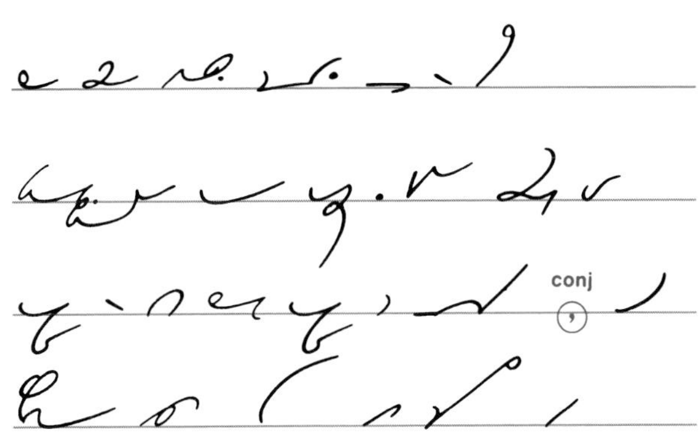

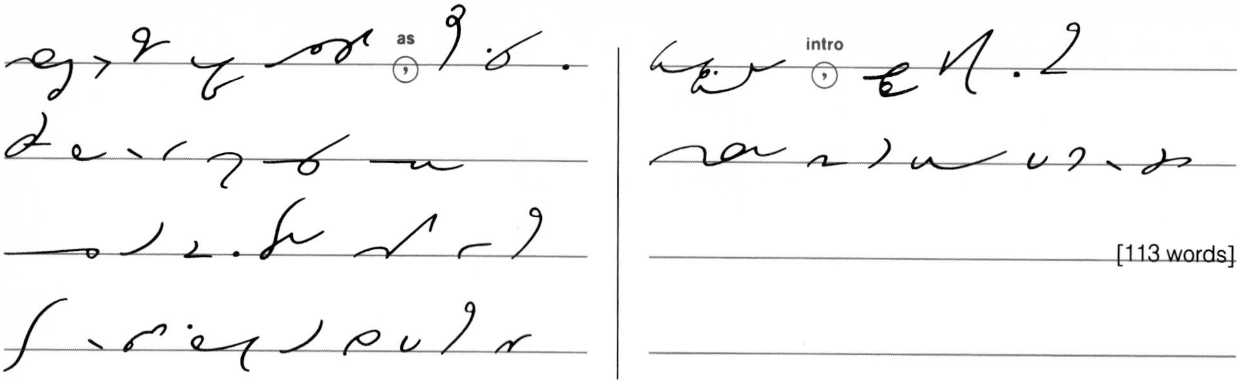

TRANSCRIPTION SKILL DEVELOPMENT

Transcription Warmup

Transcribe the following groups of words for speed and accuracy, applying transcription rules and assuring correct spelling.

10.2

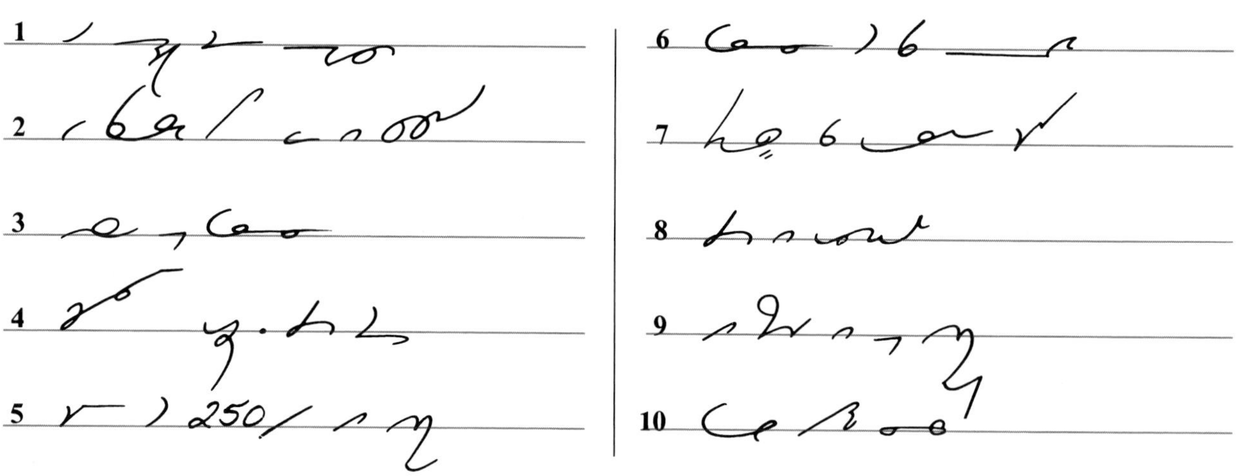

Transcription Practice

Transcribe the following letter for 2 minutes in unarranged format, applying transcription rules and assuring correct spelling. For every word not transcribed and every keyboarding error, deduct one word from the total word count.

10.3 Goal: 25 wam transcription rate

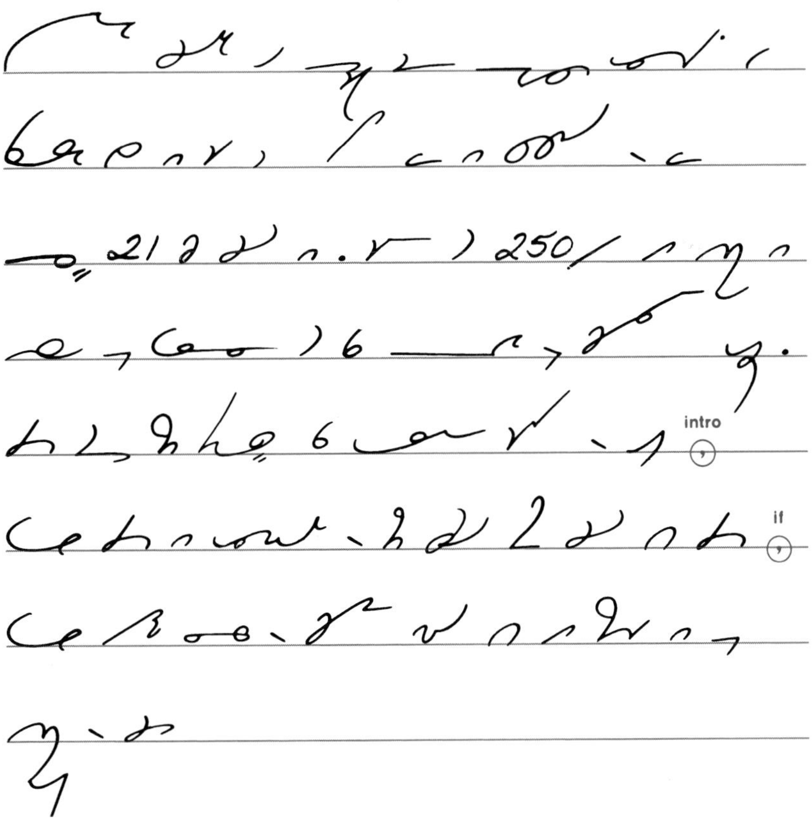

Word Count

11
21
32
44
55
69
83
88

Mailable Production

Transcribe the following mailable production letter in block style, assuring proper placement of all letter parts. Insert punctuation prior to transcribing, and capitalize proper nouns and titles. Address a large envelope with the special notation *Registered.*

10.4 Time Limit: 15 minutes

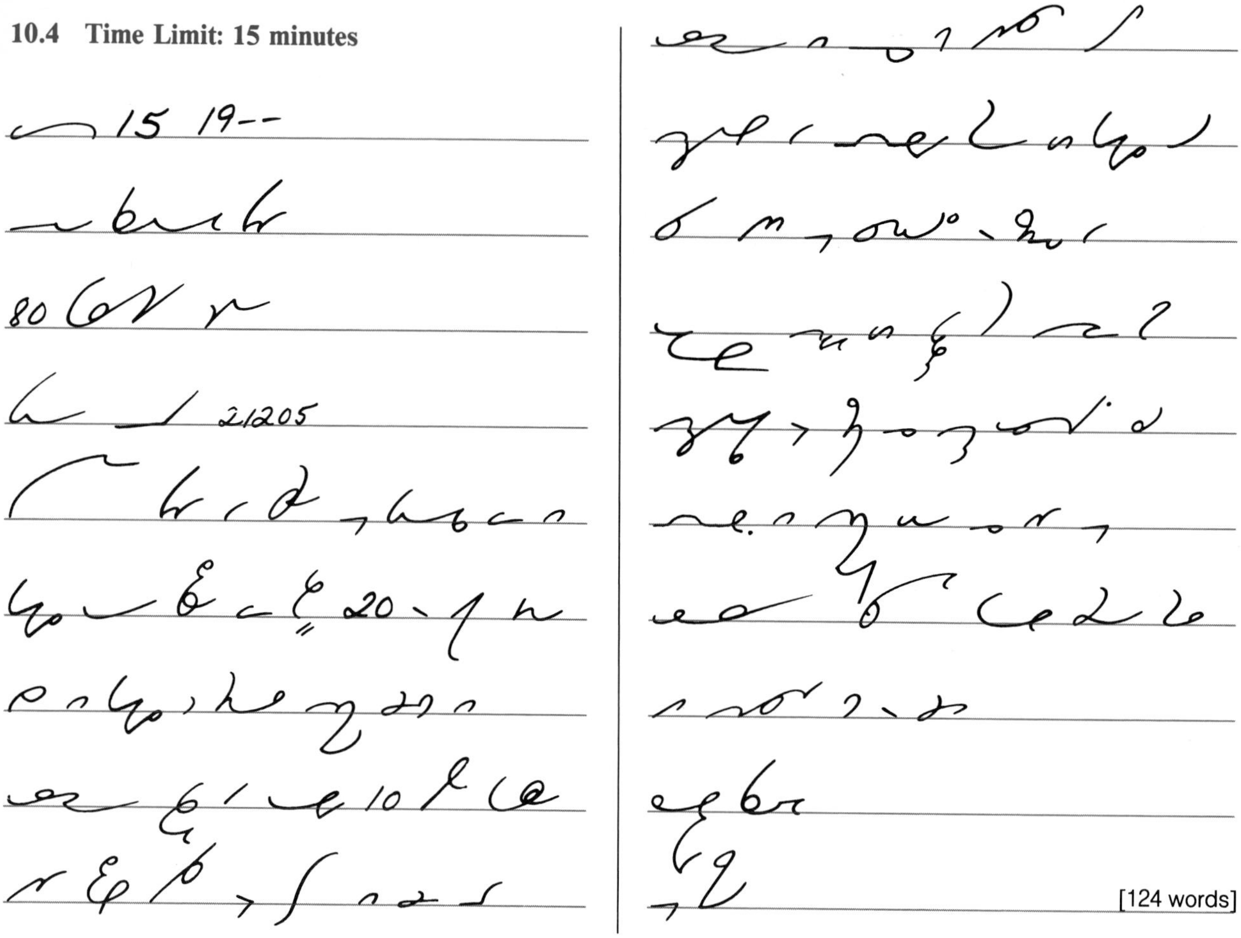

[124 words]

LESSON 11

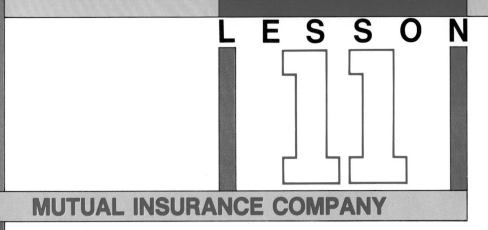

MUTUAL INSURANCE COMPANY

DICTATION SPEED BUILDING

The shorthand outlines below appear in the speed dictation practice that follows. Practice writing these words using the shorthand outlines. Then, using the key that follows, dictate the words to yourself in preparation for the speed dictation practice.

Dictation Preview

Key: Dear Ms. Garcia, health, coverage, without, described, necessary, filled, signature, contract, retain, return, I know, you have been, to me

Speed Dictation Practice

11.1 Goal: 70 wam speed dictation

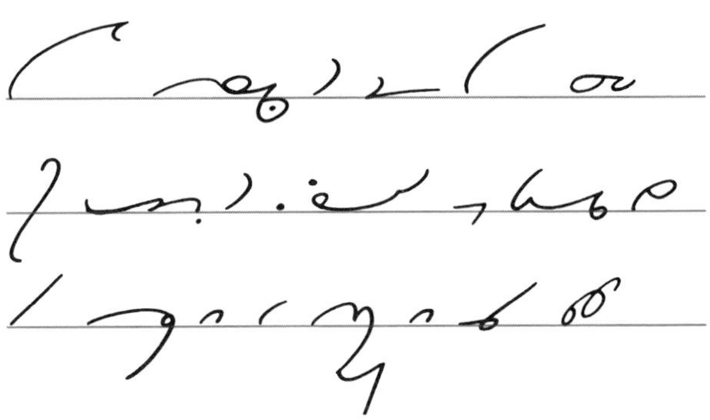

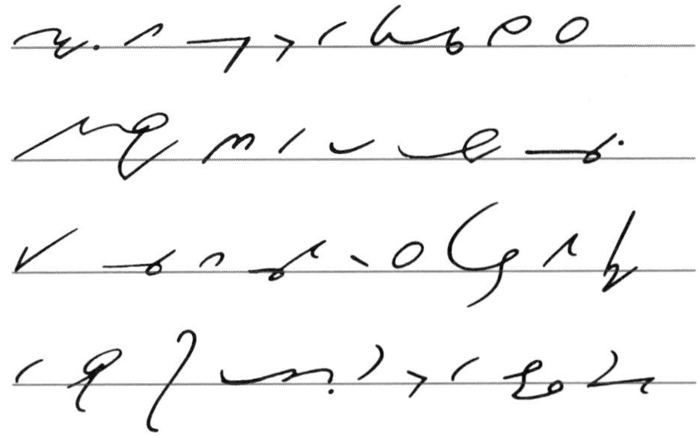

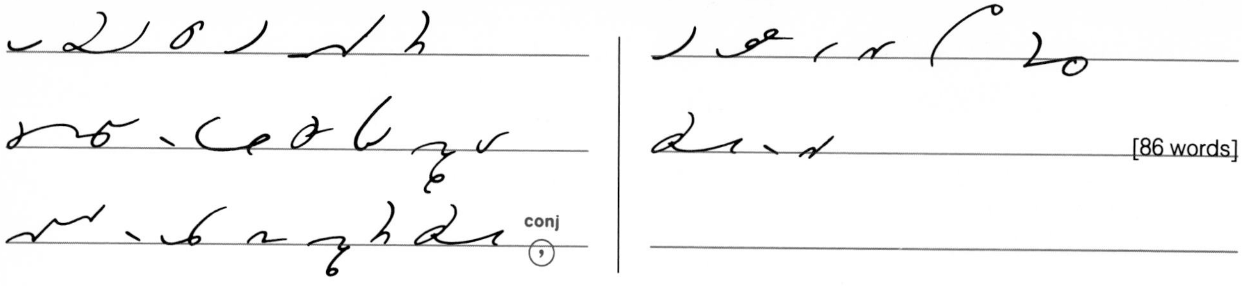

TRANSCRIPTION SKILL DEVELOPMENT

Transcription Warmup

Transcribe the following groups of words for speed and accuracy, applying transcription rules and assuring correct spelling.

11.2

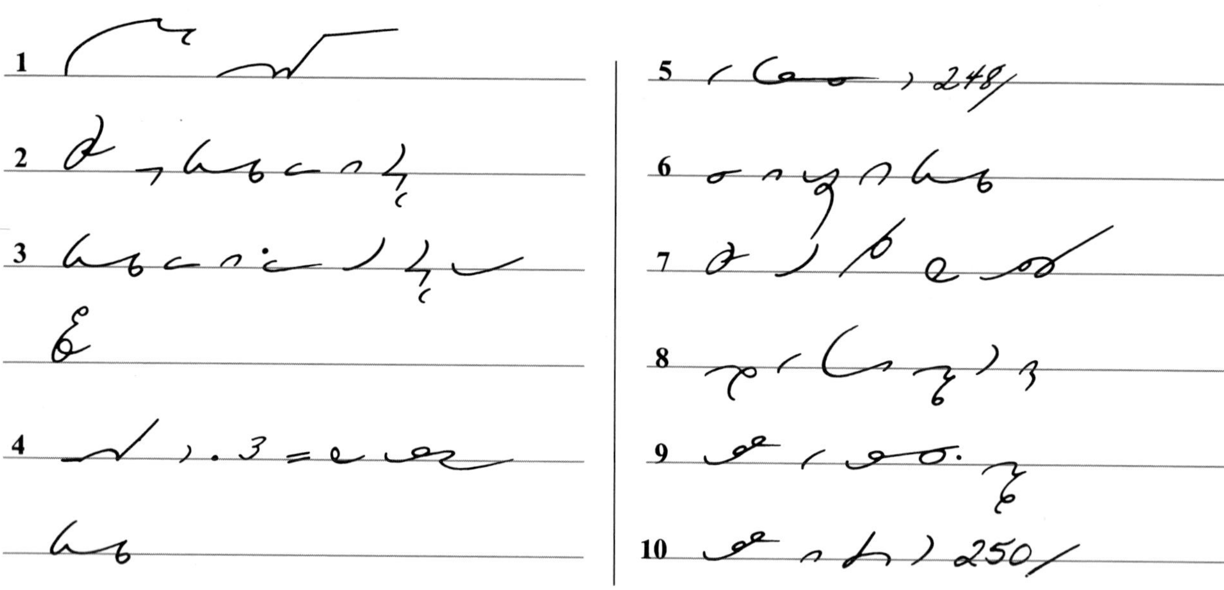

Transcription Practice

Transcribe the following letter for 2 minutes in unarranged format, applying transcription rules and assuring correct spelling. For every word not transcribed and every keyboarding error, deduct one word from the total word count.

11.3 Goal: 25 wam transcription rate

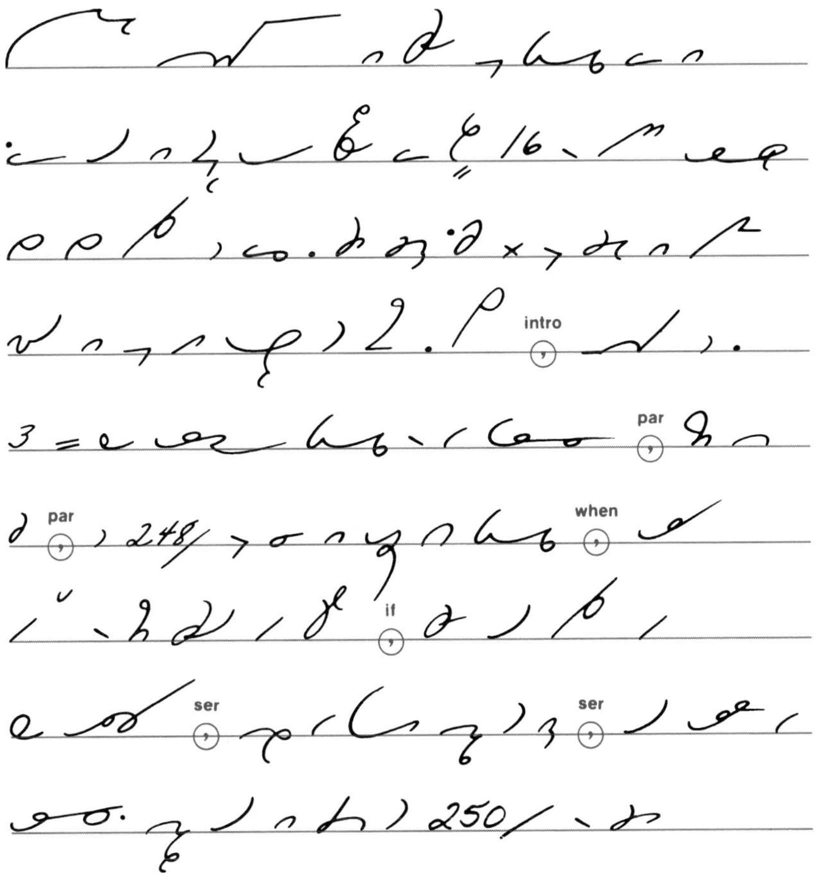

Word Count
10
24
36
48
58
68
80
92
104

Mailable Production

Transcribe the following mailable production letter in block style, assuring proper placement of all letter parts. Insert punctuation prior to transcribing, and capitalize proper nouns and titles. Address a large envelope with the special notation *Registered.*

11.4 Time Limit: 15 minutes

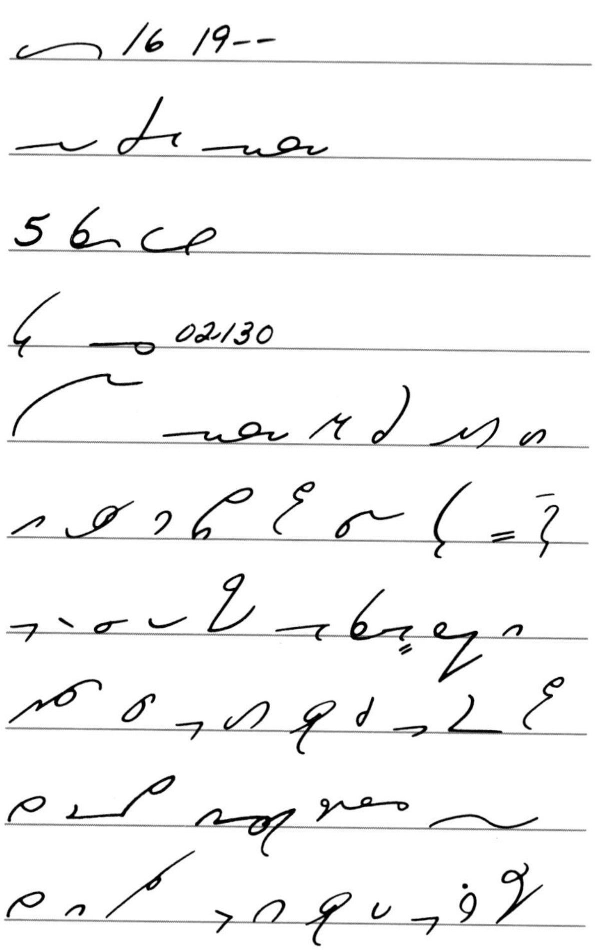

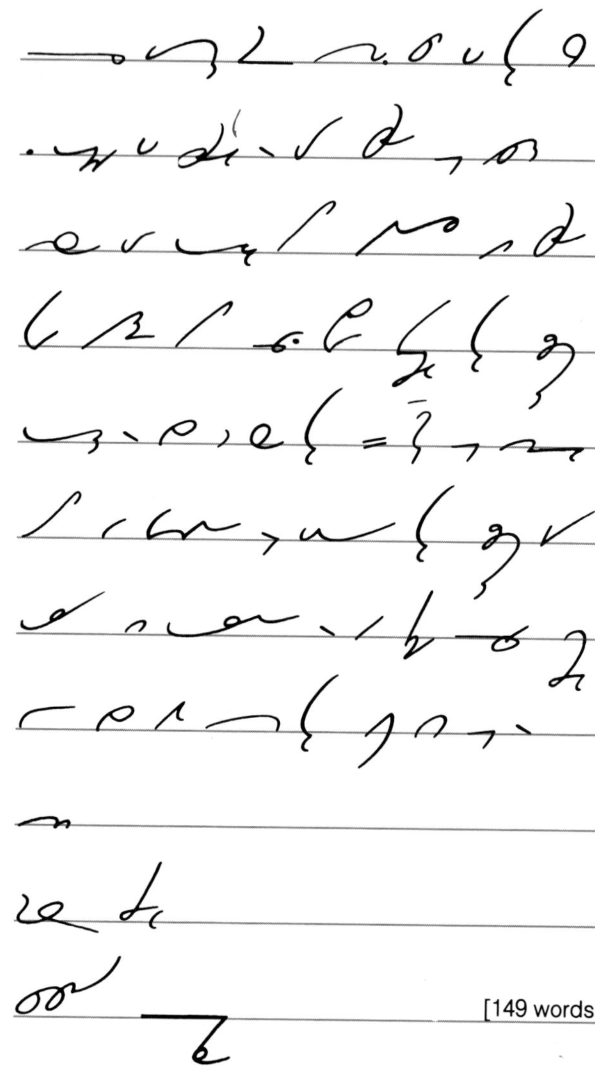

[149 words]

LESSON 12

MUTUAL INSURANCE COMPANY

DICTATION SPEED BUILDING

The shorthand outlines below appear in the speed dictation practice that follows. Practice writing these words using the shorthand outlines. Then, using the key that follows, dictate the words to yourself in preparation for the speed dictation practice.

Dictation Preview

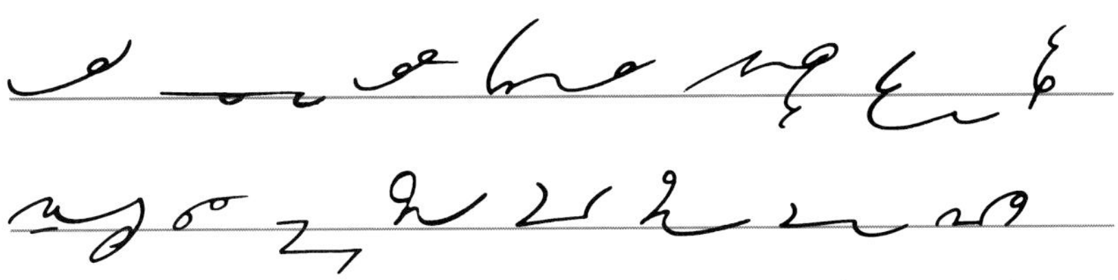

Key: leather, memorandum, return, booklet, describes, popular, special, qualify, within, information, as you will, from the, if you will, some of our, one of these

Speed Dictation Practice

12.1 Goal: 70 wam speed dictation

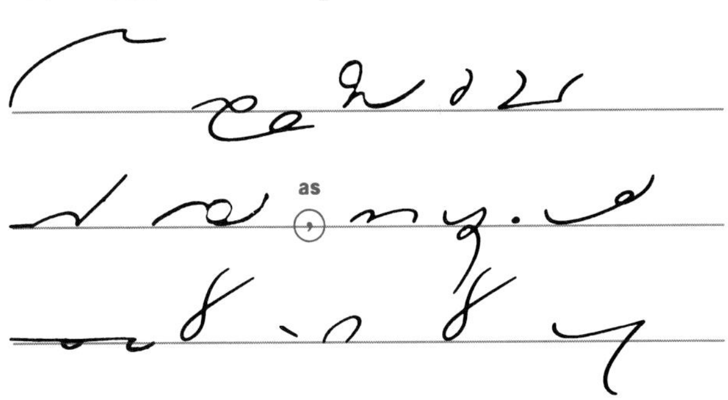

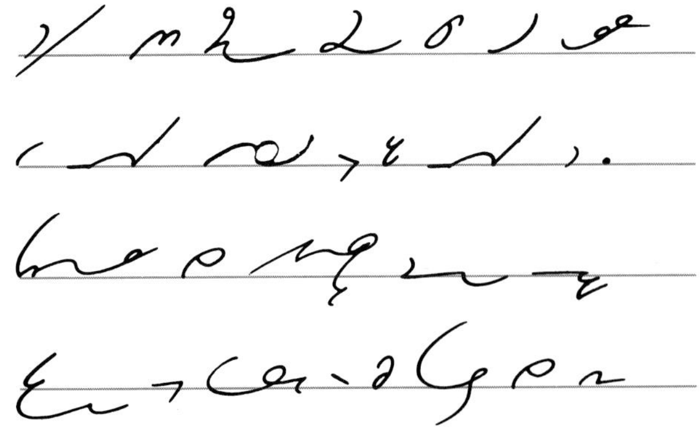

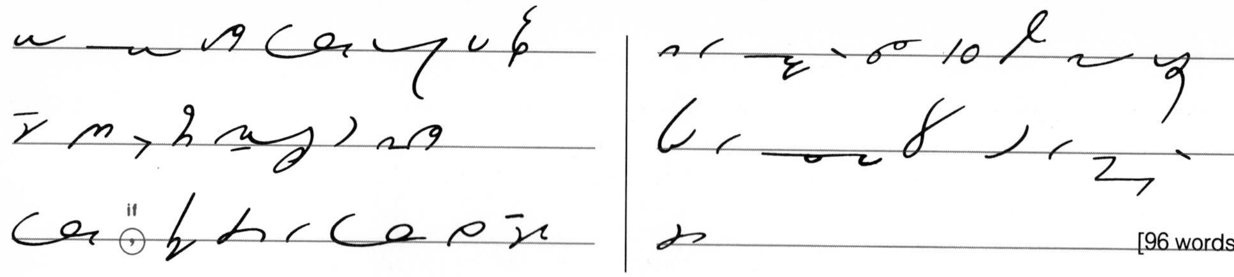

[96 words]

TRANSCRIPTION SKILL DEVELOPMENT

Transcription Warmup

Transcribe the following groups of words for speed and accuracy, applying transcription rules and assuring correct spelling.

12.2

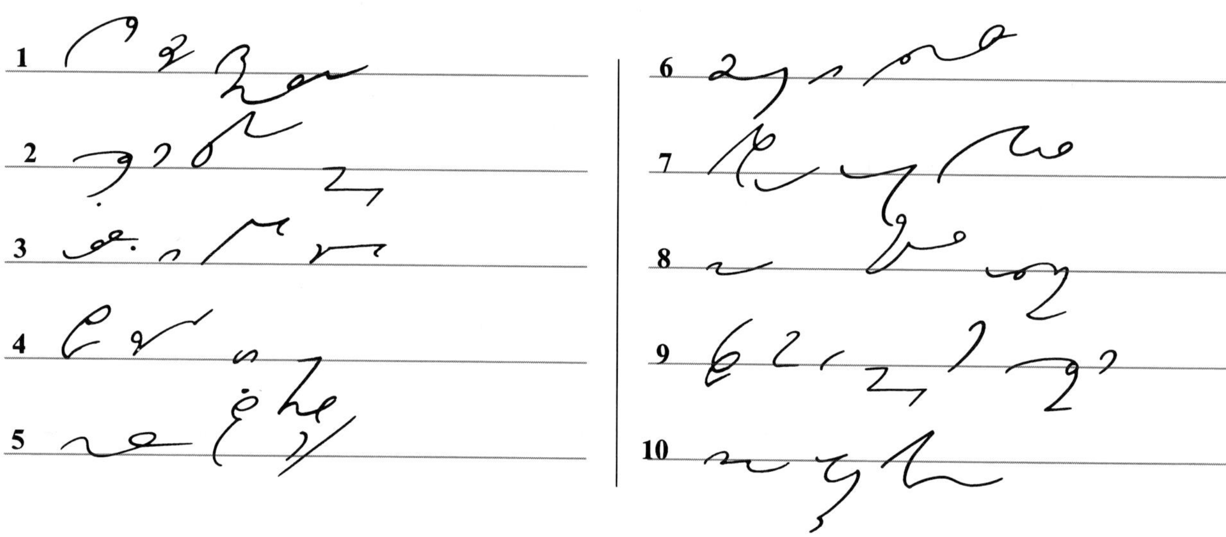

Transcription Practice

Transcribe the following letter for 2 minutes in unarranged format, applying transcription rules and assuring correct spelling. For every word not transcribed and every keyboarding error, deduct one word from the total word count.

12.3 Goal: 25 wam transcription rate

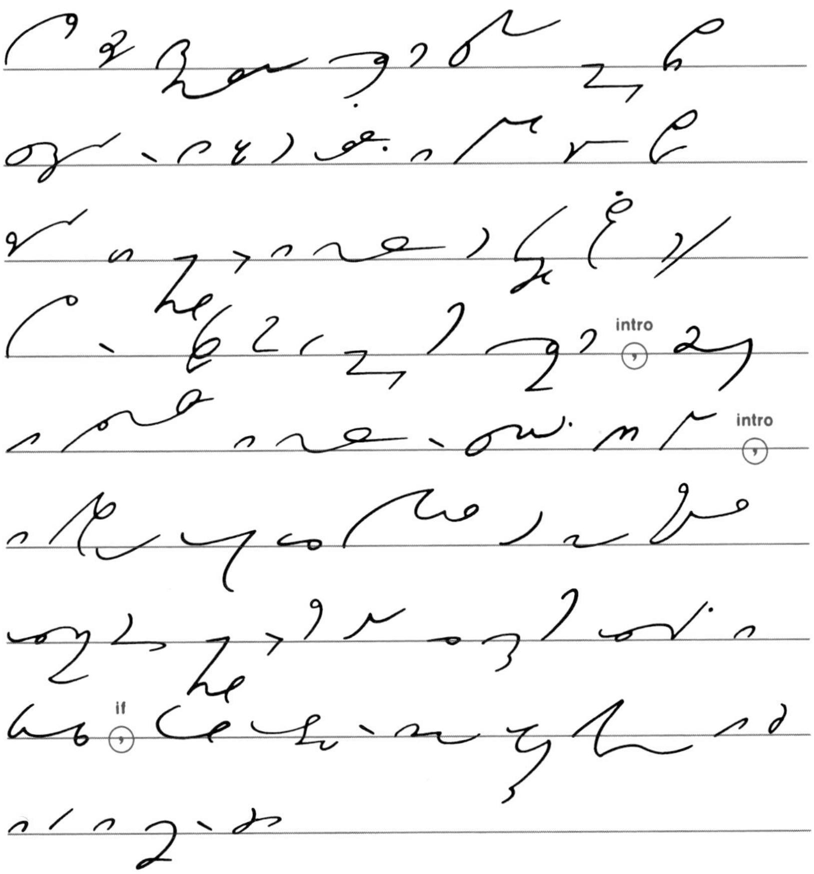

Word Count
17
32
46
59
69
81
97
112
120

Mailable Production

Transcribe the following mailable production letter in block style, assuring proper placement of all letter parts. Insert punctuation prior to transcribing, and capitalize proper nouns and titles. Address a large envelope with the special notation *Confidential.*

12.4 Time Limit: 15 minutes

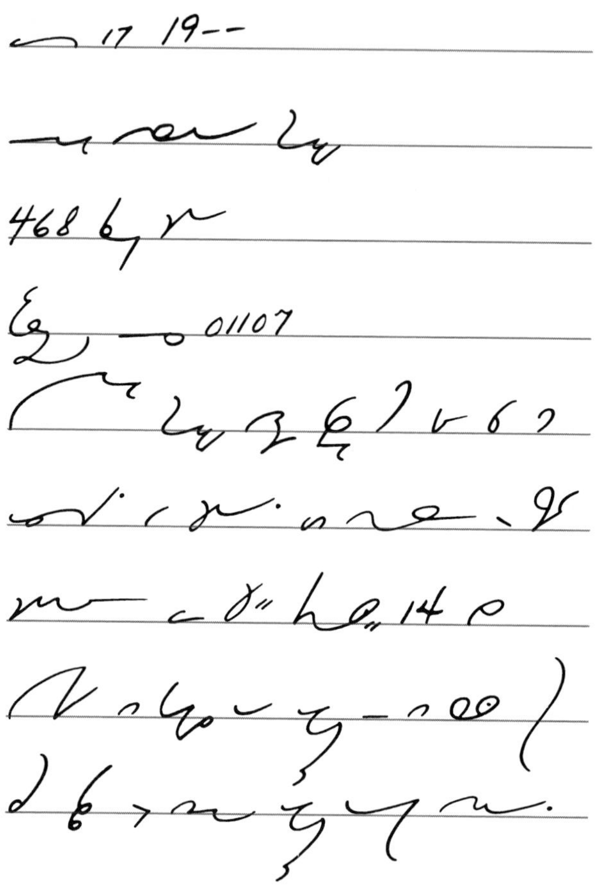

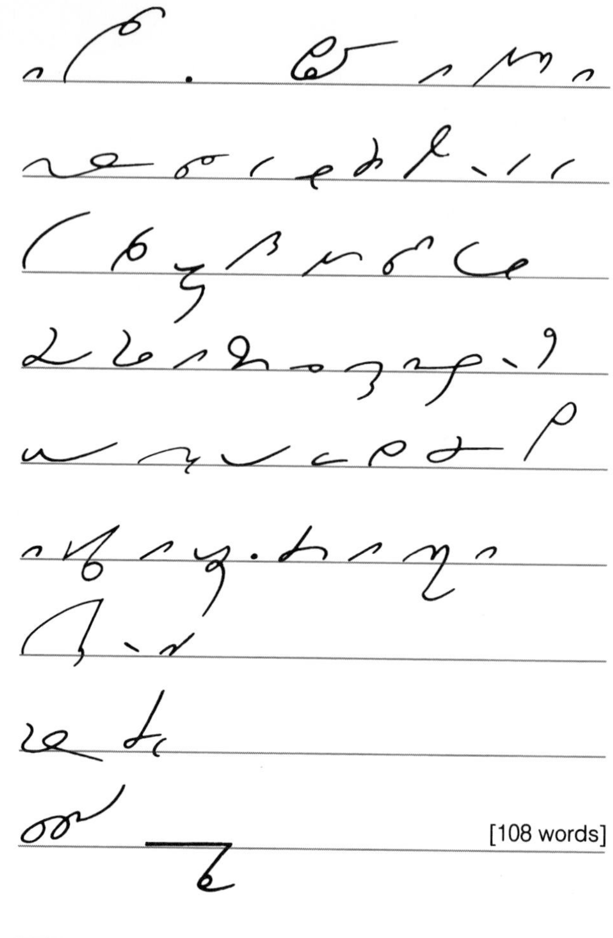

[108 words]

LESSON 13

MUTUAL INSURANCE COMPANY

DICTATION SPEED BUILDING

The shorthand outlines below appear in the speed dictation practice that follows. Practice writing these words using the shorthand outlines. Then, using the key that follows, dictate the words to yourself in preparation for the speed dictation practice.

Dictation Preview

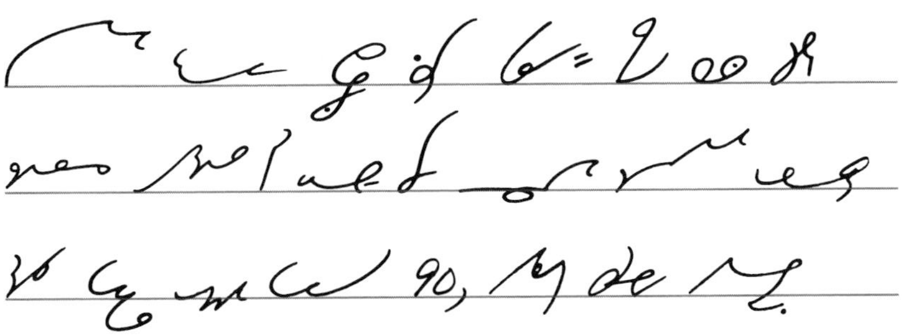

Key: Dear Mrs. Sloan, appreciate, behalf, Boyd, agent, area, satisfaction, extremely, industry, such, always, been, maintains, standards, realizes, substitute, properly, results, prompt, 90 percent, deserve, finest, delivering

Speed Dictation Practice

13.1 Goal: 70 wam dictation speed

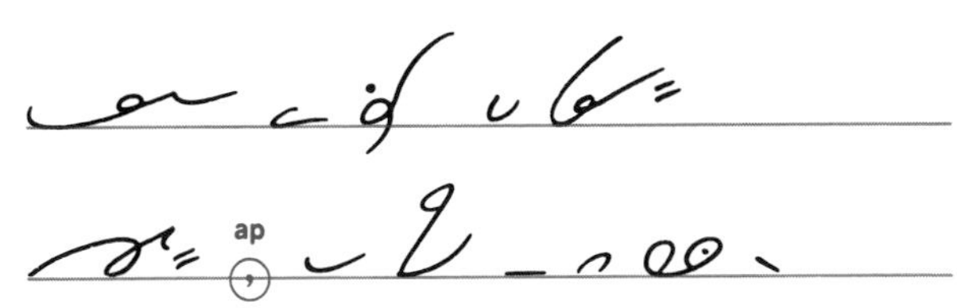

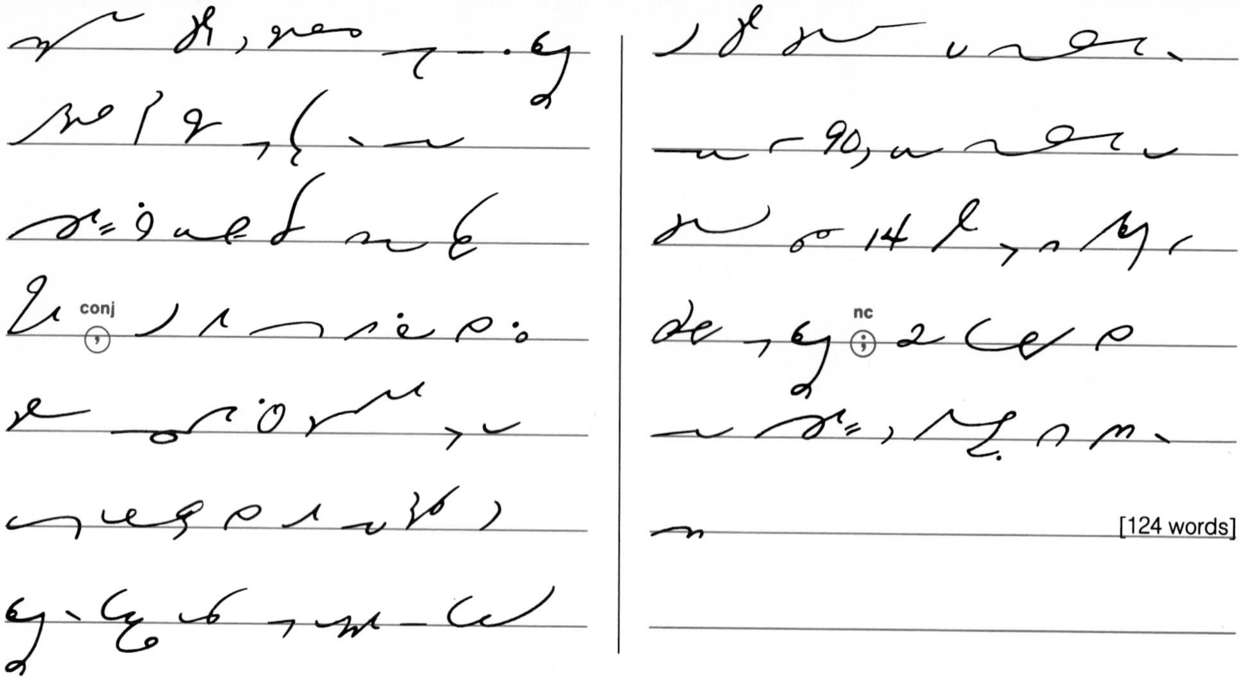

TRANSCRIPTION SKILL DEVELOPMENT

Transcription Warmup

Transcribe the following groups of words for speed and accuracy, applying transcription rules and assuring correct spelling.

13.2

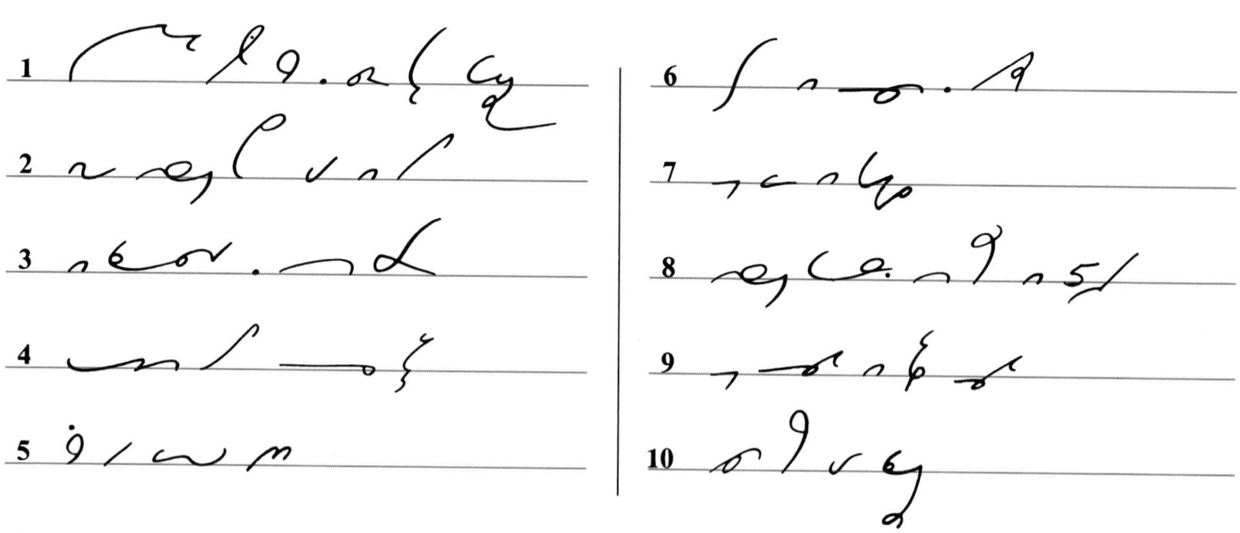

Transcription Practice

Transcribe the following letter for 2 minutes in unarranged format, applying transcription rules and assuring correct spelling. For every word not transcribed and every keyboarding error, deduct one word from the total word count.

13.3 Goal: 25 wam transcription rate

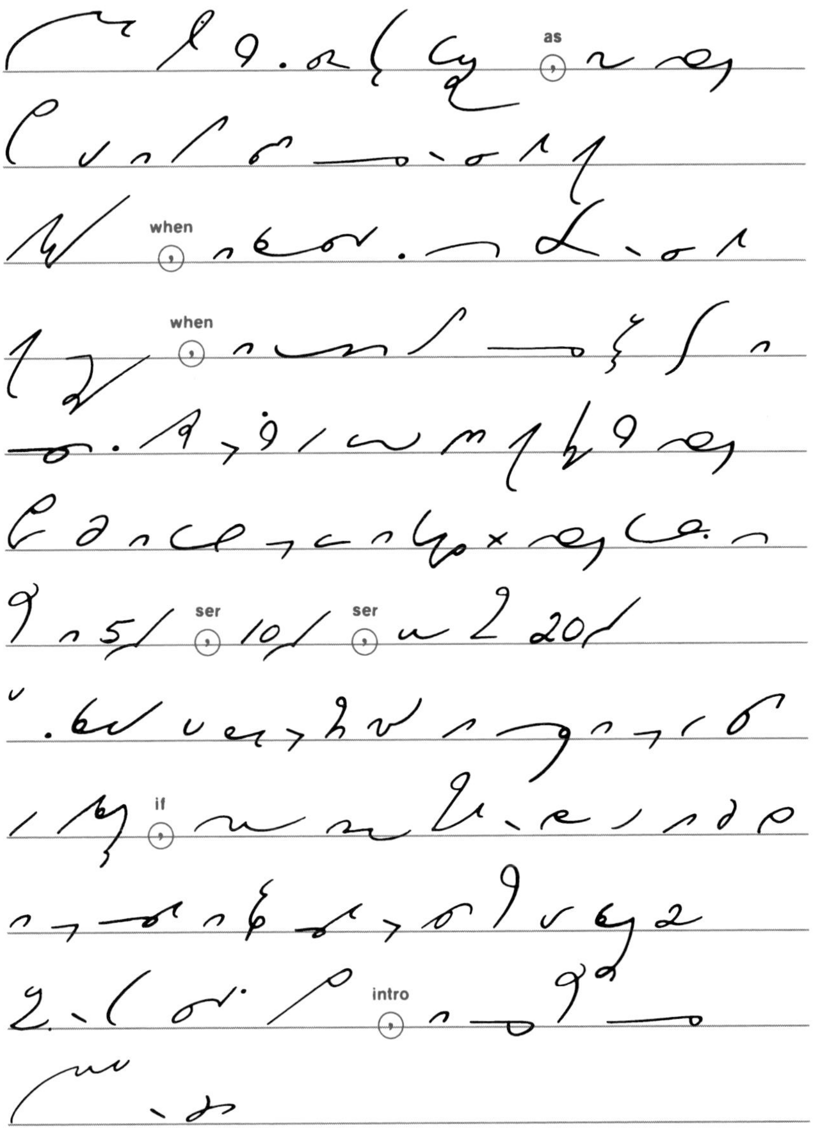

Word Count

13

23

32

43

55

70

78

93

106

122

131

136

Mailable Production

Transcribe the following mailable production letter in block style, assuring proper placement of all letter parts and special notation. Insert punctuation prior to transcribing, and capitalize proper nouns and titles. Add any special notations plus a copy notation for Joseph Baker on the letter. Address a large envelope.

13.4 Time Limit: 15 minutes

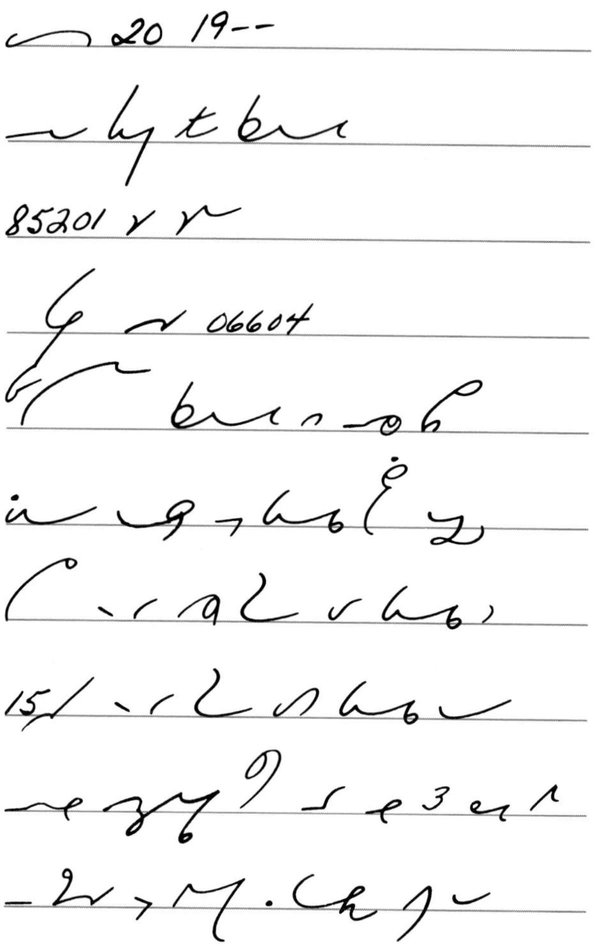

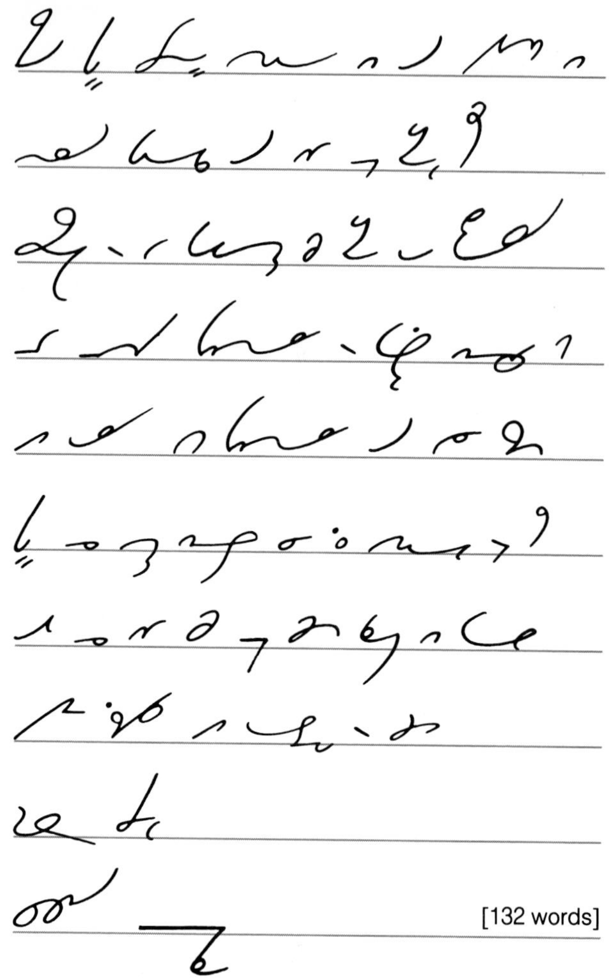

[132 words]

LESSON 14

MUTUAL INSURANCE COMPANY

DICTATION SPEED BUILDING

The shorthand outlines below appear in the speed dictation practice that follows. Practice writing these words using the shorthand outlines. Then, using the key that follows, dictate the words to yourself in preparation for the speed dictation practice.

Dictation Preview

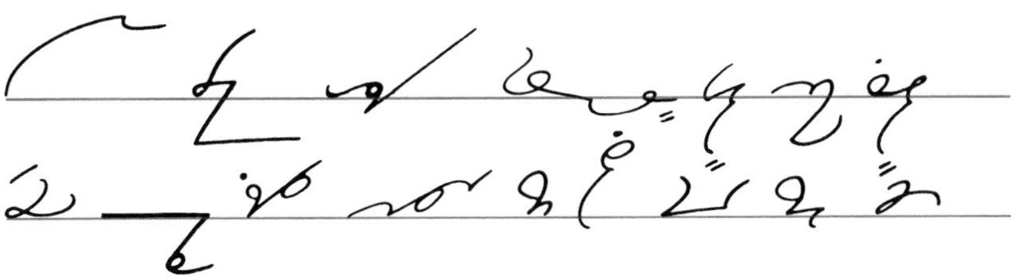

Key: Dear Mr. Benjamin, requested, Franklin, Pittsburgh, covered, Harrisburg, transferred, manager, hesitate, contact, as you, has been, from the, as soon as, we can

Speed Dictation Practice

14.1 Goal: 70 wam speed dictation

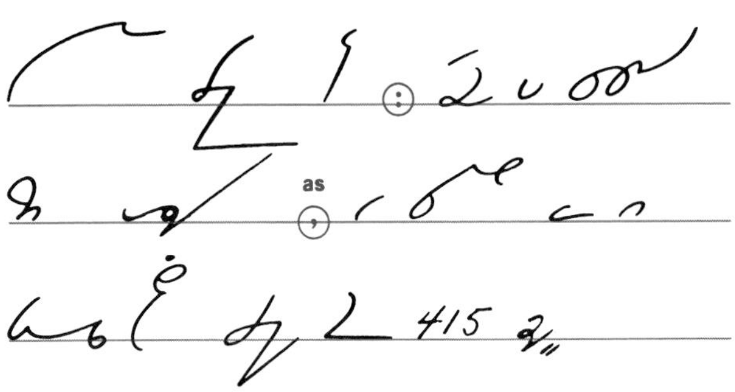

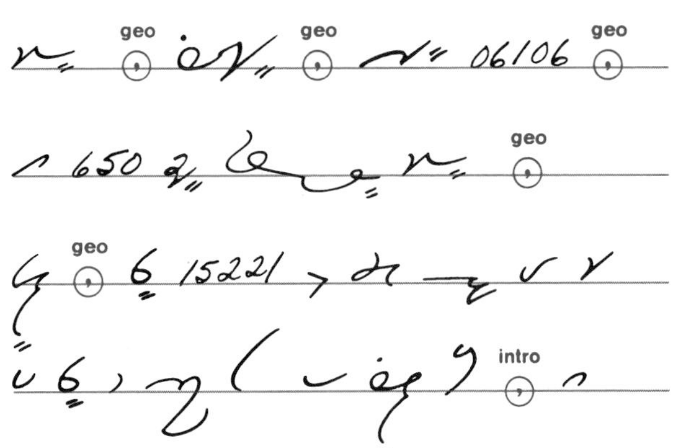

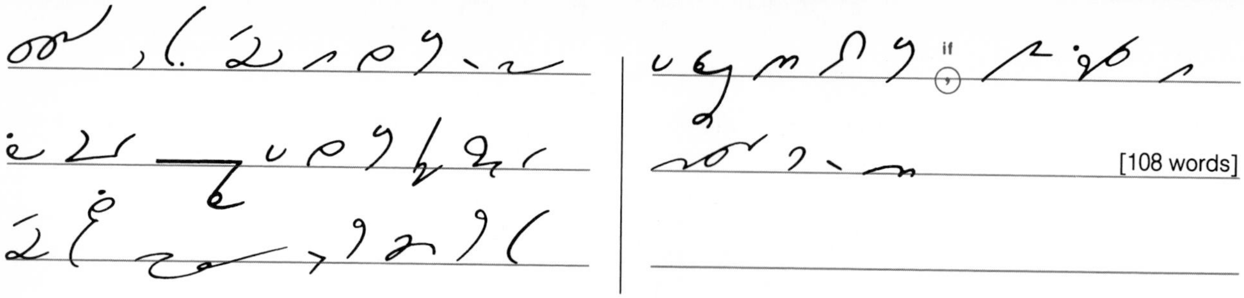

[108 words]

TRANSCRIPTION SKILL DEVELOPMENT

Transcription Warmup

Transcribe the following groups of words for speed and accuracy, applying transcription rules and assuring correct spelling.

14.2

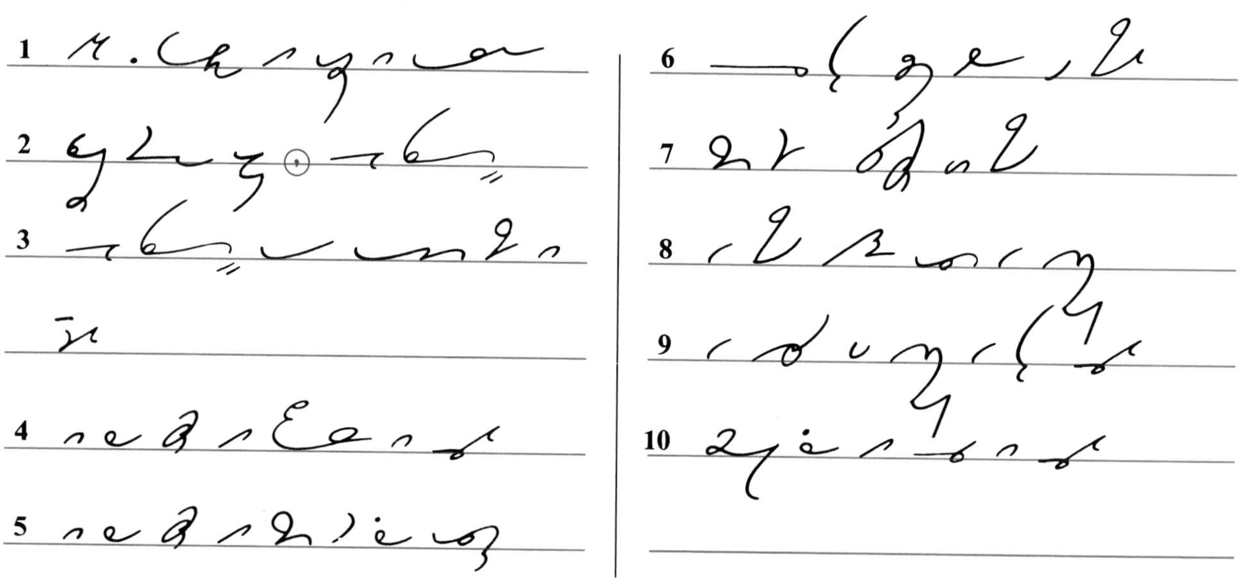

Transcription Practice

Transcribe the following letter for 2 minutes in unarranged format, applying transcription rules and assuring correct spelling. For every word not transcribed and every keyboarding error, deduct one word from the total word count.

14.3 Goal: 25 wam transcription rate

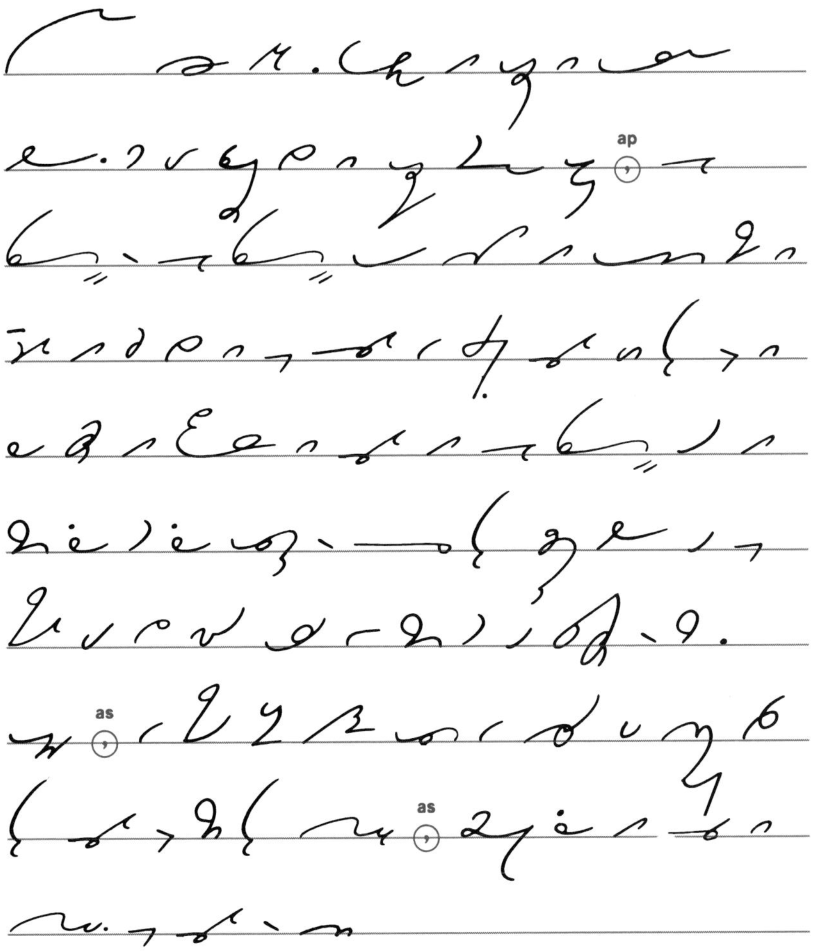

Word Count
11
26
36
53
63
79
91
106
120
128

Mailable Production

Transcribe the following mailable production letter in block style, assuring proper placement of all letter parts and special notations. Insert punctuation prior to transcribing, and capitalize proper nouns and titles. Address a large envelope.

14.4 Time Limit: 15 minutes

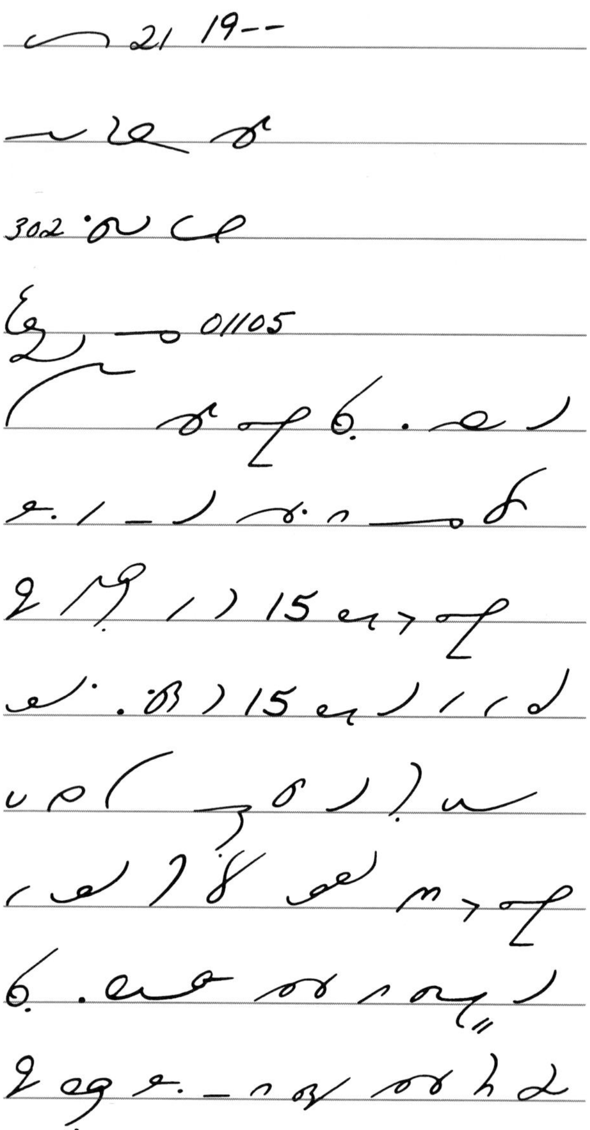

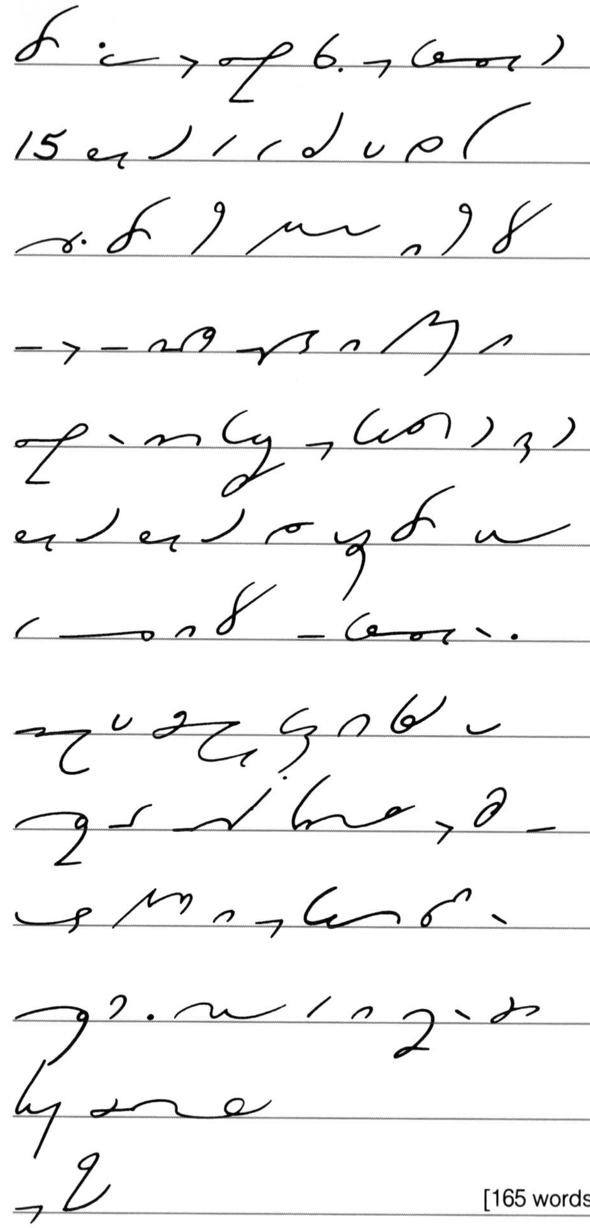

[165 words]

LESSON

15

MUTUAL INSURANCE COMPANY

DICTATION SPEED BUILDING

The shorthand outlines below appear in the speed dictation practice that follows. Practice writing these words using the shorthand outlines. Then, using the key that follows, dictate the words to yourself in preparation for the speed dictation practice.

Dictation Preview

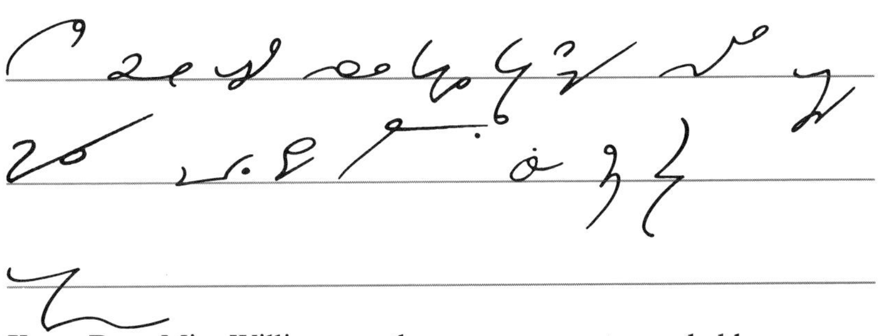

Key: Dear Miss Willis, recently, carry, property, probably, underinsured, country, reviewed, updated, something, assist, determining, higher, if you have, have not been, will be glad

Speed Dictation Practice

15.1 Goal: 70 wam speed dictation

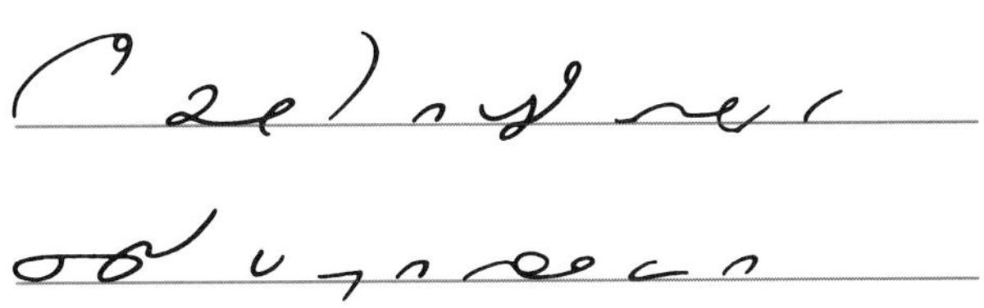

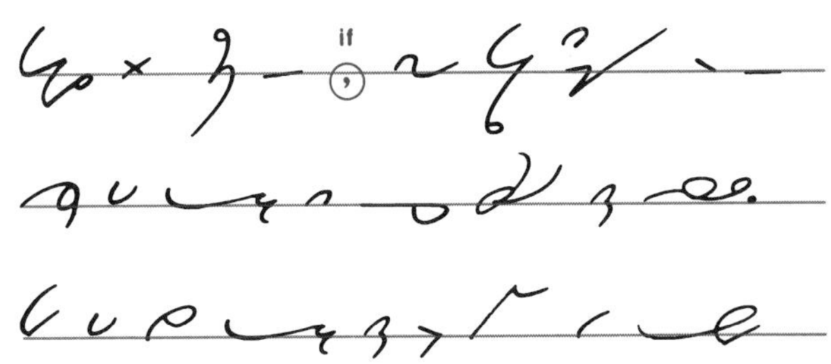

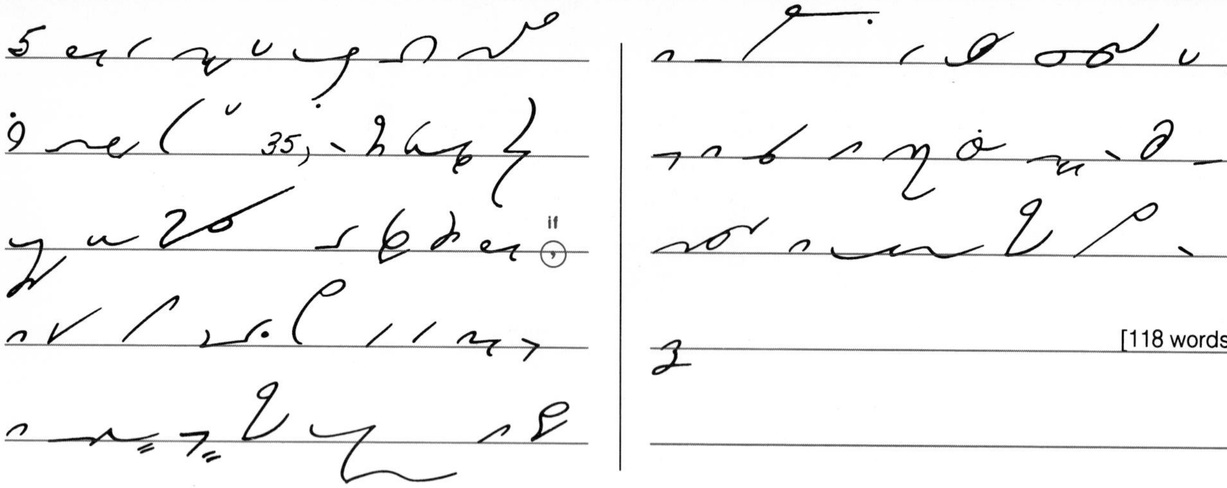

TRANSCRIPTION SKILL DEVELOPMENT

Transcription Warmup

Transcribe the following groups of words for speed and accuracy, applying transcription rules and assuring correct spelling.

15.2

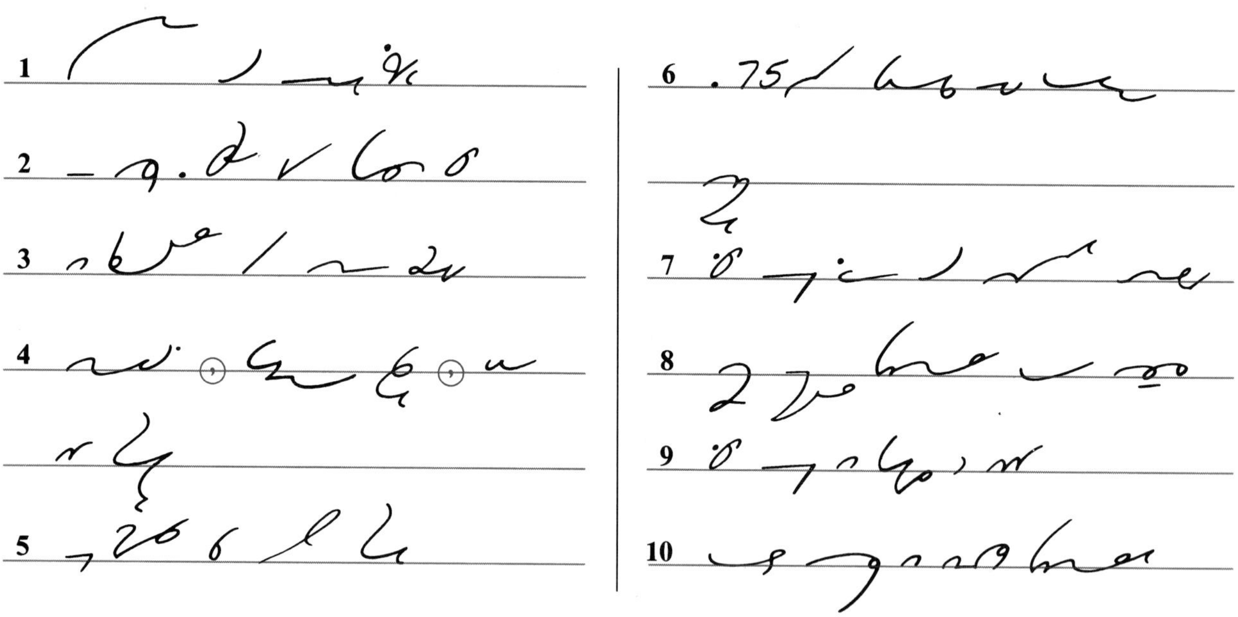

Transcription Practice

Transcribe the following letter for 2 minutes in unarranged format, applying transcription rules and assuring correct spelling. For every word not transcribed and every keyboarding error, deduct one word from the total word count.

15.3 Goal: 25 wam transcription rate

Mailable Production

Transcribe the following mailable production letter in block style, assuring proper placement of all letter parts and special notation. Insert punctuation prior to transcribing, and capitalize proper nouns and titles. Address a large envelope with the special notation *Special Delivery*.

15.4 Time Limit: 15 minutes

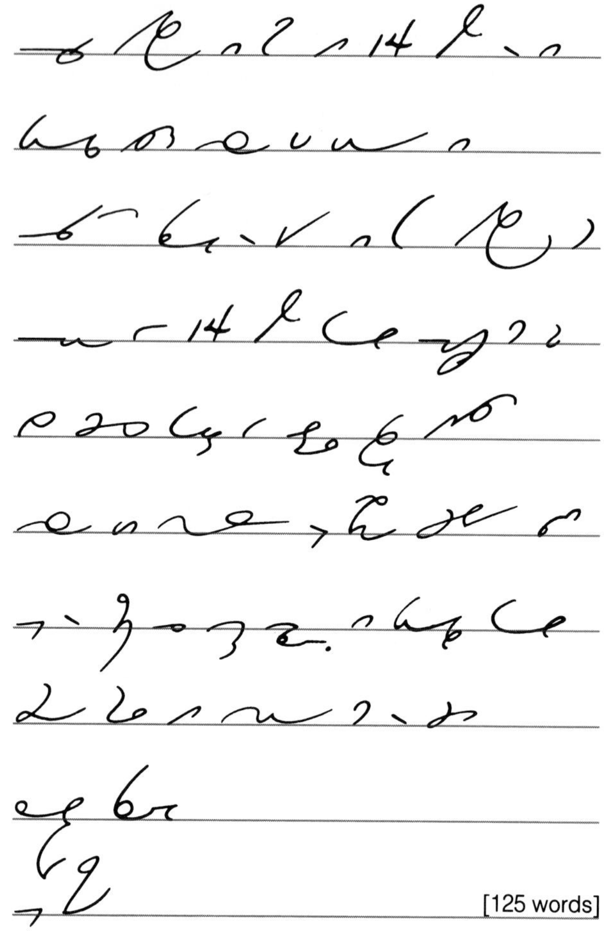

[125 words]

LESSON 16

MUTUAL INSURANCE COMPANY

DICTATION SPEED BUILDING

The shorthand outlines below appear in the speed dictation practice that follows. Practice writing these words using the shorthand outlines. Then, using the key that follows, dictate the words to yourself in preparation for the speed dictation practice.

Dictation Preview

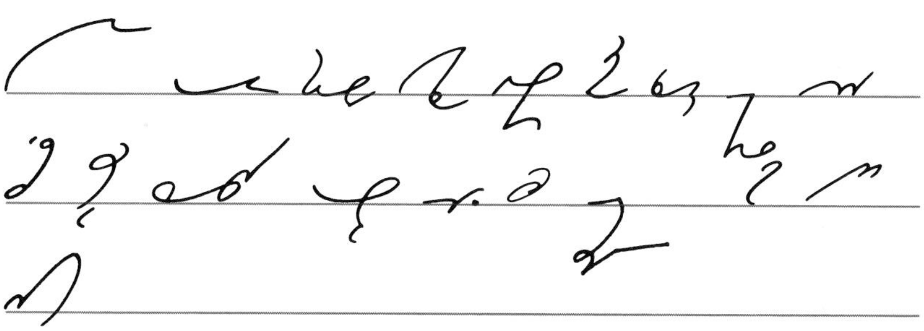

Key: Dear Mr. Long, forest, danger, tragic, suffer, serious, injury, cut, heavy, savings, allowed, lapse, nothing, why, investment, up, do you, you would have

Speed Dictation Practice

16.1 Goal: 70 wam speed dictation

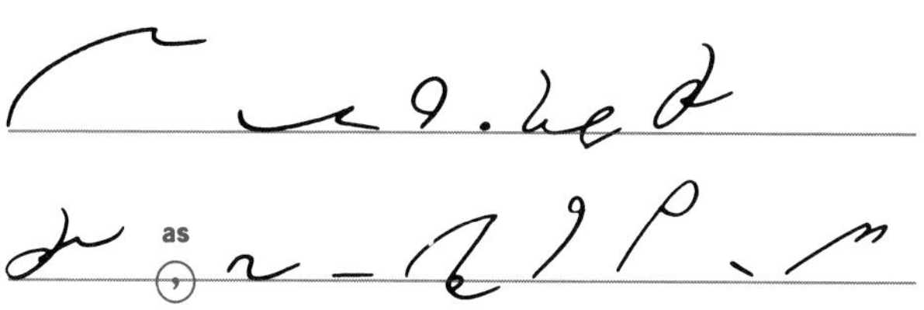

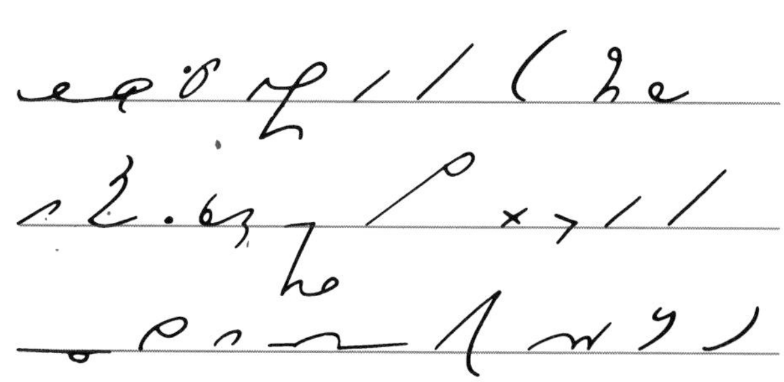

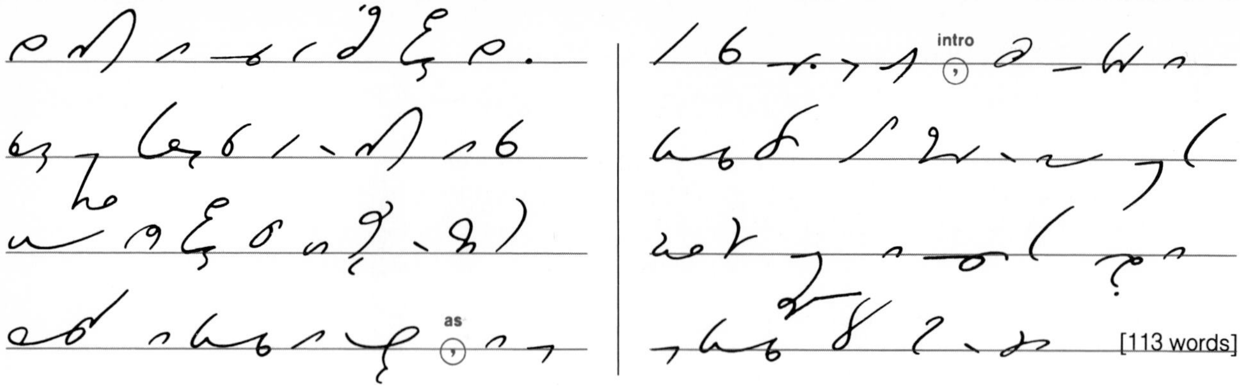

TRANSCRIPTION SKILL DEVELOPMENT

Transcription Warmup

Transcribe the following groups of words for speed and accuracy, applying transcription rules and assuring correct spelling.

16.2

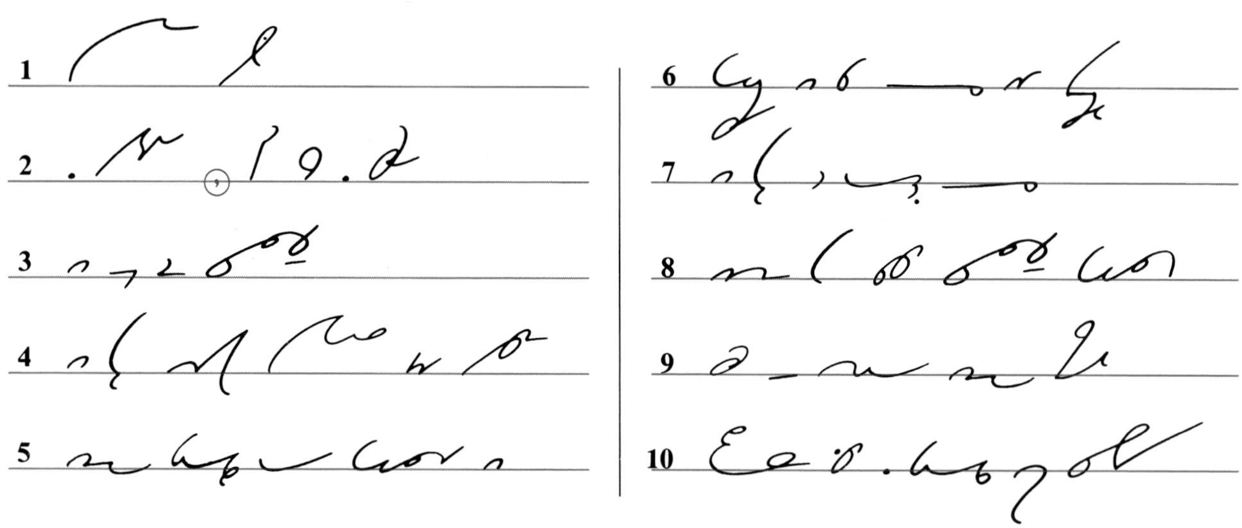

Transcription Practice

Transcribe the following letter for 2 minutes in unarranged format, applying transcription rules and assuring correct spelling. For every word not transcribed and every keyboarding error, deduct one word from the total word count.

16.3 Goal: 25 wam transcription rate

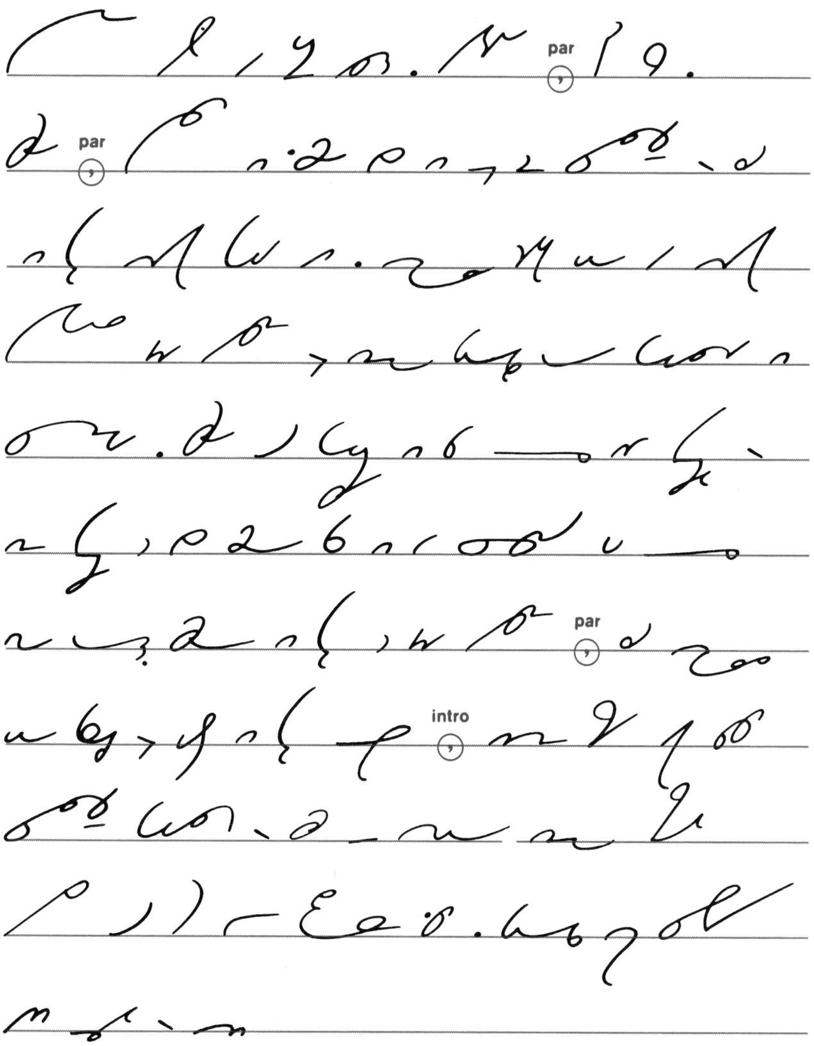

Word Count

10
24
38
50
61
72
85
100
111
122
128

Mailable Production

Transcribe the following mailable production letter in block style, assuring proper placement of all letter parts and special notation. Insert punctuation prior to transcribing, and capitalize proper nouns and titles. Address a large envelope.

16.4 Time Limit: 15 minutes

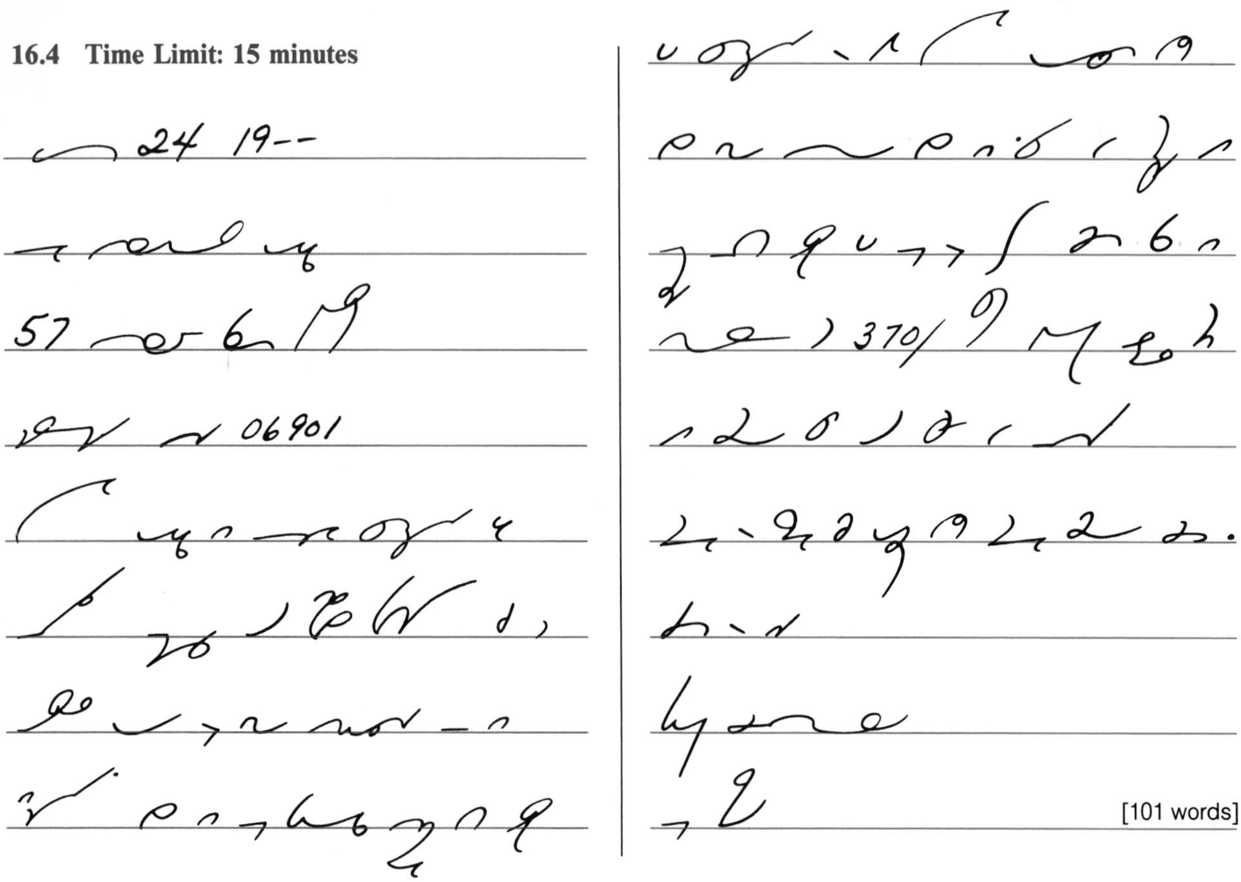

[101 words]

UNIT III

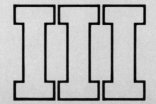

FRANKLIN REAL ESTATE AGENCY

LESSON 17

FRANKLIN REAL ESTATE AGENCY

You are employed as an administrative assistant for the Franklin Real Estate Agency in Phoenix, Arizona. In your position you will report to Philip Franklin, president. Franklin Real Estate is a privately owned real estate company with no branch offices. Mr. Franklin opened this agency in 1978 and has three sales agents on staff, Carla Clark, Sam Byrd, and Philip Pierce.

Your responsibilities are varied and include answering the telephone, replying to inquiries about property listings, setting up appointments for the agents, using database software to track property listings, taking dictation from Mr. Franklin and the three sales agents, and typing correspondence using a computer with word processing software.

As you work through the materials, you will acquire knowledge about the many facets of the real estate area, as well as develop additional proficiency in dictation speed and increase your transcription speed and accuracy. The mailable production letters in the lessons and the letters the instructor dictates will provide you with the opportunity to type correspondence for the signature of Philip Franklin, president, and the three sales agents on staff.

Below is a copy of your company letterhead. Develop the return address that you will use to type the envelope for the mailable production letters. Remember that above the return address you will add the sender's name.

FRANKLIN REAL ESTATE AGENCY

328 Indian School Road
Phoenix, AZ 85011 (602) 555-8631

Transcription Tip

Forms are used in varying degrees by business and industry. Below is a sample of a form you may be required to complete for the Franklin Real Estate Agency.

FRANKLIN REAL ESTATE AGENCY

Listing Information for House

Name of client(s): Daniel and Martha Collins

Address: 329 Indian School Road
Phoenix, AZ 85000

Telephone No.: (602) 555-7311 (home)
555-3821 (husband's office)
555-2894 (wife's office)

Number of rooms: 9	Size of lot: 2.5 acres
Dimensions of rooms:	Number of garages: 2
Kitchen 10 x 12	Other buildings on property: None
Living room 12 x 22	Special features: Fireplace in LR
Dining room 12 x 17	Deck
Family room 12 x 20	Landscaped
Study/Den 12 x 15	
Master bedroom 12 x 18	Appraised value: $280,000
Master bathroom 6 x 9	Year house was built: 1948
Bedroom 12 x 15	Type of heating system: Gas
Bedroom 11 x 14	Average monthly heating bill: $95
Bedroom 8 x 11	
Bathroom 5 x 7	
Bathroom 5 x 7	
Powder room 4 x 5	
Foyer 10 x 12	
Basement 24 x 36	
Others	

DICTATION SPEED BUILDING

The shorthand outlines below appear in the speed dictation practice that follows. Practice writing these words using the shorthand outlines. Then, using the key that follows, dictate the words to yourself in preparation for the speed dictation practice.

Dictation Preview

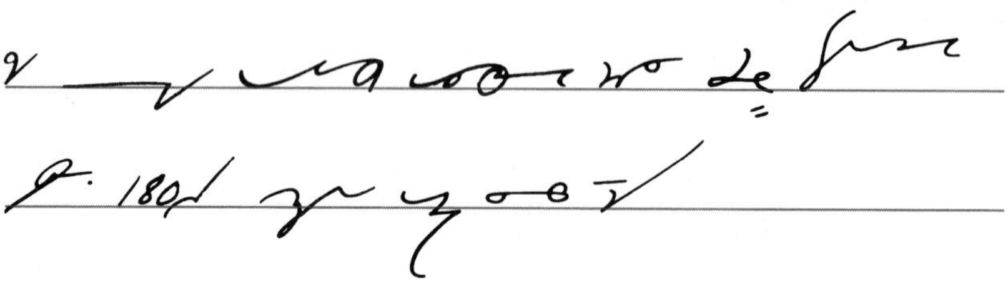

Key: yesterday, mentioned, location, requirements, southern, Phoenix, bedrooms, dining, $180,000, consider, reasonable, immediately, interested

Speed Dictation Practice

17.1 Goal: 80 wam speed dictation

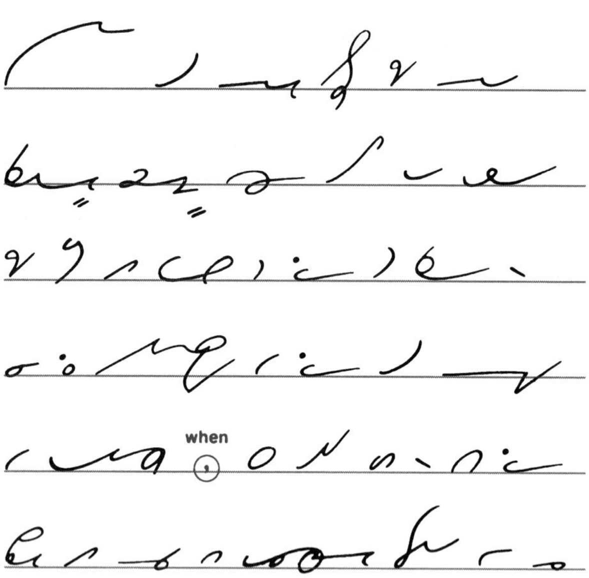

[104 words]

TRANSCRIPTION SKILL DEVELOPMENT

Transcription Warmup

Transcribe the following groups of words for speed and accuracy, applying transcription rules and assuring correct spelling.

17.2

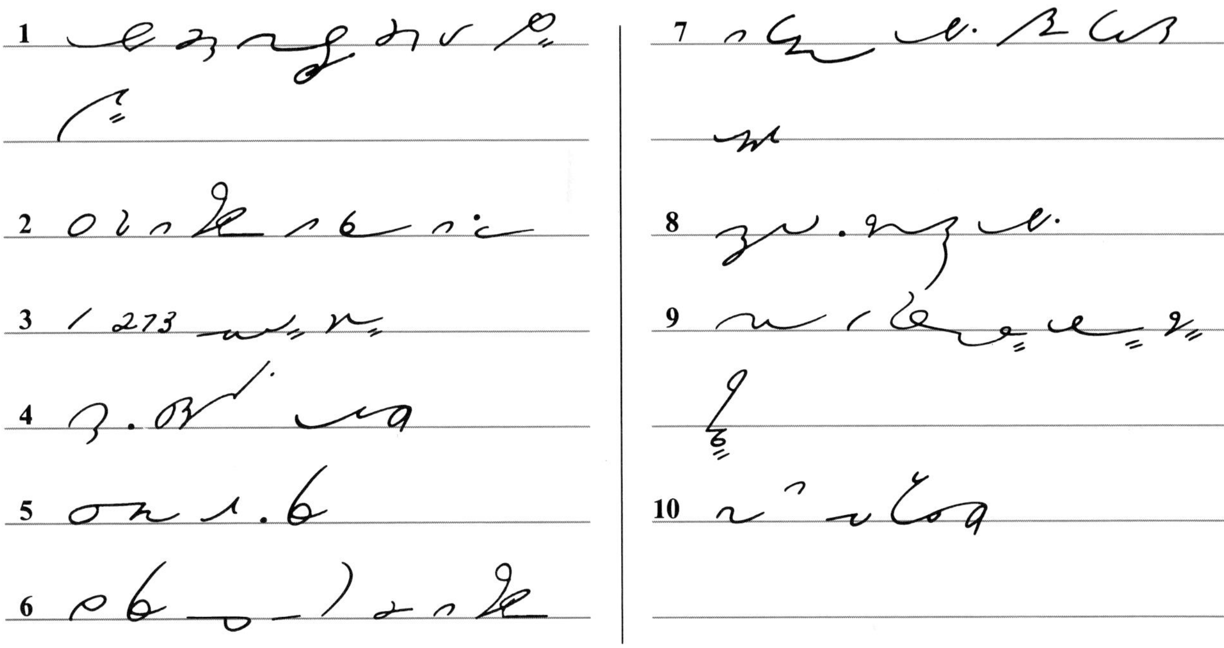

Transcription Practice

Transcribe the following letter for 2 minutes in unarranged format, applying transcription rules and assuring correct spelling. For every word not transcribed and every keyboarding error, deduct one word from the total word count.

17.3 Goal: 25 wam transcription rate

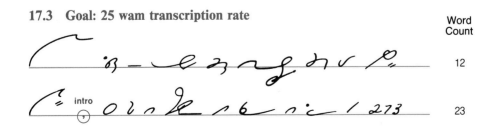

Word Count

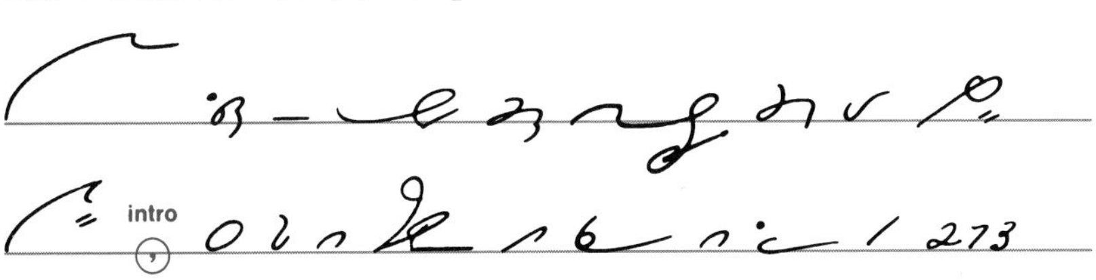

12

23

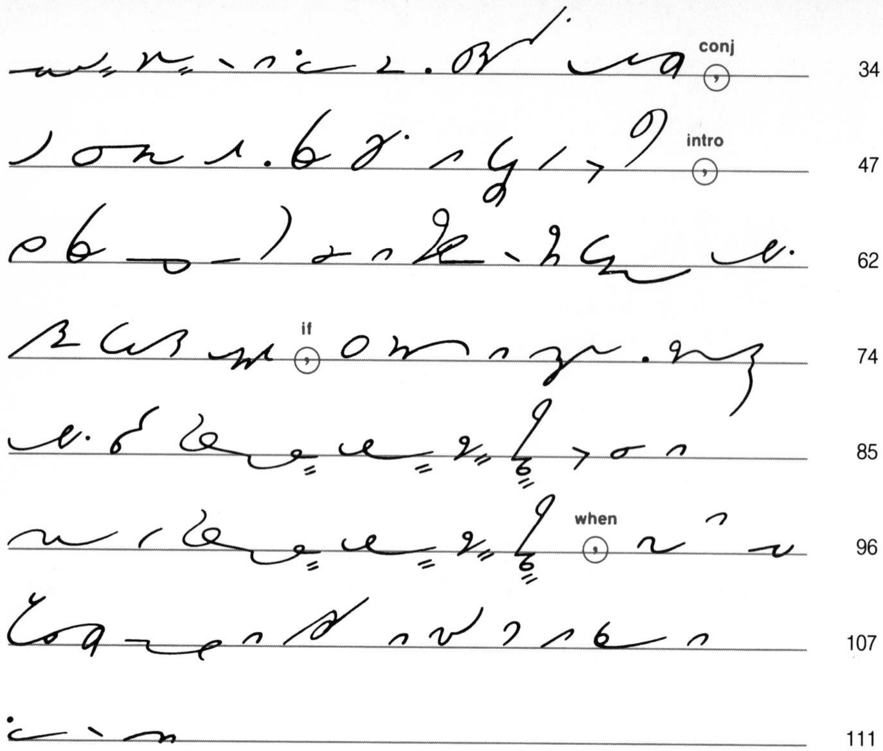
conj
34
intro
47
62
if
74
85
when
96
107
111

LESSON 18

FRANKLIN REAL ESTATE AGENCY

DICTATION SPEED BUILDING

The shorthand outlines below appear in the speed dictation practice that follows. Practice writing these words using the shorthand outlines. Then, using the key that follows, dictate the words to yourself in preparation for the speed dictation practice.

Dictation Preview

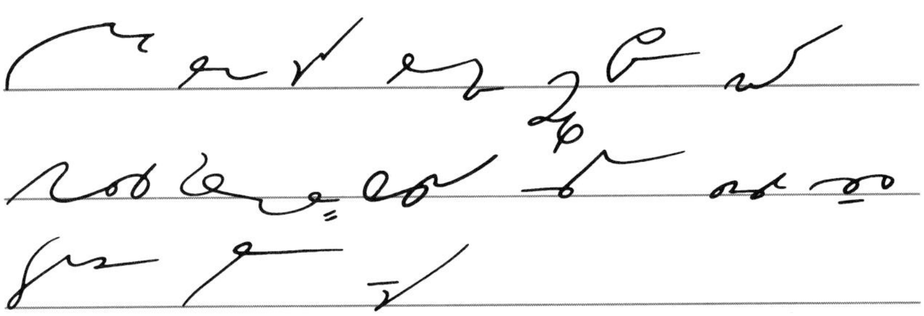

Key: Dear Mrs. Turner, stated, telephone, conversation, apartment, wanted, duplicate, Franklin, around, middle, units, quickly, bedroom, determine, interested

Speed Dictation Practice

18.1 Goal: 80 wam speed dictation

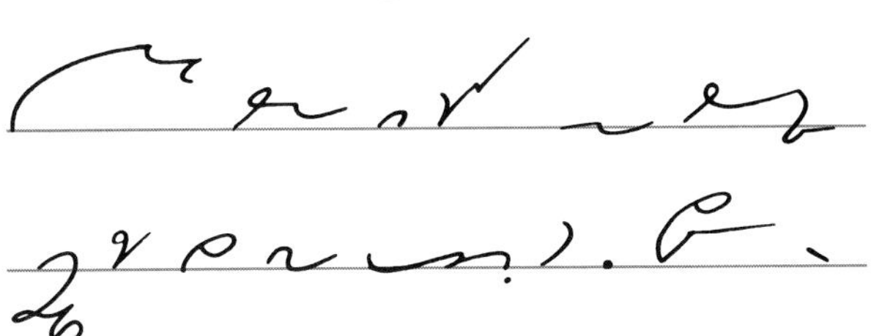

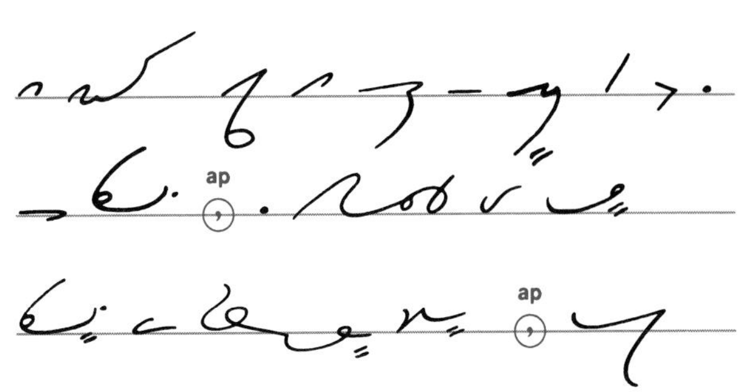

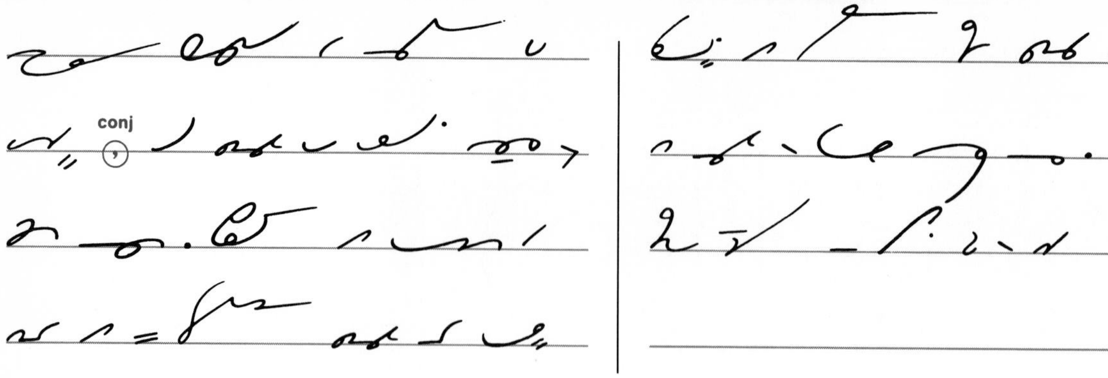

[97 words]

TRANSCRIPTION SKILL DEVELOPMENT

Transcription Warmup

Transcribe the following groups of words for speed and accuracy, applying transcription rules and assuring correct spelling.

18.2

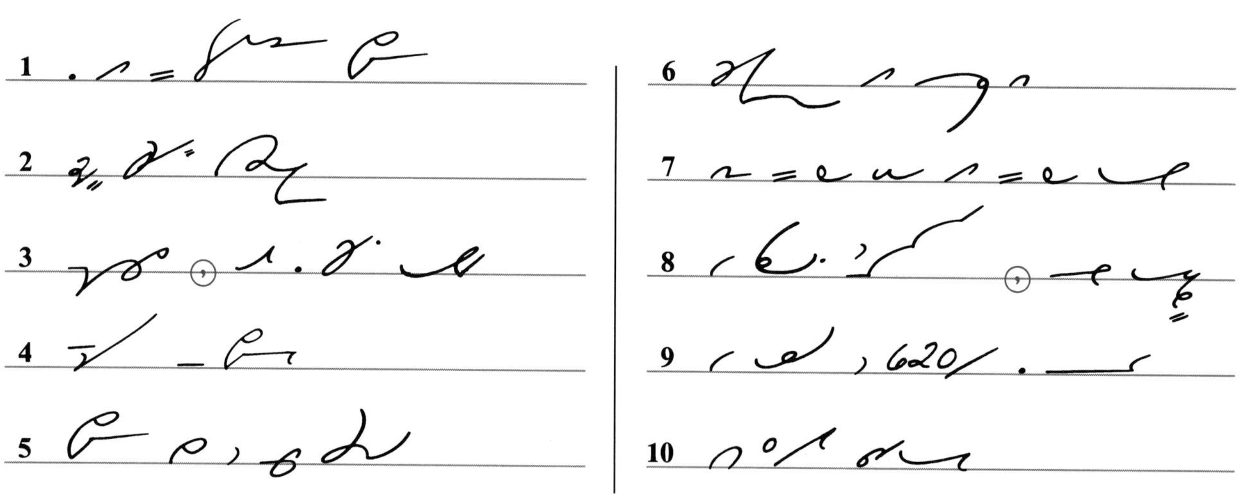

Transcription Practice

Transcribe the following letter for 2 minutes in unarranged format, applying transcription rules and assuring correct spelling. For every word not transcribed and every keyboarding error, deduct one word from the total word count.

18.3 Goal: 25 wam transcription rate

Word Count

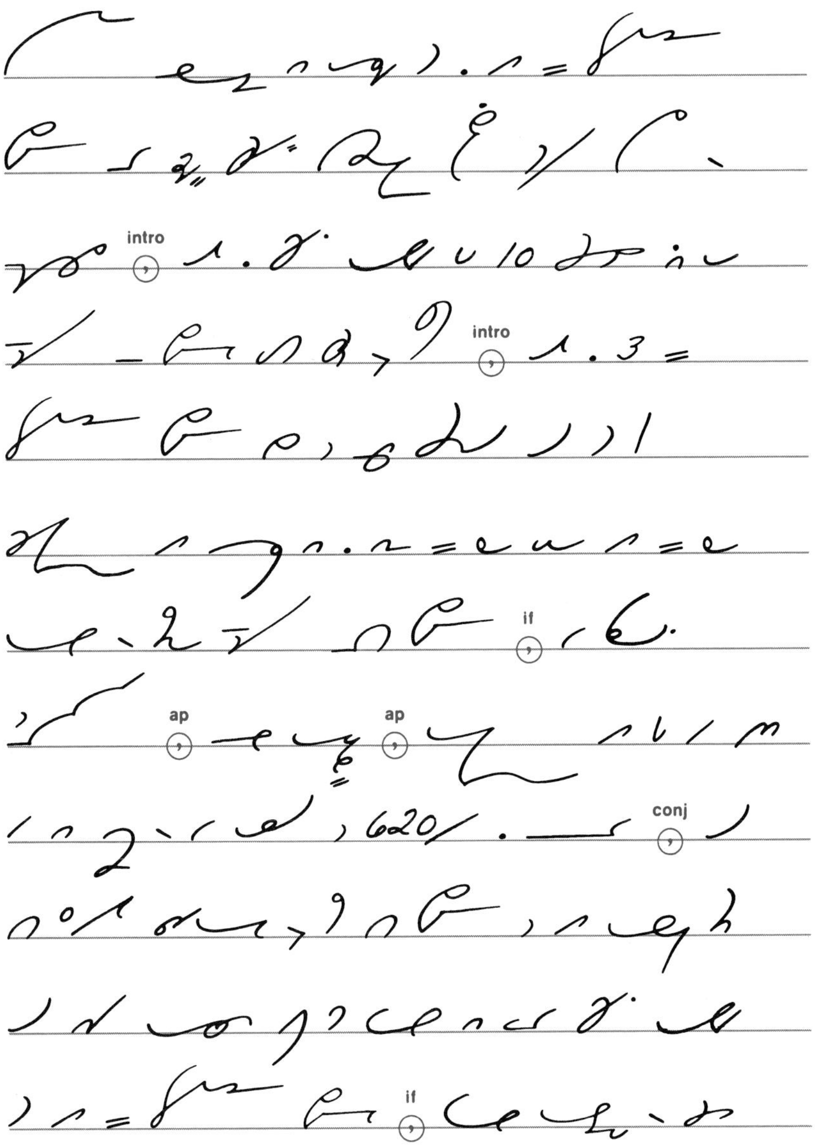

9
22
34
47
57
67
79
93
101
115
127
139

Mailable Production

Transcribe the following mailable production letter in block style, assuring proper placement of all letter parts. Insert punctuation prior to transcribing, and capitalize proper nouns and titles. Address a large envelope with the special notation *Confidential.*

18.4 Time Limit: 15 minutes

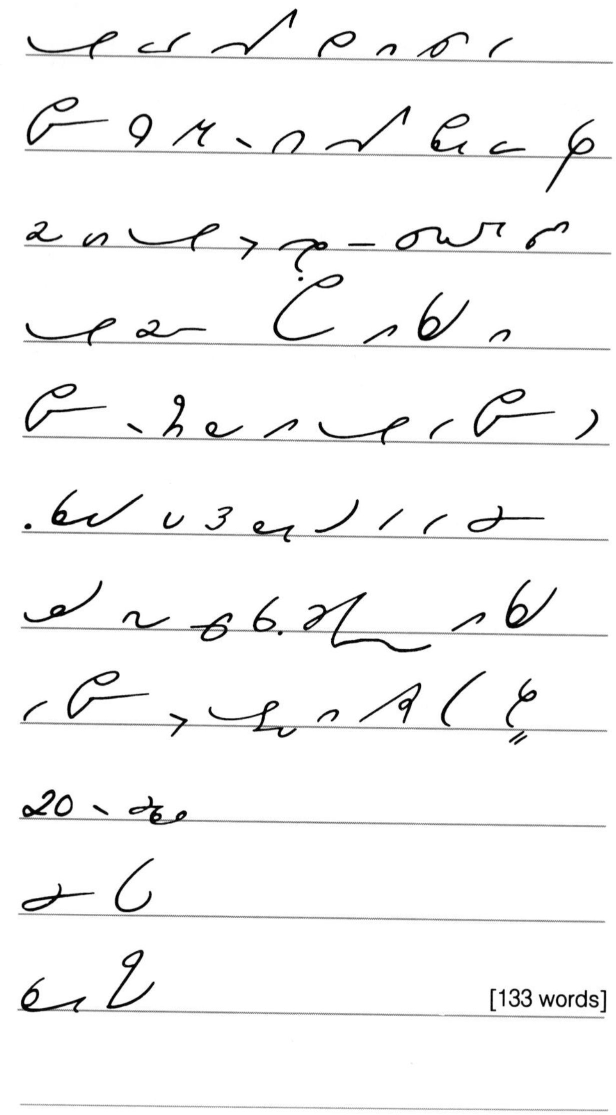

[133 words]

LESSON 19

FRANKLIN REAL ESTATE AGENCY

DICTATION SPEED BUILDING

The shorthand outlines below appear in the speed dictation practice that follows. Practice writing these words using the shorthand outlines. Then, using the key that follows, dictate the words to yourself in preparation for the speed dictation practice.

Dictation Preview

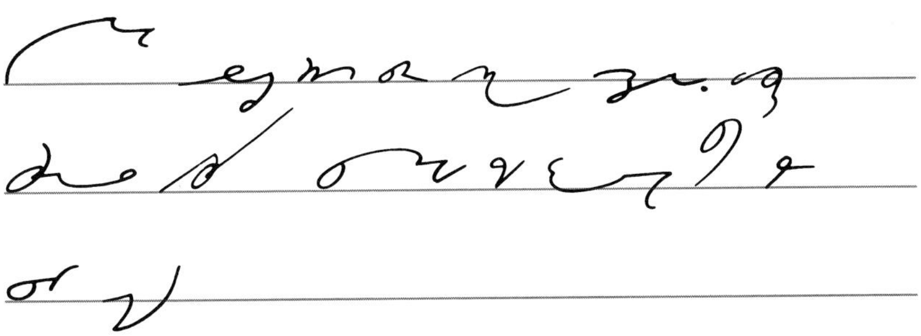

Key: Dear Mrs. Murphy, success, young, couple, considering, occasions, finally, decided, against, estate, slump, however, turn, another, informed

Speed Dictation Practice

19.1 Goal: 80 wam speed dictation

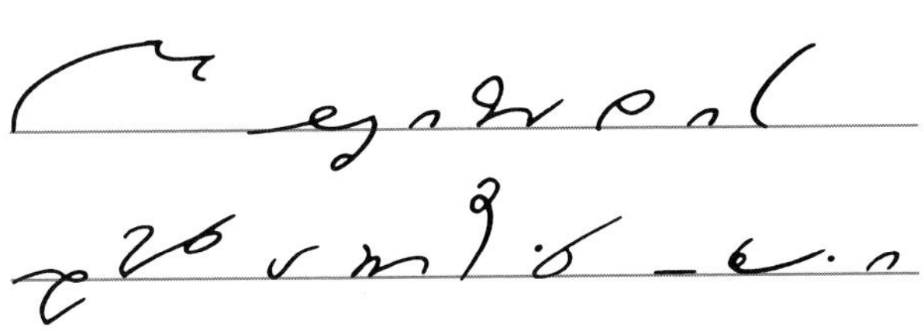

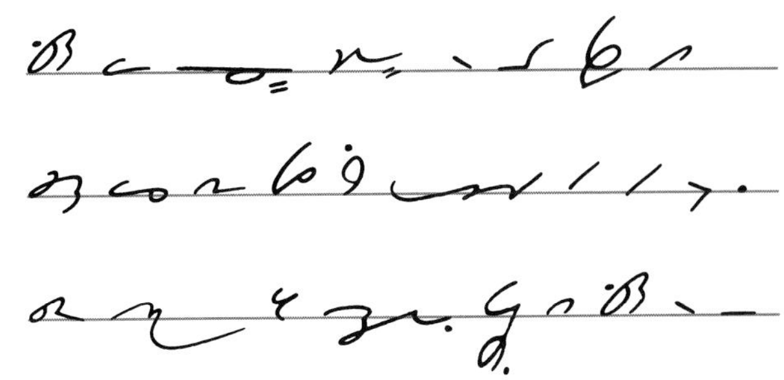

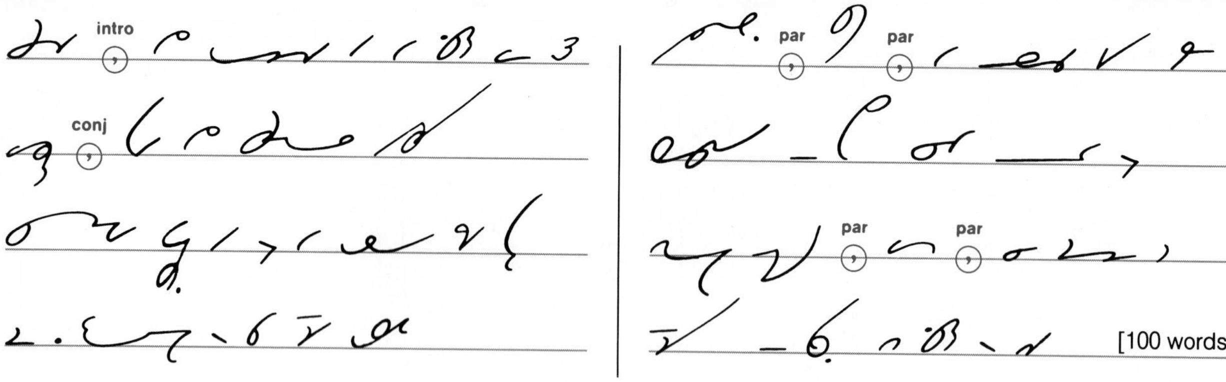

TRANSCRIPTION SKILL DEVELOPMENT

Transcription Warmup

Transcribe the following groups of words for speed and accuracy, applying transcription rules and assuring correct spelling.

19.2

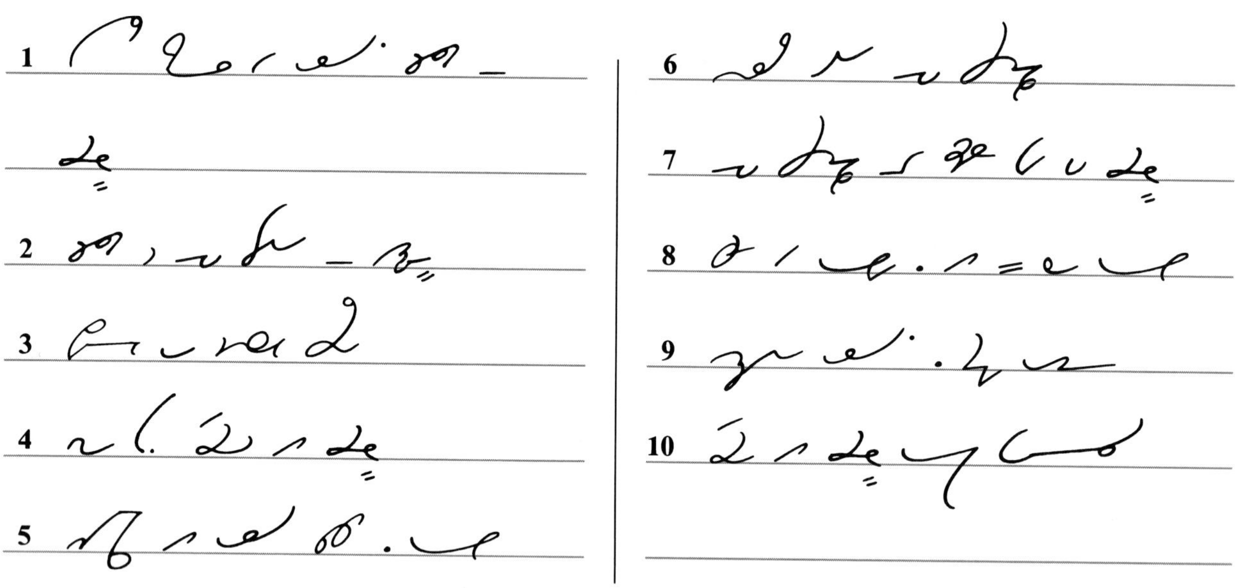

Transcription Practice

Transcribe the following letter for 2 minutes in unarranged format, applying transcription rules and assuring correct spelling. For every word not transcribed and every keyboarding error, deduct one word from the total word count.

19.3 Goal: 25 wam transcription rate

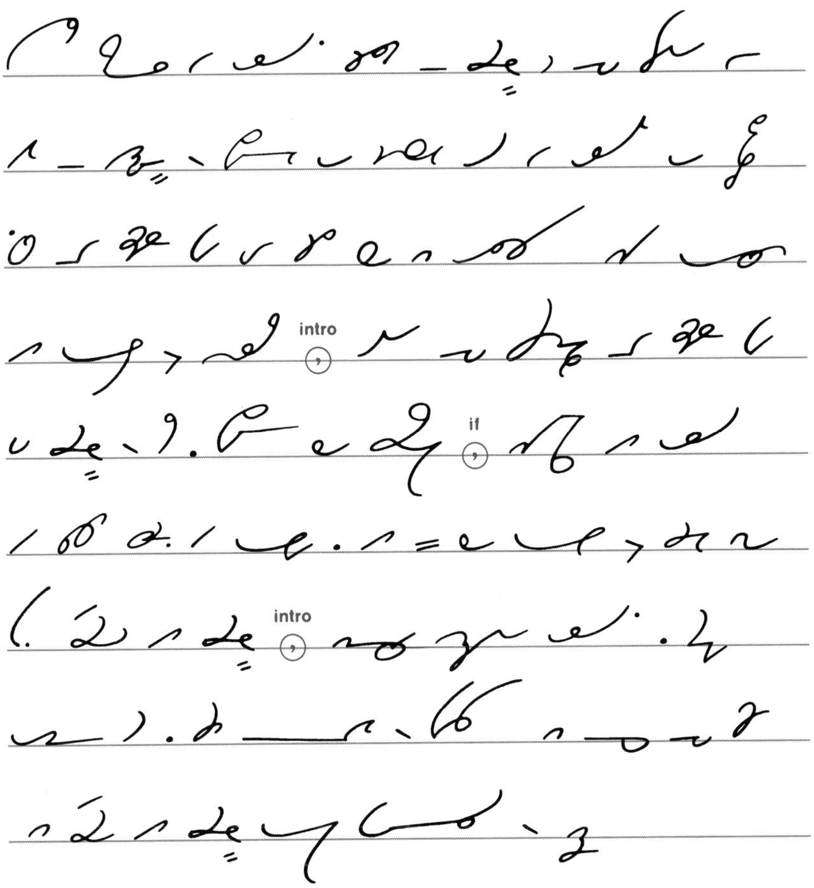

Word Count
13
27
41
54
70
82
96
107
119

Mailable Production

Transcribe the following mailable production letter in block style, assuring proper placement of all letter parts. Insert punctuation prior to transcribing, and capitalize proper nouns and titles. Address a large envelope.

19.4 Time Limit: 15 minutes

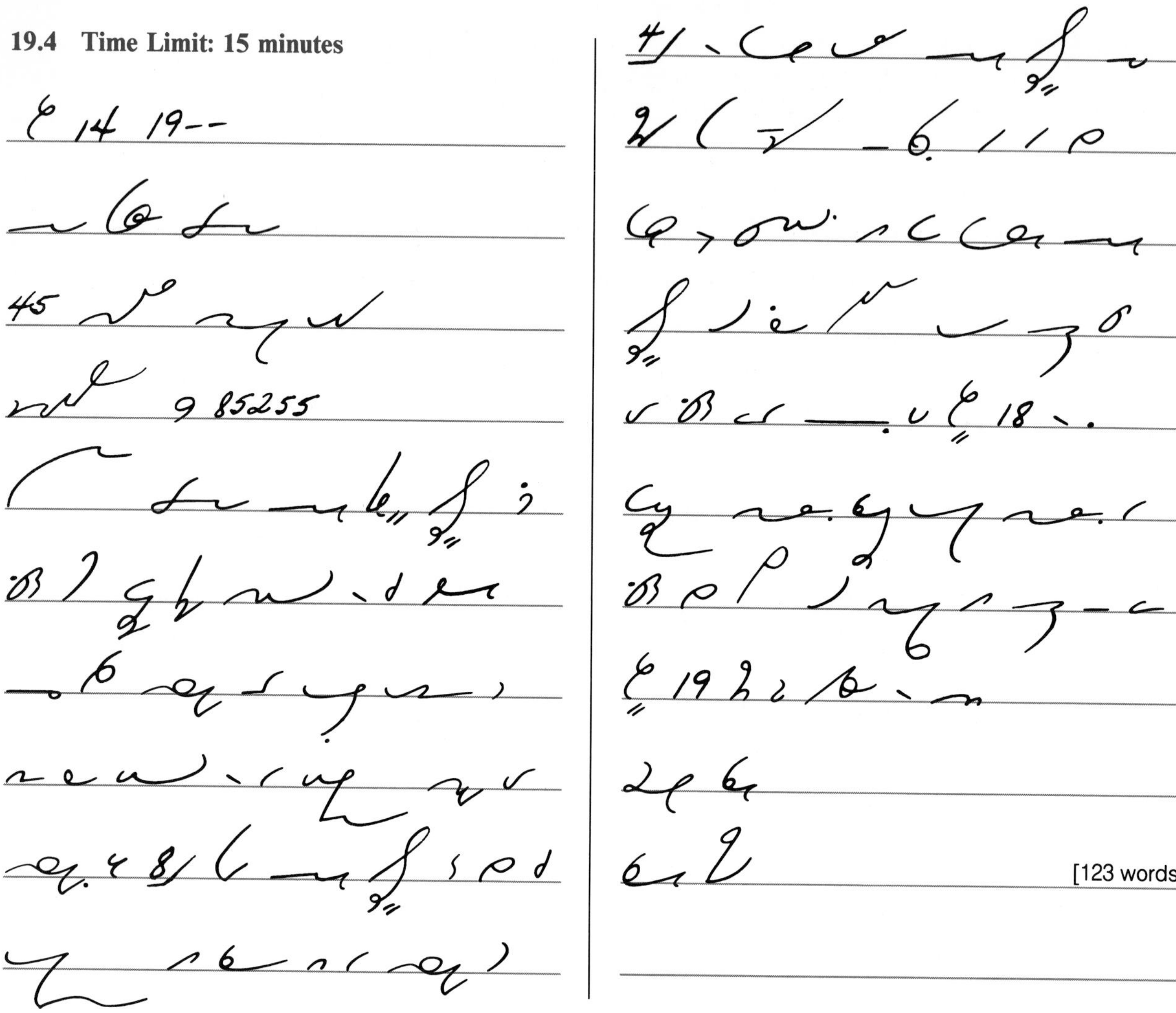

[123 words]

LESSON 20

FRANKLIN REAL ESTATE AGENCY

DICTATION SPEED BUILDING

The shorthand outlines below appear in the speed dictation practice that follows. Practice writing these words using the shorthand outlines. Then, using the key that follows, dictate the words to yourself in preparation for the speed dictation practice.

Dictation Preview

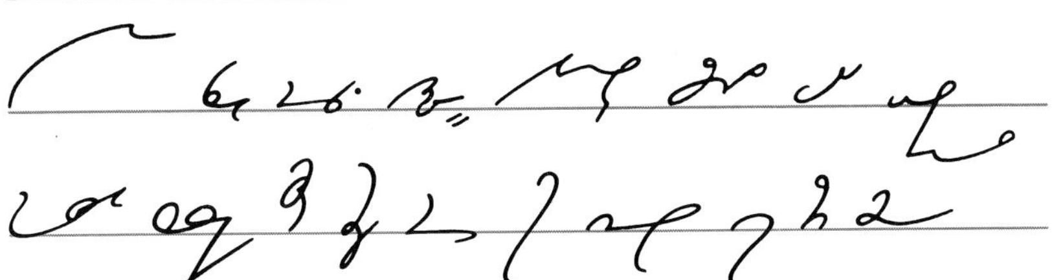

Key: Dear Mr. Pierce, submitting, Tucson, description, exactly, although, originally, flights, arranged, wife, visit, from your, you have been, you may be, can be, if you, we will

Speed Dictation Practice

20.1 Goal: 80 wam speed dictation

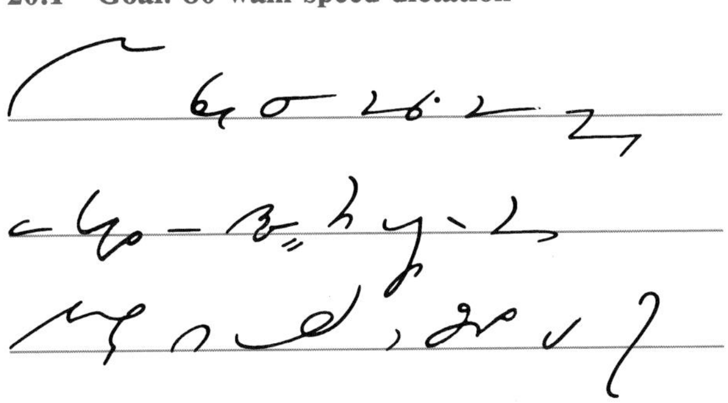

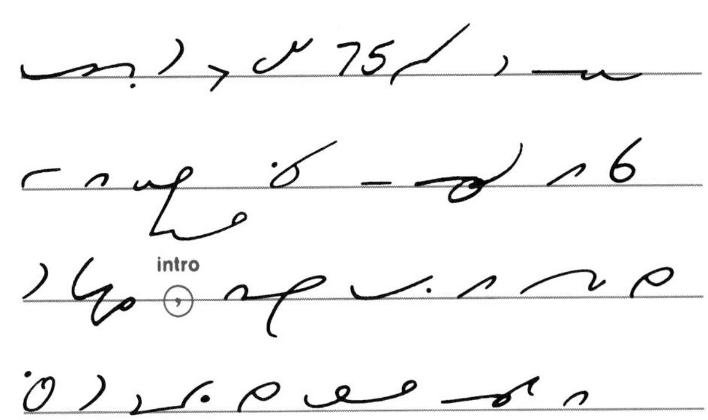

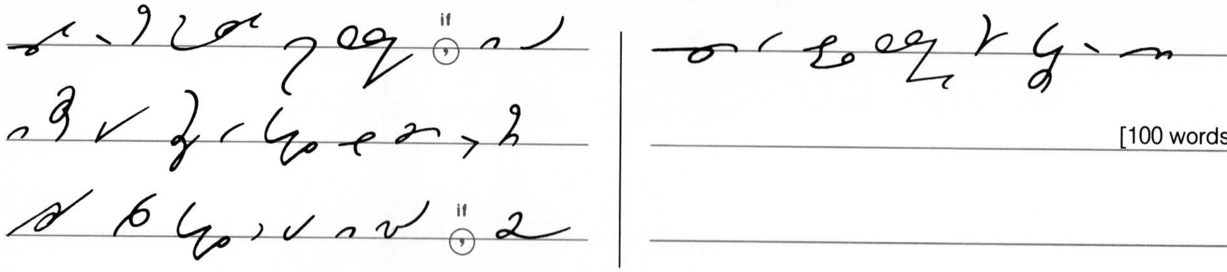

TRANSCRIPTION SKILL DEVELOPMENT

Transcription Warmup

Transcribe the following groups of words for speed and accuracy, applying transcription rules and assuring correct spelling.

20.2

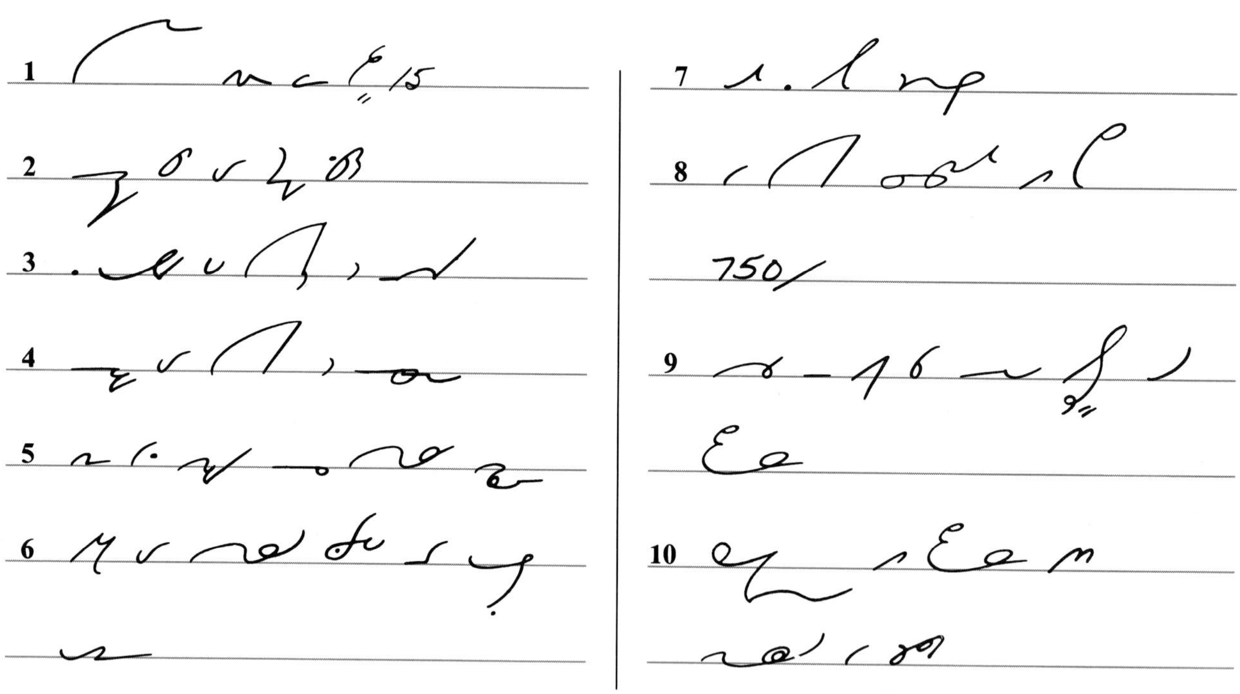

Transcription Practice

Transcribe the following letter for 2 minutes in unarranged format, applying transcription rules and assuring correct spelling. For every word not transcribed and every keyboarding error, deduct one word from the total word count.

20.3 Goal: 25 wam transcription rate

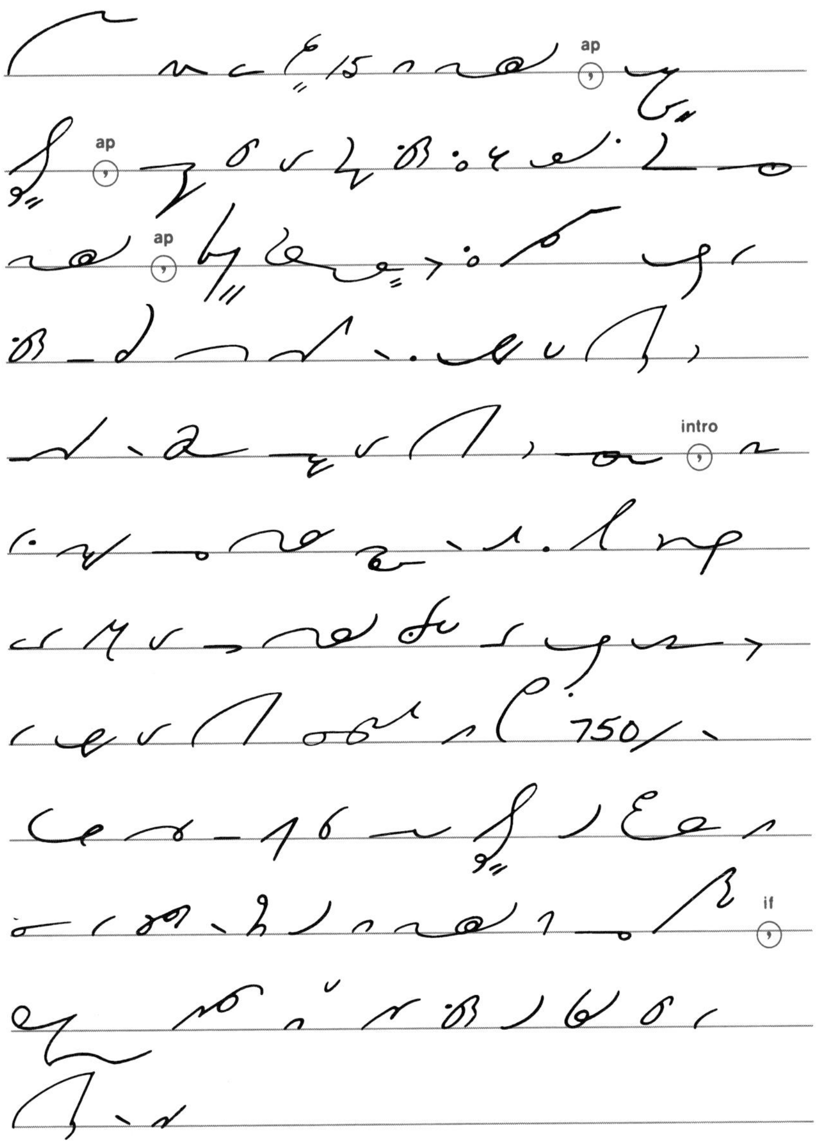

Word Count

10
22
31
41
51
62
73
82
92
104
116
120

Mailable Production

Transcribe the following mailable production letter in block style, assuring proper placement of all letter parts. Insert punctuation prior to transcribing, and capitalize proper nouns and titles. Address a large envelope.

20.4 Time Limit: 15 minutes

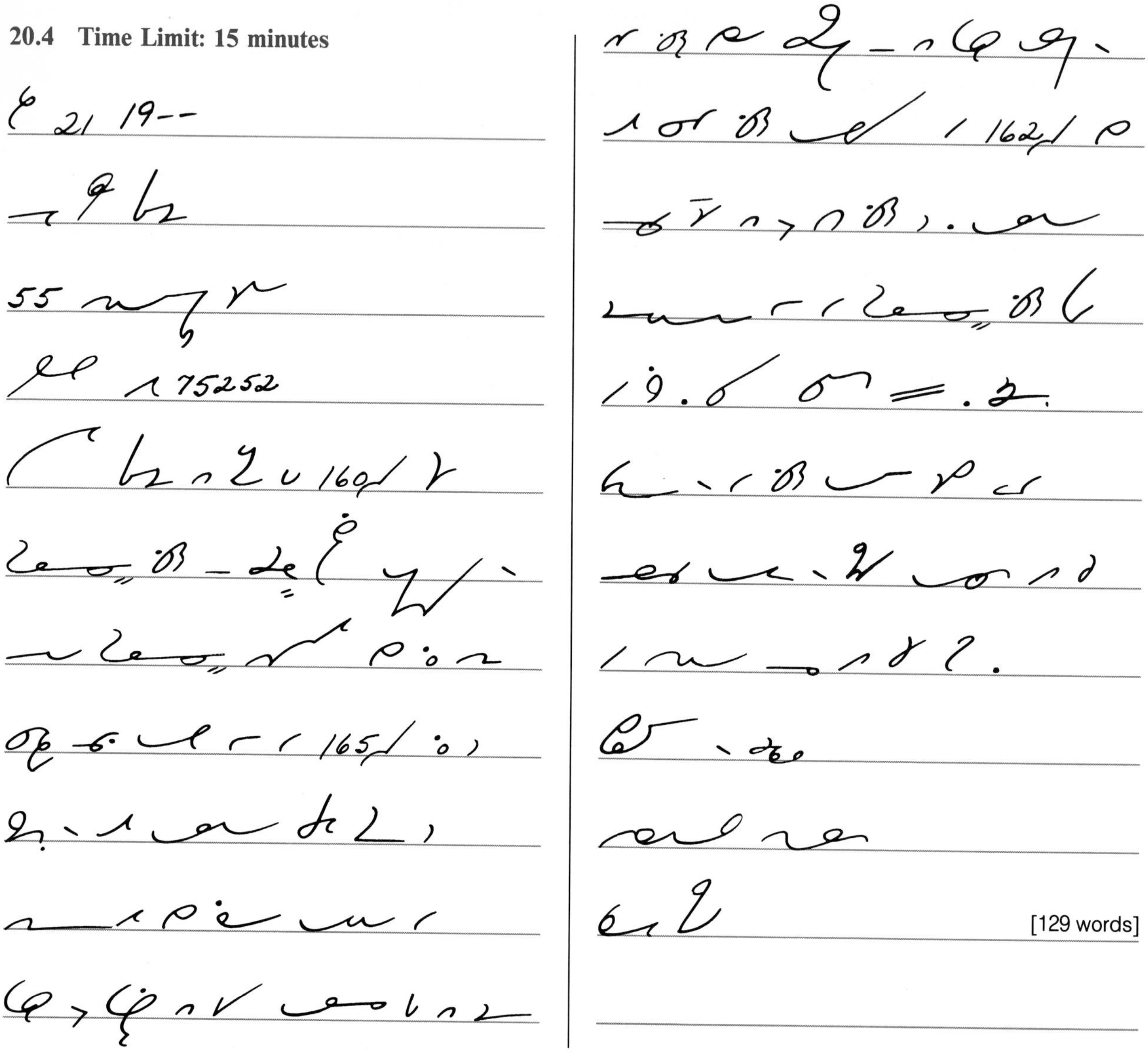

[129 words]

LESSON 21

FRANKLIN REAL ESTATE AGENCY

DICTATION SPEED BUILDING

The shorthand outlines below appear in the speed dictation practice that follows. Practice writing these words using the shorthand outlines. Then, using the key that follows, dictate the words to yourself in preparation for the speed dictation practice.

Dictation Preview

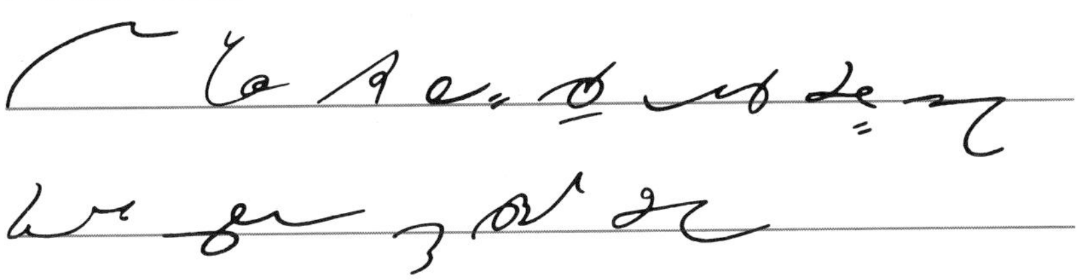

Key: Dear Mr. O'Bryan, decision, Arizona, quite, locate, Phoenix, number, folders, material, questions, thousands, example

Speed Dictation Practice

21.1 Goal: 80 wam speed dictation

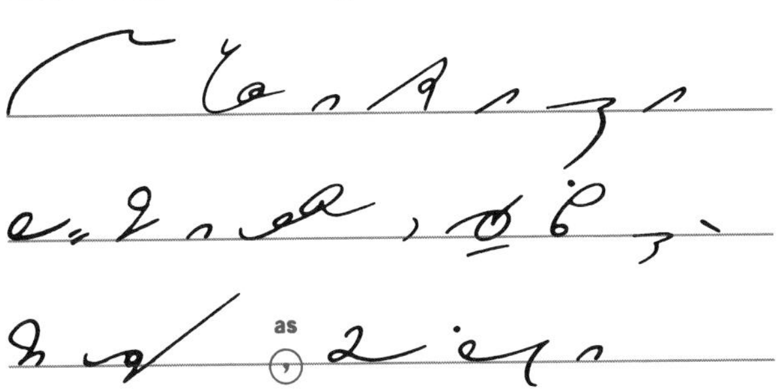

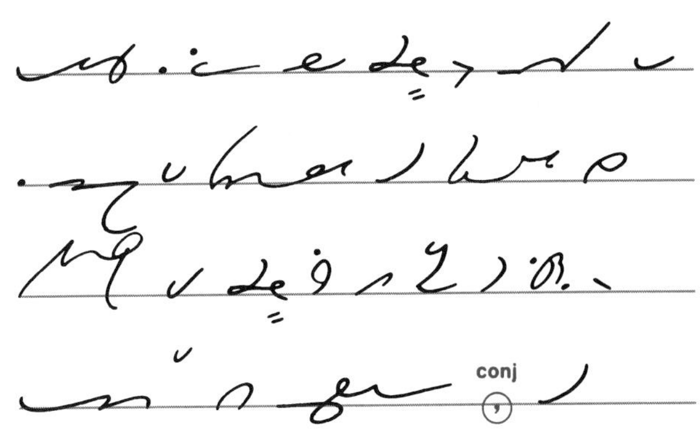

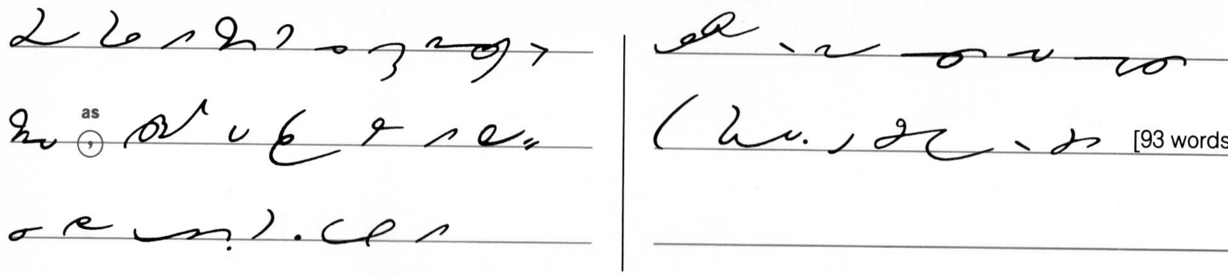

[93 words]

TRANSCRIPTION SKILL DEVELOPMENT

Transcription Warmup

Transcribe the following groups of words for speed and accuracy, applying transcription rules and assuring correct spelling.

21.2

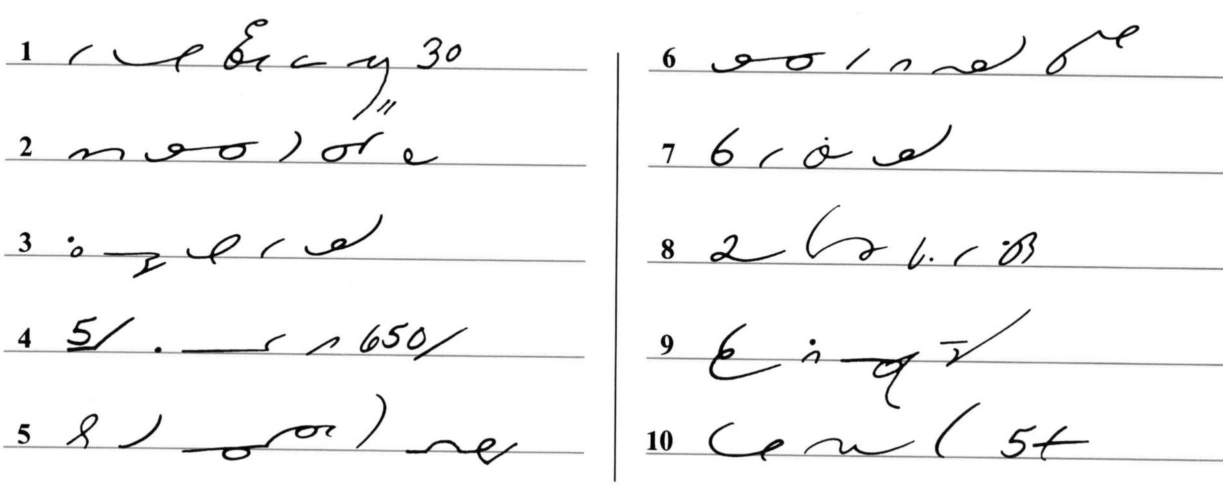

Transcription Practice

Transcribe the following letter for 2 minutes in unarranged format, applying transcription rules and assuring correct spelling. For every word not transcribed and every keyboarding error, deduct one word from the total word count.

21.3 Goal: 25 wam transcription rate

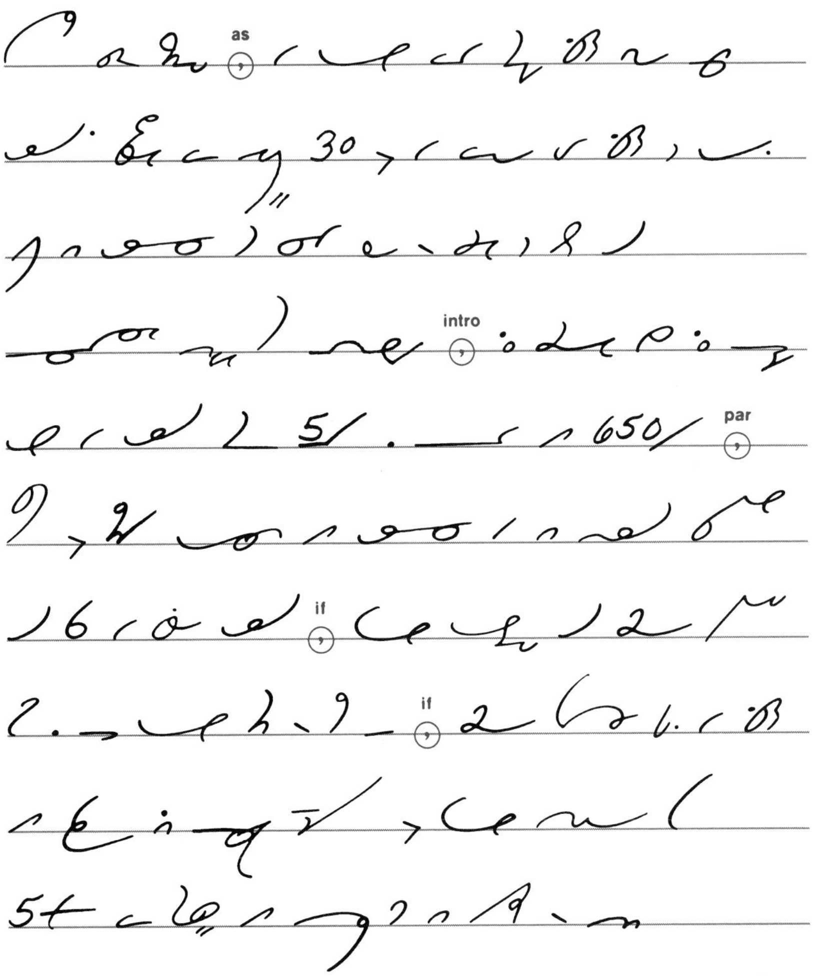

Word Count

15
28
39
50
58
70
82
94
105
116

Mailable Production

Transcribe the following mailable production letter in block style, assuring proper placement of all letter parts. Insert punctuation prior to transcribing, and capitalize proper nouns and titles. Address a large envelope.

21.4 Time Limit: 15 minutes

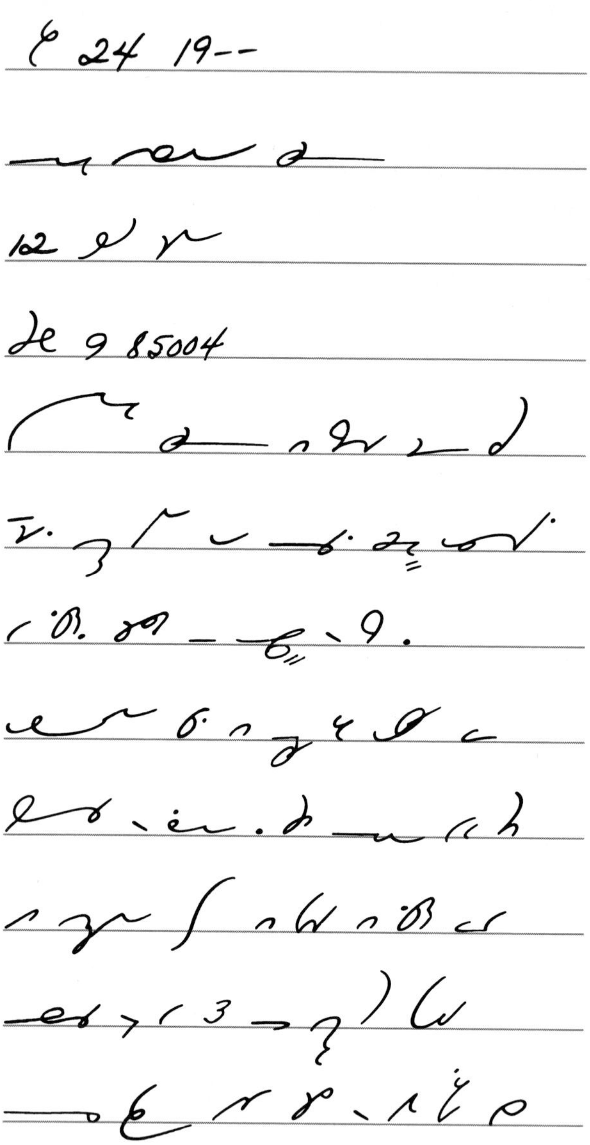

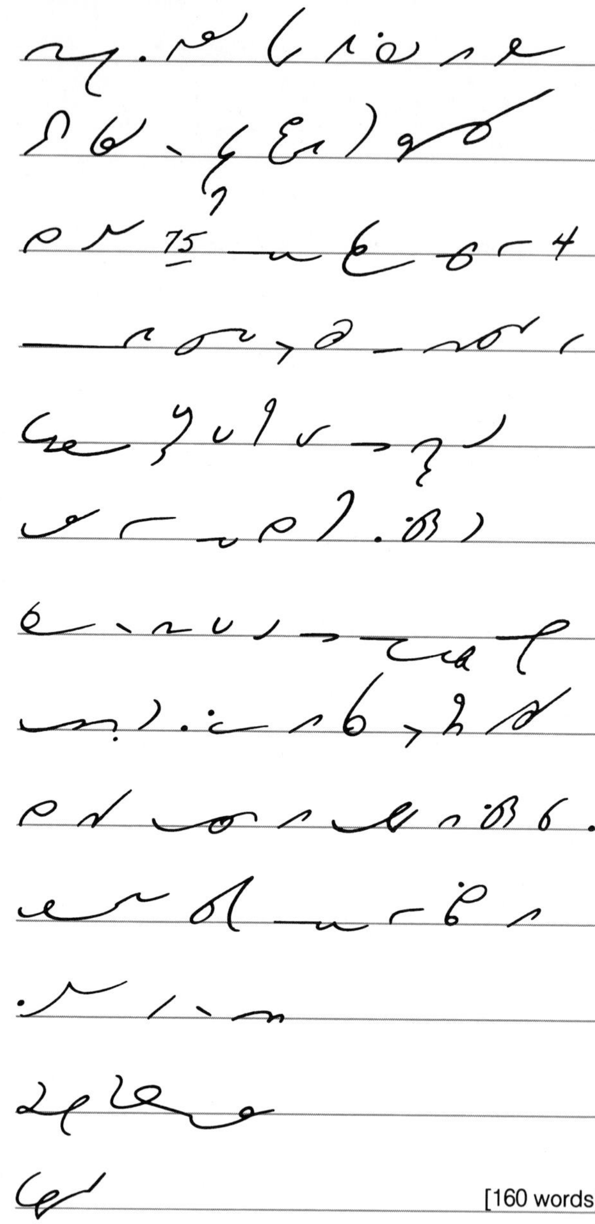

[160 words]

LESSON 22

FRANKLIN REAL ESTATE AGENCY

DICTATION SPEED BUILDING

The shorthand outlines below appear in the speed dictation practice that follows. Practice writing these words using the shorthand outlines. Then, using the key that follows, dictate the words to yourself in preparation for the speed dictation practice.

Dictation Preview

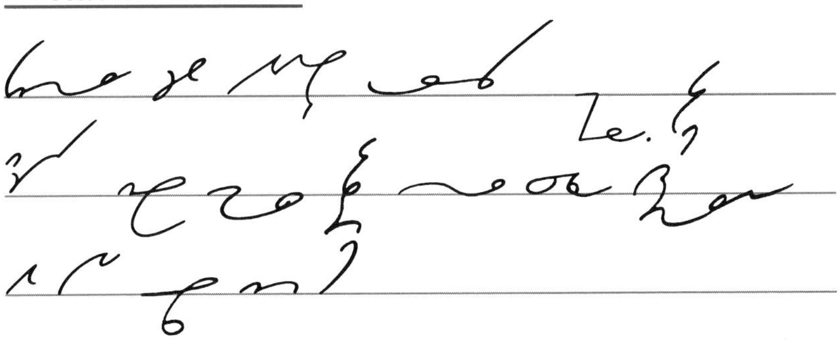

Key: booklet, cities, distribution, limited, engineering, population, understand, unable, comply, specific, gladly, answer, thank you for your letter, it is, to know, may be able, you can, you have

Speed Dictation Practice

22.1 Goal: 80 wam speed dictation

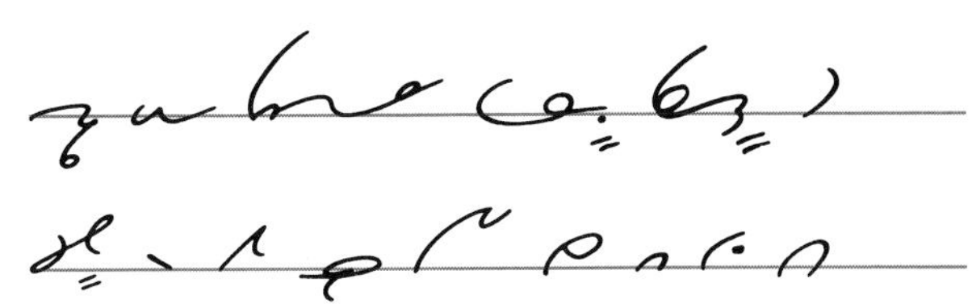

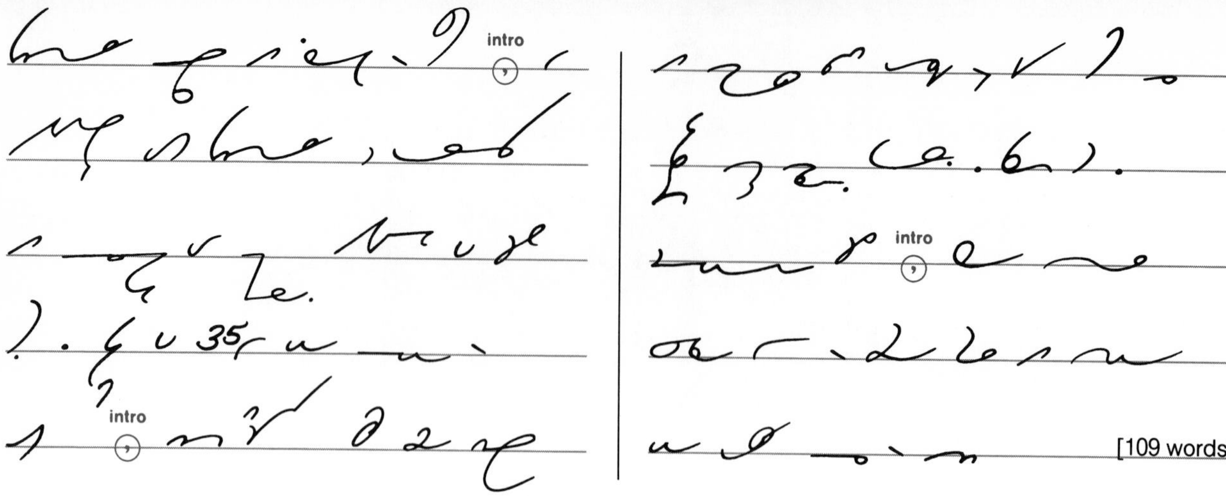

TRANSCRIPTION SKILL DEVELOPMENT

Transcription Warmup

Transcribe the following groups of words for speed and accuracy, applying transcription rules and assuring correct spelling.

22.2

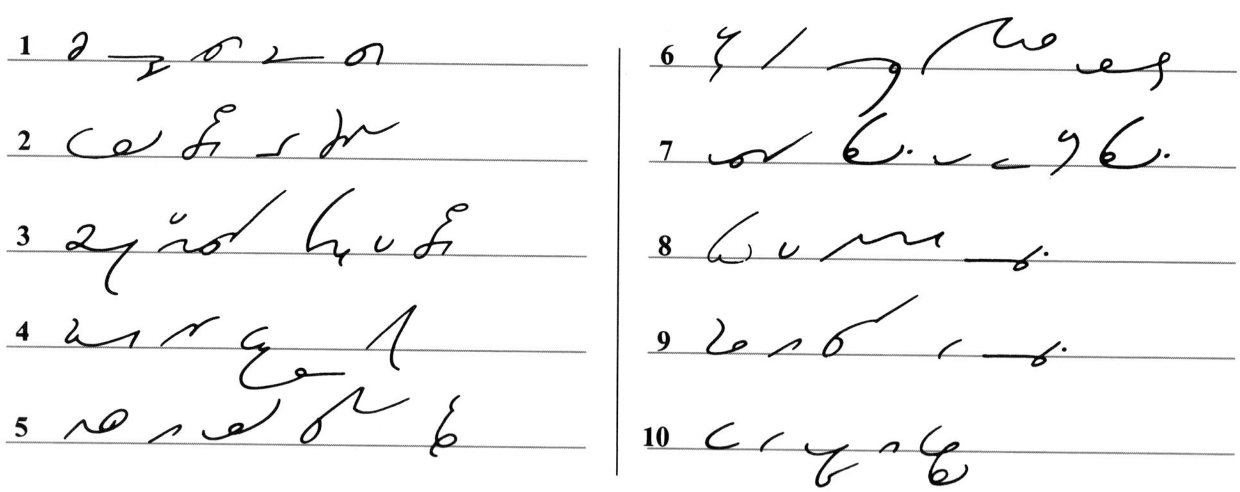

Transcription Practice

Transcribe the following note for 2 minutes in unarranged format, applying transcription rules and assuring correct spelling. For every word not transcribed and every keyboarding error, deduct one word from the total word count.

22.3 Goal: 25 wam transcription rate

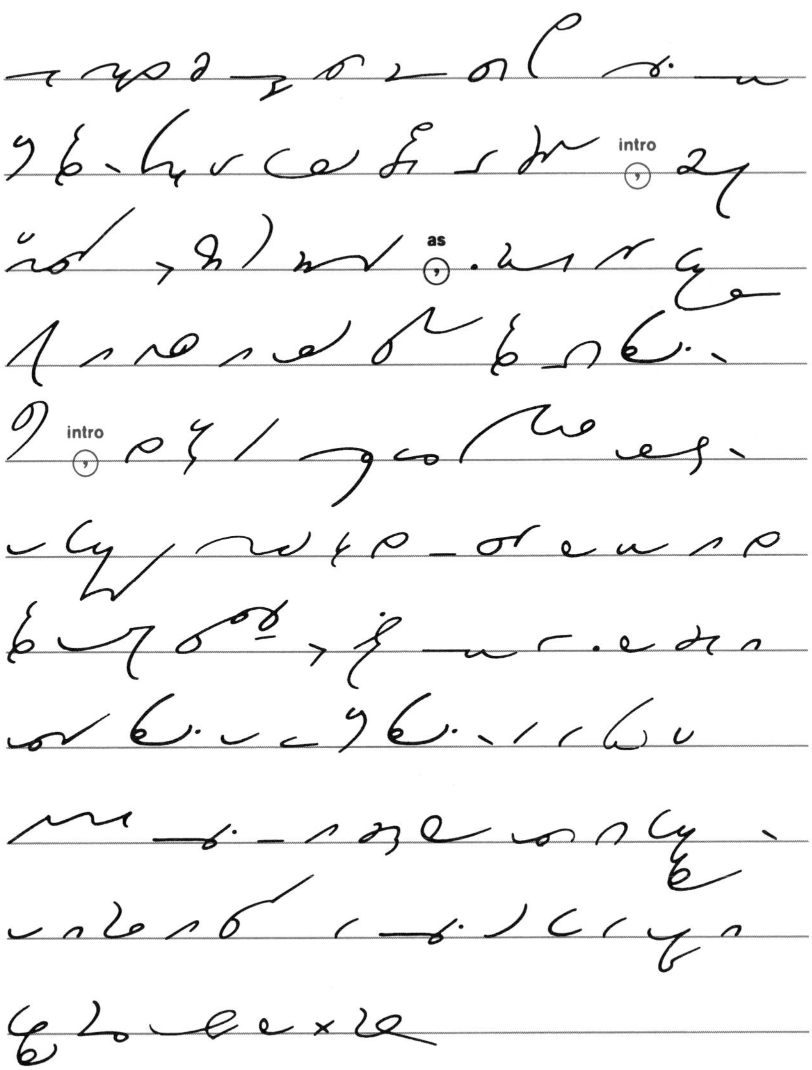

Word Count
11
25
37
49
60
71
84
96
108
120
126

Mailable Production

Transcribe the following mailable production letter in block style, assuring proper placement of all letter parts. Insert punctuation prior to transcribing, and capitalize proper nouns and titles. Address a large envelope.

22.4 Time Limit: 15 minutes

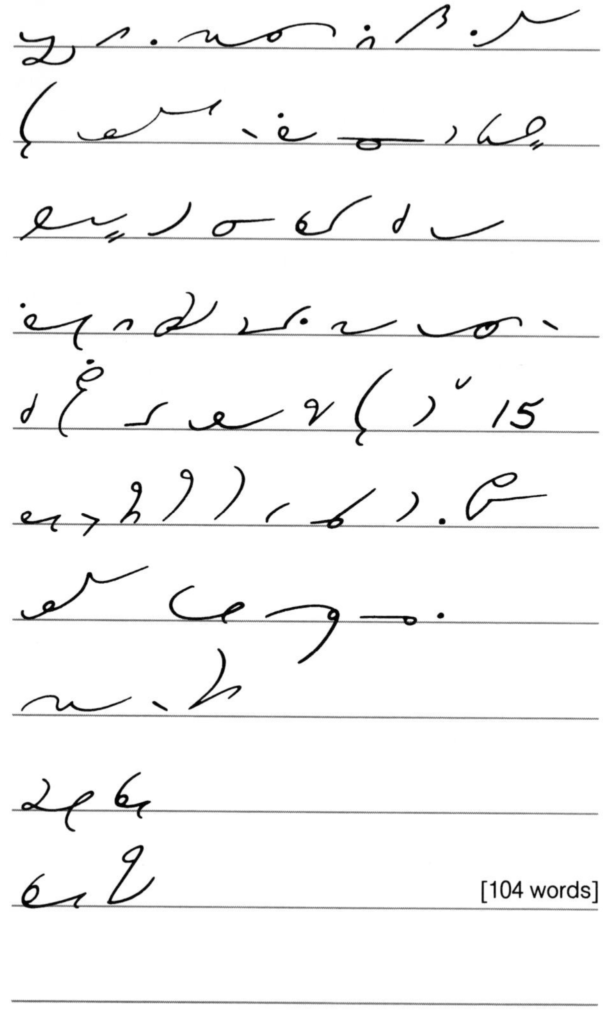

[104 words]

LESSON 23

FRANKLIN REAL ESTATE AGENCY

DICTATION SPEED BUILDING

The shorthand outlines below appear in the speed dictation practice that follows. Practice writing these words using the shorthand outlines. Then, using the key that follows, dictate the words to yourself in preparation for the speed dictation practice.

Dictation Preview

Key: Dear Ms. Howard, visited, wanted, bedrooms, baths, such, anything, market, including, available, property, you might be, has been, let me, as soon as possible

Speed Dictation Practice

23.1 Goal: 80 wam speed dictation

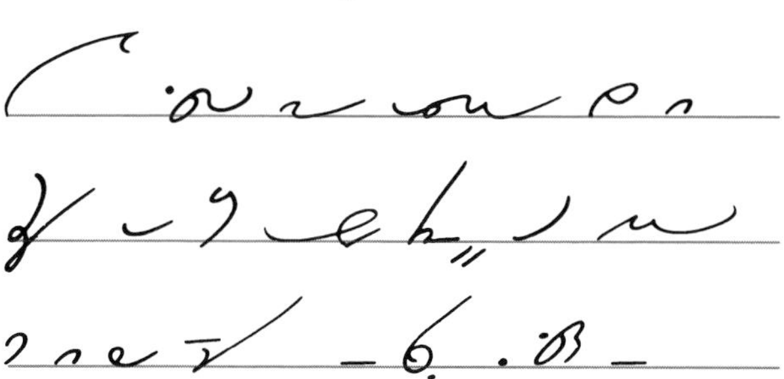

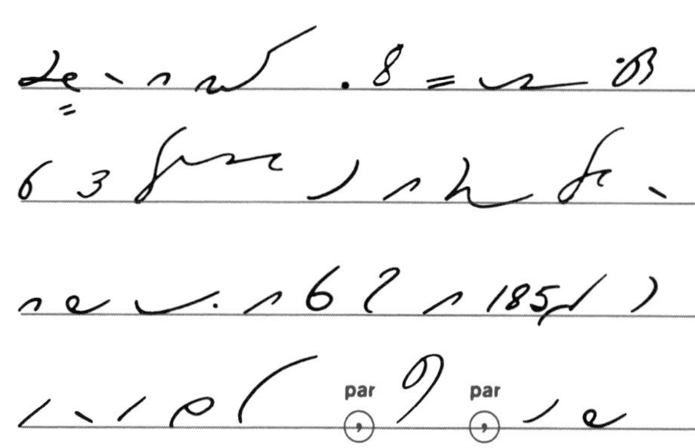

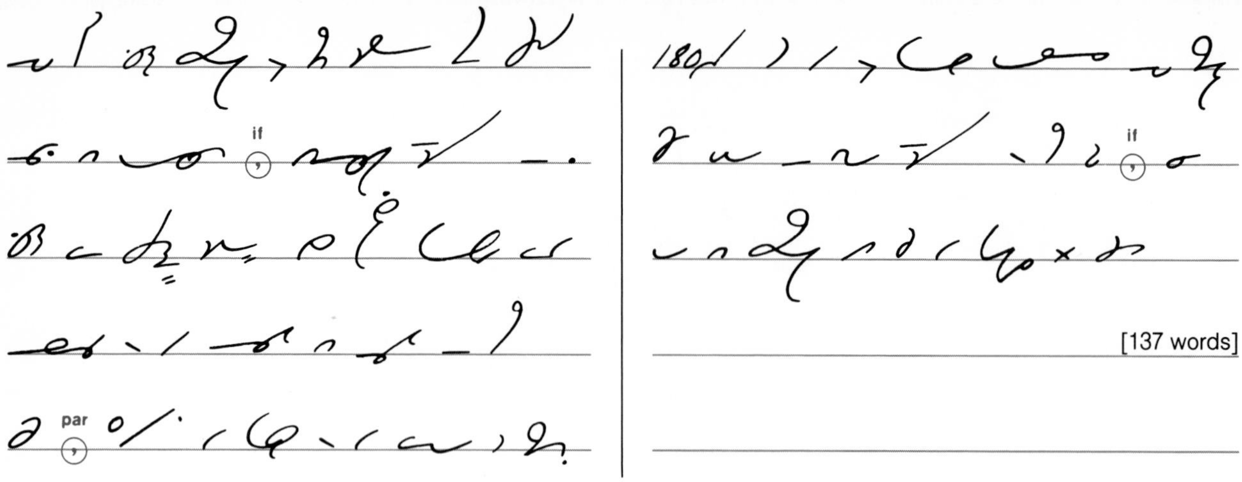

TRANSCRIPTION SKILL DEVELOPMENT

Transcription Warmup

Transcribe the following groups of words for speed and accuracy, applying transcription rules and assuring correct spelling.

23.2

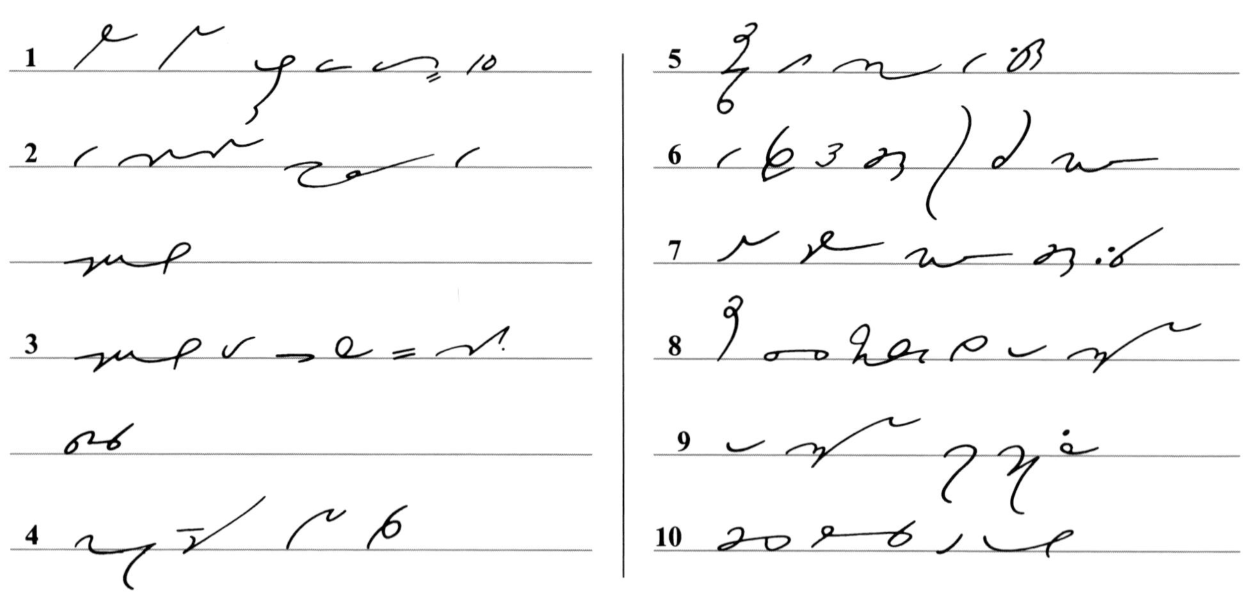

Transcription Practice

Transcribe the following letter for 2 minutes in unarranged format, applying transcription rules and assuring correct spelling. For every word not transcribed and every keyboarding error, deduct one word from the total word count.

23.3 Goal: 25 wam transcription rate

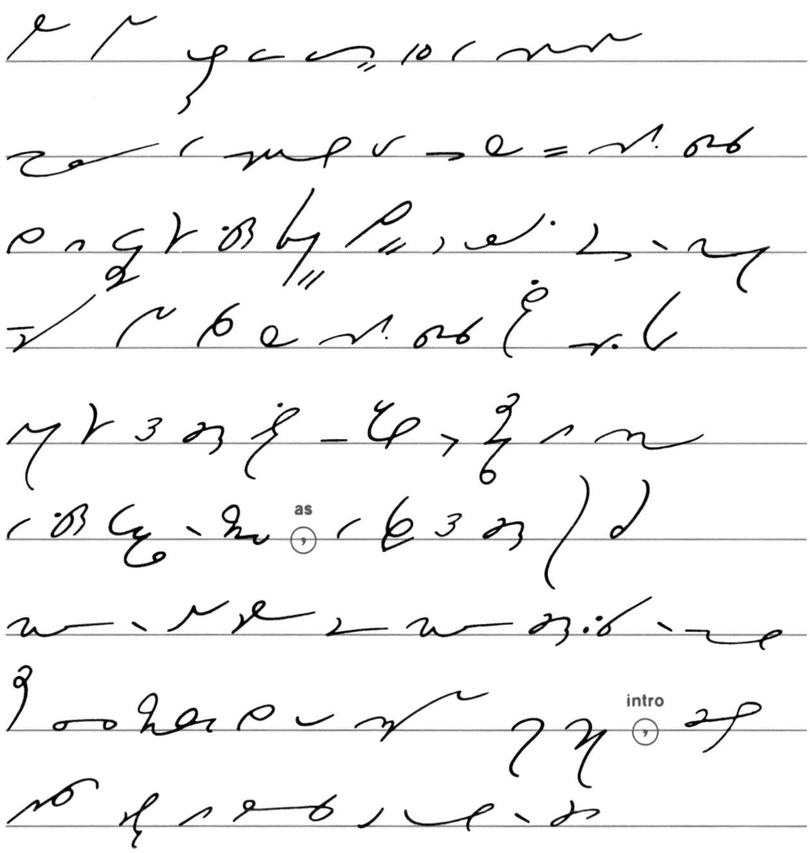

Word Count
9
21
36
50
67
81
92
107
118

Mailable Production

Transcribe the following mailable production letter in block style, assuring proper placement of all letter parts. Insert punctuation prior to transcribing, and capitalize proper nouns and titles. Address a large envelope.

23.4 Time Limit: 15 minutes

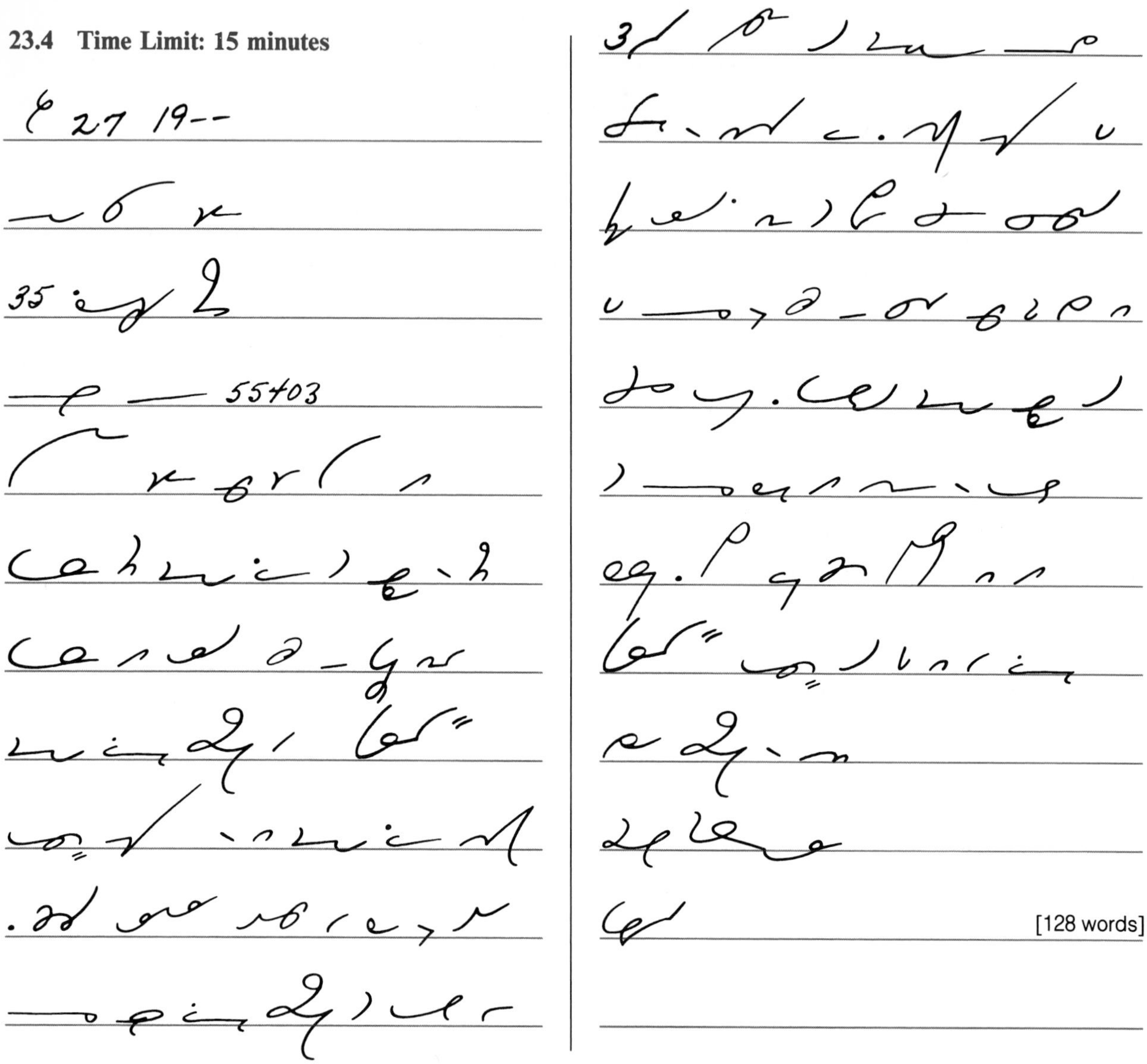

LESSON 24

FRANKLIN REAL ESTATE AGENCY

DICTATION SPEED BUILDING

The shorthand outlines below appear in the speed dictation practice that follows. Practice writing these words using the shorthand outlines. Then, using the key that follows, dictate the words to yourself in preparation for the speed dictation practice.

Dictation Preview

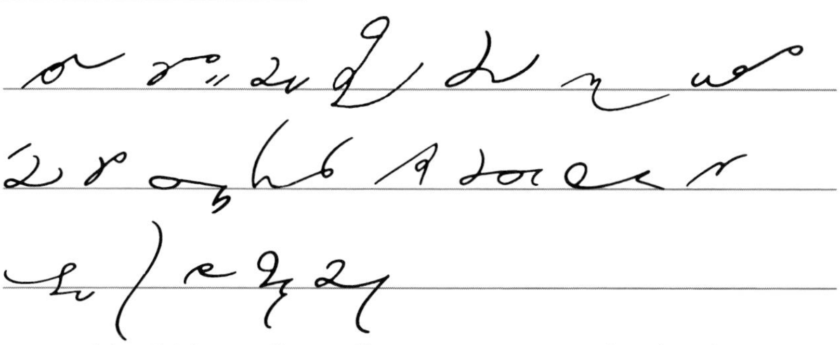

Key: title, Whitney, first, adjacent, vacant, couple, already, transferred, city, anxious, bulletin, decision, finance, along, to the, let us know, have been, they are, as soon as possible, we will be

Speed Dictation Practice

24.1 Goal: 80 wam speed dictation

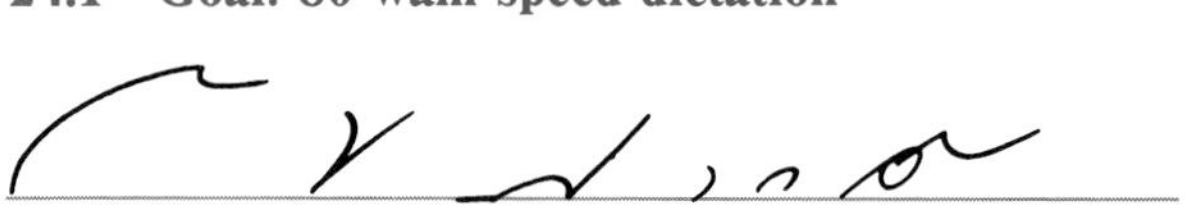

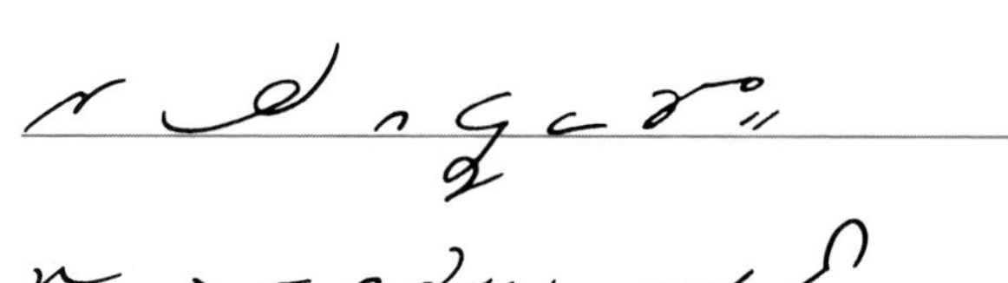

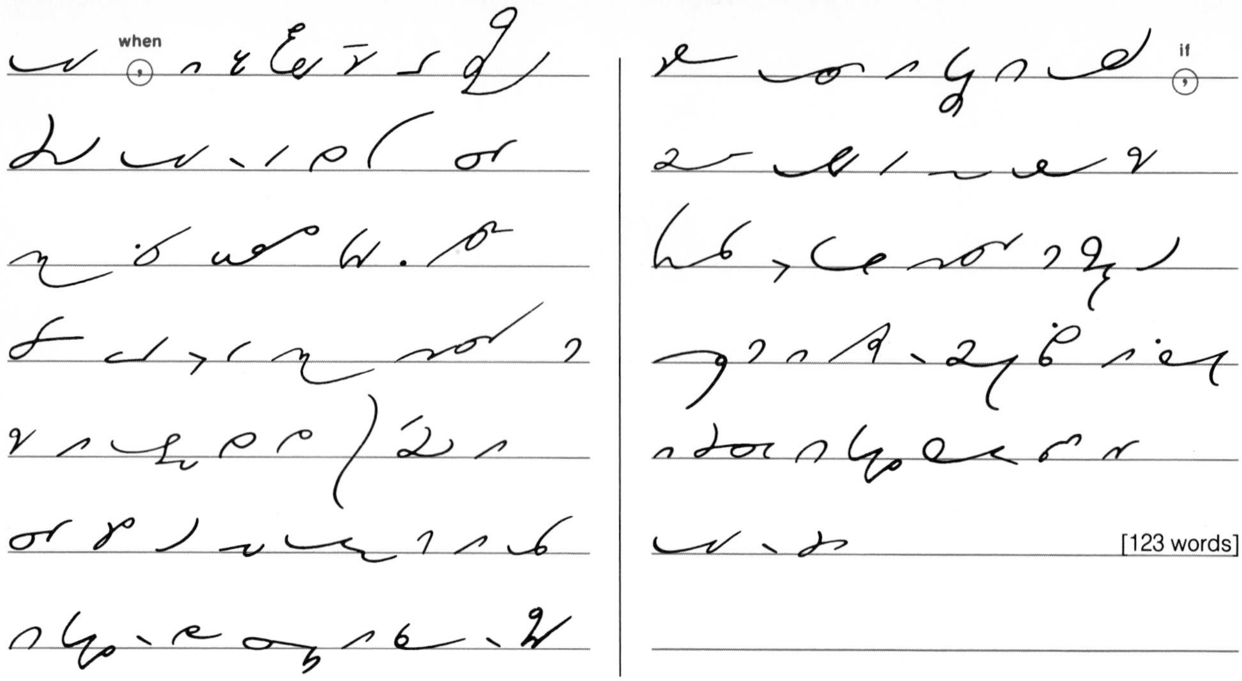

TRANSCRIPTION SKILL DEVELOPMENT

Transcription Warmup

Transcribe the following groups of words for speed and accuracy, applying transcription rules and assuring correct spelling.

24.2

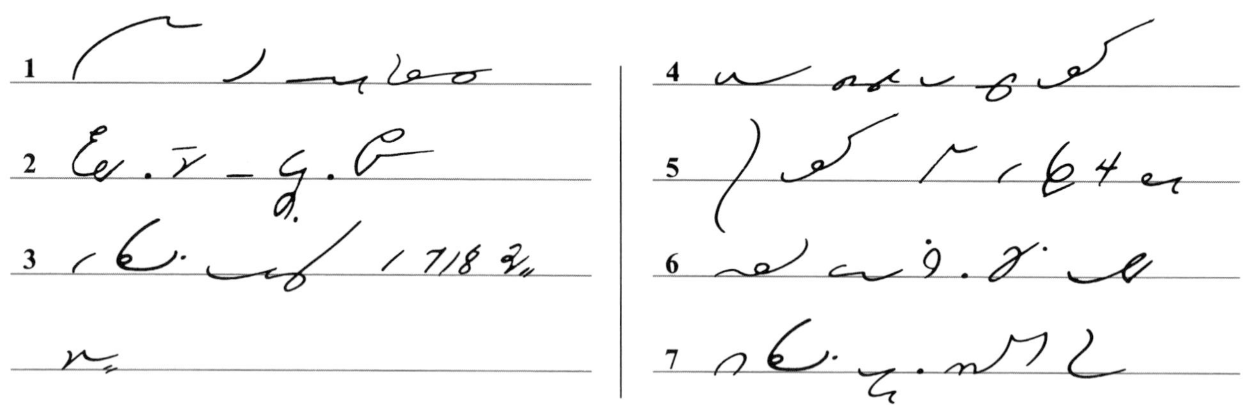

8 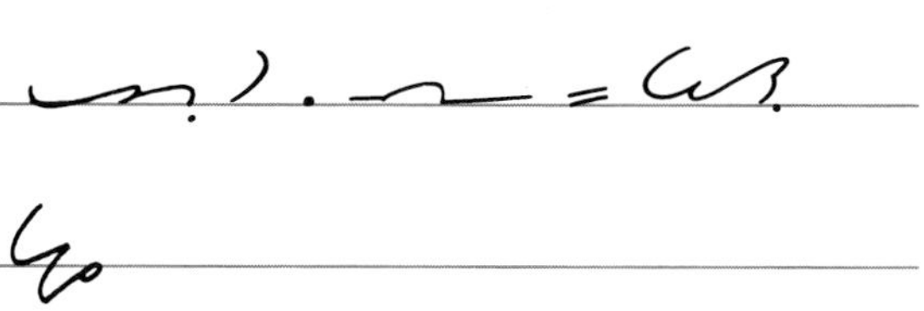

9 

10 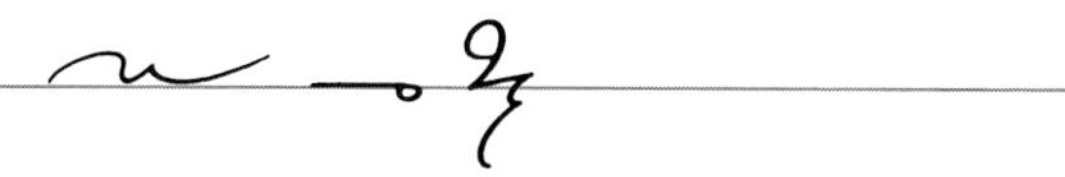

Transcription Practice

Transcribe the following letter for 2 minutes in unarranged format, applying transcription rules and assuring correct spelling. For every word not transcribed and every keyboarding error, deduct one word from the total word count.

24.3 Goal: 25 wam transcription rate

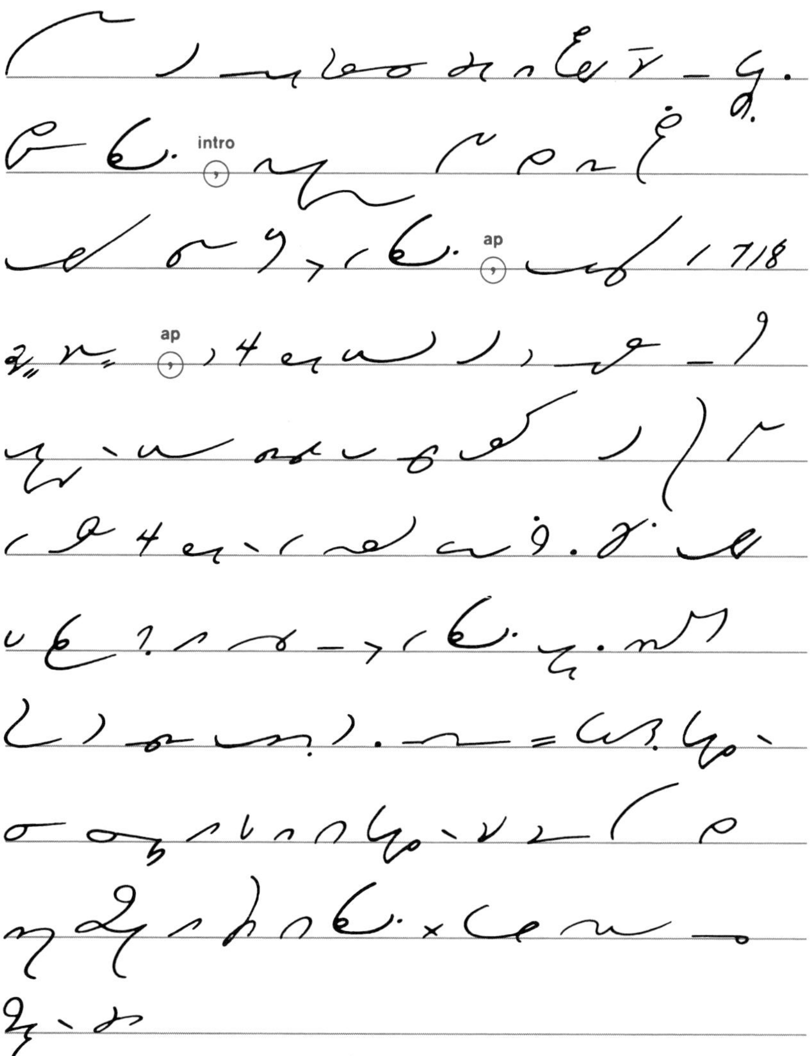

Word Count

14
26
37
48
59
71
84
96
109
121
128

Mailable Production

Transcribe the following mailable production memo and property listing, assuring proper placement of the guide words in the heading of the memo. Insert punctuation prior to transcribing.

24.4 Time Limit: 15 minutes

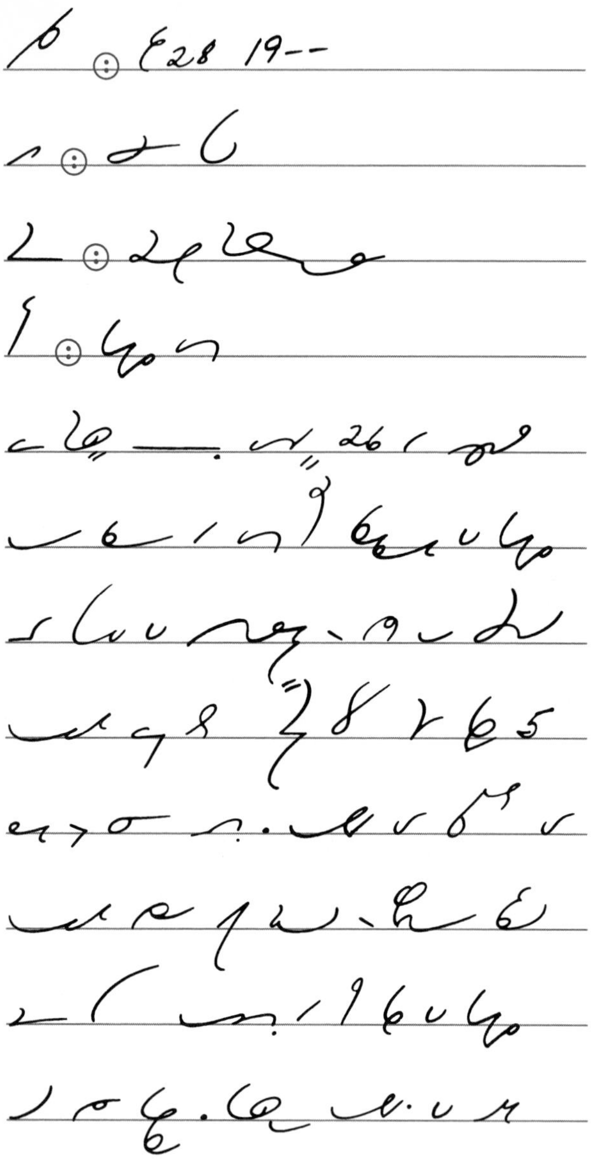

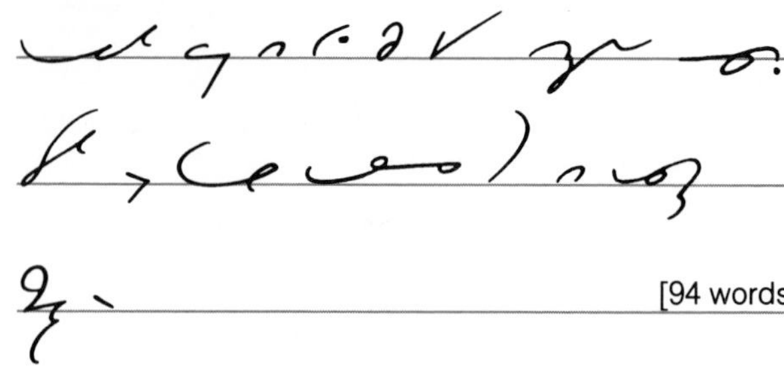

[94 words]

24.5 Time Limit: 5 minutes

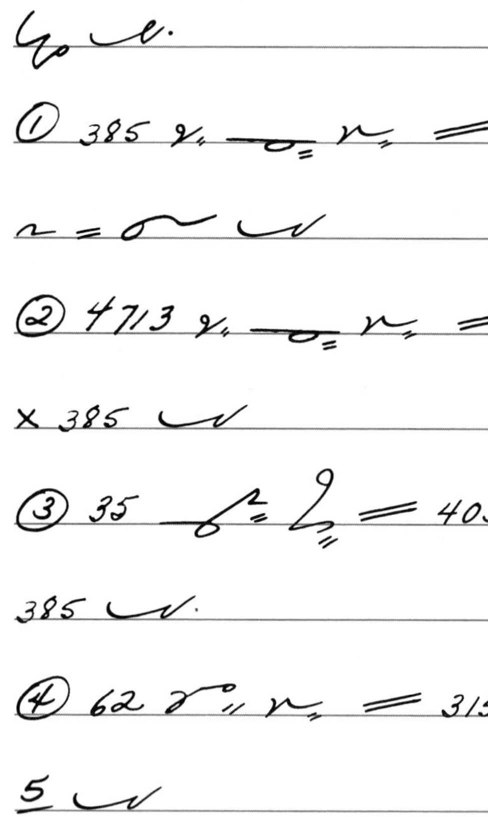

[43 words]

UNIT IV

HAMILTON PUBLISHING COMPANY

LESSON 25

HAMILTON PUBLISHING COMPANY

You are employed as an administrative assistant in the marketing area of the Hamilton Publishing Company in Boston, Massachusetts. Your company publishes several magazines—*Sports Today*, *News Magazine*, *Financial Monthly*, *Executive Journal*, and *Chemical Engineer*—as well as numerous trade books and textbooks.

In the marketing area you report to Martin Tyler and Kenneth Lopez, marketing managers for the Publications Division. When typing the mailable production letters, be sure to use the title *Marketing Manager*.

Your responsibilities will include answering the telephone, listening to customers, using word processing equipment, taking dictation, and typing correspondence and reports from various forms. Most of the correspondence will involve responding to inquiries, writing promotional letters, and giving information.

Below is a copy of your company letterhead. Develop the return address that you will use to type the envelopes for the mailable production letters.

HAMILTON
PUBLISHING
COMPANY
500 Melrose Avenue Boston, MA 02109 (617) 555-3702

In your position as an administrative assistant, you may be asked to type a listing of publications and prices and/or ISBN numbers, as well as other information to serve the needs of customers and the sales staff. Usually this information is typed in tabulation form and should be centered horizontally. The marketing managers will not instruct you on procedure; they will expect it to look "good," but "good" is determined by you. Therefore, you can use as many spaces between columns as you wish, center vertically if you wish, and center column headings. The ultimate goal is that the information be acceptable.

Of course if you center vertically, you will be assured that it will be acceptable, but time constraints might prevent doing so. A 2-inch top margin, therefore, is a good guideline.

↓ 13

TOP TEN BEST-SELLERS ↓ 3

ISBN	Book Title	Net Price ↓ 2
707882-371	Business Careers	$35.25
78218-765	Computers Today	36.20
38721-3028	Dynamics of Business Communications	24.70
373821-786	English Essentials	18.20
402866-158	Medical Assistant	35.50
715828-005	Office of Tomorrow	28.25
371285-780	Paralegal	28.60
397812-108	Principles of Accounting	25.60
473960-752	Reference Manual for Business	13.60
27385-002	Secretaries' Handbook	15.20

Titles of Books and Magazines

Underscore titles of complete works that are published as separate items, such as books, pamphlets, magazines, and newspapers.

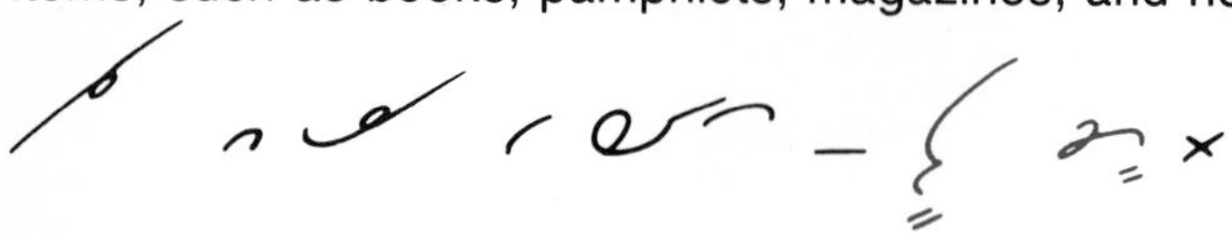

Did you read the article in Business Week?

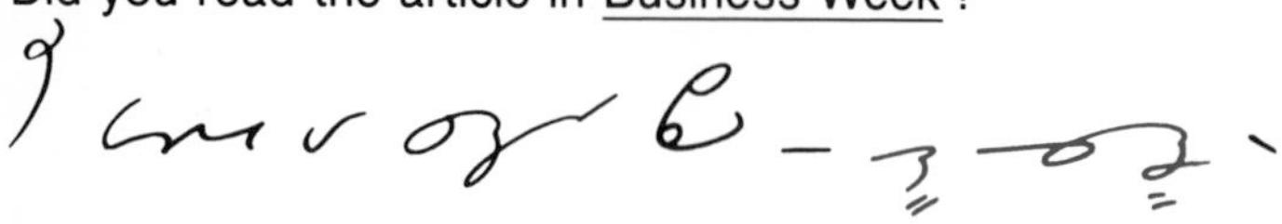

Several pictures of the accident appeared in News Magazine.

DICTATION SPEED BUILDING

The shorthand outlines below appear in the speed dictation practice that follows. Practice writing these words using the shorthand outlines. Then, using the key that follows, dictate the words to yourself in preparation for the speed dictation practice.

Dictation Preview

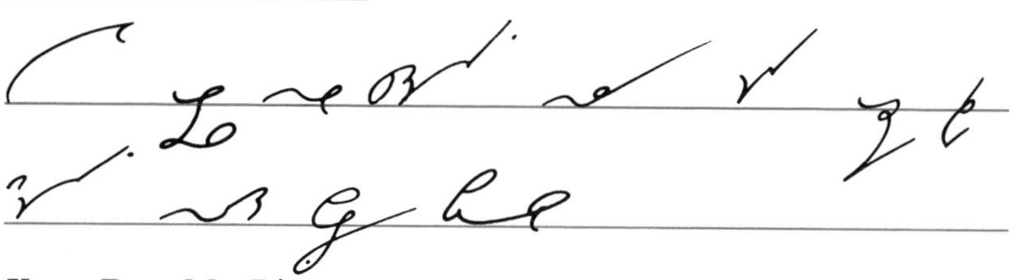

Key: Dear Ms. Rivera, correspondence, outstanding, credit, stated, received, shipped, understanding, courteous, appreciated, apologize

Speed Dictation Practice

25.1 Goal: 80 wam speed dictation

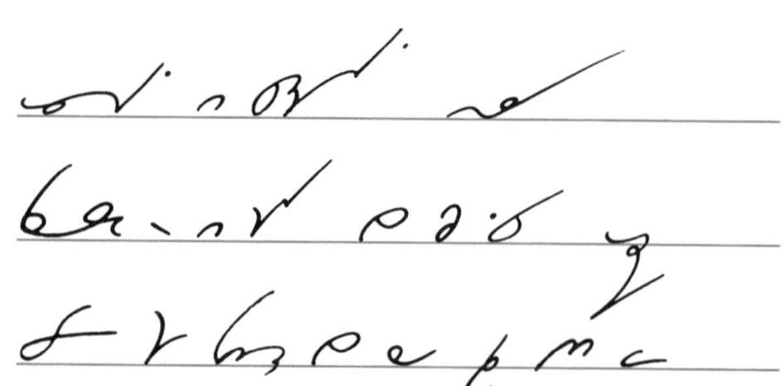

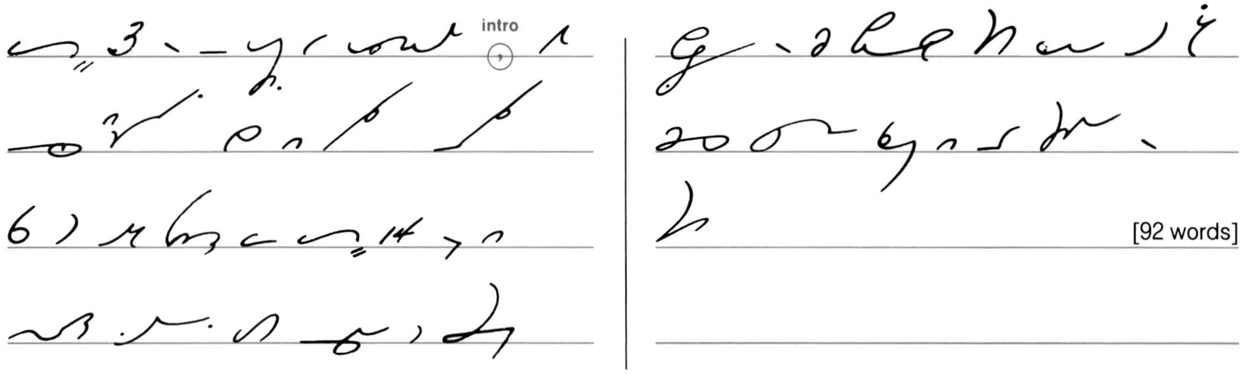

TRANSCRIPTION SKILL DEVELOPMENT

Transcription Warmup

Transcribe the following groups of words for speed and accuracy, applying transcription rules and assuring correct spelling.

25.2

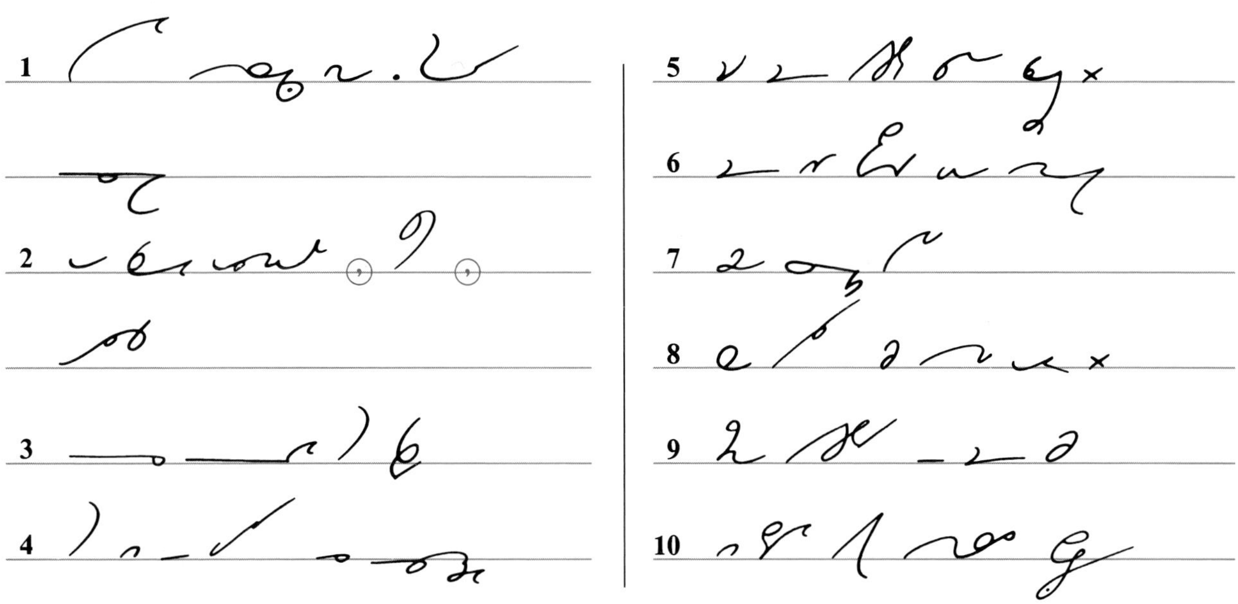

Transcription Practice

Transcribe the following letter for 2 minutes in unarranged format, applying transcription rules and assuring correct spelling. For every word not transcribed and every keyboarding error, deduct one word from the total word count.

25.3 Goal: 25 wam transcription rate

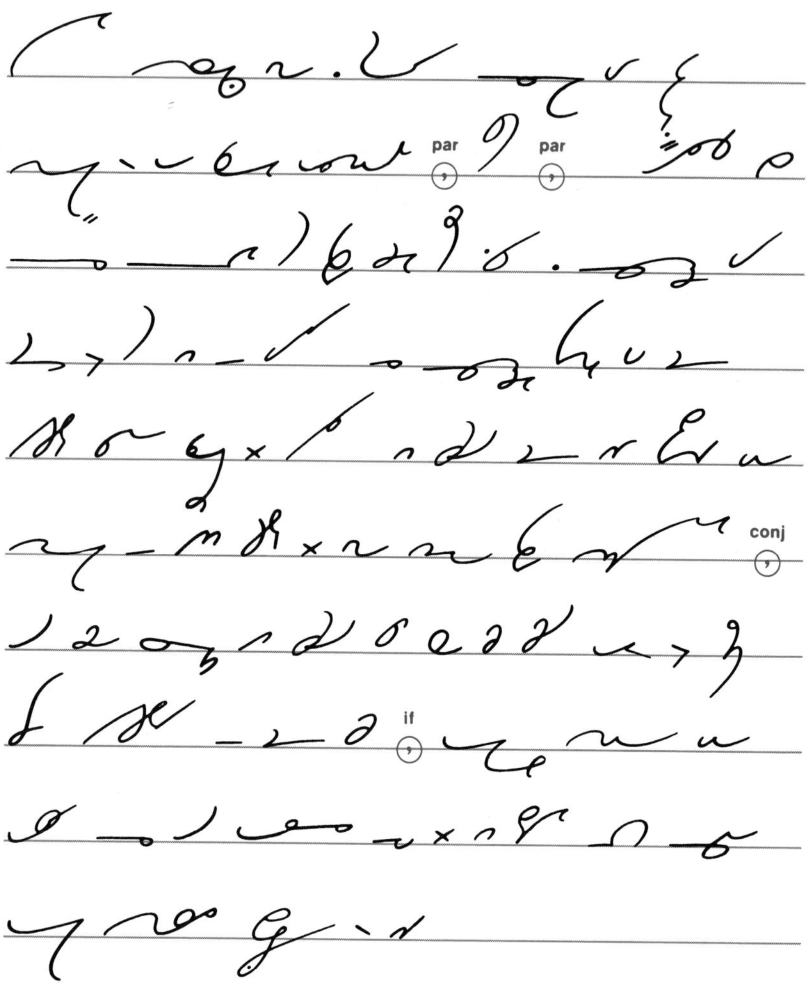

Word Count
11
21
33
45
59
72
85
96
107
115

LESSON 26

HAMILTON PUBLISHING COMPANY

DICTATION SPEED BUILDING

The shorthand outlines below appear in the speed dictation practice that follows. Practice writing these words using the shorthand outlines. Then, using the key that follows, dictate the words to yourself in preparation for the speed dictation practice.

Dictation Preview

Key: subscriptions, magazine, destination, updated, addresses, Michaels, your order, send the, with the, will you please

Speed Dictation Practice

26.1 Goal: 80 wam speed dictation

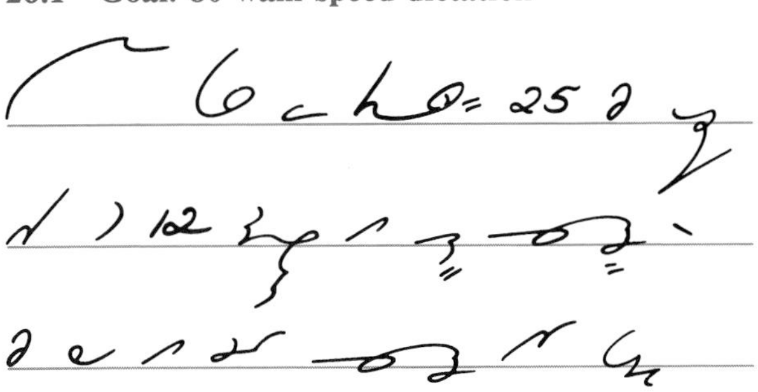

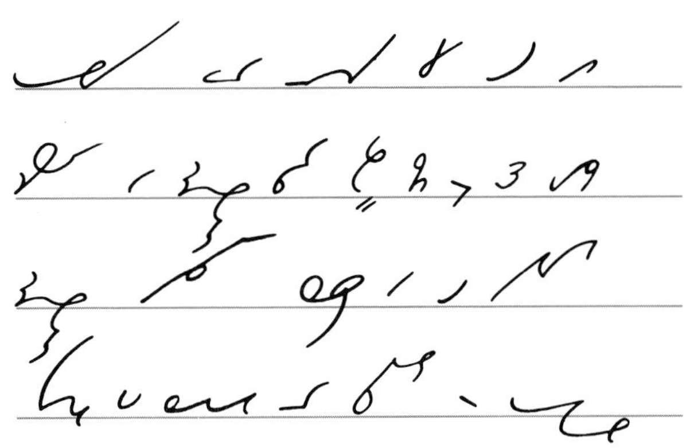

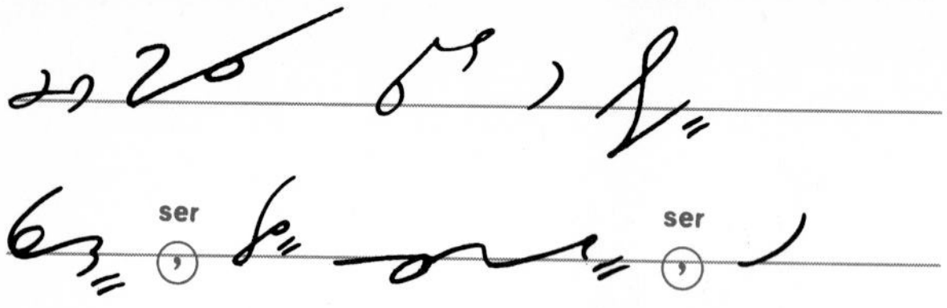

[80 words]

TRANSCRIPTION SKILL DEVELOPMENT

Transcription Warmup

Transcribe the following groups of words for speed and accuracy, applying transcription rules and assuring correct spelling.

26.2

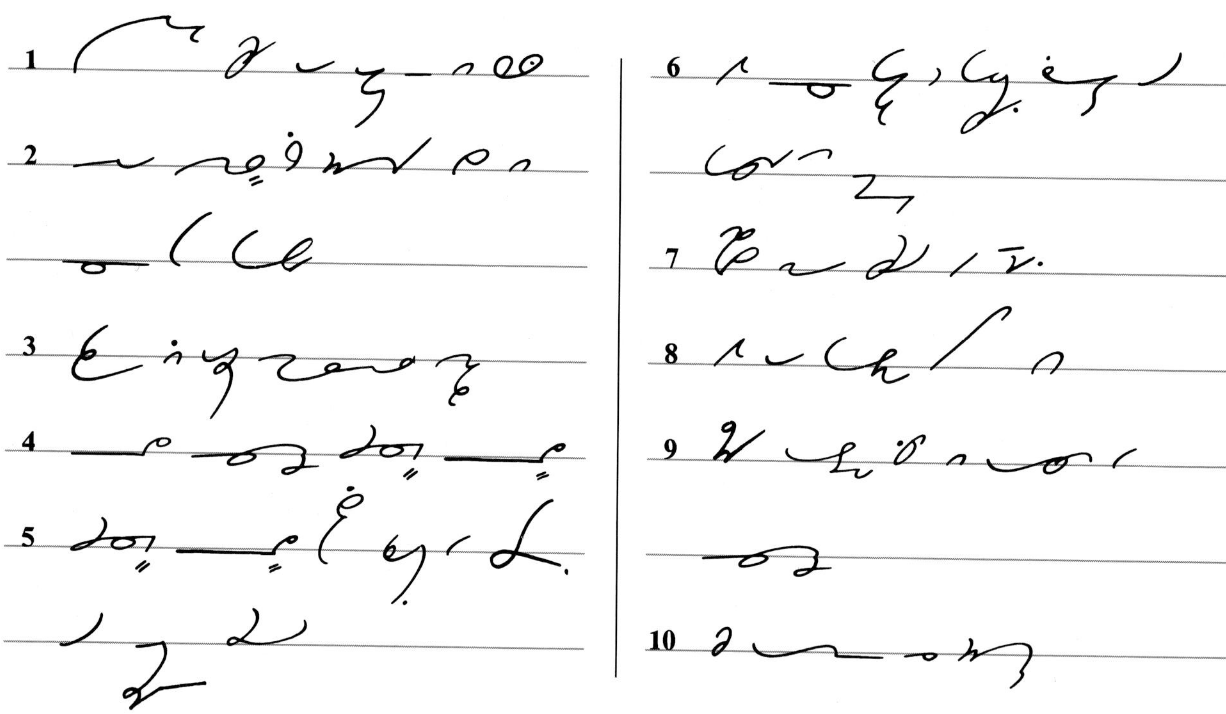

Transcription Practice

Transcribe the following letter for 2 minutes in unarranged format, applying transcription rules and assuring correct spelling. For every word not transcribed and every keyboarding error, deduct one word from the total word count.

26.3 Goal: 25 wam transcription rate

Word Count

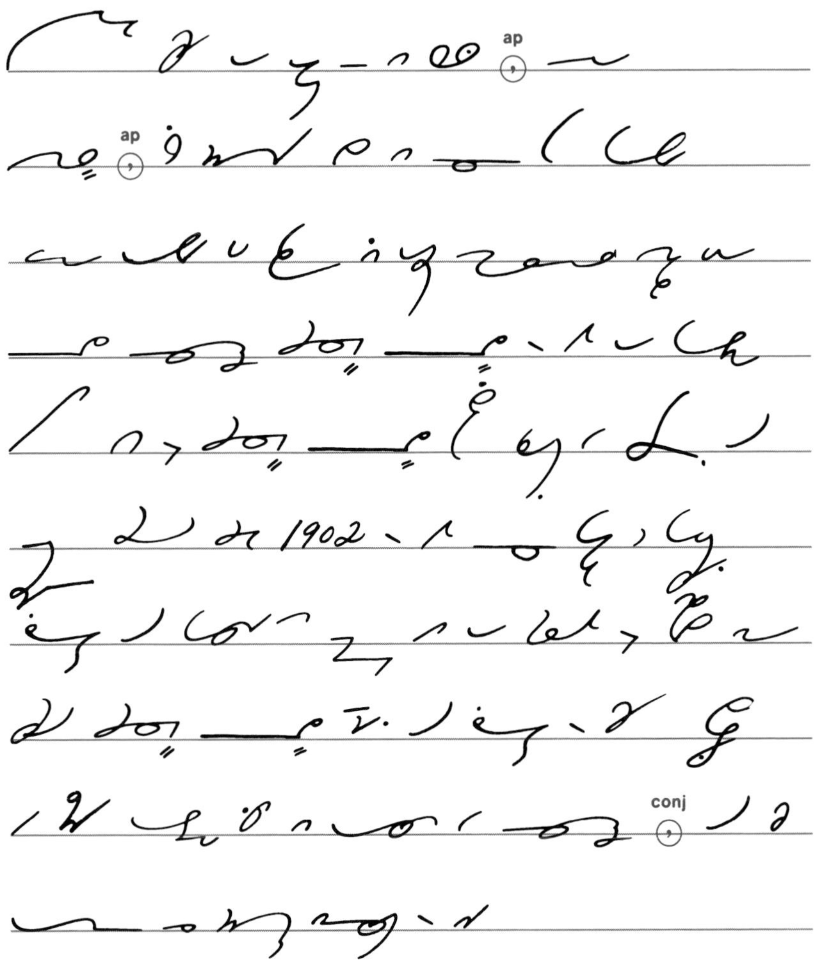

10
19
31
42
55
67
81
95
107
117

Mailable Production

Transcribe the following mailable production letter in block style, assuring proper placement of all letter parts and special notation. Insert punctuation prior to transcribing, and capitalize proper nouns and titles. Address a large envelope with the special notation *Registered.*

26.4 Time Limit: 15 minutes

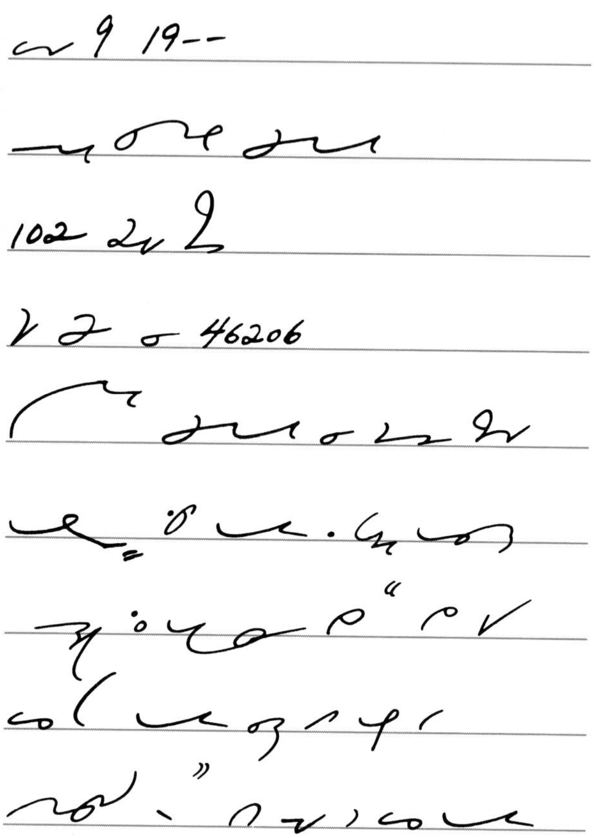

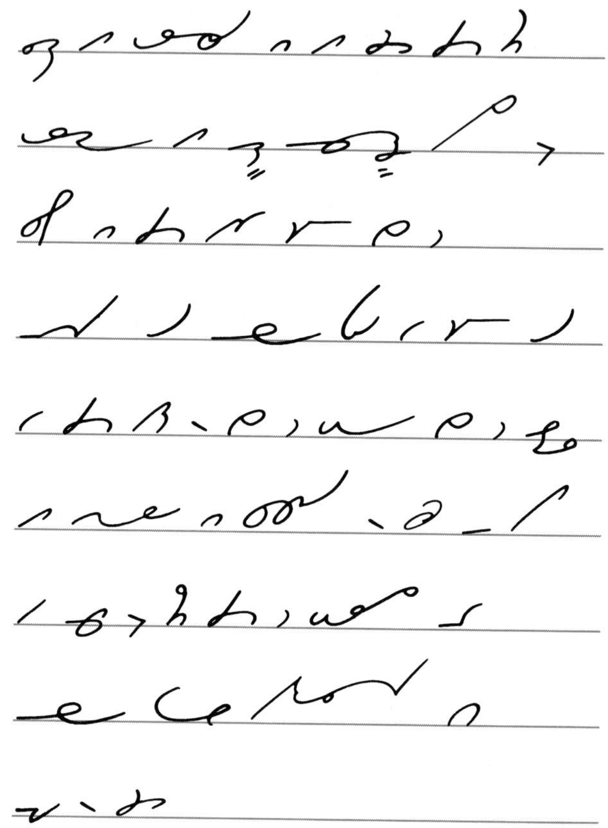

[92 words]

LESSON 27

HAMILTON PUBLISHING COMPANY

DICTATION SPEED BUILDING

The shorthand outlines below appear in the speed dictation practice that follows. Practice writing these words using the shorthand outlines. Then, using the key that follows, dictate the words to yourself in preparation for the speed dictation practice.

Dictation Preview

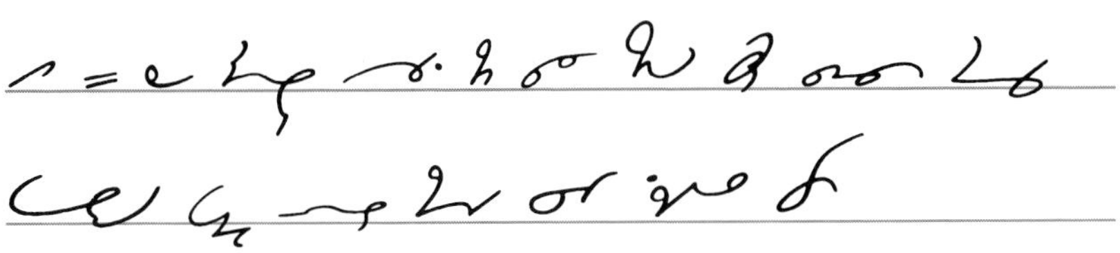

Key: two-year subscription, getting, issue, within, assured, wise, unique, format, pleasant, persons, increases, effect, another, history, back

Speed Dictation Practice

27.1 Goal: 80 wam speed dictation

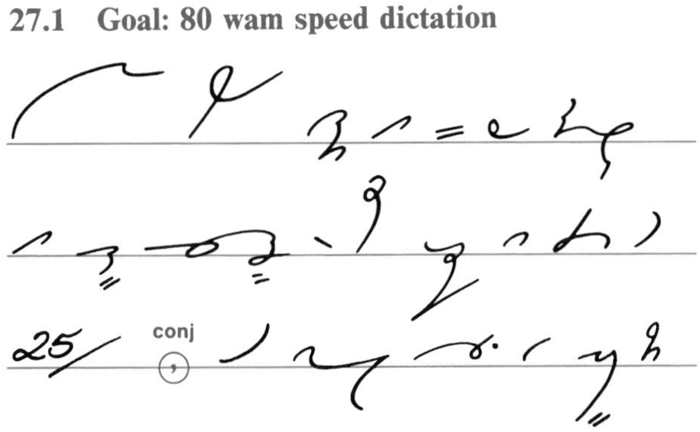

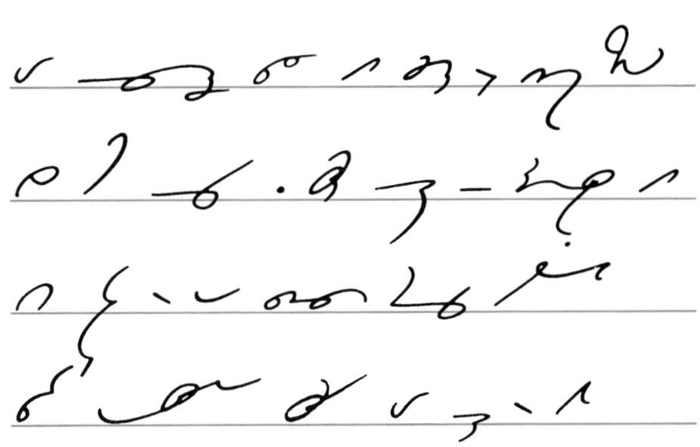

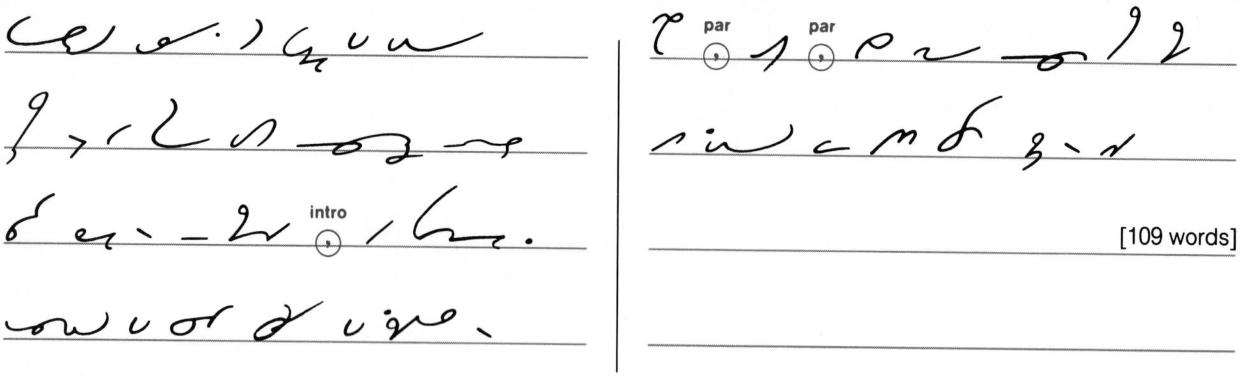

[109 words]

TRANSCRIPTION SKILL DEVELOPMENT

Transcription Warmup

Transcribe the following groups of words for speed and accuracy, applying transcription rules and assuring correct spelling.

27.2

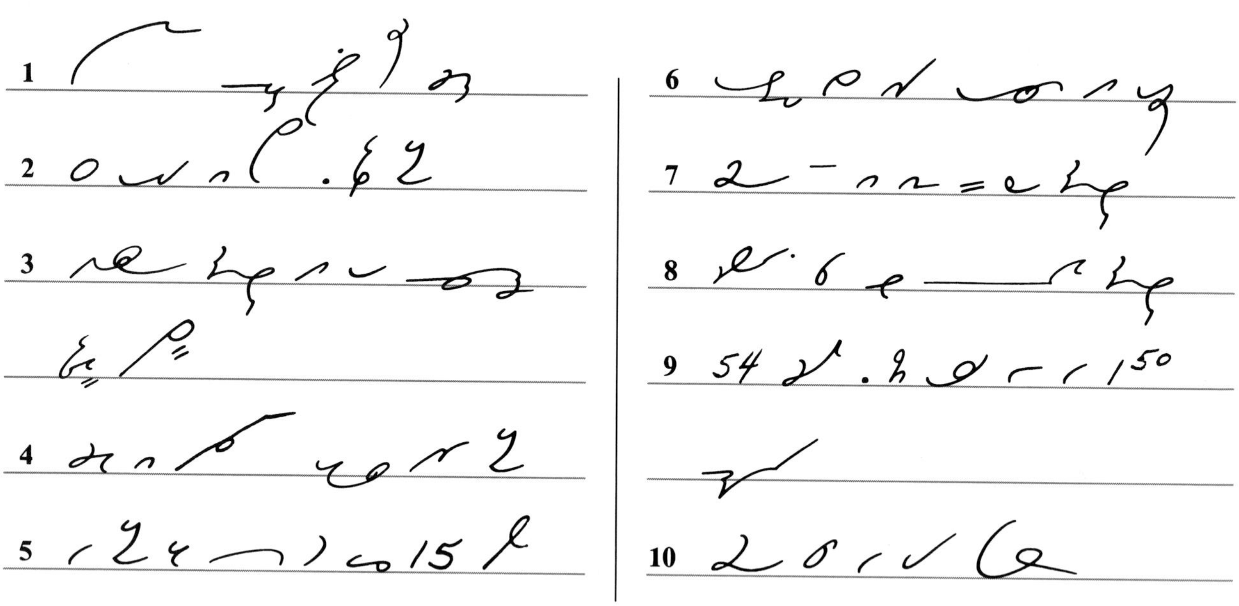

Transcription Practice

Transcribe the following letter for 2 minutes in unarranged format, applying transcription rules and assuring correct spelling. For every word not transcribed and every keyboarding error, deduct one word from the total word count.

27.3 Goal: 25 wam transcription rate

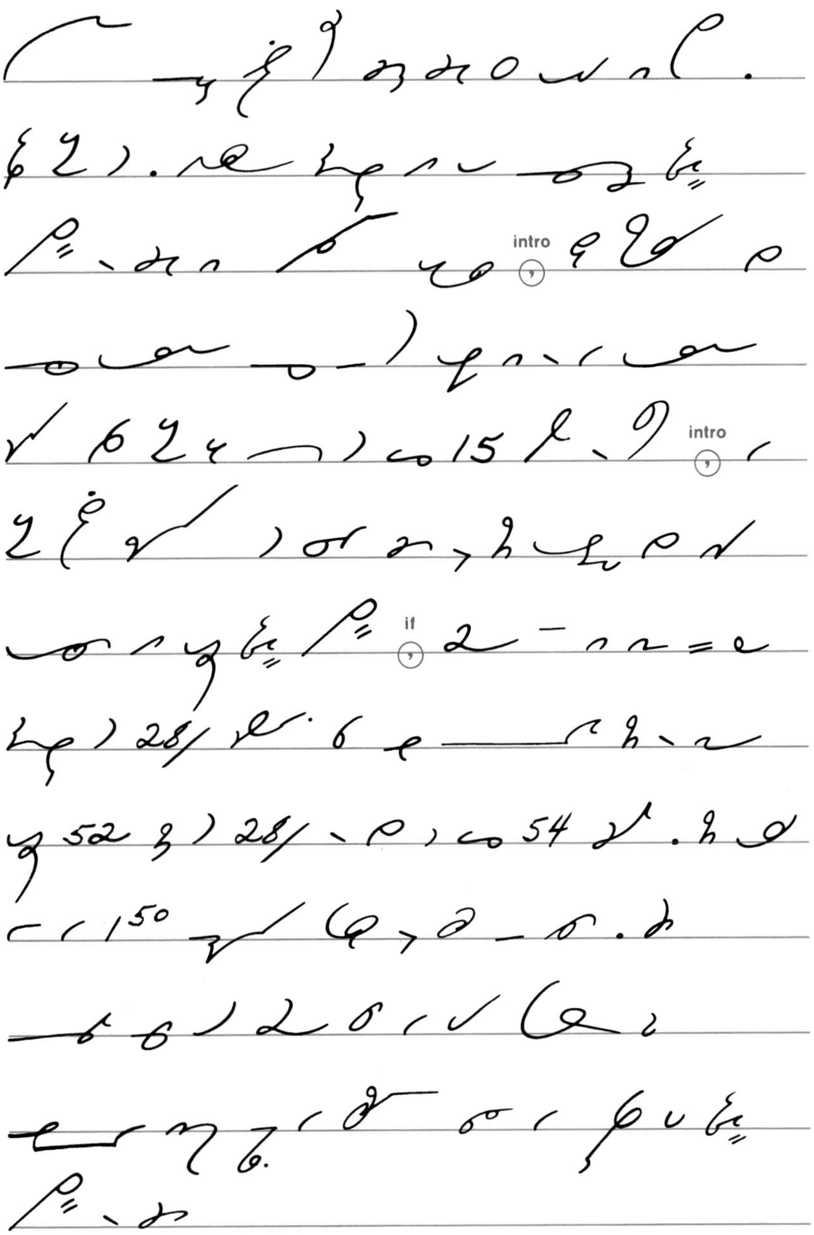

Word Count

13
25
35
44
56
71
83
96
109
119
128
142
147

Mailable Production

Transcribe the following mailable production letter in block style, assuring proper placement of all letter parts and special notation. Insert punctuation prior to transcribing, and capitalize proper nouns and titles. Address a large envelope with the special notation *Special Delivery.*

27.4 Time Limit: 15 minutes

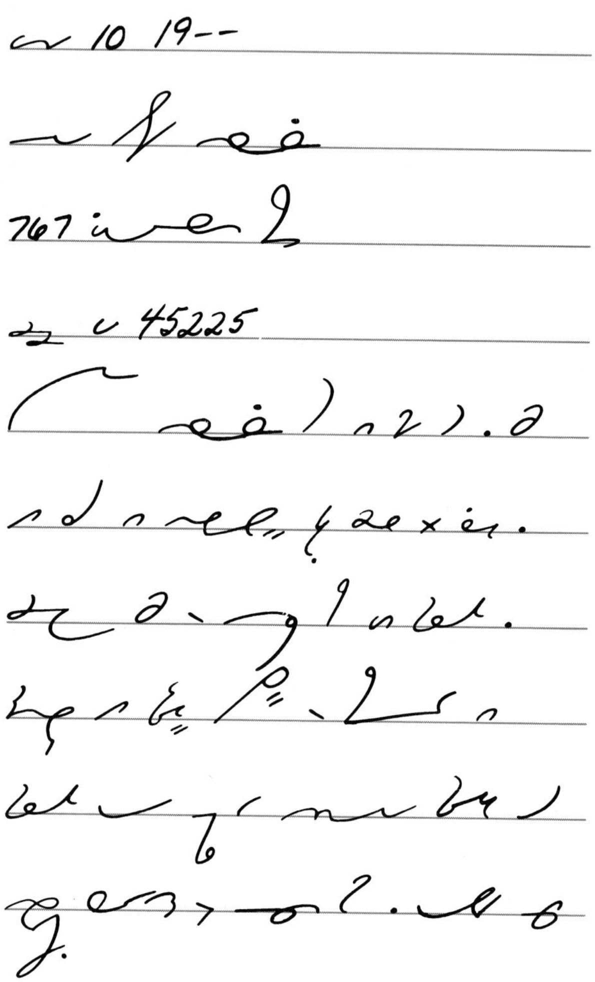

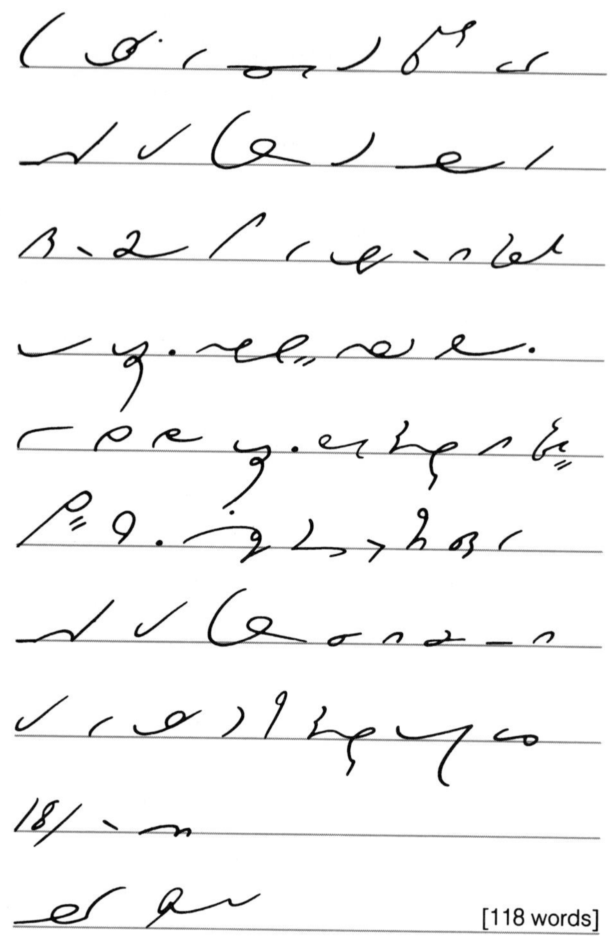

[118 words]

LESSON 28

HAMILTON PUBLISHING COMPANY

DICTATION SPEED BUILDING

The shorthand outlines below appear in the speed dictation practice that follows. Practice writing these words using the shorthand outlines. Then, using the key that follows, dictate the words to yourself in preparation for the speed dictation practice.

Dictation Preview

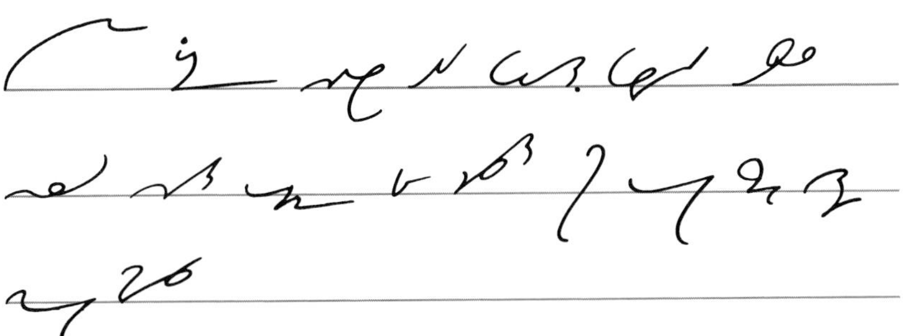

Key: Dear Mr. Hoffmann, contributor, thought, producing, president, entirely, current, conditions, resume, shown, status, you have been, will be, as soon as, thank you for the, you will be, up to date

Speed Dictation Practice

28.1 Goal: 80 wam speed dictation

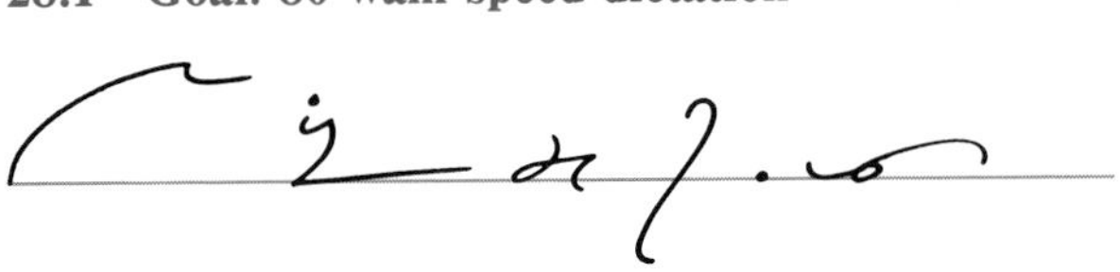

TRANSCRIPTION SKILL DEVELOPMENT

Transcription Warmup

Transcribe the following groups of words for speed and accuracy, applying transcription rules and assuring correct spelling.

28.2

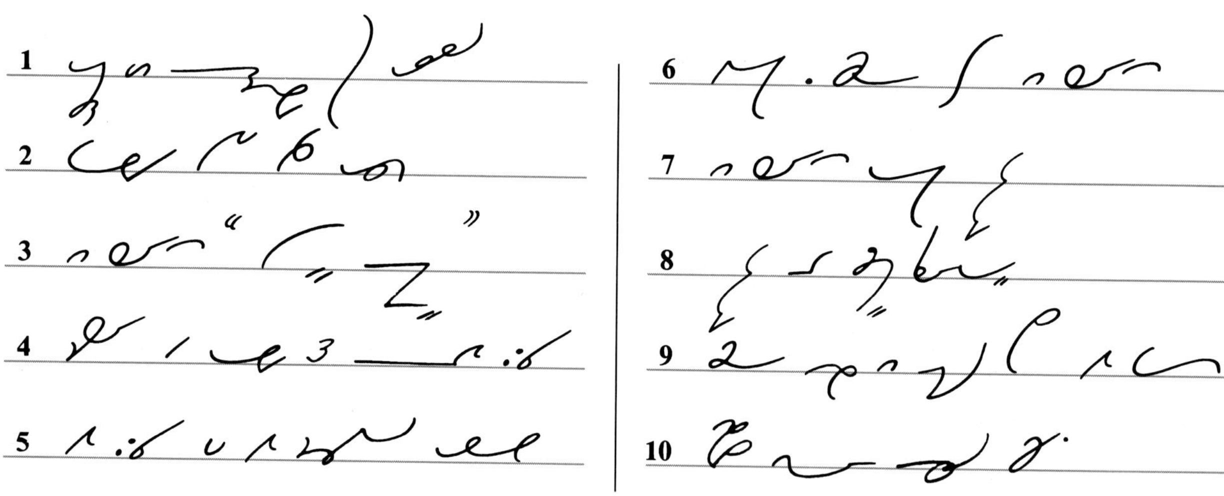

Transcription Practice

Transcribe the following letter for 2 minutes in unarranged format, applying transcription rules and assuring correct spelling. For every word not transcribed and every keyboarding error, deduct one word from the total word count.

28.3 Goal: 25 wam transcription rate

Word Count

11
25
36
49
60
72
86
96
109

Mailable Production

You may be asked to take dictation for a tabular listing. Notice that the information that appears in the tabular listing below does not contain capitalization or column headings. Also, notice that the shorthand for each unit of information—that is, ISBN, title, and net price—is separate from the next unit of information.

Type the following list of textbooks using the column headings *ISBN*, *Book Title*, and *Net Price* as illustrated in the example in Lesson 25. Use the title *New Listings*, and follow the guidelines presented in Lesson 25 for formatting this document.

28.4 Time Limit: 15 minutes

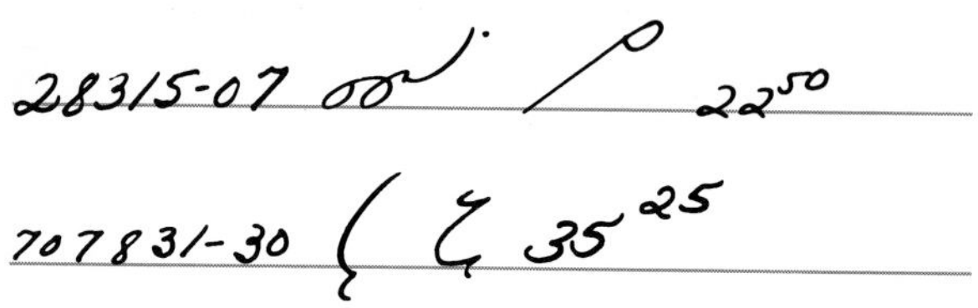

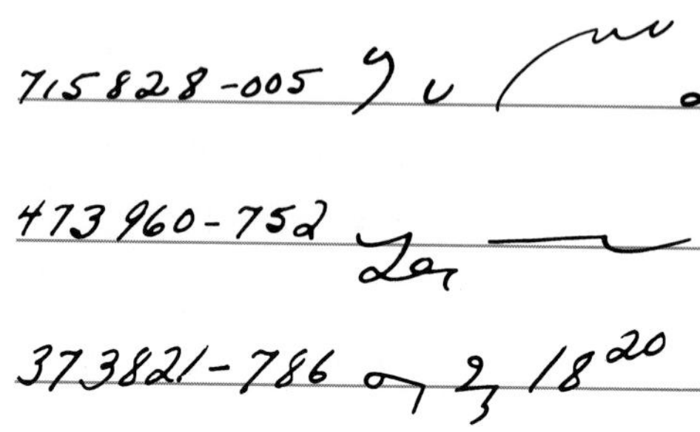

[80 words]

LESSON 29

HAMILTON PUBLISHING COMPANY

DICTATION SPEED BUILDING

The shorthand outlines below appear in the speed dictation practice that follows. Practice writing these words using the shorthand outlines. Then, using the key that follows, dictate the words to yourself in preparation for the speed dictation practice.

Dictation Preview

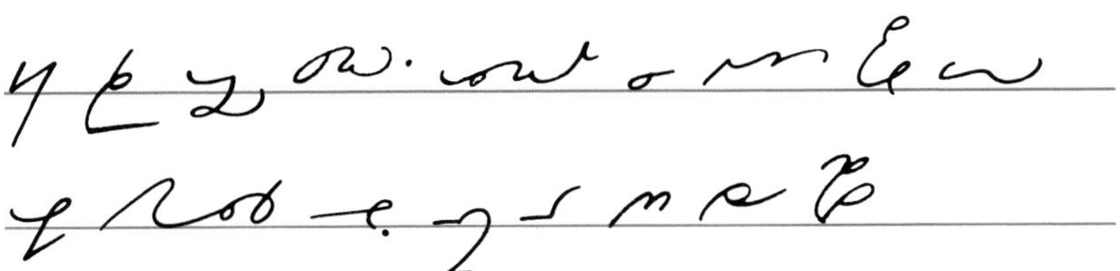

Key: shortage, shipment, referred, according, records, when, truck, express, occurred, reached, duplicate, missing, inconvenience, in the, to you, that are, we hope that

Speed Dictation Practice

29.1 Goal: 80 wam speed dictation

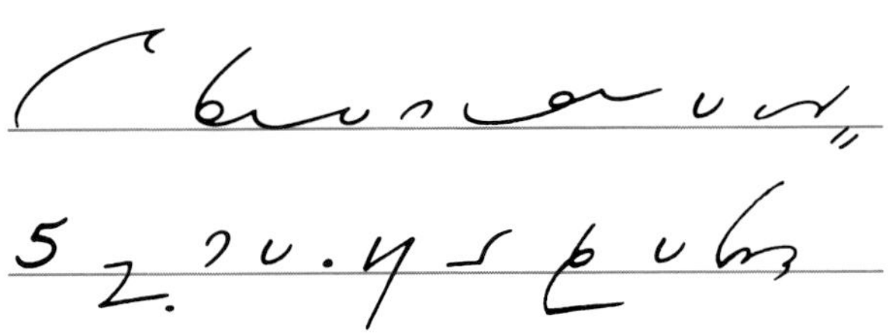

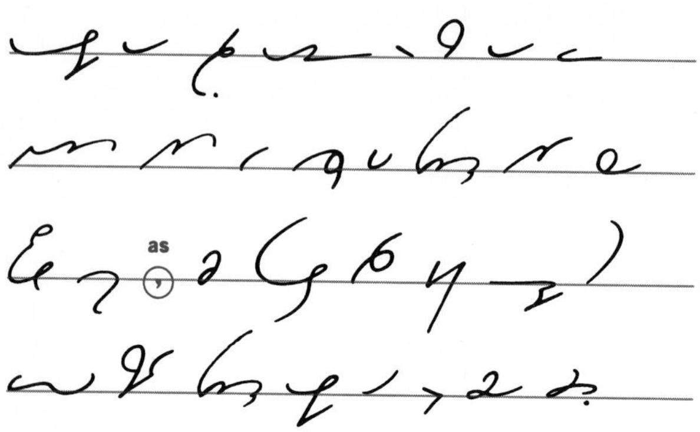

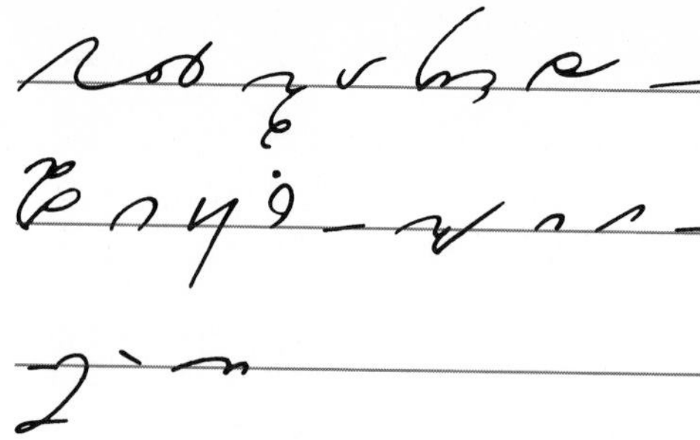

[98 words]

TRANSCRIPTION SKILL DEVELOPMENT

Transcription Warmup

Transcribe the following groups of words for speed and accuracy, applying transcription rules and assuring correct spelling.

29.2

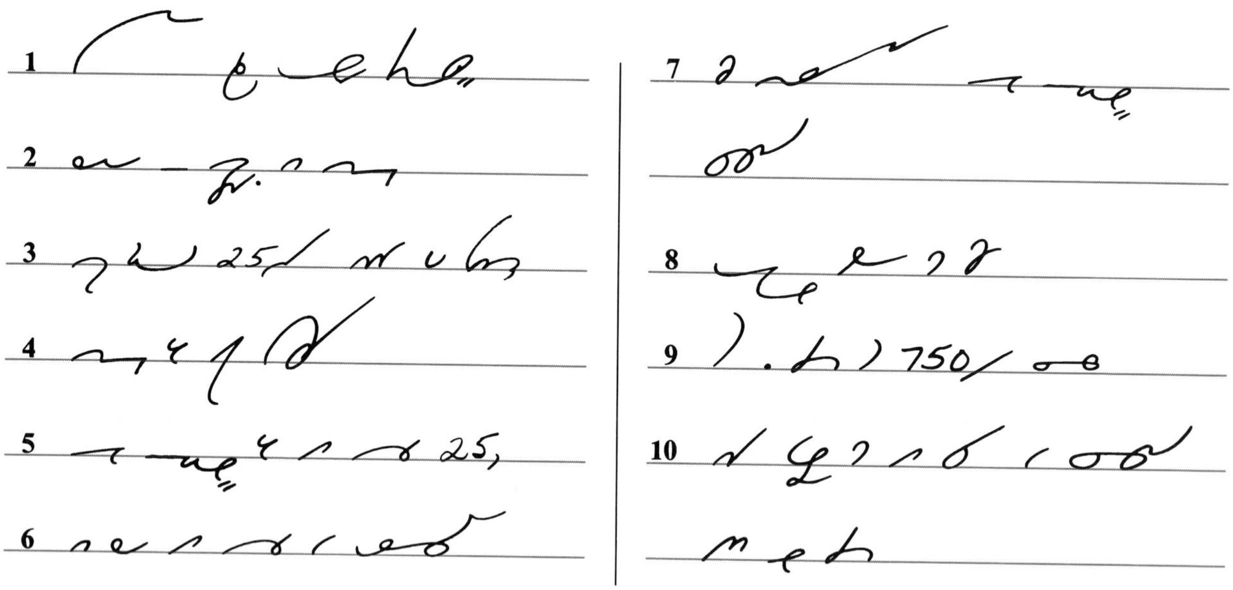

Transcription Practice

Transcribe the following letter for 2 minutes in unarranged format, applying transcription rules and assuring correct spelling. For every word not transcribed and every keyboarding error, deduct one word from the total word count.

29.3 Goal: 25 wam transcription rate

Word Count

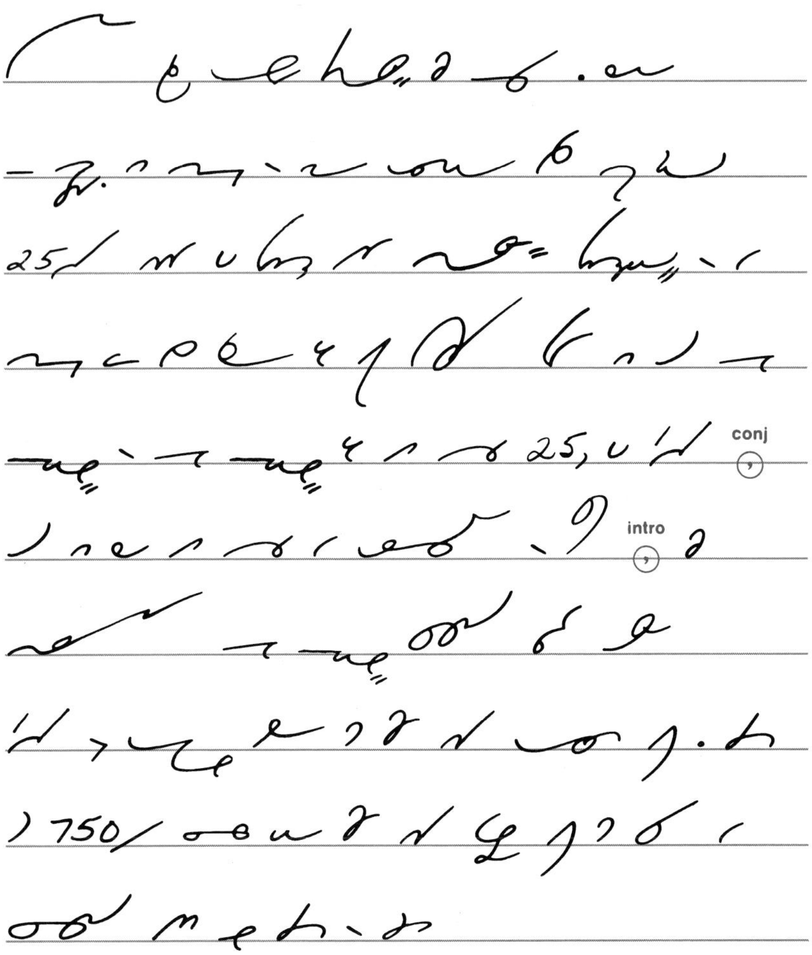

9
23
33
45
55
64
73
87
100
109

Mailable Production

Transcribe the following mailable production letter in block style, assuring proper placement of all letter parts. Insert punctuation prior to transcribing, and capitalize proper nouns and titles. Address a large envelope.

29.4 Time Limit: 15 minutes

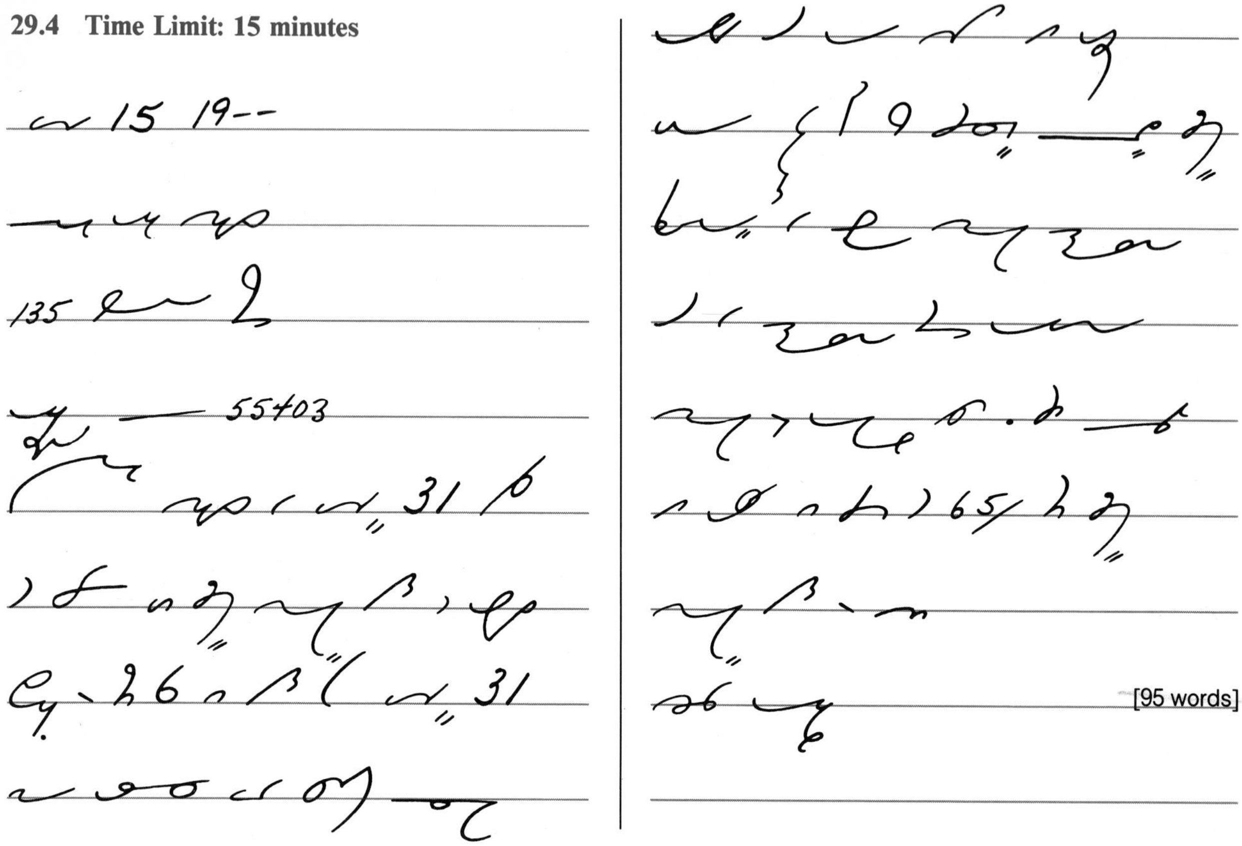

[95 words]

LESSON 30

HAMILTON PUBLISHING COMPANY

DICTATION SPEED BUILDING

The shorthand outlines below appear in the speed dictation practice that follows. Practice writing these words using the shorthand outlines. Then, using the key that follows, dictate the words to yourself in preparation for the speed dictation practice.

Dictation Preview

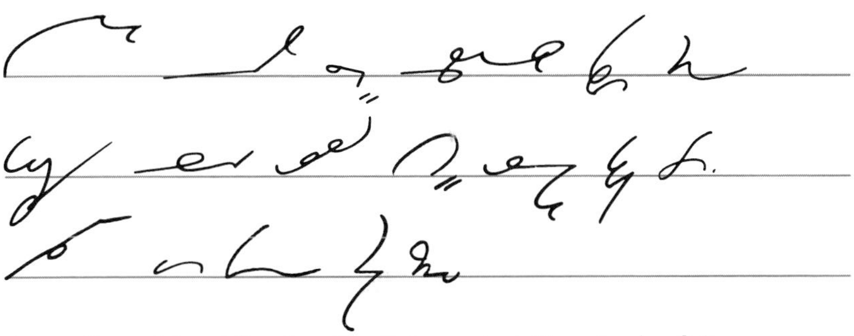

Key: Dear Mrs. Mendez, English, materialize, basic, full, provided, marked, returned, Denver, reimburse, postage, packing, did not, of course, be glad, have not been, as you know

Speed Dictation Practice

30.1 Goal: 80 wam speed dictation

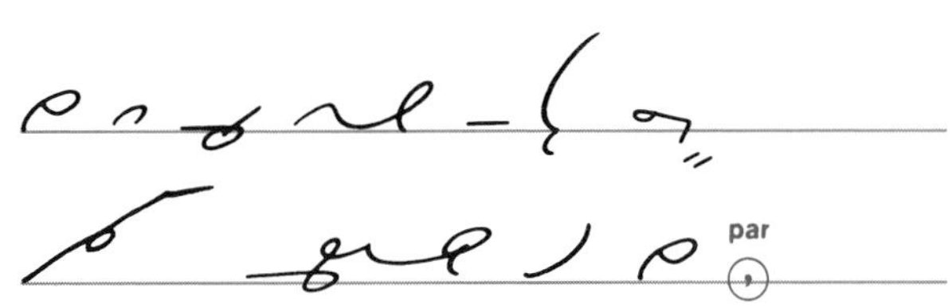

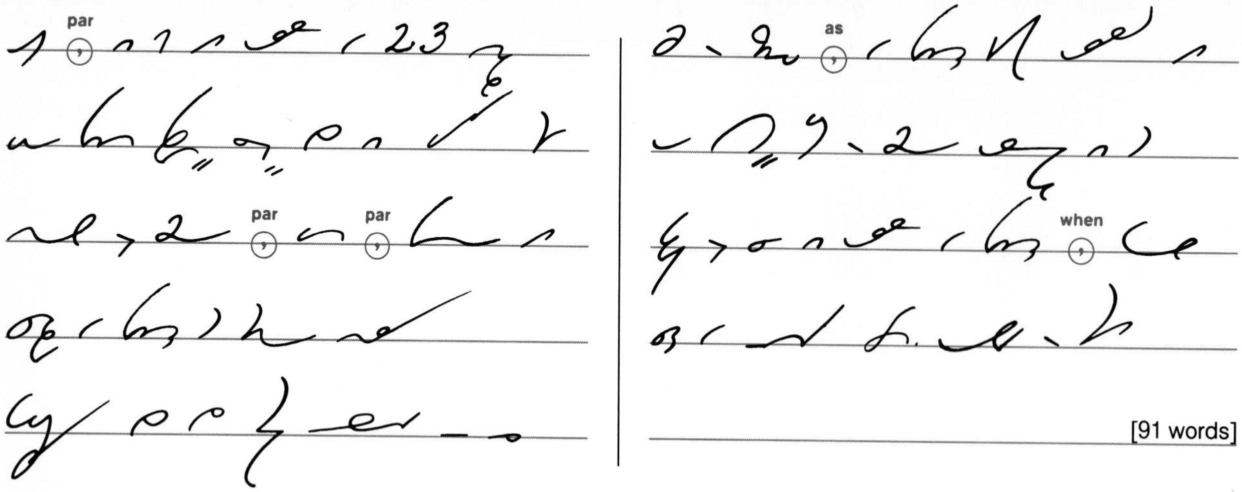

TRANSCRIPTION SKILL DEVELOPMENT

Transcription Warmup

Transcribe the following groups of words for speed and accuracy, applying transcription rules and assuring correct spelling.

30.2

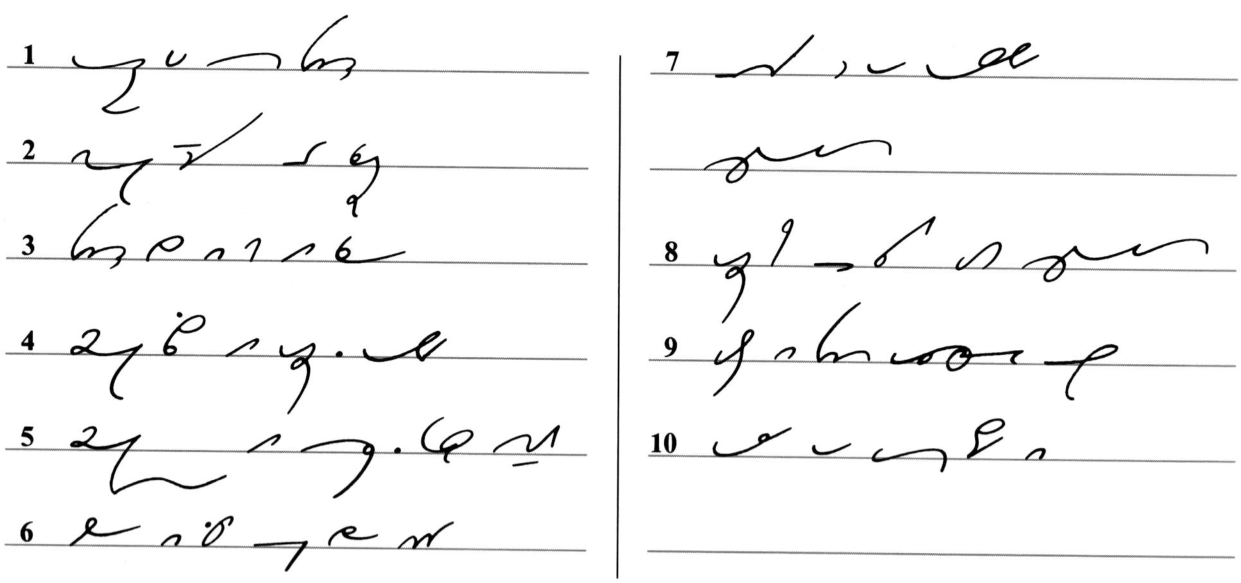

Transcription Practice

Transcribe the following letter for 2 minutes in unarranged format, applying transcription rules and assuring correct spelling. For every word not transcribed and every keyboarding error, deduct one word from the total word count.

30.3 Goal: 25 wam transcription rate

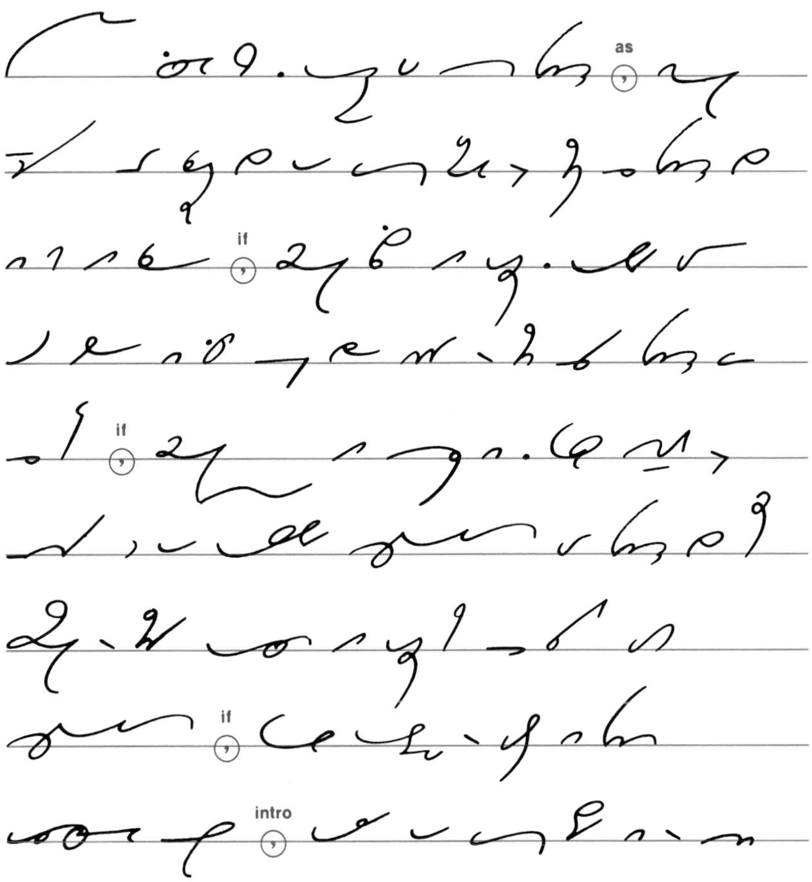

Word Count
10
27
39
51
63
74
87
97
111

Mailable Production

Transcribe the following mailable production letter in block style, assuring proper placement of all letter parts. Insert punctuation prior to transcribing, and capitalize proper nouns and titles. Address a large envelope.

30.4 Time Limit: 15 minutes

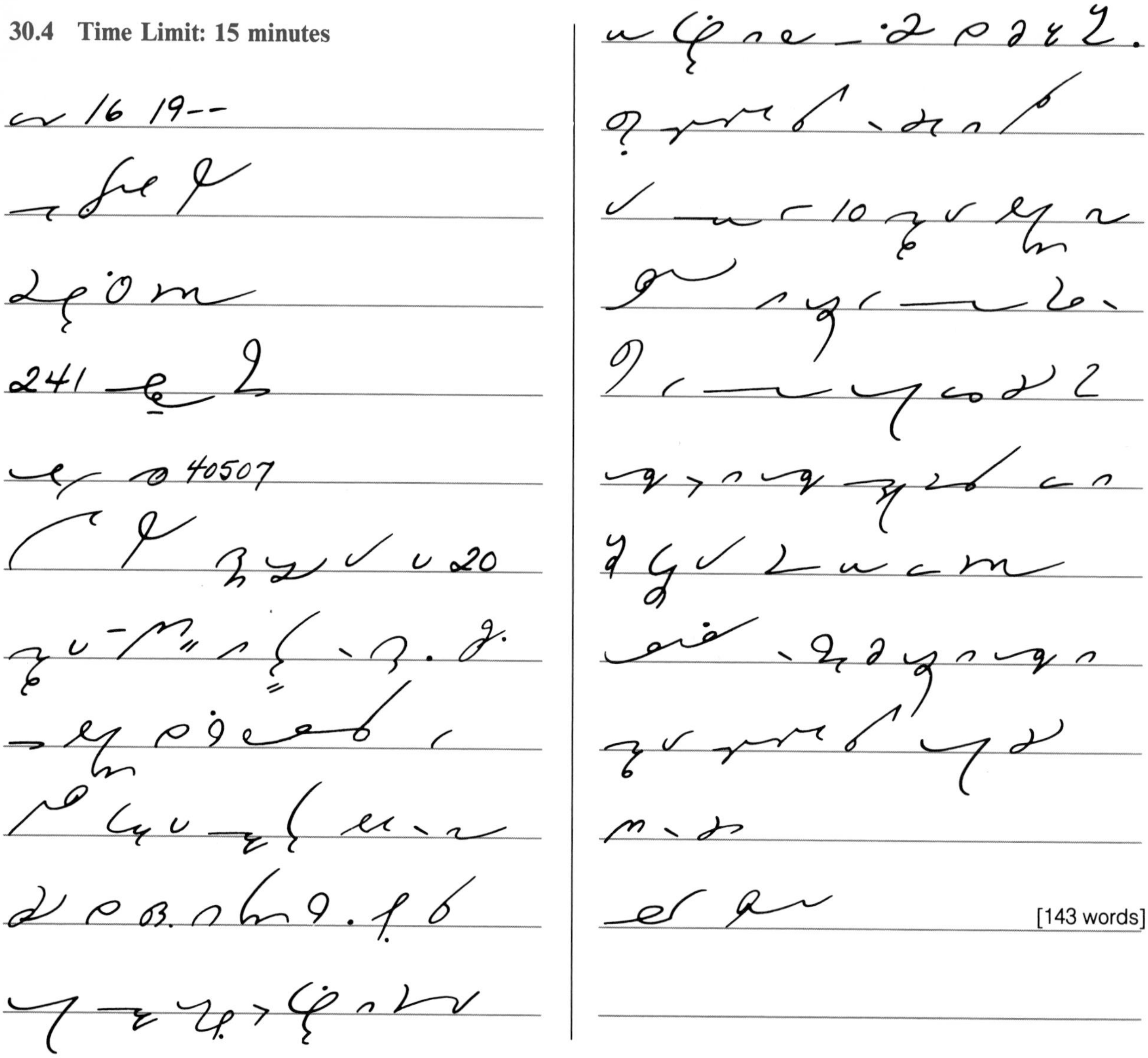

[143 words]

LESSON 31

HAMILTON PUBLISHING COMPANY

DICTATION SPEED BUILDING

The shorthand outlines below appear in the speed dictation practice that follows. Practice writing these words using the shorthand outlines. Then, using the key that follows, dictate the words to yourself in preparation for the speed dictation practice.

Dictation Preview

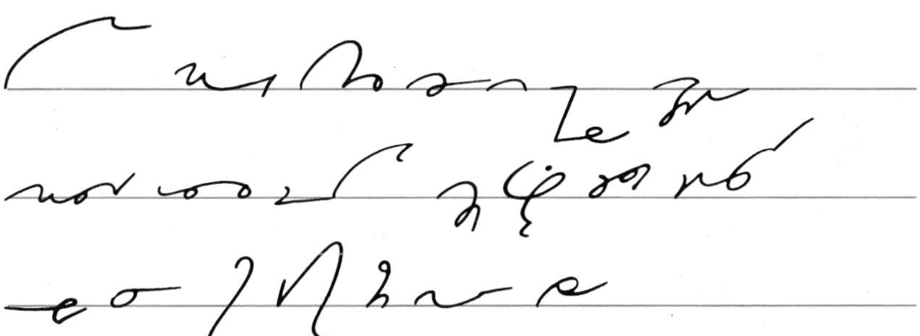

Key: Dear Mr. Walsh, difficulty, chemical, engineer, computer, correct, regularly, sometimes, confusion, perhaps, situation, straightened, missed, I am, you have been, should have been, if you, you are not, that are

Speed Dictation Practice

31.1 Goal: 80 wam speed dictation

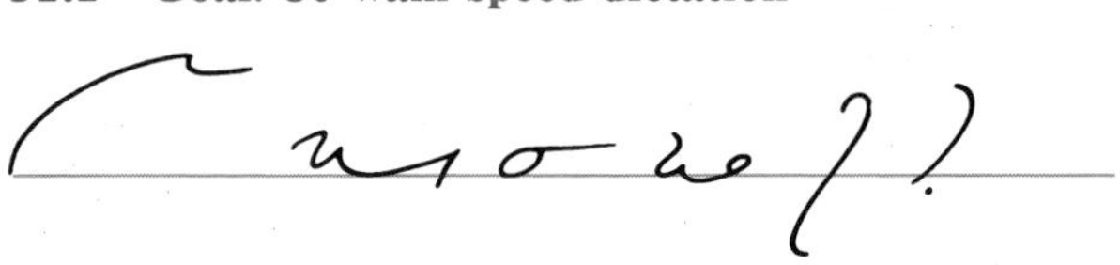

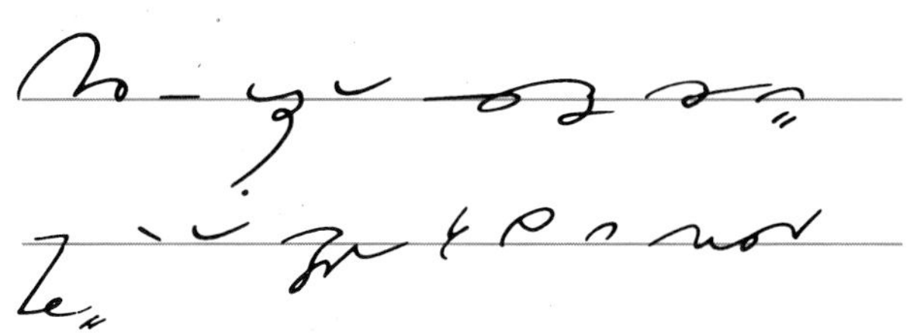

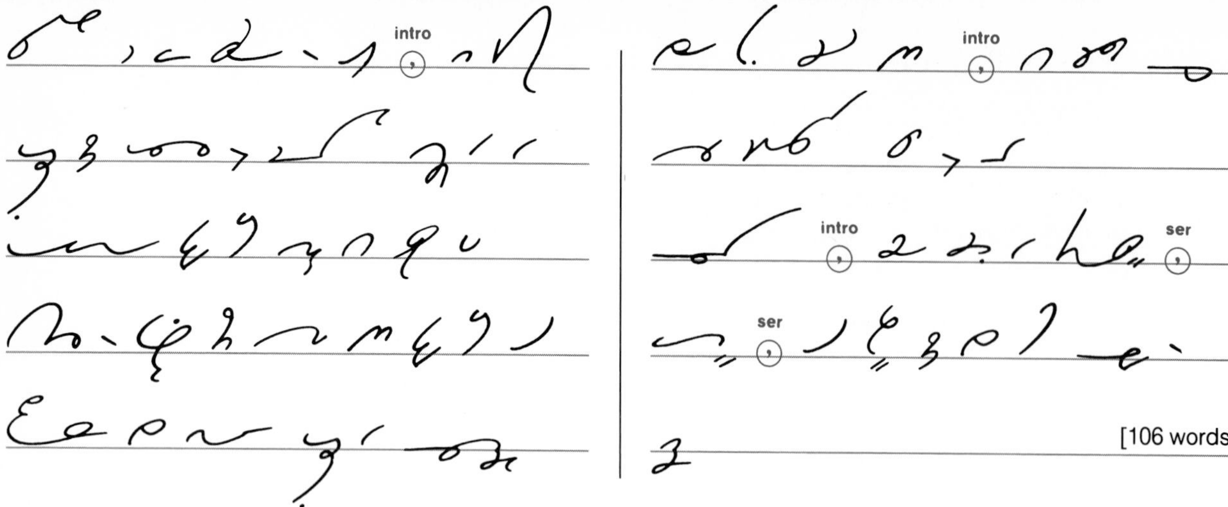

[106 words]

TRANSCRIPTION SKILL DEVELOPMENT

Transcription Warmup

Transcribe the following groups of words for speed and accuracy, applying transcription rules and assuring correct spelling.

31.2

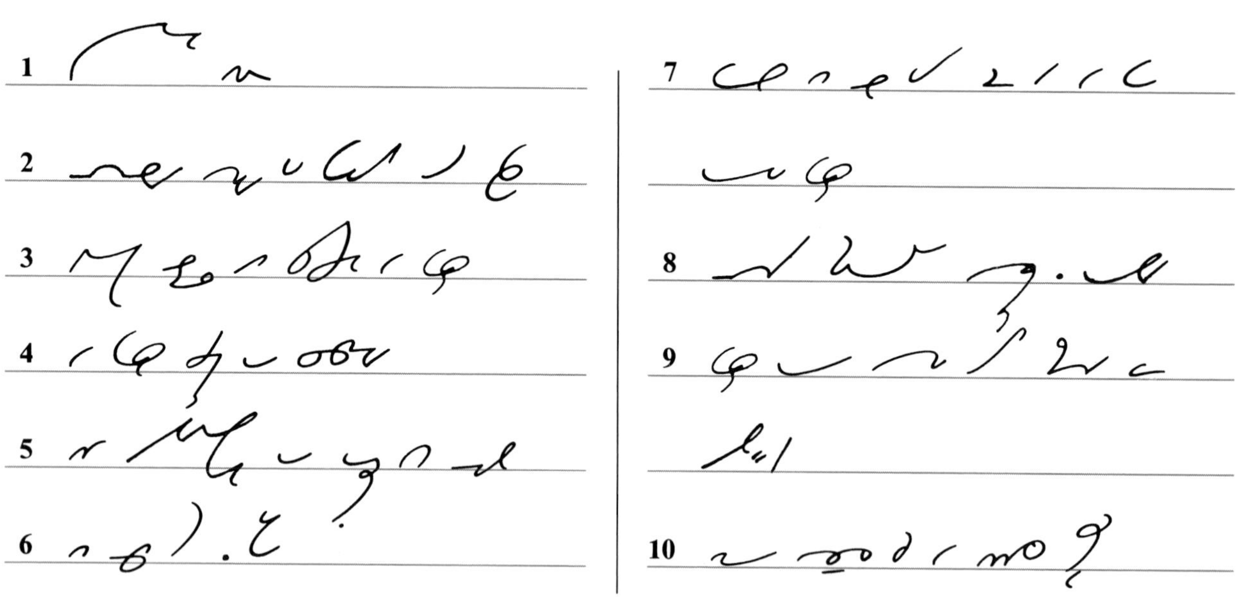

Transcription Practice

Transcribe the following letter for 2 minutes in unarranged format, applying transcription rules and assuring correct spelling. For every word not transcribed and every keyboarding error, deduct one word from the total word count.

31.3 Goal: 25 wam transcription rate

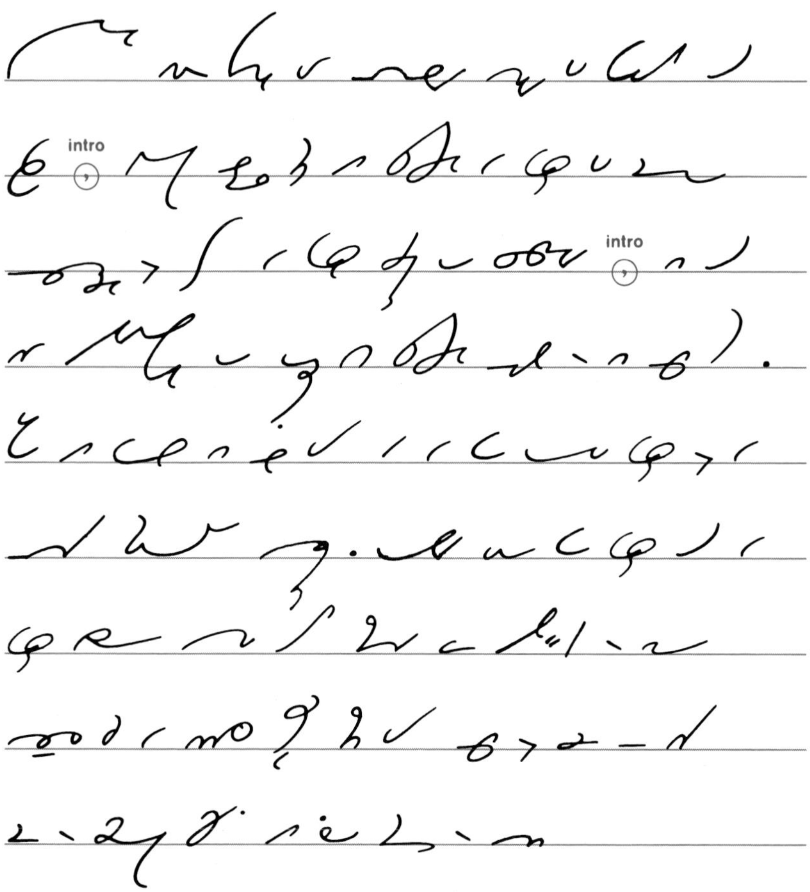

Word Count

12
26
38
52
65
77
89
103
115

Mailable Production

Transcribe the following mailable production letter in block style, assuring proper placement of all letter parts. Insert punctuation prior to transcribing, and capitalize proper nouns and titles. Address a large envelope with the special notation *Personal.*

31.4 Time Limit: 15 minutes

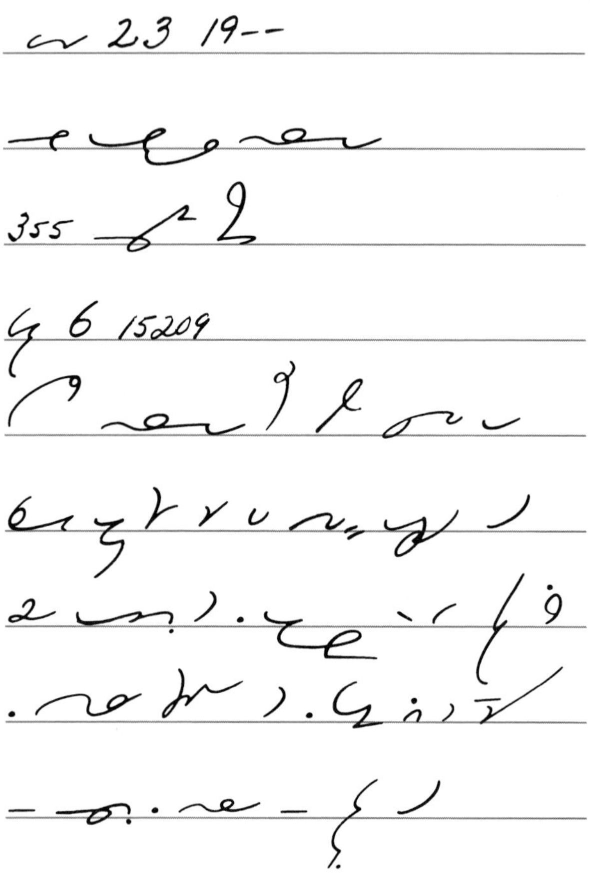

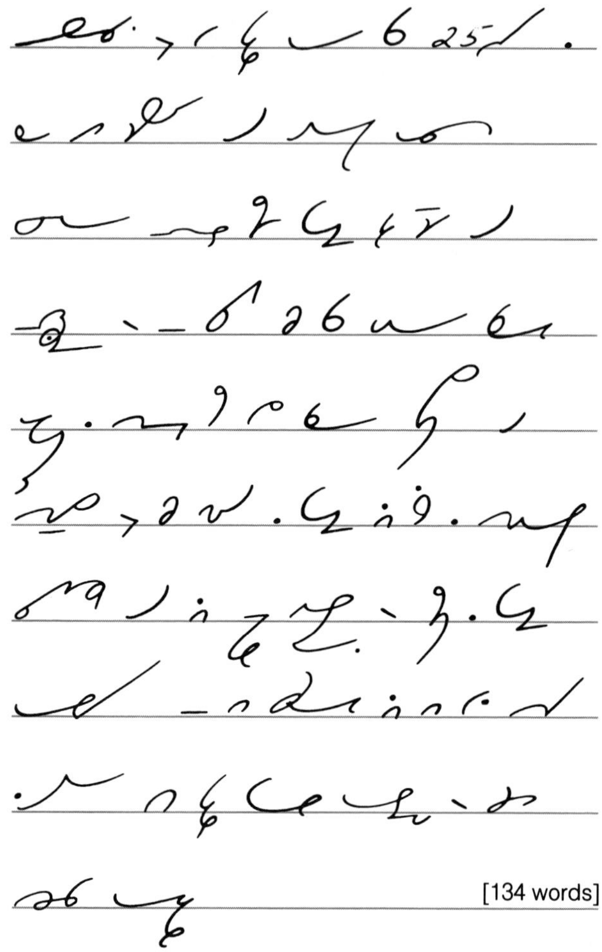

[134 words]

LESSON 32

HAMILTON PUBLISHING COMPANY

DICTATION SPEED BUILDING

The shorthand outlines below appear in the speed dictation practice that follows. Practice writing these words using the shorthand outlines. Then, using the key that follows, dictate the words to yourself in preparation for the speed dictation practice.

Dictation Preview

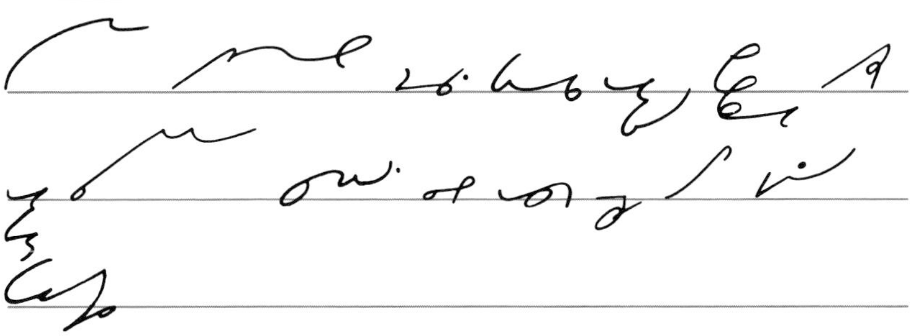

Key: Dear Mr. Douglas, submitting, policy, respond, appraisals, decision, responses, editorial, according, initial, reaction, insight, into, shorthand, productivity

Speed Dictation Practice

32.1 Goal: 80 wam speed dictation

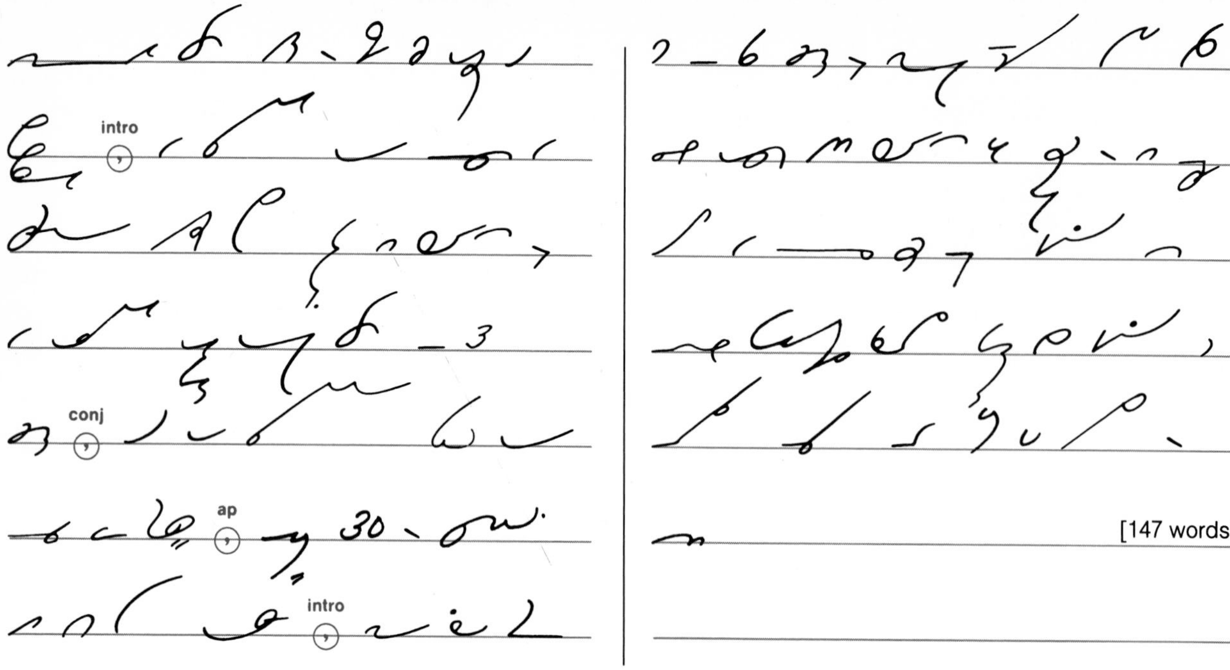

TRANSCRIPTION SKILL DEVELOPMENT

Transcription Warmup

Transcribe the following groups of words for speed and accuracy, applying transcription rules and assuring correct spelling.

32.2

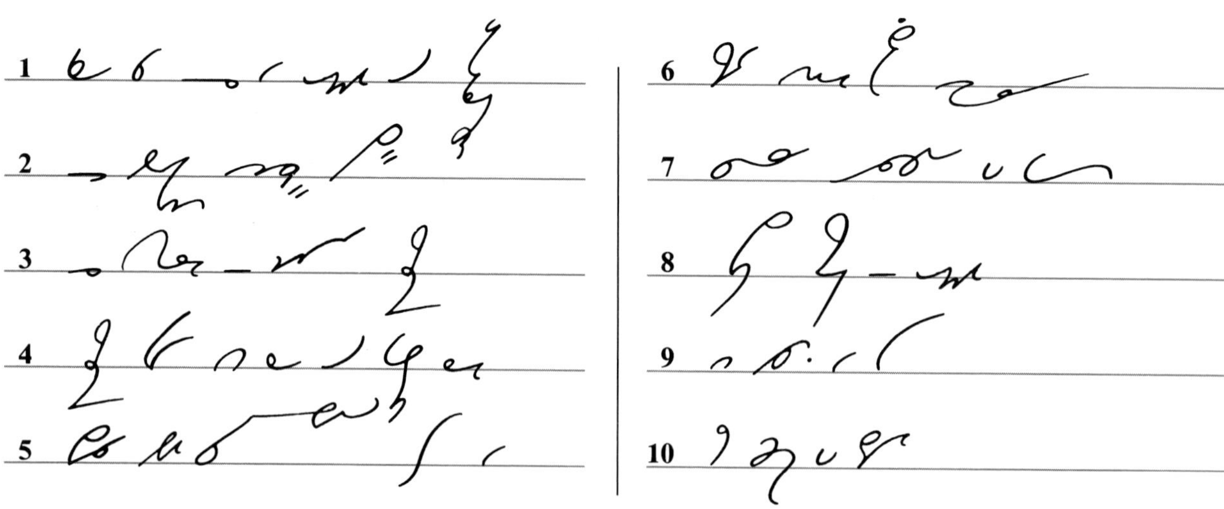

Transcription Practice

Transcribe the following letter for 2 minutes in unarranged format, applying transcription rules and assuring correct spelling. For every word not transcribed and every keyboarding error, deduct one word from the total word count.

32.3 Goal: 25 wam transcription rate

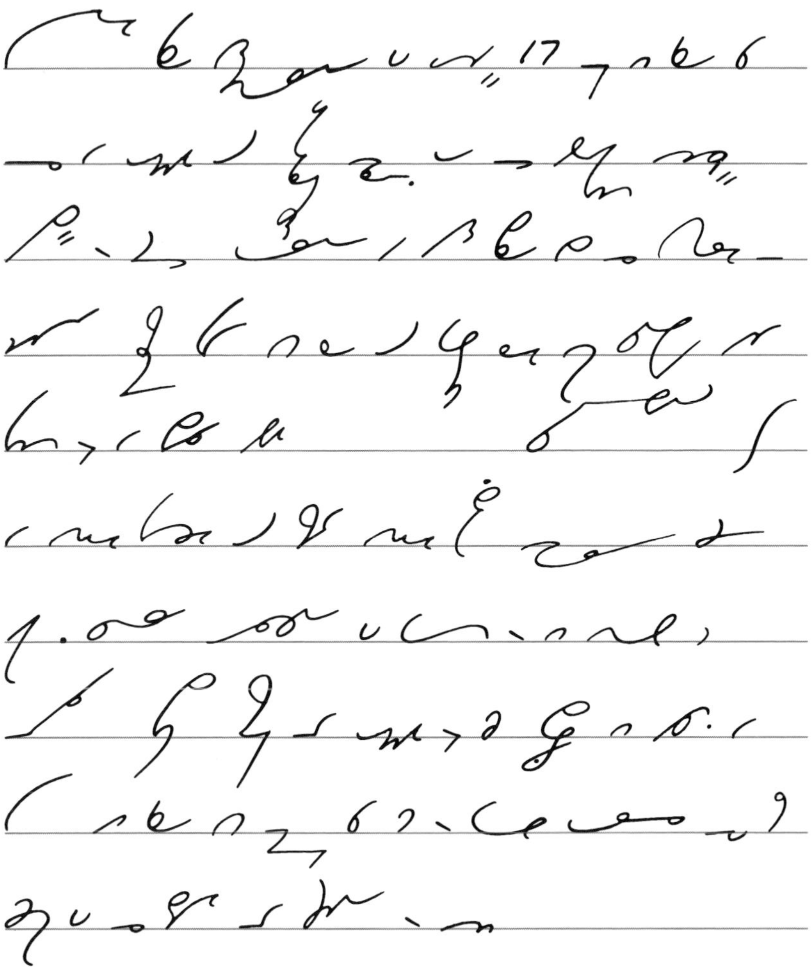

Word Count

16
31
43
59
68
80
91
104
116
128

Mailable Production

You may be asked to take dictation for a tabular listing. Notice that the information that appears in the tabular listing below does not contain capitalization or column headings. Also, notice that the shorthand for each unit of information—that is, ISBN, title, and net price—is separate from the next unit of information.

Type the following list of textbooks using the column headings *ISBN*, *Book Title*, and *Net Price* as illustrated in the example in Lesson 25. Use the title *New Listings*, and follow the guidelines presented in Lesson 25 for formatting this document.

32.4 Time Limit: 15 minutes

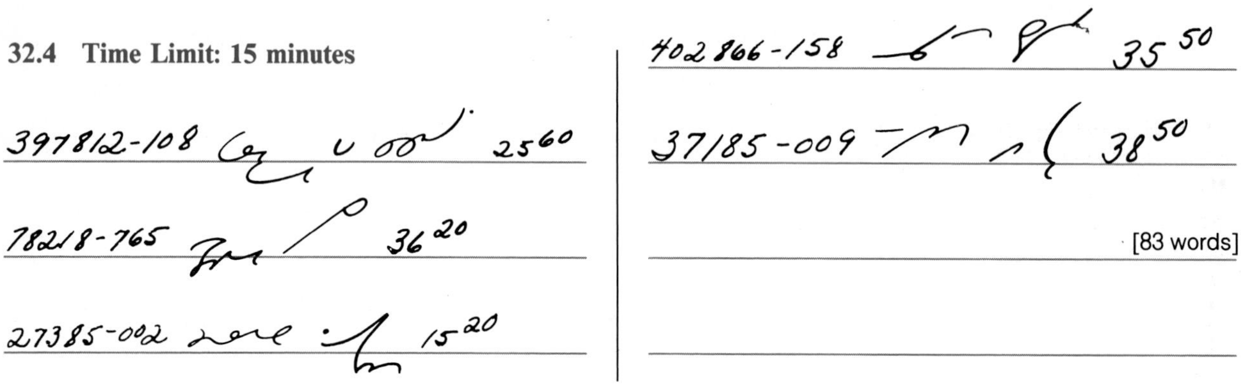

[83 words]

UNIT V

FIRST
NATIONAL
BANK

LESSON 33

FIRST NATIONAL BANK

You are employed at one of the four branch offices of the First National Bank located in Nashville, Tennessee. The main office is located in Memphis, and there are other branch offices in Chattanooga and Knoxville. The First National Bank is a full-service bank. The services include savings, checking, safe-deposit boxes, loans, estates and trusts, and investment advice.

You are employed as an administrative assistant to Elizabeth Adams, the general manager. Your administrative responsibilities are varied, including greeting customers, answering the telephone, setting up appointments, directing customers to the proper people handling the different services the bank provides, filing, taking dictation, and typing correspondence.

As you work through the lessons, you will be acquiring knowledge about banking services, as well as developing proficiency in taking dictation and increasing your transcription speed. The mailable production letters that are provided in the lessons and the letters the instructor will dictate will provide you with the opportunity to type correspondence for the signature of your manager, Elizabeth Adams.

Below is a copy of your company letterhead. Develop the return address that you will use to type the envelopes for the mailable production letters.

FIRST NATIONAL BANK

250 Woods Boulevard   Nashville, TN 37202
(615) 555-3702
Main office in Memphis
Branch offices in Nashville, Chattanooga, and Knoxville

Appointment Book

One of your responsibilities is to keep an appointment calendar for Elizabeth Adams. Below is an example of an appointment calendar.

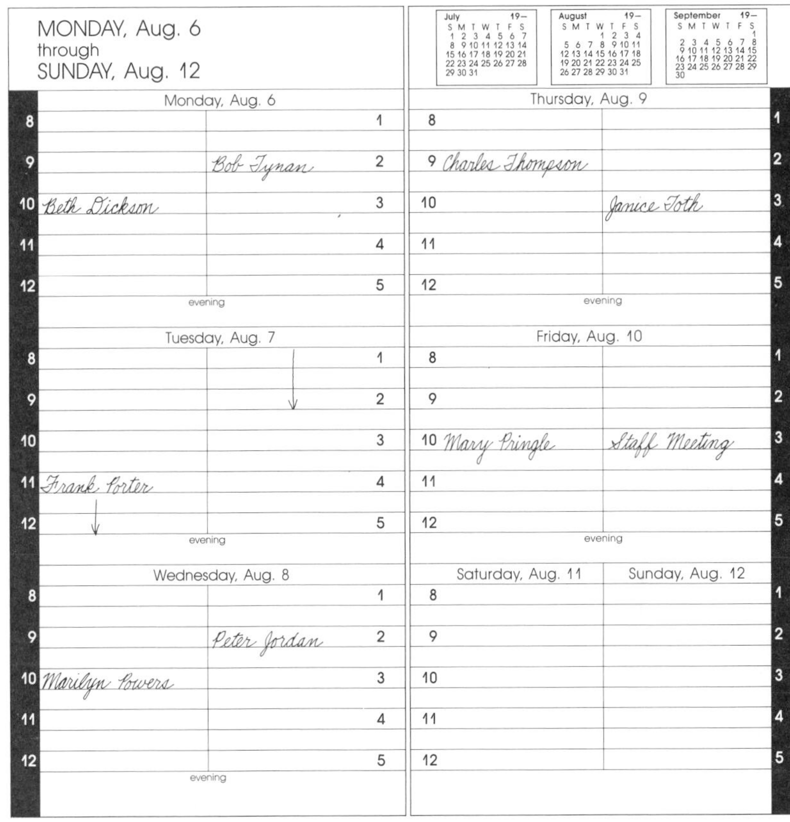

MONDAY, Aug. 6
through
SUNDAY, Aug. 12
July 19—
August 19—
September 19—
Monday, Aug. 6
Bob Tynan
Beth Dickson
evening
Tuesday, Aug. 7
Frank Porter
evening
Wednesday, Aug. 8
Peter Jordan
Marilyn Powers
evening
Thursday, Aug. 9
9 Charles Thompson
Janice Toth
evening
Friday, Aug. 10
10 Mary Pringle
Staff Meeting
evening
Saturday, Aug. 11
Sunday, Aug. 12

Transcription Tips

When two numbers come together in a sentence and both are in figures or both are in words, separate them with a comma.

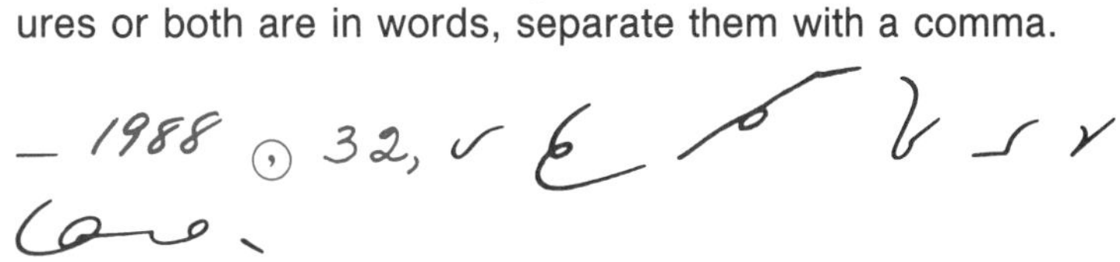

In *1988*, *32* percent of the people did not vote in the state primary.

When two numbers come together and one is part of a compound modifier, express one of the numbers in figures and the other in words. As a rule, spell out the first number unless the second number would make a shorter word.

Fifty $10 bills
500 two-page brochures

Serial numbers, such as invoice, model, and check numbers, are usually written without commas.

Invoice 38573
Model 43762
Check 37510

If the term *number* precedes a figure, express it as an abbreviation (singular: *No.*; plural: *Nos.*).

Social Security No. 149-33-1428

DICTATION SPEED BUILDING

The shorthand outlines below appear in the speed dictation practice that follows. Practice writing these words using the shorthand outlines. Then, using the key that follows, dictate the words to yourself in preparation for the speed dictation practice.

Dictation Preview

Key: Dear Mr. Knox, already, safe-deposit box, advantage, special, regular, depositors, limited, advertised, short, possession, come, to do, let us, to take

Speed Dictation Practice

33.1 Goal: 90 wam speed dictation

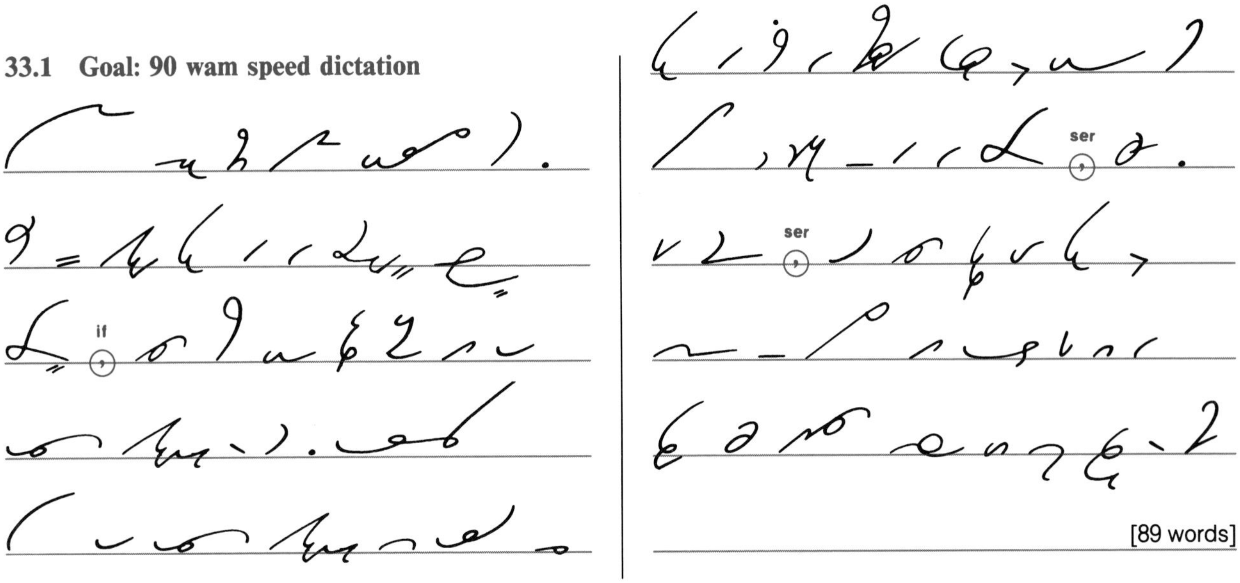

TRANSCRIPTION SKILL DEVELOPMENT

Transcription Warmup

Transcribe the following groups of words for speed and accuracy, applying transcription rules and assuring correct spelling.

33.2

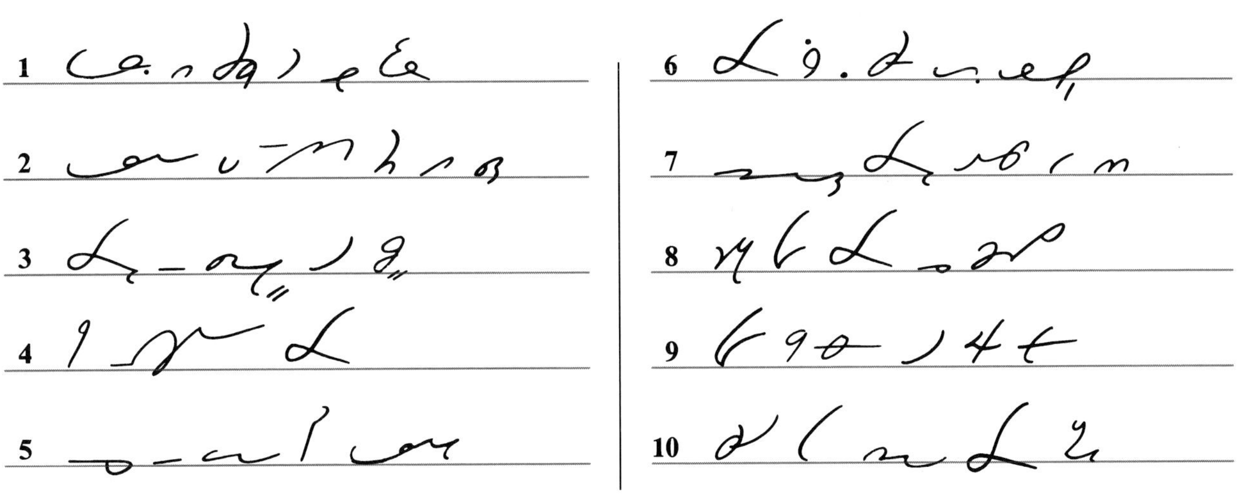

Transcription Practice

Transcribe the following letter for 2 minutes in unarranged format, applying transcription rules and assuring correct spelling. For every word not transcribed and every keyboarding error, deduct one word from the total word count.

33.3 Goal: 25 wam transcription rate

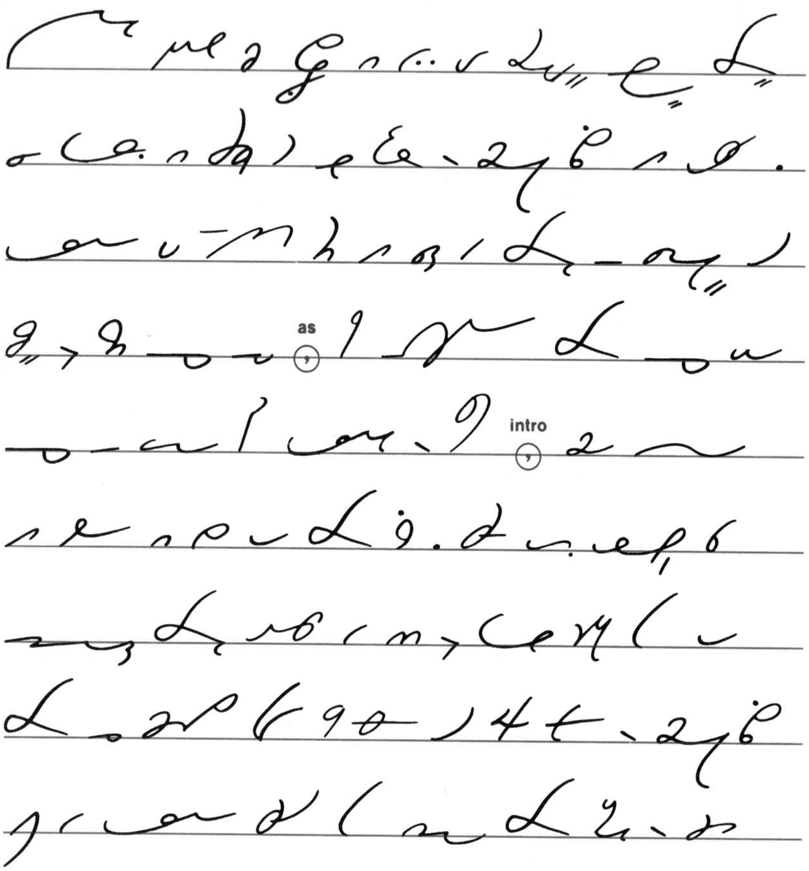

Word Count

14
29
41
51
61
73
84
96
111

LESSON 34

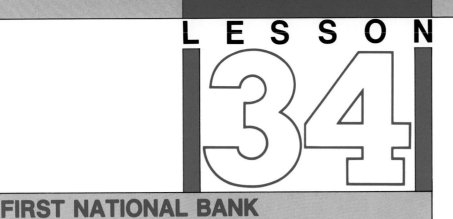

FIRST NATIONAL BANK

DICTATION SPEED BUILDING

The shorthand outlines below appear in the speed dictation practice that follows. Practice writing these words using the shorthand outlines. Then, using the key that follows, dictate the words to yourself in preparation for the speed dictation practice.

Dictation Preview

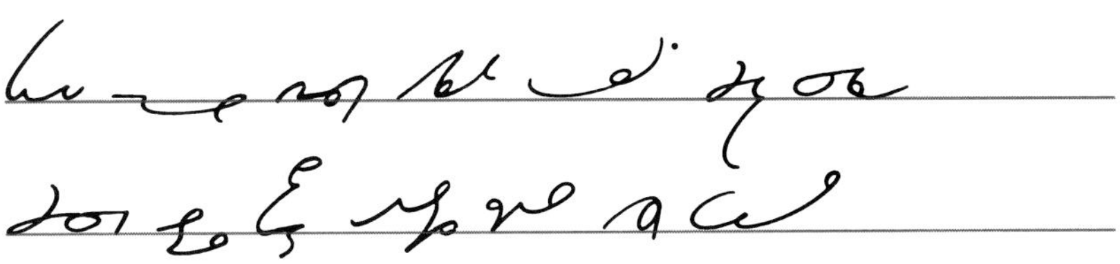

Key: borrow, unless, unusual, depends, lending, sensible, answer, financial, necessary, expenses, thrifty, extra, cash, promptly

Speed Dictation Practice

34.1 Goal: 90 wam speed dictation

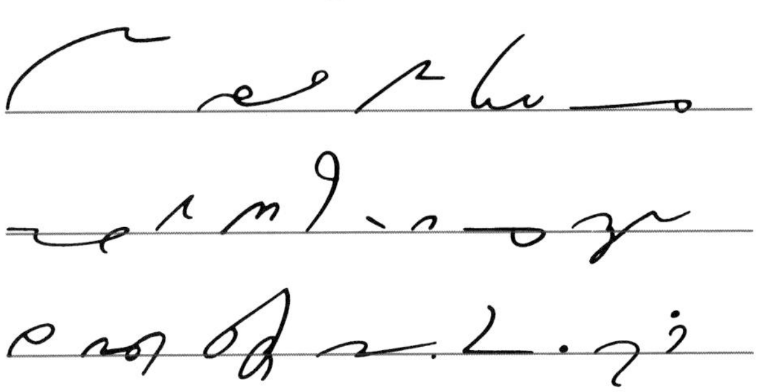

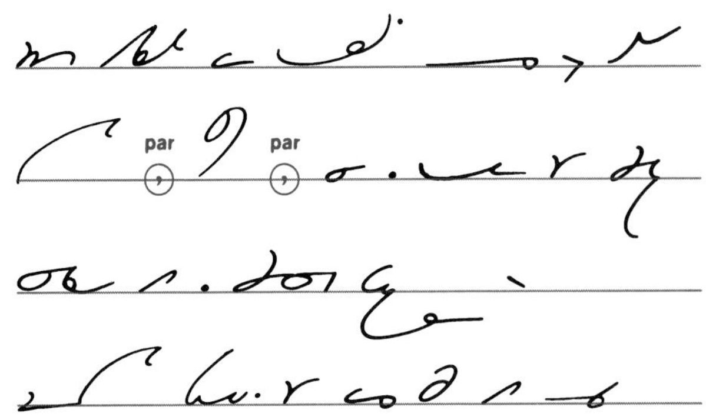

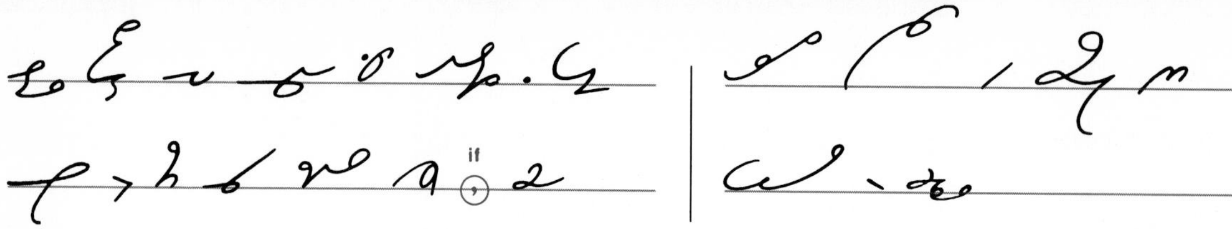

[90 words]

TRANSCRIPTION SKILL DEVELOPMENT

Transcription Warmup

Transcribe the following groups of words for speed and accuracy, applying transcription rules and assuring correct spelling.

34.2

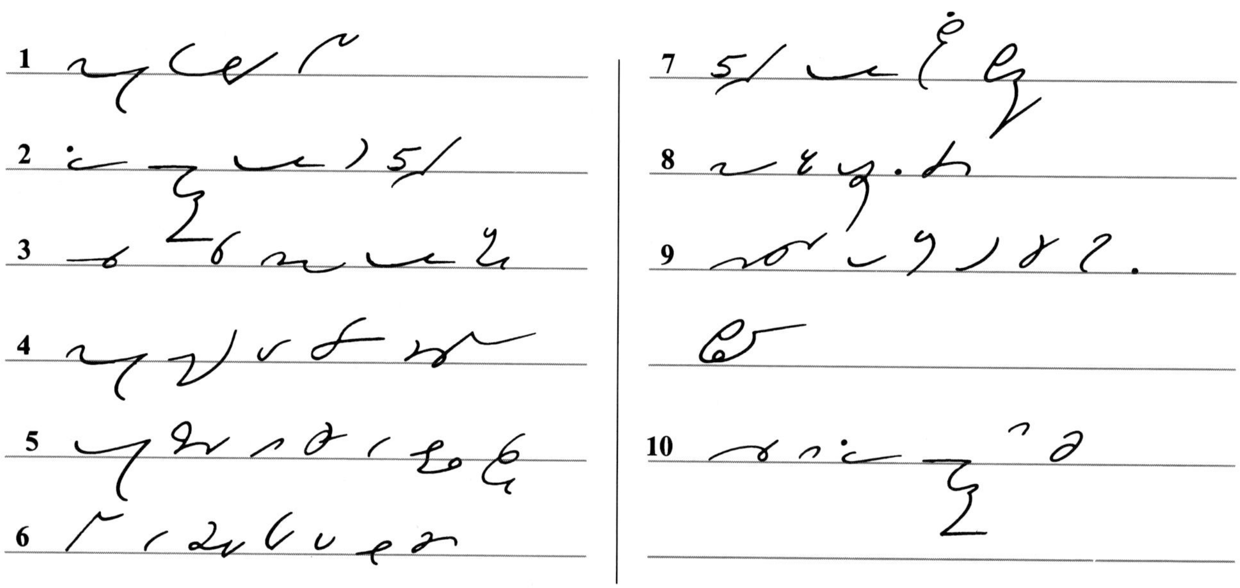

Transcription Practice

Transcribe the following letter for 2 minutes in unarranged format, applying transcription rules and assuring correct spelling. For every word not transcribed and every keyboarding error, deduct one word from the total word count.

34.3 Goal: 25 wam transcription rate

Word Count

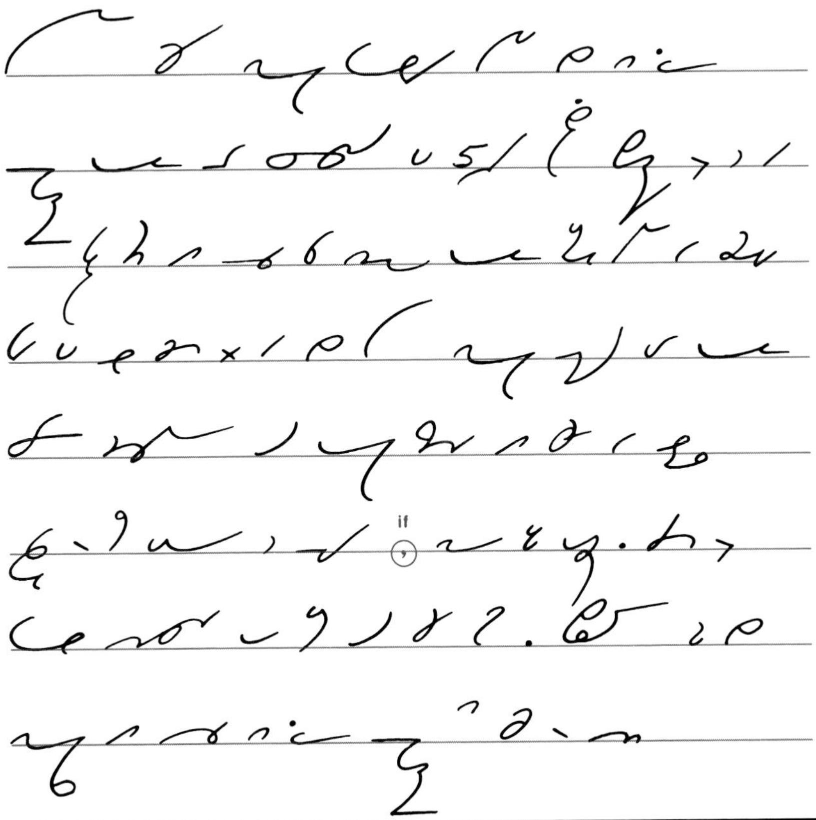

11
24
38
51
62
74
86
101

Mailable Production

Transcribe the following mailable production letter in block style, assuring proper placement of all letter parts. Insert punctuation prior to transcribing, and capitalize proper nouns and titles. Address a large envelope with the special notation *Express Mail.*

34.4 Time Limit: 15 minutes

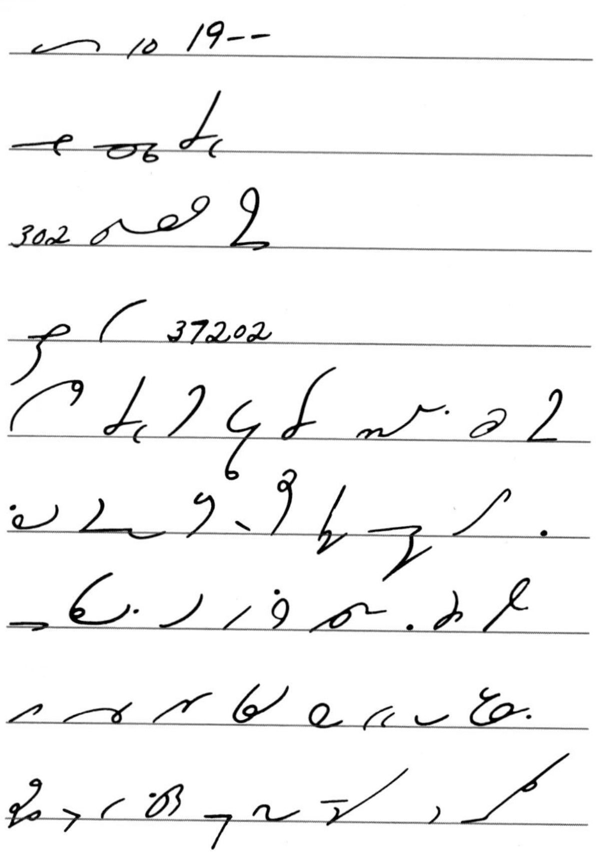

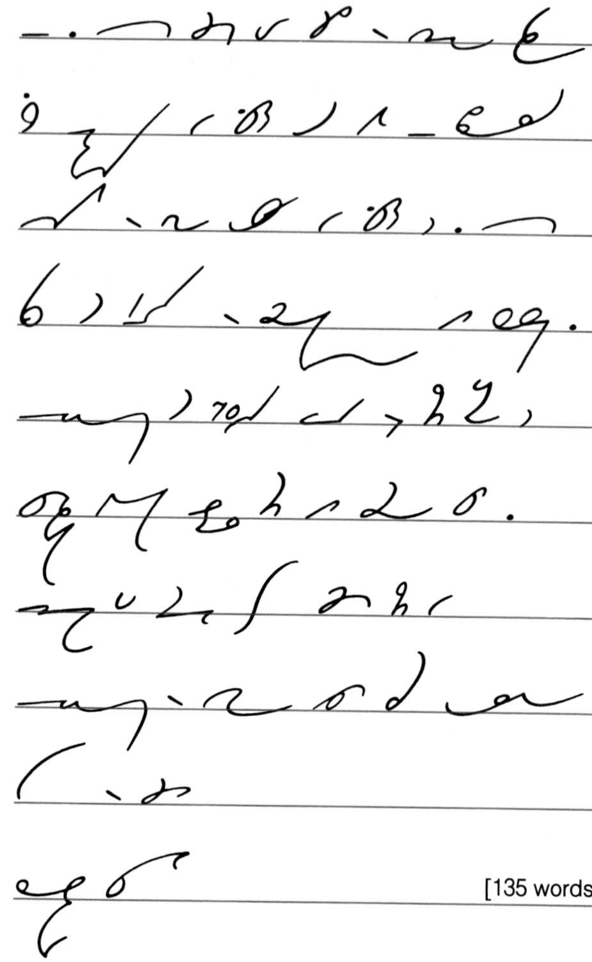

[135 words]

LESSON 35

FIRST NATIONAL BANK

DICTATION SPEED BUILDING

The shorthand outlines below appear in the speed dictation practice that follows. Practice writing these words using the shorthand outlines. Then, using the key that follows, dictate the words to yourself in preparation for the speed dictation practice.

Dictation Preview

Key: Dear Ms. Costa, welcome, Nashville, examined, report, condition, bargain, president, Chicago, highest, recommendation, institution, mortgage, to the, in which, has been, it is, if you can, you will be

Speed Dictation Practice

35.1 Goal: 90 wam speed dictation

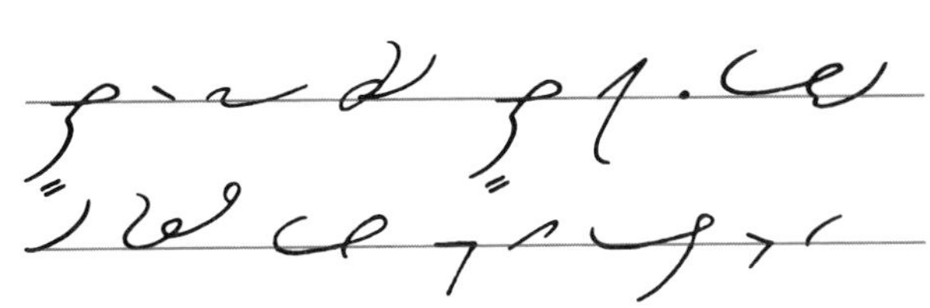

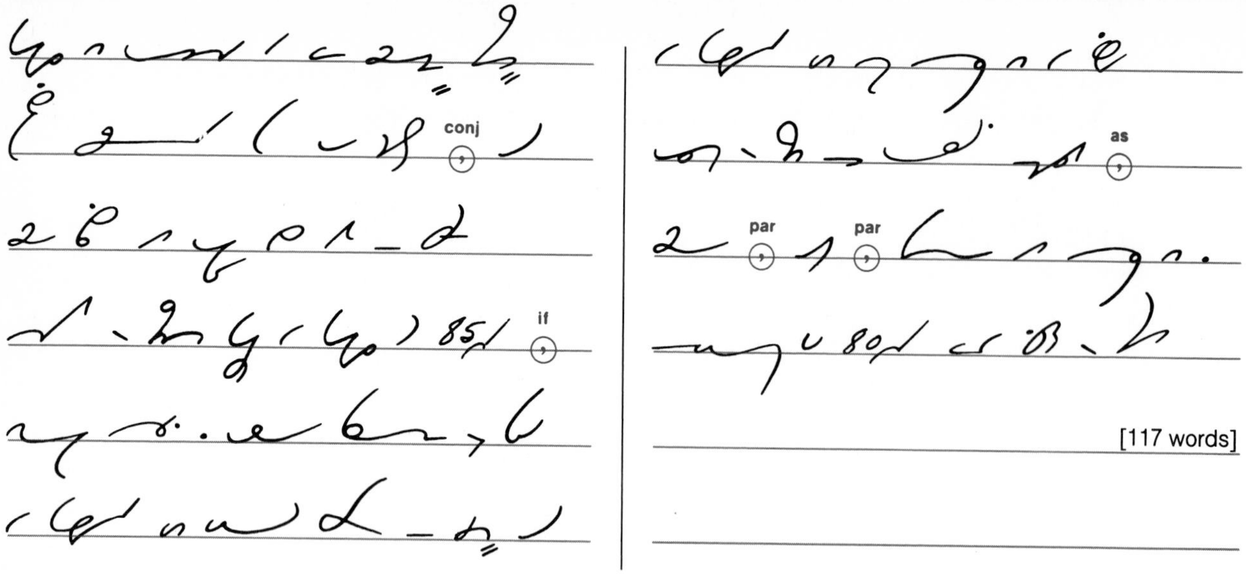

[117 words]

TRANSCRIPTION SKILL DEVELOPMENT

Transcription Warmup

Transcribe the following groups of words for speed and accuracy, applying transcription rules and assuring correct spelling.

35.2

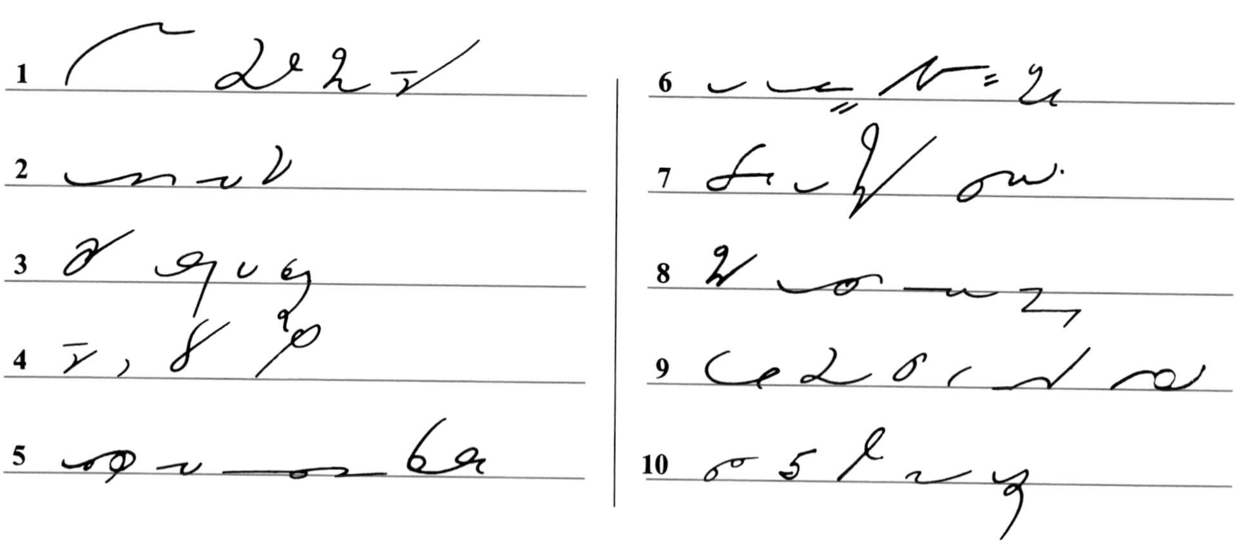

Transcription Practice

Transcribe the following letter for 2 minutes in unarranged format, applying transcription rules and assuring correct spelling. For every word not transcribed and every keyboarding error, deduct one word from the total word count.

35.3 Goal: 25 wam transcription rate

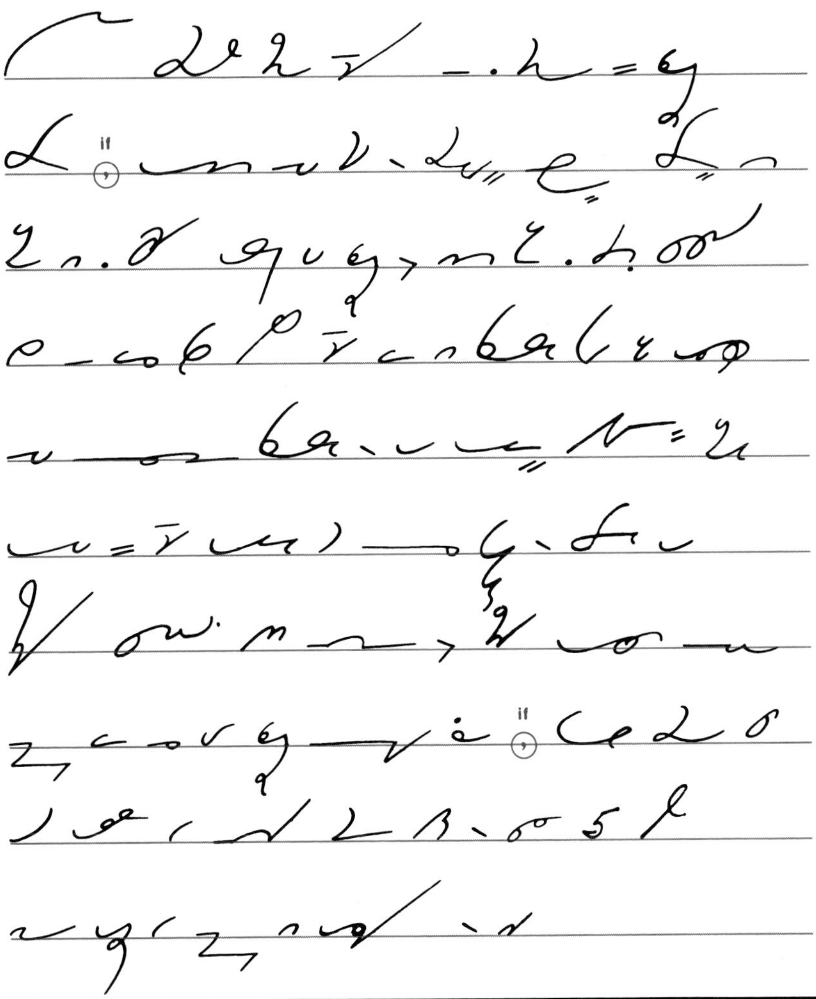

Word Count
11
20
34
48
57
67
79
92
103
115

Mailable Production

Transcribe the following mailable production letter in block style, assuring proper placement of all letter parts and adding a copy notation to Charles Hewitt. Insert punctuation prior to transcribing, and capitalize proper nouns and titles. Address a large envelope.

35.4 Time Limit: 15 minutes

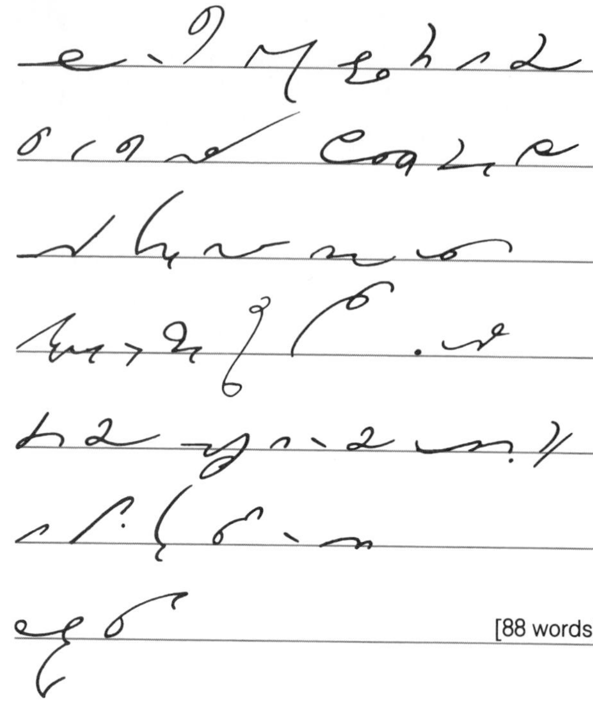

[88 words]

LESSON 36

FIRST NATIONAL BANK

DICTATION SPEED BUILDING

The shorthand outlines below appear in the speed dictation practice that follows. Practice writing these words using the shorthand outlines. Then, using the key that follows, dictate the words to yourself in preparation for the speed dictation practice.

Dictation Preview

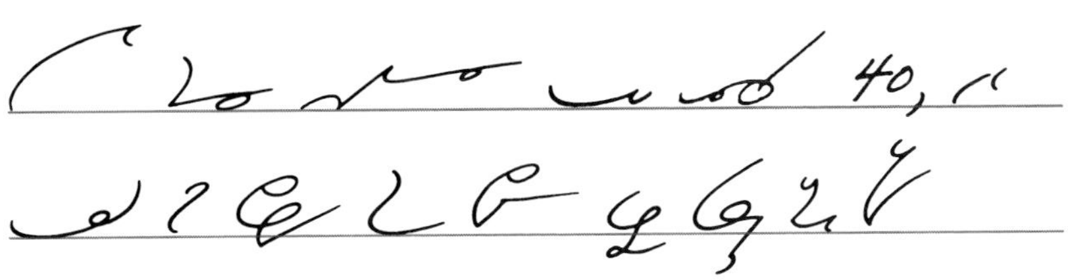

Key: Dear Ms. Foreman, condominium, law, required, 40 percent, thanks, lend, up, appraised, value, apartment, prefer, branches, officers, obtain

Speed Dictation Practice

36.1 Goal: 90 wam speed dictation

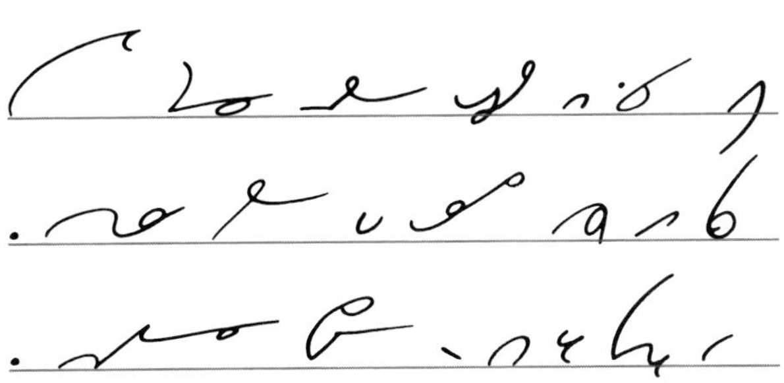

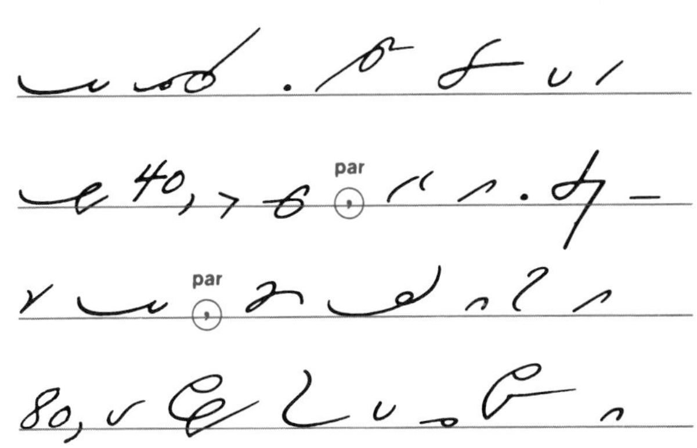

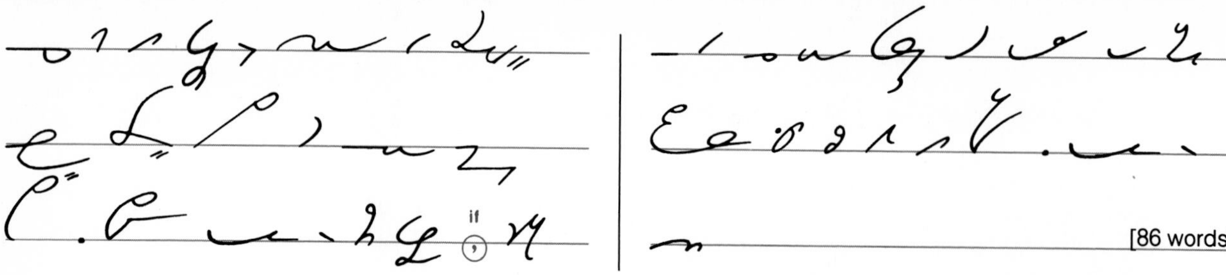

[86 words]

TRANSCRIPTION SKILL DEVELOPMENT

Transcription Warmup

Transcribe the following groups of words for speed and accuracy, applying transcription rules and assuring correct spelling.

36.2

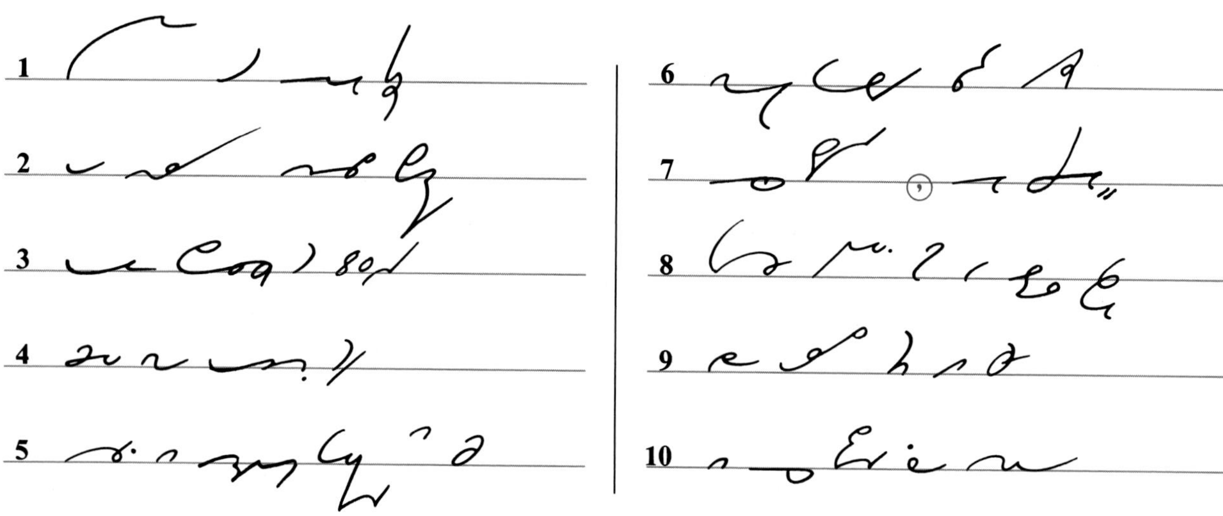

Transcription Practice

Transcribe the following letter for 2 minutes in unarranged format, applying transcription rules and assuring correct spelling. For every word not transcribed and every keyboarding error, deduct one word from the total word count.

36.3 Goal: 25 wam transcription rate

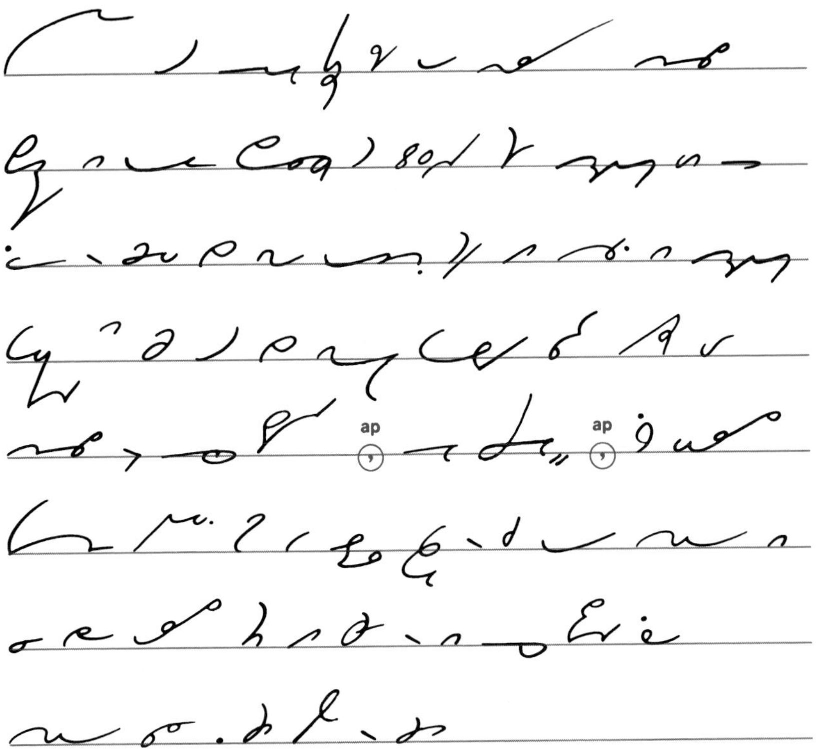

Word Count

11

26

40

54

64

75

86

94

Mailable Production

Transcribe the following mailable production letter in block style, assuring proper placement of all letter parts. Insert punctuation prior to transcribing, and capitalize proper nouns and titles. Address a large envelope.

36.4 Time Limit: 15 minutes

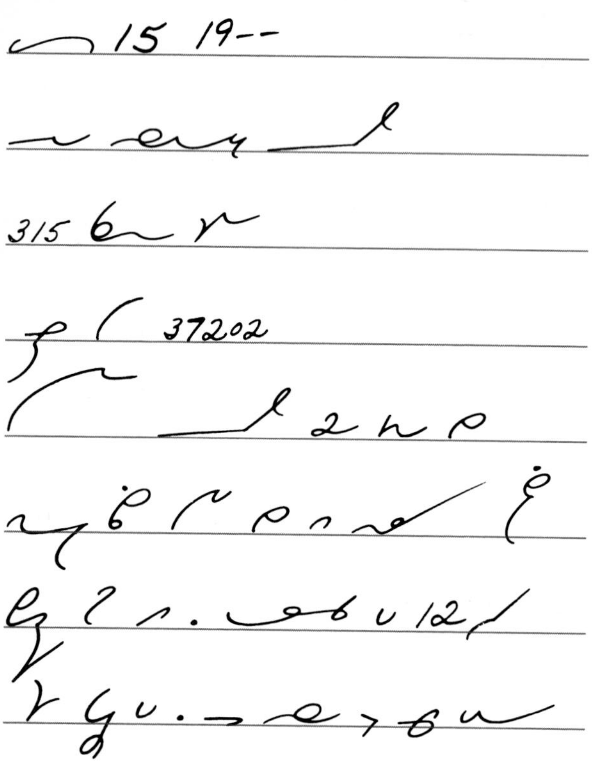

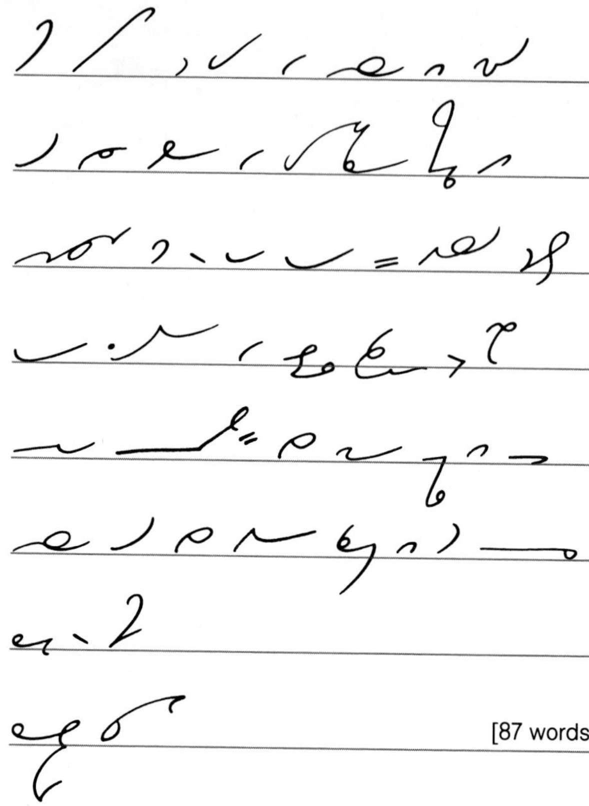

[87 words]

LESSON 37

FIRST NATIONAL BANK

DICTATION SPEED BUILDING

The shorthand outlines below appear in the speed dictation practice that follows. Practice writing these words using the shorthand outlines. Then, using the key that follows, dictate the words to yourself in preparation for the speed dictation practice.

Dictation Preview

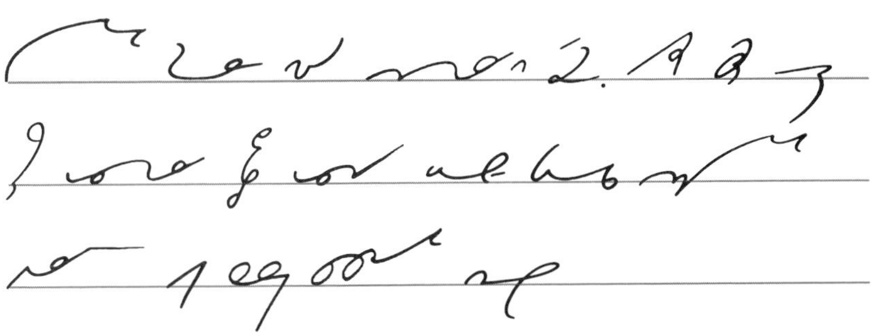

Key: Dear Mrs. Flynn, want, congratulate, transferring, decision, wise, move, advantages, regret, especially, recommended, always, policy, customers, treatment, touch, arrange, accounts, you may be

Speed Dictation Practice

37.1 Goal: 90 wam speed dictation

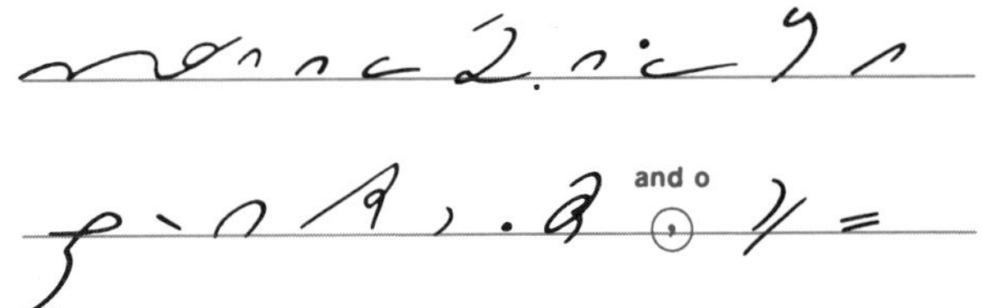

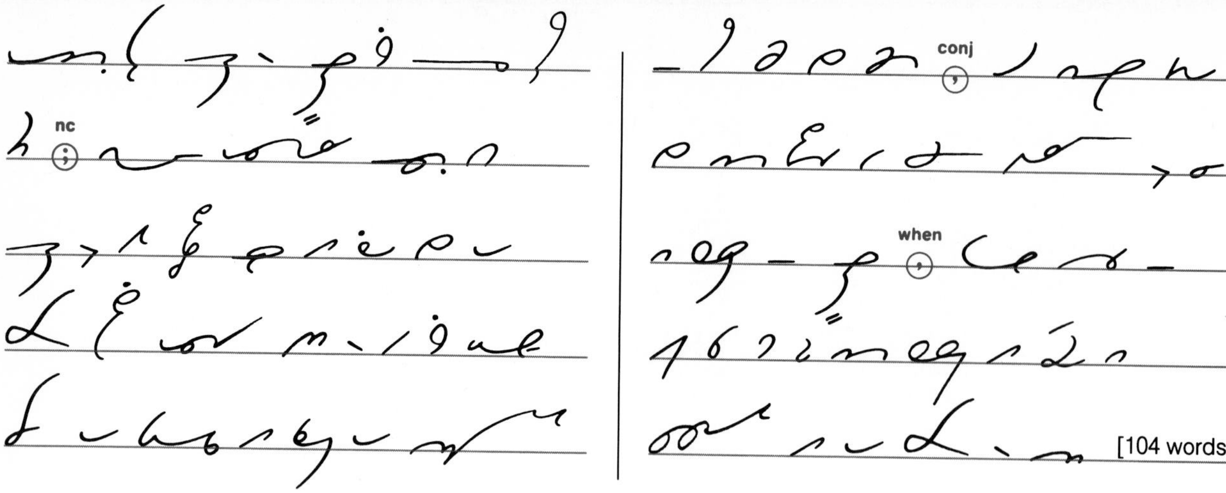

TRANSCRIPTION SKILL DEVELOPMENT

Transcription Warmup

Transcribe the following groups of words for speed and accuracy, applying transcription rules and assuring correct spelling.

37.2

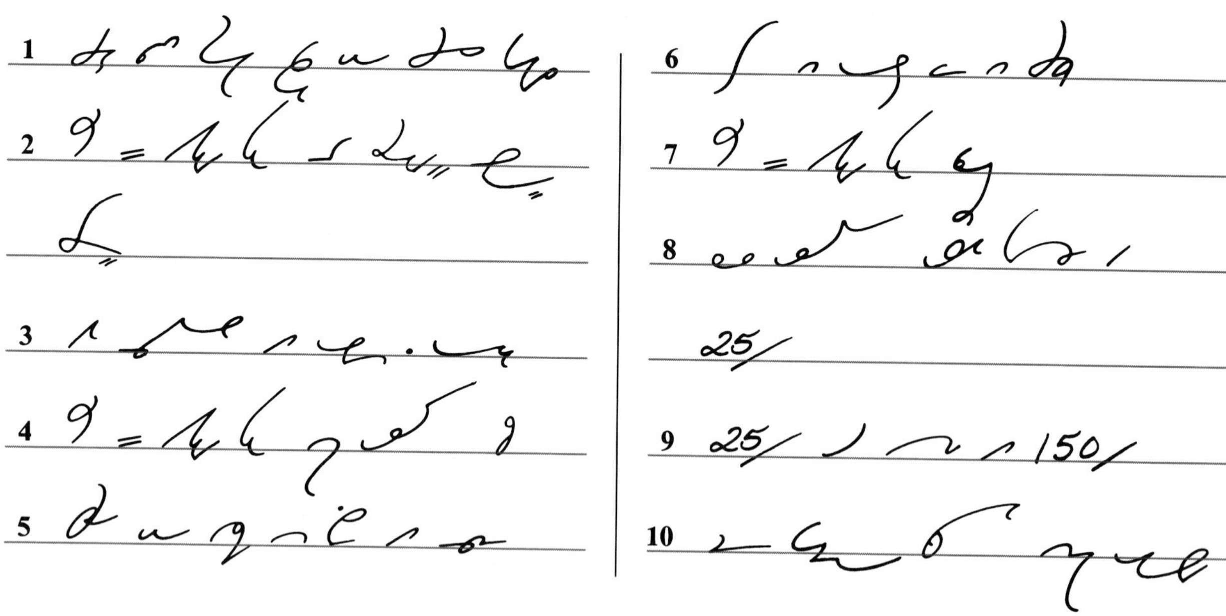

Transcription Practice

Transcribe the following letter for 2 minutes in unarranged format, applying transcription rules and assuring correct spelling. For every word not transcribed and every keyboarding error, deduct one word from the total word count.

37.3 Goal: 25 wam transcription rate

Word Count

13
24
35
46
57
68
78
88
97
107
114

Mailable Production

Transcribe the following mailable production letter in block style, assuring proper placement of all letter parts. Insert punctuation prior to transcribing, and capitalize proper nouns and titles. Address a large envelope with the special notation *Registered.*

37.4 Time Limit: 15 minutes

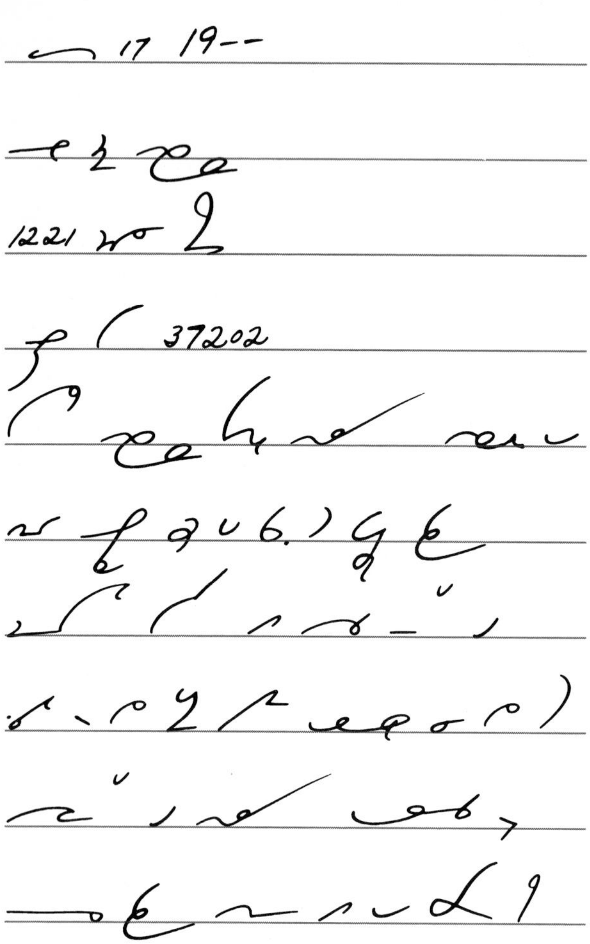

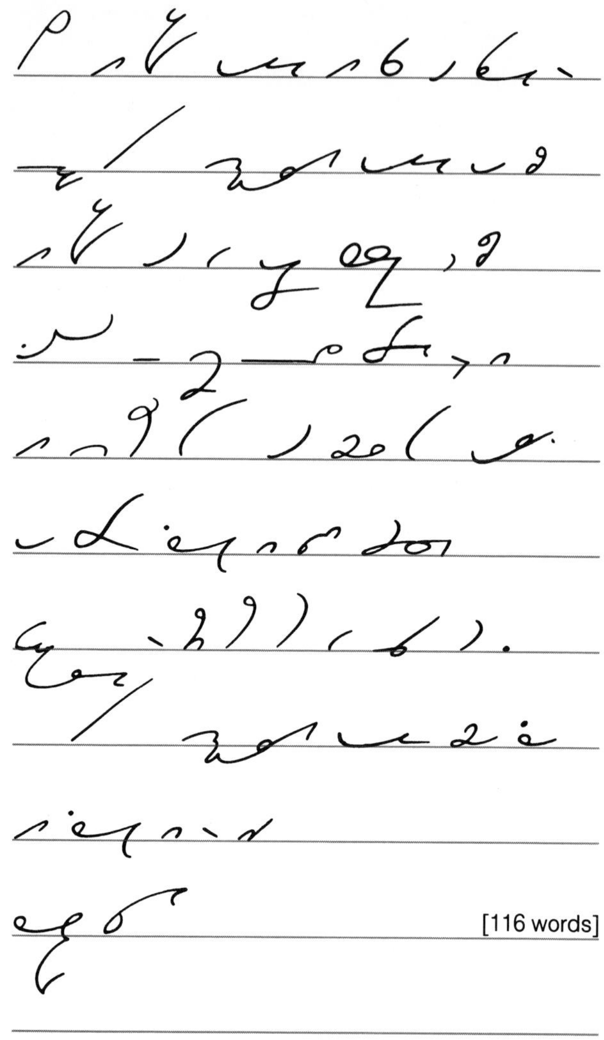

[116 words]

LESSON 38

FIRST NATIONAL BANK

DICTATION SPEED BUILDING

The shorthand outlines below appear in the speed dictation practice that follows. Practice writing these words using the shorthand outlines. Then, using the key that follows, dictate the words to yourself in preparation for the speed dictation practice.

Dictation Preview

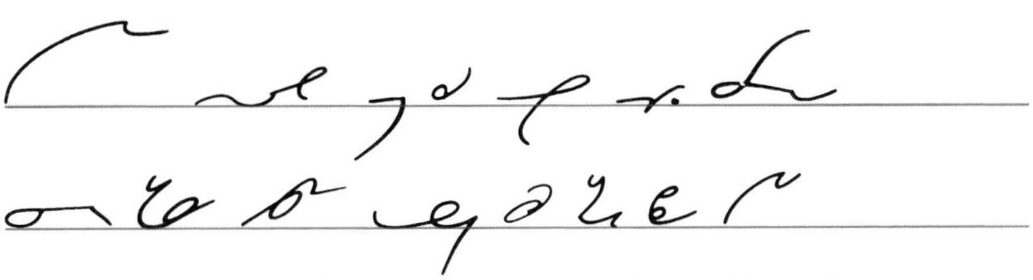

Key: Dear Mr. Curtis, never, either, maybe, nothing, banker, among, operate, town, large, why, officers, easier, to know

Speed Dictation Practice

38.1 Goal: 90 wam speed dictation

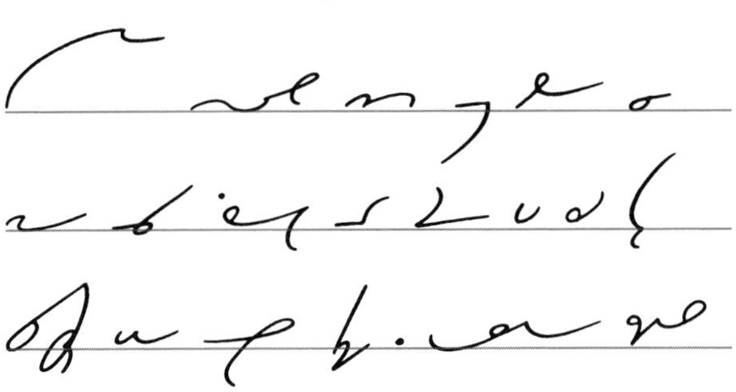

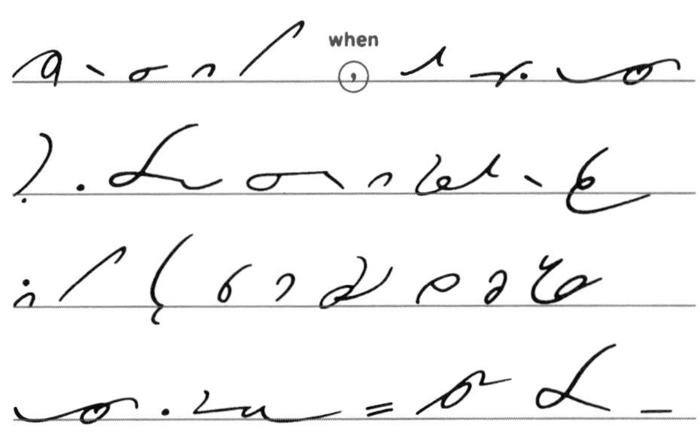

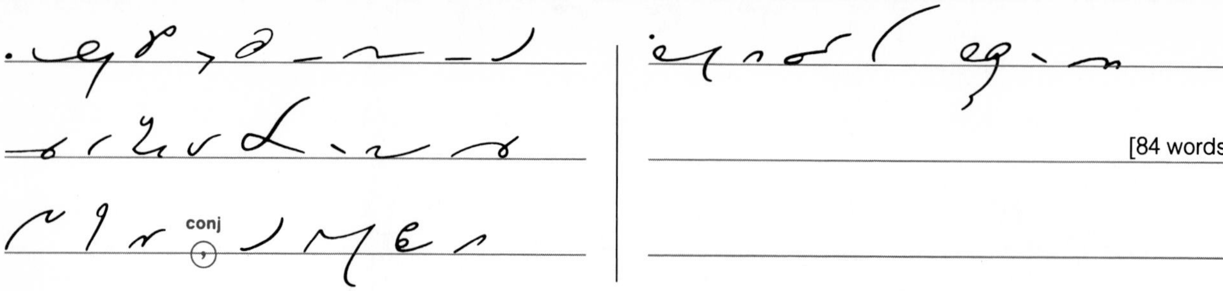

[84 words]

TRANSCRIPTION SKILL DEVELOPMENT

Transcription Warmup

Transcribe the following groups of words for speed and accuracy, applying transcription rules and assuring correct spelling.

38.2

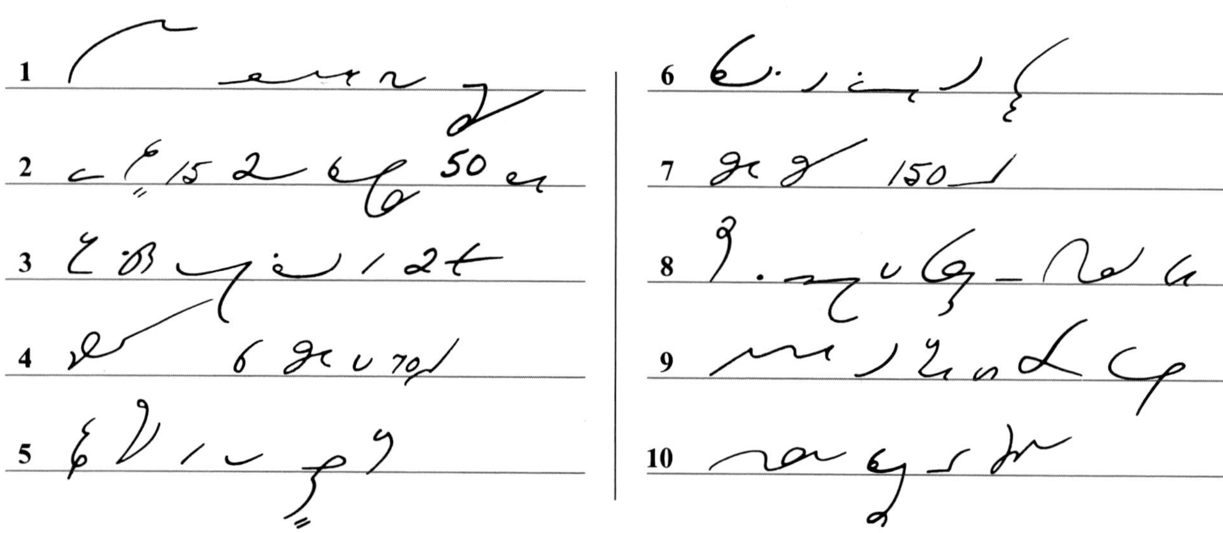

Transcription Practice

Transcribe the following letter for 2 minutes in unarranged format, applying transcription rules and assuring correct spelling. For every word not transcribed and every keyboarding error, deduct one word from the total word count.

38.3 Goal: 25 wam transcription rate

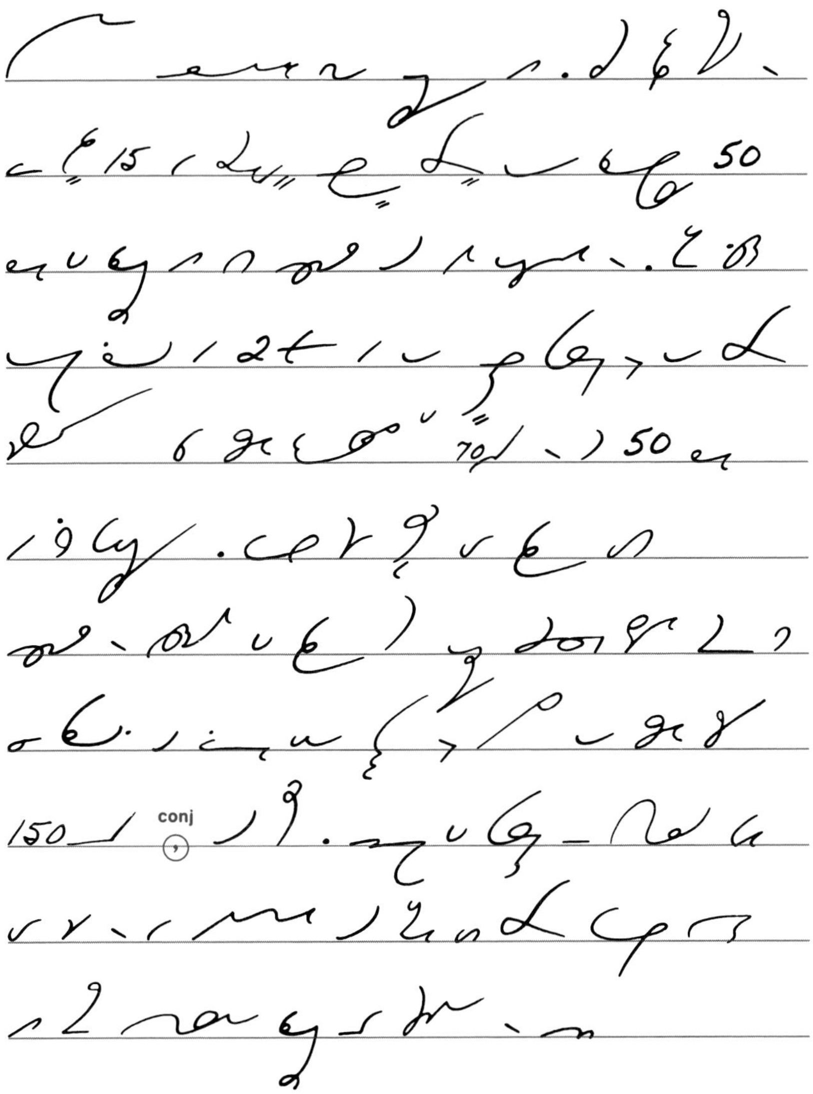

Word Count

11
22
35
46
57
69
83
96
109
123
134

Mailable Production

Transcribe the following mailable production letter in block style, assuring proper placement of all letter parts. Insert punctuation prior to transcribing, and capitalize proper nouns and titles. Address a large envelope.

38.4 Time Limit: 15 minutes

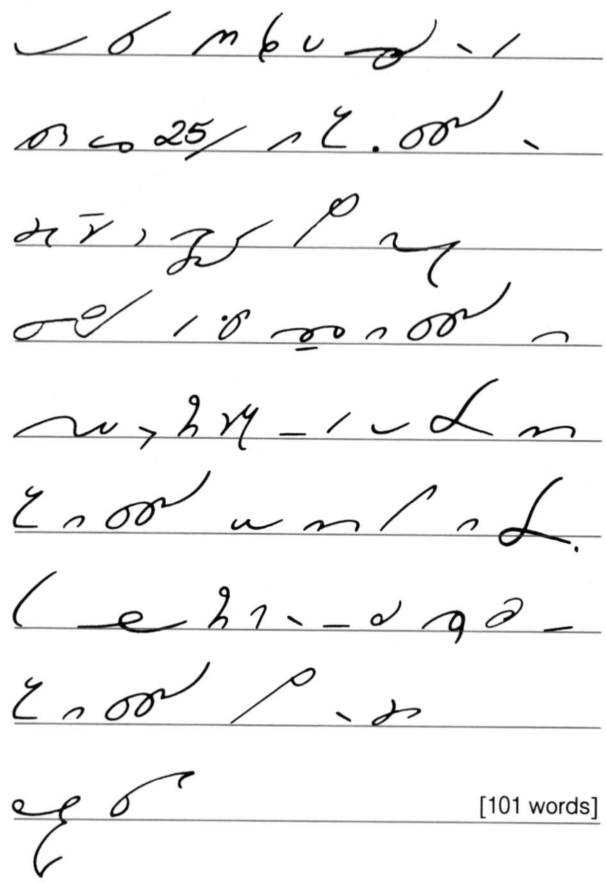

[101 words]

LESSON 39

FIRST NATIONAL BANK

DICTATION SPEED BUILDING

The shorthand outlines below appear in the speed dictation practice that follows. Practice writing these words using the shorthand outlines. Then, using the key that follows, dictate the words to yourself in preparation for the speed dictation practice.

Dictation Preview

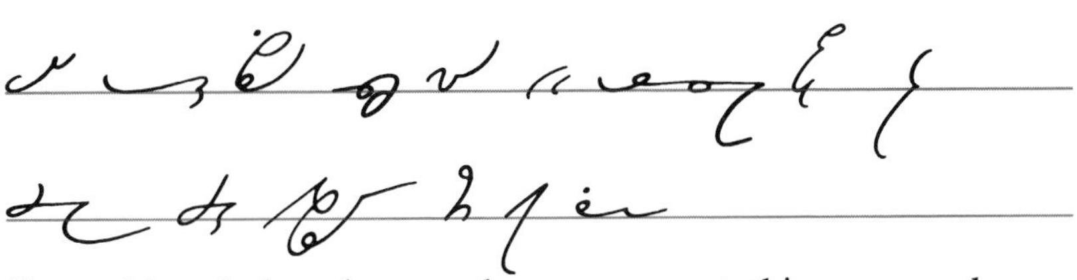

Key: although, lose, happened, anyway, want, things, remember, expose, public, simple, chances, disappointment, if you, to be, here are

Speed Dictation Practice

39.1 Goal: 90 wam speed dictation

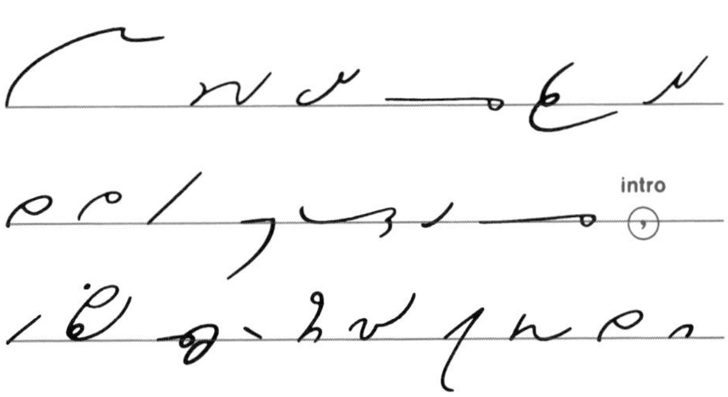

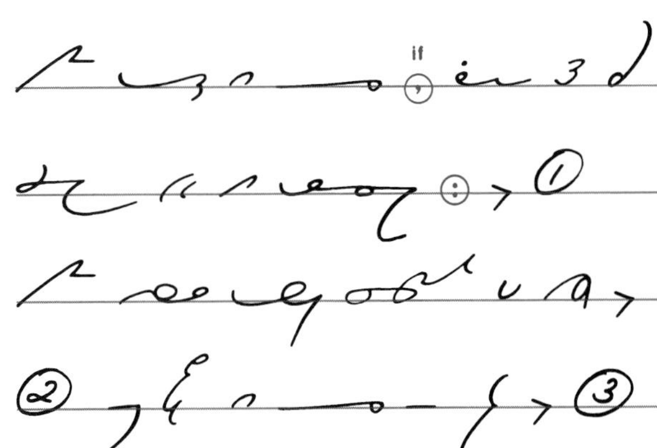

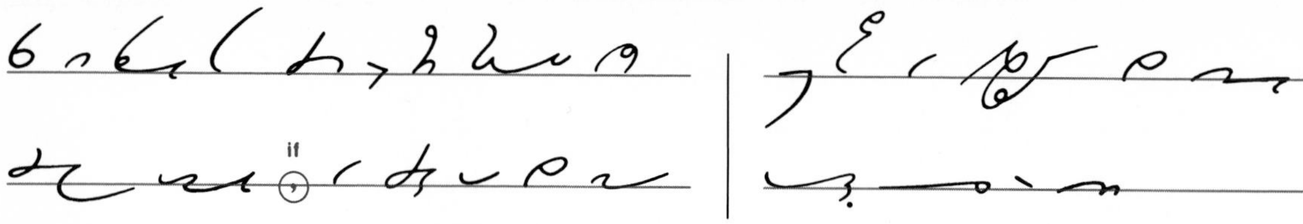

[84 words]

TRANSCRIPTION SKILL DEVELOPMENT

Transcription Warmup

Transcribe the following groups of words for speed and accuracy, applying transcription rules and assuring correct spelling.

39.2

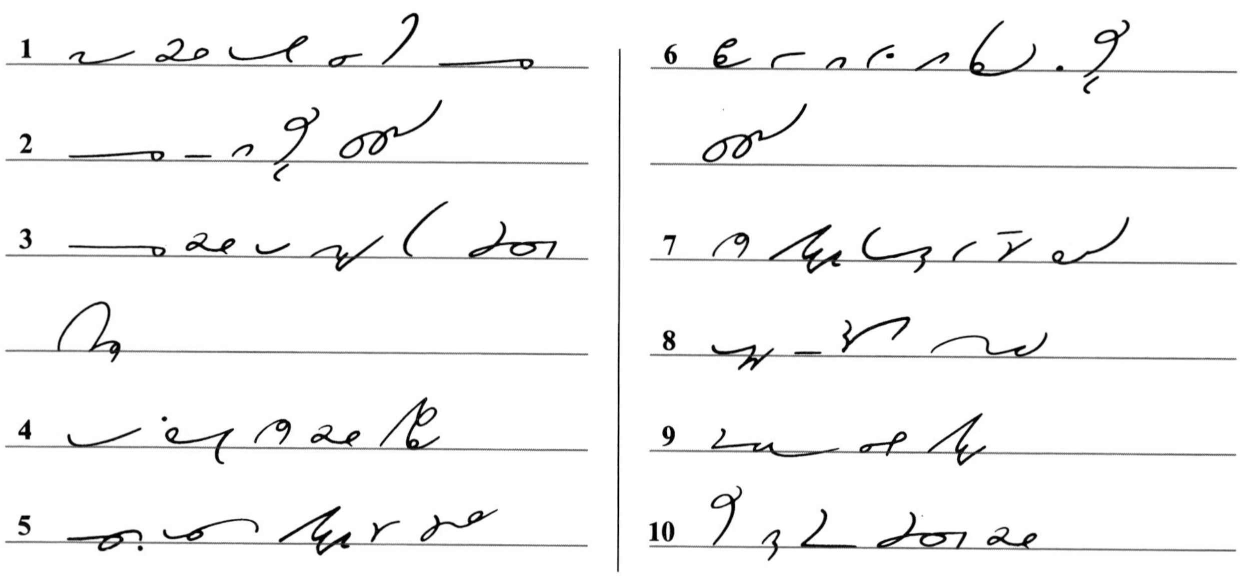

Transcription Practice

Transcribe the following letter for 2 minutes in unarranged format, applying transcription rules and assuring correct spelling. For every word not transcribed and every keyboarding error, deduct one word from the total word count.

39.3 Goal: 25 wam transcription rate

Word Count

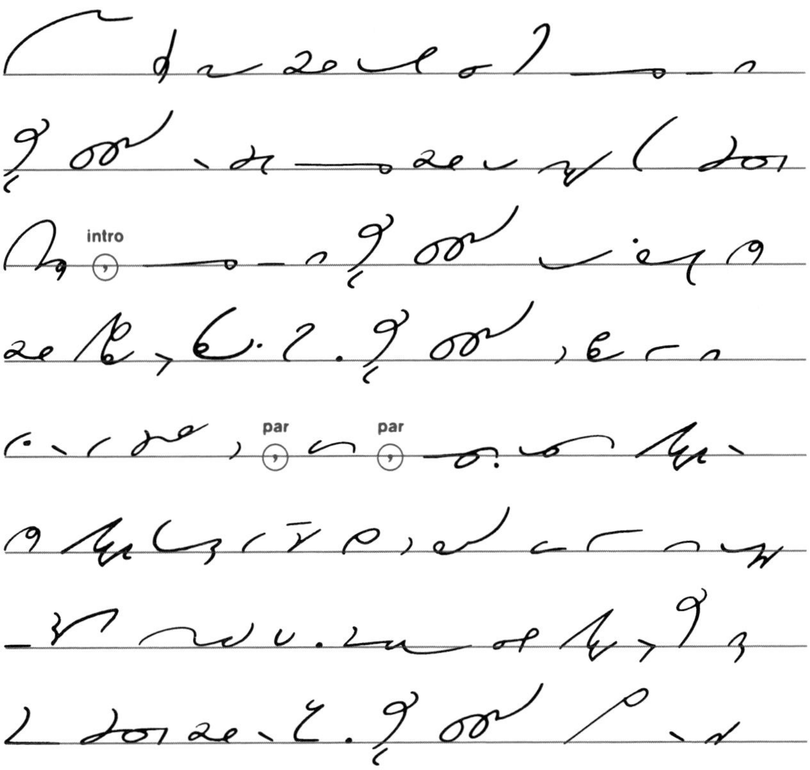

12
24
36
50
61
74
87
100

Mailable Production

Transcribe the following mailable production letter in block style, assuring proper placement of all letter parts. Insert punctuation prior to transcribing, and capitalize proper nouns and titles. Address a large envelope.

39.4 Time Limit: 15 minutes

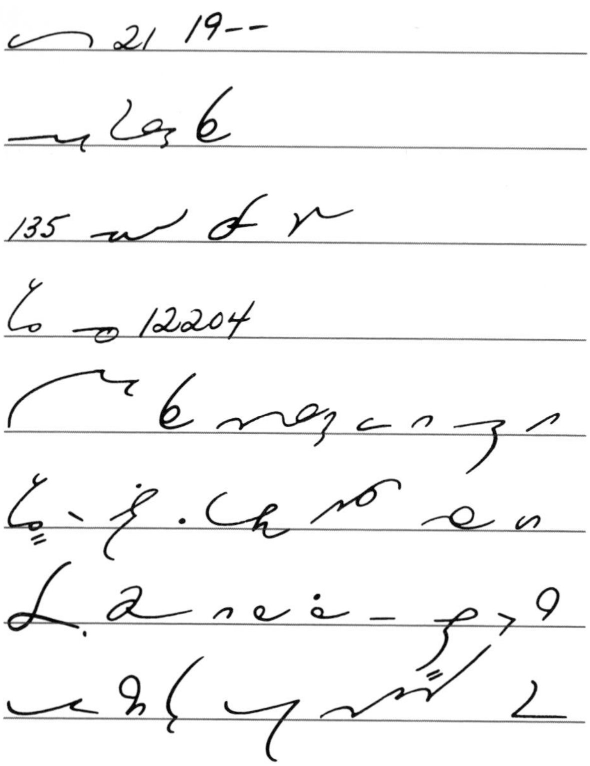

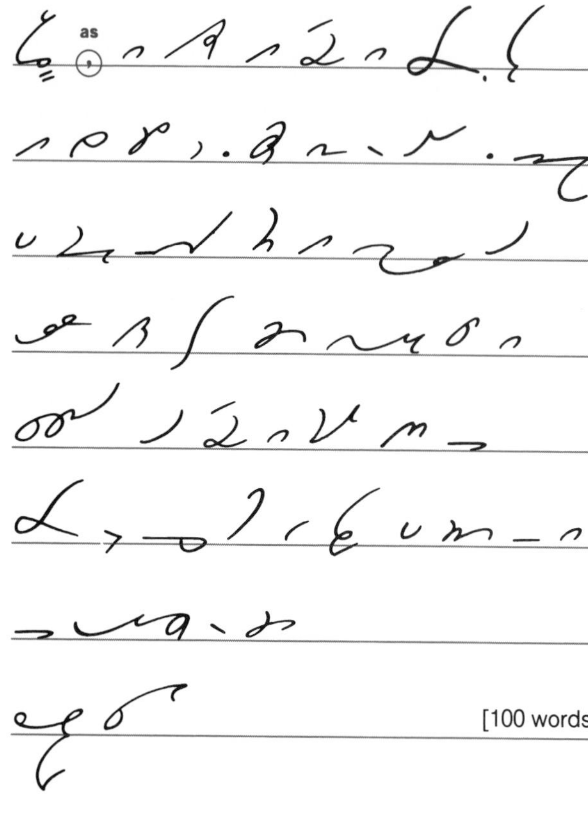

[100 words]

LESSON 40

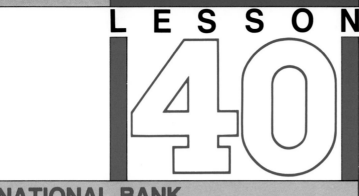

FIRST NATIONAL BANK

DICTATION SPEED BUILDING

The shorthand outlines below appear in the speed dictation practice that follows. Practice writing these words using the shorthand outlines. Then, using the key that follows, dictate the words to yourself in preparation for the speed dictation practice.

Dictation Preview

Key: protect, money, simply, aside, common, power, food, clothing, stocks, known, protection, inflation, against

Speed Dictation Practice

40.1 Goal: 90 wam speed dictation

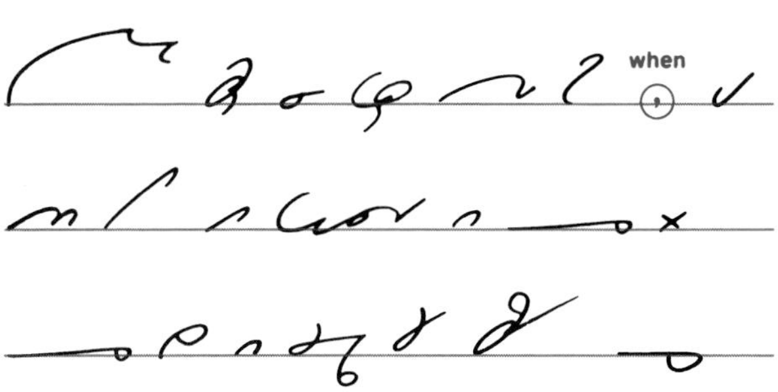

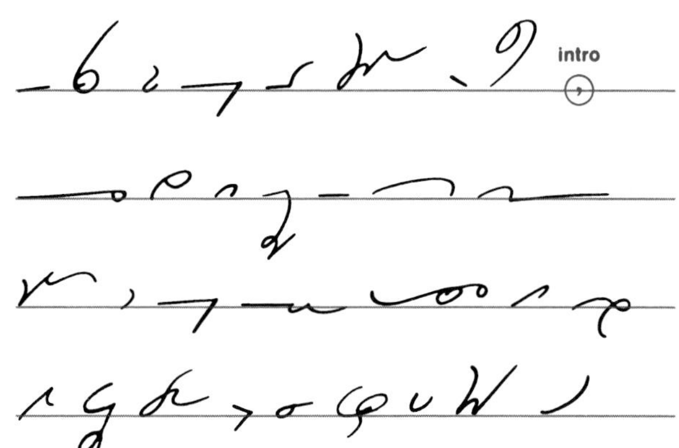

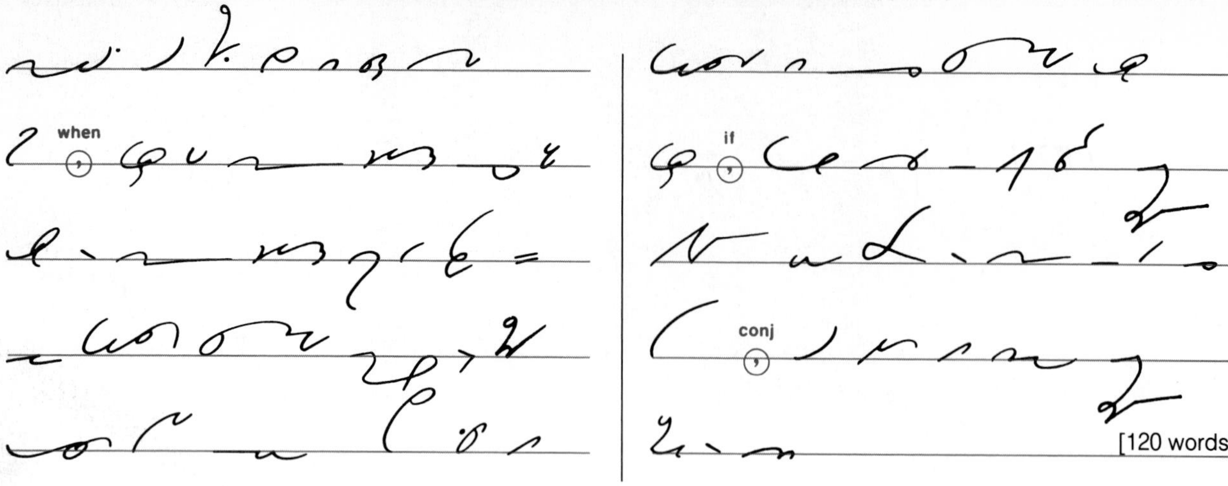

TRANSCRIPTION SKILL DEVELOPMENT

Transcription Warmup

Transcribe the following groups of words for speed and accuracy, applying transcription rules and assuring correct spelling.

40.2

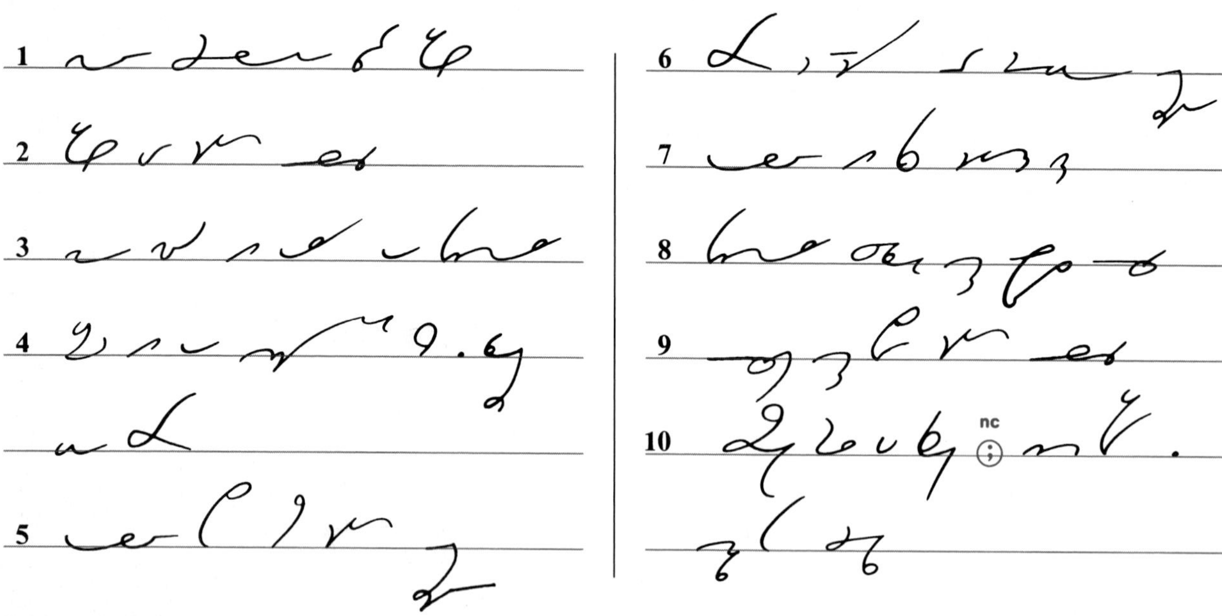

Transcription Practice

Transcribe the following letter for 2 minutes in unarranged format, applying transcription rules and assuring correct spelling. For every word not transcribed and every keyboarding error, deduct one word from the total word count.

40.3 Goal: 25 wam transcription rate

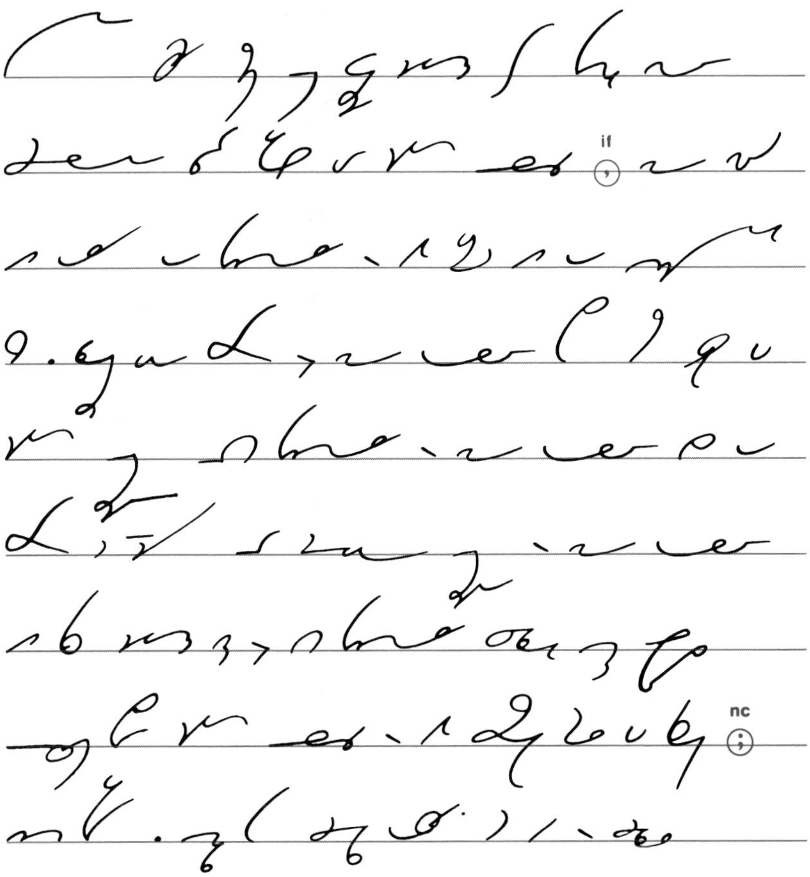

Word Count

15
27
37
49
61
72
85
98
110

Mailable Production

Transcribe the following mailable production letter in block style, assuring proper placement of all letter parts. Insert punctuation prior to transcribing, and capitalize proper nouns and titles. Address a large envelope with the special notation *Personal.*

40.4 Time Limit: 15 minutes

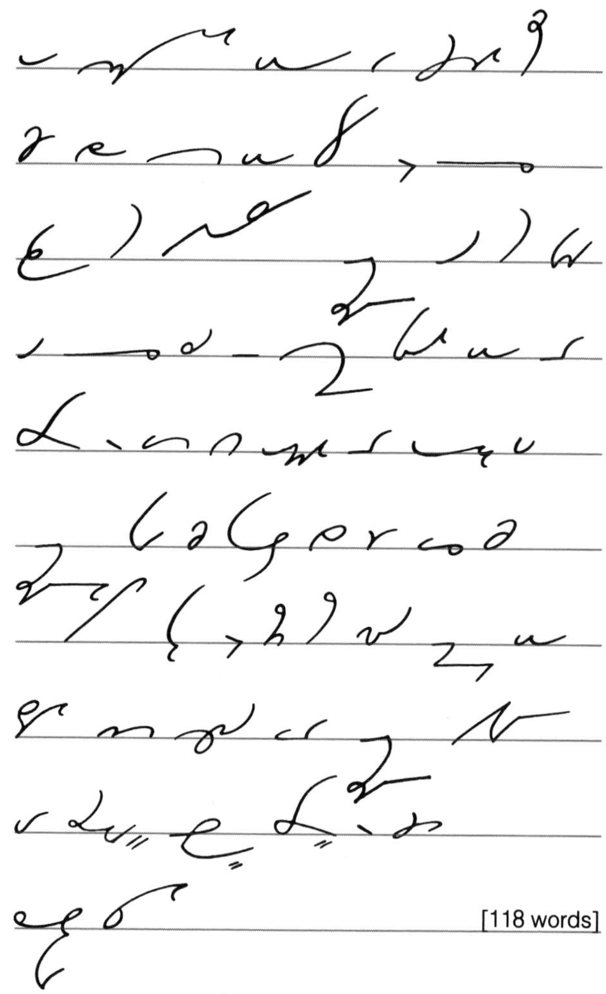

[118 words]

UNIT VI

MORRIS TRAVEL AGENCY

LESSON 41

MORRIS TRAVEL AGENCY

You are employed by the Morris Travel Agency in New York City, and you report to Nancy Johnson, a travel agent. Your responsibilities include assisting Ms. Johnson in making personal and professional travel arrangements, such as hotel and airline reservations and car rentals. In addition, you type itineraries and correspondence announcing the many exciting vacation spots and conference sites. You also handle special requests, such as arranging for conference rooms or meeting space at hotels throughout the country for major corporations.

Below is a copy of your company letterhead. Develop the return address that you will use to type the envelopes for the mailable production letters.

MORRIS TRAVEL AGENCY

511 Madison Avenue New York, NY 10022 (212) 555-1782

Itinerary

One of the items you will be providing to customers will be an itinerary outlining the travel date(s), the departure and arrival times and places, the accommodations, and rental cars. Your clients depend on the accuracy of this information. It is important to proofread the itinerary to assure that dates, flight numbers, and times of departure and arrival are correct. In addition, notice the type of information on each line and the vertical spacing between the lines.

On the following page is a sample itinerary for you to follow. Use standard (1-inch) margins, and set a tab 15 spaces from the left margin for the explanation.

↓ 13

ITINERARY OF JAMES CAMPBELL ↓ 2

December 17-19, 19-- ↓ 3

1" → Monday, December 17 ↓ 2

9:30 a.m.	Depart Newark Airport for Chicago, American Flight 25 ↓ 2
10:40 a.m.	Arrive Chicago Airport; limousine service to Madison Hotel, 371 Chestnut Street
12:30 p.m.	Luncheon in ballroom at Madison Hotel
7:30 p.m.	Dinner with Kenneth Briggs, vice president of World News in Chicago
	Overnight accommodations at Madison Hotel ↓ 3

15 → (tab) 1" ← (right margin)

Tuesday, December 18

8:15 a.m.	Depart Chicago Airport for Phoenix, American Flight 218
11:05 a.m.	Arrive Phoenix Airport
	National rental car (return December 19) Confirmation No. 380218
2:30 p.m.	Meeting with Adam Simpson, Talbott Industries
	Overnight accommodations at Phoenix Resort, 305 Capital Street ↓ 3

Wednesday, December 19

9:20 a.m.	Depart Phoenix Airport for New York, American Flight 355
2:05 p.m.	Arrive Newark Airport; limousine service to office

DICTATION SPEED BUILDING

The shorthand outlines below appear in the speed dictation practice that follows. Practice writing these words using the shorthand outlines. Then, using the key that follows, dictate the words to yourself in preparation for the speed dictation practice.

Dictation Preview

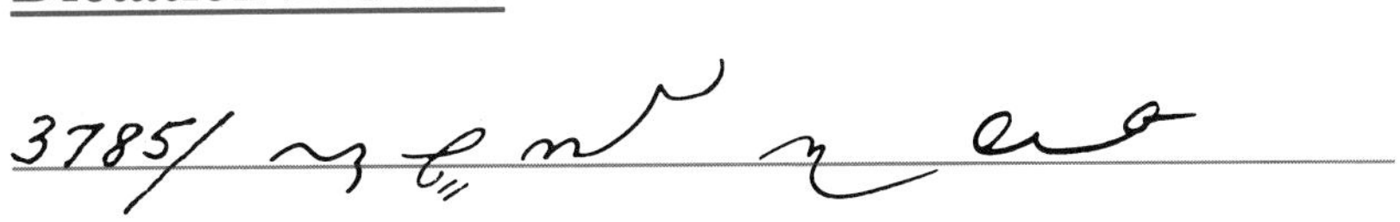

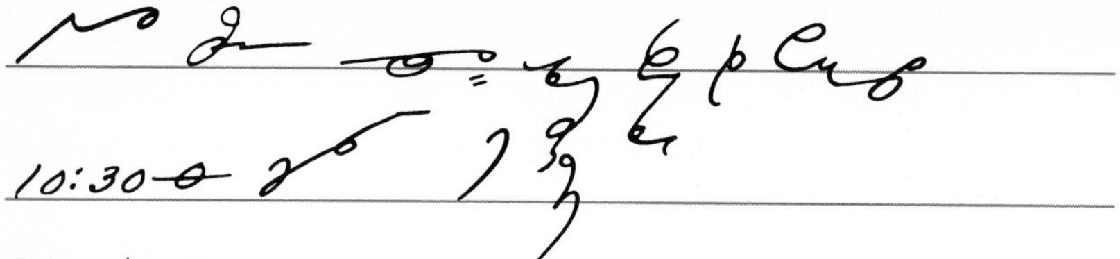

Key: $3,785, cruise, Nassau, wondered, couple, airline, directly, assignment, Miami, reservations, passengers, ship, approximately, 10:30 a.m., we did not, you have, if you have

Speed Dictation Practice

41.1 Goal: 90 wam speed dictation

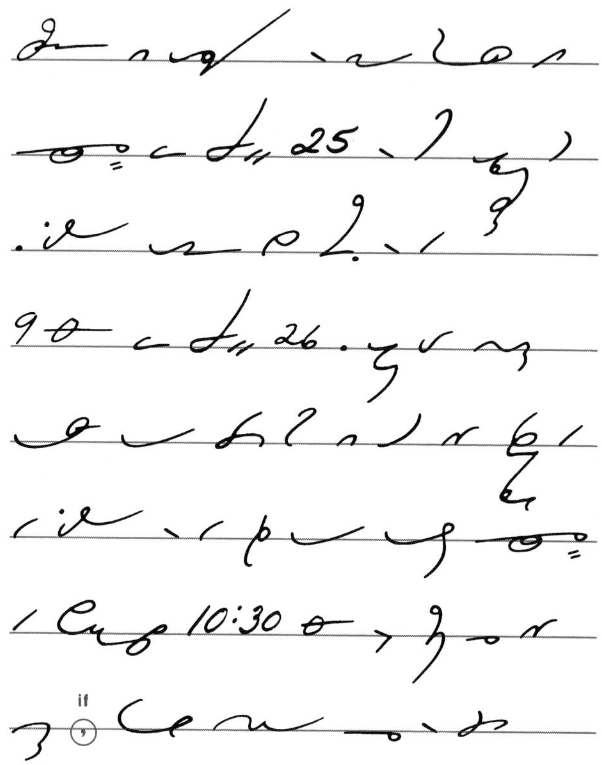

[153 words]

TRANSCRIPTION SKILL DEVELOPMENT

Transcription Warmup

Transcribe the following groups of words for speed and accuracy, applying transcription rules and assuring correct spelling.

41.2

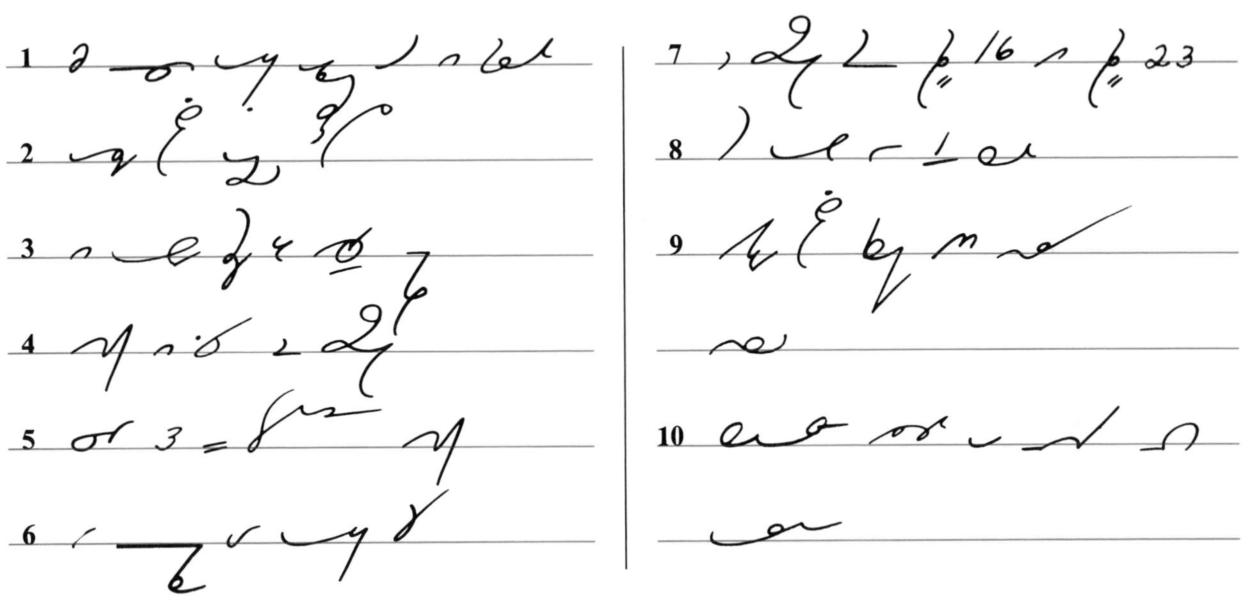

Transcription Practice

Transcribe the following letter for 2 minutes in unarranged format, applying transcription rules and assuring correct spelling. For every word not transcribed and every keyboarding error, deduct one word from the total word count.

41.3 Goal: 30 wam transcription rate

Word Count

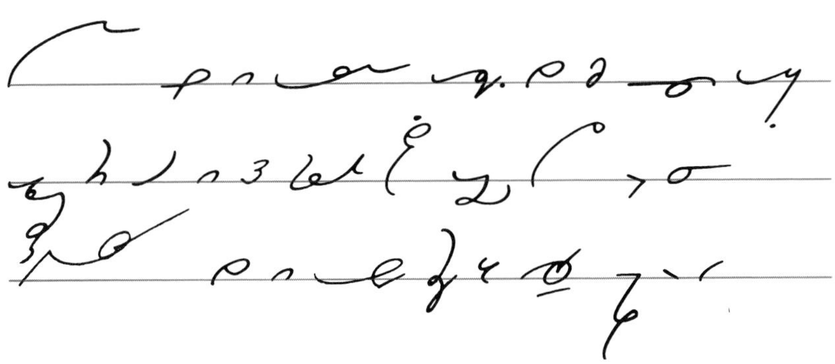

11

26

37

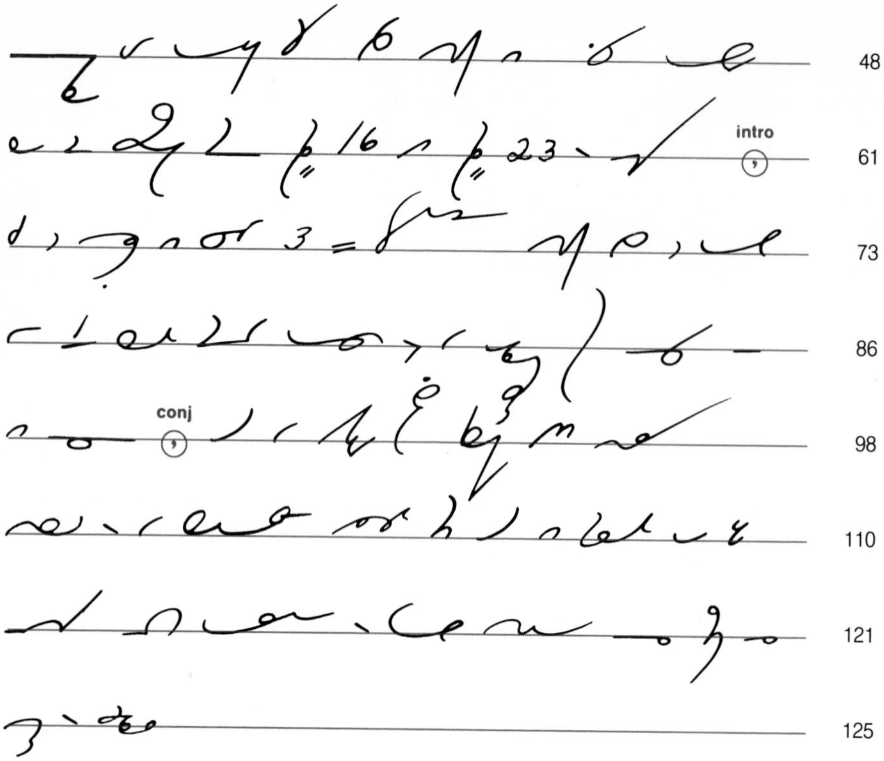
intro
conj
48
61
73
86
98
110
121
125

LESSON 42

MORRIS TRAVEL AGENCY

DICTATION SPEED BUILDING

The shorthand outlines below appear in the speed dictation practice that follows. Practice writing these words using the shorthand outlines. Then, using the key that follows, dictate the words to yourself in preparation for the speed dictation practice.

Dictation Preview

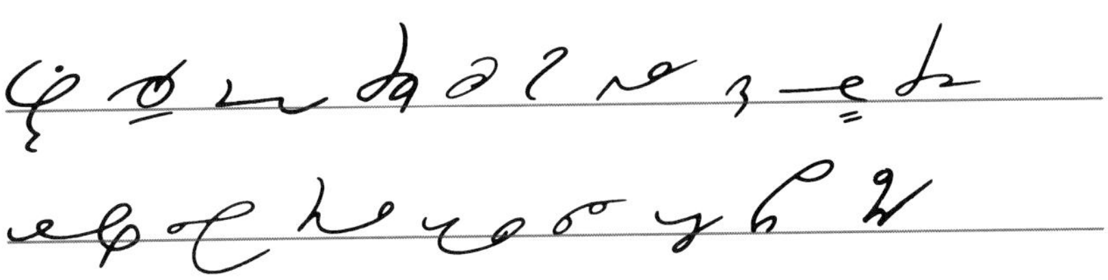

Key: perhaps, quite, summer, vacation, why, up, treat, yourself, Mexico, genuine, relaxation, enable, fully, reply, within, receipt, about your, if you would

Speed Dictation Practice

42.1 Goal: 90 wam speed dictation

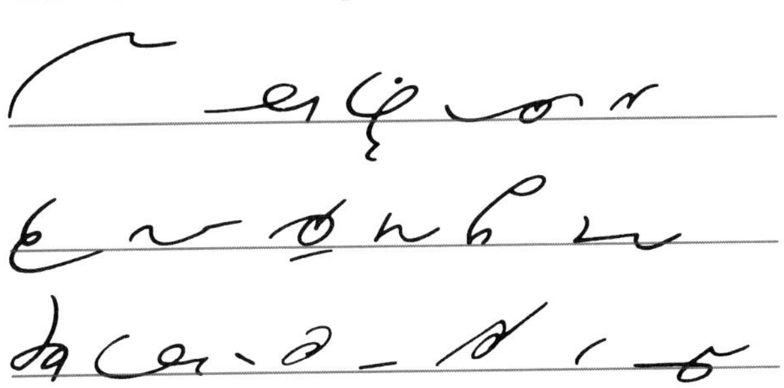

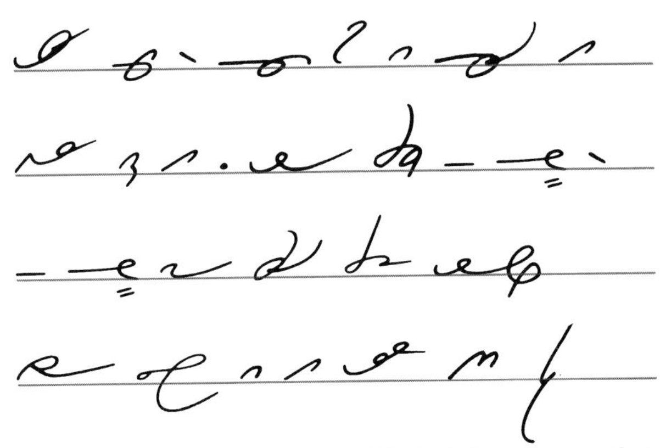

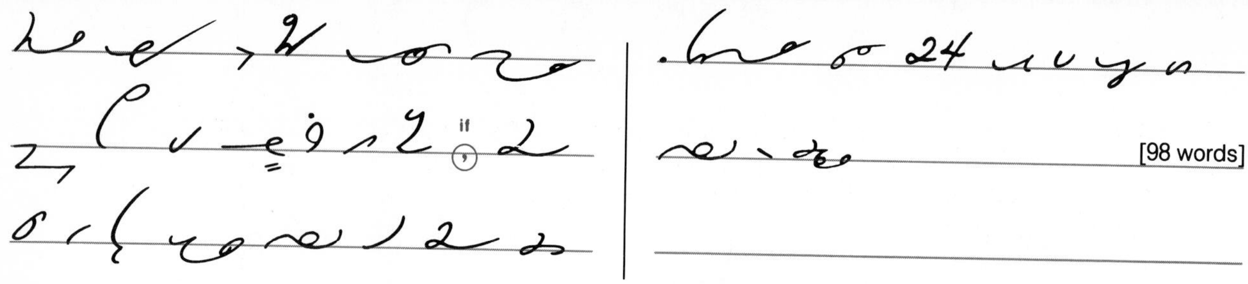

TRANSCRIPTION SKILL DEVELOPMENT

Transcription Warmup

Transcribe the following groups of words for speed and accuracy, applying transcription rules and assuring correct spelling.

42.2

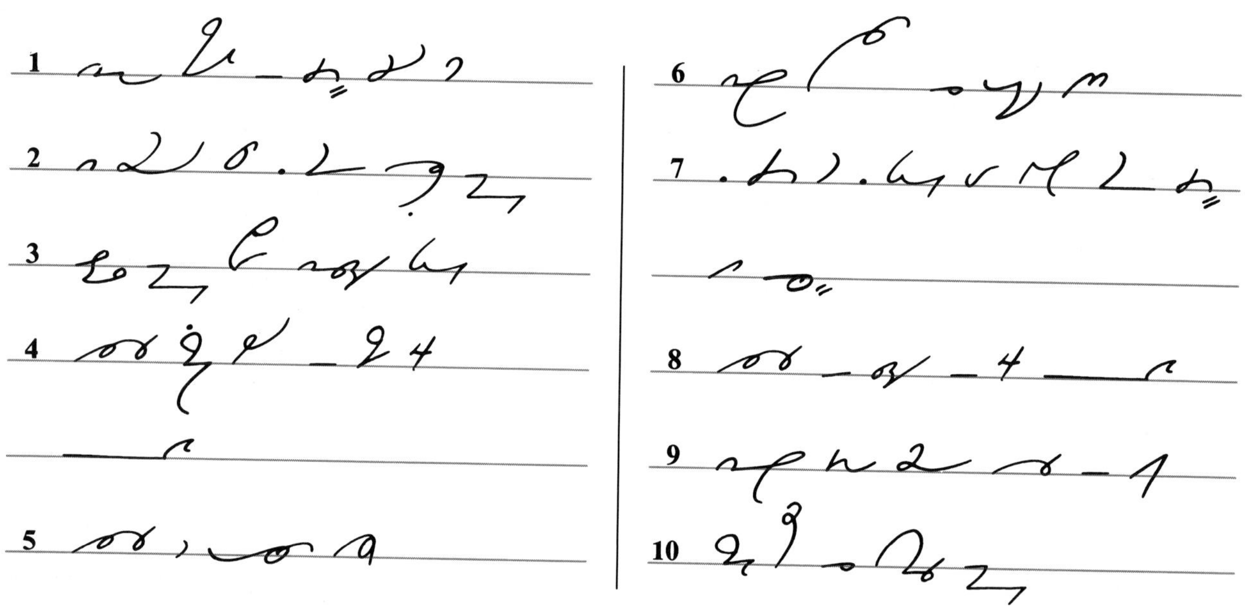

Transcription Practice

Transcribe the following letter for 2 minutes in unarranged format, applying transcription rules and assuring correct spelling. For every word not transcribed and every keyboarding error, deduct one word from the total word count.

42.3 Goal: 30 wam transcription rate

Word Count

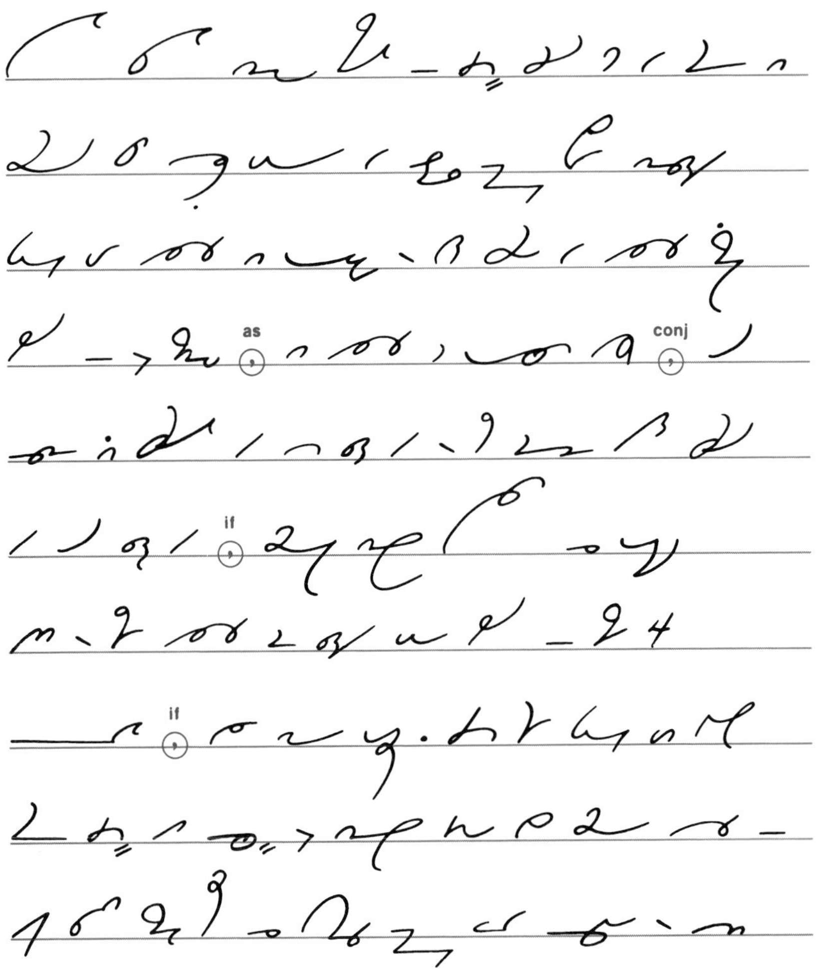

13
26
39
50
61
73
83
96
108
126

Mailable Production

Transcribe the following mailable production letter in block style, assuring proper placement of all letter parts. Insert punctuation prior to transcribing, and capitalize proper nouns and titles. Address a large envelope.

42.4 Time Limit: 15 minutes

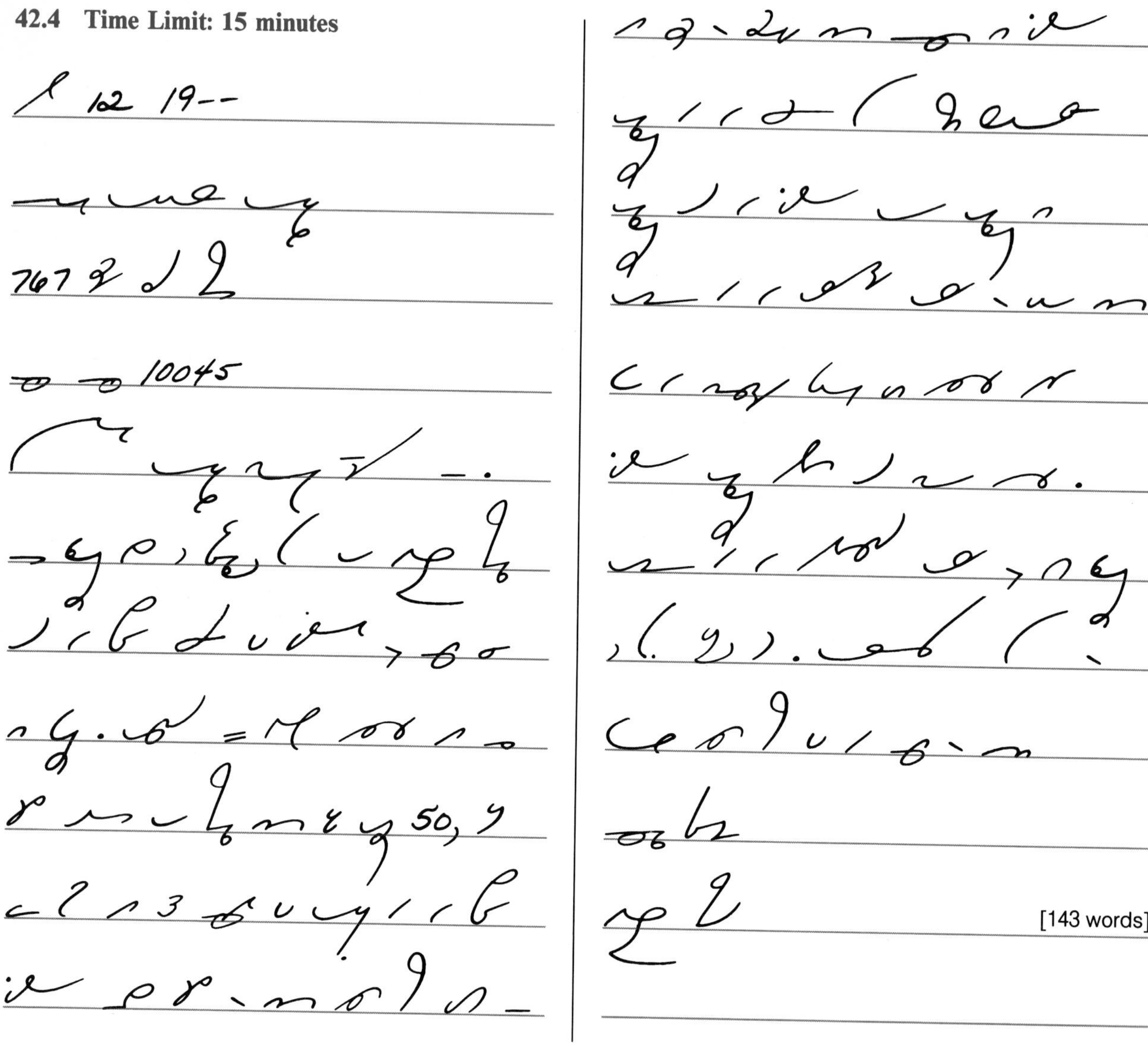

[143 words]

LESSON 43

MORRIS TRAVEL AGENCY

DICTATION SPEED BUILDING

The shorthand outlines below appear in the speed dictation practice that follows. Practice writing these words using the shorthand outlines. Then, using the key that follows, dictate the words to yourself in preparation for the speed dictation practice.

Dictation Preview

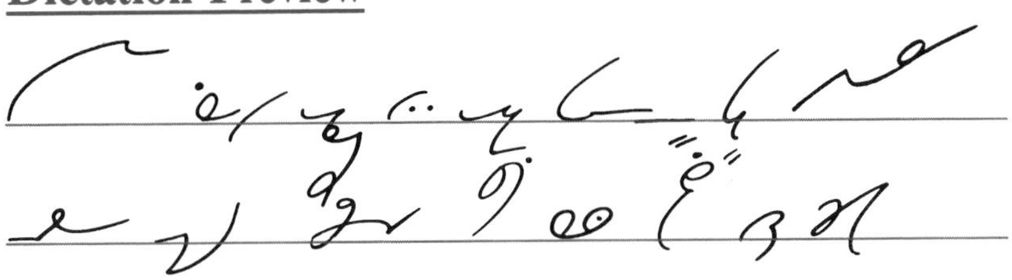

Key: Dear Mr. Harrington, reservation, thinking, reopening, Birmingham, Boston, delayed, until, informed, exact, however, area, has been, thank you for, we would be

Speed Dictation Practice

43.1 Goal: 90 wam speed dictation

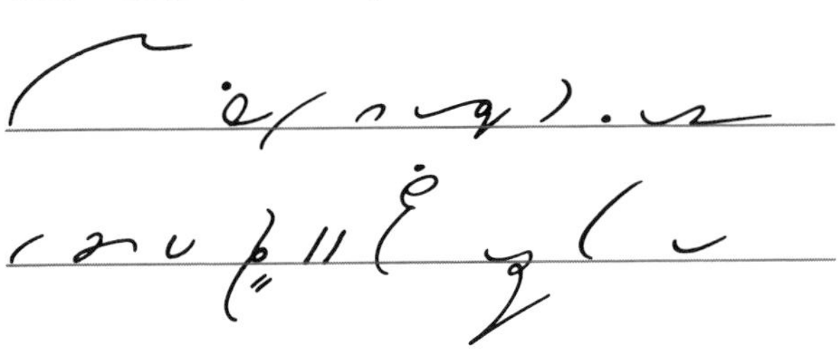

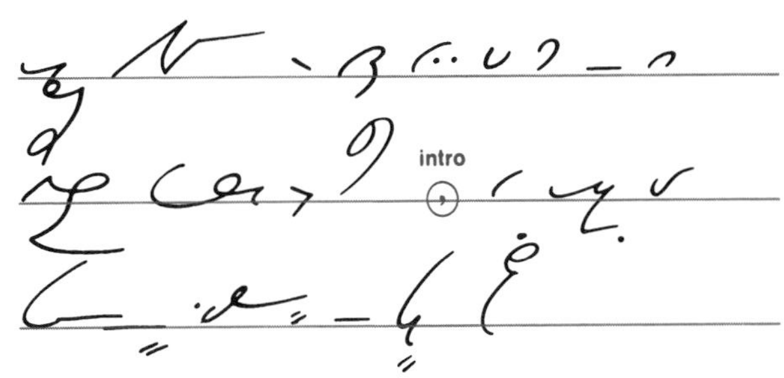

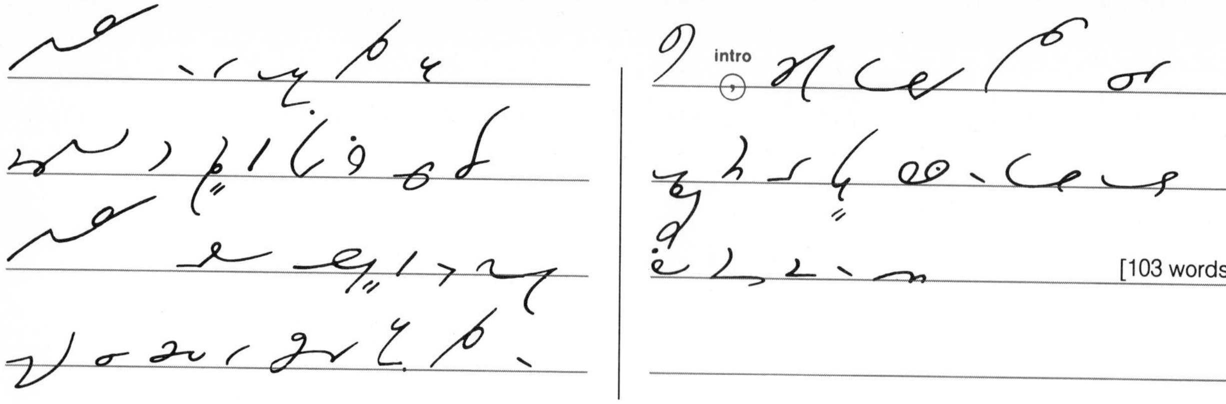

[103 words]

TRANSCRIPTION SKILL DEVELOPMENT

Transcription Warmup

Transcribe the following groups of words for speed and accuracy, applying transcription rules and assuring correct spelling.

43.2

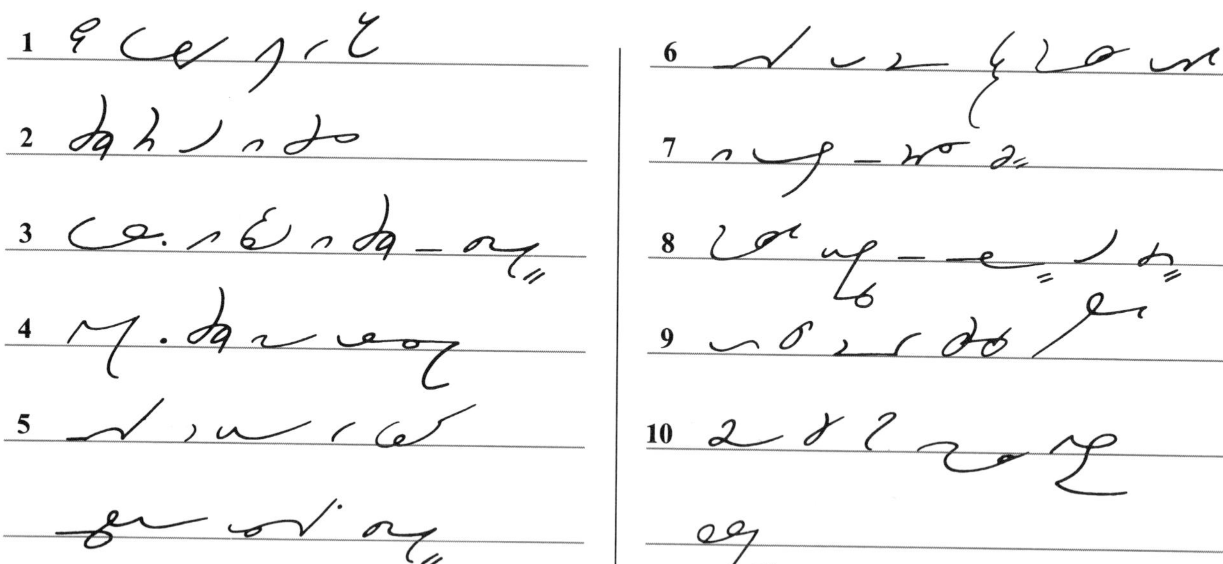

Transcription Practice

Transcribe the following letter for 2 minutes in unarranged format, applying transcription rules and assuring correct spelling. For every word not transcribed and every keyboarding error, deduct one word from the total word count.

43.3 Goal: 30 wam transcription rate

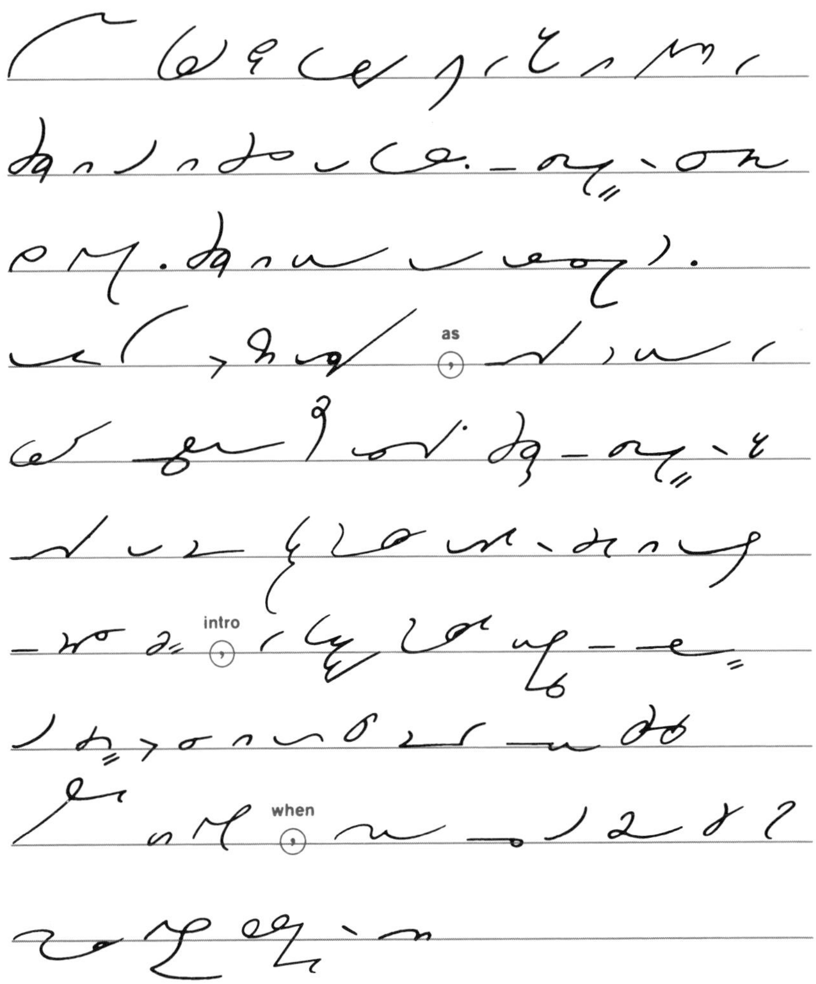

Word Count

13
26
37
47
59
70
83
94
104
113

Mailable Production

Transcribe the following itinerary. Follow the directions provided in Lesson 41. Read carefully prior to transcribing and determine the spacing between the information.

43.4 Time Limit: 15 minutes

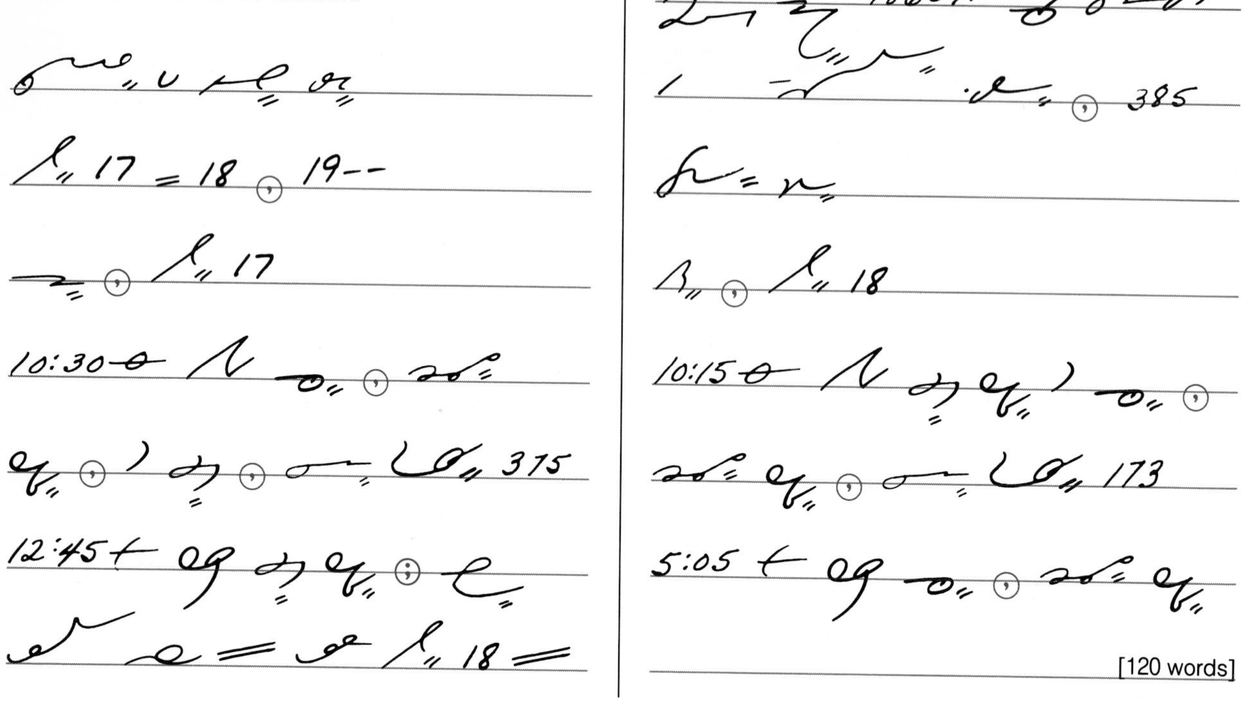

[120 words]

LESSON 44

MORRIS TRAVEL AGENCY

DICTATION SPEED BUILDING

The shorthand outlines below appear in the speed dictation practice that follows. Practice writing these words using the shorthand outlines. Then, using the key that follows, dictate the words to yourself in preparation for the speed dictation practice.

Dictation Preview

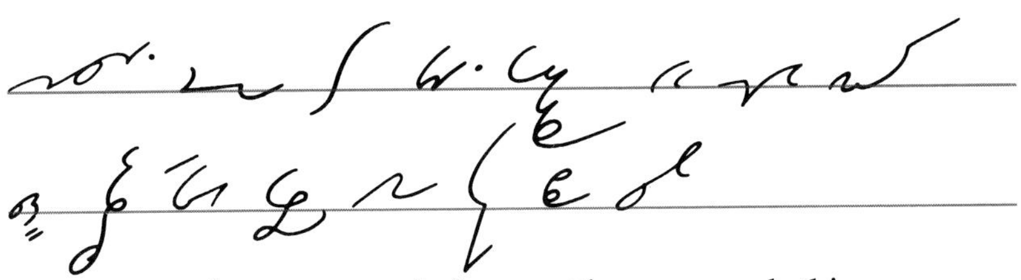

Key: contacting, summer, before, putting, proposal, things, instance, wanted, United States, specify, transportation, preferred, tour, budget, easier, ideas

Speed Dictation Practice

44.1 Goal: 90 wam speed dictation

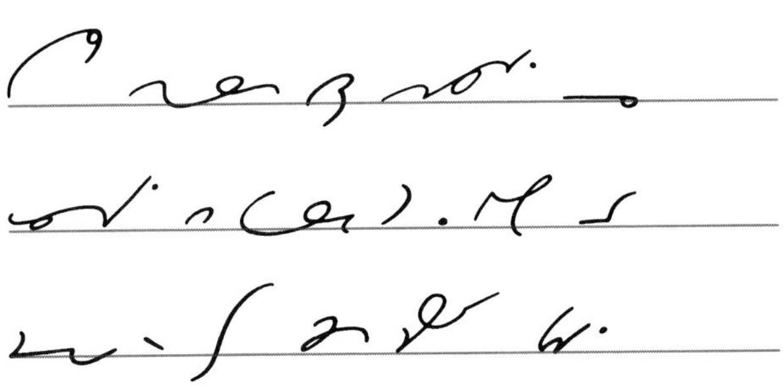

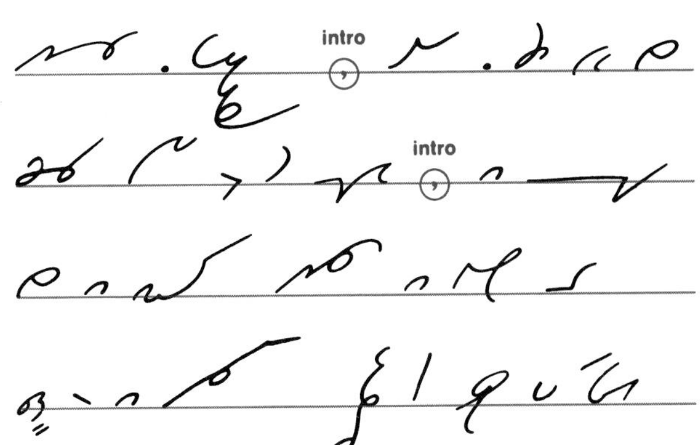

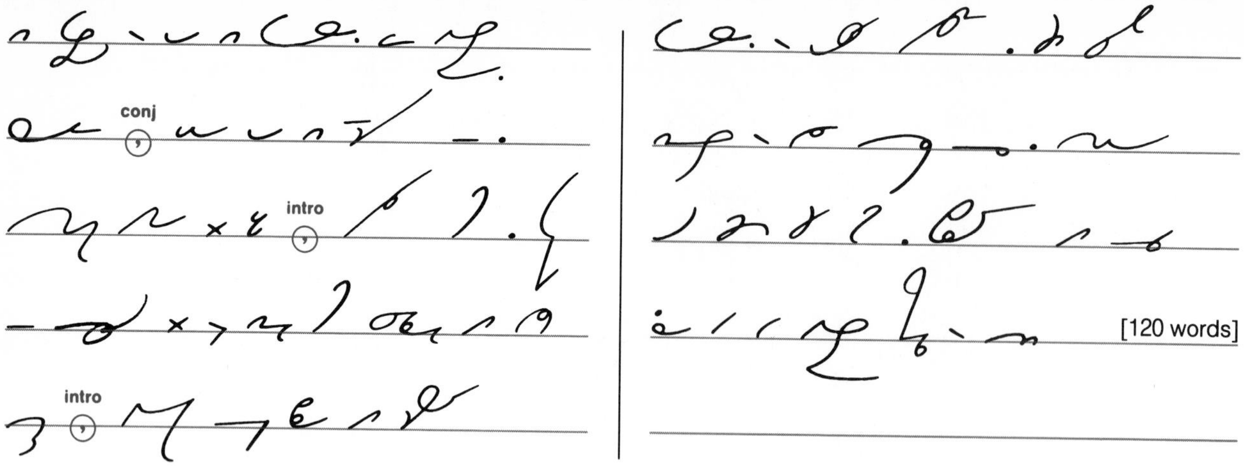

TRANSCRIPTION SKILL DEVELOPMENT

Transcription Warmup

Transcribe the following groups of words for speed and accuracy, applying transcription rules and assuring correct spelling.

44.2

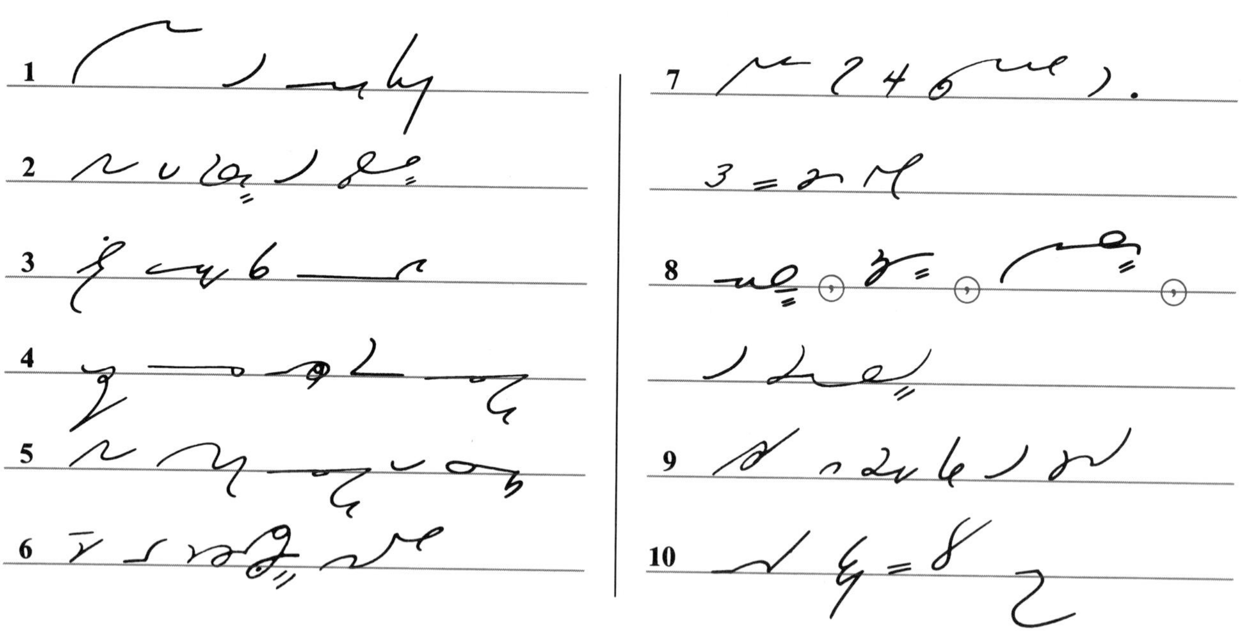

Transcription Practice

Transcribe the following letter for 2 minutes in unarranged format, applying transcription rules and assuring correct spelling. For every word not transcribed and every keyboarding error, deduct one word from the total word count.

44.3 Goal: 30 wam transcription rate

Word Count

10
21
31
45
56
66
81
94
102
113
125
140
154

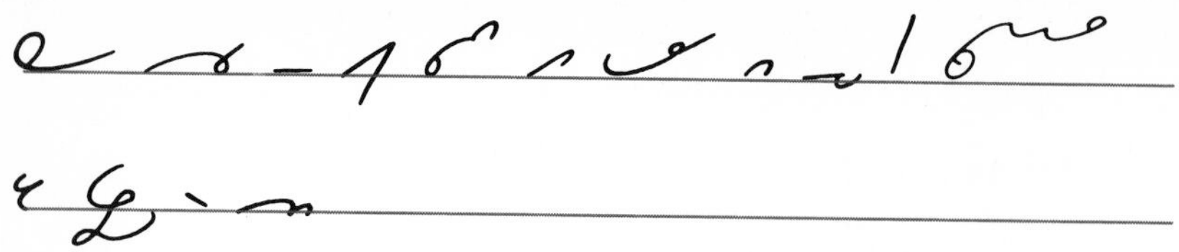

167

172

Mailable Production

Transcribe the following mailable production letter in block style, assuring proper placement of all letter parts. Insert punctuation prior to transcribing, and capitalize proper nouns and titles. Address a large envelope.

44.4 Time Limit: 15 minutes

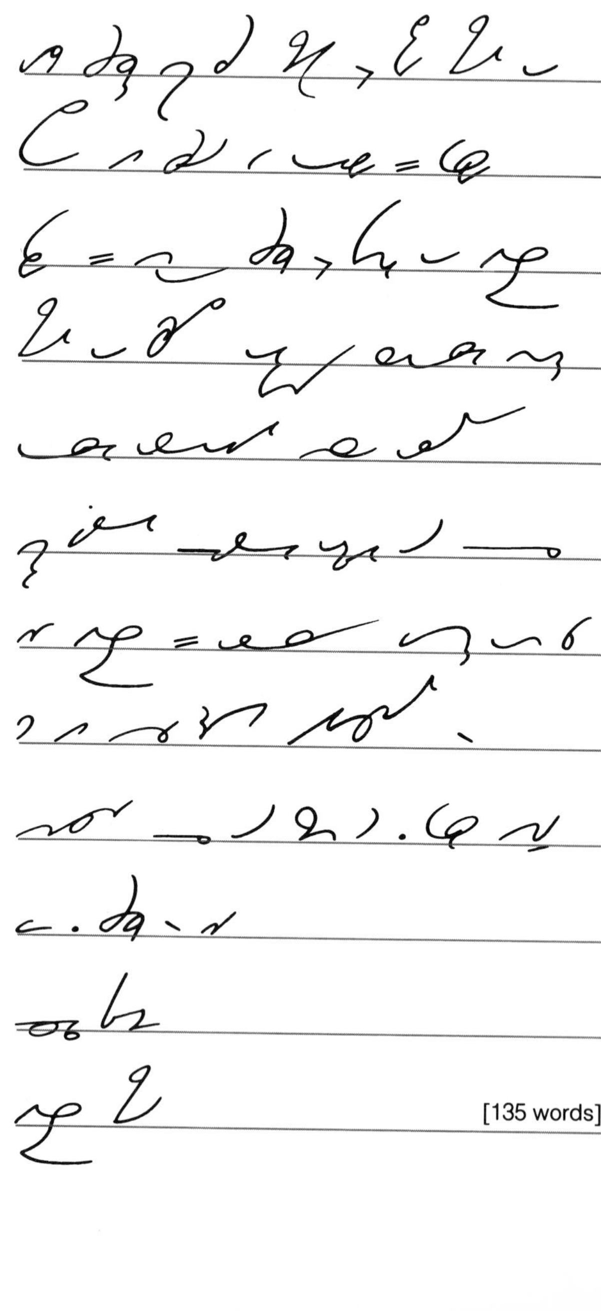

[135 words]

LESSON 45

MORRIS TRAVEL AGENCY

DICTATION SPEED BUILDING

The shorthand outlines below appear in the speed dictation practice that follows. Practice writing these words using the shorthand outlines. Then, using the key that follows, dictate the words to yourself in preparation for the speed dictation practice.

Dictation Preview

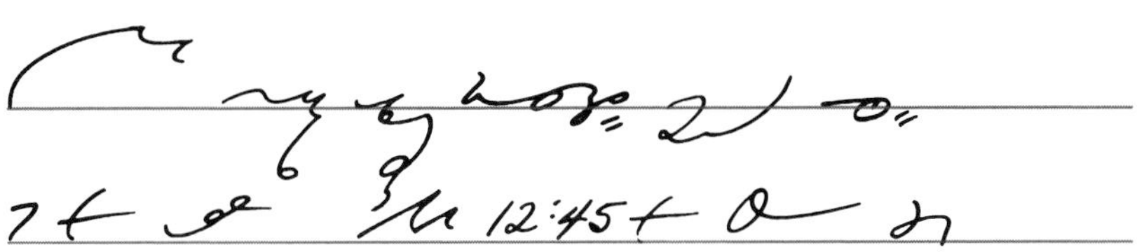

Key: Dear Mrs. Crosby, reservations, Salt Lake City, confirmed, New York, 7 p.m., return, departs, 12:45 p.m., aisle, section

Speed Dictation Practice

45.1 Goal: 90 wam speed dictation

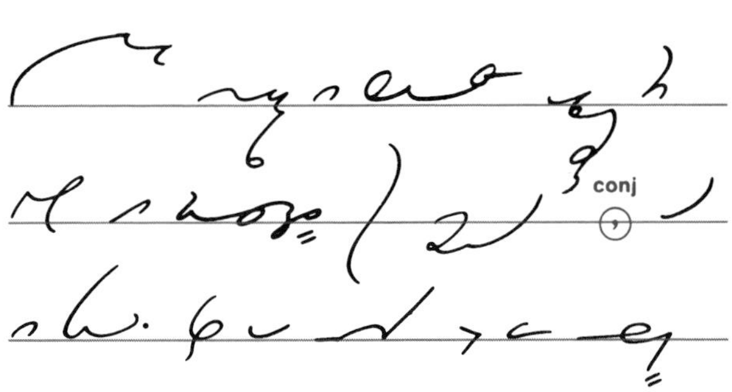

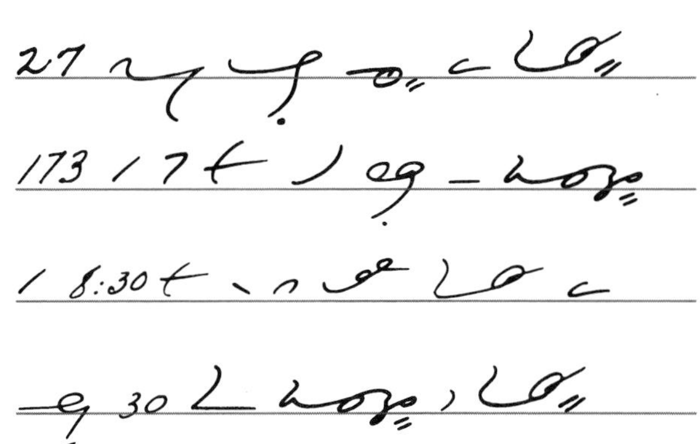

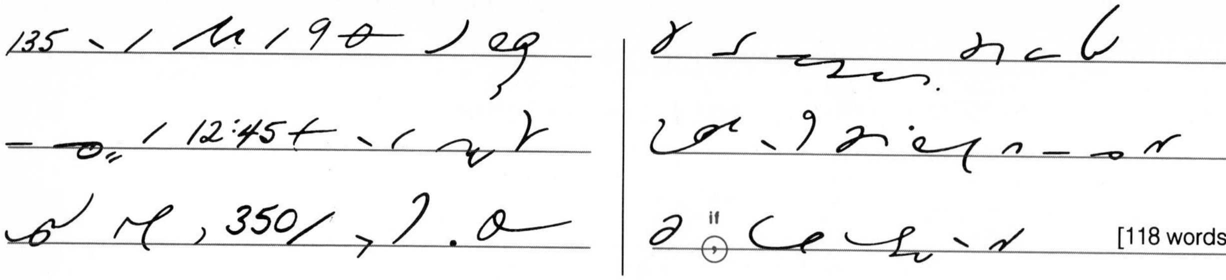

TRANSCRIPTION SKILL DEVELOPMENT

Transcription Warmup

Transcribe the following groups of words for speed and accuracy, applying transcription rules and assuring correct spelling.

45.2

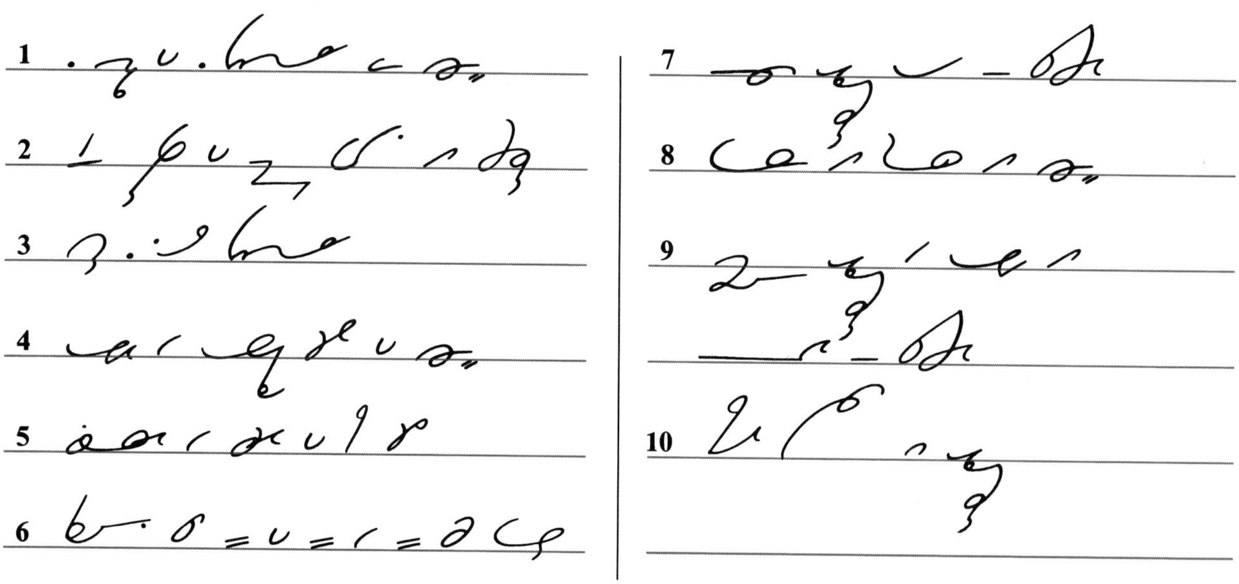

Transcription Practice

Transcribe the following letter for 2 minutes in unarranged format, applying transcription rules and assuring correct spelling. For every word not transcribed and every keyboarding error, deduct one word from the total word count.

45.3 Goal: 30 wam transcription rate

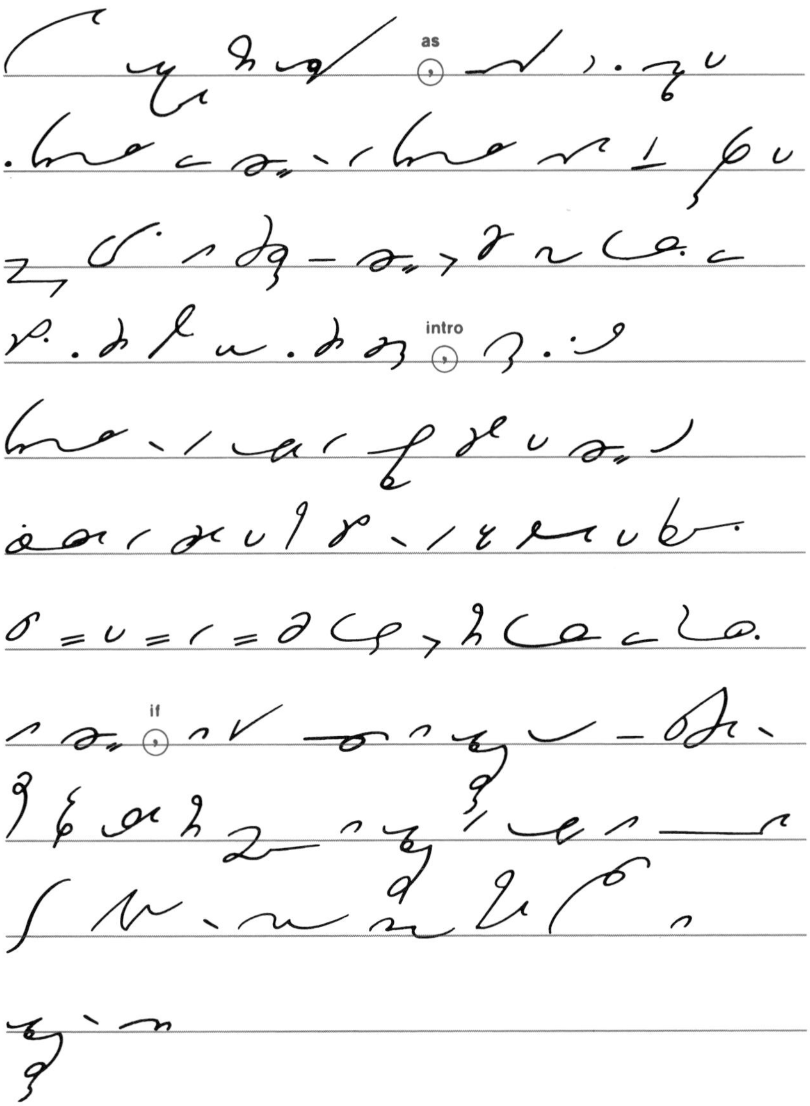

Word Count

11

22

37

47

57

69

78

90

105

116

122

Mailable Production

Transcribe the following itinerary. Follow the directions provided in Lesson 41. Read carefully prior to transcribing and determine the spacing between the information.

45.4 Time Limit: 15 minutes

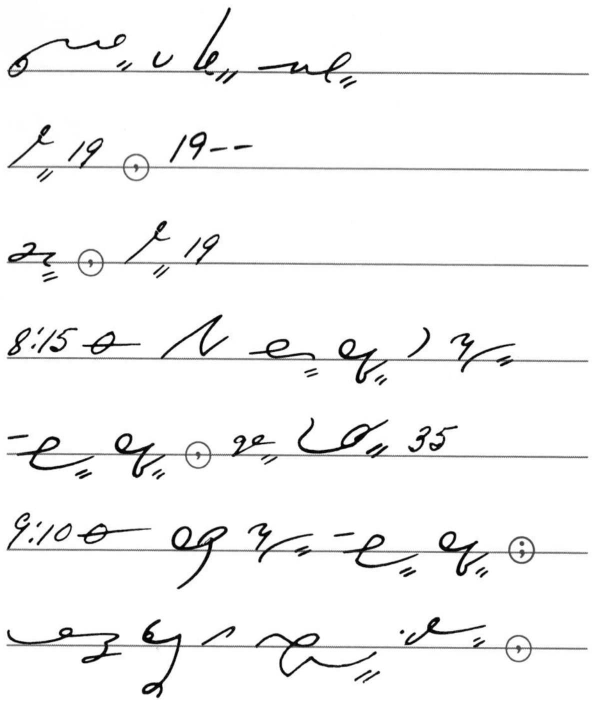

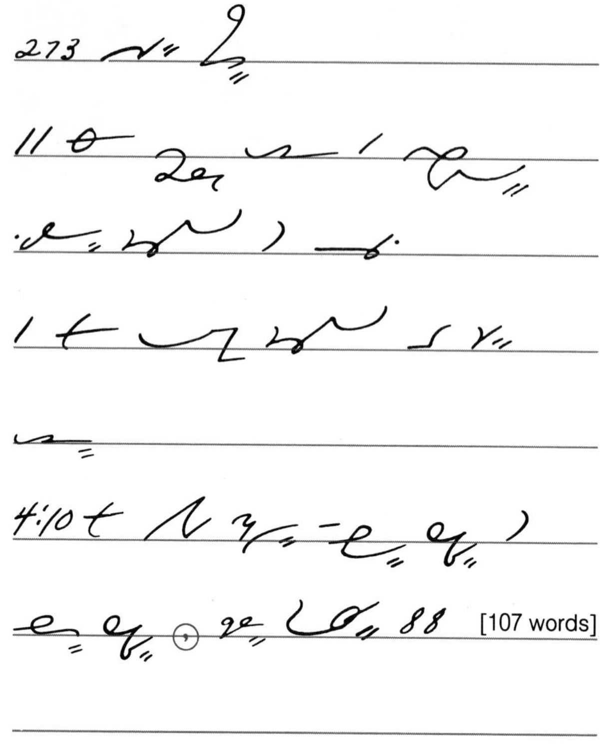

[107 words]

LESSON 46

MORRIS TRAVEL AGENCY

DICTATION SPEED BUILDING

The shorthand outlines below appear in the speed dictation practice that follows. Practice writing these words using the shorthand outlines. Then, using the key that follows, dictate the words to yourself in preparation for the speed dictation practice.

Dictation Preview

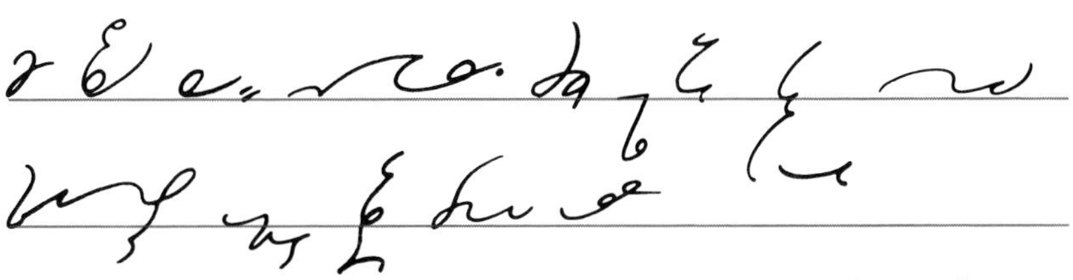

Key: whether, expand, Arizona, contemplating, vacation, enjoy, opportunities, possibilities, growth, photographs, resources, specific, bureau, return

Speed Dictation Practice

46.1 Goal: 90 wam speed dictation

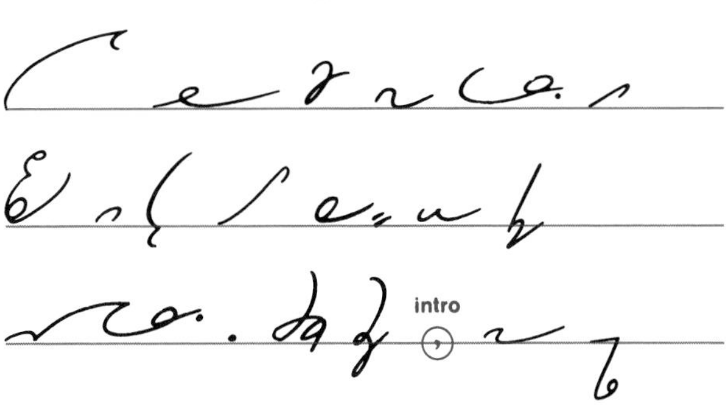

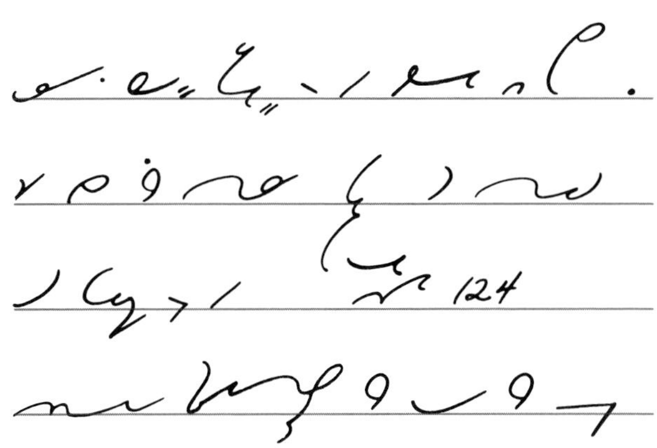

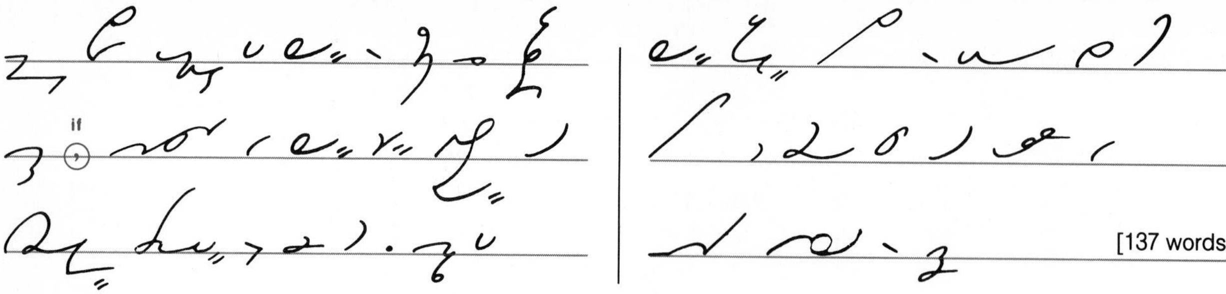

[137 words]

TRANSCRIPTION SKILL DEVELOPMENT

Transcription Warmup

Transcribe the following groups of words for speed and accuracy, applying transcription rules and assuring correct spelling.

46.2

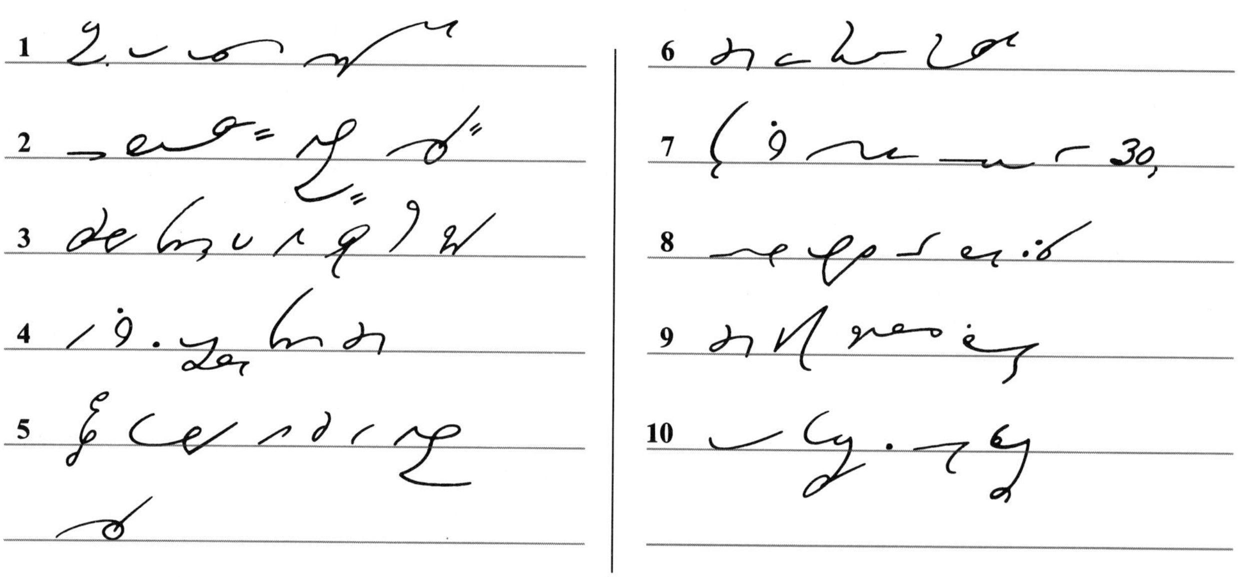

Transcription Practice

Transcribe the following letter for 2 minutes in unarranged format, applying transcription rules and assuring correct spelling. For every word not transcribed and every keyboarding error, deduct one word from the total word count.

46.3 Goal: 30 wam transcription rate

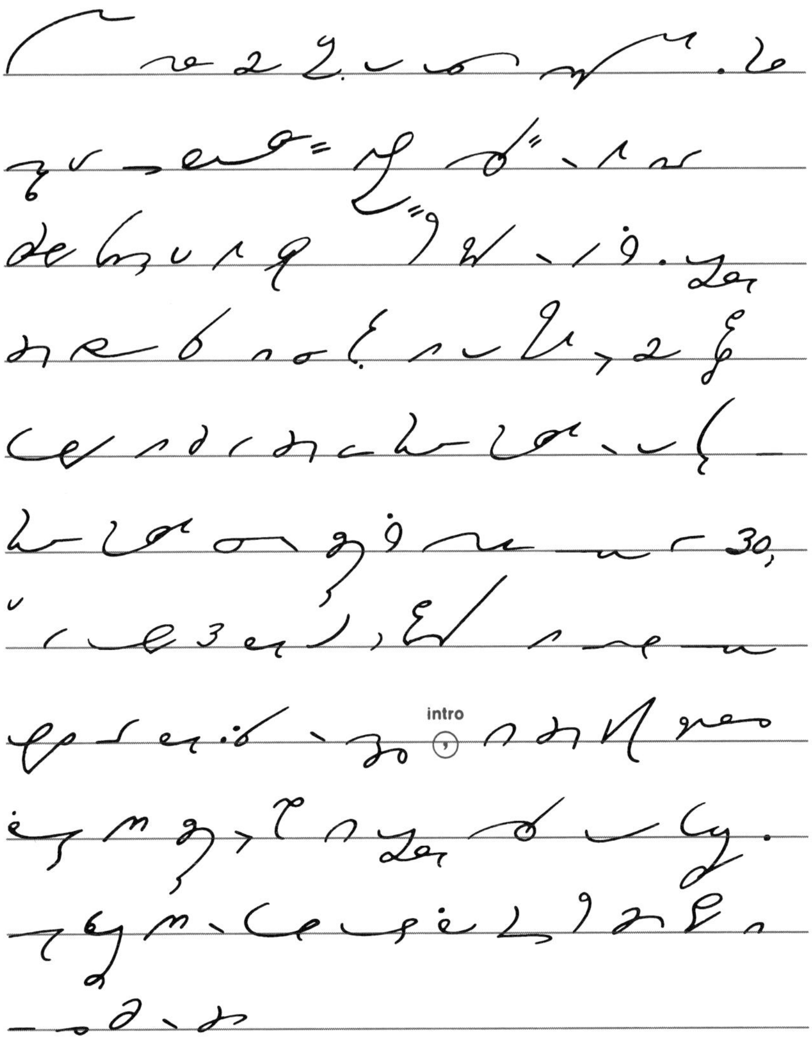

Word Count

12
23
34
49
62
75
87
102
117
132
138

Mailable Production

Transcribe the following mailable production letter in block style, assuring proper placement of all letter parts. Insert punctuation prior to transcribing, and capitalize proper nouns and titles. Address a large envelope.

46.4 Time Limit: 15 minutes

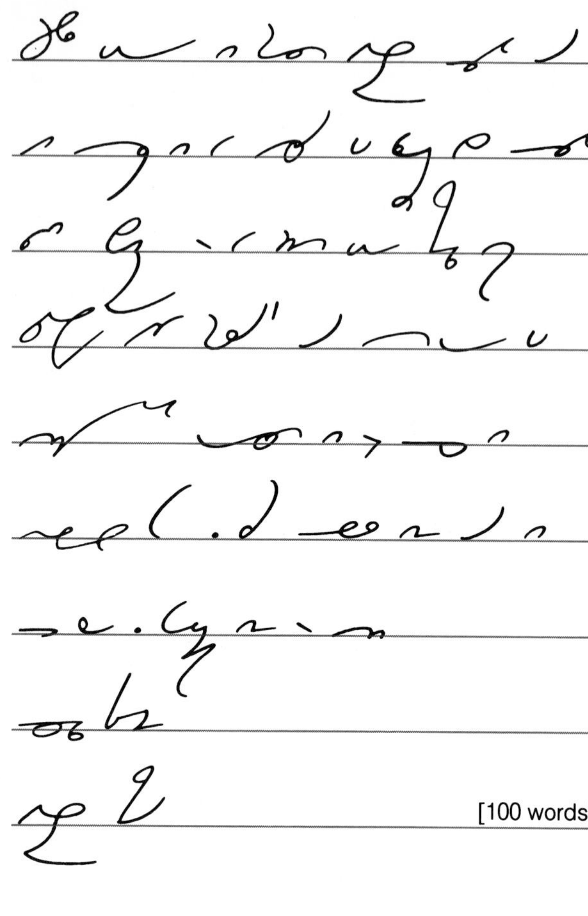

[100 words]

LESSON 47

MORRIS TRAVEL AGENCY

DICTATION SPEED BUILDING

The shorthand outlines below appear in the speed dictation practice that follows. Practice writing these words using the shorthand outlines. Then, using the key that follows, dictate the words to yourself in preparation for the speed dictation practice.

Dictation Preview

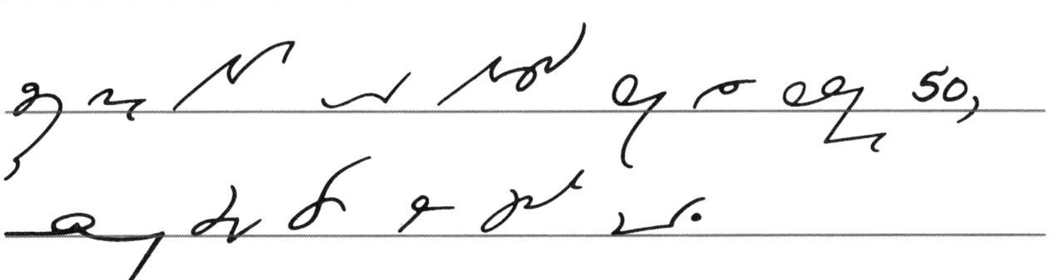

Key: executives, once, destination, worked, discount, whereby, then, arrangements, 50 percent, mileage, finished, back, turn, sounds, something

Speed Dictation Practice

47.1 Goal: 90 wam speed dictation

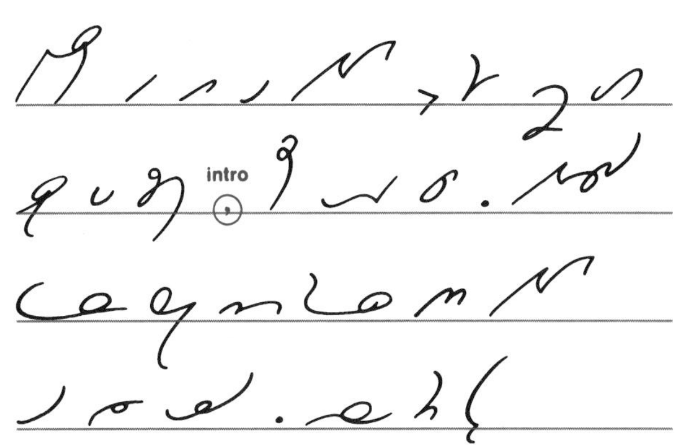

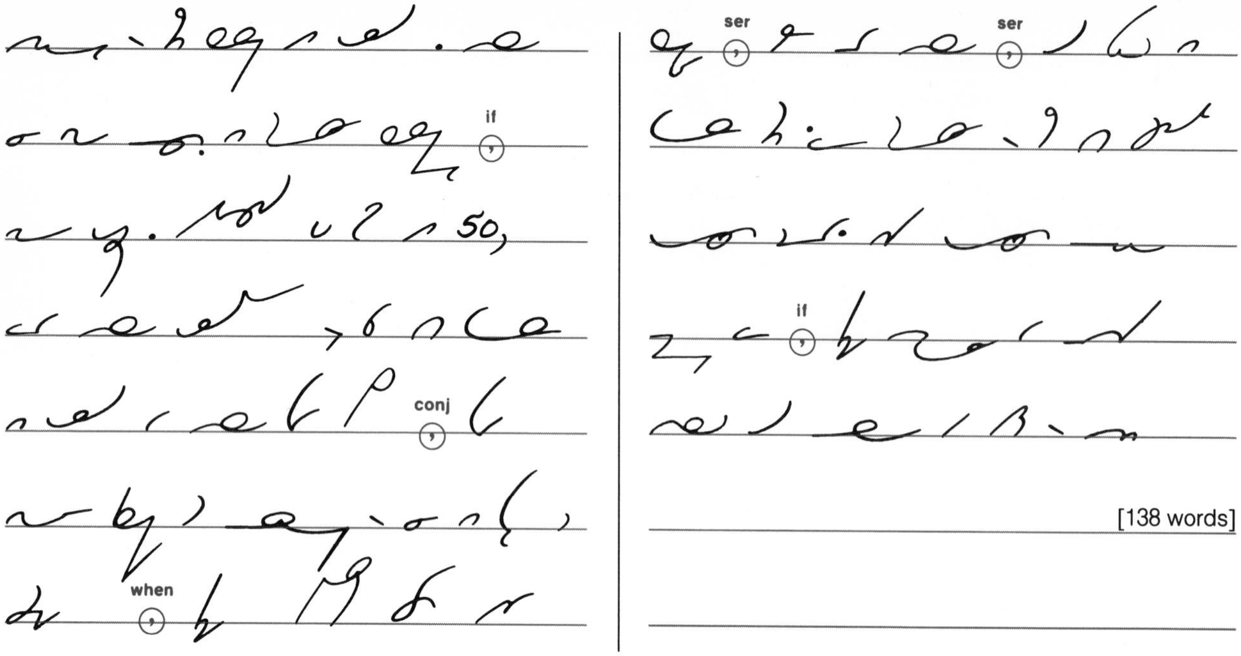

TRANSCRIPTION SKILL DEVELOPMENT

Transcription Warmup

Transcribe the following groups of words for speed and accuracy, applying transcription rules and assuring correct spelling.

47.2

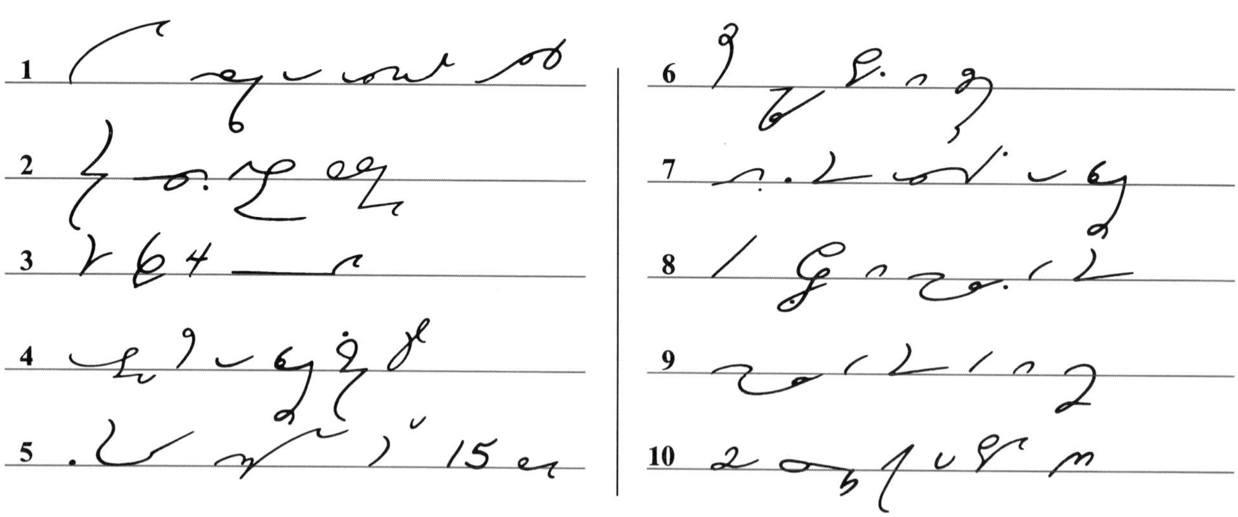

Transcription Practice

Transcribe the following letter for 2 minutes in unarranged format, applying transcription rules and assuring correct spelling. For every word not transcribed and every keyboarding error, deduct one word from the total word count.

47.3 Goal: 30 wam transcription rate

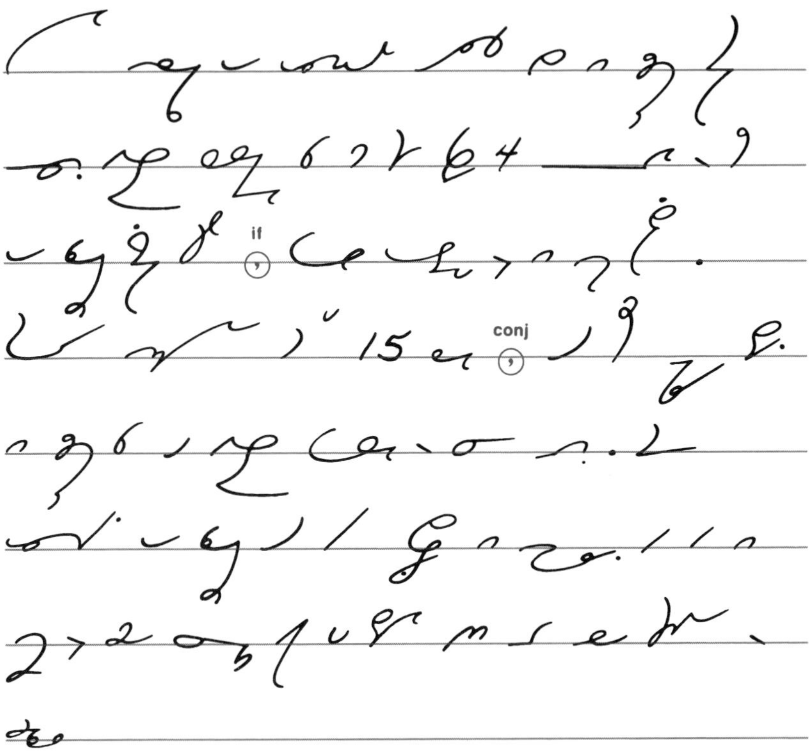

Word Count
14
27
44
57
70
84
99
101

Mailable Production

Transcribe the following itinerary. Follow the directions provided in Lesson 41. Read carefully prior to transcribing and determine the spacing between the information.

47.4 Time Limit: 15 minutes

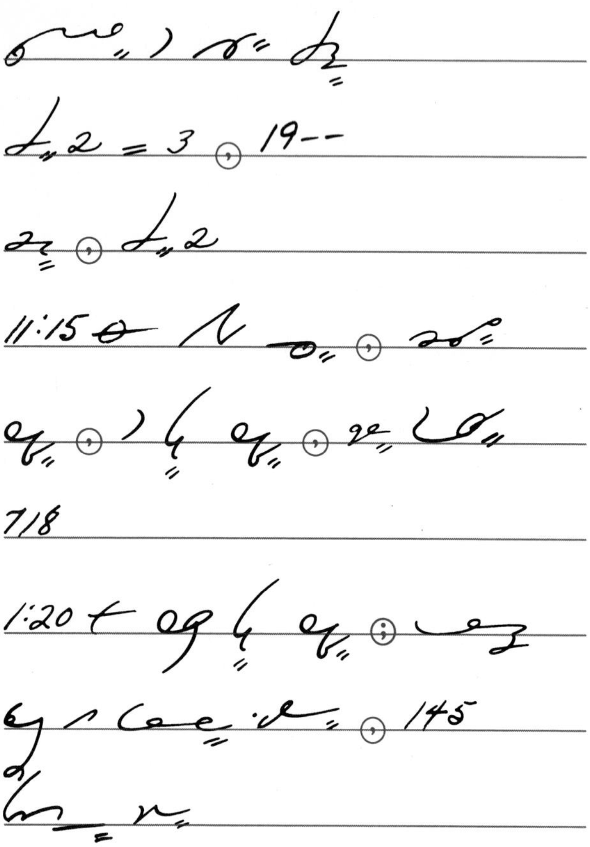

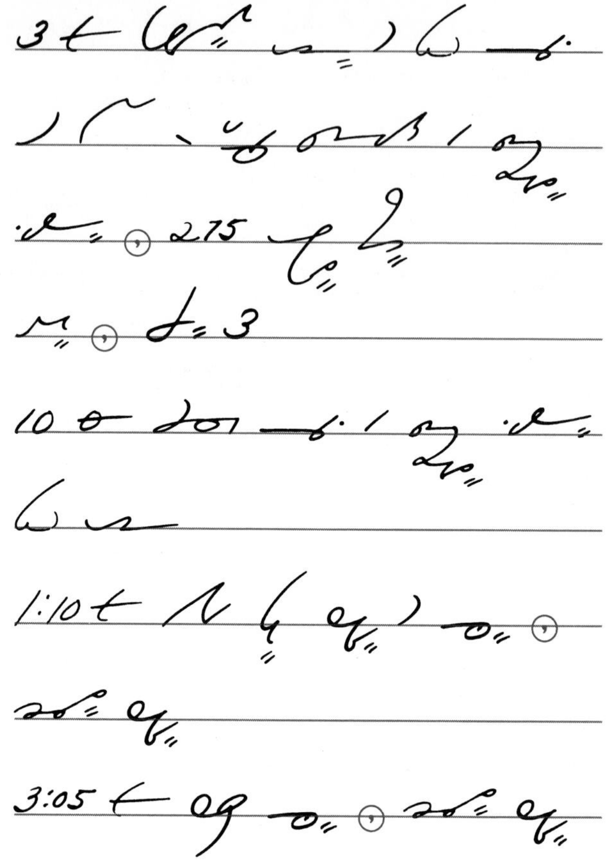

[99 words]

LESSON 48

MORRIS TRAVEL AGENCY

DICTATION SPEED BUILDING

The shorthand outlines below appear in the speed dictation practice that follows. Practice writing these words using the shorthand outlines. Then, using the key that follows, dictate the words to yourself in preparation for the speed dictation practice.

Dictation Preview

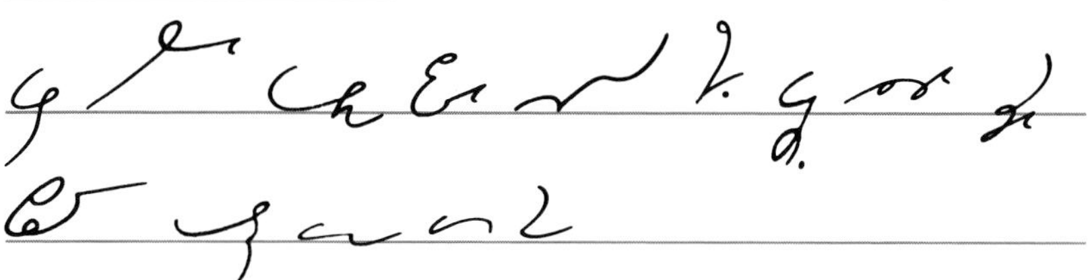

Key: privilege, details, pleasure, experts, continent, everything, purchasing, tickets, visits, appointment, let us have, on our, of course, for our

Speed Dictation Practice

48.1 Goal: 90 wam speed dictation

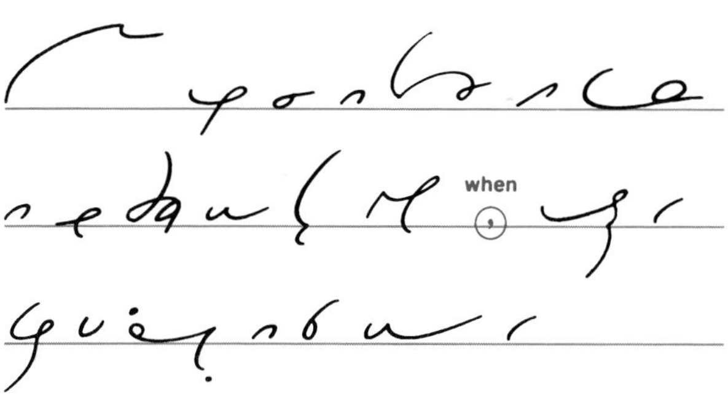

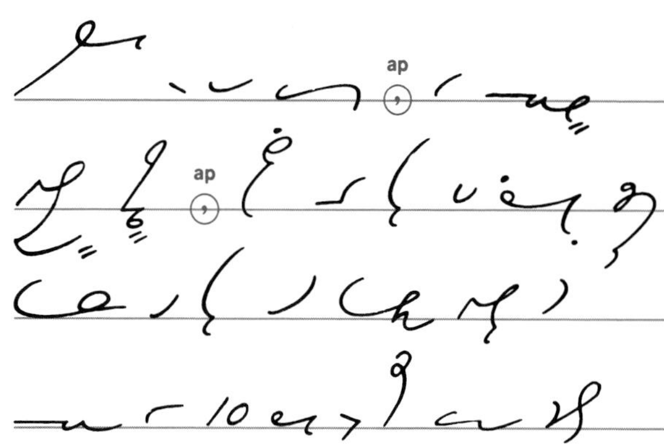

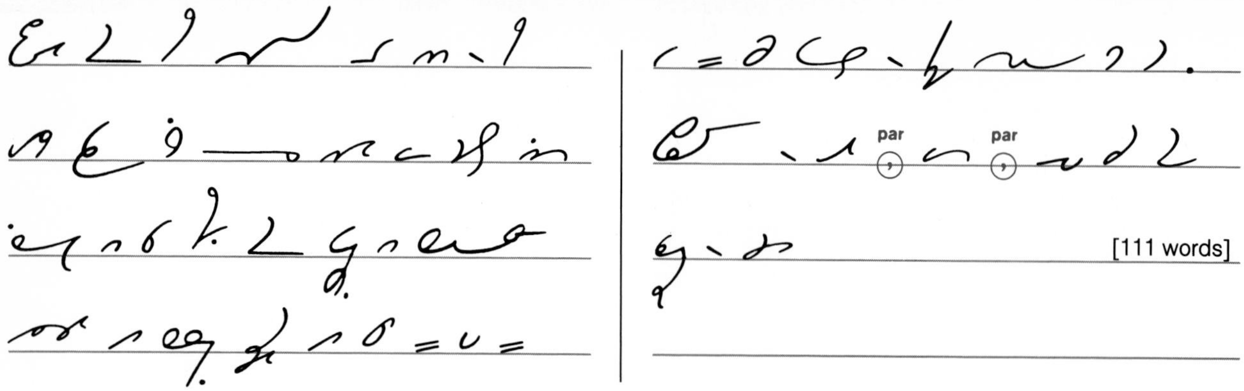

TRANSCRIPTION SKILL DEVELOPMENT

Transcription Warmup

Transcribe the following groups of words for speed and accuracy, applying transcription rules and assuring correct spelling.

48.2

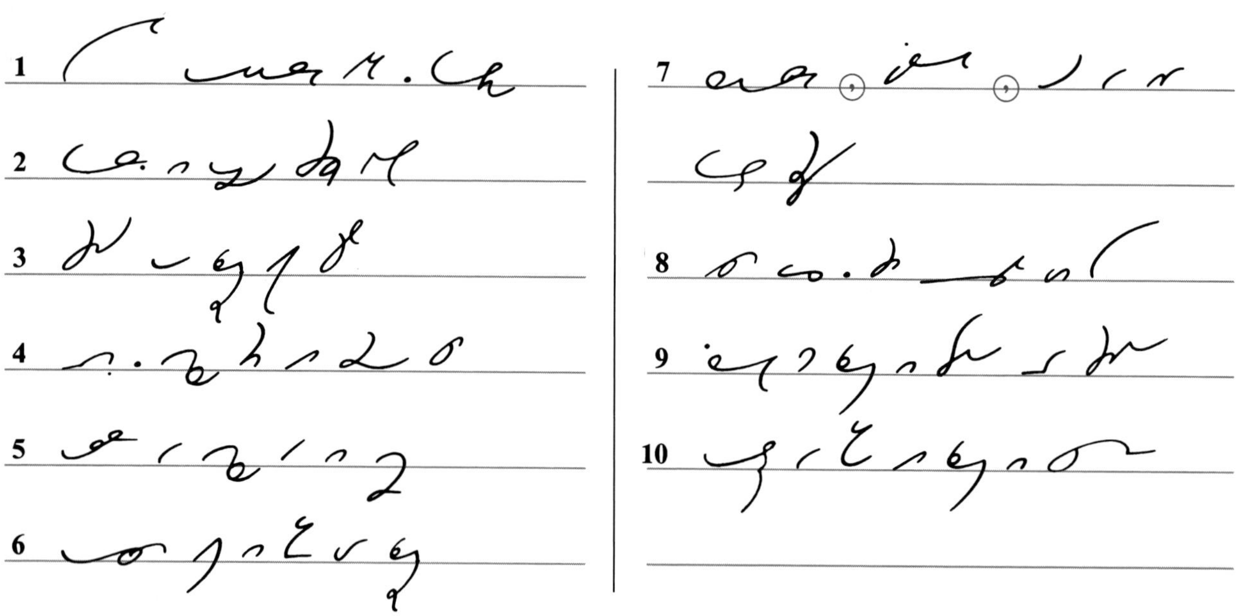

Transcription Practice

Transcribe the following letter for 2 minutes in unarranged format, applying transcription rules and assuring correct spelling. For every word not transcribed and every keyboarding error, deduct one word from the total word count.

48.3 Goal: 30 wam transcription rate

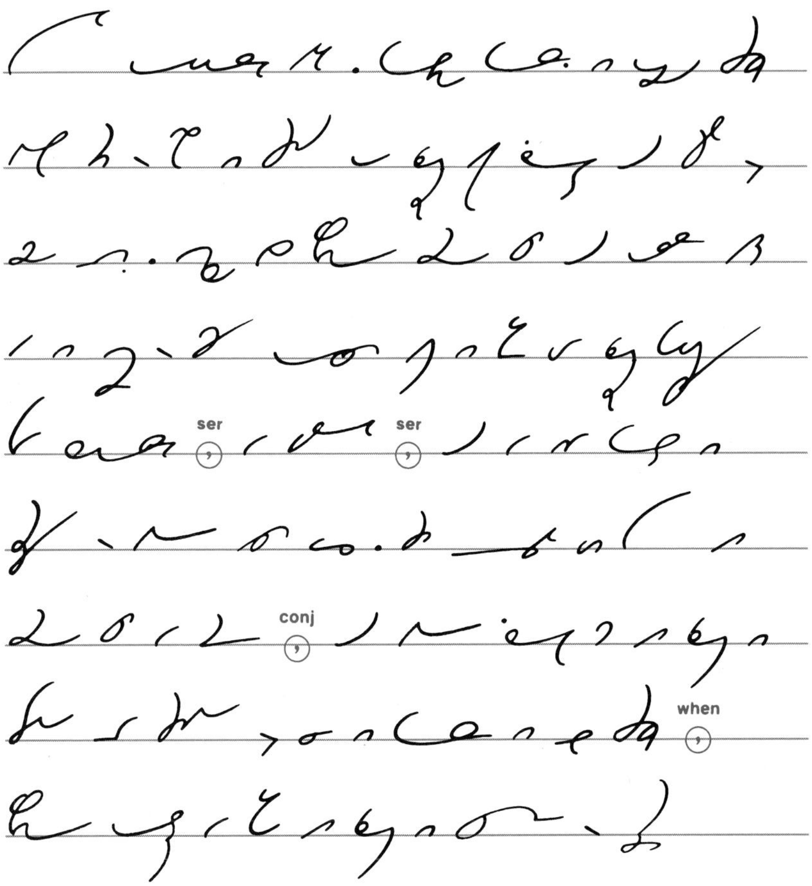

Word Count
13
28
44
60
71
82
92
103
120

Mailable Production

Transcribe the following mailable production memo, inserting punctuation prior to transcribing. Capitalize proper nouns and titles. Do not address a letter envelope. A memo would be placed in an interoffice envelope, and the information requested would be handwritten.

48.4 Time Limit: 15 minutes

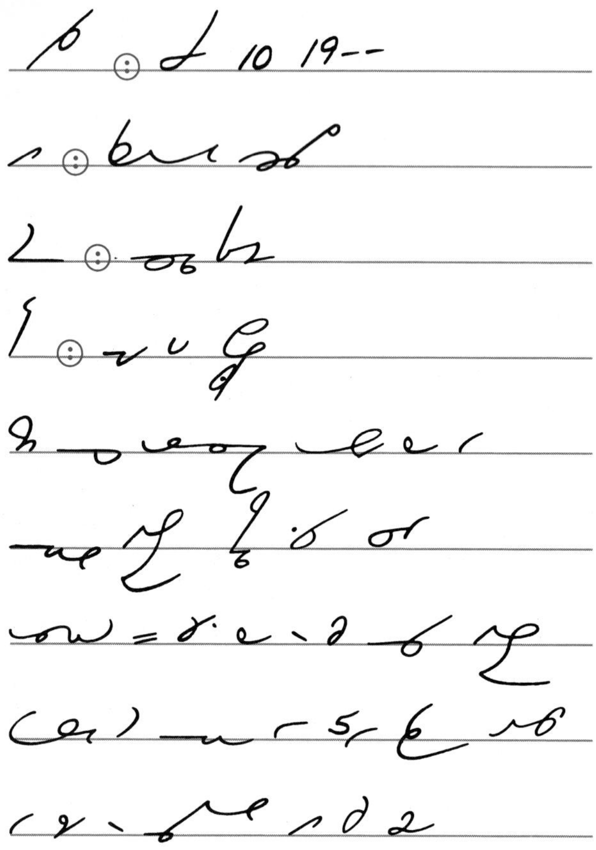

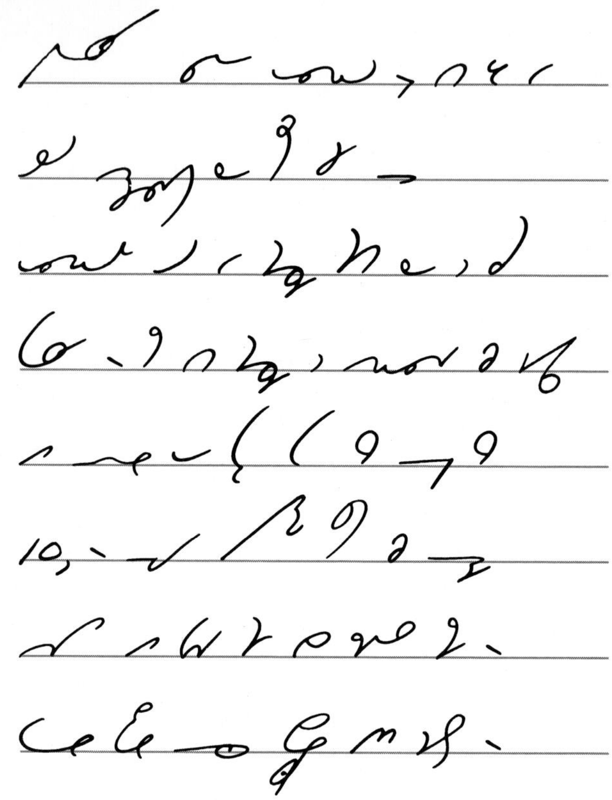

[120 words]

UNIT

VII

TAYLOR DEPARTMENT STORE

LESSON 49

TAYLOR DEPARTMENT STORE

If you are interested in retailing and marketing, you are going to enjoy your job as administrative assistant to Philip Walters, marketing manager for the Taylor Department Store chain located in Chicago, Illinois.

The advertising staff here originates its own advertising materials or uses those supplied by an advertising firm. Taylor Department Store advertises in local newspapers and on television and radio. It also sends out promotional advertisements weekly.

The department store carries clothes for men, women, and children; major appliances; home furnishings; and numerous other items to meet the everyday needs of its customers.

Below is a copy of your company letterhead. Develop the return address that you will use to type the envelopes for the mailable production letters.

TAYLOR

DEPARTMENT STORE

375 SPRING STREET CHICAGO IL 60607 (312) 555-1678

DICTATION SPEED BUILDING

The shorthand outlines below appear in the speed dictation practice that follows. Practice writing these words using the shorthand outlines. Then, using the key that follows, dictate the words to yourself in preparation for the speed dictation practice.

Dictation Preview

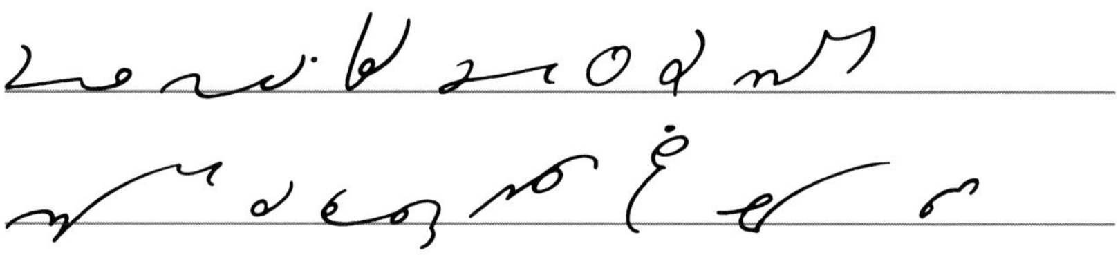

Key: formerly, clothing, joined, women's, eye, fashion, wonderful, customers, either, selections, to take, has been, next time, with your

Speed Dictation Practice

49.1 Goal: 100 wam speed dictation

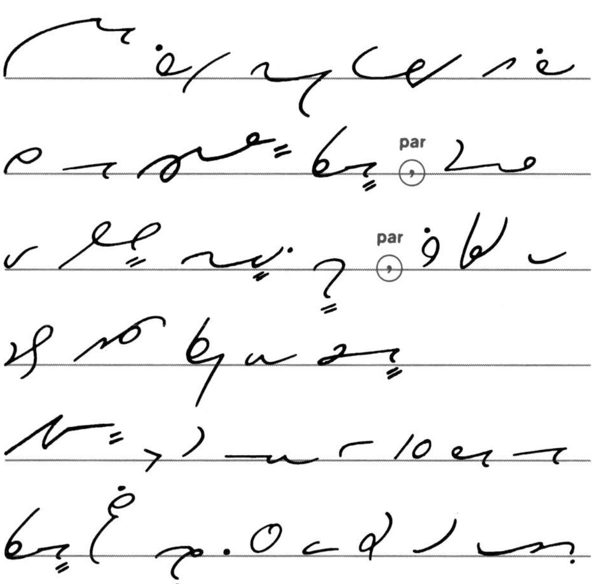

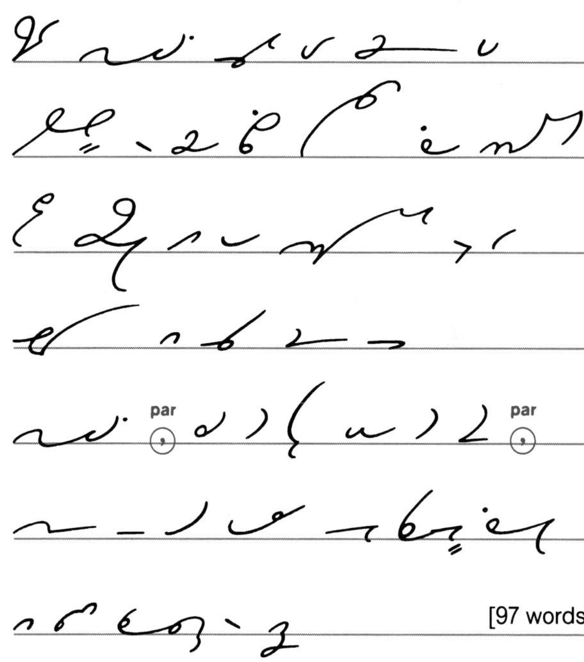

[97 words]

TRANSCRIPTION SKILL DEVELOPMENT

Transcription Warmup

Transcribe the following groups of words for speed and accuracy, applying transcription rules and assuring correct spelling.

49.2

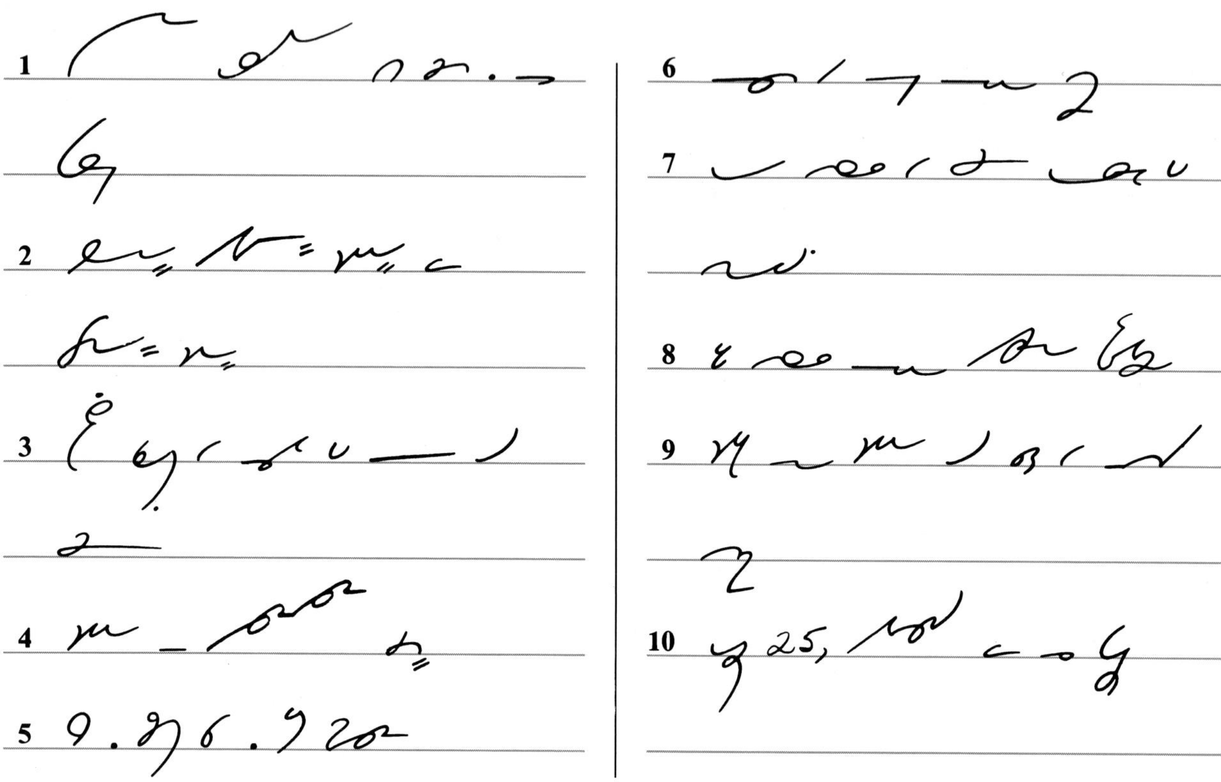

Transcription Practice

Transcribe the following letter for 2 minutes in unarranged format, applying transcription rules and assuring correct spelling. For every word not transcribed and every keyboarding error, deduct one word from the total word count.

49.3 Goal: 30 wam transcription rate

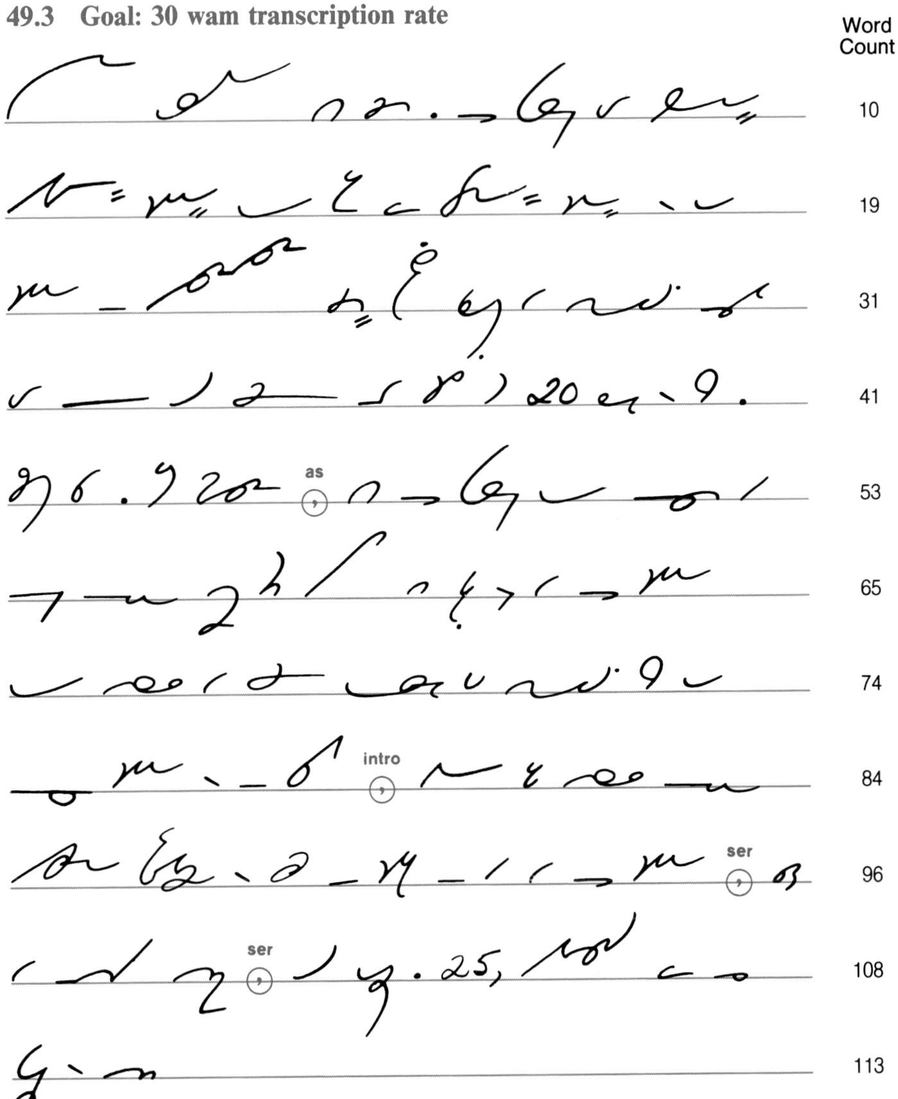

LESSON 50

TAYLOR DEPARTMENT STORE

DICTATION SPEED BUILDING

The shorthand outlines below appear in the speed dictation practice that follows. Practice writing these words using the shorthand outlines. Then, using the key that follows, dictate the words to yourself in preparation for the speed dictation practice.

Dictation Preview

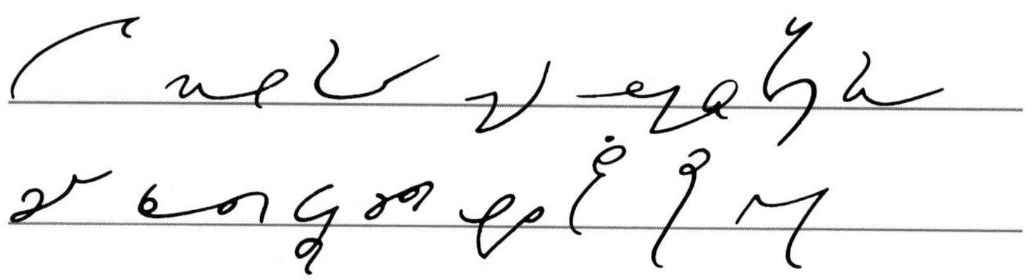

Key: Dear Ms. Wallace, valued, informed, merchandise, objective, fall, winter, selection, purchases, situation, rapidly, has been, we have been, it will be

Speed Dictation Practice

50.1 Goal: 100 wam speed dictation

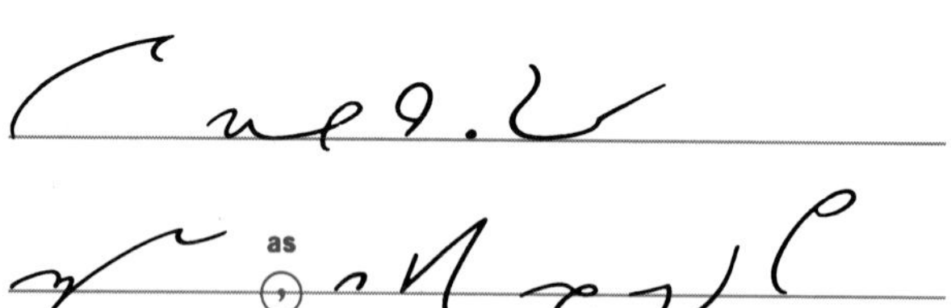

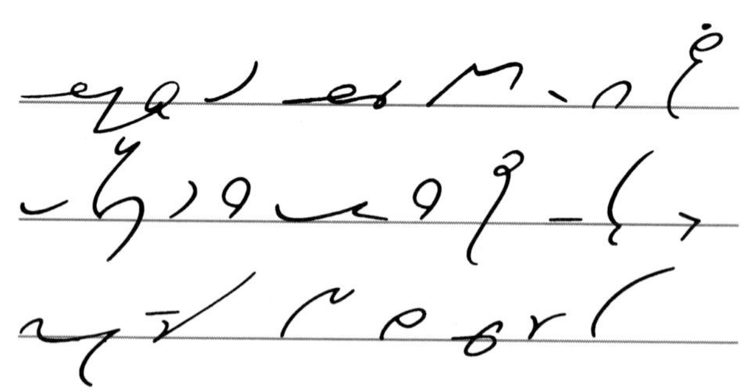

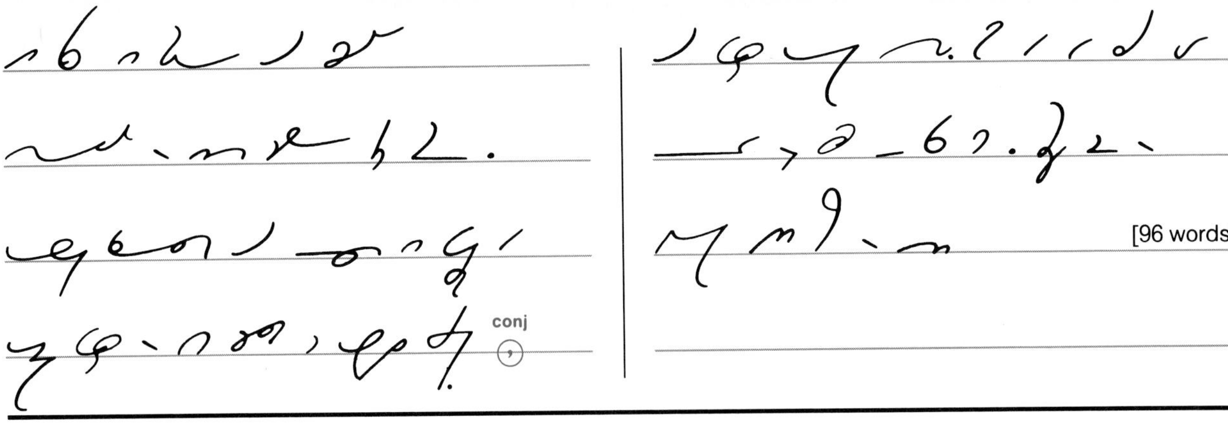

TRANSCRIPTION SKILL DEVELOPMENT

Transcription Warmup

Transcribe the following groups of words for speed and accuracy, applying transcription rules and assuring correct spelling.

50.2

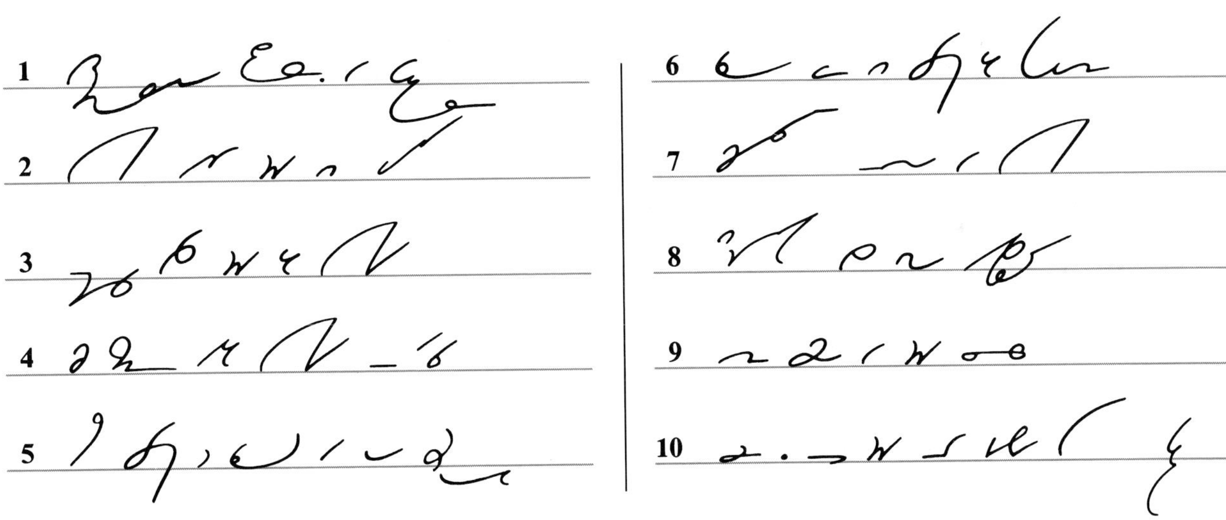

Transcription Practice

Transcribe the following letter for 2 minutes in unarranged format, applying transcription rules and assuring correct spelling. For every word not transcribed and every keyboarding error, deduct one word from the total word count.

50.3 Goal: 30 wam transcription rate

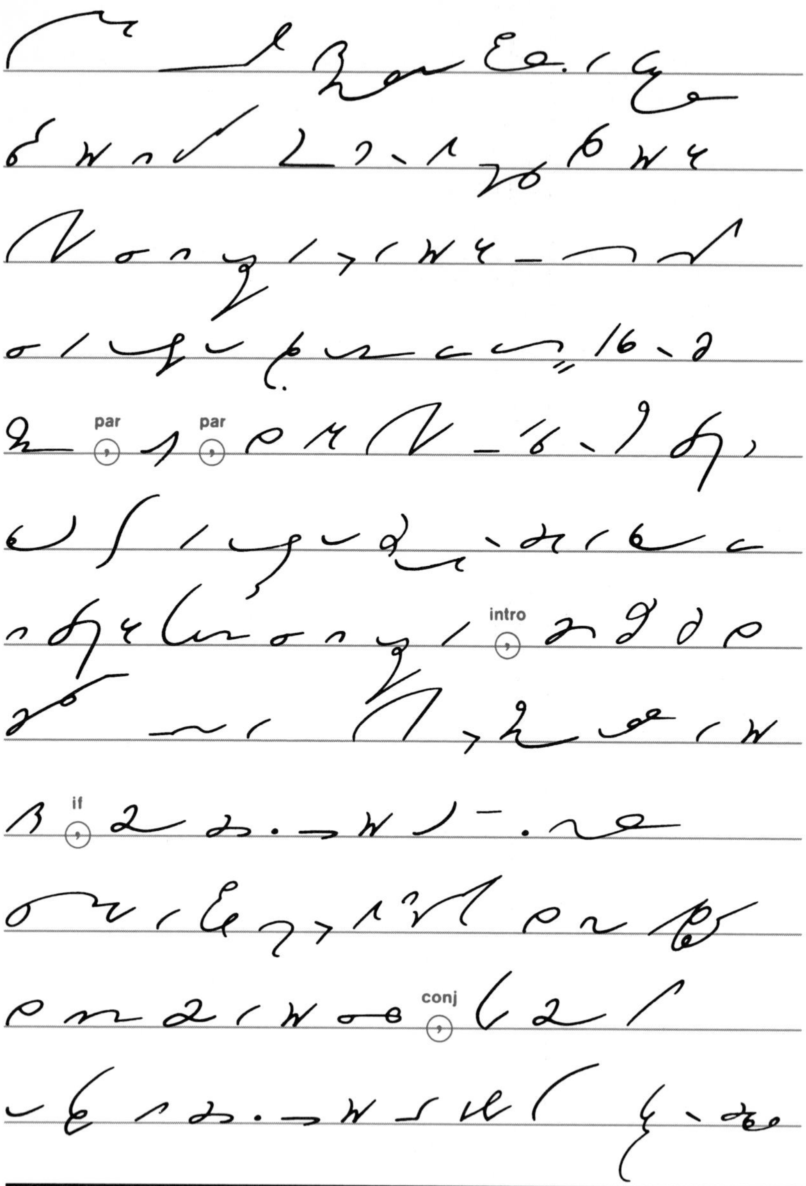

Word Count

13
27
39
49
62
73
86
97
108
123
136
150

Mailable Production

Transcribe the following mailable production letter in block style, assuring proper placement of all letter parts. Insert punctuation prior to transcribing, and capitalize proper nouns and titles. Address a large envelope.

50.4 Time Limit: 15 minutes

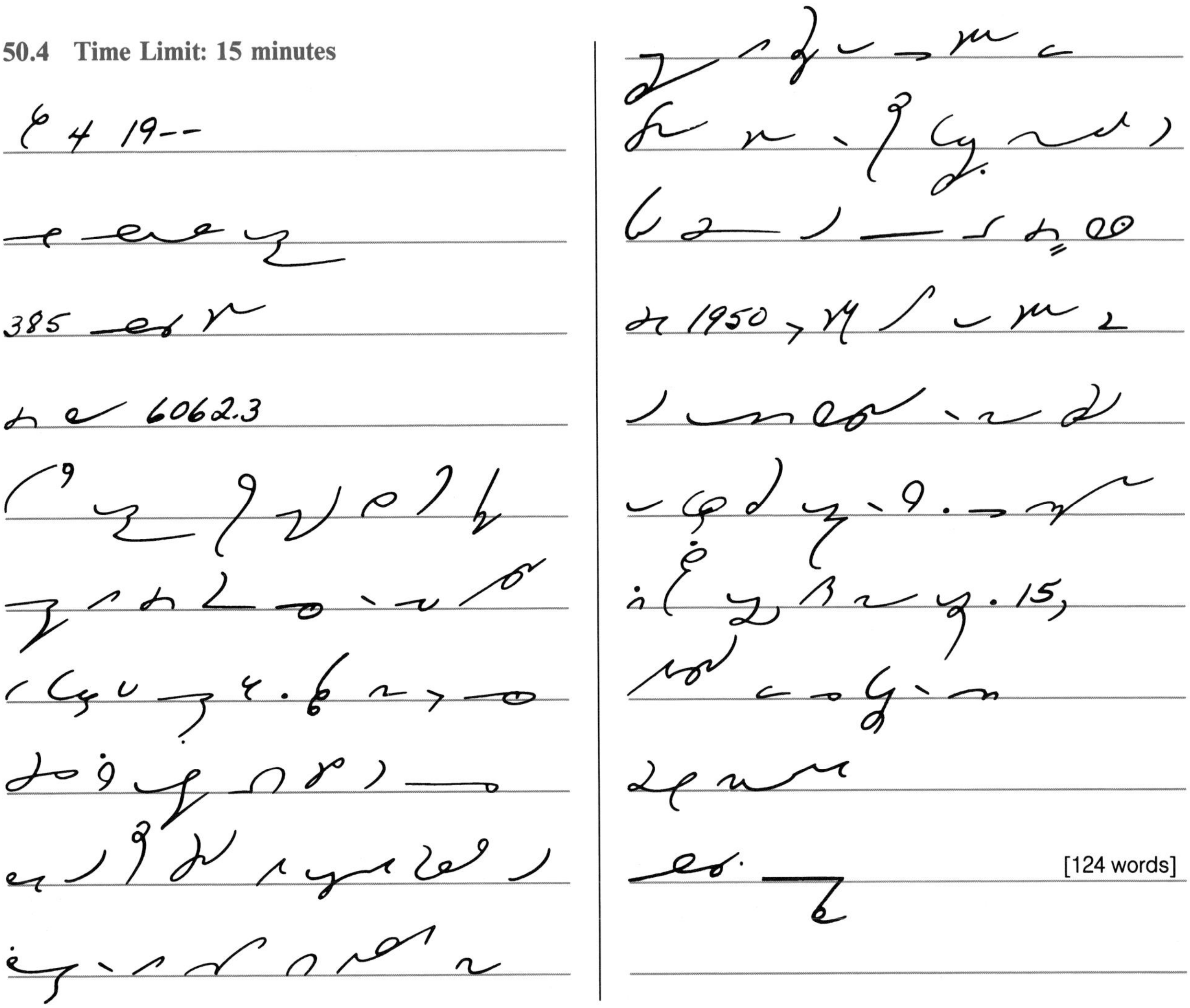

[124 words]

LESSON 51

TAYLOR DEPARTMENT STORE

DICTATION SPEED BUILDING

The shorthand outlines below appear in the speed dictation practice that follows. Practice writing these words using the shorthand outlines. Then, using the key that follows, dictate the words to yourself in preparation for the speed dictation practice.

Dictation Preview

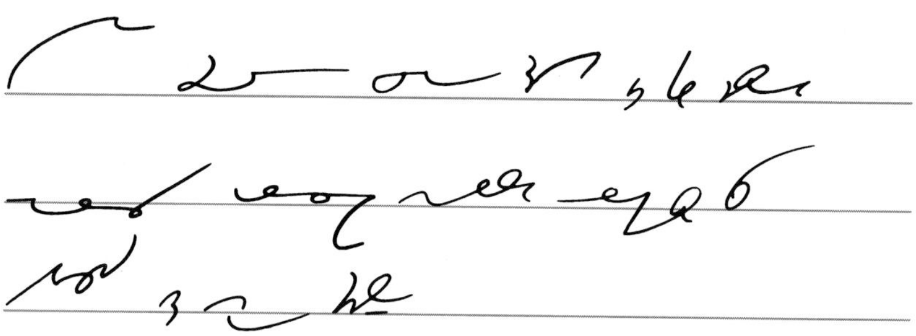

Key: Dear Mr. Feldman, annual, substantial, shoes, choice, styles, unlimited, remember, clearance, merchandise, item, discount, yourself, quality, footwear

Speed Dictation Practice

51.1 Goal: 100 wam speed dictation

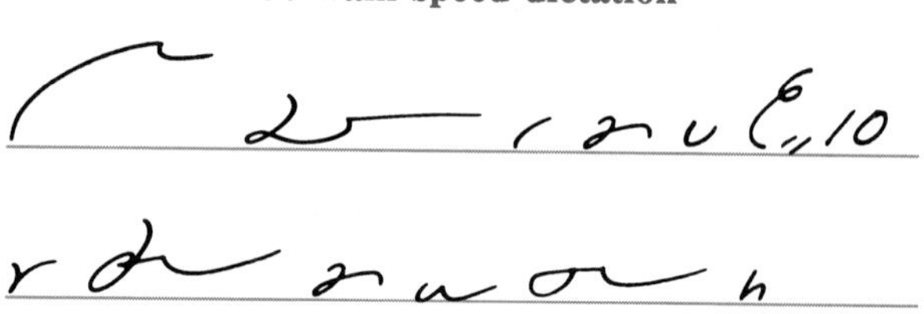

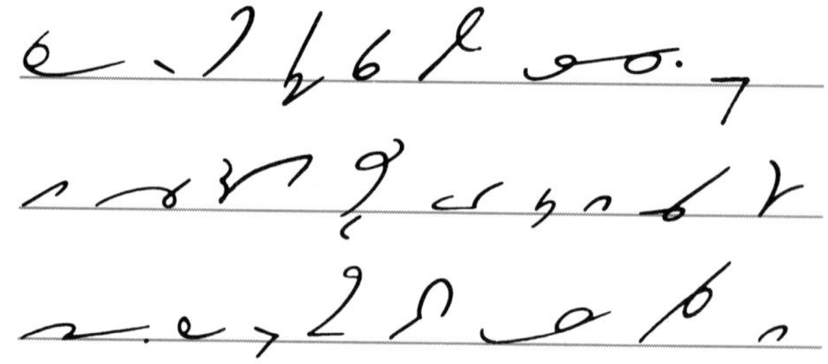

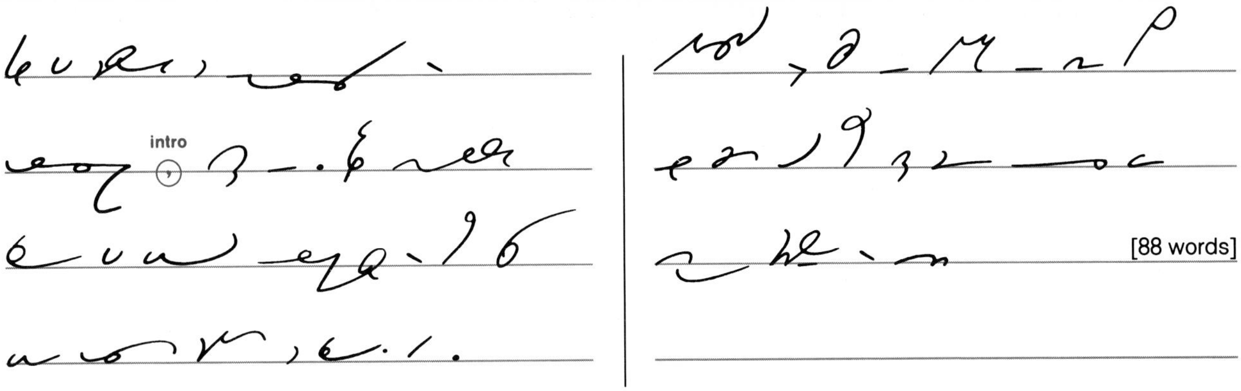

TRANSCRIPTION SKILL DEVELOPMENT

Transcription Warmup

Transcribe the following groups of words for speed and accuracy, applying transcription rules and assuring correct spelling.

51.2

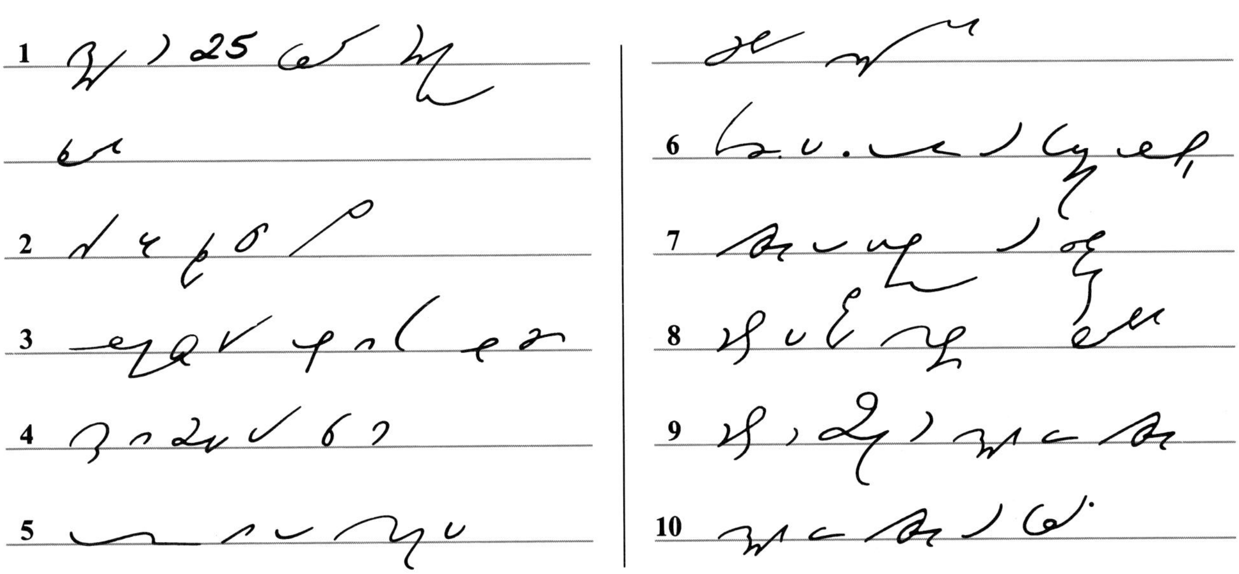

Transcription Practice

Transcribe the following letter for 2 minutes in unarranged format, applying transcription rules and assuring correct spelling. For every word not transcribed and every keyboarding error, deduct one word from the total word count.

51.3 Goal: 30 wam transcription rate

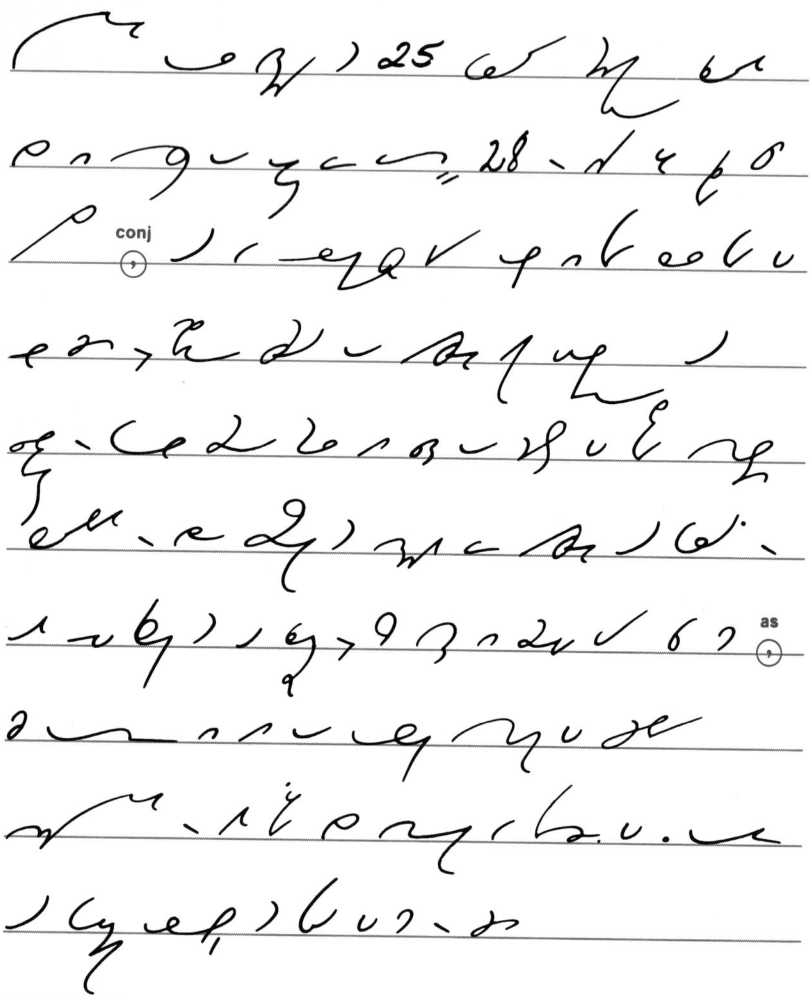

Word Count
14
28
41
54
68
82
97
106
118
129

Mailable Production

Transcribe the following mailable production letter in block style, assuring proper placement of all letter parts. Insert punctuation prior to transcribing, and capitalize proper nouns and titles. Address a large envelope.

51.4 Time Limit: 15 minutes

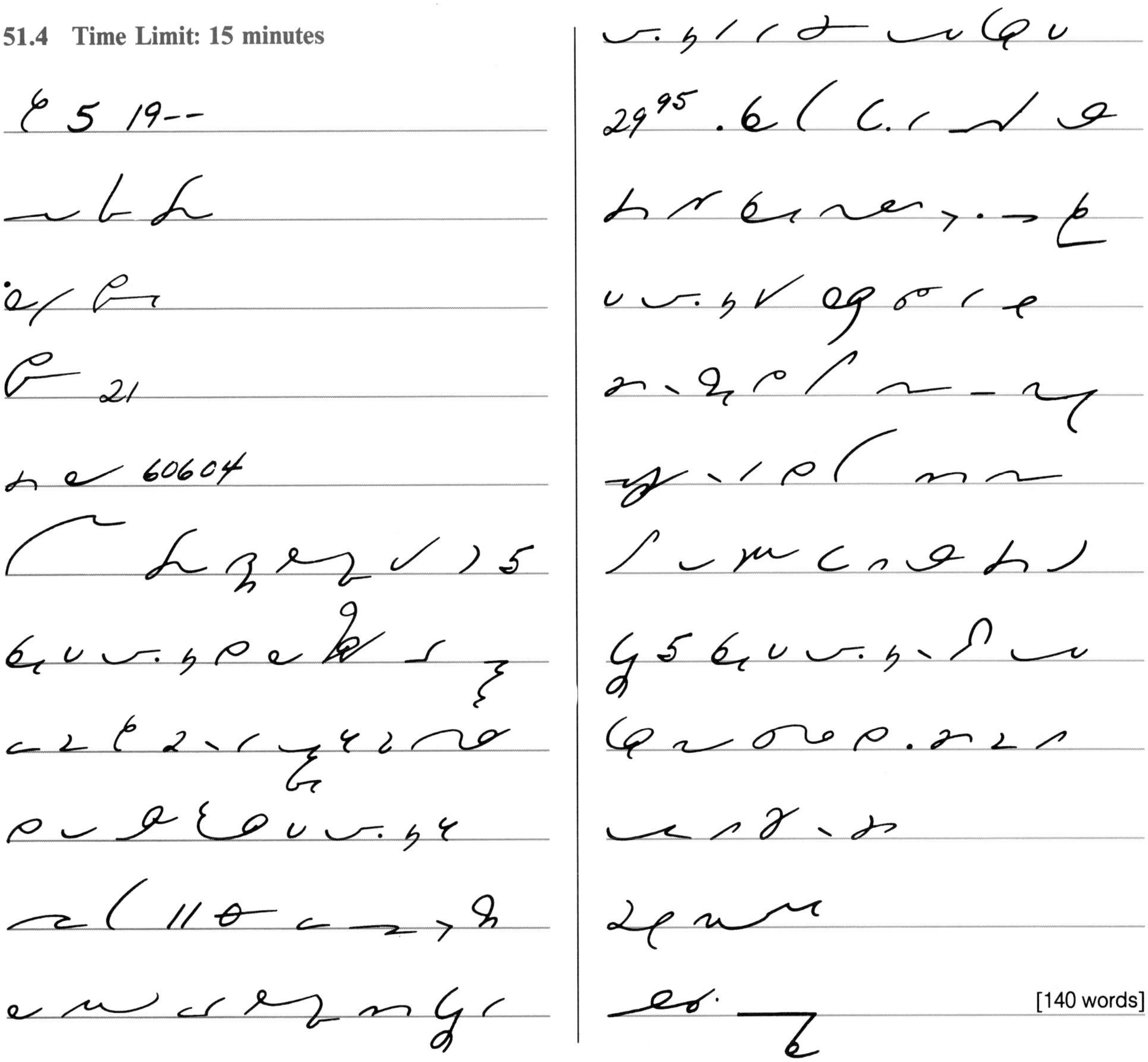

[140 words]

LESSON 52

TAYLOR DEPARTMENT STORE

DICTATION SPEED BUILDING

The shorthand outlines below appear in the speed dictation practice that follows. Practice writing these words using the shorthand outlines. Then, using the key that follows, dictate the words to yourself in preparation for the speed dictation practice.

Dictation Preview

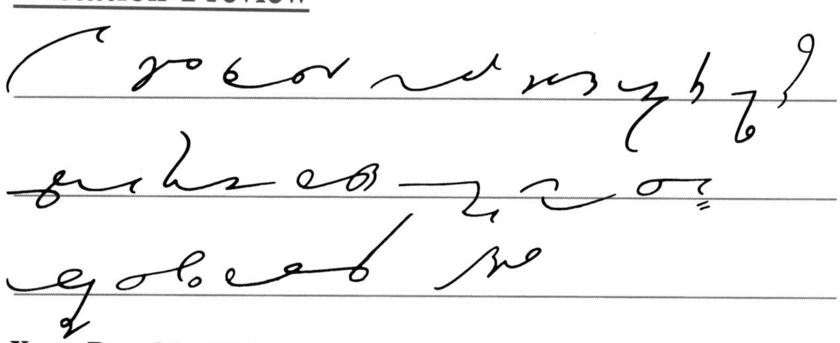

Key: Dear Ms. Whitney, select, clothes, stocks, reasonable, choose, enjoy, advantages, materials, volume, allows, manufacturers, quality, America's, largest, amazingly, eliminated, industry

Speed Dictation Practice

52.1 Goal: 100 wam speed dictation

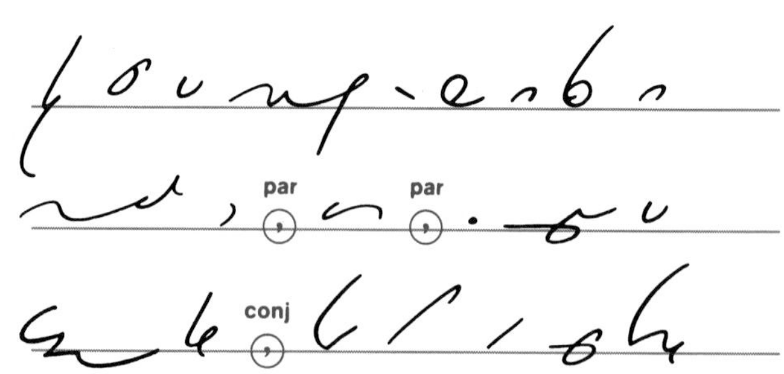

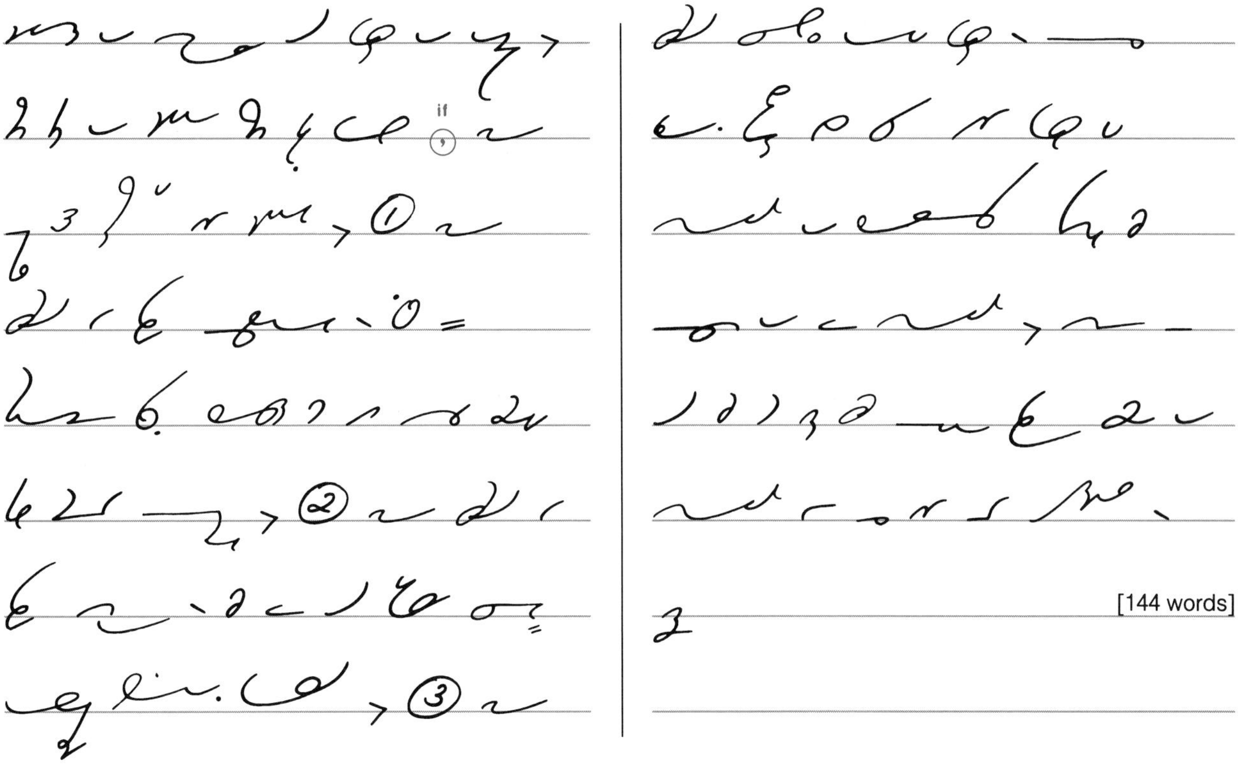

TRANSCRIPTION SKILL DEVELOPMENT

Transcription Warmup

Transcribe the following groups of words for speed and accuracy, applying transcription rules and assuring correct spelling.

52.2

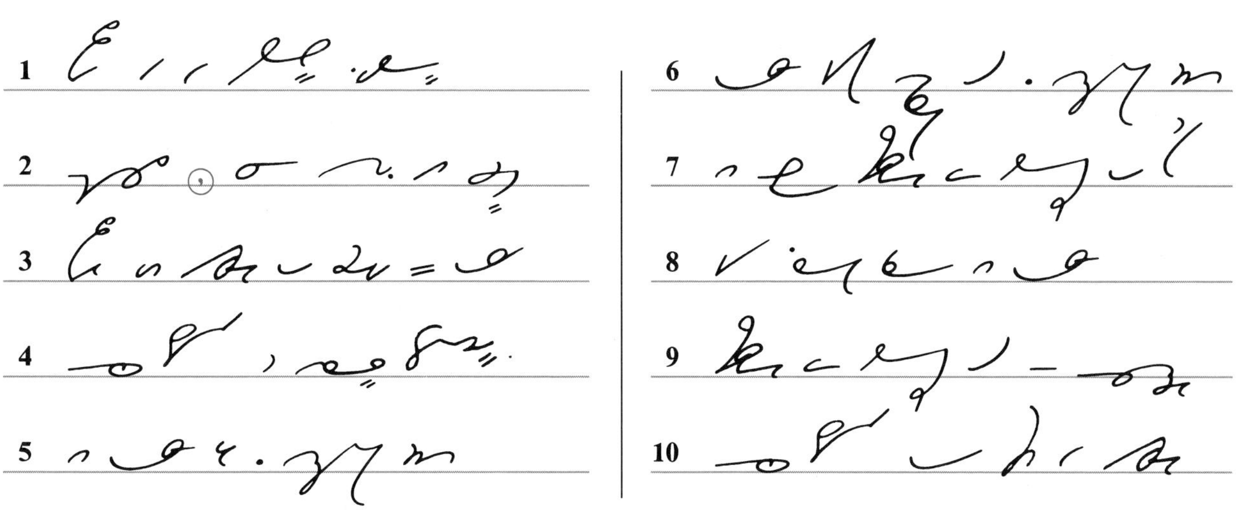

Transcription Practice

Transcribe the following letter for 2 minutes in unarranged format, applying transcription rules and assuring correct spelling. For every word not transcribed and every keyboarding error, deduct one word from the total word count.

52.3 Goal: 30 wam transcription rate

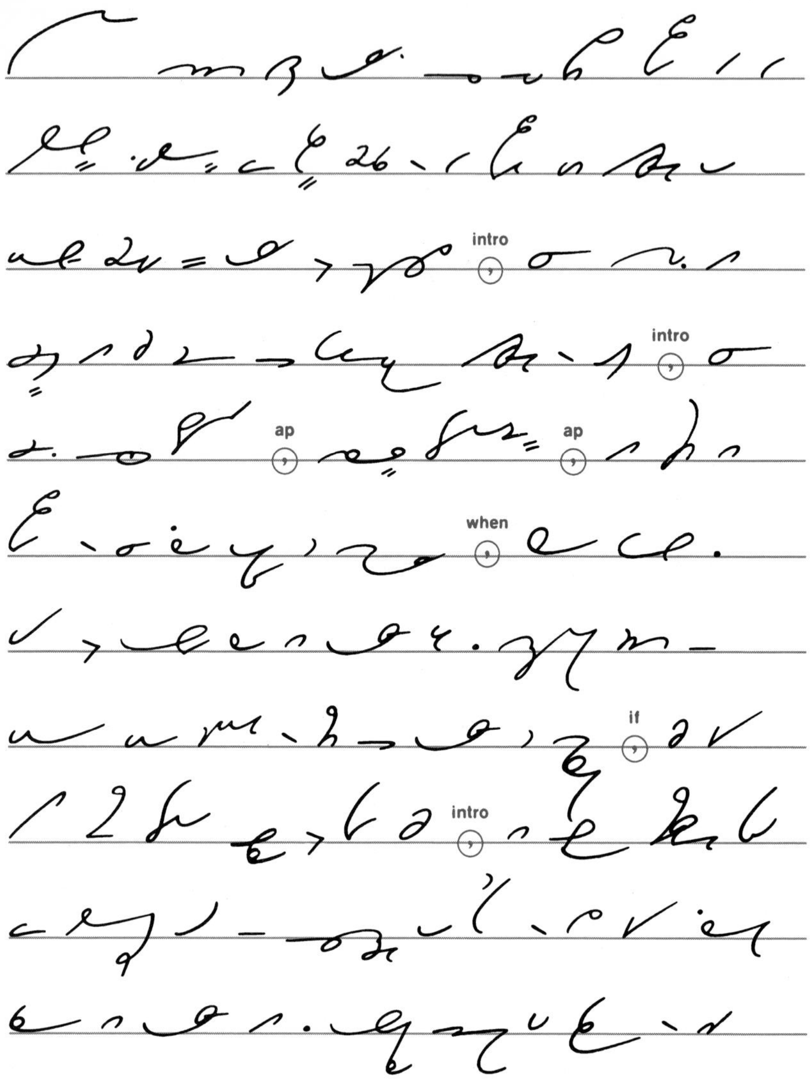

Word Count

14
27
36
49
59
70
81
93
107
119
131

Mailable Production

Transcribe the following mailable production letter in block style, assuring proper placement of all letter parts. Insert punctuation prior to transcribing, and capitalize proper nouns and titles. Address a large envelope.

52.4 Time Limit: 15 minutes

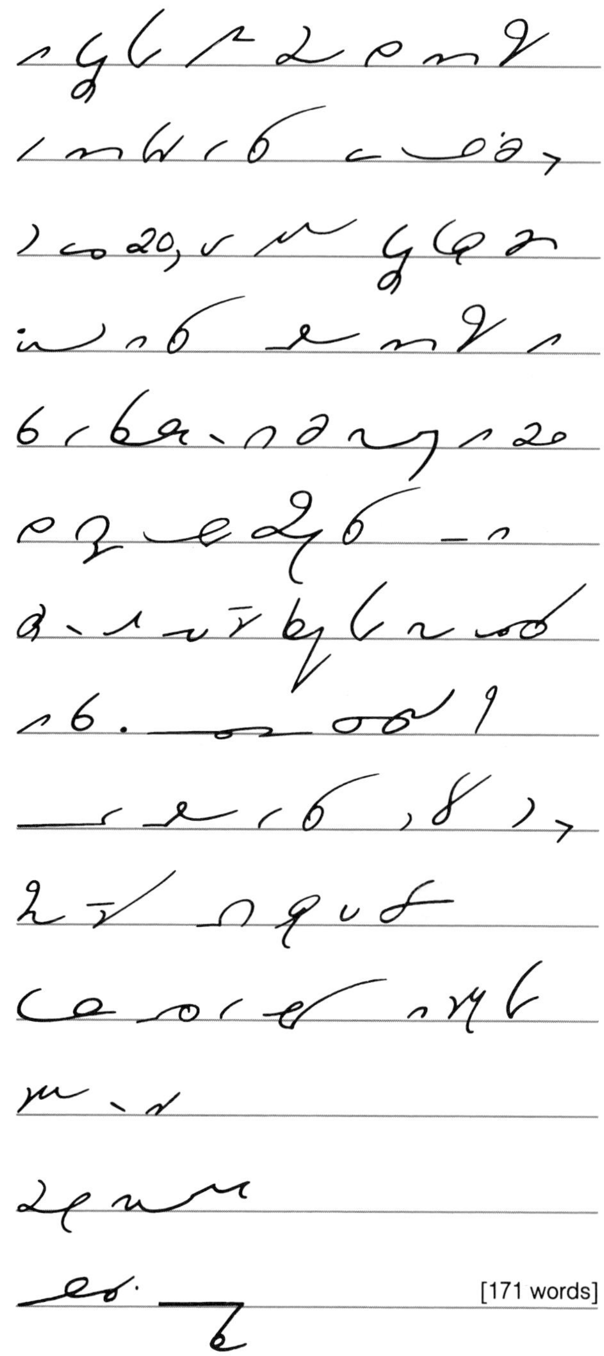

[171 words]

LESSON 53

TAYLOR DEPARTMENT STORE

DICTATION SPEED BUILDING

The shorthand outlines below appear in the speed dictation practice that follows. Practice writing these words using the shorthand outlines. Then, using the key that follows, dictate the words to yourself in preparation for the speed dictation practice.

Dictation Preview

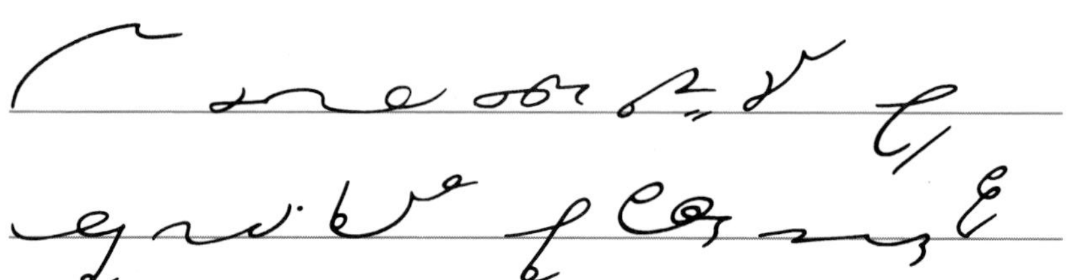

Key: Dear Mr. Sinclair, announce, Edison, center, neighborhood, largest, clothing, children, major, appliances, numerous, except

Speed Dictation Practice

53.1 Goal: 100 wam speed dictation

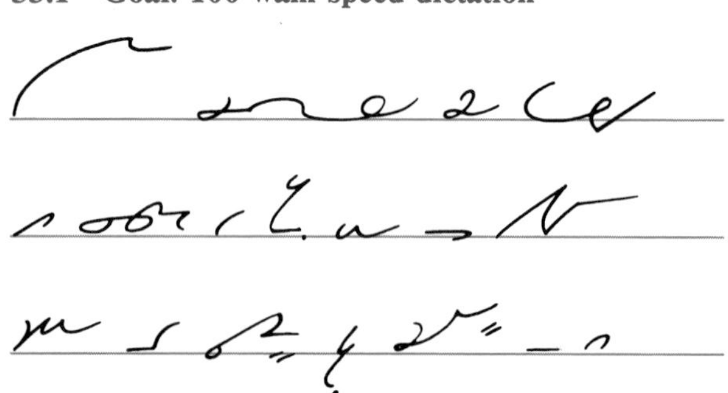

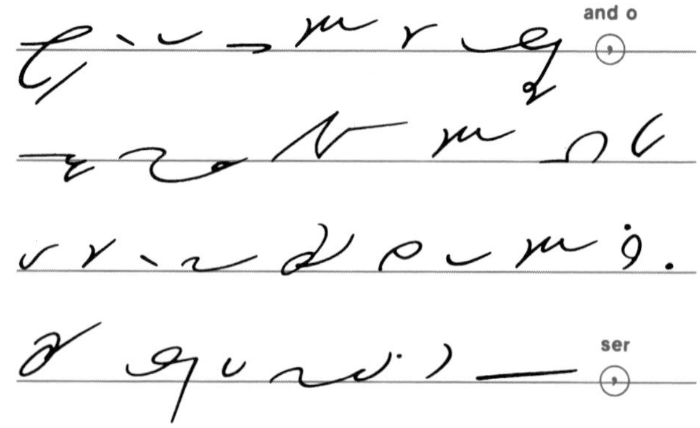

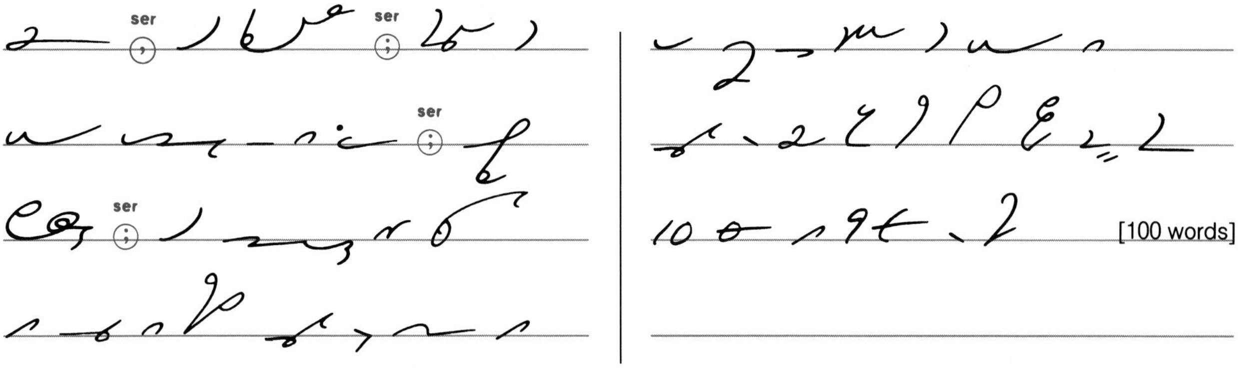

TRANSCRIPTION SKILL DEVELOPMENT

Transcription Warmup

Transcribe the followi groups of words for speed and accuracy, applying transcription rules and assuring correct spelling.

53.2

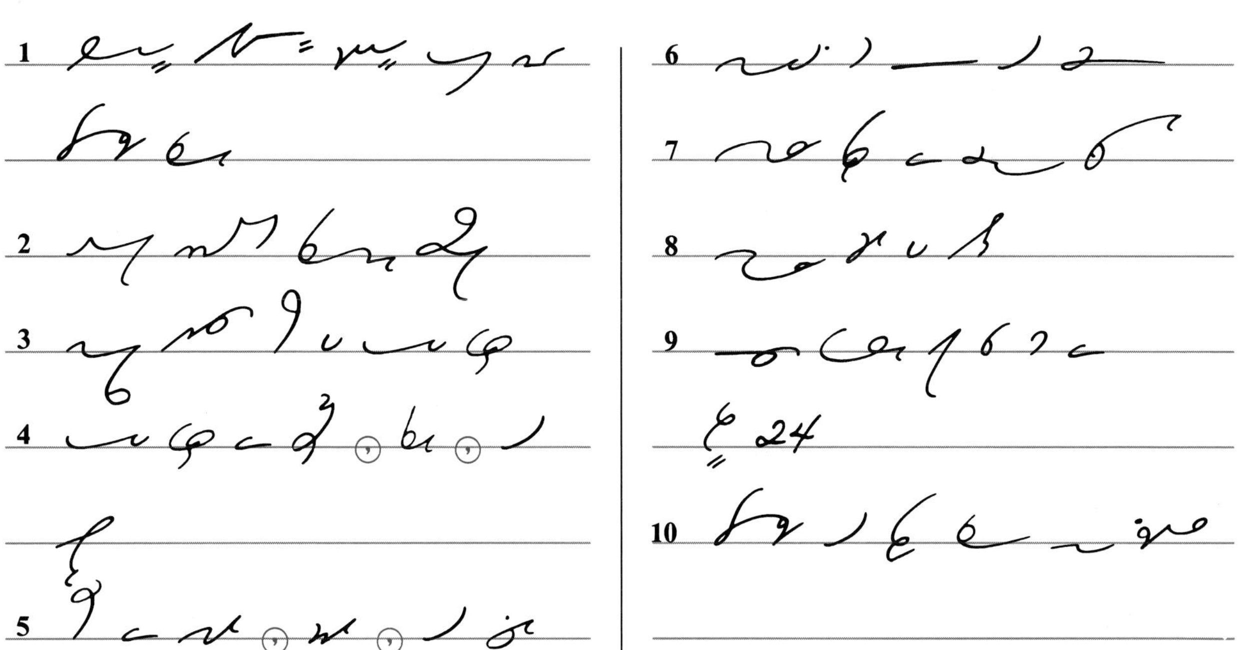

Transcription Practice

Transcribe the following letter for 2 minutes in unarranged format, applying transcription rules and assuring correct spelling. For every word not transcribed and every keyboarding error, deduct one word from the total word count.

53.3 Goal: 30 wam transcription rate

Word Count

10
22
34
48
60
73
85
97
106
118
125

Mailable Production

Transcribe the following mailable production memo, inserting punctuation prior to transcribing. Capitalize proper nouns and titles. Do not address a letter envelope. A memo would be placed in an interoffice envelope, and the information requested would be handwritten.

53.4 Time Limit: 15 minutes

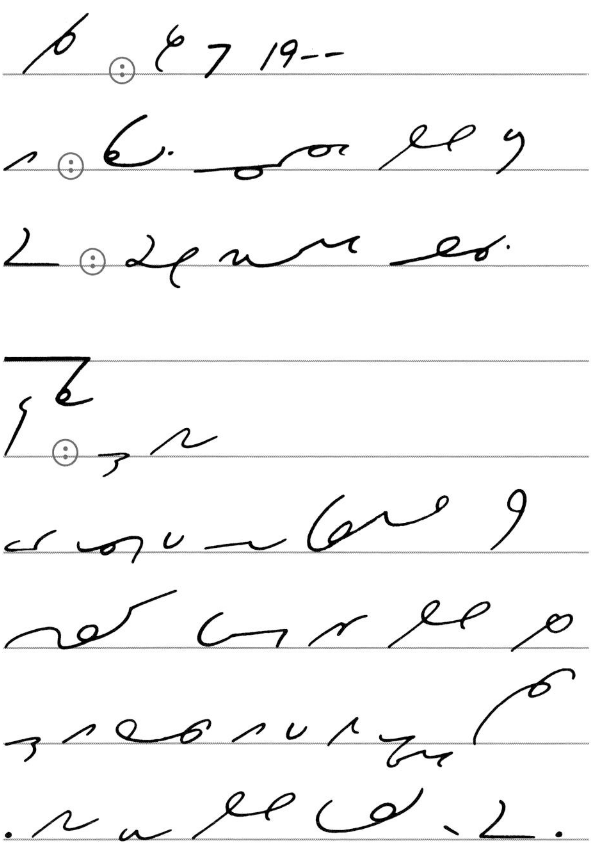

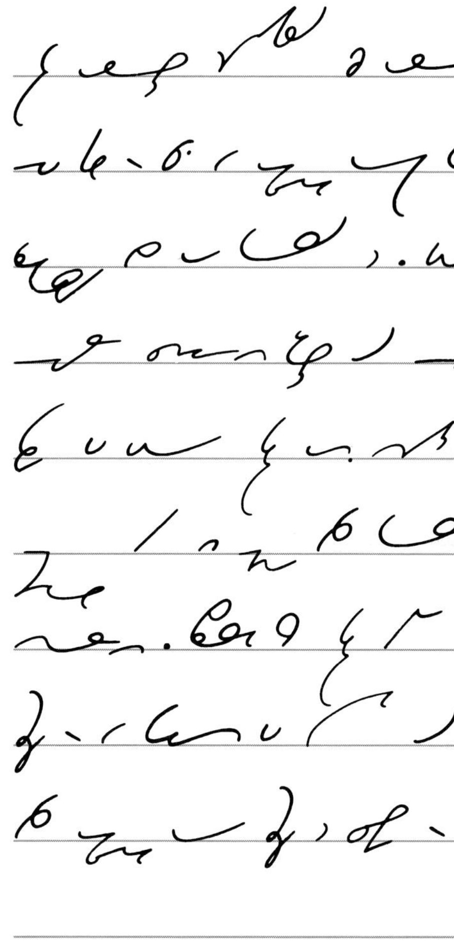

[134 words]

LESSON 54

TAYLOR DEPARTMENT STORE

DICTATION SPEED BUILDING

The shorthand outlines below appear in the speed dictation practice that follows. Practice writing these words using the shorthand outlines. Then, using the key that follows, dictate the words to yourself in preparation for the speed dictation practice.

Dictation Preview

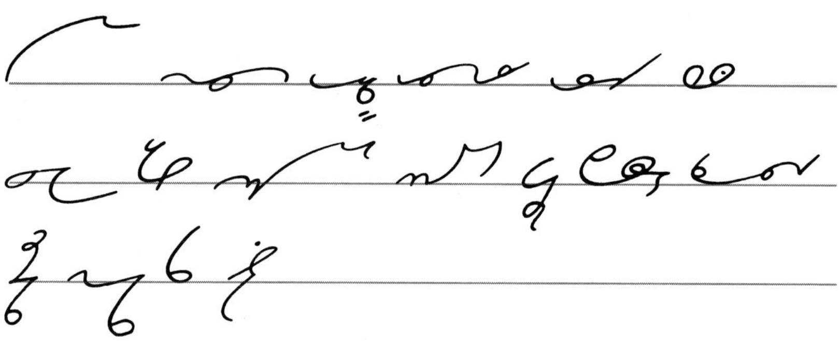

Key: Dear Mr. Craig, Los Angeles, regret, renewed, area, ample, operation, customers, wonderful, purchases, appliances, select, we have not been able, you will be able, be able, it has been

Speed Dictation Practice

54.1 Goal: 100 wam speed dictation

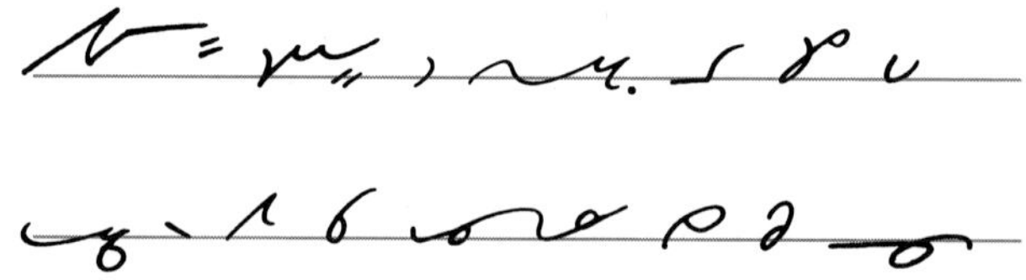

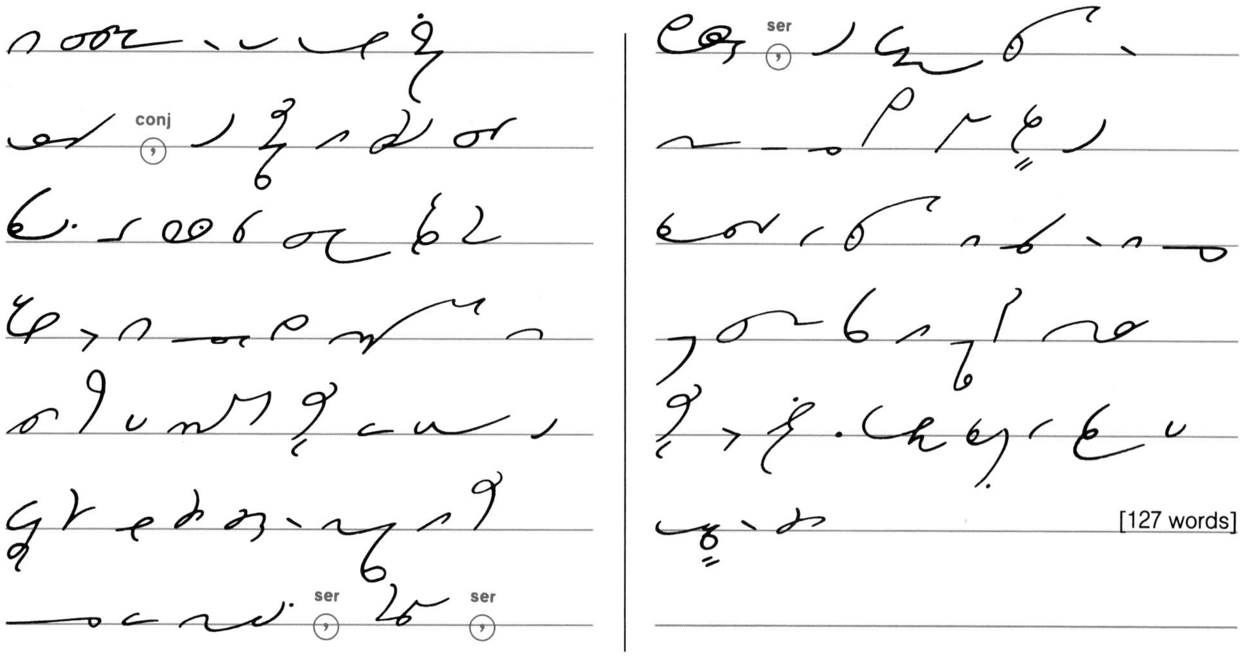

TRANSCRIPTION SKILL DEVELOPMENT

Transcription Warmup

Transcribe the following groups of words for speed and accuracy, applying transcription rules and assuring correct spelling.

54.2

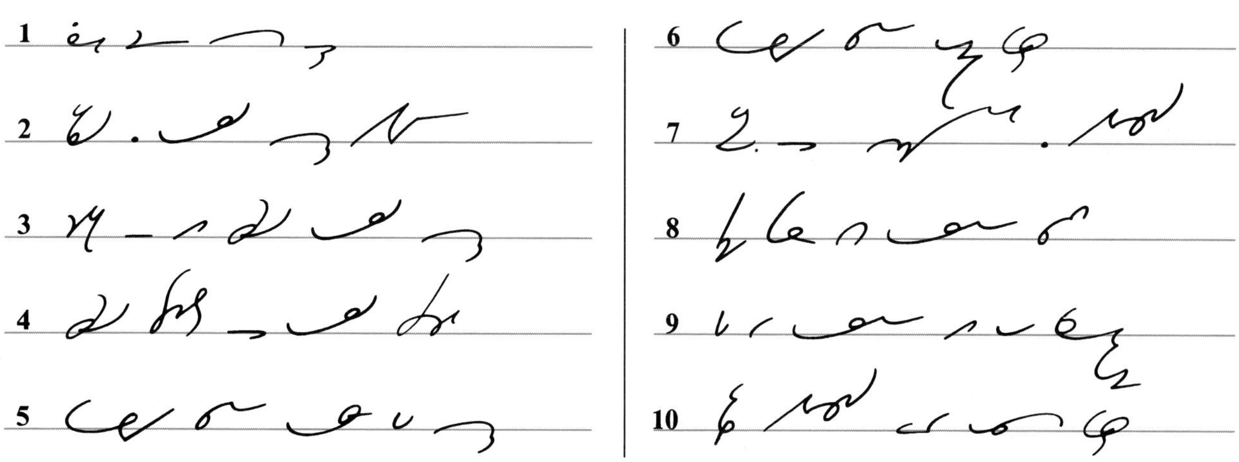

Transcription Practice

Transcribe the following letter for 2 minutes in unarranged format, applying transcription rules and assuring correct spelling. For every word not transcribed and every keyboarding error, deduct one word from the total word count.

54.3 Goal: 30 wam transcription rate

Word Count

13
25
37
49
61
76
88
100
112
126
134

Mailable Production

Transcribe the following mailable production letter in block style, assuring proper placement of all letter parts. Insert punctuation prior to transcribing, and capitalize proper nouns and titles. Address a large envelope.

54.4 Time Limit: 15 minutes

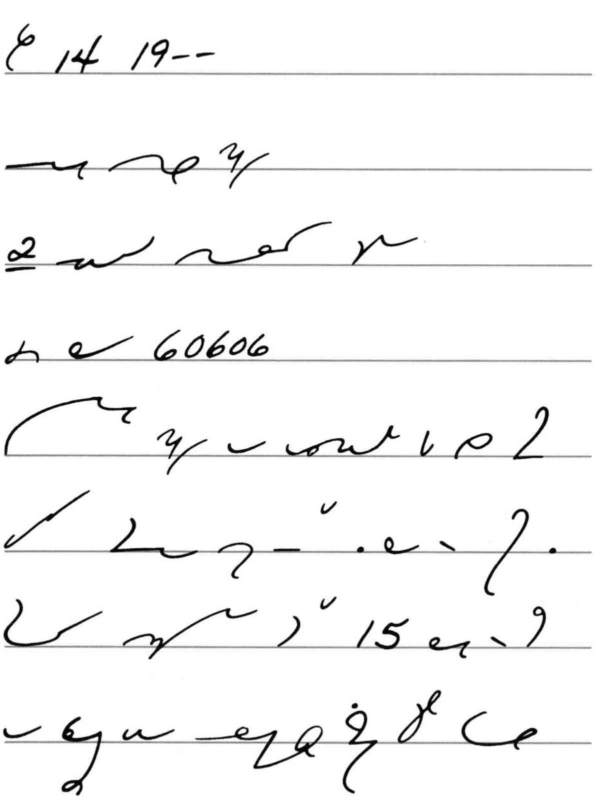

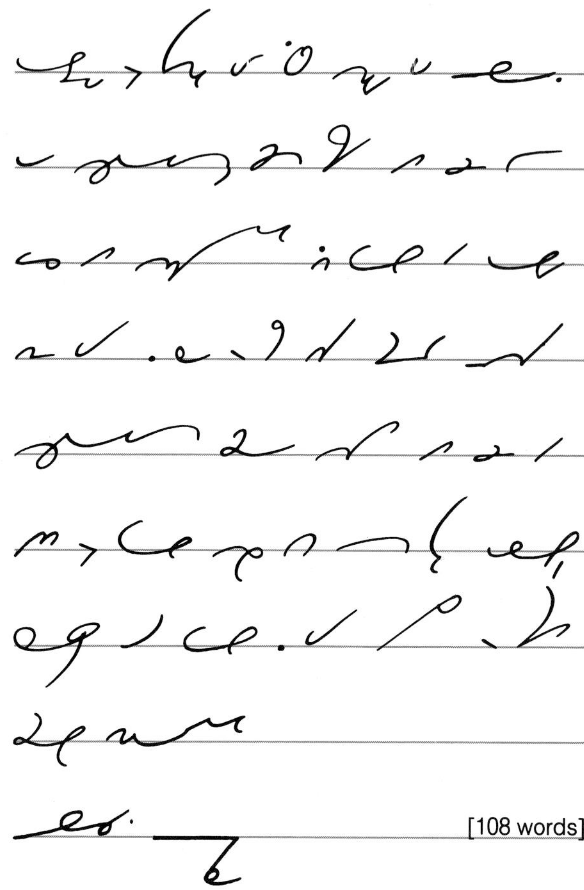

[108 words]

LESSON 55

TAYLOR DEPARTMENT STORE

DICTATION SPEED BUILDING

The shorthand outlines below appear in the speed dictation practice that follows. Practice writing these words using the shorthand outlines. Then, using the key that follows, dictate the words to yourself in preparation for the speed dictation practice.

Dictation Preview

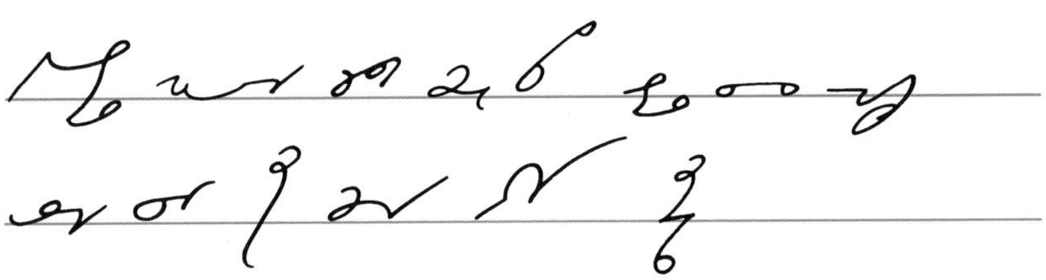

Key: delivery, walnut, situation, worse, idea, necessary, immediate, notify, reinstate, another, we have been, we could, at this time, we have not been able

Speed Dictation Practice

55.1 Goal: 100 wam speed dictation

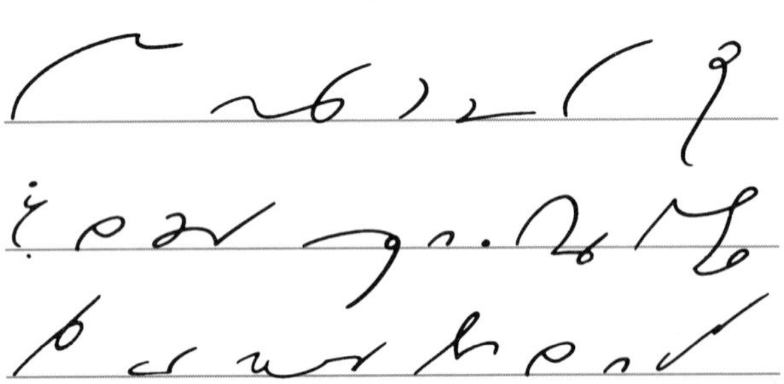

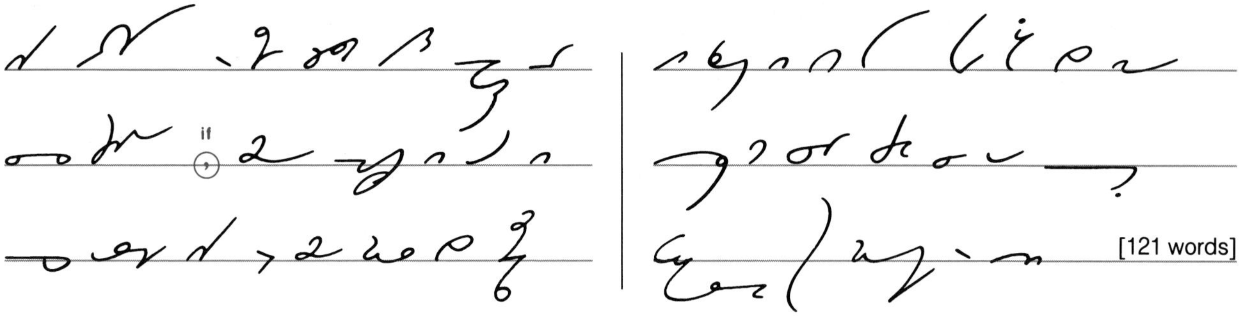

[121 words]

TRANSCRIPTION SKILL DEVELOPMENT

Transcription Warmup

Transcribe the following groups of words for speed and accuracy, applying transcription rules and assuring correct spelling.

55.2

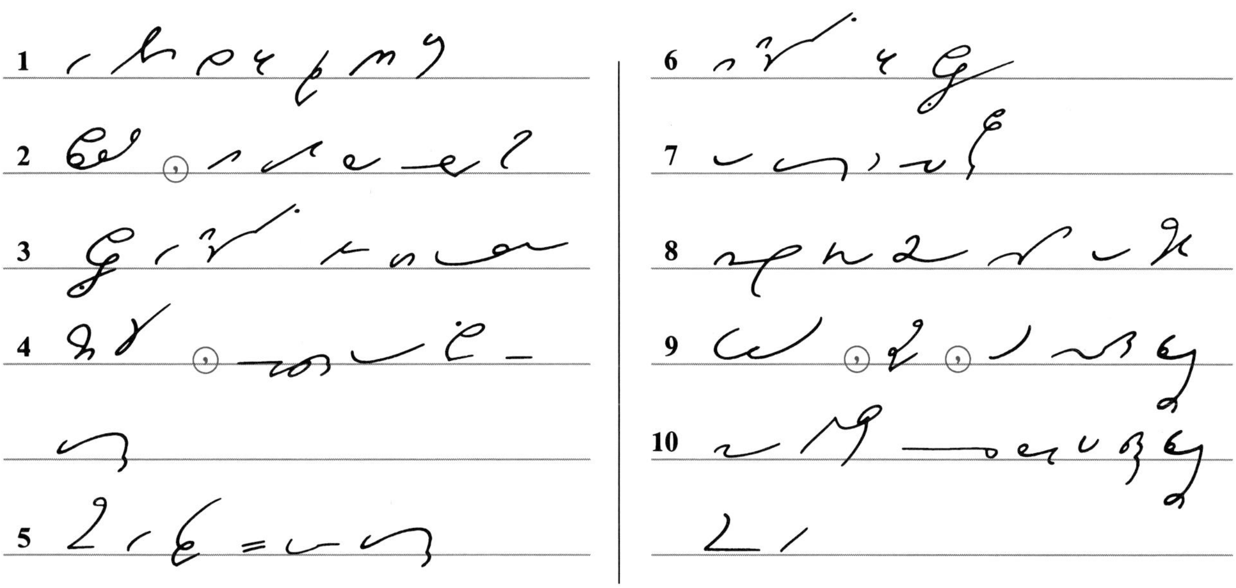

Transcription Practice

Transcribe the following letter for 2 minutes in unarranged format, applying transcription rules and assuring correct spelling. For every word not transcribed and every keyboarding error, deduct one word from the total word count.

55.3 Goal: 30 wam transcription rate

Word Count

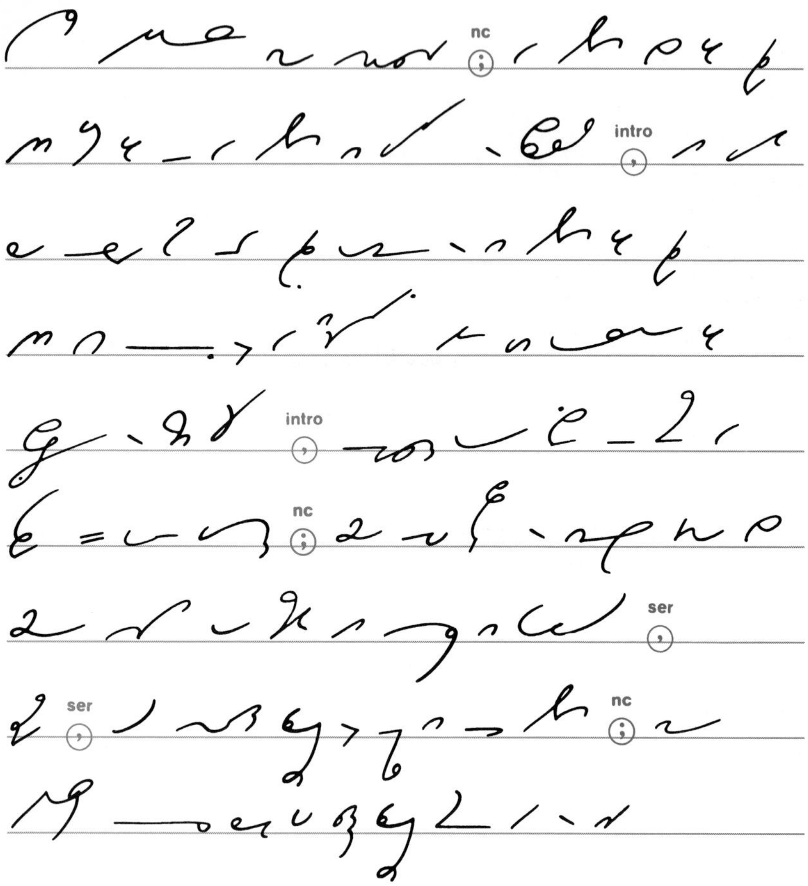

12
25
37
50
62
75
85
98
109

Mailable Production

Transcribe the following mailable production memo, inserting punctuation prior to transcribing. Capitalize proper nouns and titles. Do not address a letter envelope. A memo would be placed in an interoffice envelope, and the information requested would be handwritten.

55.4 Time Limit: 15 minutes

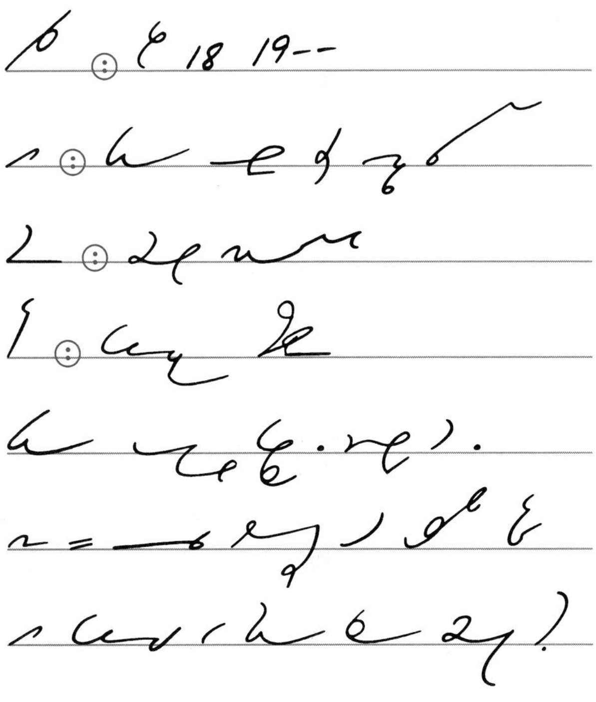

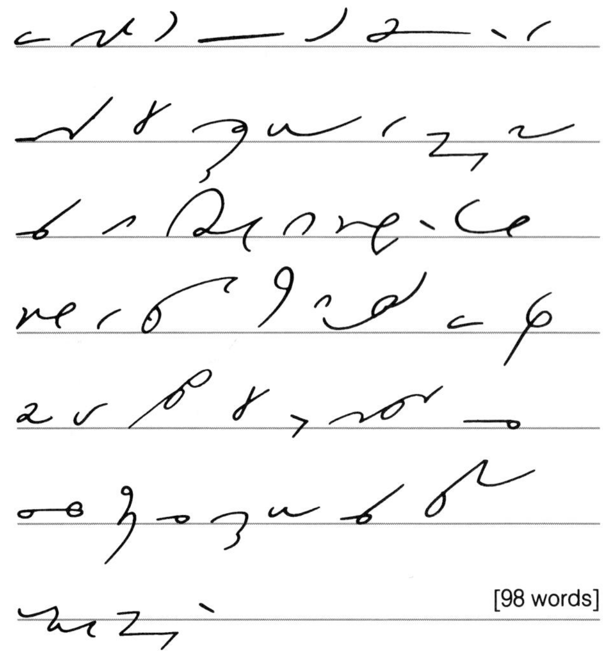

[98 words]

LESSON 56

TAYLOR DEPARTMENT STORE

DICTATION SPEED BUILDING

The shorthand outlines below appear in the speed dictation practice that follows. Practice writing these words using the shorthand outlines. Then, using the key that follows, dictate the words to yourself in preparation for the speed dictation practice.

Dictation Preview

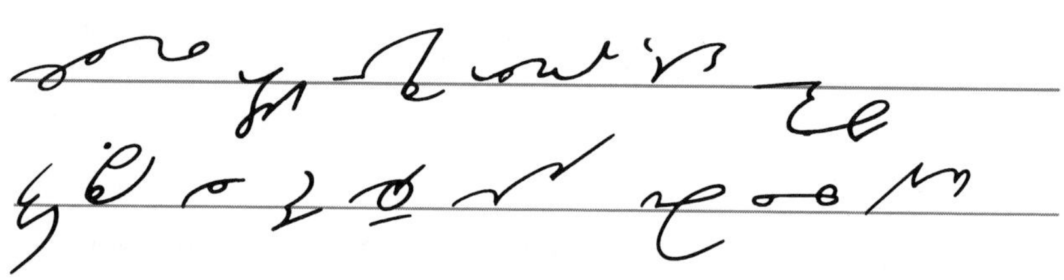

Key: category, reputation, endanger, records, circumstances, misplaced, positive, happened, then, forced, quite, continued, unable, immediately, discuss

Speed Dictation Practice

56.1 Goal: 100 wam speed dictation

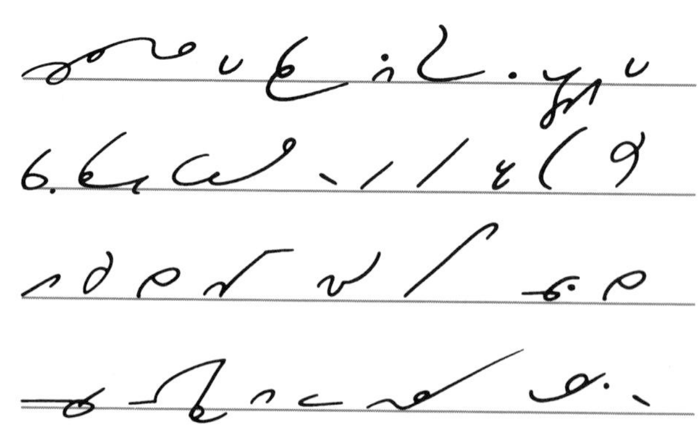

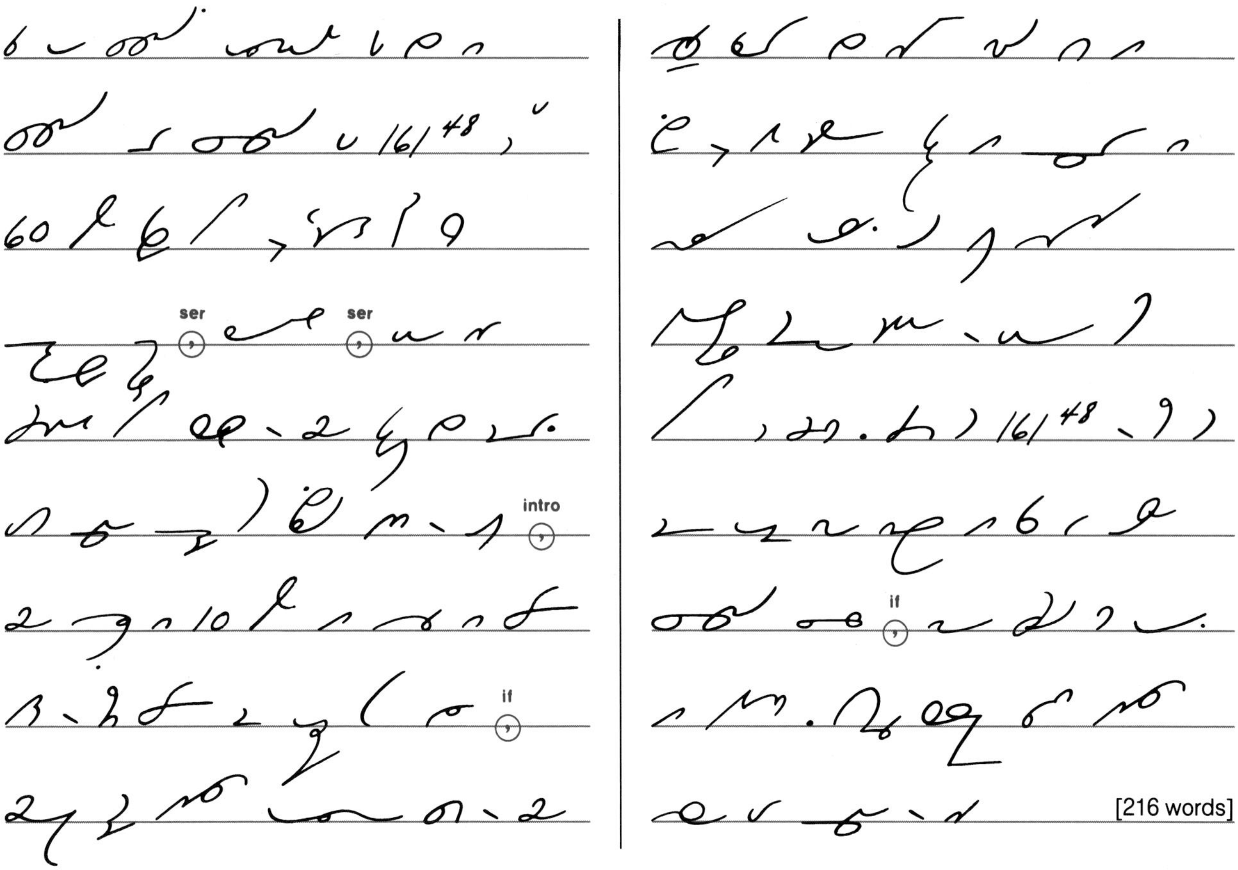

TRANSCRIPTION SKILL DEVELOPMENT

Transcription Warmup

Transcribe the following groups of words for speed and accuracy, applying transcription rules and assuring correct spelling.

56.2

1 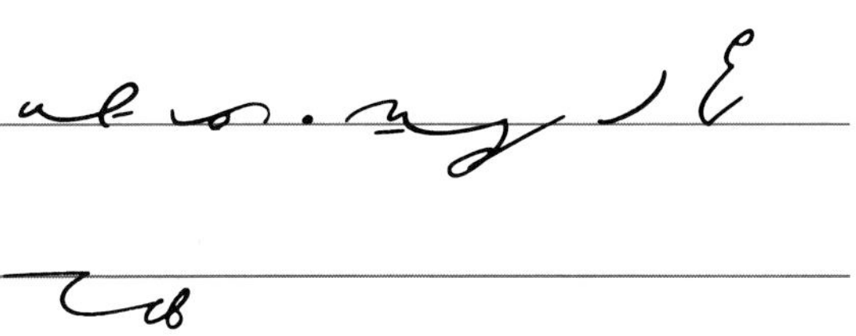

2 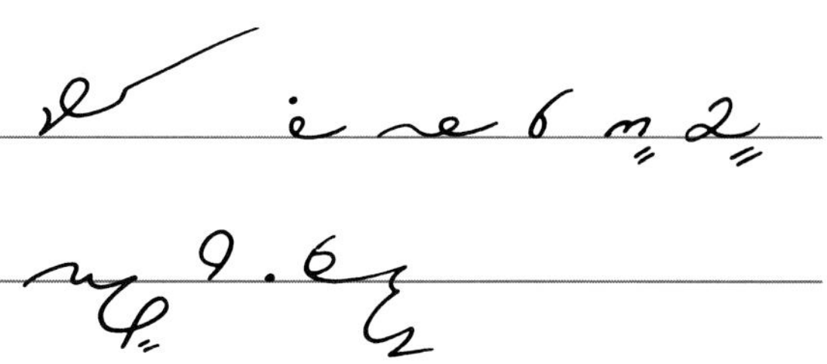

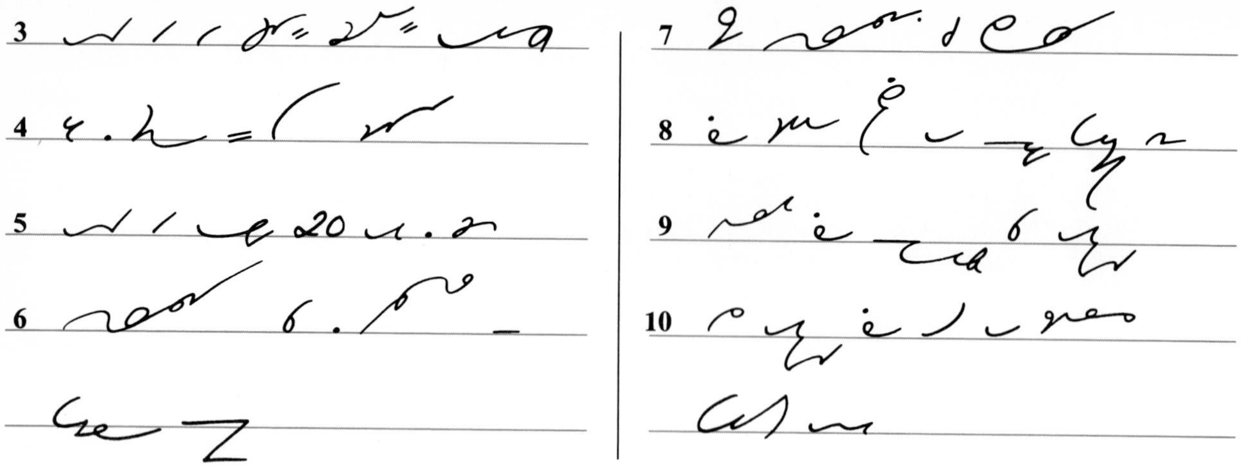

Transcription Practice

Transcribe the following letter for 2 minutes in unarranged format, applying transcription rules and assuring correct spelling. For every word not transcribed and every keyboarding error, deduct one word from the total word count.

56.3 Goal: 30 wam transcription rate

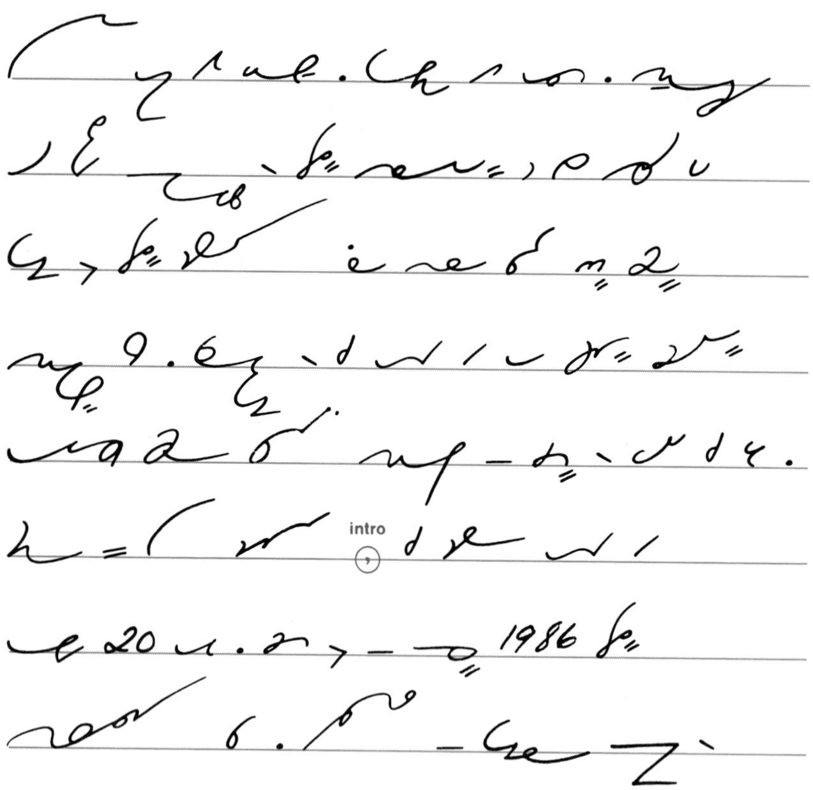

Word Count

13

23

34

46

59

67

75

85

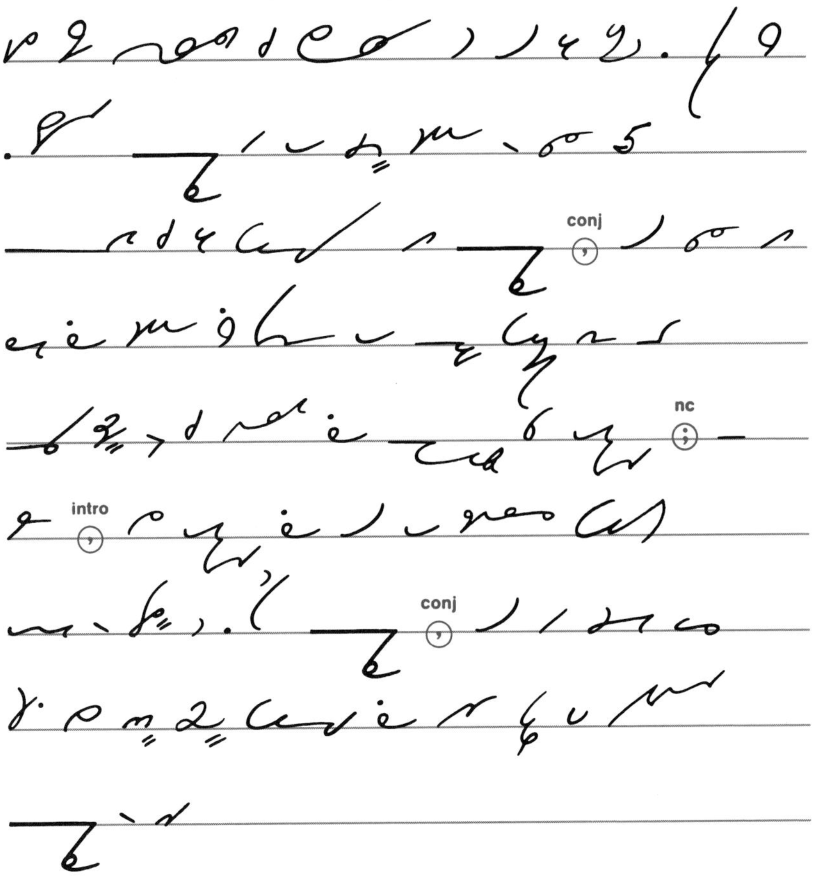

98
109
119
130
140
150
161
174
178

Mailable Production

Transcribe the following mailable production letter in block style, assuring proper placement of all letter parts. Insert punctuation prior to transcribing, and capitalize proper nouns and titles. Address a large envelope.

56.4 Time Limit: 15 minutes

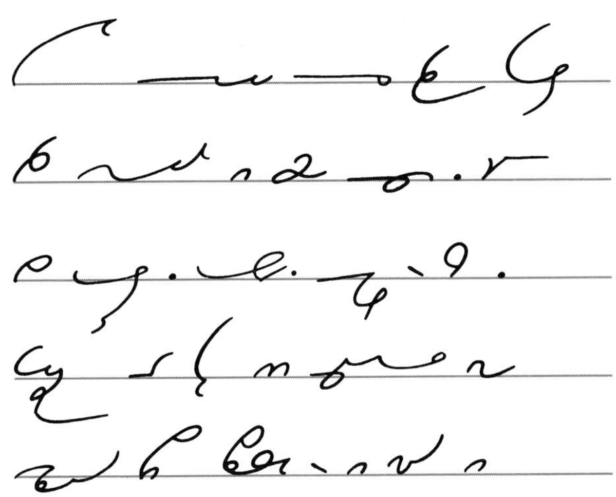

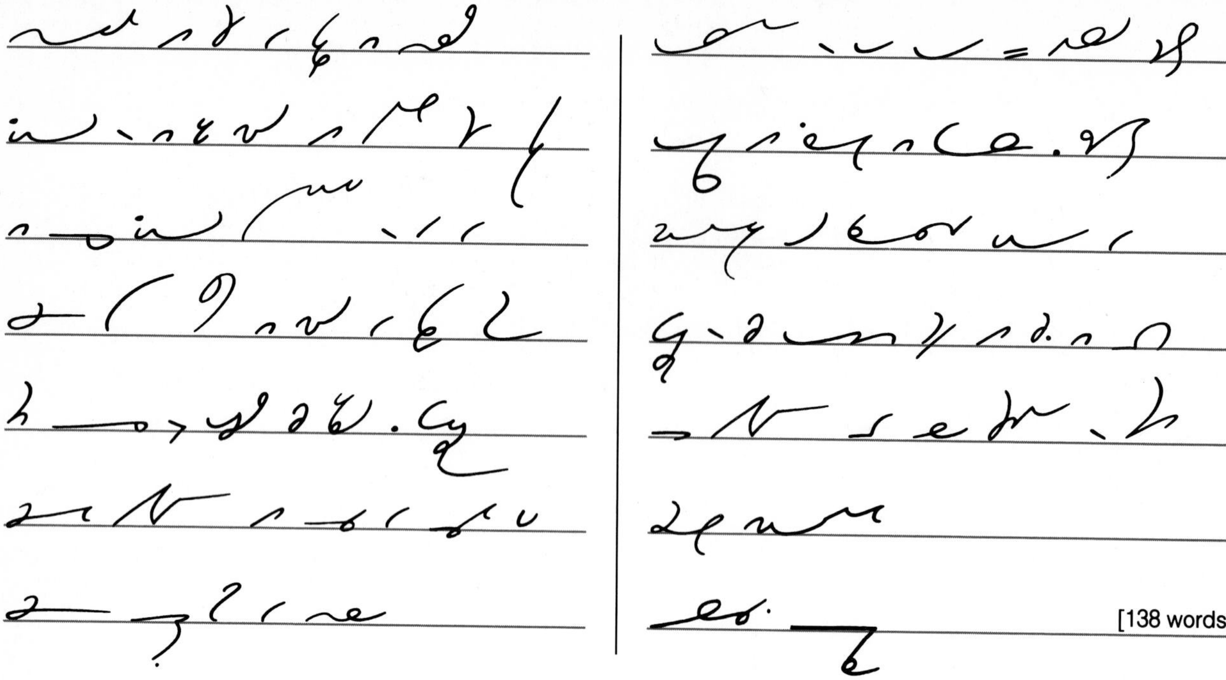

[138 words]

UNIT VIII

SAMUELS,
KEELEY,
AND
FRANK
attorneys-at-law

LESSON 57

SAMUELS, KEELEY, AND FRANK

You are employed by the law firm of Samuels, Keeley, and Frank in Greensburg, Pennsylvania. You are one of three secretaries, and you report to George Frank, a junior partner in the firm. Your duties are numerous and varied, including researching legal problems, answering the telephone, greeting clients, scheduling appointments, and typing correspondence and legal documents.

You use your shorthand to take dictation for correspondence, but you also are called into depositions to record testimony and into meetings to take down pertinent information or changes needed in documents such as wills and agreements. In addition, you work closely with the personnel in the courthouse and have begun to research legal problems and, therefore, use your shorthand to record information.

Below is a copy of your company letterhead. Develop the return address that you will use to type the envelopes for the mailable production letters.

SAMUELS,
KEELEY,
AND
FRANK
attorneys-at-law

365 Pennsylvania Avenue
Greensburg, PA 15601 (412) 555-5715

Preparing Legal Documents

Types of legal documents prepared by the administrative assistant include leases, powers of attorney, wills, and buy and sell agreements.

1 Center the title in all capitals on line 13, leaving a 2-inch top margin. Subsequent pages have 1 1/2-inch top margins.
2 Triple-space after the title and double-space the body of the document.
3 Indent paragraphs ten spaces.

4 Express money amounts first in words that are capitalized, followed by figures in parentheses.
5 Use a 1 1/2-inch left margin and a 1-inch right margin if paper is not ruled.
6 Begin signature lines in the center of the page and end at the right margin. Leave at least three line spaces to accommodate the handwritten signatures.
7 Do not number the first page. Pages after the first page are numbered three lines up from the bottom of the page and centered.

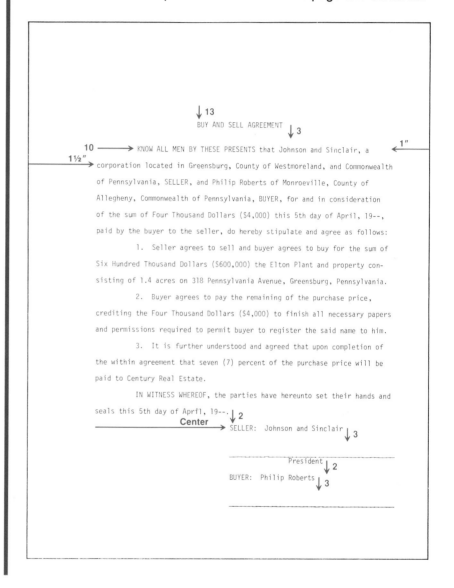

↓ 13

BUY AND SELL AGREEMENT ↓ 3

1½″ 10 → KNOW ALL MEN BY THESE PRESENTS that Johnson and Sinclair, a corporation located in Greensburg, County of Westmoreland, and Commonwealth of Pennsylvania, SELLER, and Philip Roberts of Monroeville, County of Allegheny, Commonwealth of Pennsylvania, BUYER, for and in consideration of the sum of Four Thousand Dollars ($4,000) this 5th day of April, 19--, paid by the buyer to the seller, do hereby stipulate and agree as follows: ← 1″

1. Seller agrees to sell and buyer agrees to buy for the sum of Six Hundred Thousand Dollars ($600,000) the Elton Plant and property consisting of 1.4 acres on 318 Pennsylvania Avenue, Greensburg, Pennsylvania.

2. Buyer agrees to pay the remaining of the purchase price, crediting the Four Thousand Dollars ($4,000) to finish all necessary papers and permissions required to permit buyer to register the said name to him.

3. It is further understood and agreed that upon completion of the within agreement that seven (7) percent of the purchase price will be paid to Century Real Estate.

IN WITNESS WHEREOF, the parties have hereunto set their hands and seals this 5th day of April, 19--. ↓ 2

Center → SELLER: Johnson and Sinclair ↓ 3

____

President ↓ 2

BUYER: Philip Roberts ↓ 3

____

Addressing an Attorney

For a male attorney, address the attorney as *Mr.* before the name. Place *Attorney-at-Law* on the following line.

If the attorney is a woman, address her as *Miss*, *Ms.*, or *Mrs.*

If the title *Esquire* or *Esq.* is used, place it following the name and do not use the title *Mr.*, *Ms.*, *Miss*, or *Mrs.* Also, omit *Attorney-at-Law*.

Frank Simpson, Esquire

Subject Lines

Subject lines are used frequently in law-office correspondence. They are typed two lines below the salutation. The expression *Re* (pronounced *ra*) or *In Re* is usually used to introduce the subject.

Re: File No. 382198
In Re: George Sinclair v. Mason Real Estate

DICTATION SPEED BUILDING

The shorthand outlines below appear in the speed dictation practice that follows. Practice writing these words using the shorthand outlines. Then, using the key that follows, dictate the words to yourself in preparation for the speed dictation practice.

Dictation Preview

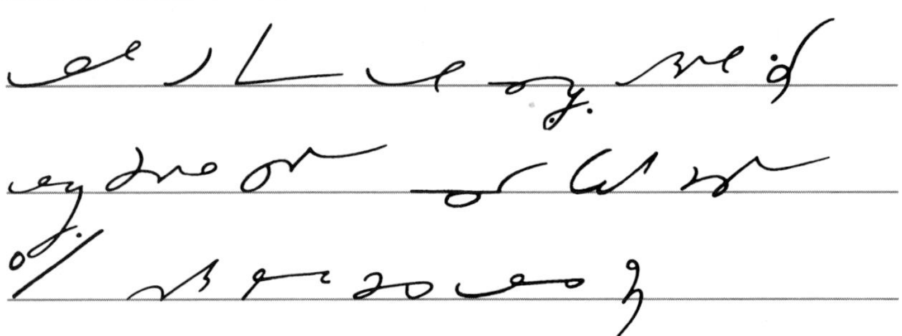

Key: Ladies and Gentlemen, lease, negotiating, industries, behalf, renovating, factory, actual, maintain, production, schedule, included, conditions, terms, we may, let me, if you have

Speed Dictation Practice

57.1 Goal: 100 wam speed dictation

[133 words]

TRANSCRIPTION SKILL DEVELOPMENT

Transcription Warmup

Transcribe the following groups of words for speed and accuracy, applying transcription rules and assuring correct spelling.

57.2

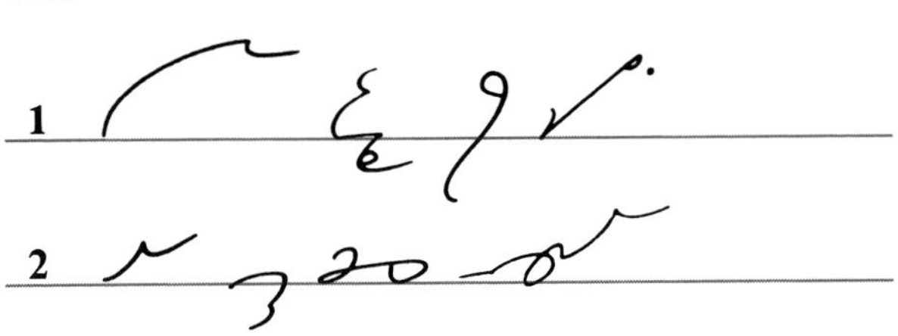

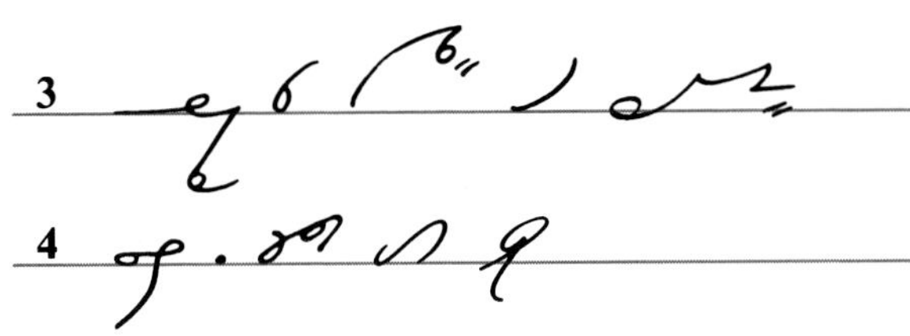

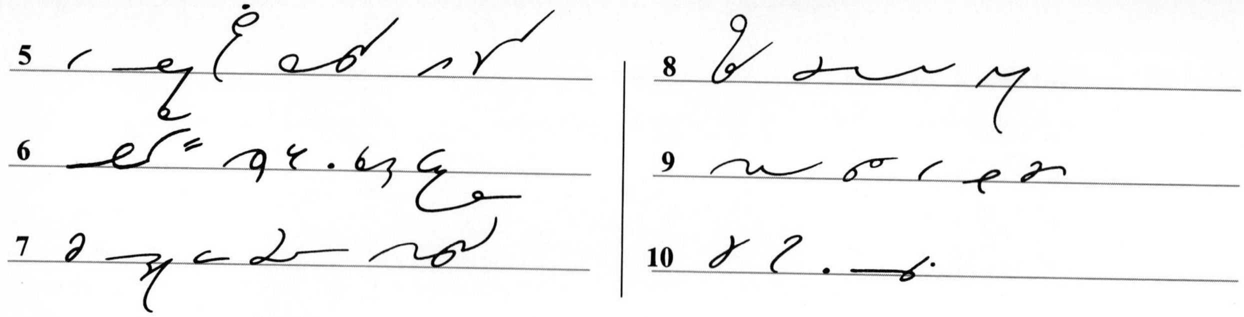

Transcription Practice

Transcribe the following letter for 2 minutes in unarranged format, applying transcription rules and assuring correct spelling. For every word not transcribed and every keyboarding error, deduct one word from the total word count.

57.3 Goal: 35 wam transcription rate

Word Count

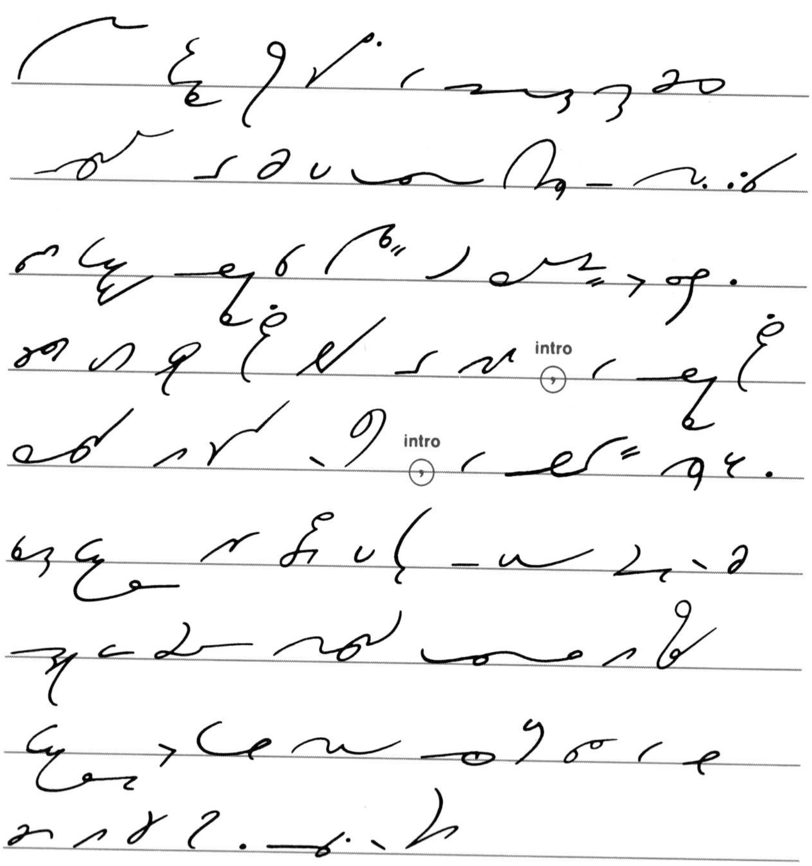

13
24
37
52
62
74
82
90
99

LESSON 58

SAMUELS, KEELEY, AND FRANK

DICTATION SPEED BUILDING

The shorthand outlines below appear in the speed dictation practice that follows. Practice writing these words using the shorthand outlines. Then, using the key that follows, dictate the words to yourself in preparation for the speed dictation practice.

Dictation Preview

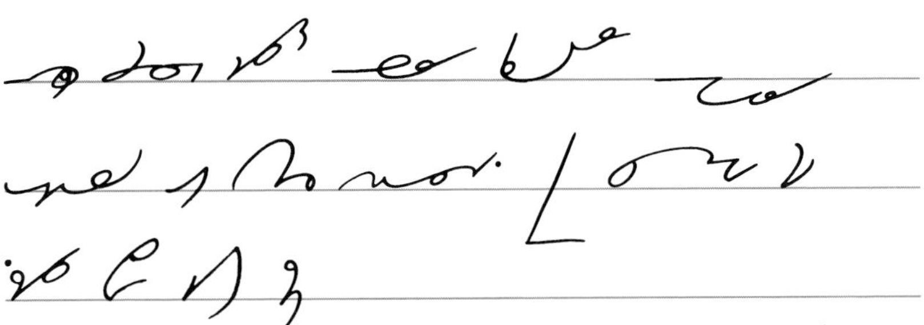

Key: inquiries, financial, status, married, children, employed, restaurant, therefore, difficulty, collecting, judgment, against, further, hesitate, about the, should have, if you have

Speed Dictation Practice

58.1 Goal: 100 wam speed dictation

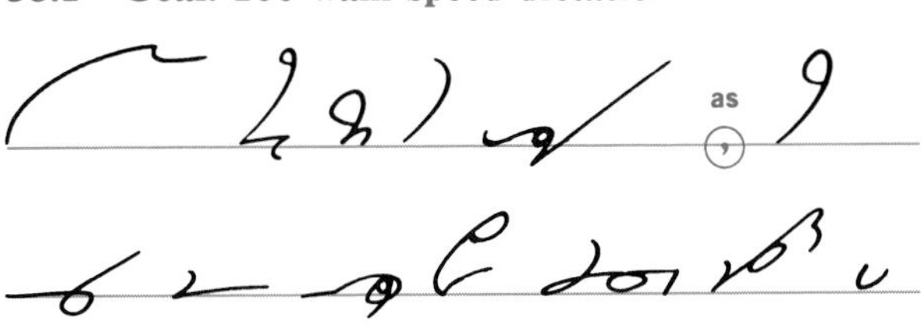

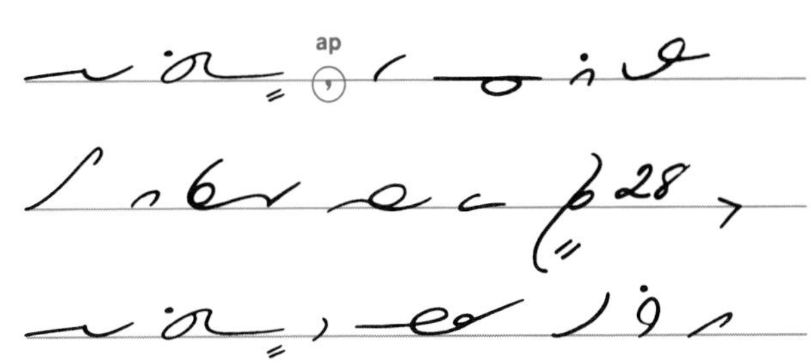

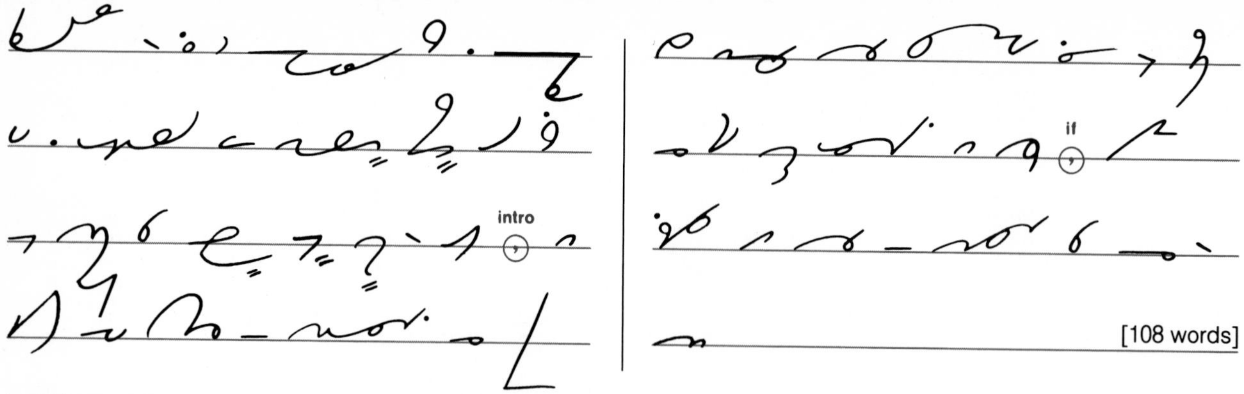

TRANSCRIPTION SKILL DEVELOPMENT

Transcription Warmup

Transcribe the following groups of words for speed and accuracy, applying transcription rules and assuring correct spelling.

58.2

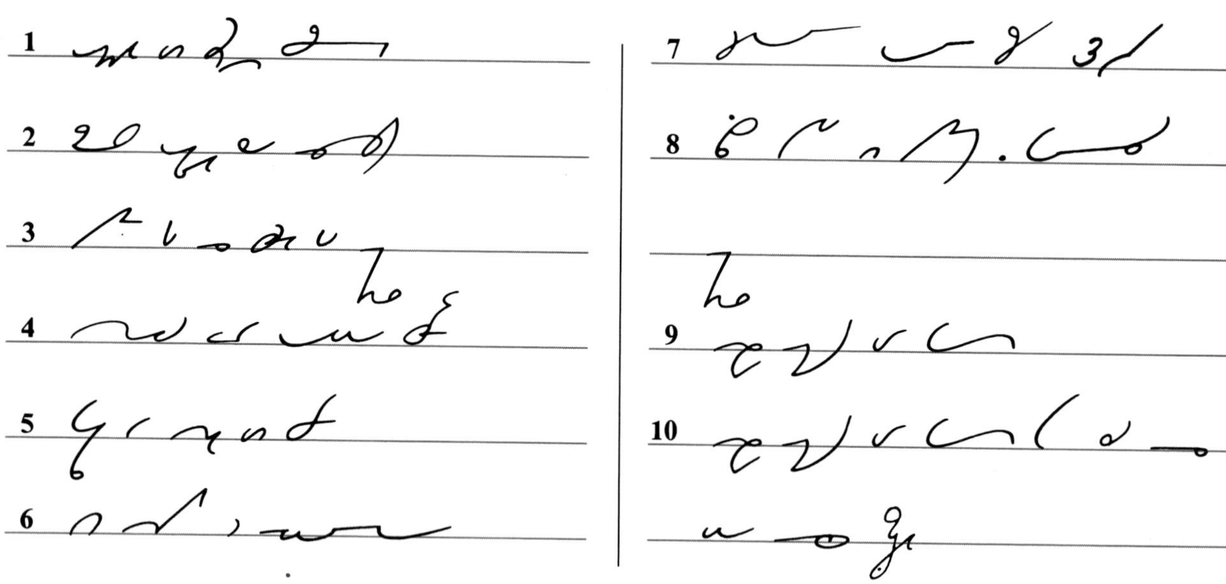

Transcription Practice

Transcribe the following letter for 2 minutes in unarranged format, applying transcription rules and assuring correct spelling. For every word not transcribed and every keyboarding error, deduct one word from the total word count.

58.3 Goal: 35 wam transcription rate

Word Count

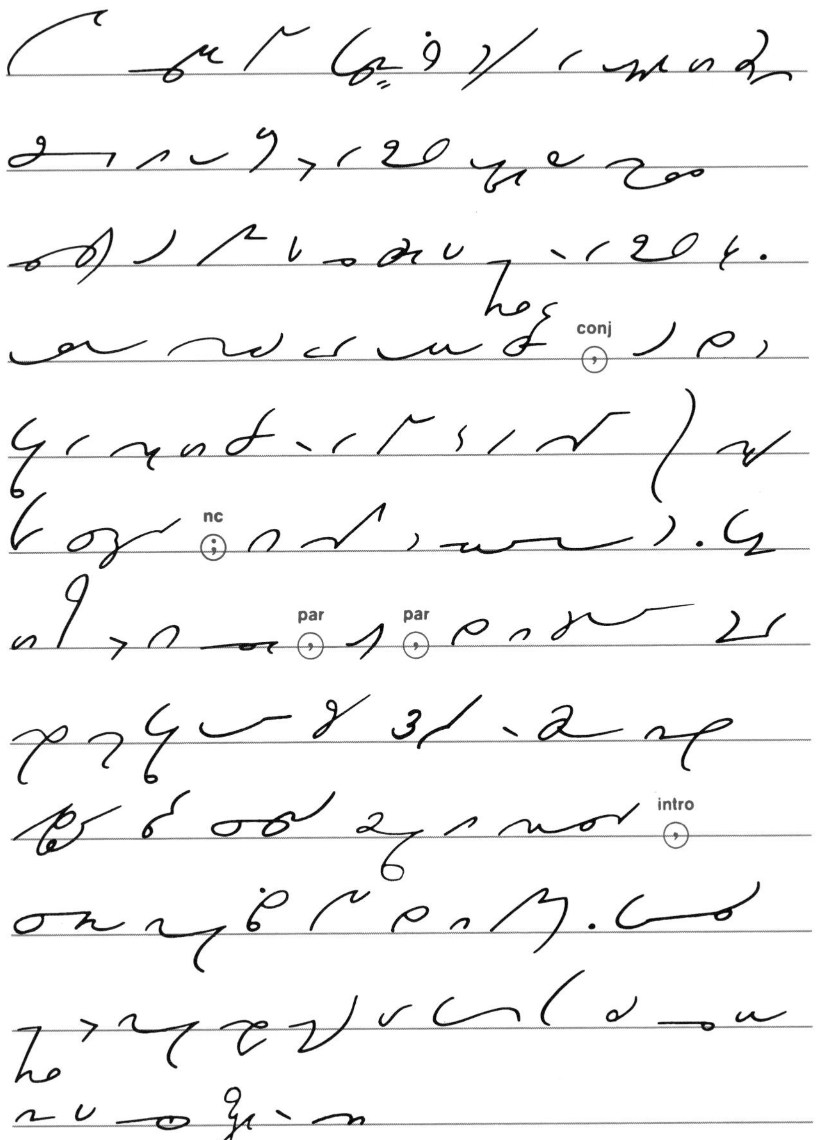

14
26
39
48
64
75
88
108
111
125
138
146

Mailable Production

Transcribe the following mailable production letter in block style, assuring proper placement of all letter parts. Insert punctuation prior to transcribing, and capitalize proper nouns and titles. Address a large envelope with the special notation *Registered.*

58.4 Time Limit: 15 minutes

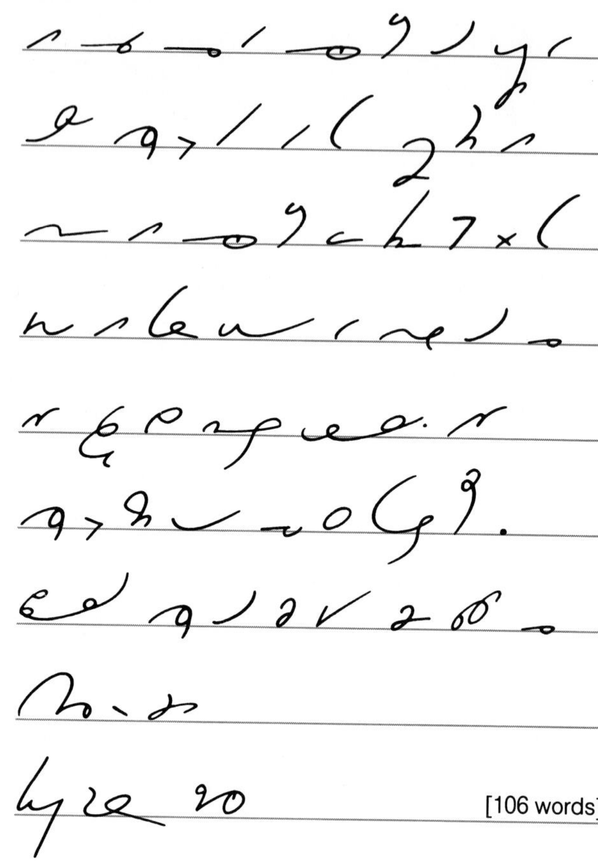

[106 words]

LESSON 59

SAMUELS, KEELEY, AND FRANK

DICTATION SPEED BUILDING

The shorthand outlines below appear in the speed dictation practice that follows. Practice writing these words using the shorthand outlines. Then, using the key that follows, dictate the words to yourself in preparation for the speed dictation practice.

Dictation Preview

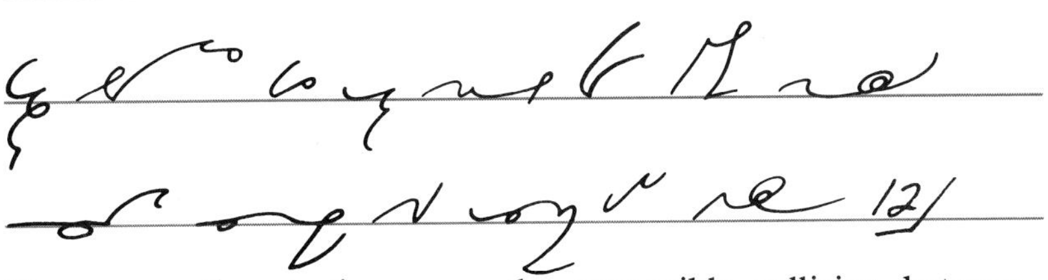

Key: perception, testimony, partly, responsible, collision, between, driven, client, maintains, negligent, court, recover, auto, trial, $1,200

Speed Dictation Practice

59.1 Goal: 100 wam speed dictation

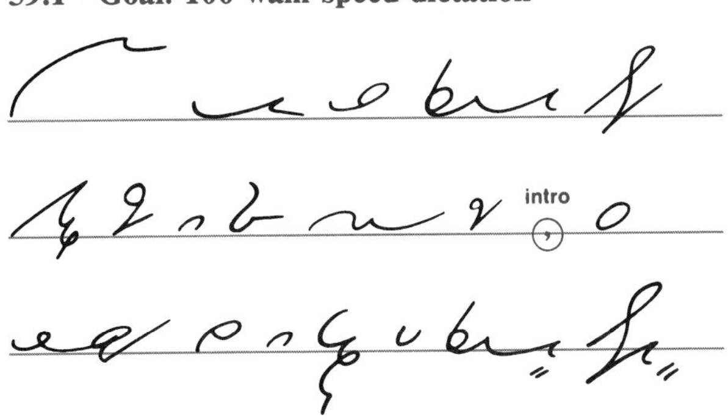

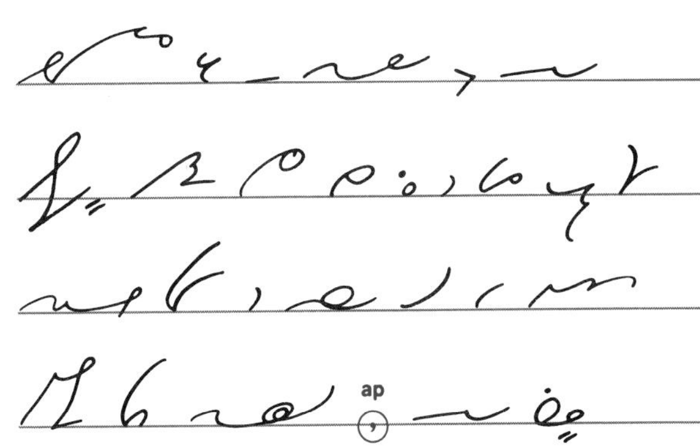

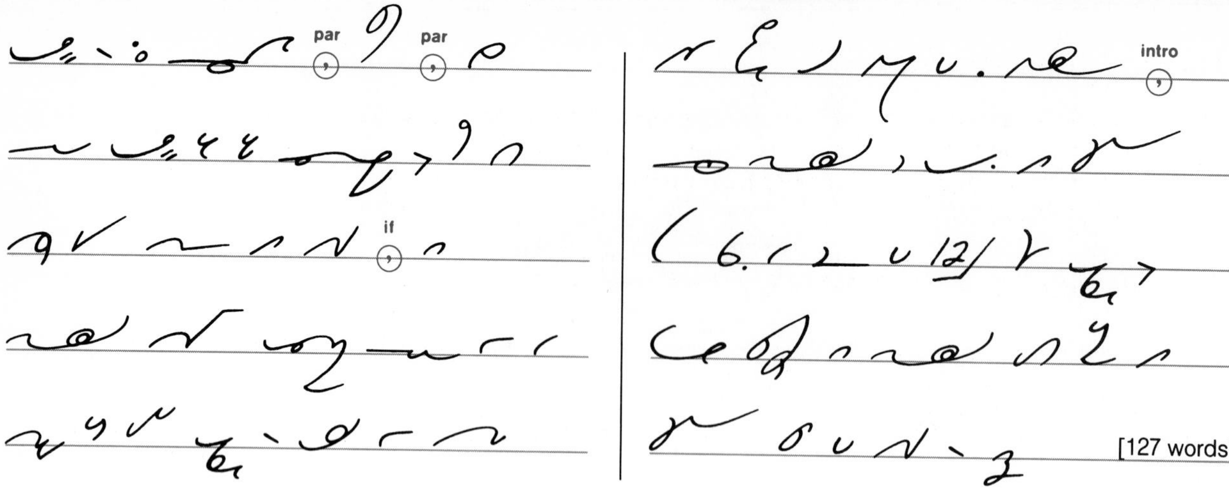

TRANSCRIPTION SKILL DEVELOPMENT

Transcription Warmup

Transcribe the following groups of words for speed and accuracy, applying transcription rules and assuring correct spelling.

59.2

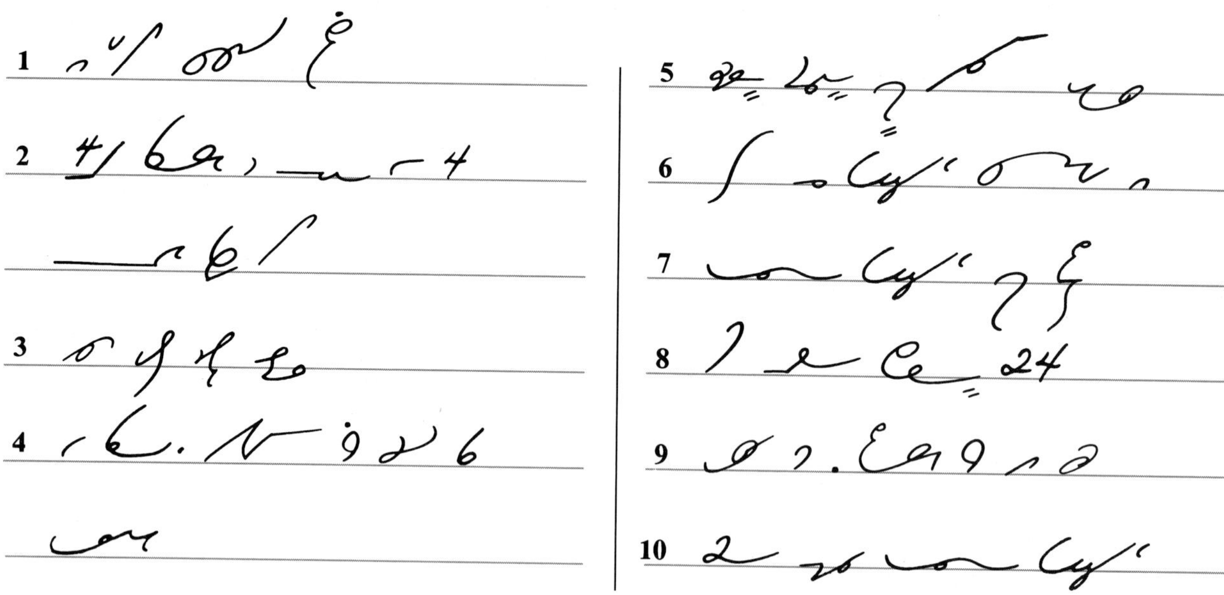

Transcription Practice

Transcribe the following letter for 2 minutes in unarranged format, applying transcription rules and assuring correct spelling. For every word not transcribed and every keyboarding error, deduct one word from the total word count.

59.3 Goal: 35 wam transcription rate

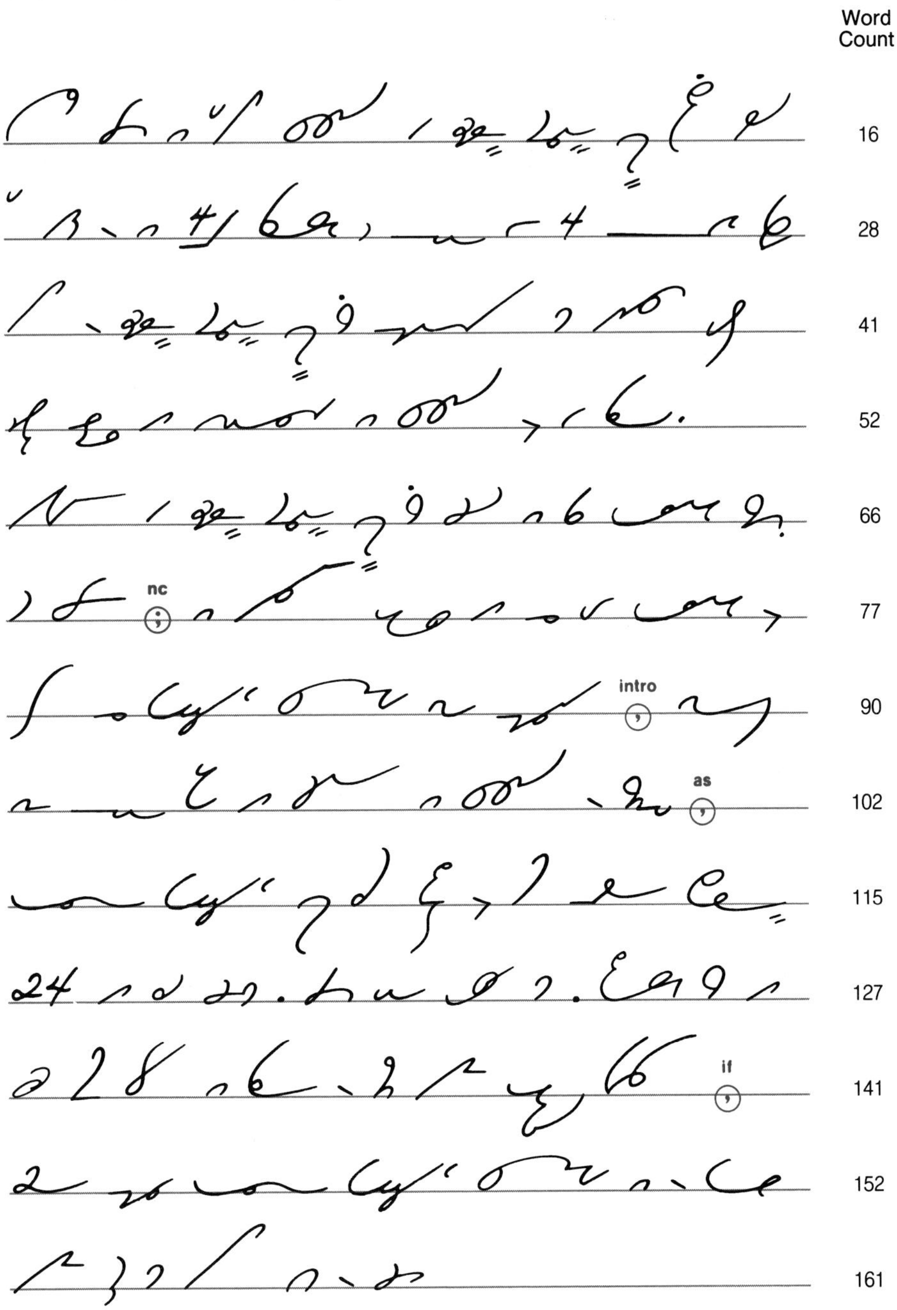

Mailable Production

Type the following deposition on a plain sheet of paper, 8 1/2 x 11. Double-space the body, center the word *Deposition* in all capitals, and triple-space after the title. Indent ten spaces for enumerations and paragraphs. Be sure to add the signature line. Refer to Lesson 57 for additional directions. Capitalize all proper nouns and titles.

59.4 Time Limit: 15 minutes

[123 words]

LESSON 60

SAMUELS, KEELEY, AND FRANK

DICTATION SPEED BUILDING

The shorthand outlines below appear in the speed dictation practice that follows. Practice writing these words using the shorthand outlines. Then, using the key that follows, dictate the words to yourself in preparation for the speed dictation practice.

Dictation Preview

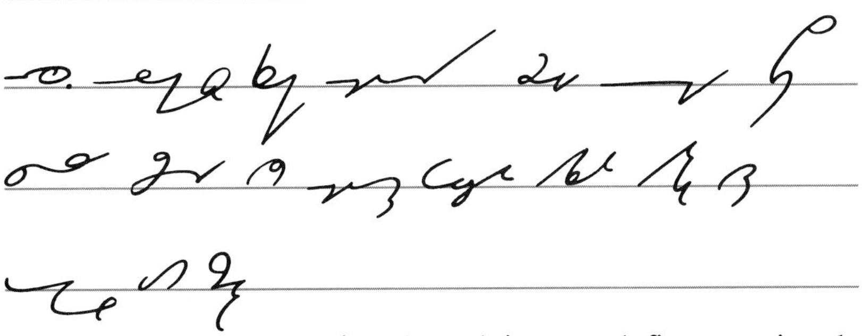

Key: inquiring, merchandise, charged, instructed, first, mentioned, above, accurate, exact, these, instructions, proceeds, depends, dispose, thank you for, will you please, of this, as soon as possible

Speed Dictation Practice

60.1 Goal: 100 wam speed dictation

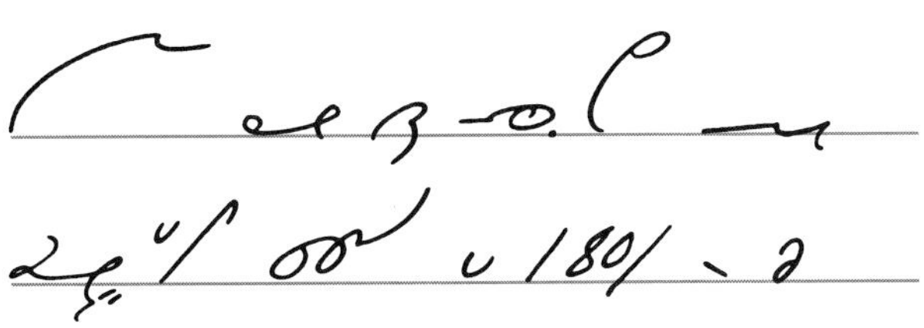

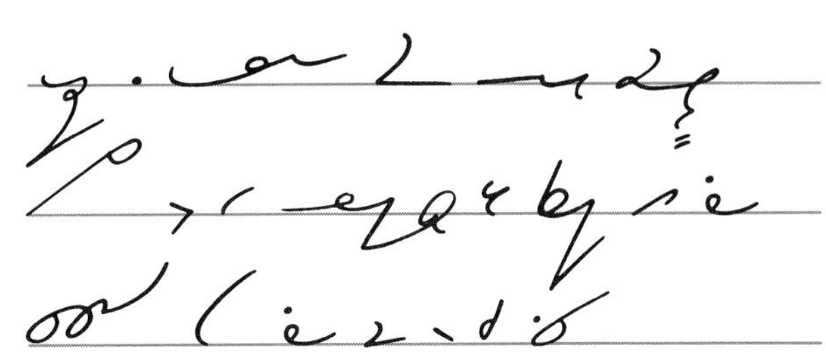

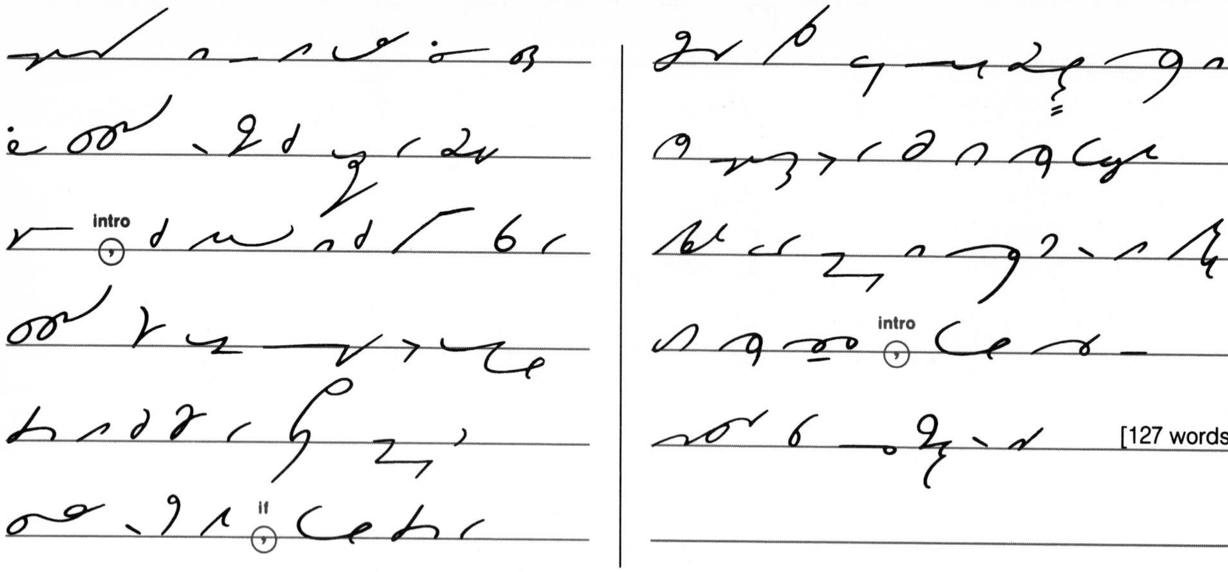

[127 words]

TRANSCRIPTION SKILL DEVELOPMENT

Transcription Warmup

Transcribe the following groups of words for speed and accuracy, applying transcription rules and assuring correct spelling.

60.2

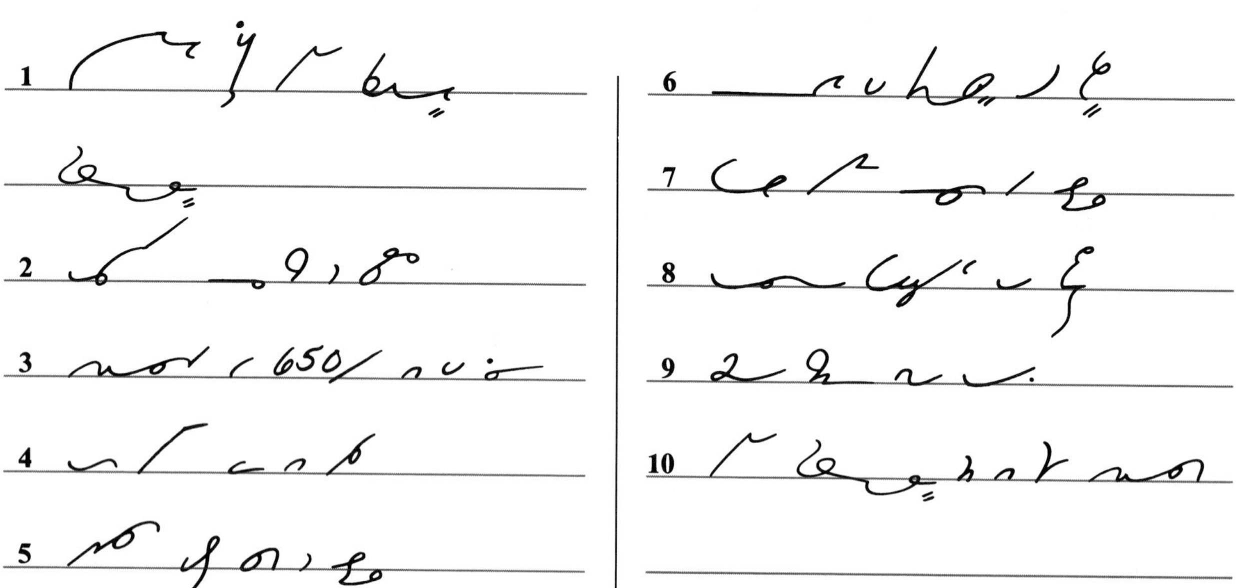

Transcription Practice

Transcribe the following letter for 2 minutes in unarranged format, applying transcription rules and assuring correct spelling. For every word not transcribed and every keyboarding error, deduct one word from the total word count.

60.3 Goal: 35 wam transcription rate

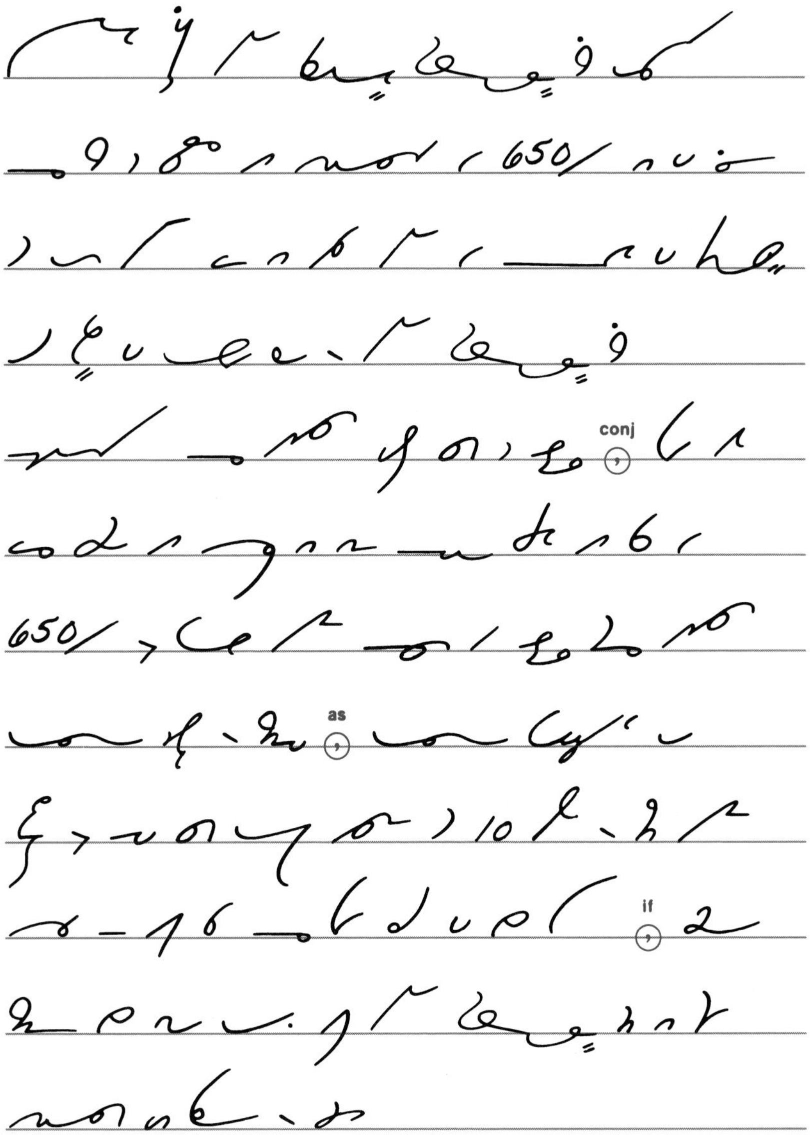

Word Count

10
20
29
38
58
68
80
90
103
114
127
135

Mailable Production

Transcribe the following mailable production letter in block style, assuring proper placement of all letter parts. Insert punctuation prior to transcribing, and capitalize proper nouns and titles. Address a large envelope with the special notation *Personal.*

60.4 Time Limit: 15 minutes

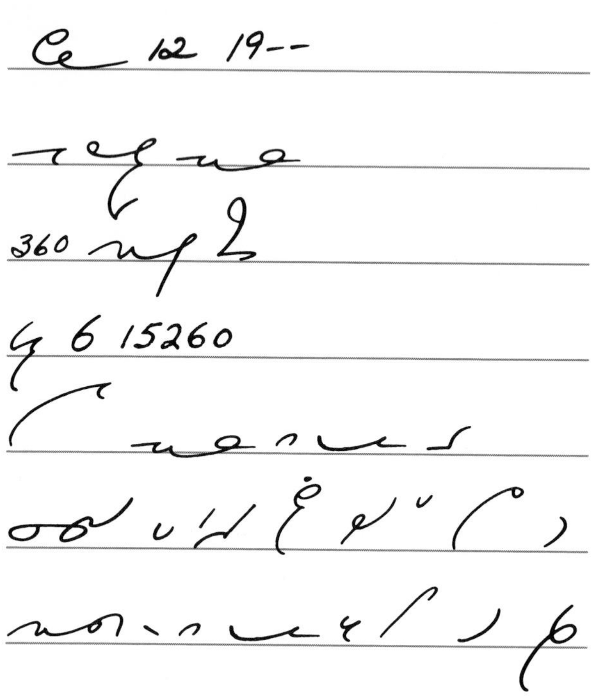

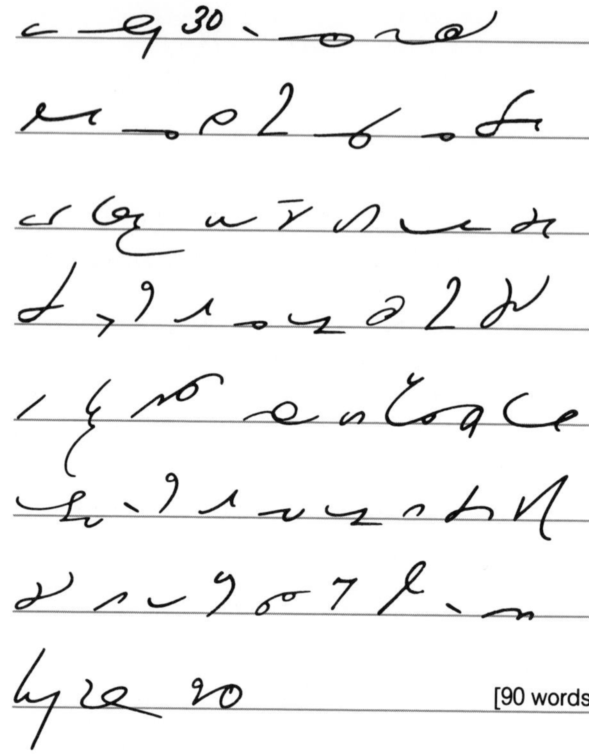

[90 words]

LESSON 61

SAMUELS, KEELEY, AND FRANK

DICTATION SPEED BUILDING

The shorthand outlines below appear in the speed dictation practice that follows. Practice writing these words using the shorthand outlines. Then, using the key that follows, dictate the words to yourself in preparation for the speed dictation practice.

Dictation Preview

Key: partner, justified, used, related, denied, proof, discuss, options, guidelines, drawn, determine, specific, violations, to do

Speed Dictation Practice

61.1 Goal: 100 wam speed dictation

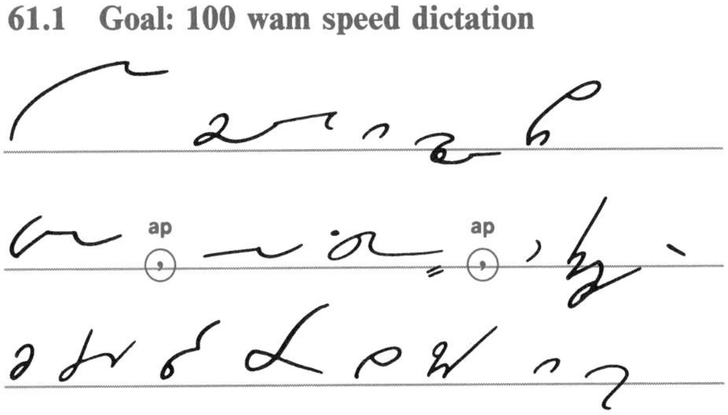

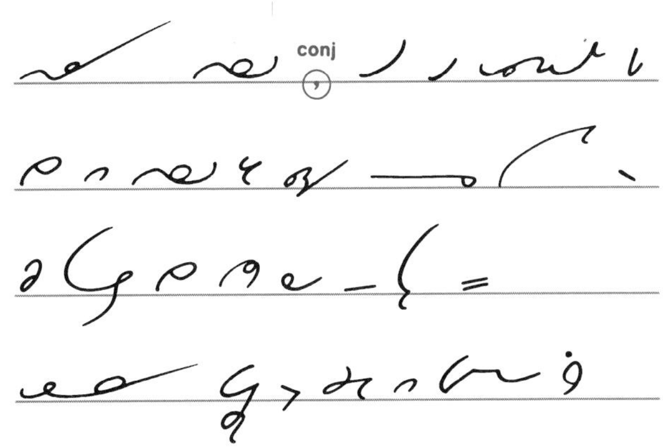

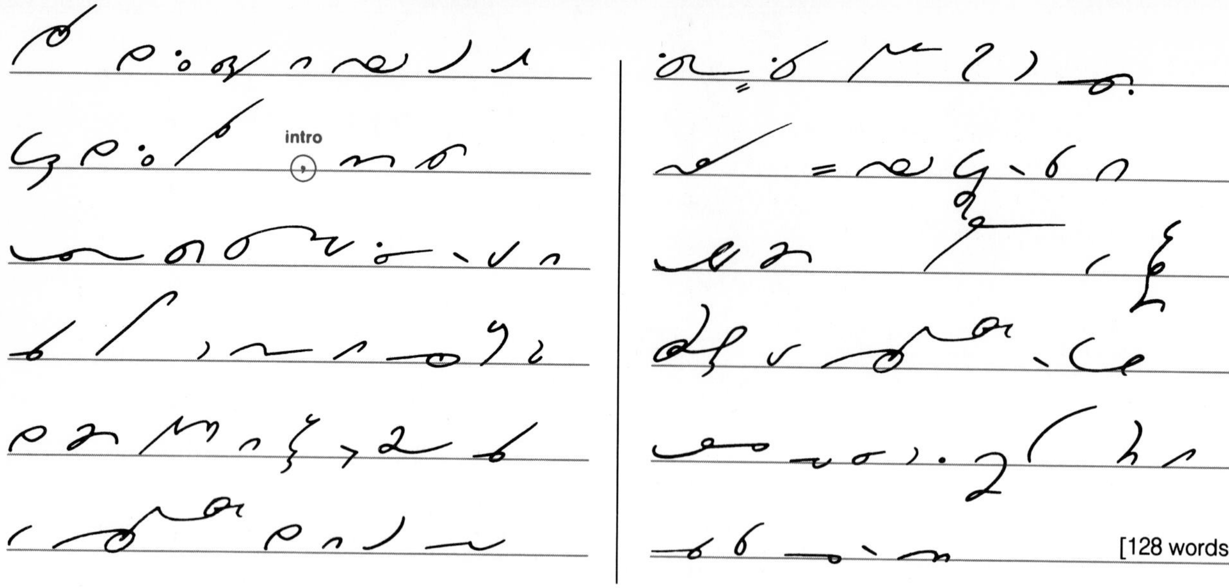

[128 words]

TRANSCRIPTION SKILL DEVELOPMENT

Transcription Warmup

Transcribe the following groups of words for speed and accuracy, applying transcription rules and assuring correct spelling.

61.2

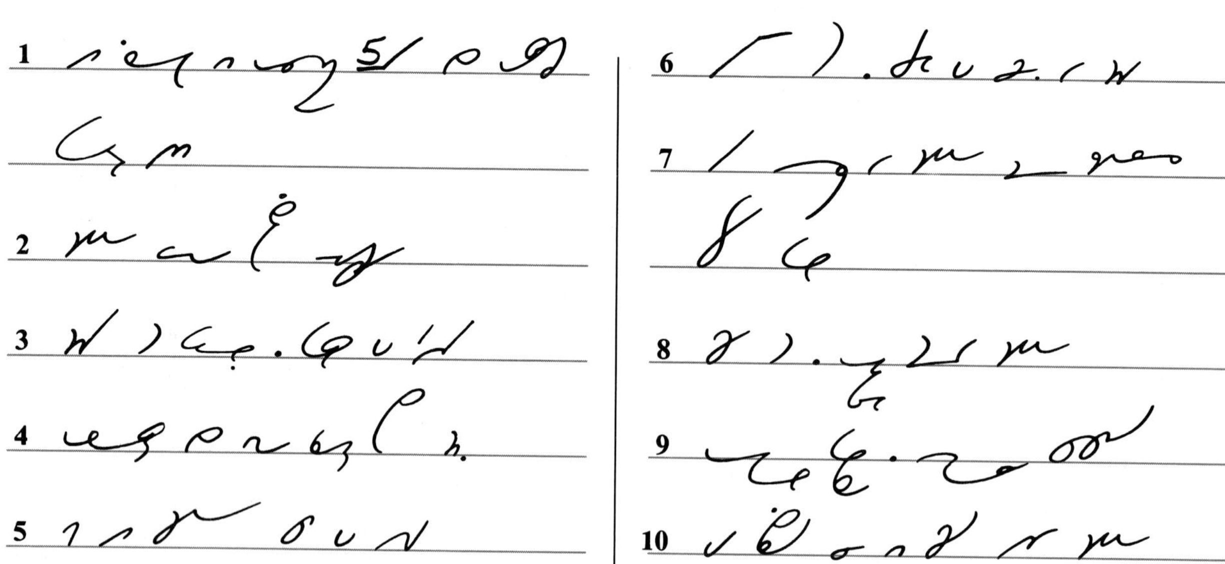

Transcription Practice

Transcribe the following letter for 2 minutes in unarranged format, applying transcription rules and assuring correct spelling. For every word not transcribed and every keyboarding error, deduct one word from the total word count.

61.3 Goal: 35 wam transcription rate

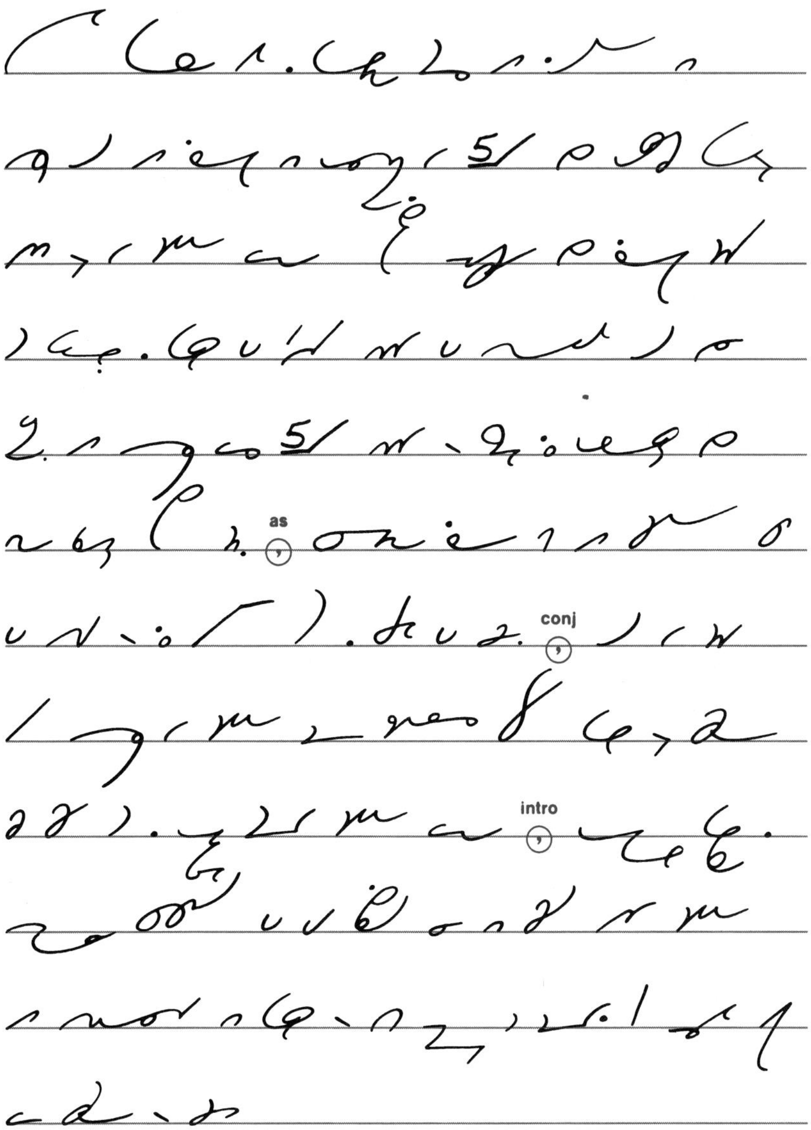

Word Count

11
23
36
47
59
72
84
95
109
121
135
140

Mailable Production

Type the following agreement, known as an *Assignment*, between Frank T. Carlson and Donald S. Cohen on a plain sheet of paper, 8 1/2 x 11. Use the guidelines set forth in Lesson 57 for agreements. Capitalize and punctuate where necessary, and use appropriate margins and spacing. Be sure to add the signature lines for Frank T. Carlson and Donald S. Cohen.

61.4 Time Limit: 15 minutes

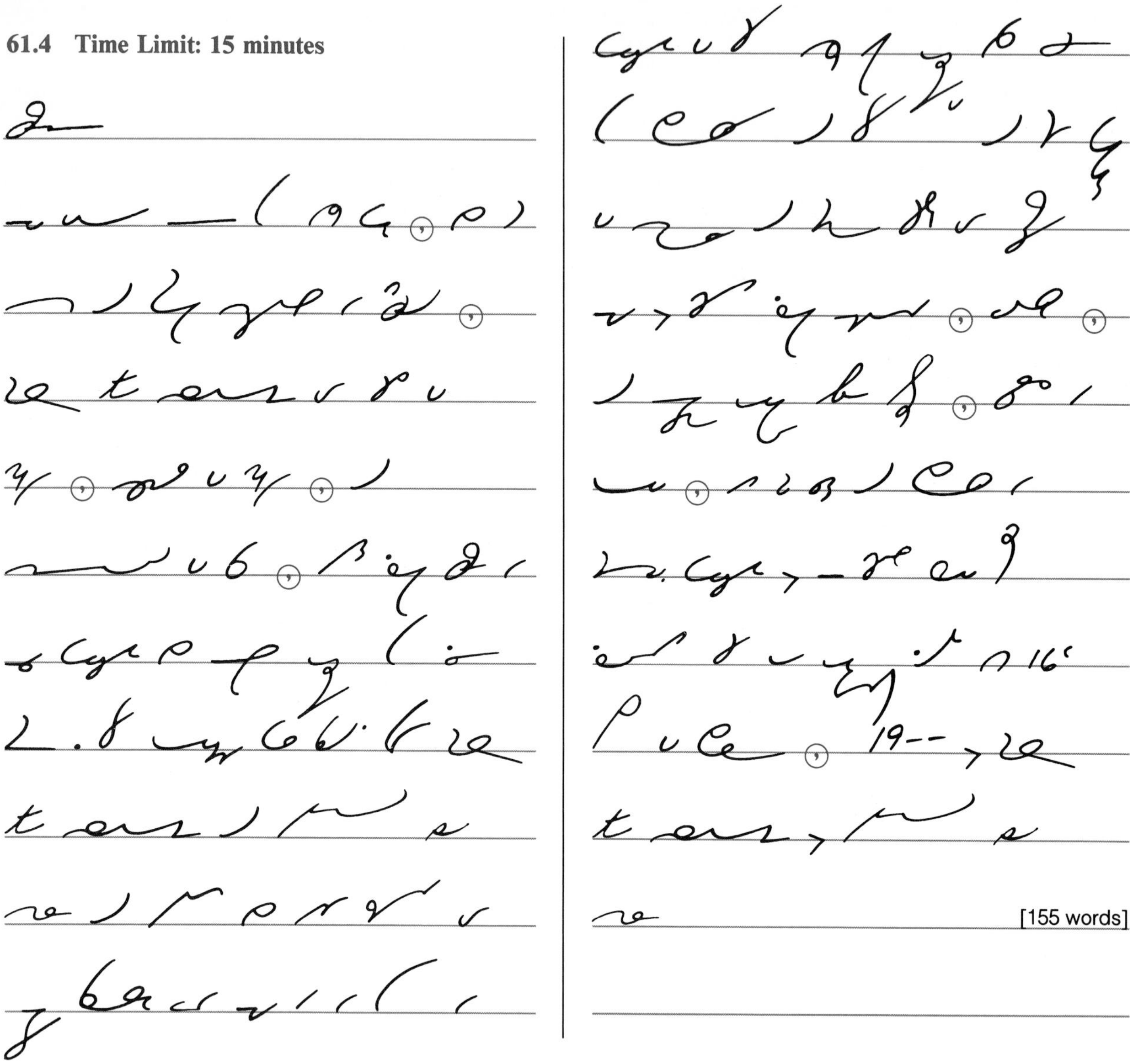

[155 words]

LESSON 62

SAMUELS, KEELEY, AND FRANK

DICTATION SPEED BUILDING

The shorthand outlines below appear in the speed dictation practice that follows. Practice writing these words using the shorthand outlines. Then, using the key that follows, dictate the words to yourself in preparation for the speed dictation practice.

Dictation Preview

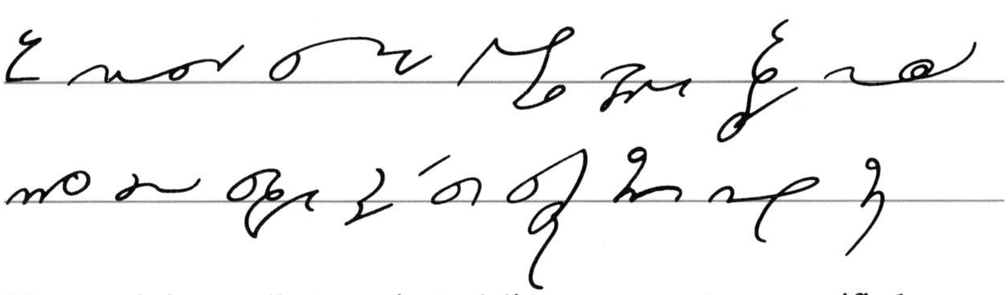

Key: opinion, collect, against, delivery, computers, specified, client, worthwhile, secure, acceptance, forced, transaction, advisable, if you can, you may be, if you have

Speed Dictation Practice

62.1 Goal: 100 wam speed dictation

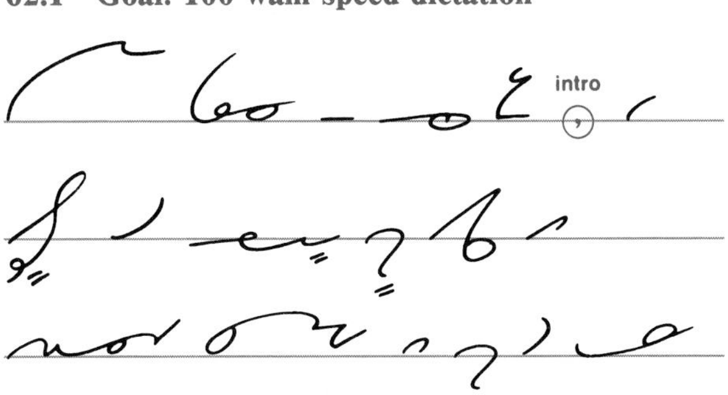

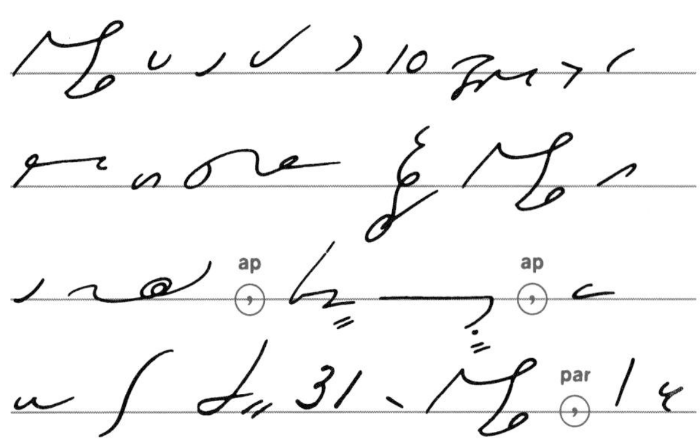

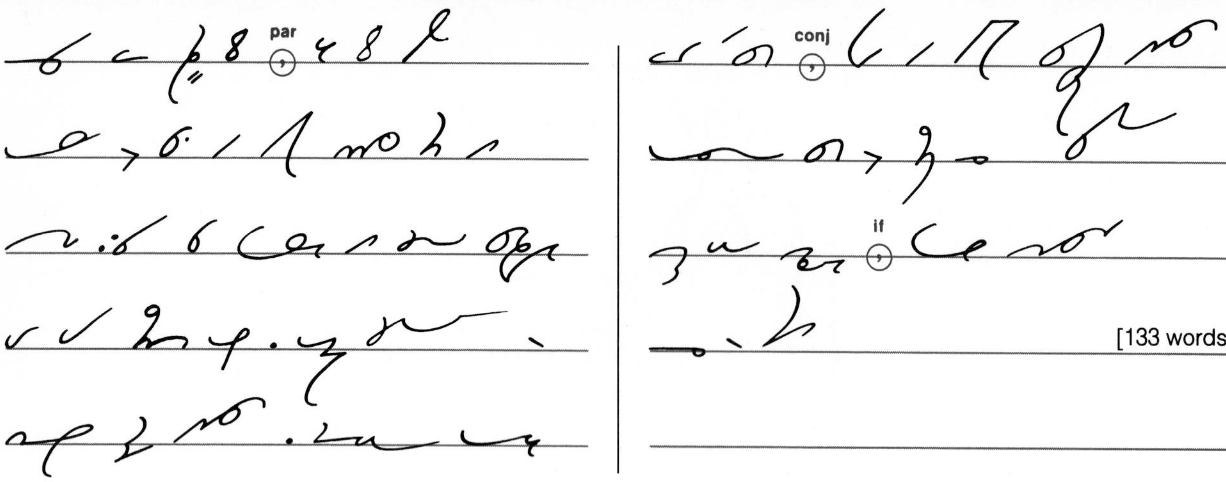

TRANSCRIPTION SKILL DEVELOPMENT

Transcription Warmup

Transcribe the following groups of words for speed and accuracy, applying transcription rules and assuring correct spelling.

62.2

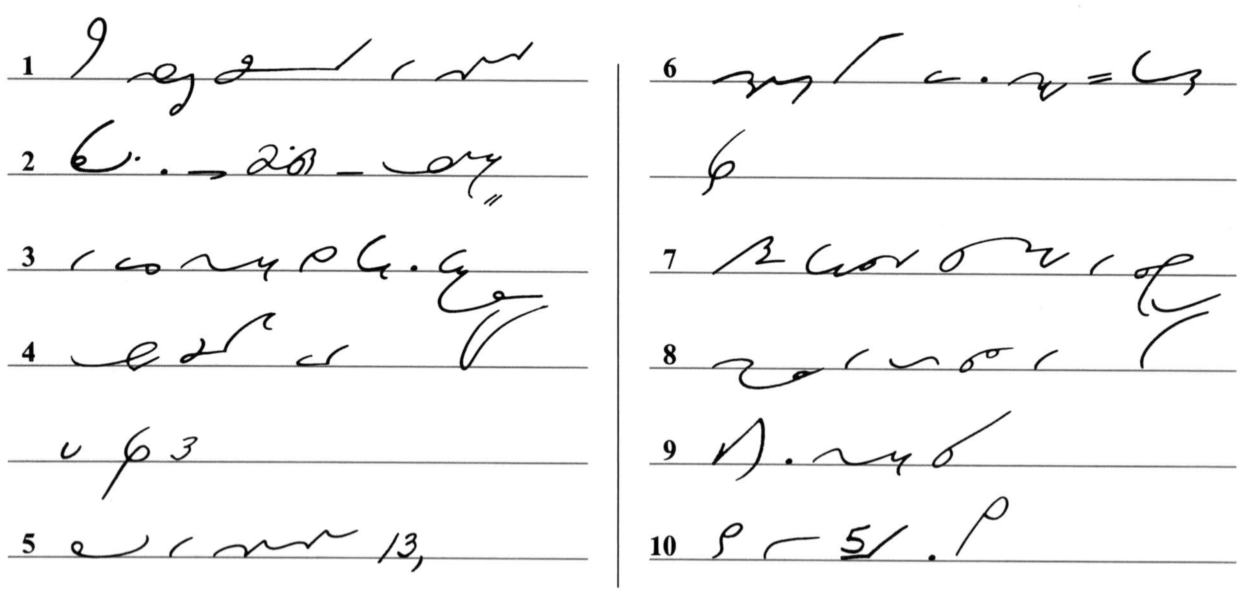

Transcription Practice

Transcribe the following letter for 2 minutes in unarranged format, applying transcription rules and assuring correct spelling. For every word not transcribed and every keyboarding error, deduct one word from the total word count.

62.3 Goal: 35 wam transcription rate

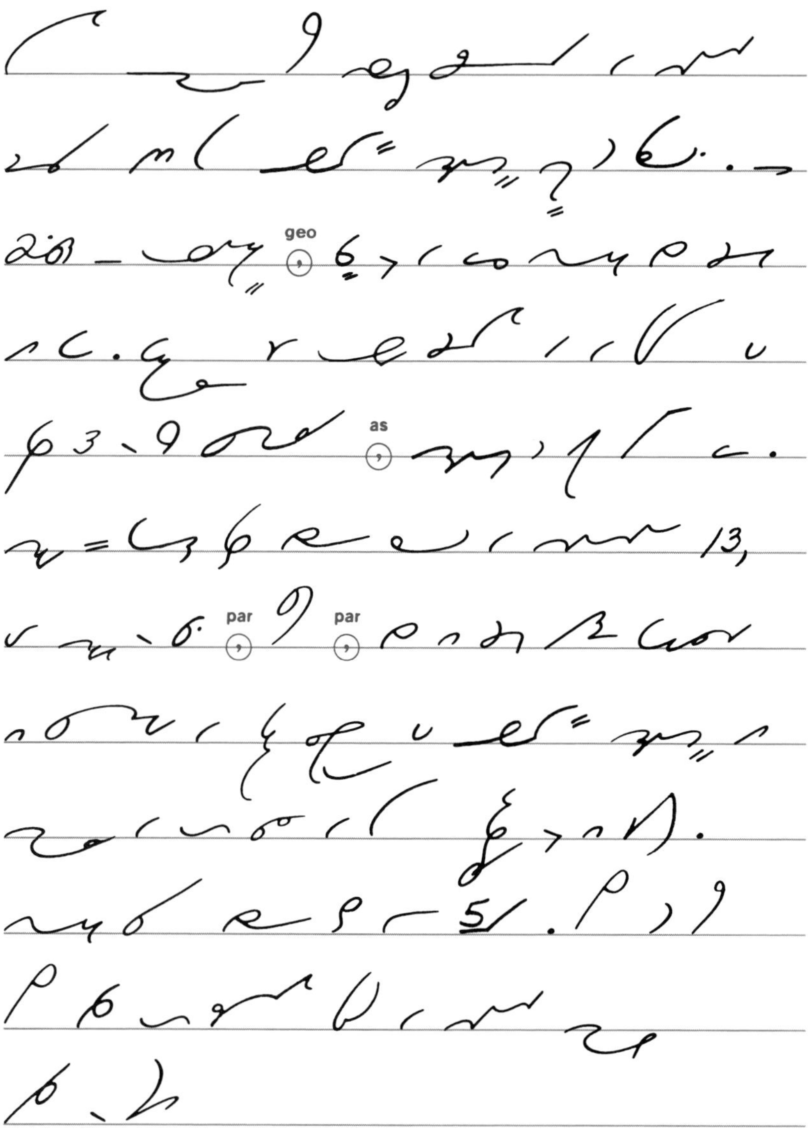

Word Count

11
24
35
47
57
68
81
93
106
117
128
133

Mailable Production

Type the following Certificate of Incorporation for the signature of Christine Parker on a plain sheet of paper, 8 1/2 x 11. Use the guidelines set forth in Lesson 57 for agreements. Capitalize and punctuate where necessary and use appropriate margins and spacing.

62.4 Time Limit: 15 minutes

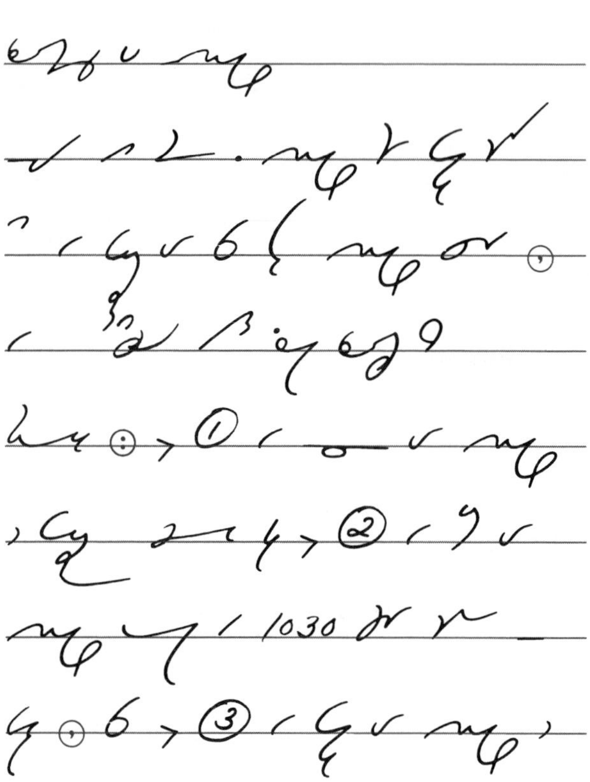

[151 words]

LESSON 63

SAMUELS, KEELEY, AND FRANK

DICTATION SPEED BUILDING

The shorthand outlines below appear in the speed dictation practice that follows. Practice writing these words using the shorthand outlines. Then, using the key that follows, dictate the words to yourself in preparation for the speed dictation practice.

Dictation Preview

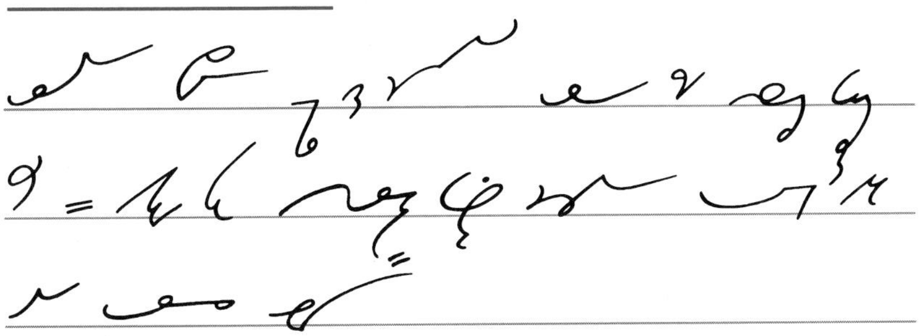

Key: rental, apartment, enjoy, yourself, standard, real estate, carefully, provisions, safe-deposit box, Greensburg, perhaps, schedule, lunch, it was, there are, let me, next time

Speed Dictation Practice

63.1 Goal: 100 wam speed dictation

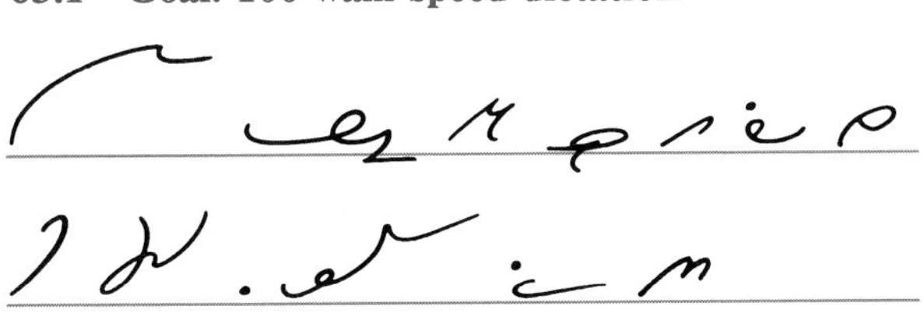

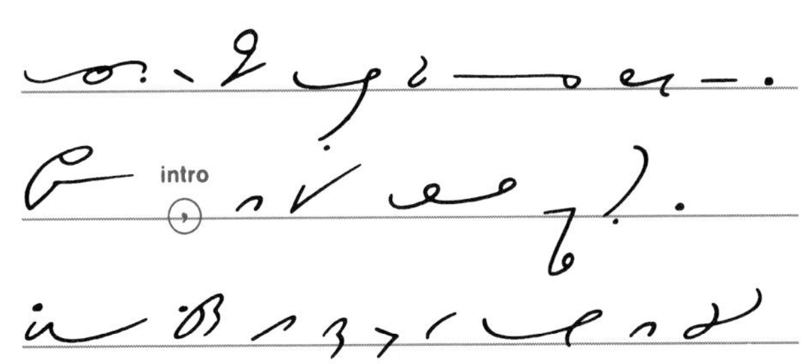

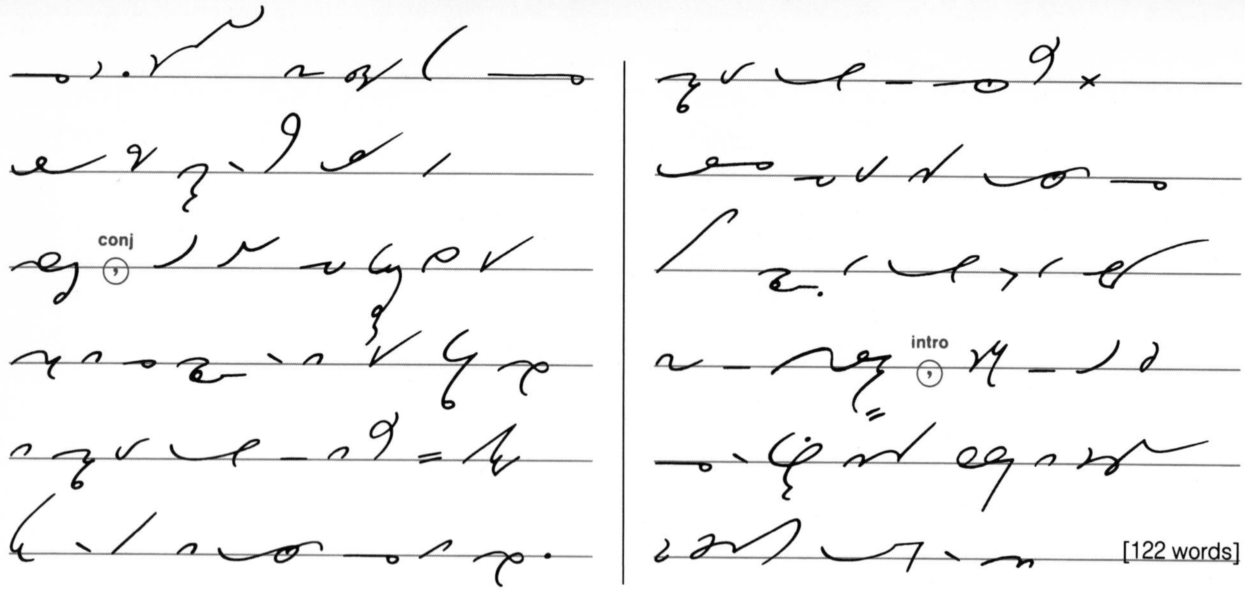

TRANSCRIPTION SKILL DEVELOPMENT

Transcription Warmup

Transcribe the following groups of words for speed and accuracy, applying transcription rules and assuring correct spelling.

63.2

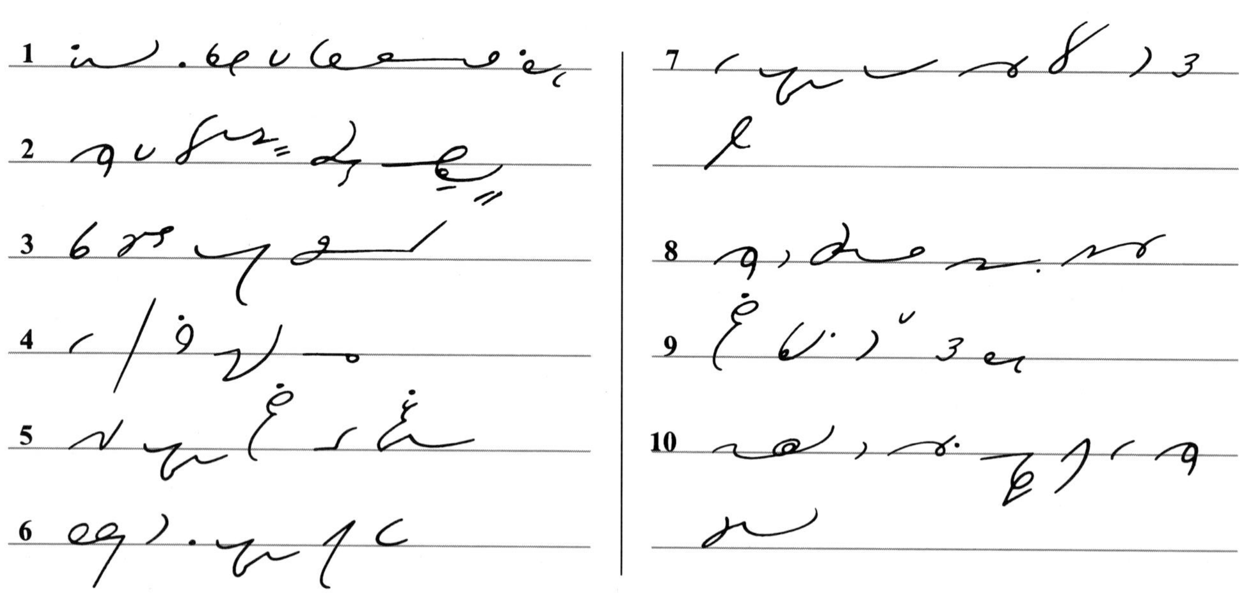

Transcription Practice

Transcribe the following letter for 2 minutes in unarranged format, applying transcription rules and assuring correct spelling. For every word not transcribed and every keyboarding error, deduct one word from the total word count

63.3 Goal: 35 wam transcription rate

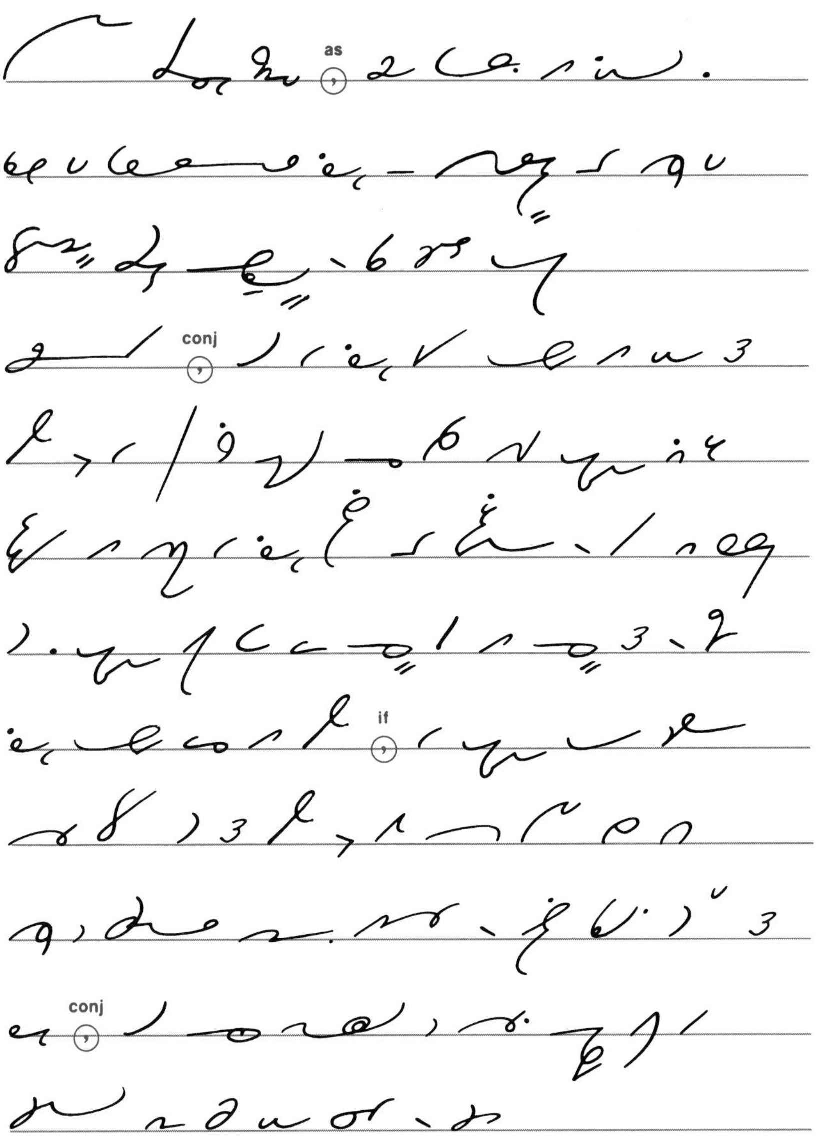

Word Count

11

21

32

42

55

70

81

91

102

116

126

135

Mailable Production

Transcribe the following mailable production letter in block style, assuring proper placement of all letter parts. Insert punctuation prior to transcribing, and capitalize proper nouns and titles. Address a large envelope with the special notation *Registered.*

63.4 Time Limit: 15 minutes

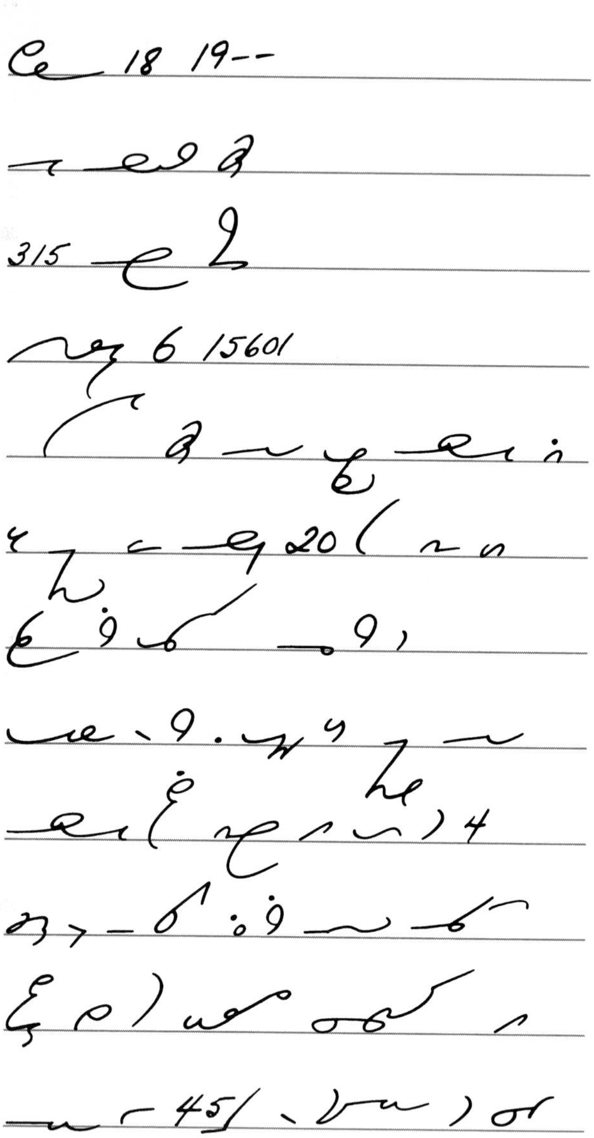

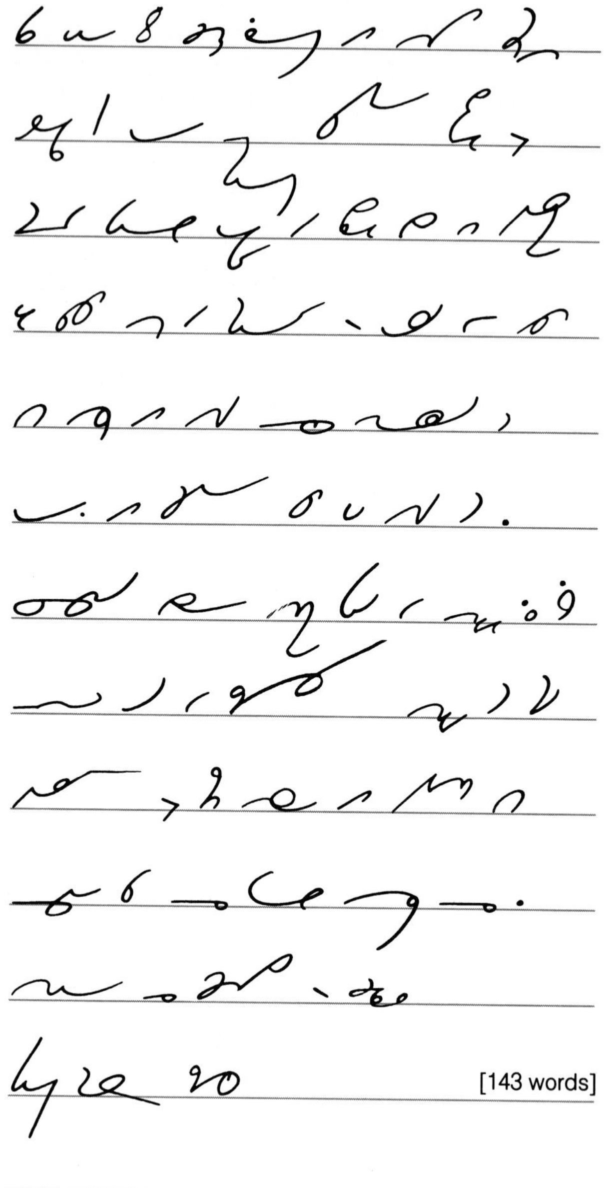

[143 words]

LESSON 64

SAMUELS, KEELEY, AND FRANK

DICTATION SPEED BUILDING

The shorthand outlines below appear in the speed dictation practice that follows. Practice writing these words using the shorthand outlines. Then, using the key that follows, dictate the words to yourself in preparation for the speed dictation practice.

Dictation Preview

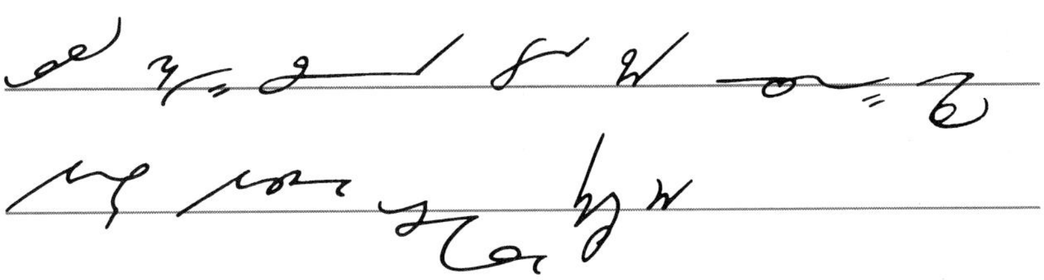

Key: returned, Washington, examined, patent, issued, Michael, compared, description, documents, resemblance, justify, suit

Speed Dictation Practice

64.1 Goal: 100 wam speed dictation

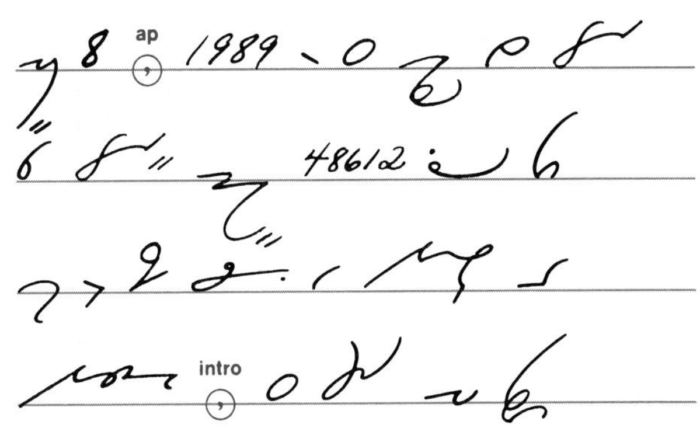

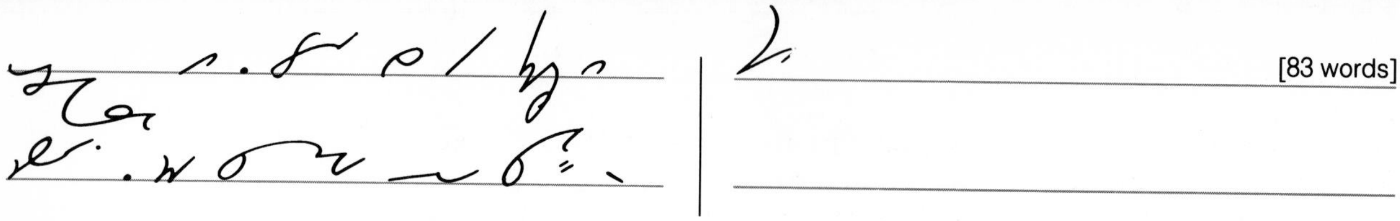

[83 words]

TRANSCRIPTION SKILL DEVELOPMENT

Transcription Warmup

Transcribe the following groups of words for speed and accuracy, applying transcription rules and assuring correct spelling.

64.2

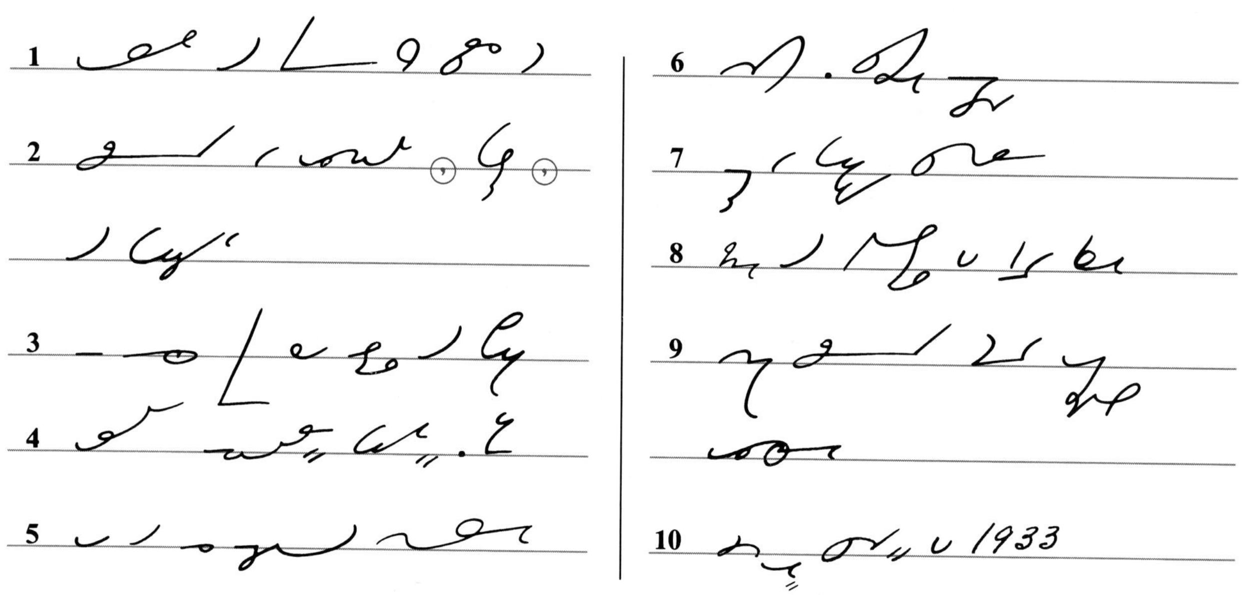

Transcription Practice

Transcribe the following letter for 2 minutes in unarranged format, applying transcription rules and assuring correct spelling. For every word not transcribed and every keyboarding error, deduct one word from the total word count.

64.3 Goal: 35 wam transcription rate

Word Count

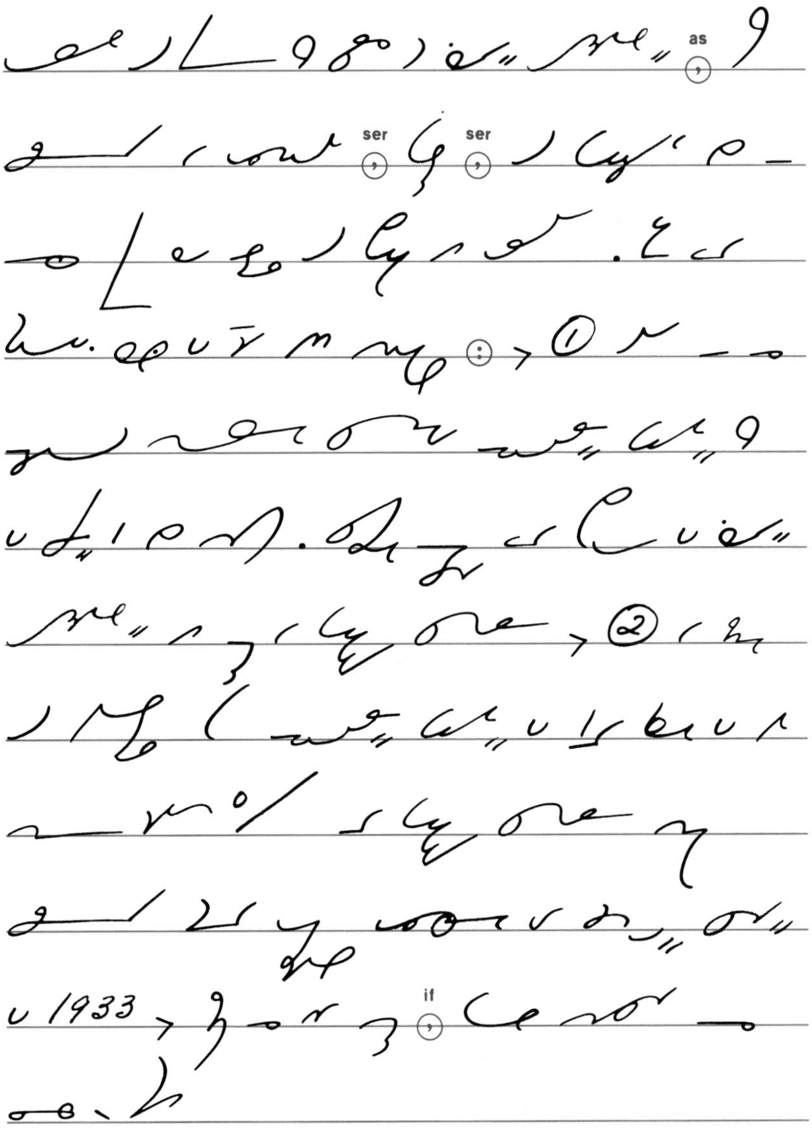

12
22
36
50
59
73
86
98
108
121
133
139

Mailable Production

Type the following deposition for the signature of Leon H. James on a plain sheet of paper, 8 1/2 x 11. Use the guidelines set forth in Lesson 57 for agreements. Capitalize and punctuate where necessary, and use appropriate margins and spacing. Be sure to add the signature line for Leon H. James.

64.4 Time Limit: 15 minutes

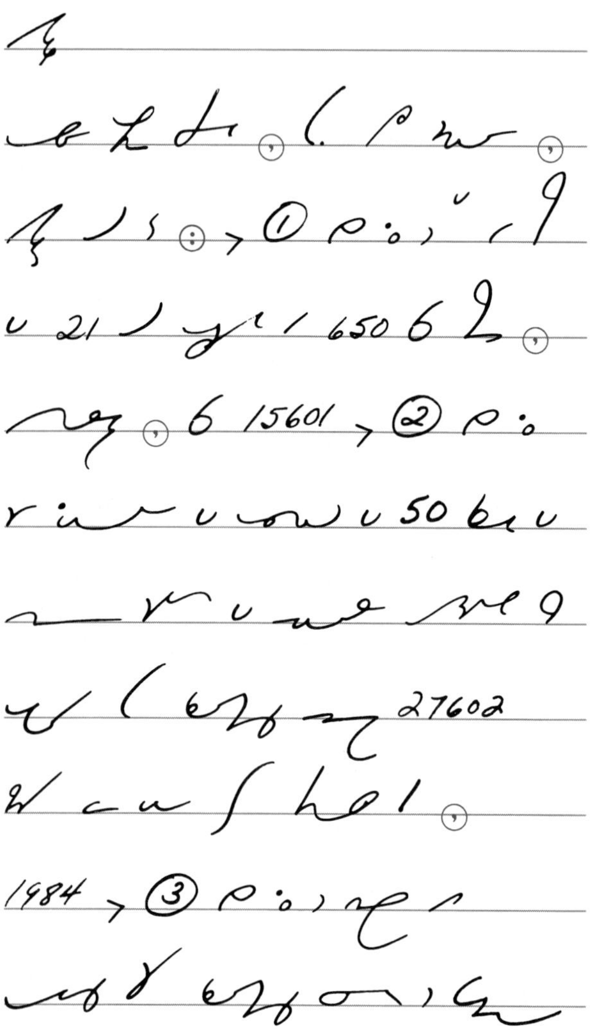

[178 words]

UNIT IX

WCAC-TV

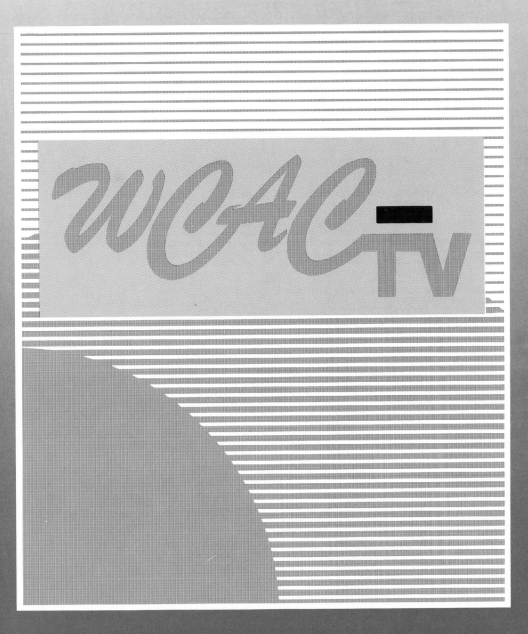

LESSON 65

WCAC-TV

You are an administrative assistant to A. H. Kirkpatrick, general manager of television station WCAC-TV in San Antonio, Texas. Ms. Kirkpatrick is the chief executive officer of this company. All letters are signed by her, and all memos are initialed by her.

Being the administrative assistant to the chief executive of a firm entails many responsibilities. First of all, it carries a high degree of various skills. A top-level administrative assistant needs not only excellent shorthand and typing skills but also such skills as the ability to make decisions, the ability to work independently, and the ability to set priorities and to follow through to see that a job is done correctly and on time.

All administrative assistants need good human relations skills. Because the chief executive corresponds and meets with many important people, the administrative assistant needs to be at ease with these people and to know how to introduce and address them.

Being an administrative assistant to the chief executive officer of a firm also has its rewards. Because of the level of skills required, such assistants are generally highly paid. In addition, the opportunity to meet and work with important people and to be personally involved in top-level decisions that affect the future of the company all combine to make the job exciting, challenging, and rewarding.

Below is a copy of your company letterhead. Develop the return address that you will use to type the envelopes for the mailable production letters.

WCAC-TV
2982 Powell Street
San Antonio, TX 78205 (512) 555-3210

DICTATION SPEED BUILDING

The shorthand outlines below appear in the speed dictation practice that follows. Practice writing these words using the shorthand outlines. Then, using the key that follows, dictate the words to yourself in preparation for the speed dictation practice.

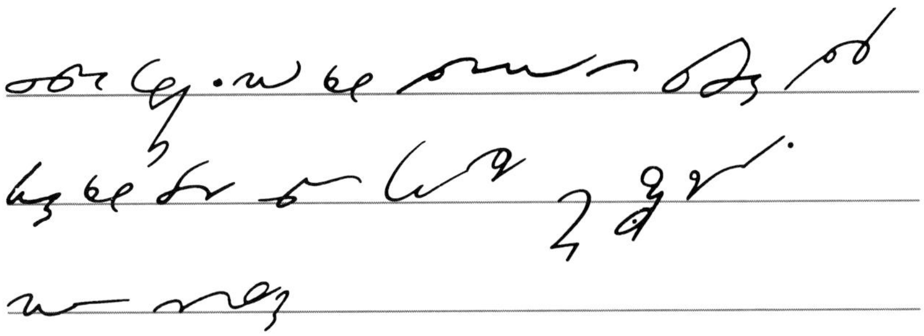

Key: announce, prestigious, award, series, technological, advances, decade, portions, series, picked, network, broadcast, convention, association, extending, warm, congratulations

Speed Dictation Practice

65.1 Goal: 110 wam speed dictation

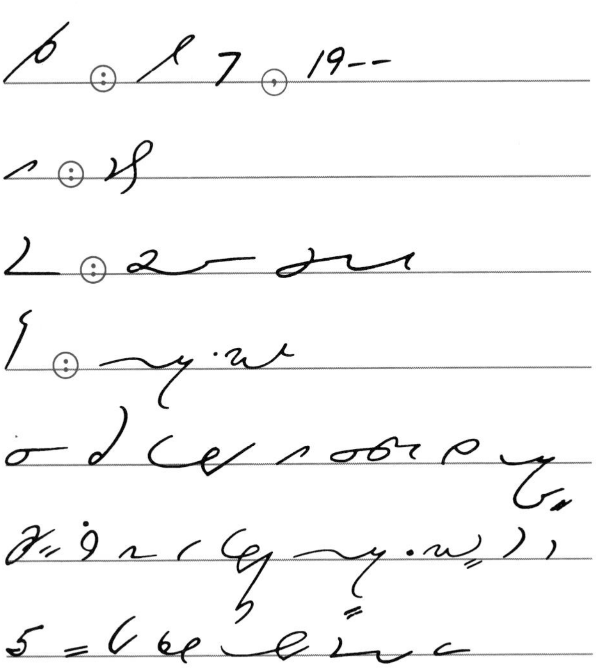

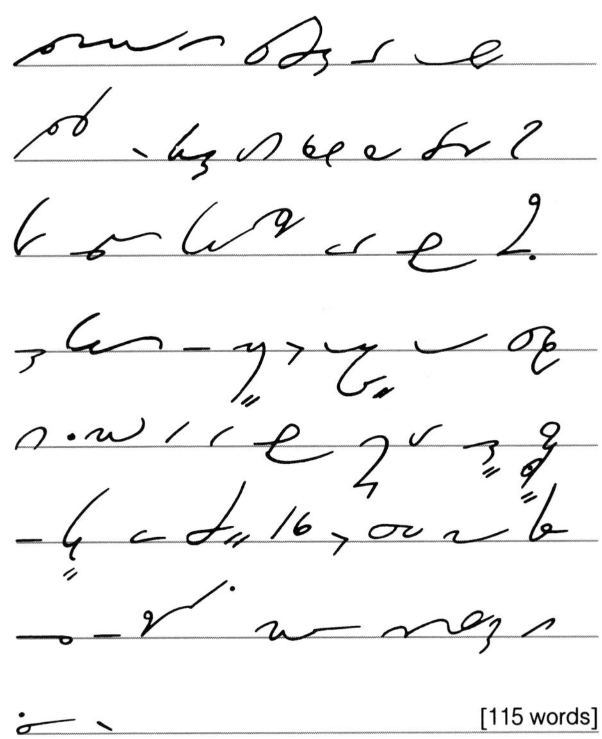

[115 words]

TRANSCRIPTION SKILL DEVELOPMENT

Transcription Warmup

Transcribe the following groups of words for speed and accuracy, applying transcription rules and assuring correct spelling.

65.2

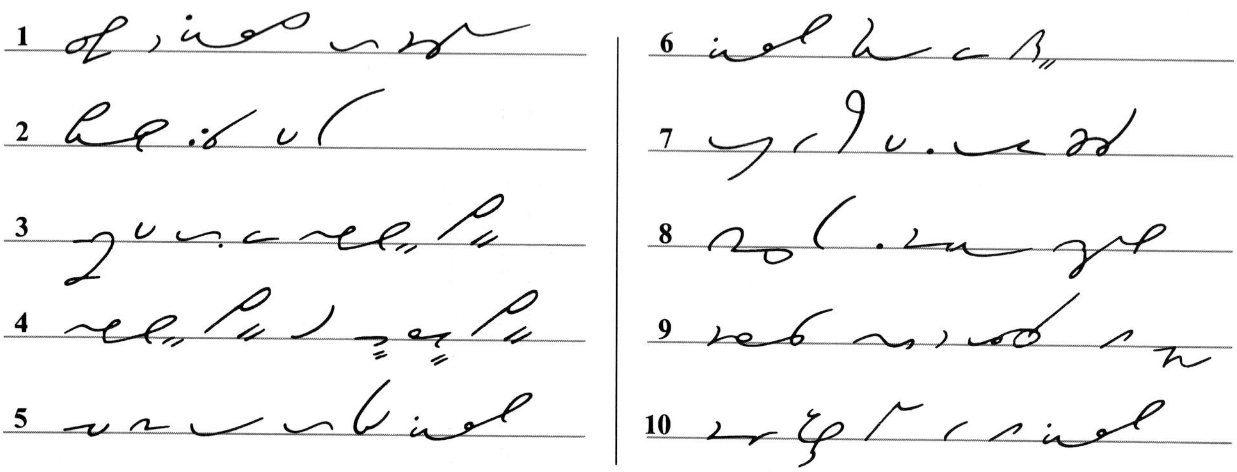

Transcription Practice

Transcribe the following memo for 2 minutes in unarranged format, applying transcription rules and assuring correct spelling. For every word not transcribed and every keyboarding error, deduct one word from the total word count.

65.3 Goal: 35 wam transcription rate

Word Count

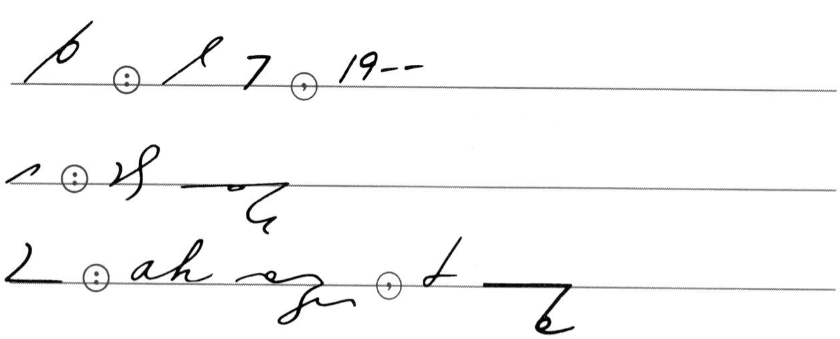

5

9

17

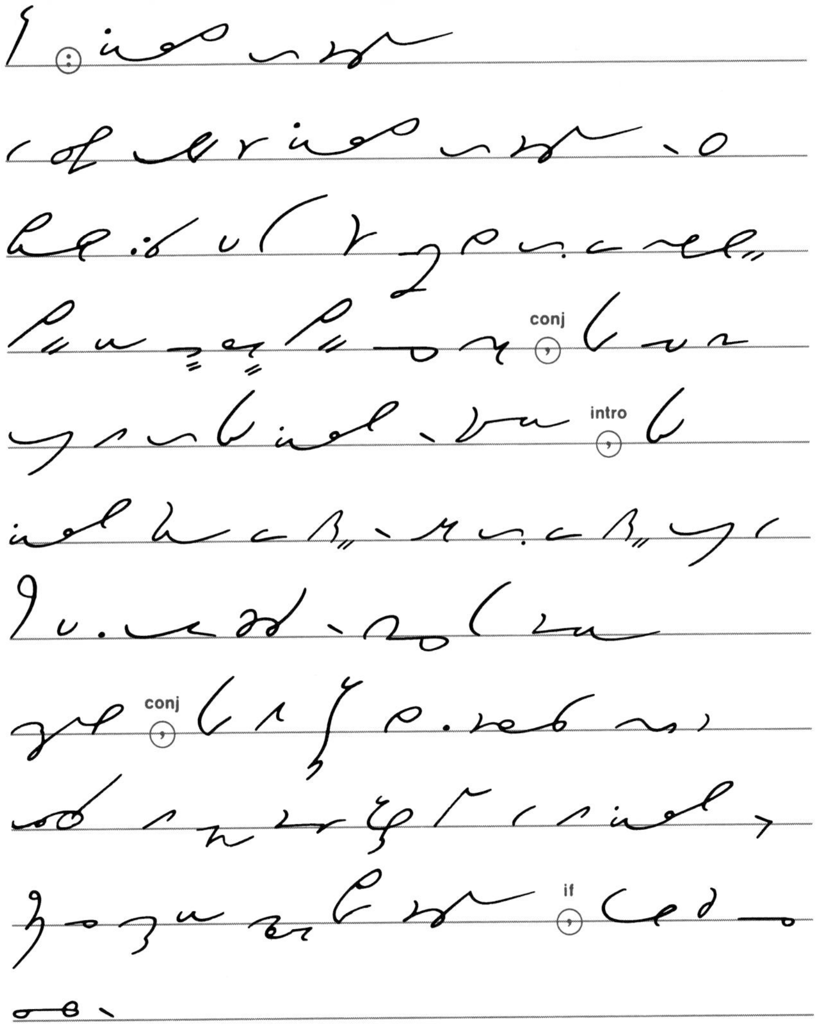

23
33
47
56
66
79
88
99
111
125
127

LESSON 66

WCAC-TV

DICTATION SPEED BUILDING

The shorthand outlines below appear in the speed dictation practice that follows. Practice writing these words using the shorthand outlines. Then, using the key that follows, dictate the words to yourself in preparation for the speed dictation practice.

Dictation Preview

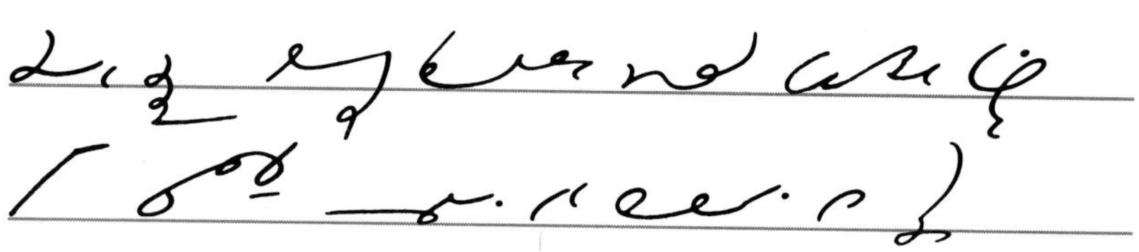

Key: feelings, sexism, television, children's, screened, producers, perhaps, done, adequate, monitoring, thanks, alerting, thank you, Very sincerely yours

Speed Dictation Practice

66.1 Goal: 110 wam speed dictation

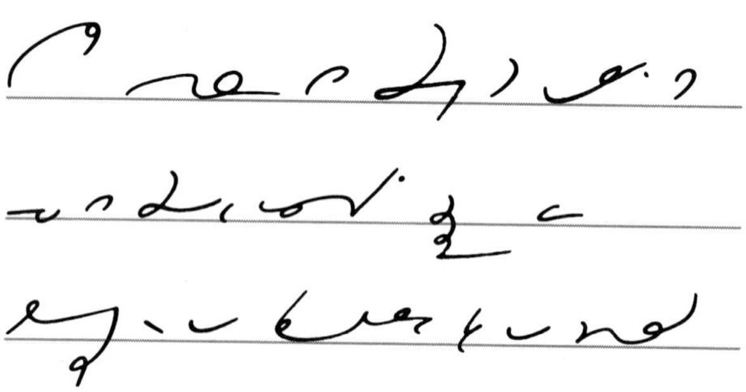

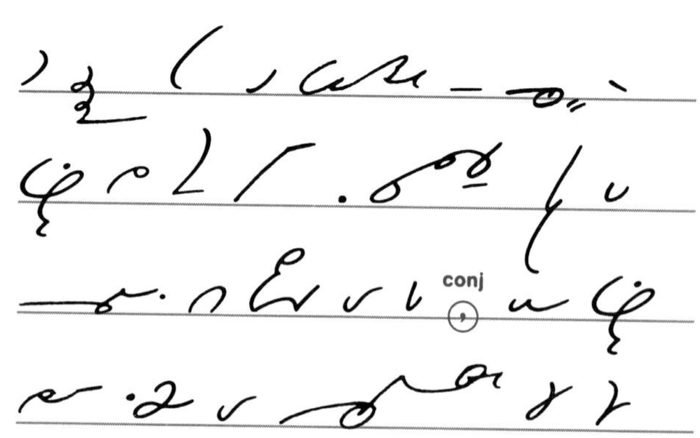

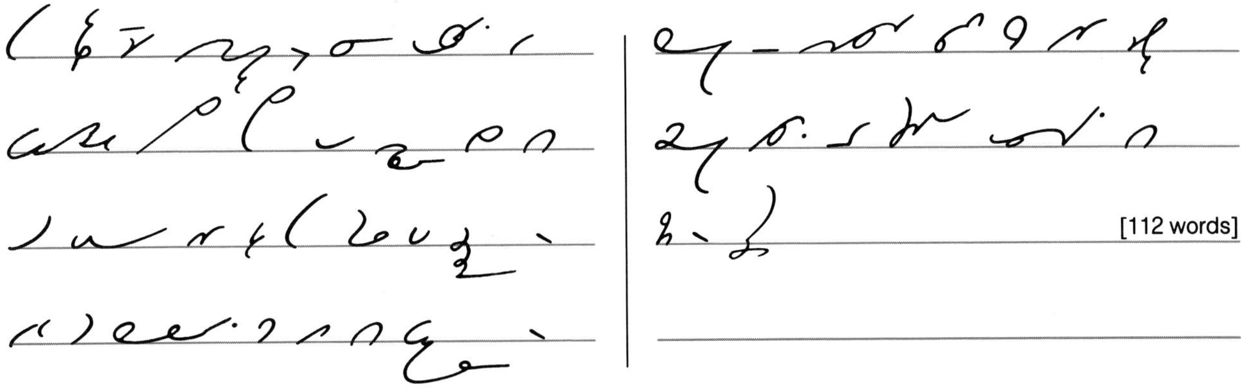

[112 words]

TRANSCRIPTION SKILL DEVELOPMENT

Transcription Warmup

Transcribe the following groups of words for speed and accuracy, applying transcription rules and assuring correct spelling.

66.2

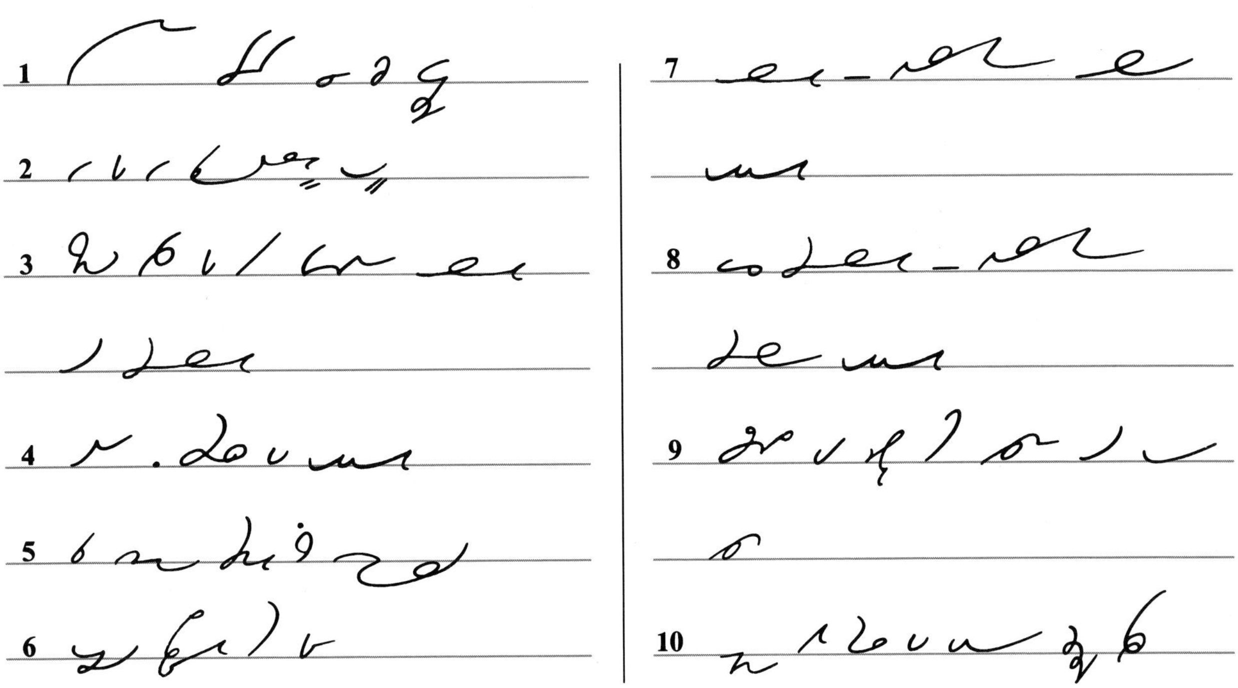

Transcription Practice

Transcribe the following letter for 2 minutes in unarranged format, applying transcription rules and assuring correct spelling. For every word not transcribed and every keyboarding error, deduct one word from the total word count.

66.3 Goal: 35 wam transcription rate

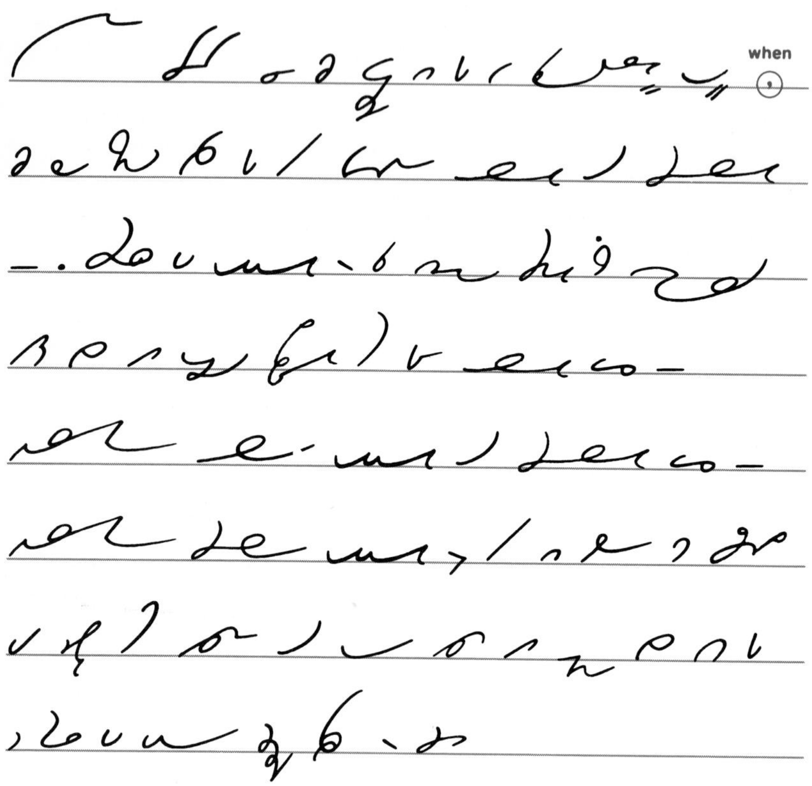

Word Count

13
25
37
48
56
66
79
88

Mailable Production

Transcribe the following mailable production memo, inserting punctuation prior to transcribing. Capitalize proper nouns and titles. Do not address a letter envelope. A memo would be placed in an interoffice envelope, and the information requested would be handwritten.

66.4 Time Limit: 15 minutes

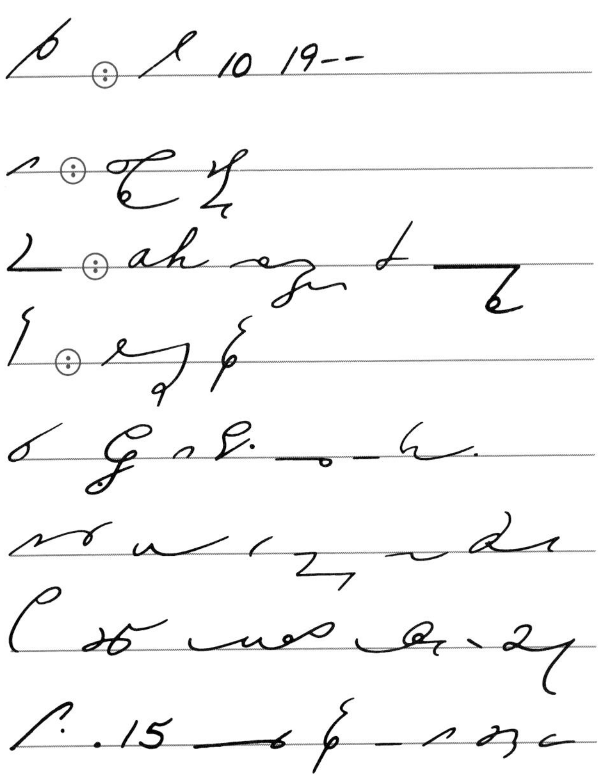

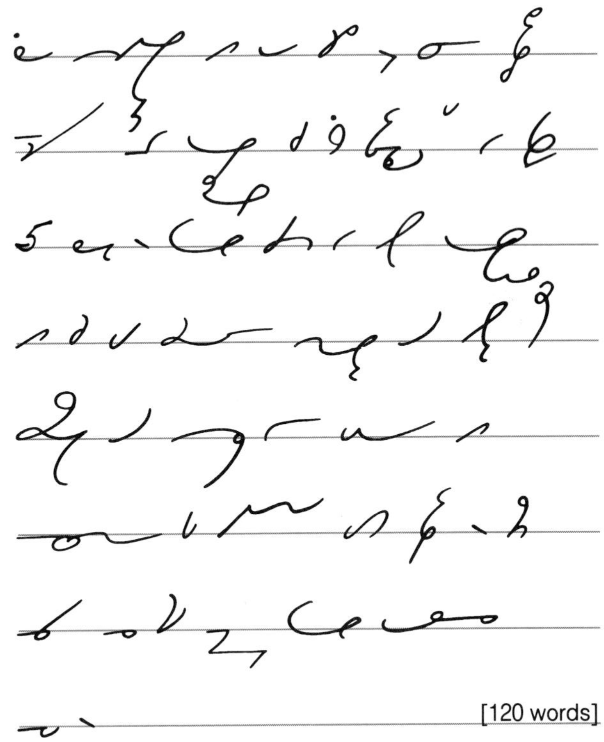

[120 words]

LESSON 67

WCAC-TV

DICTATION SPEED BUILDING

The shorthand outlines below appear in the speed dictation practice that follows. Practice writing these words using the shorthand outlines. Then, using the key that follows, dictate the words to yourself in preparation for the speed dictation practice.

Dictation Preview

Key: Ladies and Gentlemen, New York, developed, guidelines, equal, using, monitor, textbooks, university, stated, available, station, resources, appreciated, valuable, media, industry, send us

Speed Dictation Practice

67.1 Goal: 110 wam speed dictation

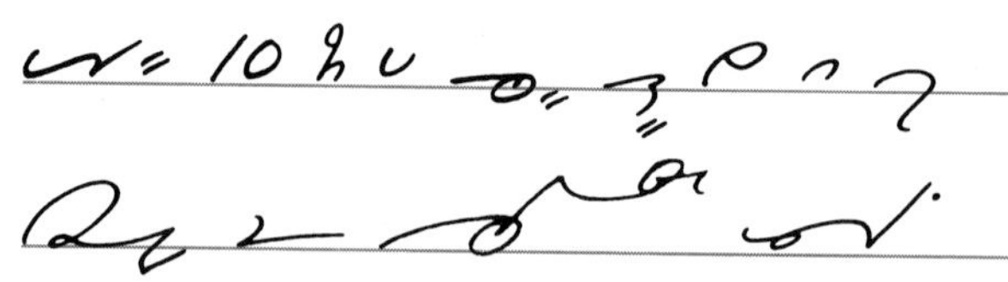

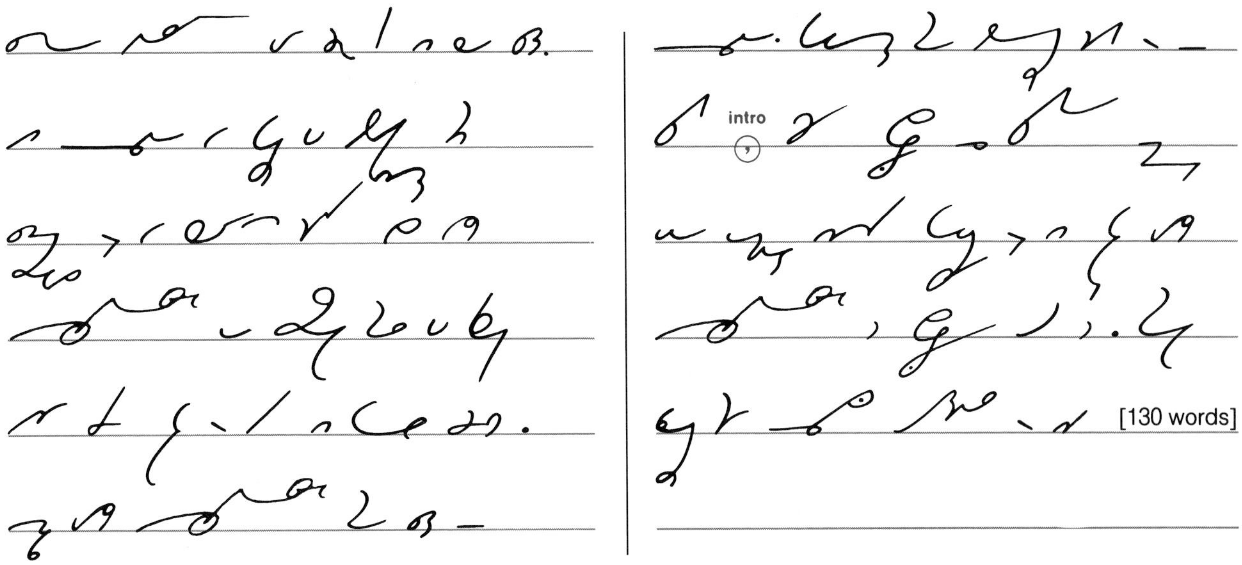

TRANSCRIPTION SKILL DEVELOPMENT

Transcription Warmup

Transcribe the following groups of words for speed and accuracy, applying transcription rules and assuring correct spelling.

67.2

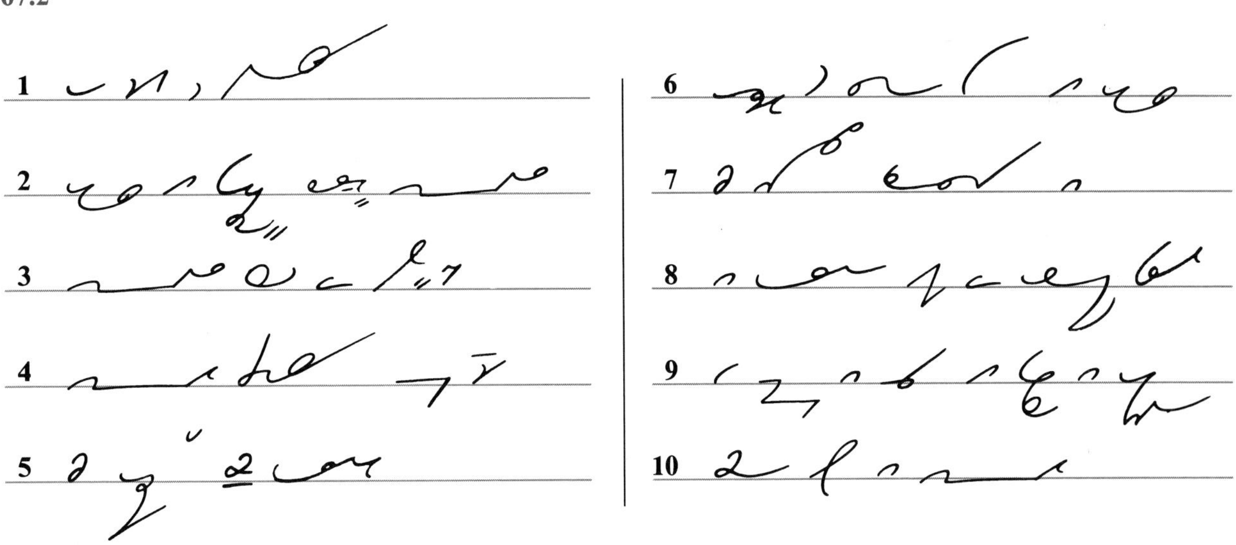

Transcription Practice

Transcribe the following letter for 2 minutes in unarranged format, applying transcription rules and assuring correct spelling. For every word not transcribed and every keyboarding error, deduct one word from the total word count.

67.3 Goal: 35 wam transcription rate

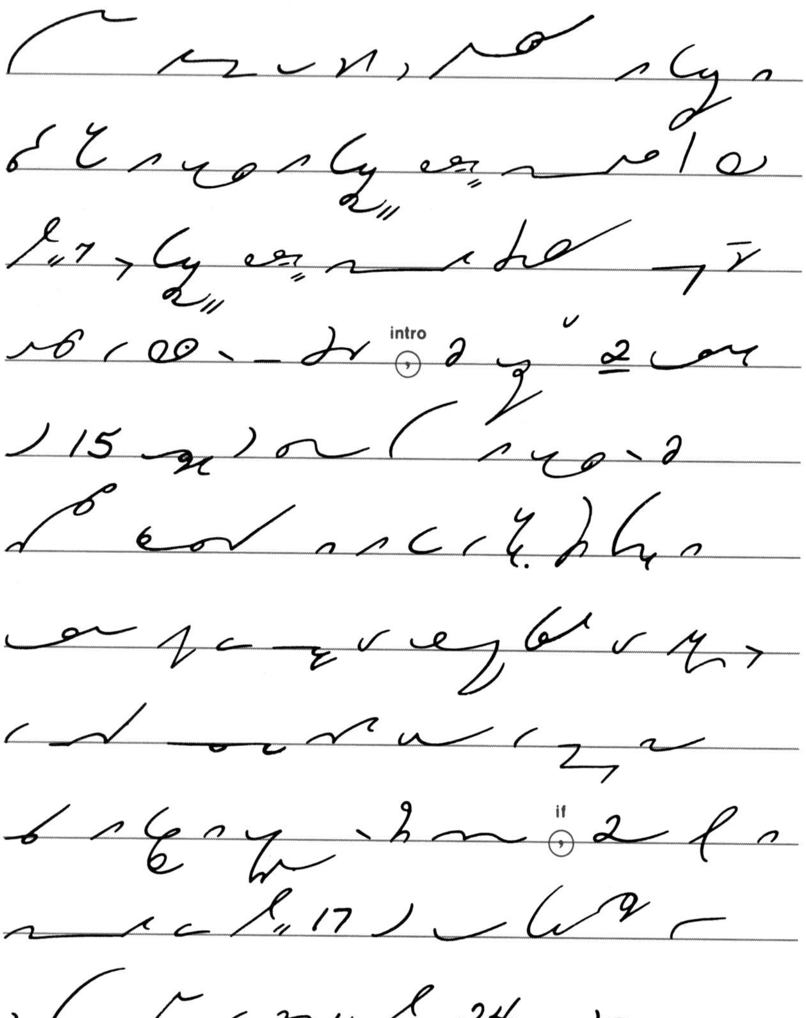

Word Count

11
26
38
51
60
73
85
97
110
119
131

Mailable Production

Transcribe the following mailable production letter in block style, assuring proper placement of all letter parts. Insert punctuation prior to transcribing, and capitalize proper nouns and titles. Address a large envelope with the special notation *Personal.*

67.4 Time Limit: 15 minutes

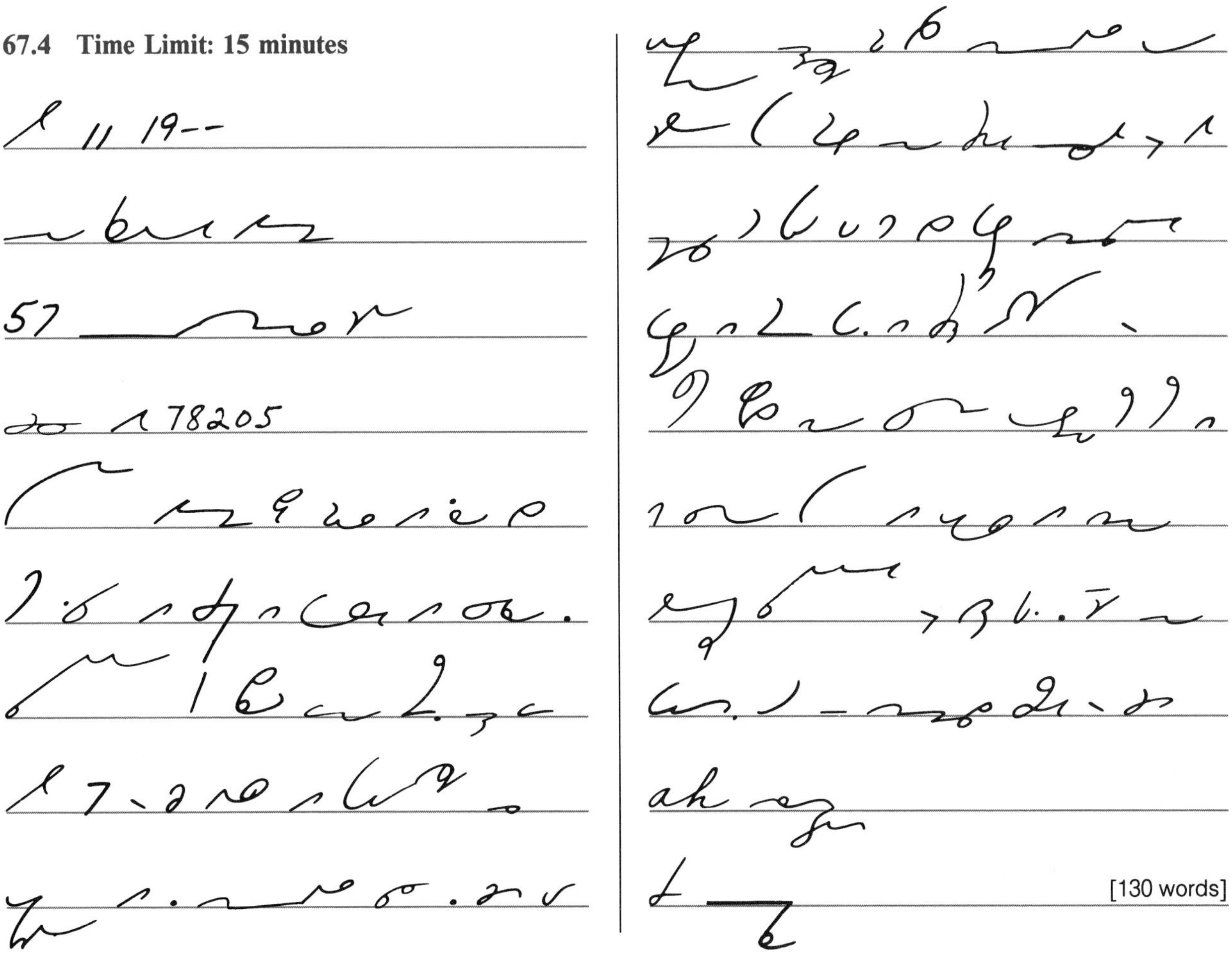

[130 words]

LESSON 68

WCAC-TV

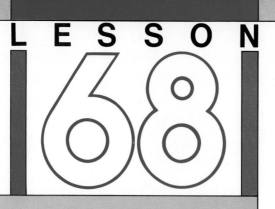

DICTATION SPEED BUILDING

The shorthand outlines below appear in the speed dictation practice that follows. Practice writing these words using the shorthand outlines. Then, using the key that follows, dictate the words to yourself in preparation for the speed dictation practice.

Dictation Preview

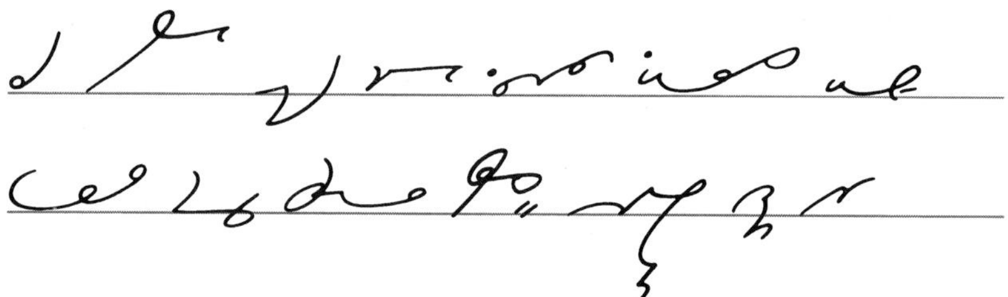

Key: end, details, informed, statements, hectic, holiday, always, plenty, format, finally, Diana, contributions, thank you for your, to the

Speed Dictation Practice

68.1 Goal: 110 wam speed dictation

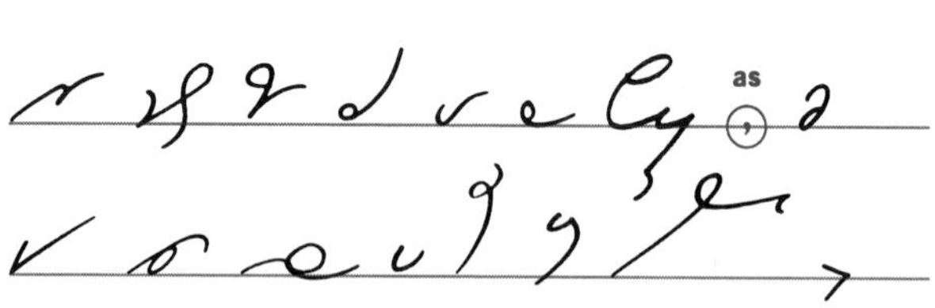

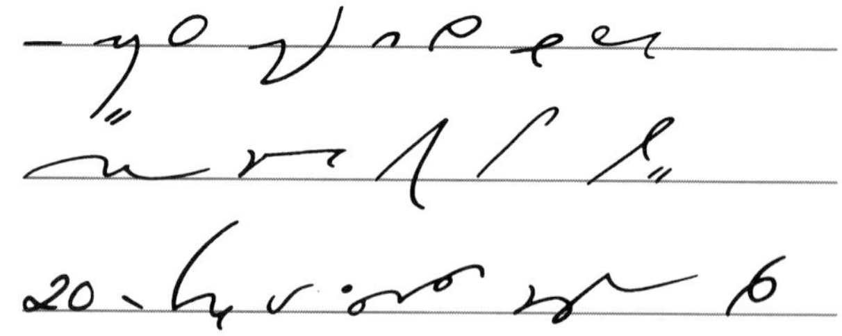

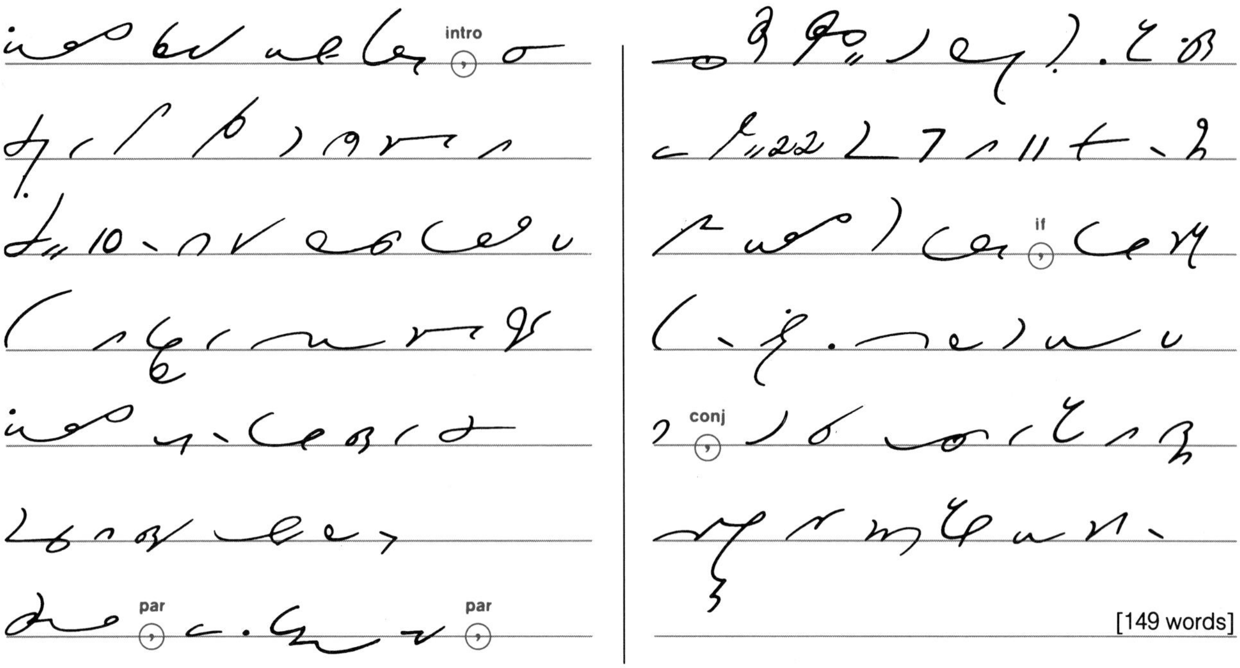

TRANSCRIPTION SKILL DEVELOPMENT

Transcription Warmup

Transcribe the following groups of words for speed and accuracy, applying transcription rules and assuring correct spelling.

68.2

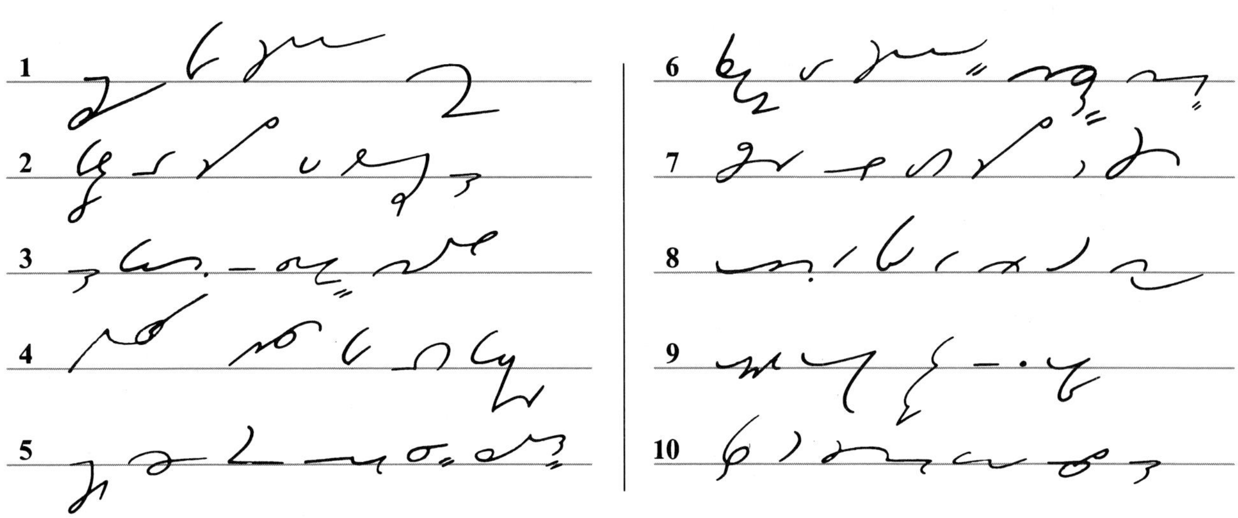

Transcription Practice

Transcribe the following memo for 2 minutes in unarranged format, applying transcription rules and assuring correct spelling. For every word not transcribed and every keyboarding error, deduct one word from the total wor count.

68.3 Goal: 35 wam transcription rate

Word Count
5
12
20
28
43
55
68
78
92
102
114
127
138

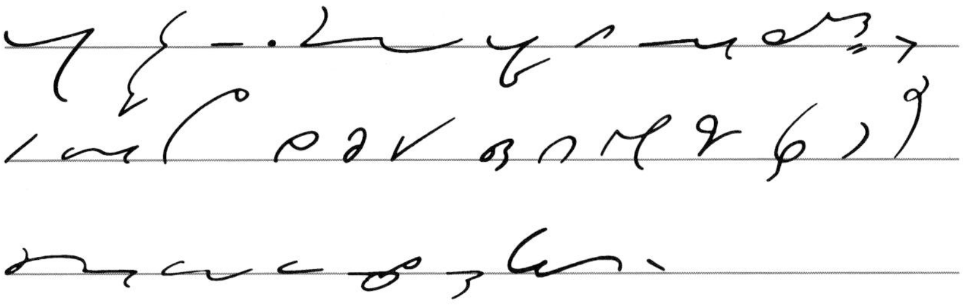

149

163

171

Mailable Production

Transcribe the following mailable production memo, inserting punctuation prior to transcribing. Capitalize proper nouns and titles. Do not address a letter envelope. A memo would be placed in an interoffice envelope, and the information requested would be handwritten.

68.4 Time Limit: 15 minutes

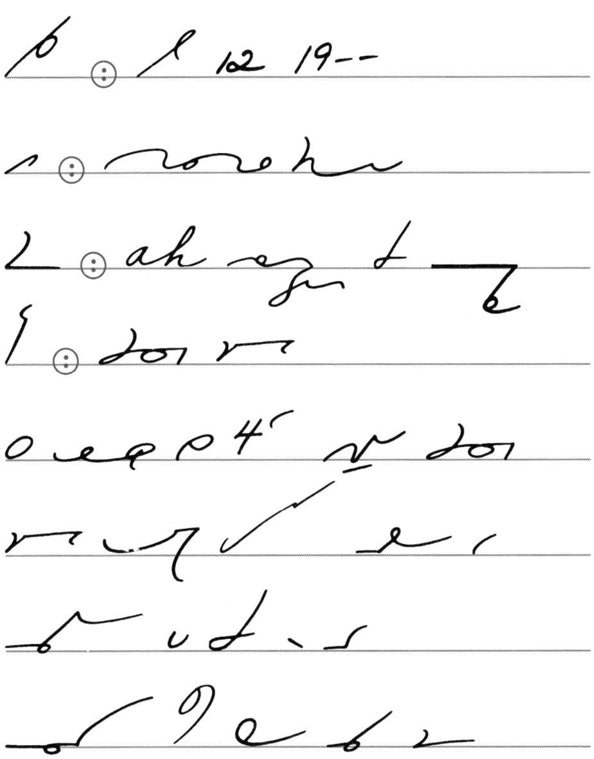

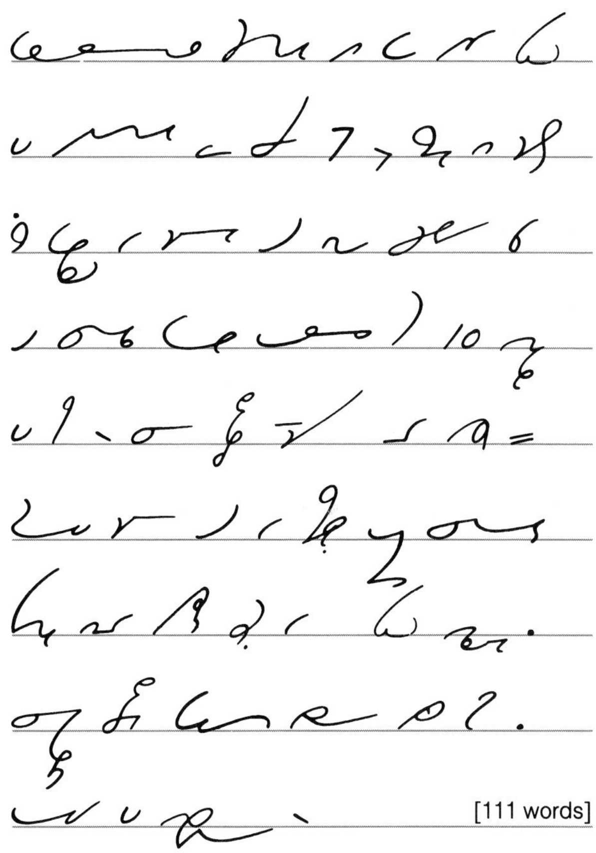

[111 words]

LESSON 69

WCAC-TV

DICTATION SPEED BUILDING

The shorthand outlines below appear in the speed dictation practice that follows. Practice writing these words using the shorthand outlines. Then, using the key that follows, dictate the words to yourself in preparation for the speed dictation practice.

Dictation Preview

Key: Anderson, associates, consulting, innovative, assess, potential, tremendous, station, imperative, identifying, candidates, feedback, strengths

Speed Dictation Practice

69.1 Goal: 110 wam speed dictation

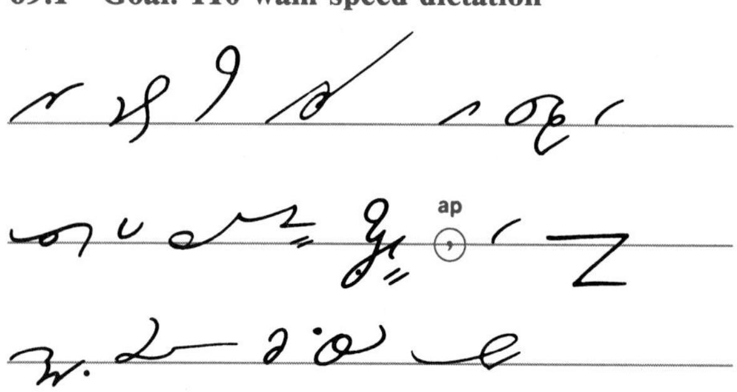

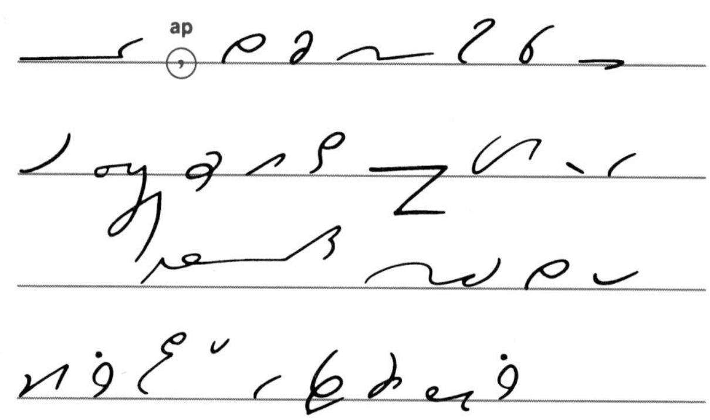

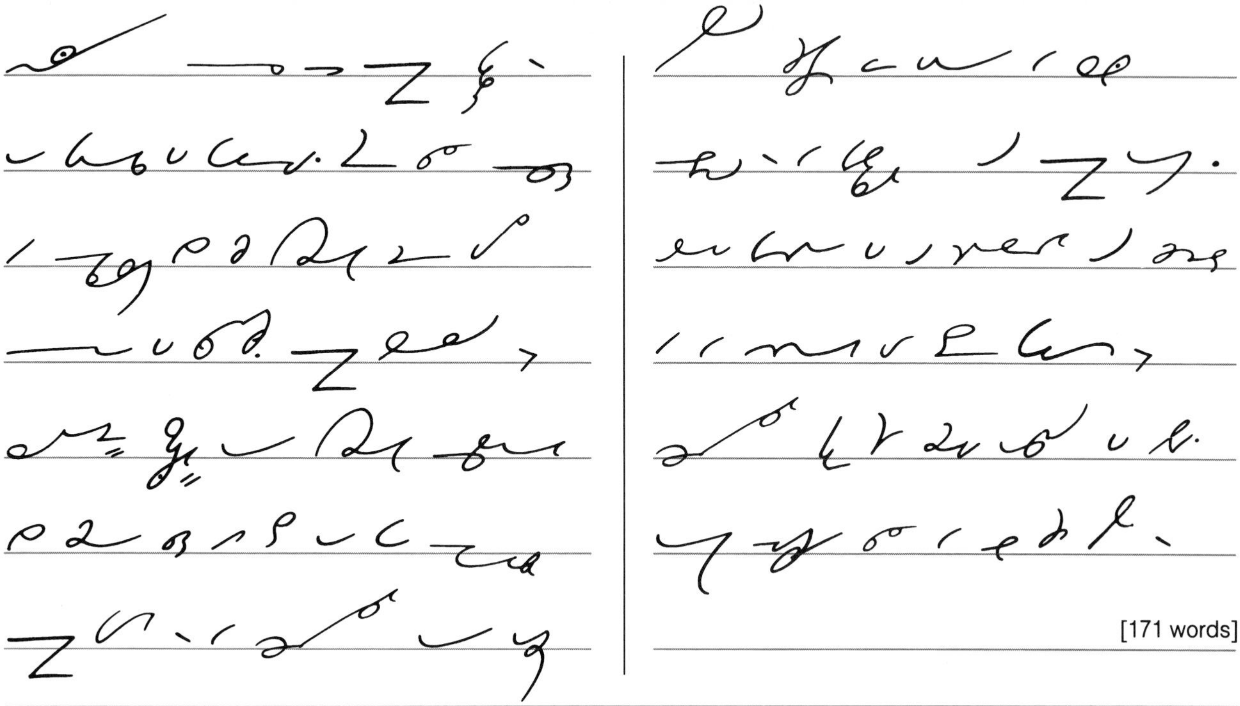

[171 words]

TRANSCRIPTION SKILL DEVELOPMENT

Transcription Warmup

Transcribe the following groups of words for speed and accuracy, applying transcription rules and assuring correct spelling.

69.2

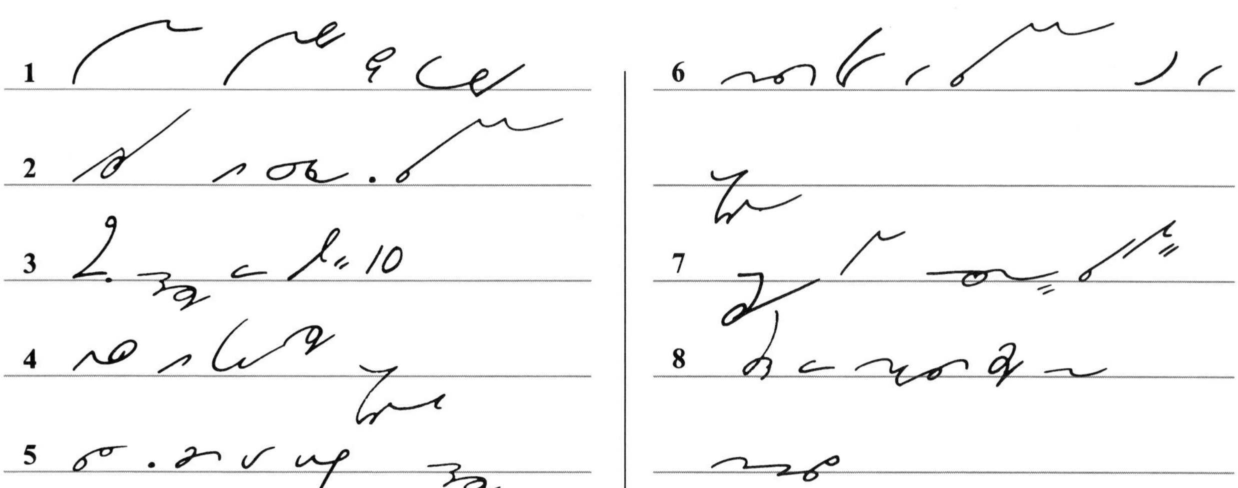

9 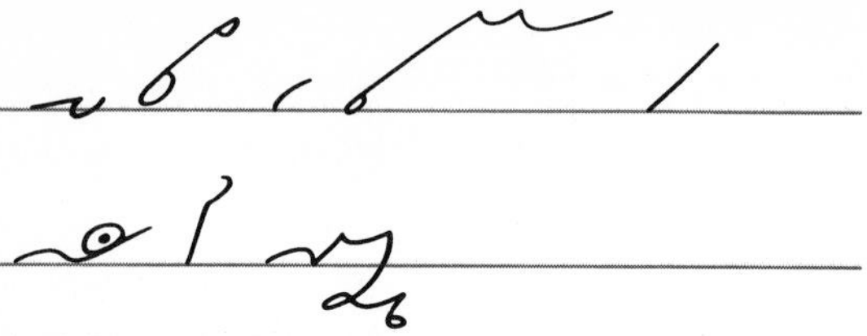

10 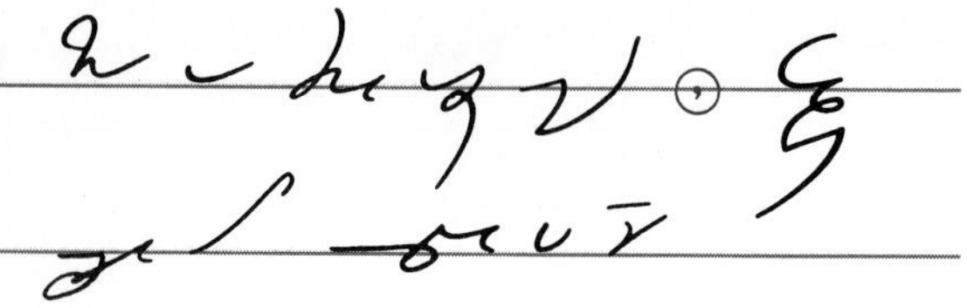

Transcription Practice

Transcribe the following letter for 2 minutes in unarranged format, applying transcription rules and assuring correct spelling. For every word not transcribed and every keyboarding error, deduct one word from the total word count.

69.3 Goal: 35 wam transcription rate

	Word Count
	11
	23
	34
	45
	59
	71
	81
	91
	103
	114
	124

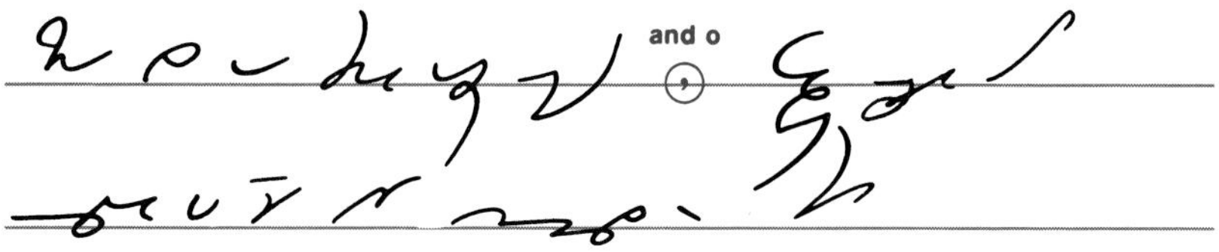

137

148

Mailable Production

Transcribe the following mailable production memo, inserting punctuation prior to transcribing. Capitalize proper nouns and titles. Do not address a letter envelope. A memo would be placed in an interoffice envelope, and the information requested would be handwritten.

69.4 Time Limit: 15 minutes

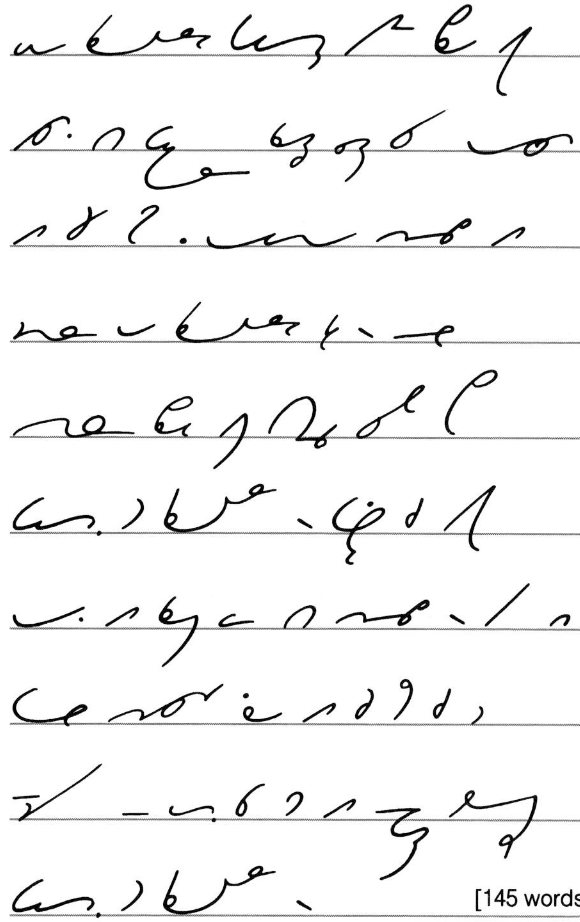

[145 words]

LESSON 70

WCAC-TV

DICTATION SPEED BUILDING

The shorthand outlines below appear in the speed dictation practice that follows. Practice writing these words using the shorthand outlines. Then, using the key that follows, dictate the words to yourself in preparation for the speed dictation practice.

Dictation Preview

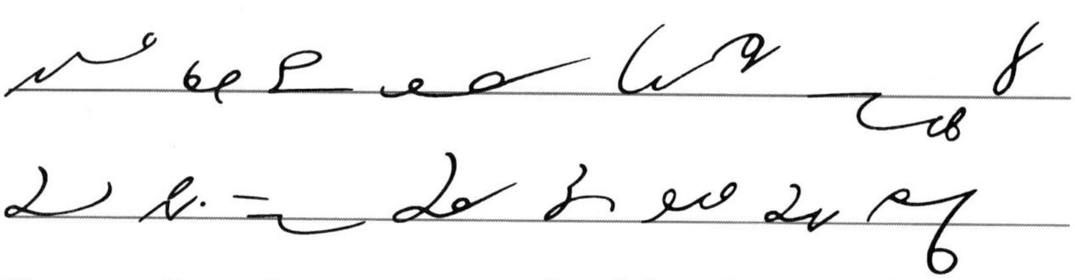

Key: totally, series, assessment, related, broadcast, employee, particular, field testing, internal, varied, subsequent, thoroughly, first, they will be able

Speed Dictation Practice

70.1 Goal: 110 wam speed dictation

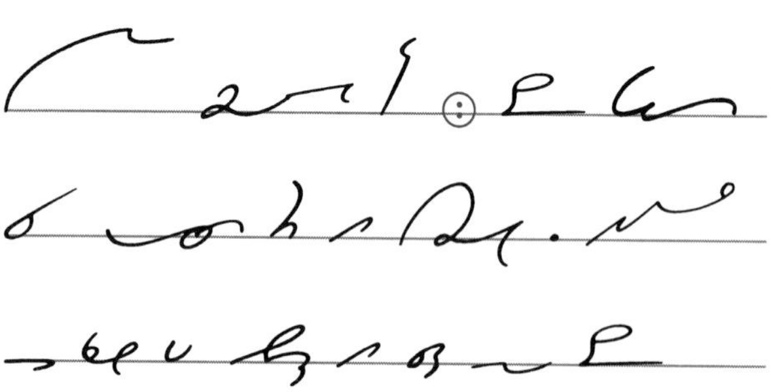

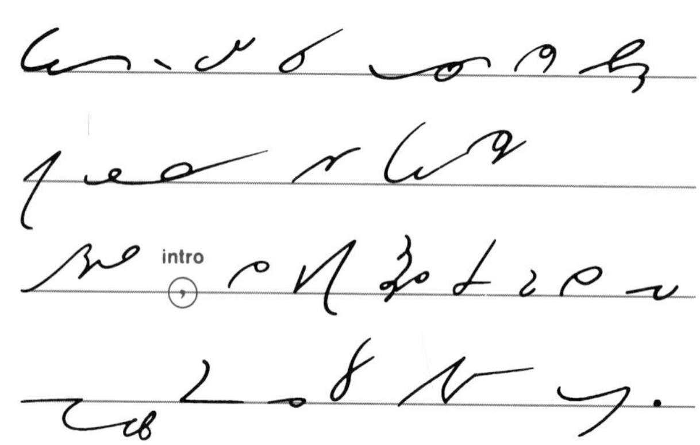

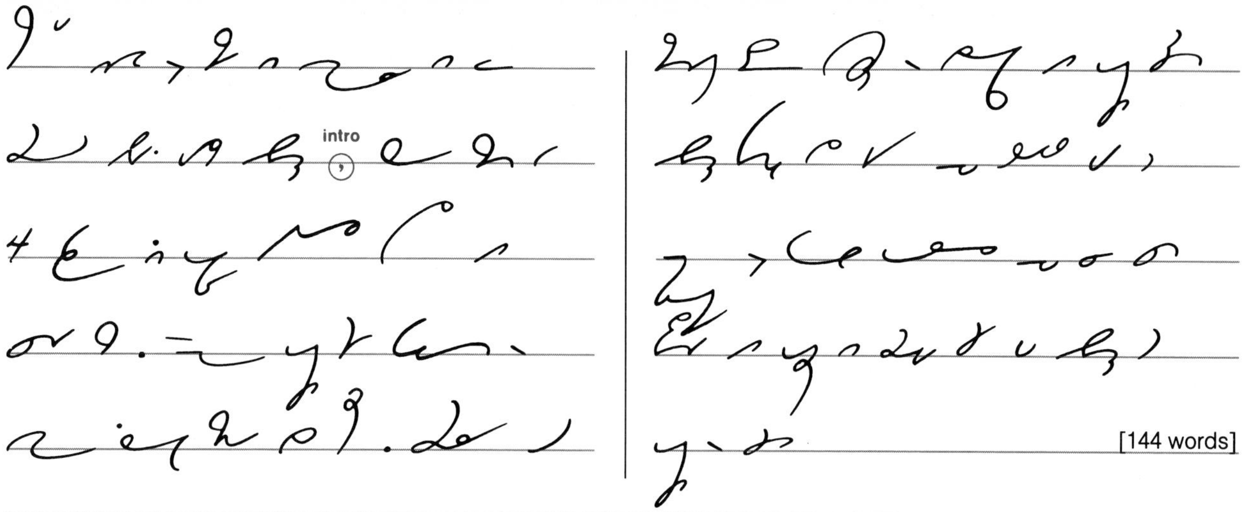

TRANSCRIPTION SKILL DEVELOPMENT

Transcription Warmup

Transcribe the following groups of words for speed and accuracy, applying transcription rules and assuring correct spelling.

70.2

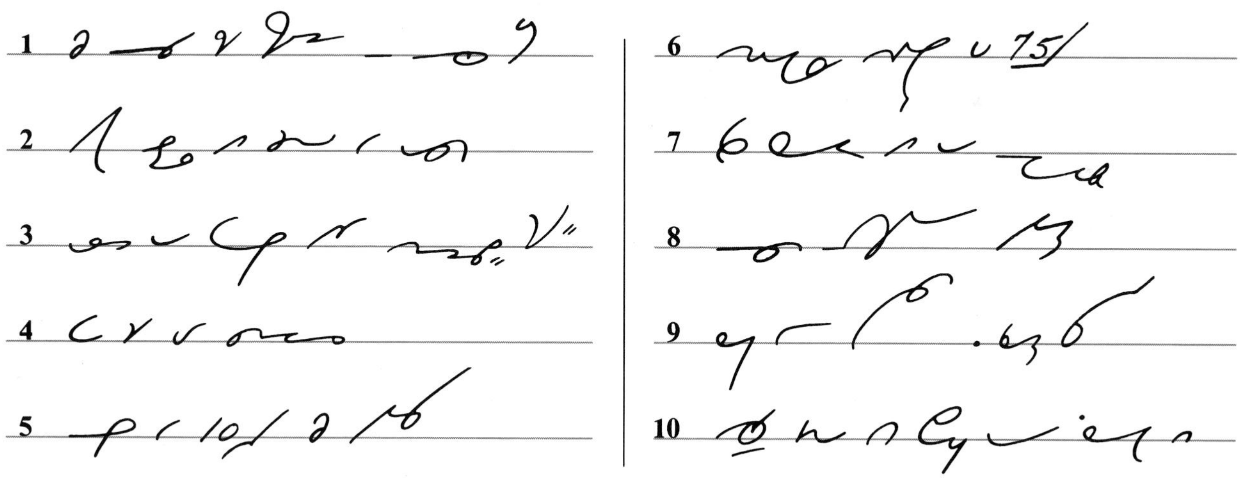

Transcription Practice

Transcribe the following letter for 2 minutes in unarranged format, applying transcription rules and assuring correct spelling. For every word not transcribed and every keyboarding error, deduct one word from the total word count.

70.3 Goal: 35 wam transcription rate

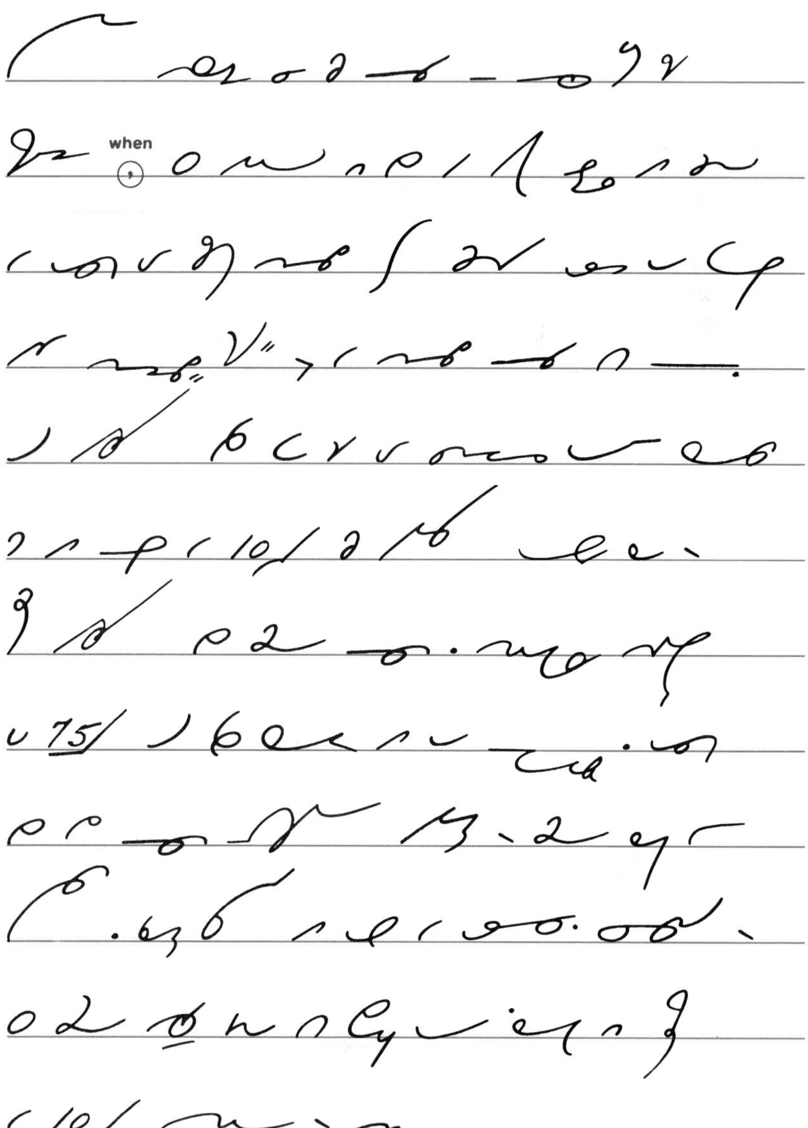

Word Count

10
22
36
47
60
69
81
93
104
115
126
133

Mailable Production

Transcribe the following mailable production memo, inserting punctuation prior to transcribing. Capitalize proper nouns and titles. Do not address a letter envelope. A memo would be placed in an interoffice envelope, and the information requested would be handwritten.

70.4 Time Limit: 15 minutes

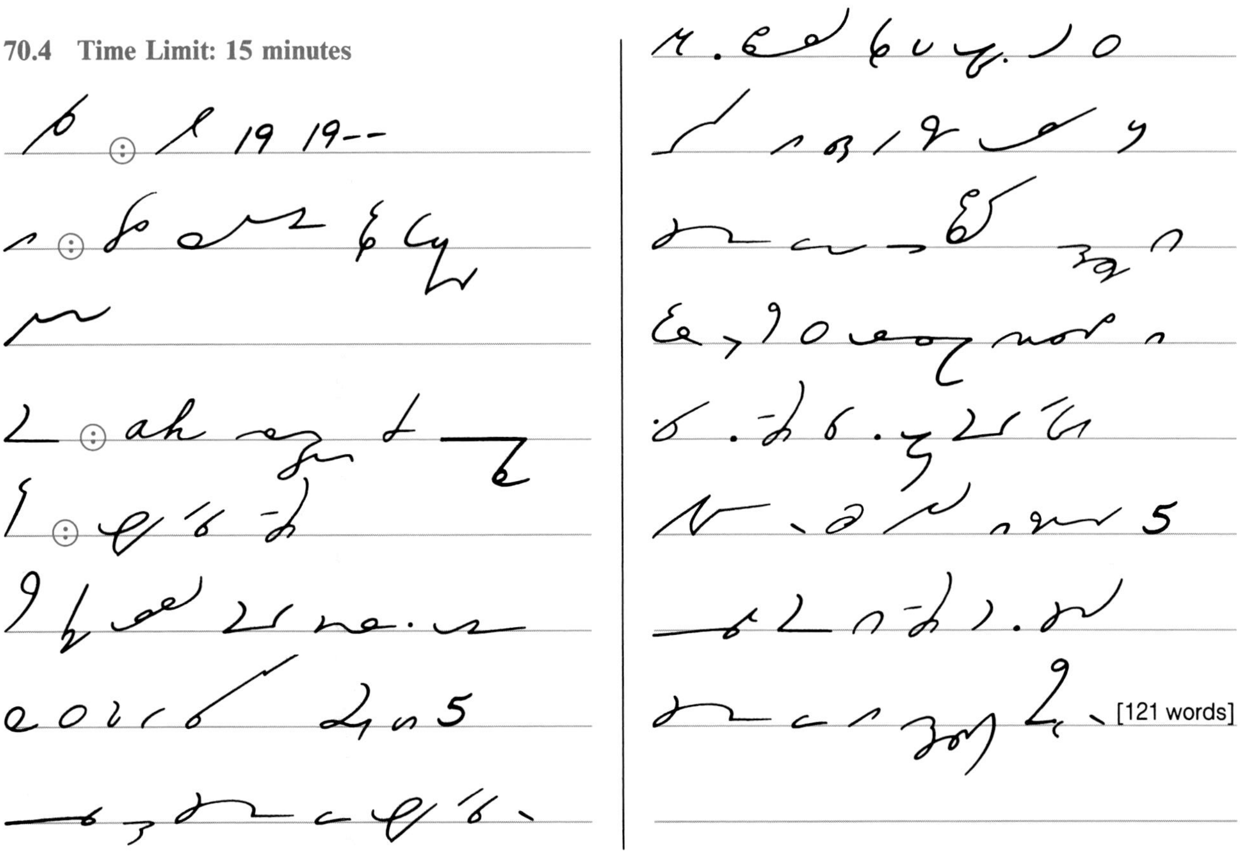

[121 words]

LESSON 71

WCAC-TV

DICTATION SPEED BUILDING

The shorthand outlines below appear in the speed dictation practice that follows. Practice writing these words using the shorthand outlines. Then, using the key that follows, dictate the words to yourself in preparation for the speed dictation practice.

Dictation Preview

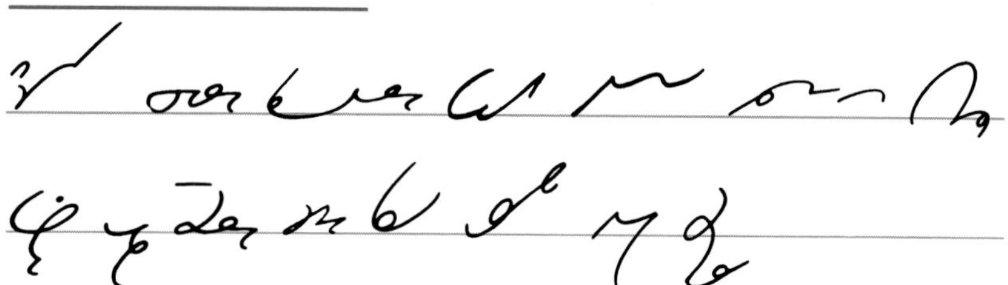

Key: understand, annoyance, children's, production, director, technical, difficulties, perhaps, reception, interference, citizen's band radio, trouble, favorite

Speed Dictation Practice

71.1 Goal: 110 wam speed dictation

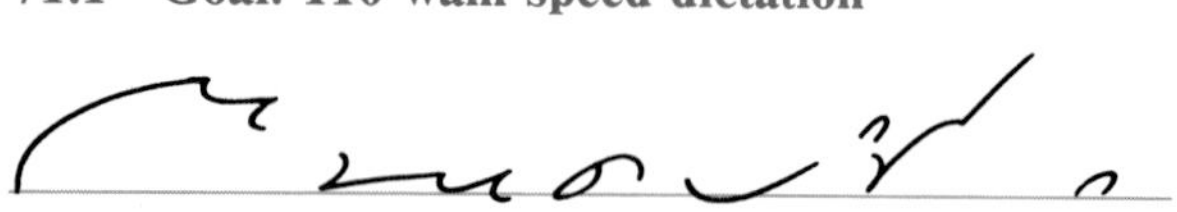

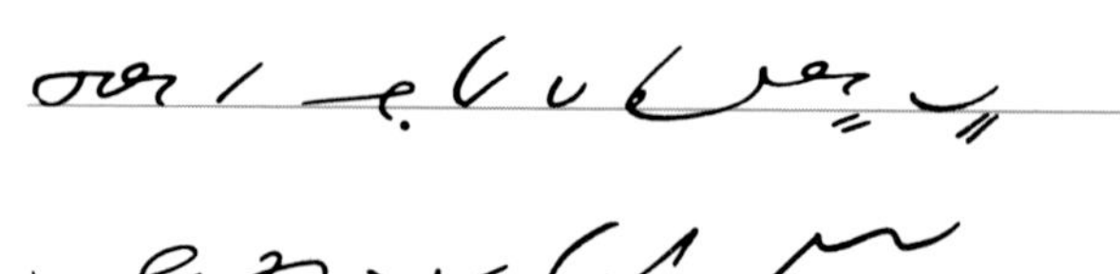

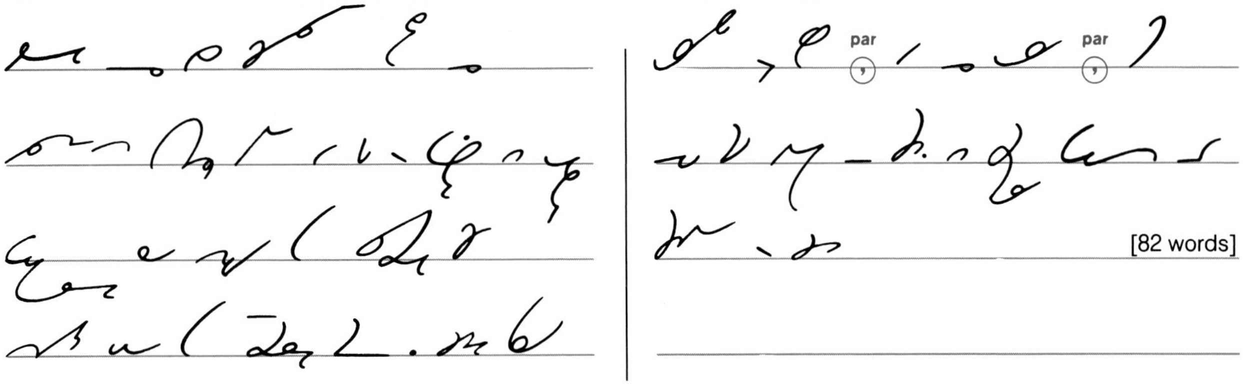

TRANSCRIPTION SKILL DEVELOPMENT

Transcription Warmup

Transcribe the following groups of words for speed and accuracy, applying transcription rules and assuring correct spelling.

71.2

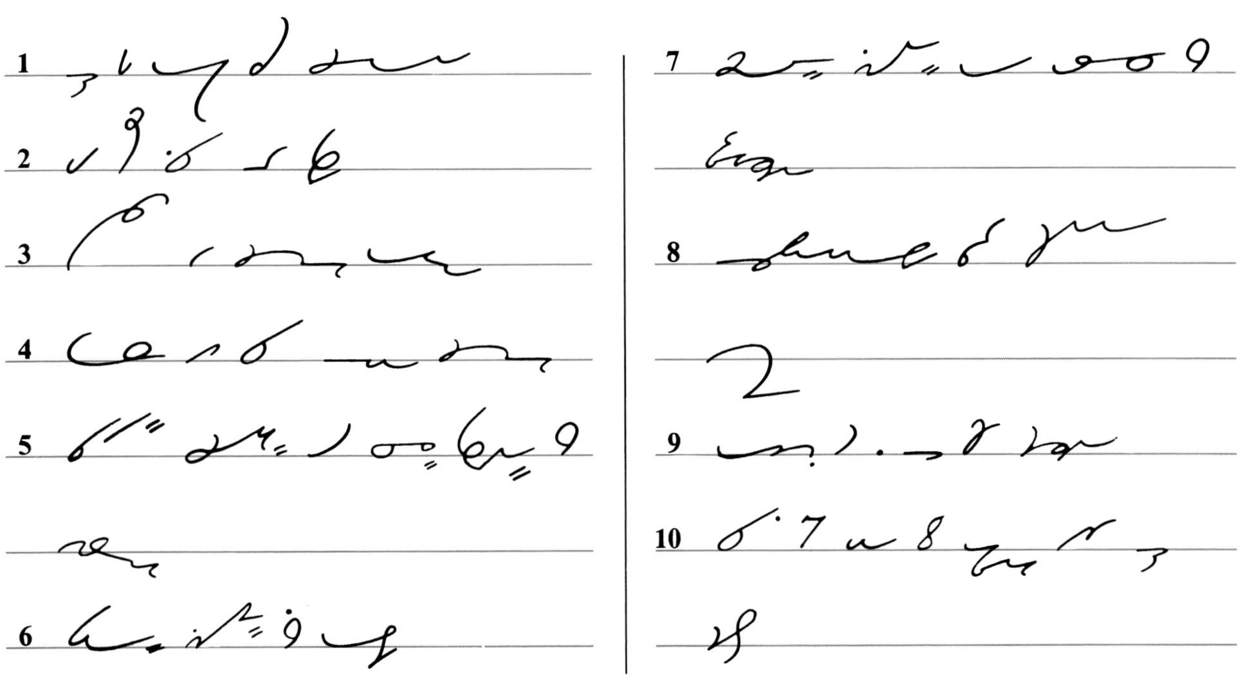

Transcription Practice

Transcribe the following memo for 2 minutes in unarranged format, applying transcription rules and assuring correct spelling. For every word not transcribed and every keyboarding error, deduct one word from the total word count.

71.3 Goal: 35 wam transcription rate

Word Count

5
9
17
23
35
47
56
65
74
83
92
103
116

Mailable Production

Transcribe the following mailable production letter in block style, assuring proper placement of all letter parts. Insert punctuation prior to transcribing, and capitalize proper nouns and titles. Address a large envelope.

71.4 Time Limit: 15 minutes

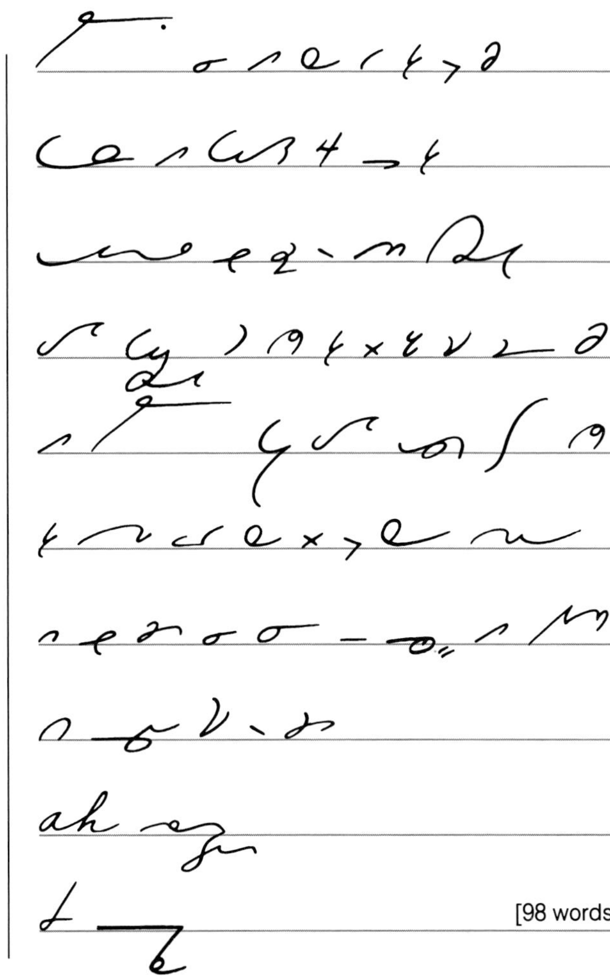

[98 words]

LESSON 72

WCAC-TV

DICTATION SPEED BUILDING

The shorthand outlines below appear in the speed dictation practice that follows. Practice writing these words using the shorthand outlines. Then, using the key that follows, dictate the words to yourself in preparation for the speed dictation practice.

Dictation Preview

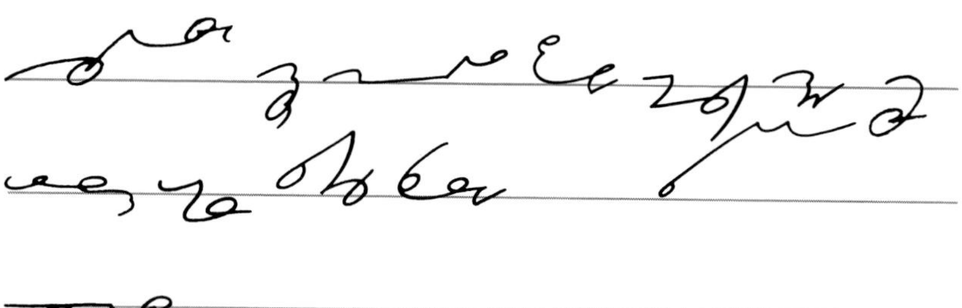

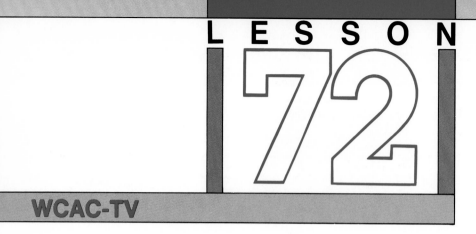

Key: guidelines, concise, commentary, explicit, informative, consult, confine, remarks, refrain, advocate, balanced, editorial, memorize

Speed Dictation Practice

72.1 Goal: 110 wam speed dictation

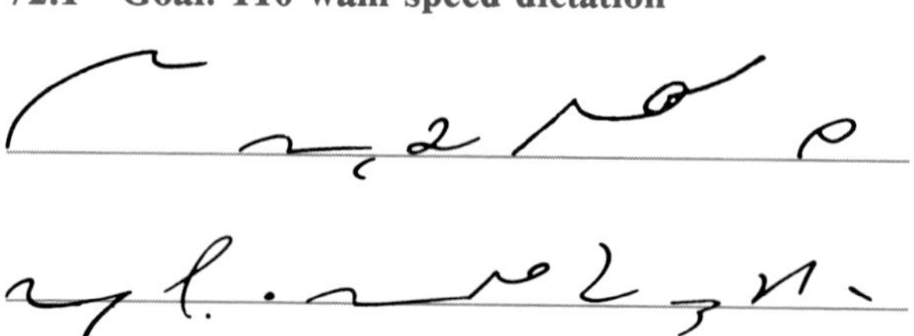

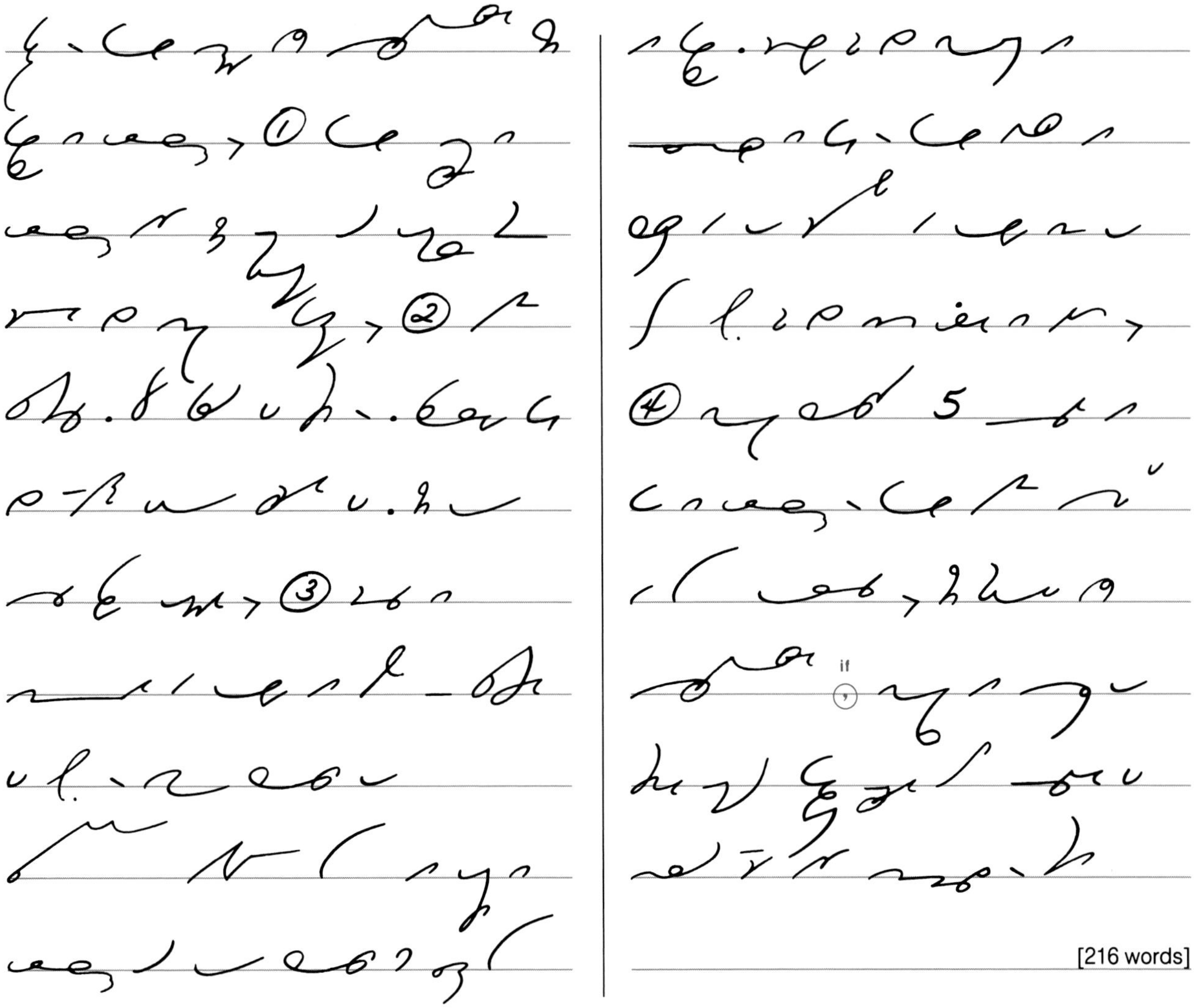

[216 words]

TRANSCRIPTION SKILL DEVELOPMENT

Transcription Warmup

Transcribe the following groups of words for speed and accuracy, applying transcription rules and assuring correct spelling.

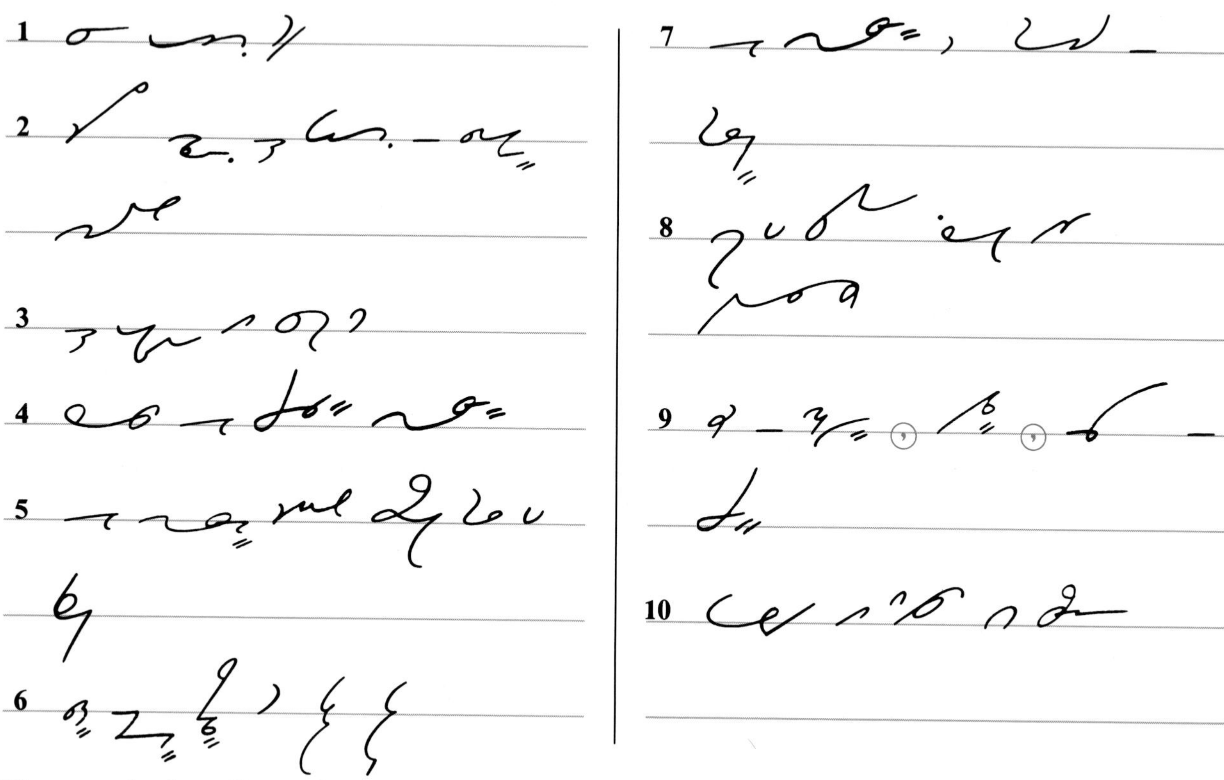

Transcription Practice

Transcribe the following letter for 2 minutes in unarranged format, applying transcription rules and assuring correct spelling. For every word not transcribed and every keyboarding error, deduct one word from the total word count.

72.3 Goal: 35 wam transcription rate

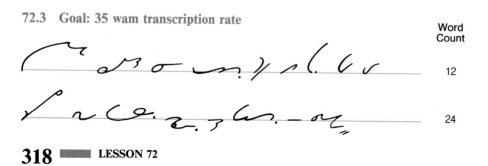

Word Count

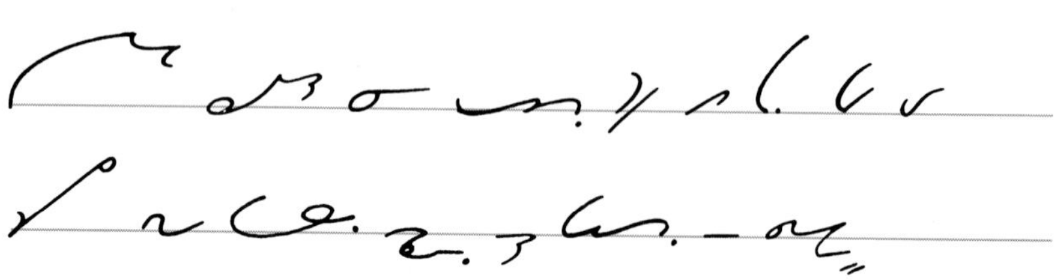

12

24

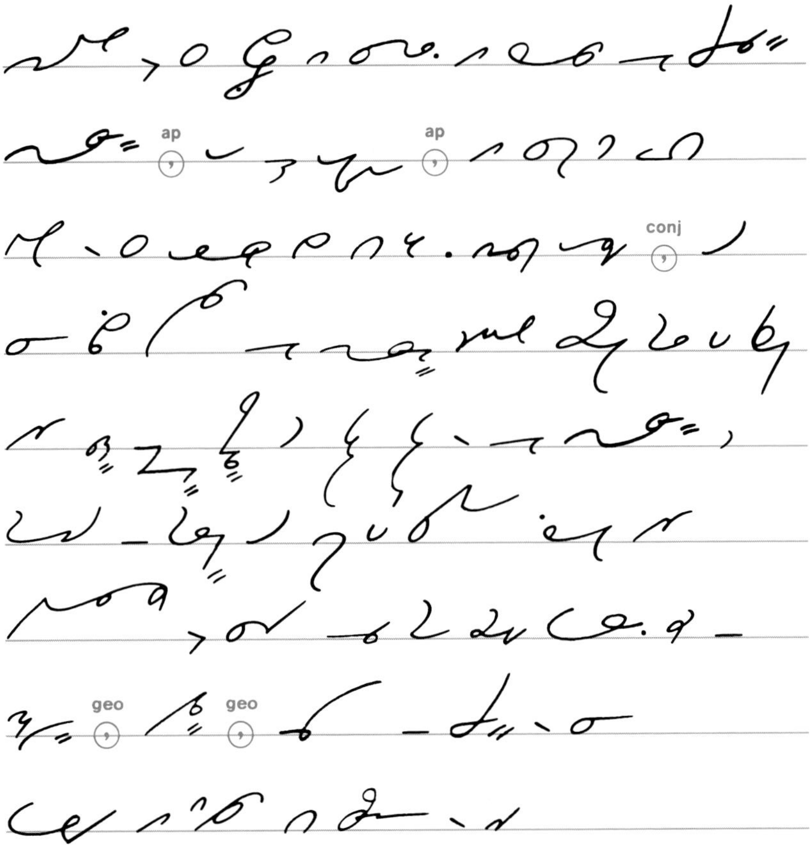

36

46

56

69

85

96

108

116

126

Mailable Production

Transcribe the following mailable production memo, inserting punctuation prior to transcribing. Capitalize proper nouns and titles. Do not address a letter envelope. A memo would be placed in an interoffice envelope, and the information requested would be handwritten.

72.4 Time Limit: 15 minutes

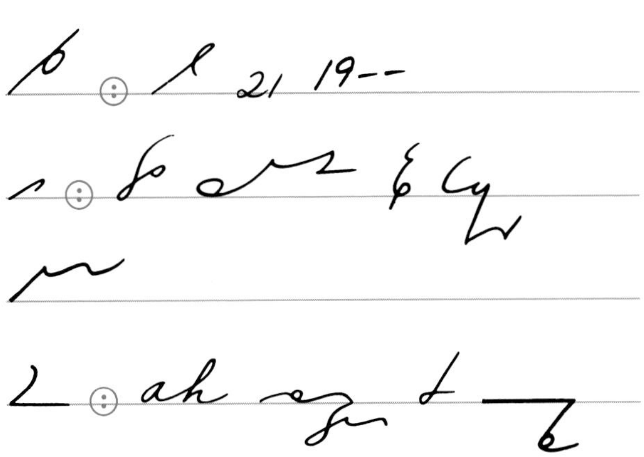

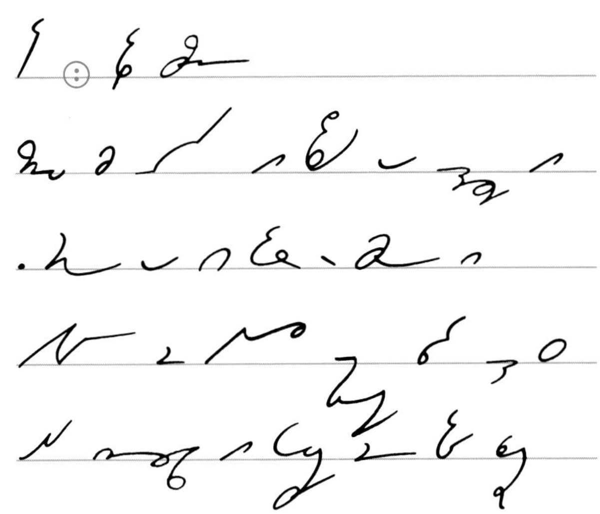

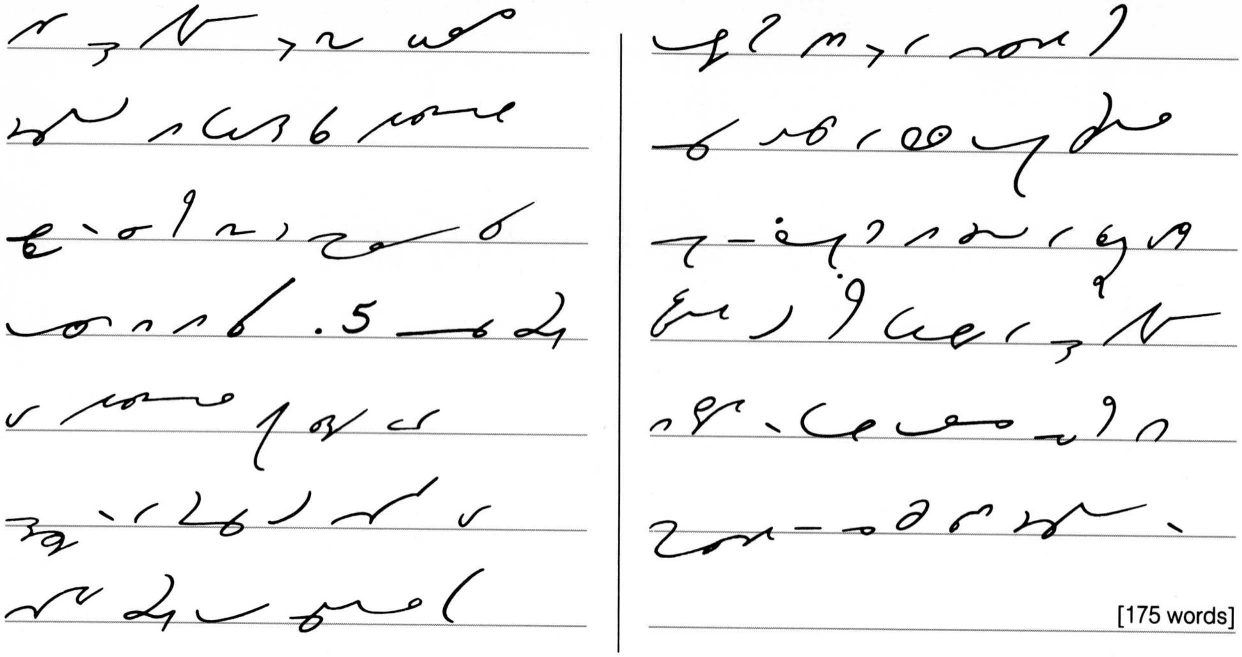

[175 words]

UNIT X

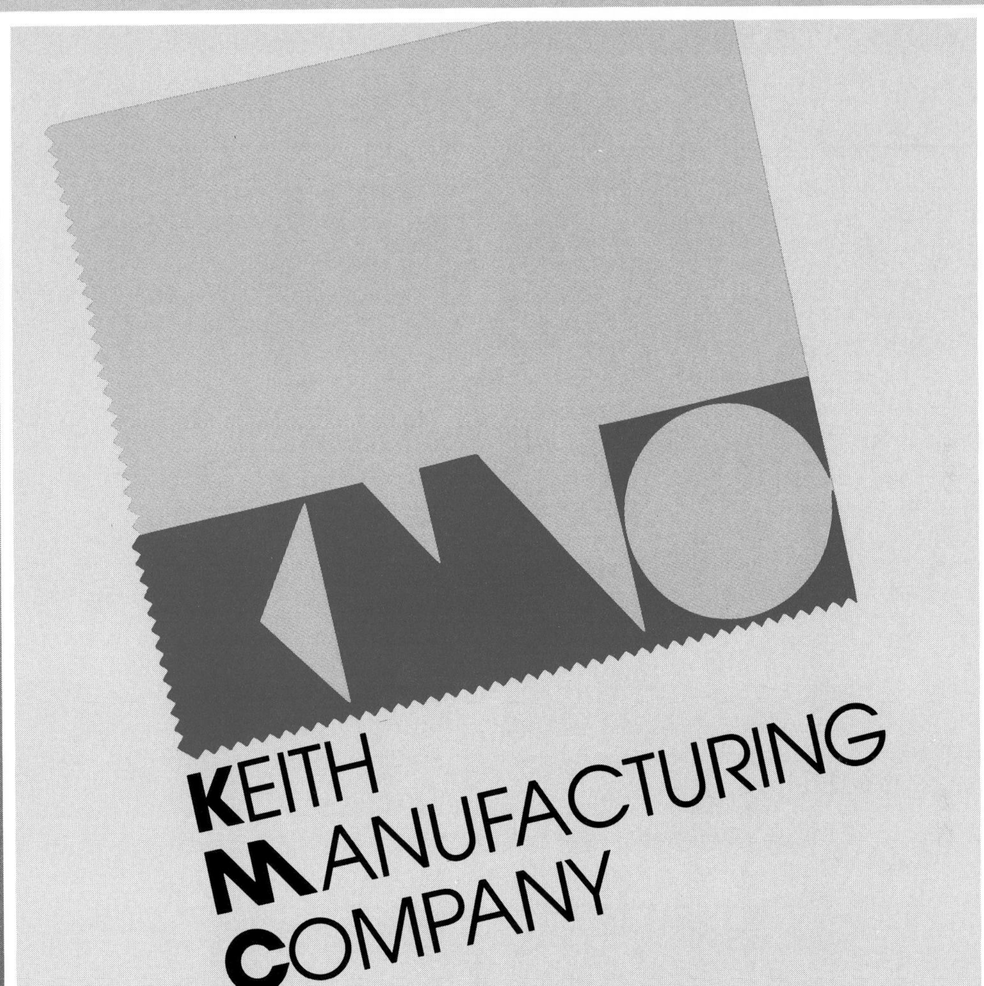

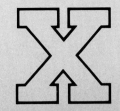

LESSON 73

KEITH MANUFACTURING COMPANY

You are employed as an administrative assistant for Keith Manufacturing Company, a textile manufacturing company located in Sacramento, California. You work in the health services area and report to Dr. Doris Graham, director of the Medical Department at Keith Manufacturing.

Dr. Graham has general responsibility for handling employees' medical problems. She conducts emergency treatment of minor illnesses and injuries incurred on the job, and she refers employees to specialists for medical problems. Dr. Graham also maintains all medical records and reviews claims of employees seeking indemnity from the company for job-related illnesses.

Your duties include speaking with employees from all departments of the company who have various injuries or illnesses, keeping an up-to-date medical history of each employee, taking dictation, and typing correspondence. The records for each employee are stored on database software, and correspondence is typed with word processing software using a microcomputer.

Interoffice Memos

Most of the correspondence you will type in this unit will be in the form of interoffice memos. Sometimes the lines containing *To* and *From* information may contain a person's name, title, and department. Below is an example of how these lines should appear.

```
  1"
-----> Date:     March 5, 19-- ↓ 2

       To:       David Baxter, Director
                 Personnel Department ↓ 2

       From:     Dr. Doris Graham, Director
                 Medical Department

       Subject:  Medical Treatment
```

DICTATION SPEED BUILDING

The shorthand outlines below appear in the speed dictation practice that follows. Practice writing these words using the shorthand outlines. Then, using the key that follows, dictate the words to yourself in preparation for the speed dictation practice.

Dictation Preview

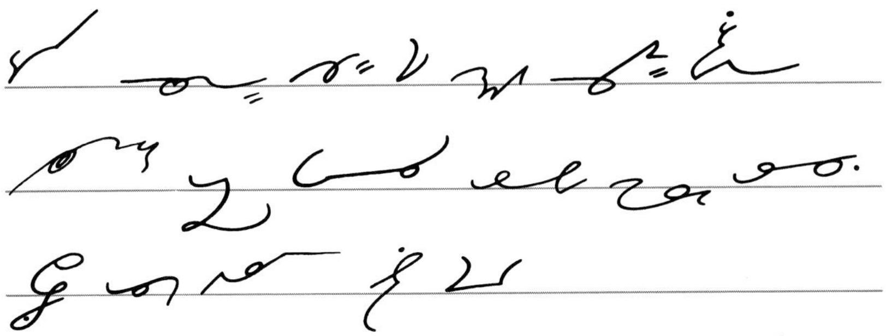

Key: sustained, Michael, Keith, further, consultation, Madison, hospital, diagnosis, revealed, permanent, released, complains, remaining, appreciate, recommendation, treatment, it has been, from the

Speed Dictation Practice

73.1 Goal: 110 wam speed dictation

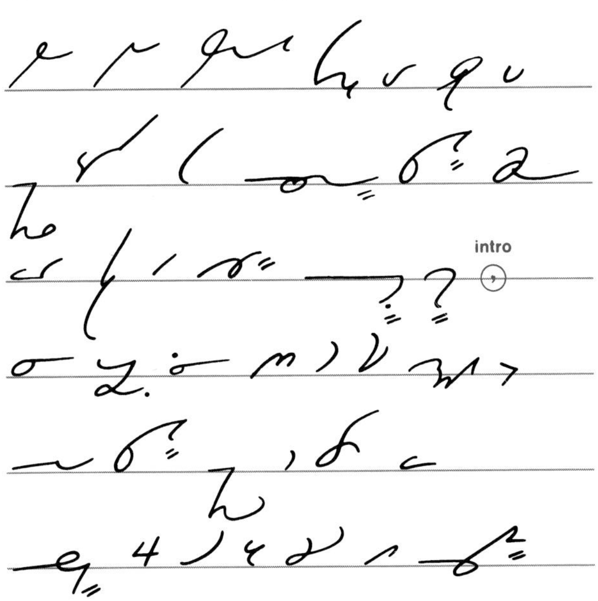

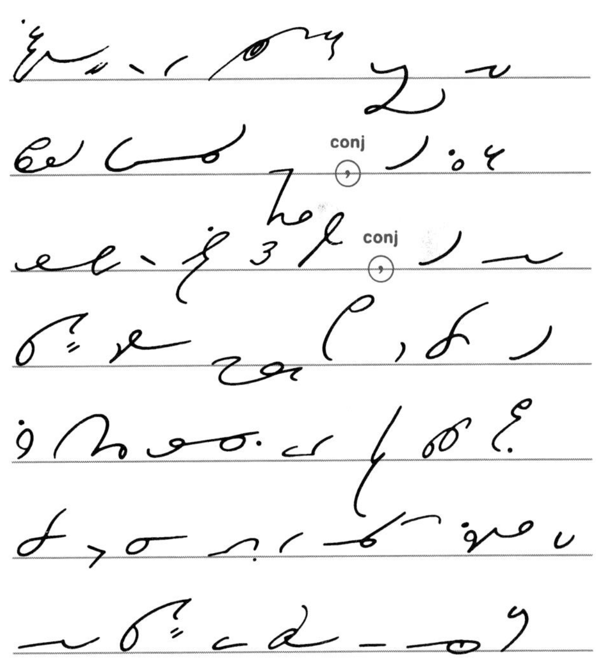

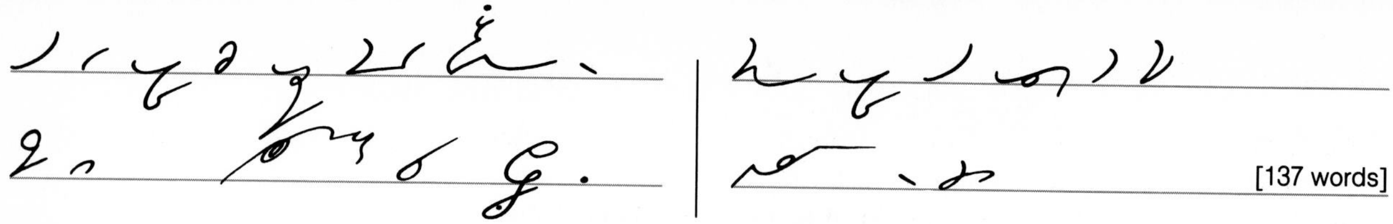

[137 words]

TRANSCRIPTION SKILL DEVELOPMENT

Transcription Warmup

Transcribe the following groups of words for speed and accuracy, applying transcription rules and assuring correct spelling.

73.2

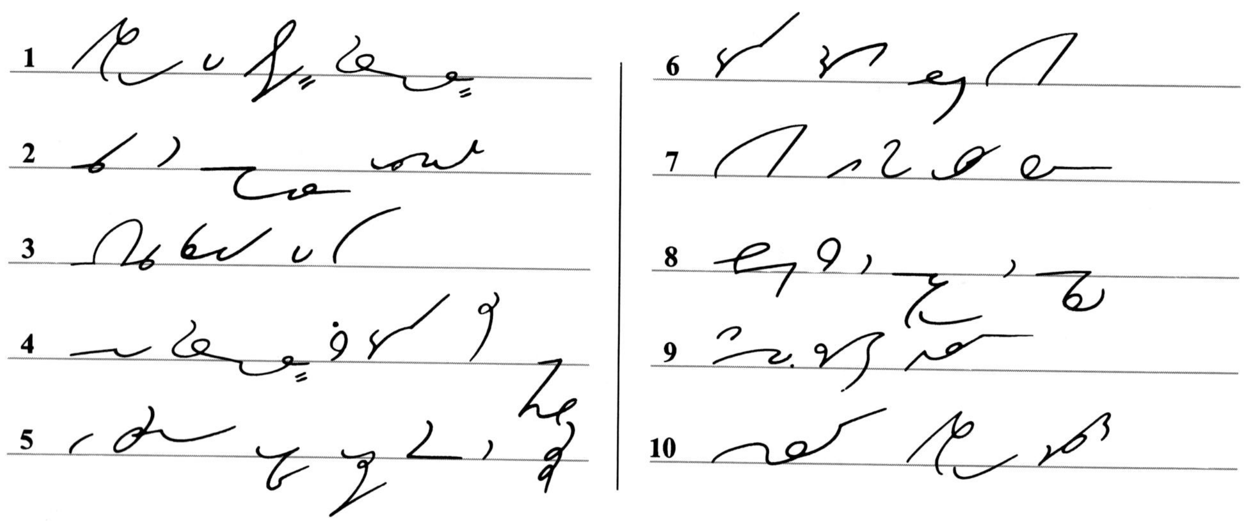

Transcription Practice

Transcribe the following memo for 2 minutes in unarranged format, applying transcription rules and assuring correct spelling. For every word not transcribed and every keyboarding error, deduct one word from the total word count.

73.3 Goal: 40 wam transcription rate

Word Count

133

139

LESSON 74

KEITH MANUFACTURING COMPANY

DICTATION SPEED BUILDING

The shorthand outlines below appear in the speed dictation practice that follows. Practice writing these words using the shorthand outlines. Then, using the key that follows, dictate the words to yourself in preparation for the speed dictation practice.

Dictation Preview

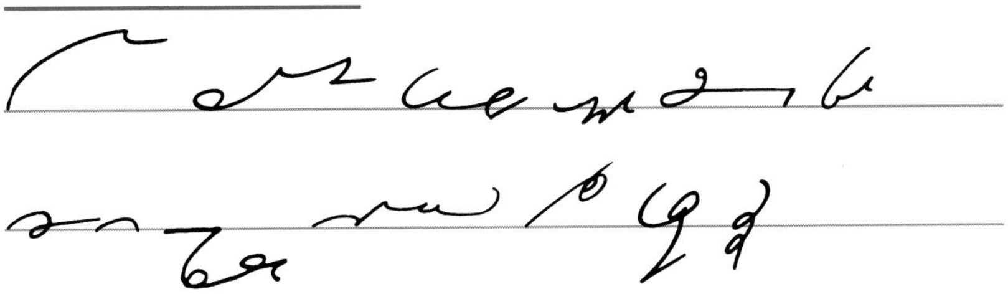

Key: Dear Mr. Anderson, promised, results, examination, bothers, chemical, imbalance, controlled, diet, private, physician

Speed Dictation Practice

74.1 Goal: 110 wam speed dictation

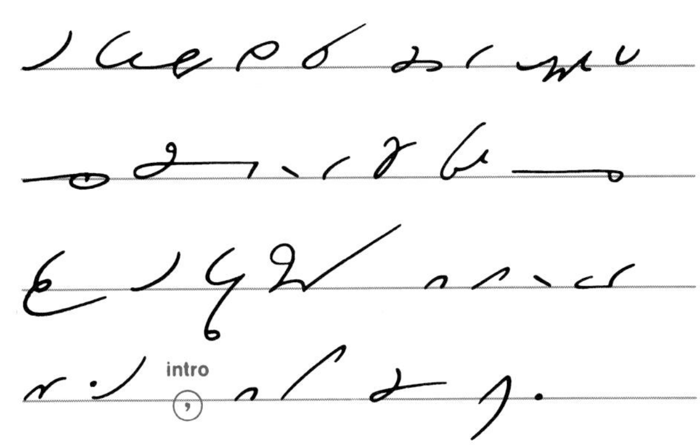

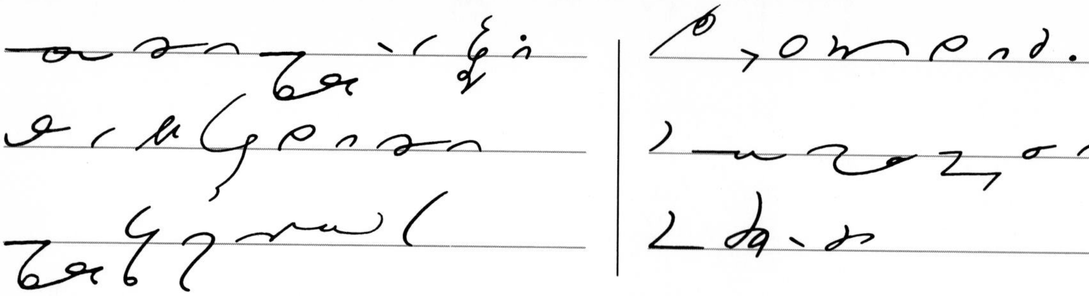

[112 words]

TRANSCRIPTION SKILL DEVELOPMENT

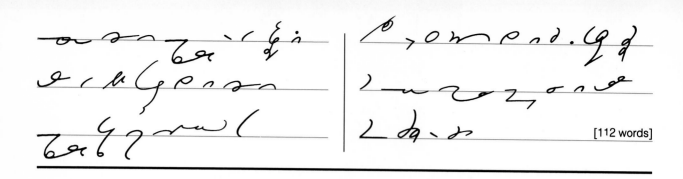

Transcription Warmup

Transcribe the following groups of words for speed and accuracy, applying transcription rules and assuring correct spelling.

74.2

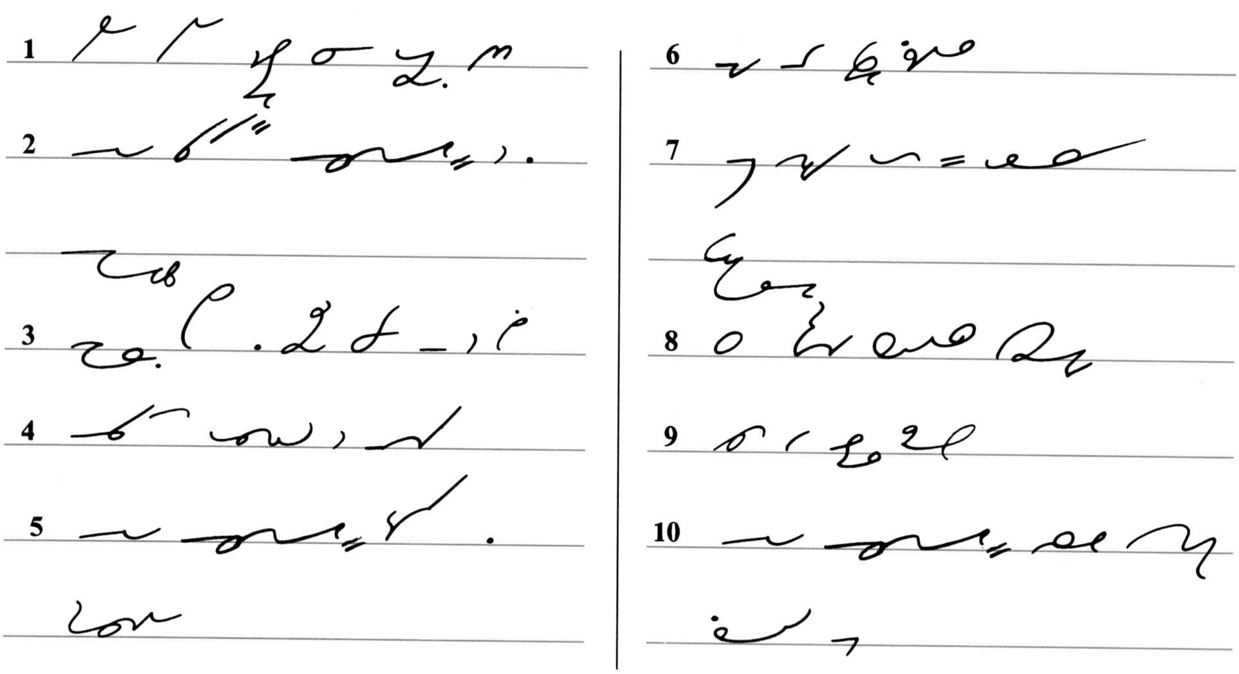

Transcription Practice

Transcribe the following letter for 2 minutes in unarranged format, applying transcription rules and assuring correct spelling. For every word not transcribed and every keyboarding error, deduct one word from the total word count.

74.3 Goal: 40 wam transcription rate

Word Count

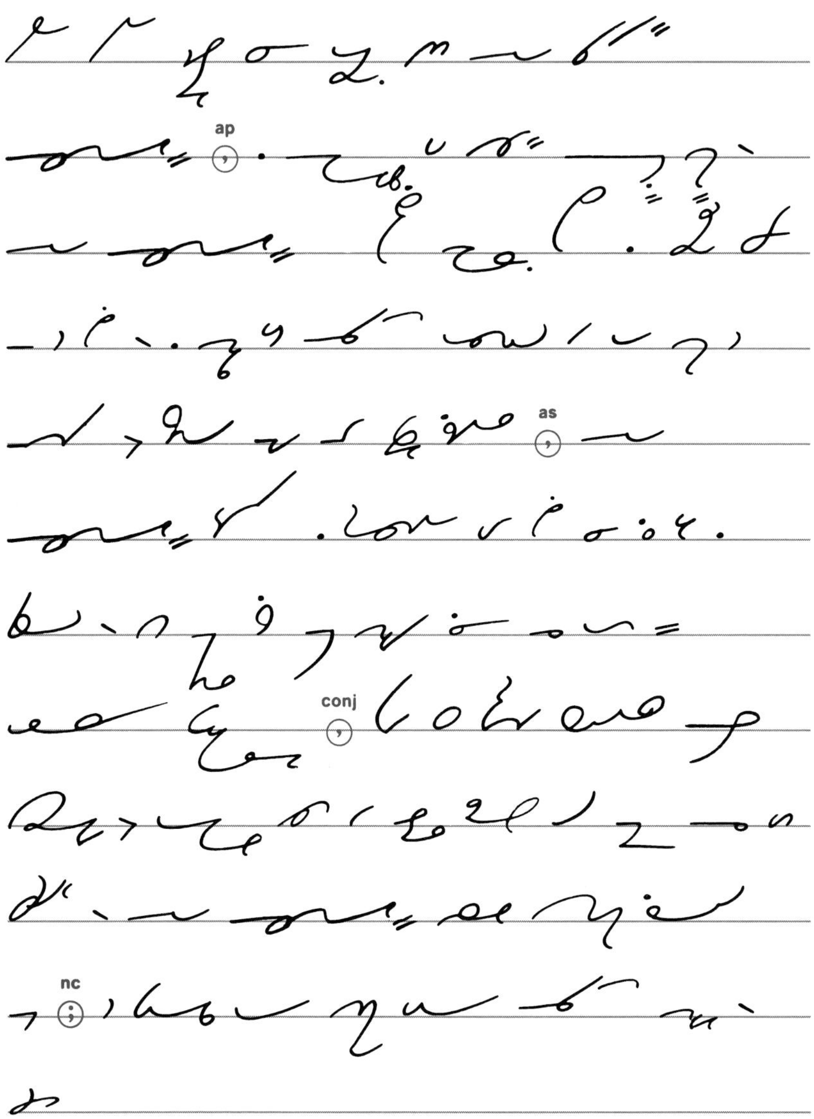

10
21
31
43
54
65
75
85
95
104
114
117

Mailable Production

Transcribe the following mailable production memo, inserting punctuation prior to transcribing. Capitalize proper nouns and titles. Do not address a letter envelope. A memo would be placed in an interoffice envelope, and the information requested would be handwritten.

74.4 Time Limit: 15 minutes

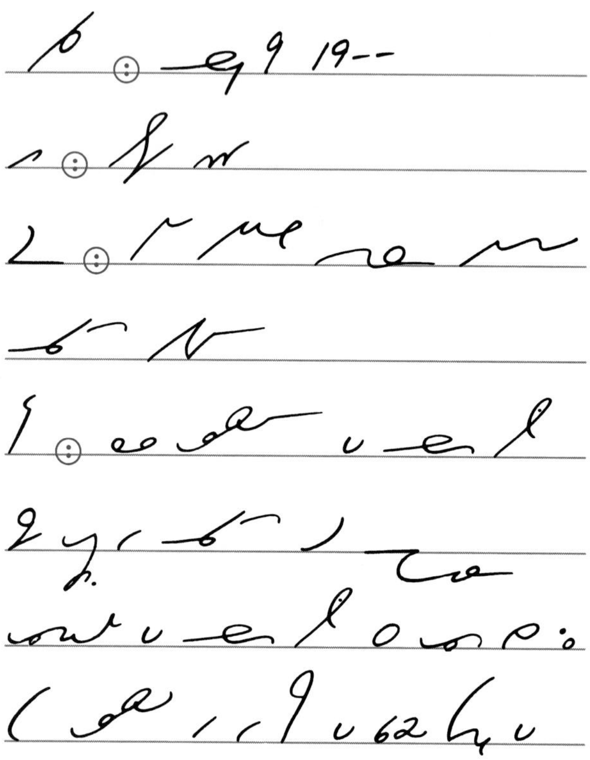

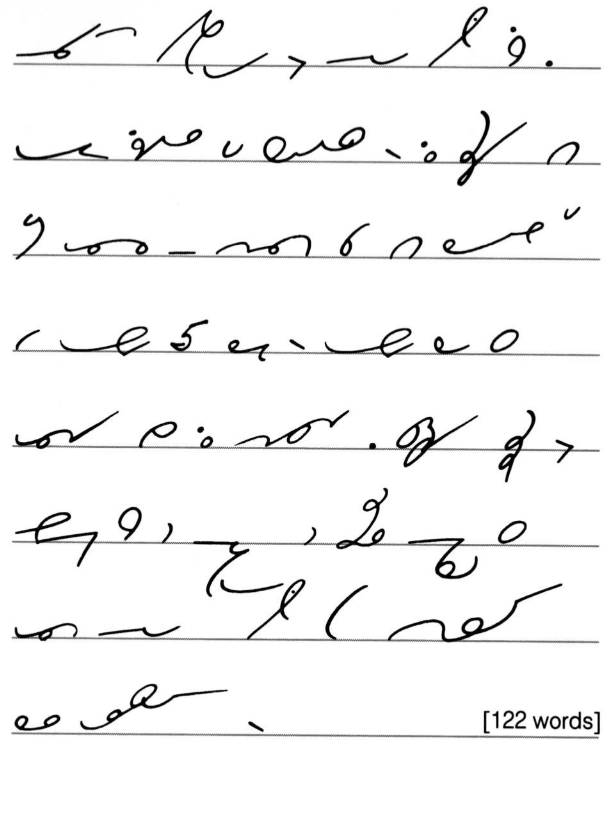

[122 words]

LESSON 75

KEITH MANUFACTURING COMPANY

DICTATION SPEED BUILDING

The shorthand outlines below appear in the speed dictation practice that follows. Practice writing these words using the shorthand outlines. Then, using the key that follows, dictate the words to yourself in preparation for the speed dictation practice.

Dictation Preview

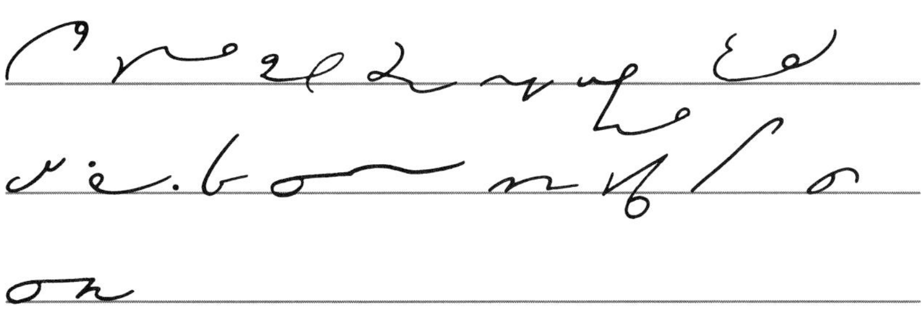

Key: Dear Miss Stanley, X rays, finger, crushed, originally, splint, although, healing, bone, I am glad, you cannot, should be able, to do, I can, I am sure

Speed Dictation Practice

75.1 Goal: 110 wam speed dictation

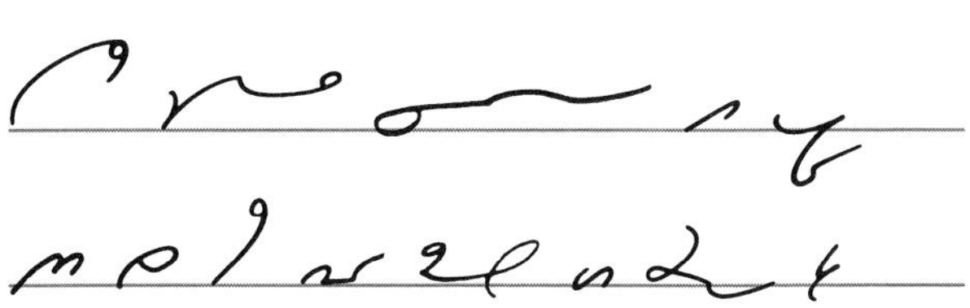

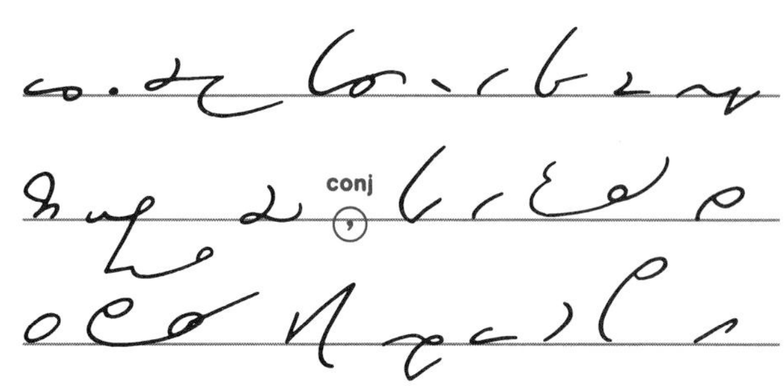

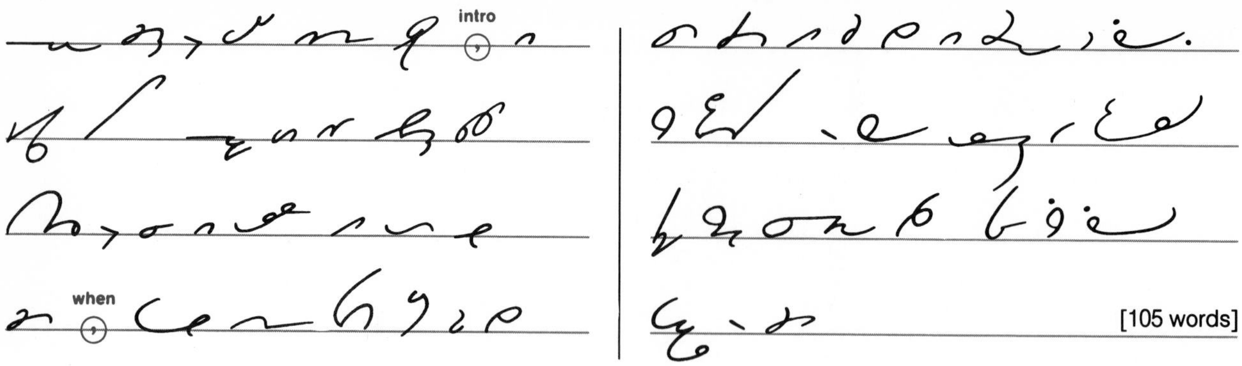

TRANSCRIPTION SKILL DEVELOPMENT

Transcription Warmup

Transcribe the following groups of words for speed and accuracy, applying transcription rules and assuring correct spelling.

75.2

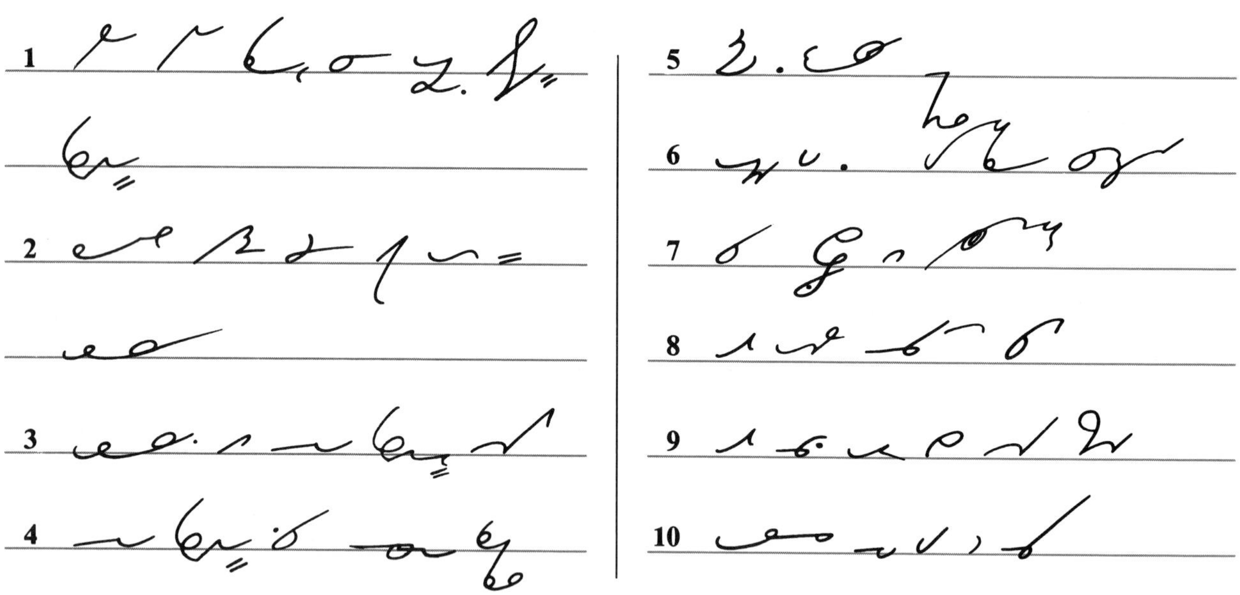

Transcription Practice

Transcribe the following letter for 2 minutes in unarranged format, applying transcription rules and assuring correct spelling. For every word not transcribed and every keyboarding error, deduct one word from the total word count.

75.3 Goal: 40 wam transcription rate

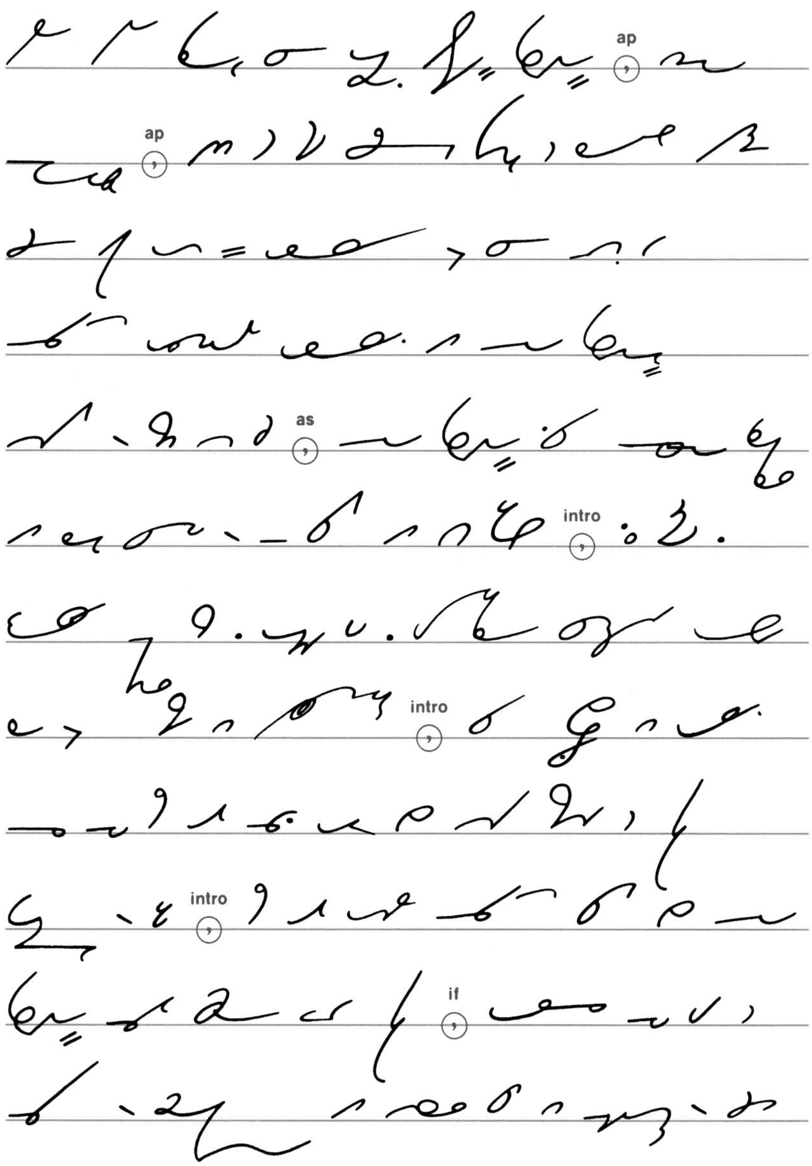

Word Count
11
25
34
42
53
65
76
88
100
113
123
138

Mailable Production

Transcribe the following mailable production memo, inserting punctuation prior to transcribing. Capitalize proper nouns and titles. Do not address a letter envelope. A memo would be placed in an interoffice envelope, and the information requested would be handwritten.

75.4 Time Limit: 15 minutes

[157 words]

LESSON 76

KEITH MANUFACTURING COMPANY

DICTATION SPEED BUILDING

The shorthand outlines below appear in the speed dictation practice that follows. Practice writing these words using the shorthand outlines. Then, using the key that follows, dictate the words to yourself in preparation for the speed dictation practice.

Dictation Preview

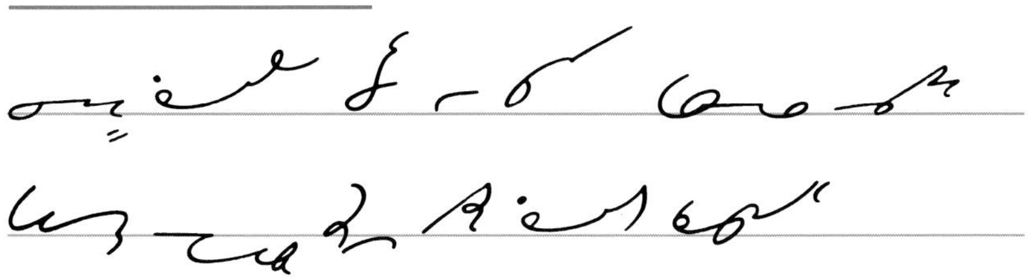

Key: Americans, healthier, span, than, attained, primarily, medicines, programs, employees, physical, diseases, healthful, surroundings

Speed Dictation Practice

76.1 Goal: 110 wam speed dictation

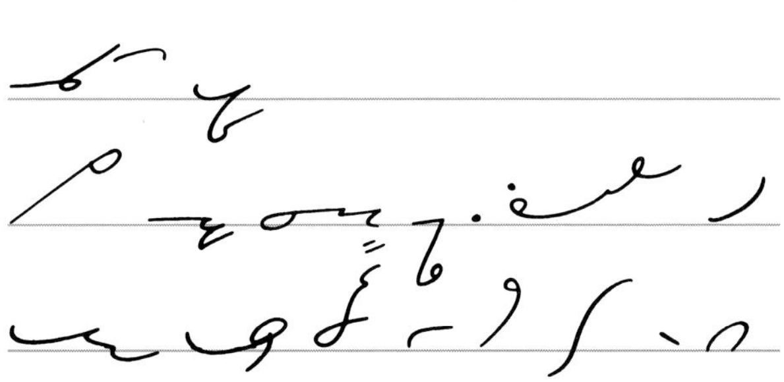

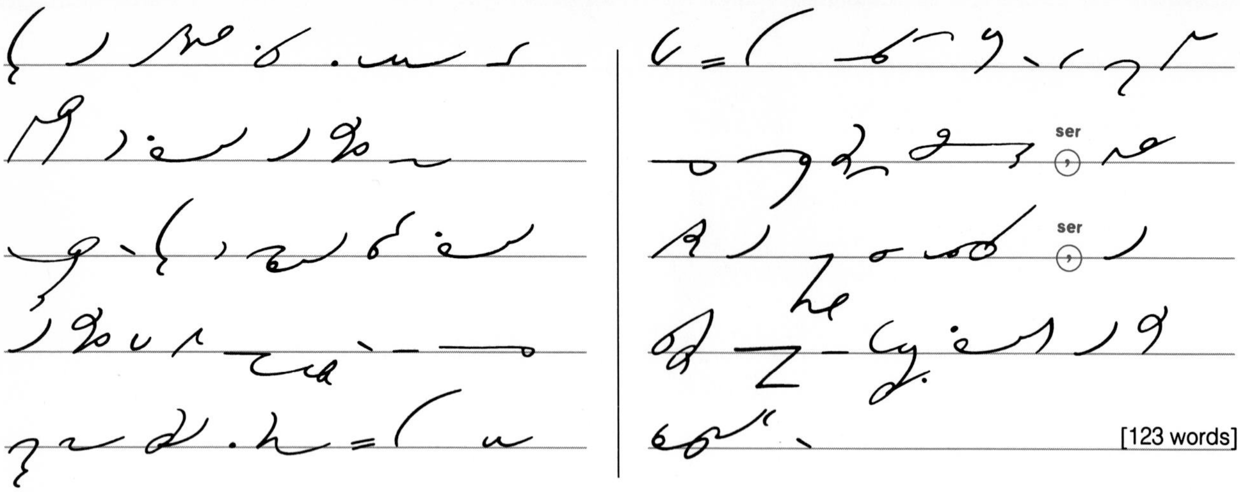

[123 words]

TRANSCRIPTION SKILL DEVELOPMENT

Transcription Warmup

Transcribe the following groups of words for speed and accuracy, applying transcription rules and assuring correct spelling.

76.2

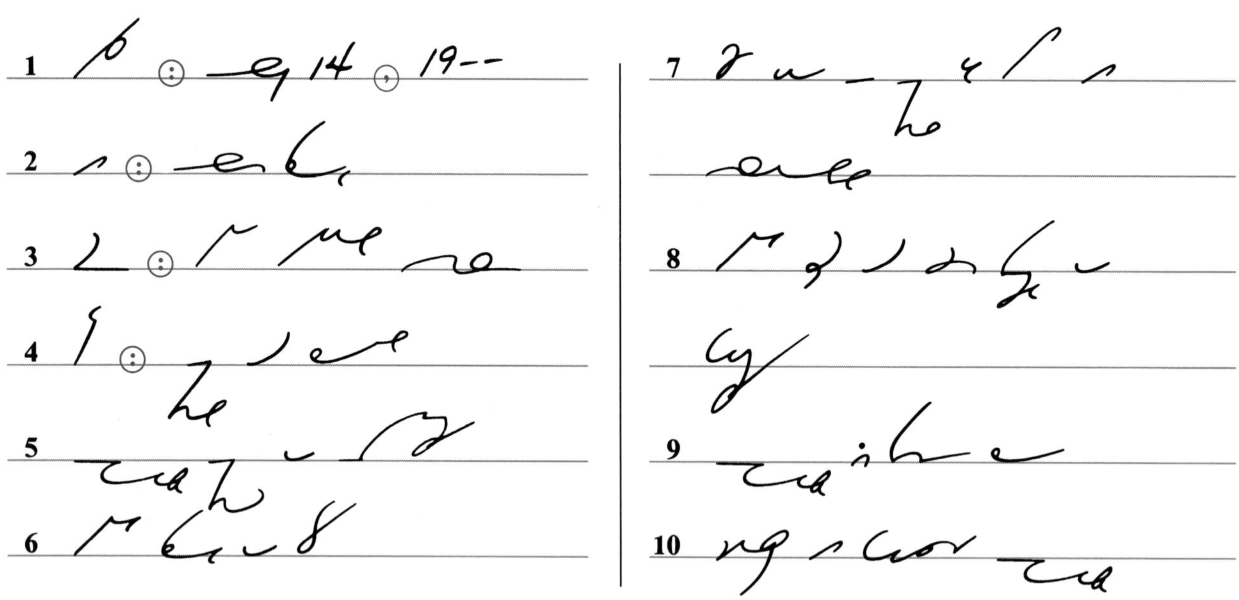

Transcription Practice

Transcribe the following memo for 2 minutes in unarranged format, applying transcription rules and assuring correct spelling. For every word not transcribed and every keyboarding error, deduct one word from the total word count.

76.3 Goal: 40 wam transcription rate

Word Count

4
8
13
19
33
43
54
66
77
87
98
108
119

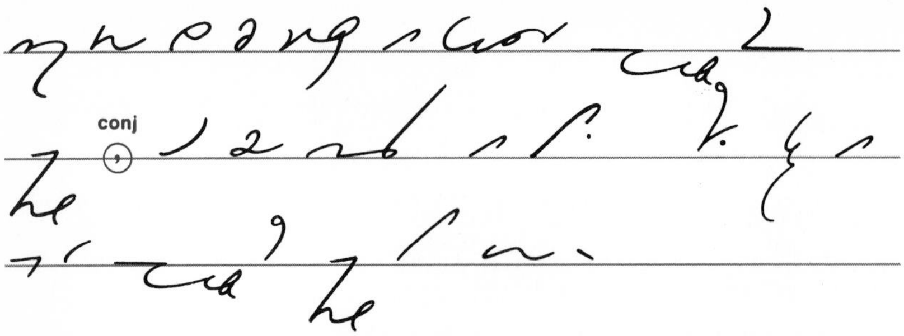

Mailable Production

Transcribe the following mailable production memo, inserting punctuation prior to transcribing. Capitalize proper nouns and titles. Do not address a letter envelope. A memo would be placed in an interoffice envelope, and the information requested would be handwritten.

76.4 Time Limit: 15 minutes

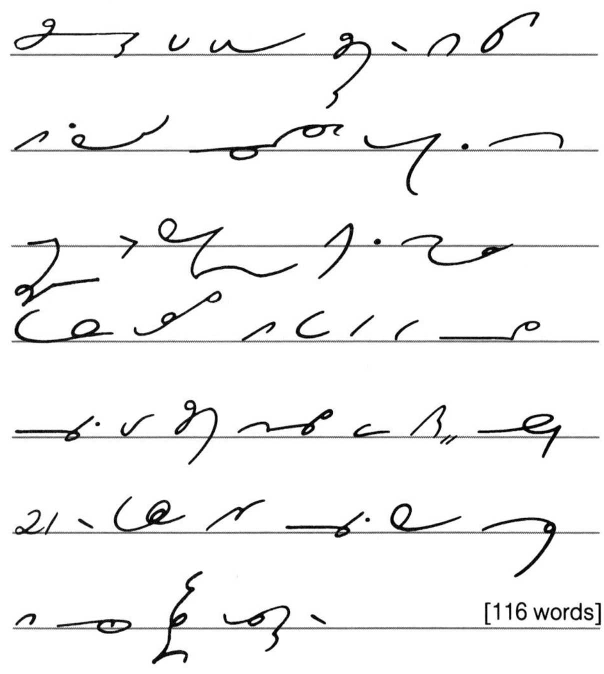

[116 words]

LESSON 77

KEITH MANUFACTURING COMPANY

DICTATION SPEED BUILDING

The shorthand outlines below appear in the speed dictation practice that follows. Practice writing these words using the shorthand outlines. Then, using the key that follows, dictate the words to yourself in preparation for the speed dictation practice.

Dictation Preview

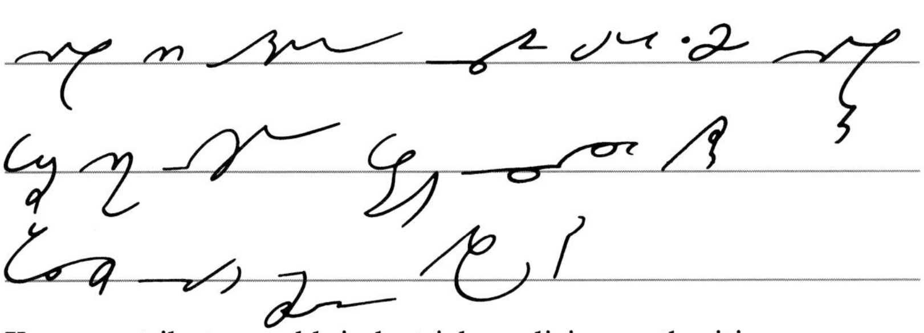

Key: contribute, world, industrial, medicine, authorities, aware, contributions, profession, cover, individual, preventive, maintenance, decisions, obligation, modification, environment, disabled, such

Speed Dictation Practice

77.1 Goal: 110 wam speed dictation

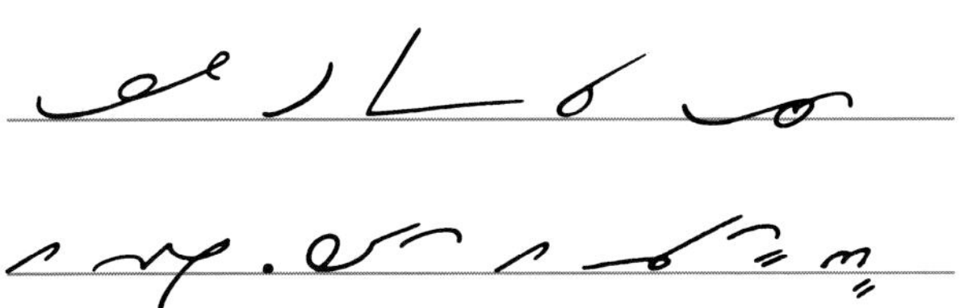

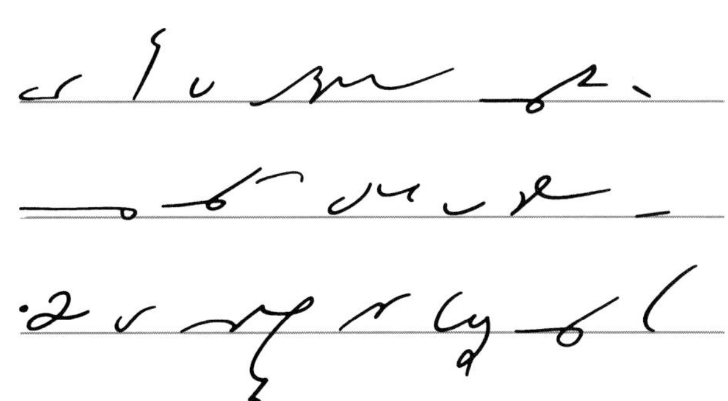

TRANSCRIPTION SKILL DEVELOPMENT

Transcription Warmup

Transcribe the following groups of words for speed and accuracy, applying transcription rules and assuring correct spelling.

77.2

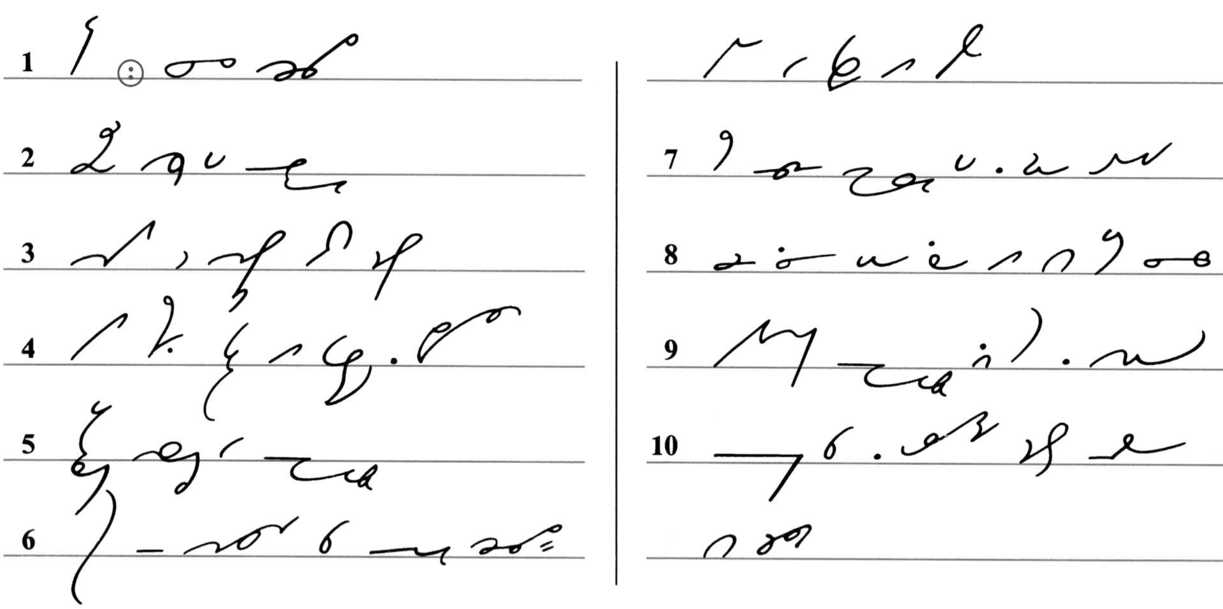

Transcription Practice

Transcribe the following memo for 2 minutes in unarranged format, applying transcription rules and assuring correct spelling. For every word not transcribed and every keyboarding error, deduct one word from the total word count.

77.3 Goal: 40 wam transcription rate

Word Count

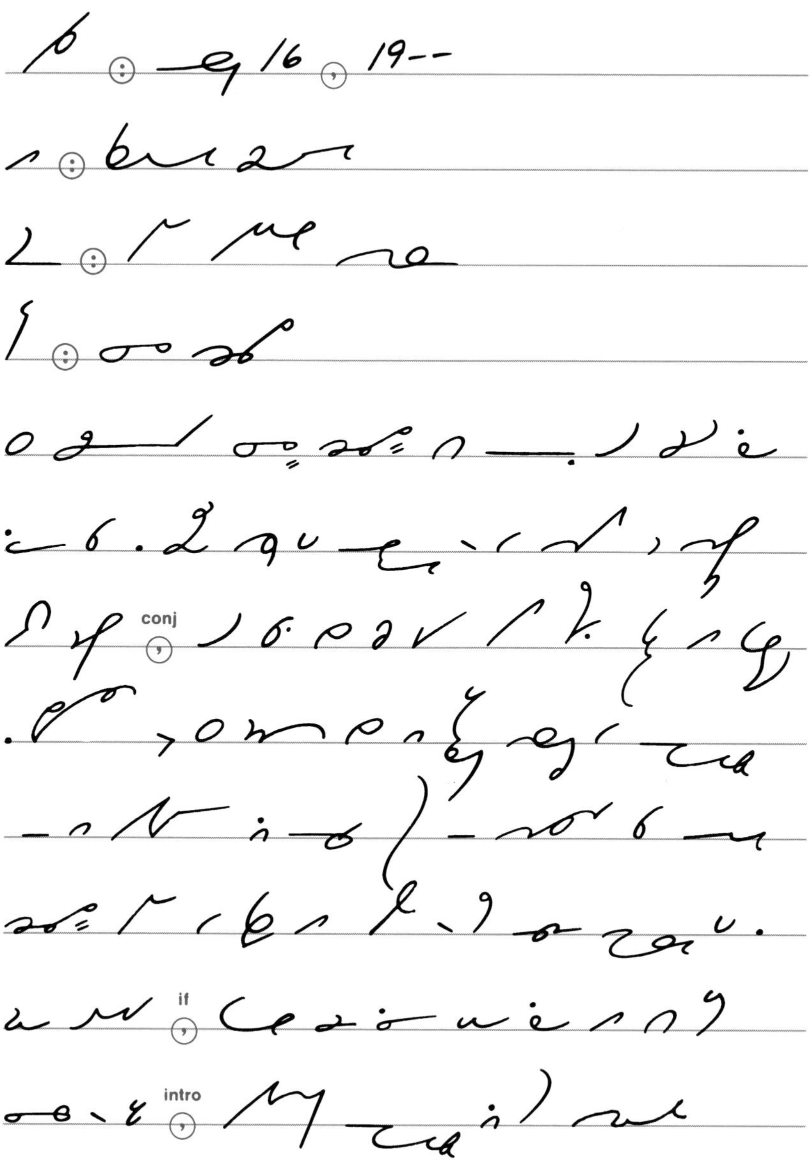

4
8
13
17
27
40
55
68
80
92
102
115

125

134

Mailable Production

Transcribe the following mailable production memo, inserting all punctuation prior to transcribing. Capitalize proper nouns and titles. Do not address a letter envelope. A memo would be placed in an interoffice envelope, and the information requested would be handwritten.

77.4 Time Limit: 15 minutes

[179 words]

LESSON 78

KEITH MANUFACTURING COMPANY

DICTATION SPEED BUILDING

The shorthand outlines below appear in the speed dictation practice that follows. Practice writing these words using the shorthand outlines. Then, using the key that follows, dictate the words to yourself in preparation for the speed dictation practice.

Dictation Preview

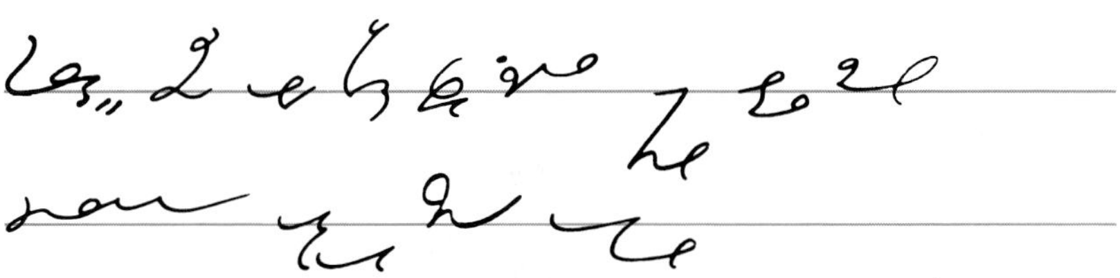

Key: Frances, severe, wrist, objects, patient's, history, injuries, necessary, X rays, secretarial, responsibilities, as you will, will you please

Speed Dictation Practice

78.1 Goal: 110 wam speed dictation

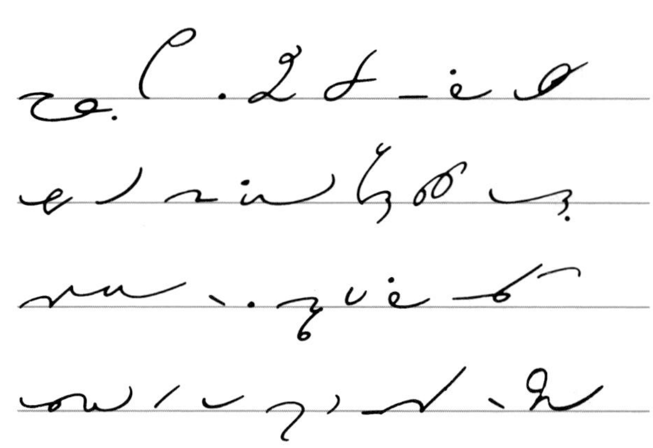

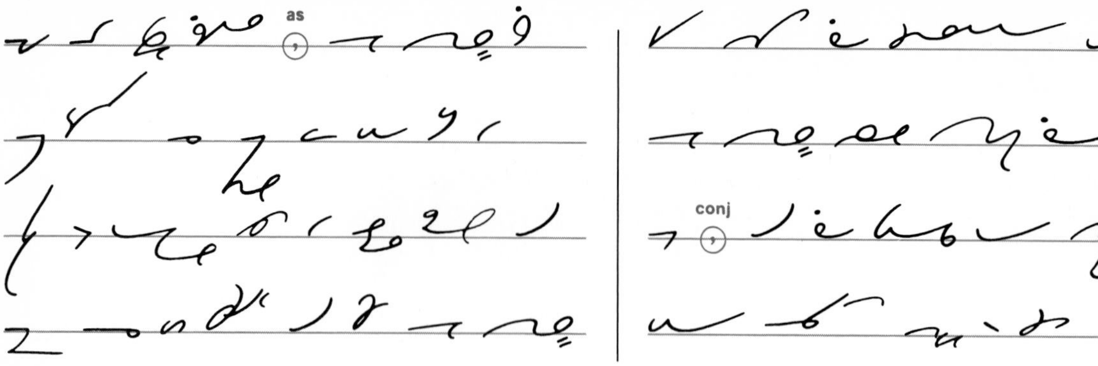

[122 words]

TRANSCRIPTION SKILL DEVELOPMENT

Transcription Warmup

Transcribe the following groups of words for speed and accuracy, applying transcription rules and assuring correct spelling.

78.2

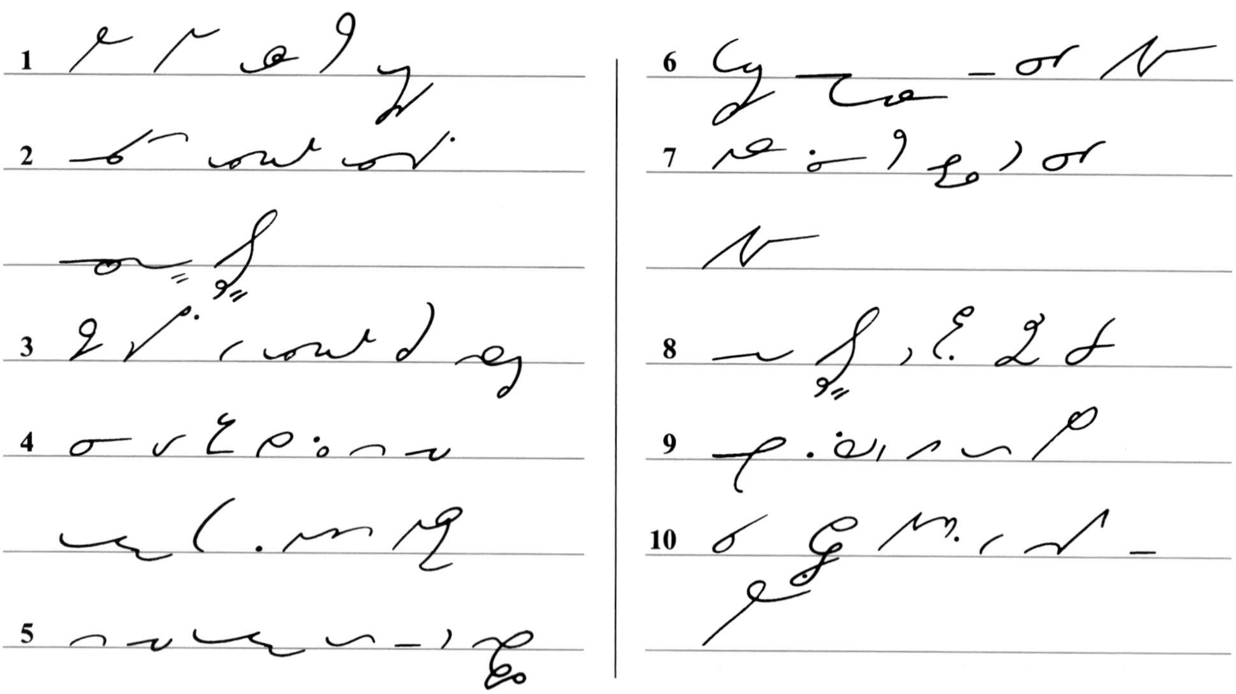

Transcription Practice

Transcribe the following letter for 2 minutes in unarranged format, applying transcription rules and assuring correct spelling. For every word not transcribed and every keyboarding error, deduct one word from the total word count.

78.3 Goal: 40 wam transcription rate

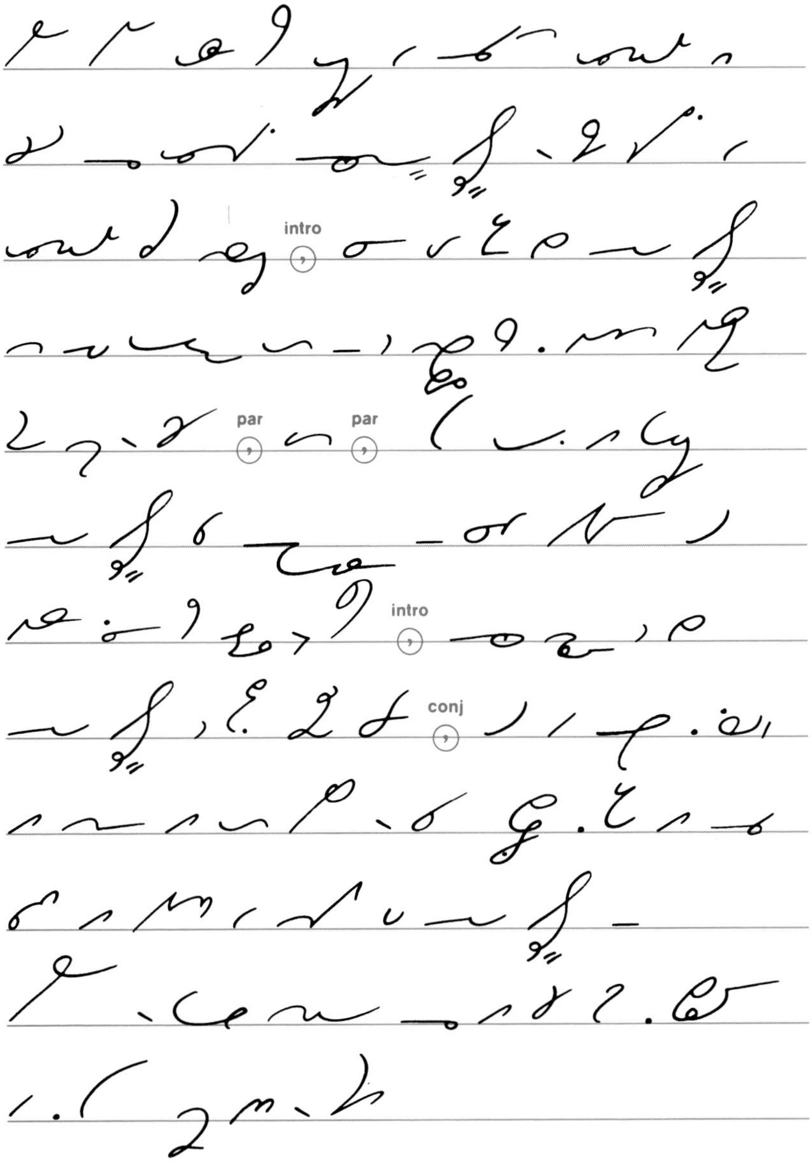

Word Count

11
21
33
43
55
65
75
88
101
111
121
130

Mailable Production

Transcribe the following mailable production memo, inserting punctuation prior to transcribing. Capitalize proper nouns and titles. Do not address a letter envelope. A memo would be placed in an interoffice envelope, and the information requested would be handwritten.

78.4 Time Limit: 15 minutes

[158 words]

LESSON 79

KEITH MANUFACTURING COMPANY

DICTATION SPEED BUILDING

The shorthand outlines below appear in the speed dictation practice that follows. Practice writing these words using the shorthand outlines. Then, using the key that follows, dictate the words to yourself in preparation for the speed dictation practice.

Dictation Preview

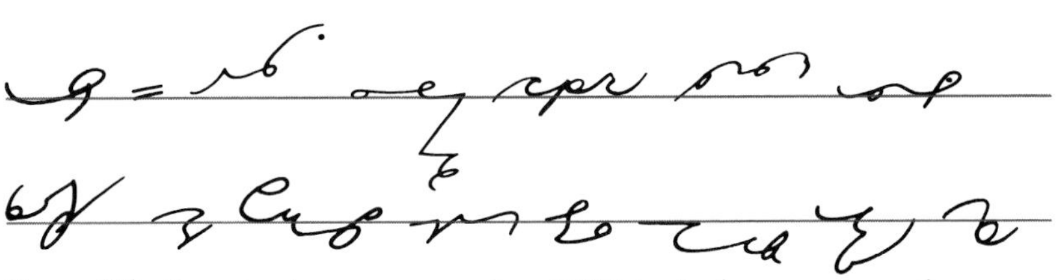

Key: life-threatening emergencies, CPR techniques, recreation, certified, consist, approximately, instruction, necessary, employees, respond, questionnaire

Speed Dictation Practice

79.1 Goal: 110 wam speed dictation

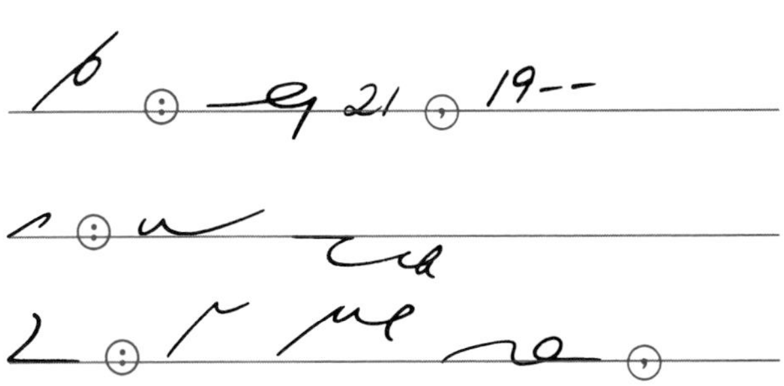

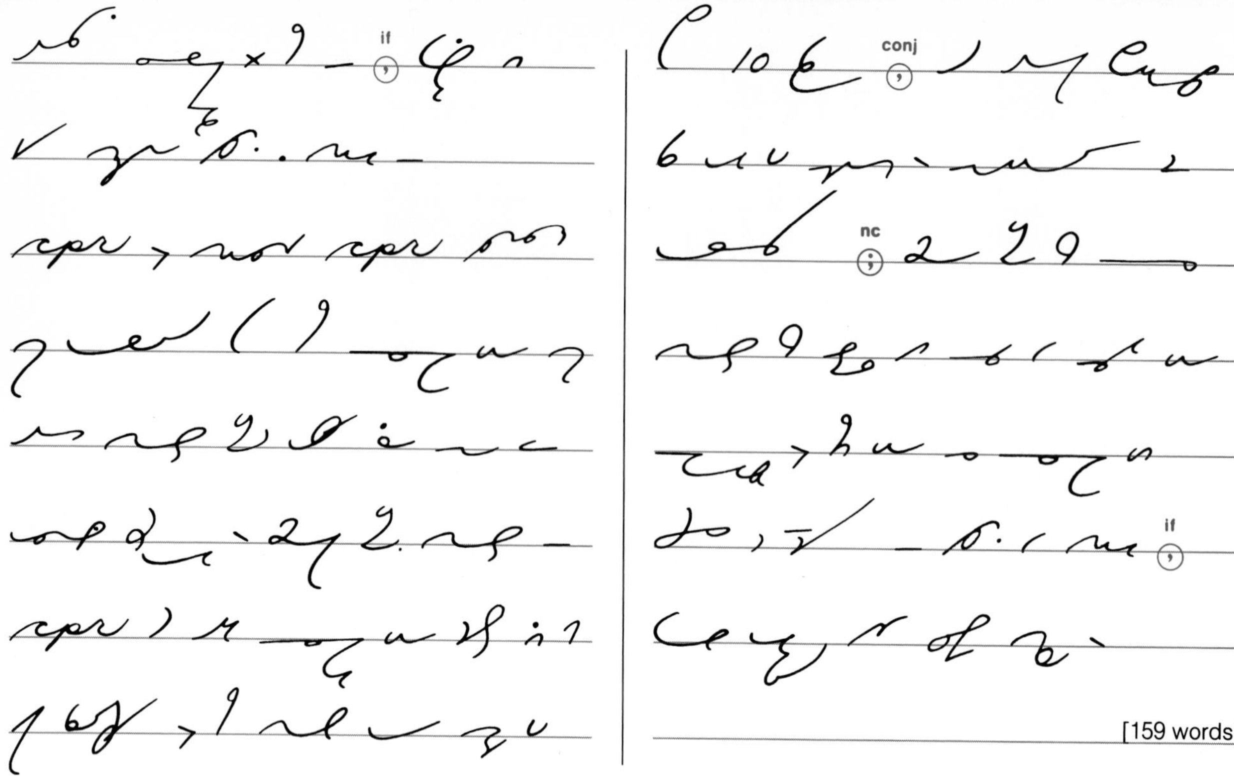

[159 words]

TRANSCRIPTION SKILL DEVELOPMENT

Transcription Warmup

Transcribe the following groups of words for speed and accuracy, applying transcription rules and assuring correct spelling.

79.2

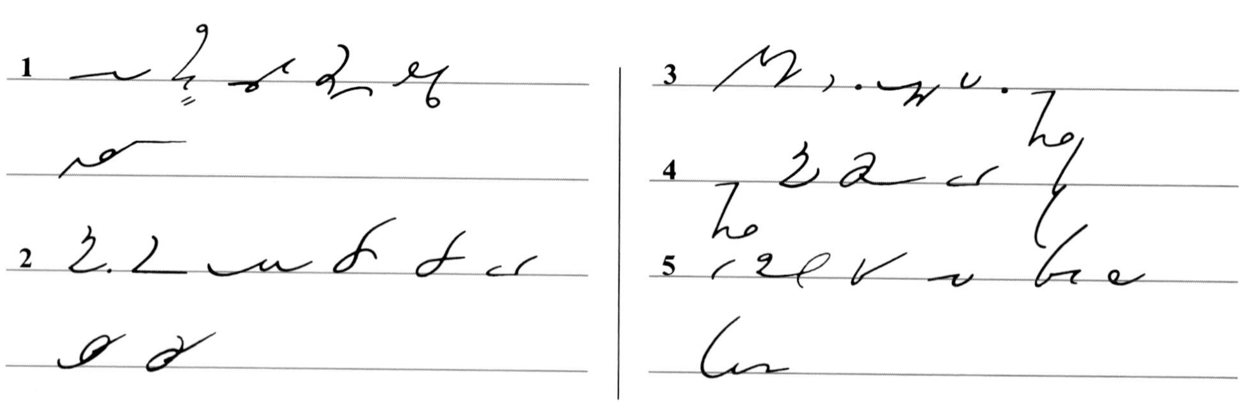

6 7 8 9 10

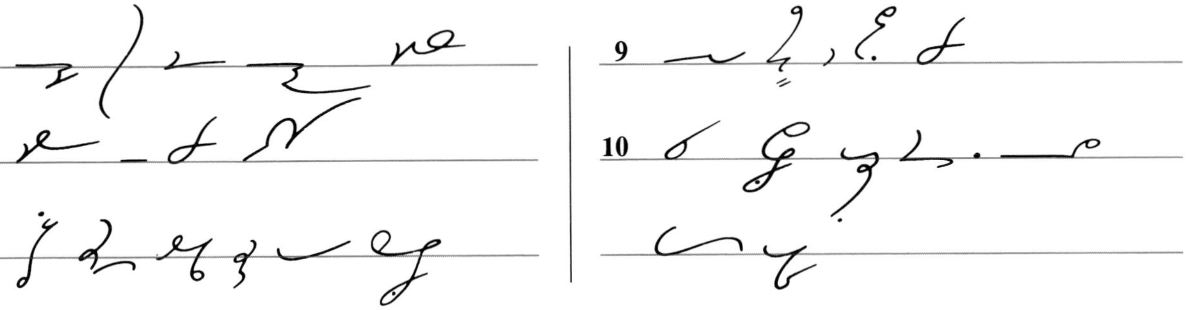

Transcription Practice

Transcribe the following letter for 2 minutes in unarranged format, applying transcription rules and assuring correct spelling. For every word not transcribed and every keyboarding error, deduct one word from the total word count.

79.3 Goal: 40 wam transcription rate

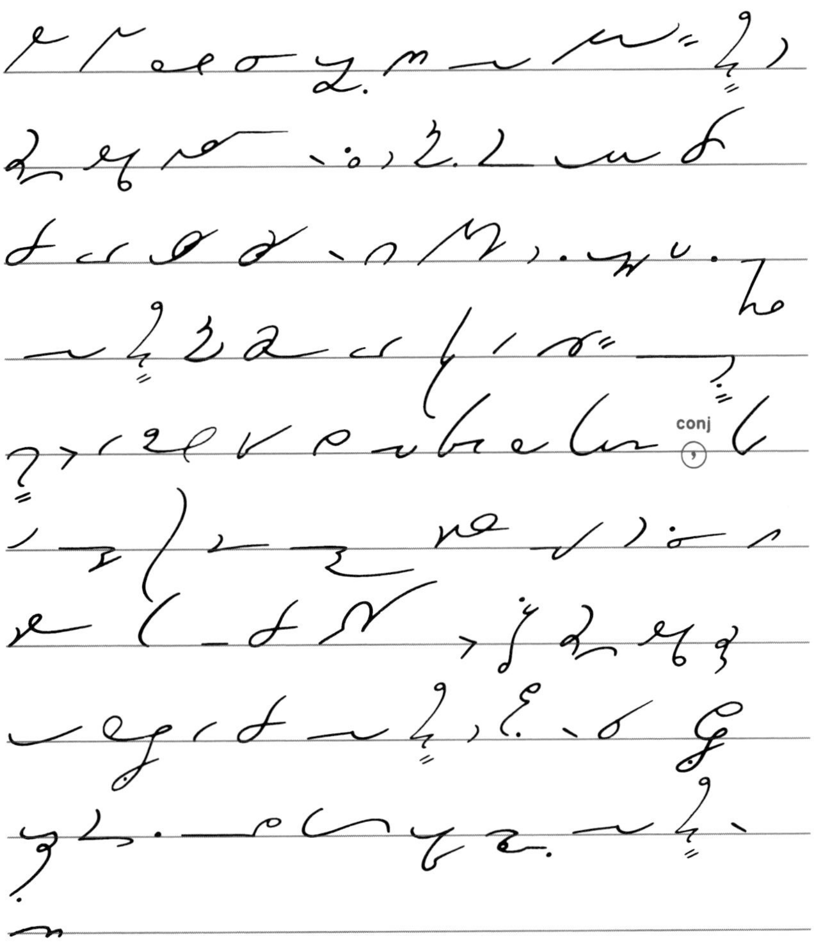

Word Count

11
23
36
48
60
72
85
99
112
115

Mailable Production

Transcribe the following mailable production memo, inserting punctuation prior to transcribing. Capitalize proper nouns and titles. Do not address a letter envelope. A memo would be placed in an interoffice envelope, and the information requested would be handwritten.

79.4 Time Limit: 15 minutes

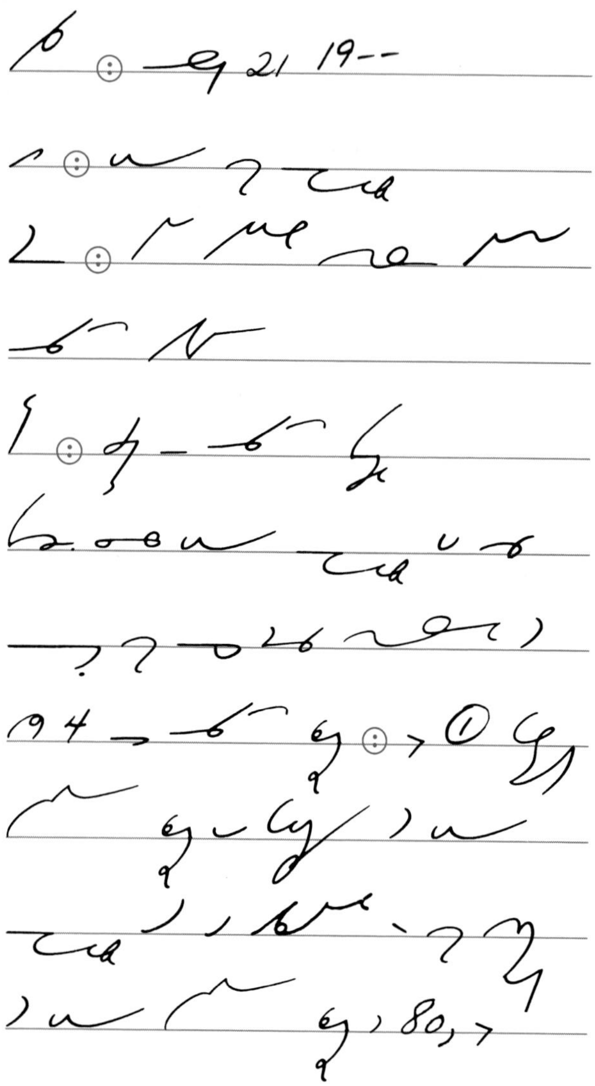

[166 words]

LESSON 80

KEITH MANUFACTURING COMPANY

DICTATION SPEED BUILDING

The shorthand outlines below appear in the speed dictation practice that follows. Practice writing these words using the shorthand outlines. Then, using the key that follows, dictate the words to yourself in preparation for the speed dictation practice.

Dictation Preview

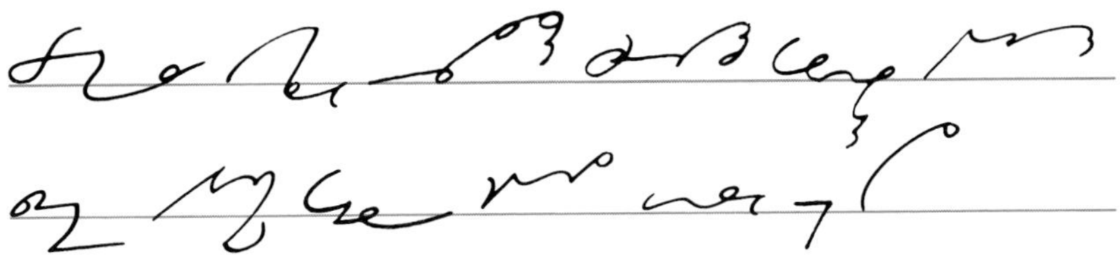

Key: pamphlet, dangers, medications, simultaneously, prescriptions, drugs, uniform, discovered, personnel, strictly, occurrence, in which, to me

Speed Dictation Practice

80.1 Goal: 110 wam speed dictation

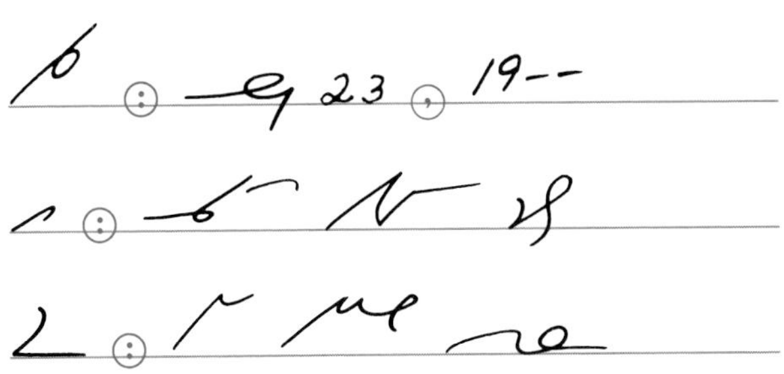

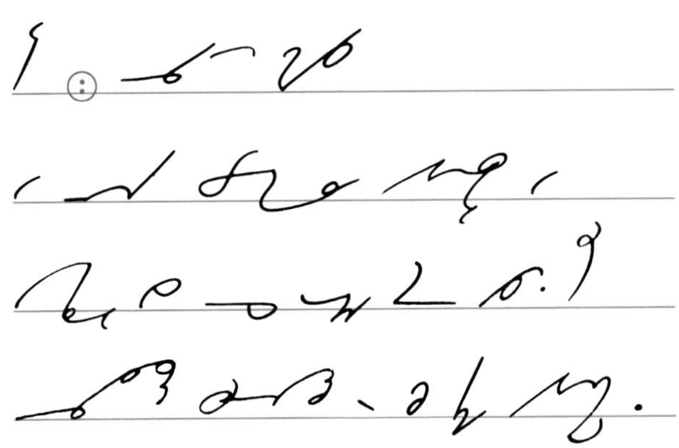

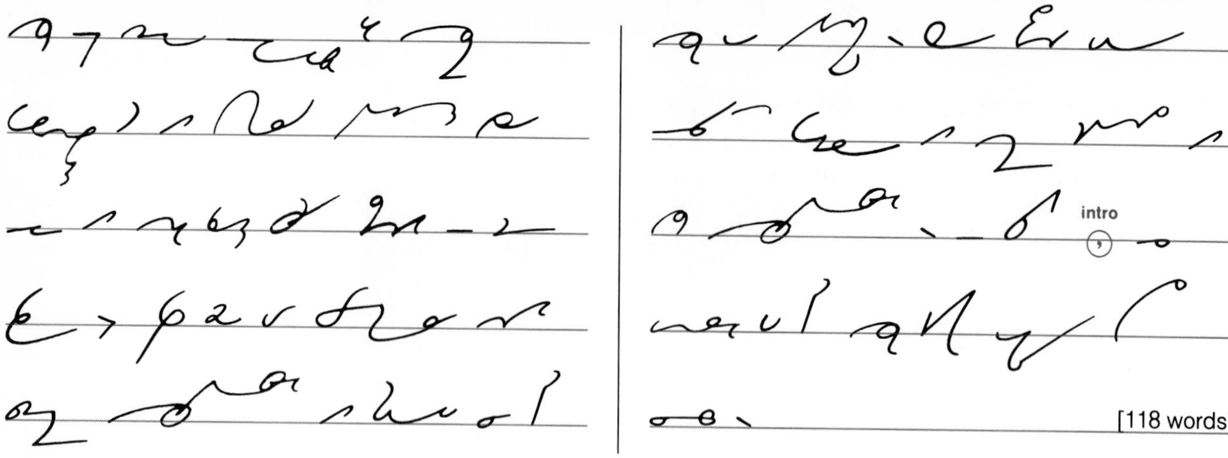

TRANSCRIPTION SKILL DEVELOPMENT

Transcription Warmup

Transcribe the following groups of words for speed and accuracy, applying transcription rules and assuring correct spelling.

80.2

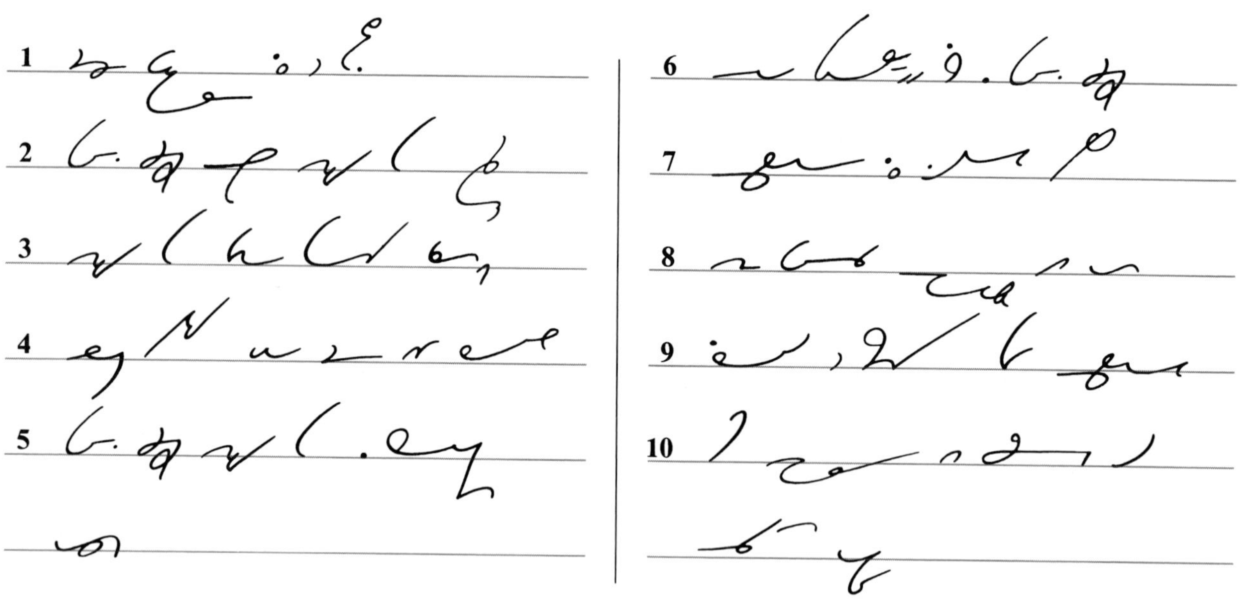

Transcription Practice

Transcribe the following letter for 2 minutes in unarranged format, applying transcription rules and assuring correct spelling. For every word not transcribed and every keyboarding error, deduct one word from the total word count.

80.3 Goal: 40 wam transcription rate

Word Count

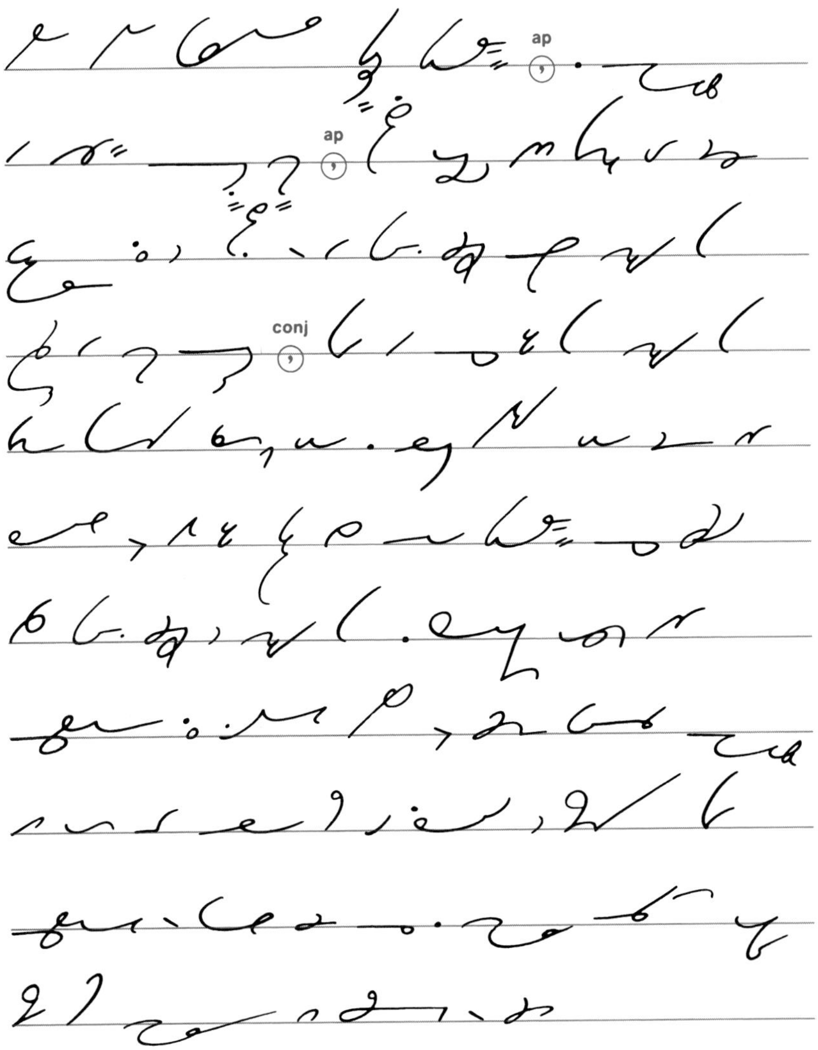

Word Count
9
24
37
49
60
71
84
95
106
116
128

Mailable Production

Transcribe the following mailable production memo, inserting punctuation prior to transcribing. Capitalize proper nouns and titles. Do not address a letter envelope. A memo would be placed in an interoffice envelope, and the information requested would be handwritten.

80.4 Time Limit: 15 minutes

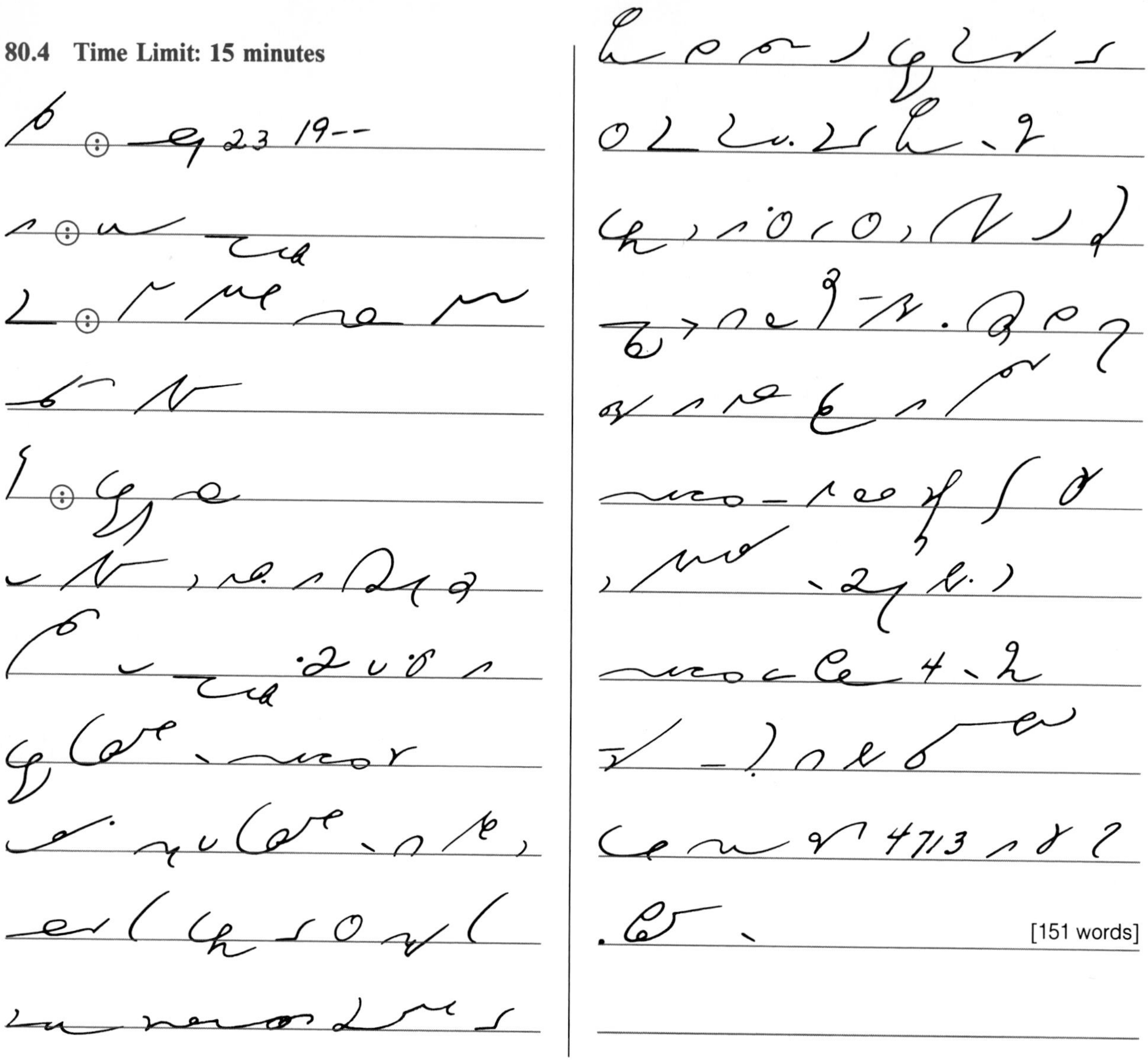

[151 words]

TRANSCRIPT

The material is counted in groups of 20 standard words or 28 syllables for convenience in timing the reading or dictation.

LESSON 1

1.1 Goal: 70 wam speed dictation

Dear Ms. Brady It is a pleasure to include your name as the satisfied user of the World Travel card.[1] We hope that you will continue to use this charge account service frequently.

If our service should ever fail to meet[2] your standards, feel free to offer us your comments and suggestions. It is our desire that your satisfaction[3] with your World Travel card will continue for many years. Cordially yours [73 words]

1.2 Goal: 25 wam transcription rate

Dear Mr. Mendez It was good to see you again in North Carolina. I sincerely appreciate everything you did in order to help my visit go more smoothly. It was nice that we had a few minutes to visit, to have dinner, and to enjoy the superb scenery.

Please let me know when you are going to be in this area again. If you will be giving presentations, I would be glad to help you. I always enjoy working with you. Cordially yours

1.3 Brief-Form Letter

Dear Ms. Davis Because you are a member of the management team of your organization, you will be[1] interested in my personal experience with the National Management Seminar. My organization[2] had all supervisory personnel take this course. I attended this seminar with great expectations and[3] was not disappointed. I feel that this seminar has helped me solve some of my most frustrating management problems.[4]

By applying the principles and information I learned at the seminar, I find that I can really[5] motivate and encourage people to do quality work. I think you will be making a wise investment of your time and[6] energy to take this seminar. Sincerely yours [130 words]

1.4 Theory Letter

Dear Dr. Watson During the past six months an announcement was sent to all our depositors regarding their[1] banking needs.

We have installed new automatic teller machine equipment in all our branch offices. These[2] machines will make it possible for you to handle your accounts with greater speed and accuracy.

Our new[3] equipment is now fully operational. Come in to one of our branch offices and pick up your new[4] automatic teller machine card today. We are sure you will enjoy this new convenience. Sincerely yours[5] [100 words]

LESSON 2

2.1 Goal: 70 wam speed dictation

Dear Dr. Carter I wish to extend to you my sincere congratulations, Dr. Carter, on your being[1]

named chancellor of Johnson College. Your appointment comes as a real boost to faculty and student morale.[2]

People are looking forward to an administration characterized by candor, fairness, and dignity. It[3] will certainly be a pleasure working with you. Enjoy your well-deserved career advancement.[4] Very truly yours [81 words]

2.2 Goal: 25 wam transcription rate

Dear Ms. Warner Subject: Computer Software Thank you for your letter about the computer software that you say you sent us last month.

After checking our records carefully, we are unable to find any trace of these items. We can find no record that indicates that we received them.

Since you sent these items through an air express company, someone at that company should be able to trace the route of the package. We would appreciate it if you would start a search for the package and let us know the results as soon as possible. Cordially yours

2.3 Brief-Form Letter

Dear Mr. Nelson One of the major factors that make a sales force effective is a positive attitude.[1] Successful executives agree that this is an important issue, particularly at the start of a year.[2] If the sales force has a positive attitude, sales boom. If it does not, the company is in for a difficult[3] year.

To help produce a positive attitude in salespeople, our Human Resources Department prepared a[4] training film last year. The purpose of the film is to make salespeople understand and appreciate the important[5] part that selling plays in the economic well-being of business.

If you would like a copy of our film on[6] a trial basis, please fill out the enclosed form and mail it to us. We will then get in touch with you. Sincerely yours[7] [140 words]

2.4 Theory Letter

Dear Mr. King Every year thousands of people fly to see friends at Christmas. Consequently,[1] the demand for a seat is much greater at that time of the year than at any other. Some people each year are[2] disappointed because a seat is not available. There are people, however, who make a reservation on a[3] flight and then fail to show up without canceling their reservation. As a result, there is an empty seat on the[4] flight and a disappointed passenger at the airline terminal.

Are you planning to have Christmas with friends or[5] relatives out of town? If you are and they live in one of the cities our airline serves, we suggest that you make[6] your reservations now. Our latest schedule is enclosed for your convenience. Sincerely yours [137 words]

LESSON 3

3.1 Goal: 70 wam speed dictation

Dear Mr. Martin Sometimes an unfortunate event makes it difficult to pay bills when they are due. If you have[1] experienced an unexpected financial strain that has made it impossible for you to send us a[2] check for $65, will you please contact our office and let us know.

You will find us more than willing to[3] cooperate with you in every way possible. We do not want to see you lose your line of credit over such[4] a small amount. We hope to hear from you soon. Yours very truly [91 words]

3.2 Goal: 25 wam transcription rate

Dear Mr. Rich It is with great pleasure we announce that Janice Stone has joined our staff. Ms. Stone is an expert in computer application and has the reputation of being an efficient, courteous worker. She has had more than ten years of experience in this field, and we are glad to place her knowledge and experience at your disposal.

Ms. Stone is available to develop software especially for your business. Last year she developed a database for a distributing company similar to yours. Please let us know if you would like to have more information about this service. We would be happy to meet with you. Cordially yours

3.3 Brief-Form Letter

Dear Ms. Matthews At one time product liability was just another form of insurance coverage. It was[1] something that a manufacturer or producer turned to when somebody got hurt using his product. The cost[2] of this coverage was small.

Over the past 20 years product liability cases began to increase at[3] a very rapid rate. If this trend continues, the results could prove disastrous for the people who make the product[4] and for the people who buy and use it.

Our reason for sharing this information with you is that we stand a[5] better chance of solving this problem if we understand it. Please let us hear from you. Just drop a note at the[6] Office of Consumer Information on 102 Washington Street in Hartford, Connecticut 16115.[7] Sincerely yours

[142 words]

3.4 Theory Letter

Dear Dr. Smith We were delighted to receive your letter requesting information about a possible tour[1] your senior class might take in June. I assure you that our entire staff will be happy to cooperate with you[2] in arranging a trip that will be both educational and recreational. We have been arranging trips[3] of this type for many years, and the people on our staff understand the problems involved in summer trips.

Enclosed[4] are several folders describing the various trips that are available this summer. The rates for each tour are also[5] included. When you decide on a particular tour, please let me know. I will have one of our representatives[6] discuss arrangements with you. Yours truly [128 words]

LESSON 4

4.1 Goal: 70 wam speed dictation

Dear Ms. Ortiz On January 25 we issued a bulletin establishing an allowance of[1] 20 cents a mile for all sales representatives who use their own cars on company business.

As a result[2] of a recent inquiry, we have decided to increase this allowance to 25 cents a mile for the[3] first 15,000 miles during the year and 15 cents a mile for all additional miles.

Please give this[4] information to all representatives who must use their cars for company business. Sincerely yours [98 words]

4.2 Goal: 25 wam transcription rate

Dear Mr. Chase We will be glad to change the listing of Mr. Green's telephone number to your name. Please ask Mr. Green to give us written permission to transfer his contract and number to you.

We are enclosing an application for your signature. Please sign the application in the proper place and return it in the envelope we have provided. The charge for changing service from one name to another is $25. This amount will appear as a service charge on your first bill. Very sincerely yours

4.3 Brief-Form Letter

Dear Ms. James One of the things we have learned during more than half a century in the airline business is that our[1] success is based on meeting your needs more often and more promptly than our competitors. As a means of getting[2] the facts we need, we have established a program whereby we can gather worthwhile information about the[3] feelings of frequent business travelers like you. One of the features of this program is our use of a survey[4] on board the plane in which you give us data about our service and make suggestions. From this survey we have been able[5] to change and improve service.

We appreciate your past business and hope that we may continue to serve[6] your travel needs in the future. Very truly yours [130 words]

4.4 Theory Letter

Dear Mr. and Mrs. Fenton Most parents feel they do not have the ability to choose the right books for their[1] young children who are just beginning to read. That is why parents are happy to turn this problem over to the highly[2] skilled and qualified editors of the National Parents Magazine by enrolling their children in our reading[3] program.

Membership brings to your home each month an outstanding, carefully selected book that you may read to your[4] child. Each book will charm your child with its colorful cover, its illustrated pages, and its appealing story[5] that is understandable to even the youngest mind.

If your child is a beginning reader, enroll him or[6] her now. You will receive the five books that are described in the enclosed folder. If you are not satisfied with our[7] product, you may return the books within ten days and owe us nothing. Sincerely yours [156 words]

LESSON 5

5.1 Goal: 70 wam speed dictation

Dear Ms. Brady I am planning to make a trip to Denver late in August. Since I will be out west, it seems I could[1] arrange to spend 10 percent of my time to include Salt Lake City in my schedule.

Would you call me and let me[2] know whether your branches will have completed their market surveys. If they have, I would like to know if the surveys[3] indicate that there is a market for our products in Salt Lake City. I would appreciate hearing from you[4] as soon as possible as my plane fare might be as much as $250 if I do not make my[5] reservation now.

If you or anyone at your organization could pass this information on to me,[6] it would be very much appreciated. Very truly yours [132 words]

5.2 Goal: 25 wam transcription rate

To: Sales Staff
From: Bill Dean, Marketing Director
Subject: Advertising Campaign
Date: April 2, 19--

We are running a large advertisement in a number of national magazines for the month of May. These magazines should reach about 8 million people. If you would like to receive reprints of this advertisement to give to prospective customers, let me know.

Considering our new advertising campaign and increased sales efforts, the next few months should see a big increase in the sale of our products.

5.3 Brief-Form Letter

Dear Mr. Lester May I extend to you on behalf of the management of Worth and Company our sincere[1] thanks for the support you have given us from the very first stages of our reorganization. We have[2] received correspondence and telephone calls imploring us to keep our fine stores open and to continue to[3] serve the special needs of our satisfied customers.

We are doing just that. We are organizing our business[4] on a strong and progressive foundation and have obtained substantial backing and interim financing from[5] several sources.

Worth and Company is being established with the traditional strength we have enjoyed for[6] so many years. We look forward to your continued support. Very truly yours [134 words]

5.4 Theory Letter

Dear Mr. West If the enclosed sports catalog is the first one you have ever received from us, we would like[1] to explain to you why it is different from the others.

Its major purpose is to add to your enjoyment of[2] sports by bringing you a carefully selected collection of quality sporting apparel, equipment, and[3] other items. We hope to save you a great deal of time and effort that you might otherwise spend looking for what you want.[4]

We are proud of our catalog and its contents. If you have any questions about any of the items[5] in the catalog, do not hesitate to call us. We would be happy to assist you in any possible way.[6] Sincerely yours [124 words]

LESSON 6

6.1 Goal: 70 wam speed dictation

Dear Dr. Lee Thank you so much for speaking to the Student Marketing Association last Thursday night. We[1] appreciate your time and effort.

Many members commented to me a few days after your speech that they left[2] the meeting feeling motivated and ready to take on the rest of the semester. Your presentation[3] touched on so many issues that there is no way anybody could leave without some new insight.

Since most of our[4] members are presently going through the interviewing process, your inspiring talk was just what[5] we needed. Sincerely [104 words]

6.2 Goal: 25 wam transcription rate

Dear Ms. Bowen Since the closing of your house is rapidly approaching, I wanted to remind you of a few things. As you know, the closing is scheduled for 10:30 a.m., June 14, at First National Bank. The mortgage loan that you will be getting to purchase the property will be in your name only. Therefore, it is necessary for you to attend the closing and sign the mortgage papers. Enclosed is a closing statement that indicates the amount due the seller and the amounts credited to you. This closing statement will be compared with the final closing statement being prepared by the seller.

If you have any questions between now and the closing, please call me. Sincerely

6.3 Brief-Form Letter

Dear Mrs. Michaels Did you know that there is a way to stop undesired advertising mail? Just get in touch with the[1] Direct Mail Control Service. They are a group of businesses that use mail to advertise their products and services,[2] and they will send you a name-removal form. Once you have returned this form you will notice a substantial decrease[3] in the amount of mail advertising you receive.

Act now and you will begin receiving less mail every day.[4] Sincerely yours [83 words]

6.4 Theory Letter

Dear Ms. Grace Has any member of your family subscribed to the Investment Guide in the past two years? If not,[1] we would like to offer you a subscription for 26 weeks of the Investment Guide for only \$35.[2] We do so because we have found that a high percentage of new subscribers who try the Investment Guide stay[3] with us on a long-term basis. The increased circulation enables us to keep our subscription fees lower[4] than would otherwise be possible.

To take advantage of this special offer, fill out and mail the enclosed form.[5] You will start receiving your magazine as soon as we process your subscription. Sincerely yours [117 words]

LESSON 7

7.1 Goal: 70 wam speed dictation

Dear Mrs. Young You called our office last Friday requesting that you be put back on our list of graduates[1] actively seeking employment. You will be pleased to know that we received a listing for an opening in your[2] field only minutes after I completed my conversation with you.

The contact person is listed on the job[3] description. Because this position needs to be filled immediately, you should apply as soon as possible.[4] We also took the liberty of sending two copies of your resume. Please let us know if we can be of[5] any more assistance. Cordially yours [107 words]

7.2 Goal: 25 wam transcription rate

Dear Mrs. Moore As we are the agents for the Drake Manufacturing Company in this territory, your recent letter has been referred to us.

At the present time we do not have in stock the type of camping equipment that you want, but we are expecting a shipment within the next week or two. We hope this still affords you enough time to plan your camping trip with your children. As soon as this shipment arrives, we will get in touch with you.

We have a full line of outdoor equipment, and I am sure that you will be interested in what we have to offer. Sincerely yours

7.3 Brief-Form Letter

Dear Ms. King Would you like to enter the exciting and challenging world of international business? More and[1] more large companies of the United States are expanding their operations into the international[2] market and are looking for capable men and women who can manage those operations.

You can obtain this[3] training and a degree in international business during two years of evening study at the Wilson School[4] of Business. Our program offers the kind of information that people in international business will expect[5] you to know.

For complete information about our program of international business and an application[6] form, fill out and mail the enclosed card. Sincerely yours [131 words]

7.4 Theory Letter

Dear Mrs. Brennan Heat that is steady and dependable in your home is important for the health and well-being[1] of your family. That is one of the reasons why natural gas is the choice of thousands of homeowners who live[2] in the western part of the United States. More households are converting to natural gas heat every day.

Gas heat[3] is clean. It is also less expensive than other heating systems. See your local gas heat dealer as soon as possible[4] to find out how easy and quick it will be to put gas heat in your home. You will find your local dealer listed[5] on the enclosed circular. Sincerely yours [108 words]

LESSON 8

8.1 Goal: 70 wam speed dictation

Dear Mr. Barnes Quality manufacturing is important in any item of clothing. It is especially[1] important in a gift.

The Williams line of clothing is quality clothing. People who receive Williams clothing[2] as a gift can be sure that they are receiving the finest style, the finest materials, and the finest[3] workmanship.

This year give that someone special a gift for the holidays that says "Williams" on the label.[4] Very sincerely yours [84 words]

8.2 Goal: 25 wam transcription rate

Dear Mr. Garcia As a preferred charge account customer, you are invited to our annual clothing sale. It will be held during the week of June 11. As usual, charge account customers will get first choice in the selection of the many bargains offered.

June 11 and 12 are reserved for charge account customers. On June 13, 14, and 15 the sale will be open to the general public.

Be sure to stop in. You will be delighted at the fine bargains on excellent quality merchandise during this sale. Cordially yours

8.3 Brief-Form Letter

Dear Reader If you are hesitant about subscribing to another magazine, we can understand your feeling.[1] It makes good sense to think about buying anything that is going to make new demands on your budget. However,[2] we want you to try the News Magazine and are, therefore, making you an offer to receive this magazine without[3] an initial payment.

As soon as we receive the enclosed card, we will place your name on our list of subscribers.[4] After you have received and read copies of our new publication for one month, you can decide whether you wish[5] to continue receiving it. When you get your bill, indicate your choice of keeping the subscription or[6] canceling it. Sincerely yours [125 words]

8.4 Theory Letter

Dear Mr. and Mrs. Morris The time has once again come when we must appeal to parents for generous[1] contributions to the Bennett School Fund.

As parents of children in Bennett School, you will be interested to know[2] that last year the fund made it possible to build an indoor swimming pool, to modernize and enlarge the library,[3] and to refurnish the reception room. The Bennett School Fund was responsible for these changes and would like[4] to do more.

We hope this year you will be able to make a contribution to our cause. For your convenience[5] we have enclosed a self-addressed envelope. Sincerely yours [110 words]

LESSON 9

9.1 Goal: 70 wam speed dictation

Dear Ms. Lang Are you paying too much for health insurance? If your answer to this question is yes, it will be worth[1] your time to return the enclosed reply form now.

Write down your answers to the few questions on the reply form. You will[2] receive valuable information about our insurance plans, and you can see for yourself what you should be[3] getting for your health insurance dollars.

You, as an individual, may obtain this important coverage.[4] Your request for information does not obligate you at all. Find out how you can have protection from Mutual[5] Life — the people you can depend on.

Mail your reply today in the enclosed envelope; no postage is needed.[6] Cordially yours

[123 words]

9.2

1 Dear Mrs. Lopez Three health insurance
2 June, July, and August coverage

3 when you went on maternity leave
4 January, February, and March
5 May coverage was raised to $161.48
6 premiums of $10.48 each
7 an additional $10.48 should have been taken out
8 you paid the $151 before you left
9 an adjustment of $10.48 will be taken out
10 everything will be back on schedule

9.3 Goal: 25 wam transcription rate

Dear Mrs. Lopez Three health insurance premiums of $10.48 each have been taken out of your July pay. This pays for June, July, and August coverage.

When you went on maternity leave, your health insurance was continued for five months. January, February, and March coverage was at the low rate, and April and May coverage was at the full cost of $151 per month.

The full cost of the coverage beginning in May was raised to $161.48. Therefore, since you paid the $151 before you left, an additional $10.48 should have been taken out of your July paycheck. An adjustment of $10.48 will be taken out of your August paycheck, and everything will be back on schedule.

If you have any questions, feel free to call me. Sincerely

LESSON 10

10.1 Goal: 70 wam speed dictation

Dear Mr. Bailey You have been a policyholder of Mutual Insurance for the past 12 years, and every[1] year we have issued an annual report. This year we are trying something new. Every policyholder will receive a[2] shorter version of the report. This year's report is enclosed, and I hope you will take time to study it carefully.[3]

As the report indicates, we have had a fine year. The company made more money and is in a better[4] condition than ever before. With your help and that of every other policyholder, next year should be[5] an even greater one for all of us. Sincerely yours

[113 words]

10.2

1 there must be some mistake
2 the balance due on your account
3 car insurance premium
4 we did not receive a check from you
5 statement for $250 to cover
6 premium for six months
7 July 6 letter stated
8 check your records
9 to affect your insurance coverage
10 please do so immediately

10.3 Goal: 25 wam transcription rate

Dear Mrs. Santos There must be some mistake regarding the balance that you state is due on your account. On May 21 we sent you a statement for $250 to cover your car insurance premium for six months.

We did not receive a check from you as your July 6 letter stated. Therefore, please check your records. If you find you have not sent this check, please do so immediately. We do not want this to affect your insurance coverage. Sincerely yours

10.4 Time Limit: 15 minutes

August 15, 19--
Mr. Charles Booth
80 Bradford Street
Baltimore, MD 21205
Dear Mr. Booth The fire insurance policy on your property will expire on September 20. To be[1] sure that your property is fully covered, send us your renewal papers at least ten days prior to the[2] expiration date.

Before you send in the renewal, you may wish to take into consideration the increased[3] value of your property and add to your insurance accordingly. As you know, the replacement costs of your[4] possessions have gone up considerably.

If you have any questions regarding either increasing your coverage[5] or any other insurance related items, please feel free to contact us. Sincerely yours
Elizabeth Barnes[6]
Insurance Agent

[124 words]

LESSON 11

11.1 Goal: 70 wam speed dictation

Dear Ms. Garcia For some time I know you have been looking for a health insurance policy that would give you[1] the coverage you need without costing too much.

The policy that I described to you at our last meeting should[2] meet your needs. I believe it is just the type you have been looking for.

The necessary forms are filled out and enclosed[3] for your signature. Please sign both copies of the contract. Retain one copy for your files, and return the other[4] to me for my files. Yours truly

[86 words]

11.2

1 Dear Mrs. Goodman
2 fire insurance policy on your furnishings
3 policy on your home and furnishings will expire
4 enclosed is a three-year renewal policy
5 the premium is $248
6 when you receive this policy
7 sign and date where indicated
8 keep the blue copy for yourself
9 return the remaining copies
10 return your check for $250

11.3 Goal: 25 wam transcription rate

Dear Mrs. Goodman Your fire insurance policy on your home and your furnishings will expire on September 16. Do you realize that that date is only a few weeks away?

Since you do not want your insurance to lapse for even a day, enclosed is a three-year renewal policy. The premium, as you can see, is $248.

When you receive this policy, read it over. If you find it satisfactory, sign and date it where indicated, keep the blue copy for yourself, and return the remaining copies and your check for $250. Sincerely yours

11.4 Time Limit: 15 minutes

August 16, 19--
Mr. James Moreno
5 Park Place
Boston, MA 02130

Dear Mr. Moreno It was very thoughtful of you to write us about your experience with our[1] business-interruption insurance. When our agent, Ms. Barnes, urged you to take out insurance of this type,[2] she knew from experience that someday you might be extremely glad that you did.

This type of insurance has saved[3] many organizations from going out of business as a result of fires. Ordinary fire insurance[4] takes care of the loss due directly to fire but does not do anything about the benefits business[5] executives lose. That is where business-interruption insurance comes into the picture.

All business[6] executives should read your letter. It just might convince them that it is good business to have this insurance.[7] Cordially yours
Frank Jennings
Account Manager [149 words]

LESSON 12

12.1 Goal: 70 wam speed dictation

Dear Mr. Kaplan As you will see from the enclosed card, you can receive a leather memorandum pad. This pad[1] will be forwarded to you if you will fill out and return the enclosed card.

Also enclosed is a booklet that[2] describes some of our most popular insurance plans. We believe that one or more of these plans will be of special[3] interest to you.

If you qualify for one of these plans, just check the plan that interests you the most. Within[4] ten days you will receive both the memorandum pad and the information. Sincerely yours [96 words]

12.2

1 Dear Miss West Thank you for your letter
2 giving us additional information
3 returning your doctor's statements
4 about the extent of your injuries
5 claim has been forwarded
6 we will have to decline
7 disability will be temporary
8 you will eventually recover
9 based upon the information you have given us
10 one of our representatives would be glad

12.3 Goal: 25 wam transcription rate

Dear Miss West Thank you for your letter giving us additional information about your accident. Thank you also for returning your doctor's statement about the extent of your injuries.

Your claim for benefits has been forwarded to me. Based upon the information you have given us, we will have to decline your claim. According to your doctor, your disability will be only temporary and you will eventually recover from your injuries.

If there are any questions you have regarding your policy, please let us know. One of our representatives would be glad to see you at your convenience. Sincerely yours

12.4 Time Limit: 15 minutes

August 17, 19--
Mrs. Carol Frost
468 Church Street
Springfield, MA 01107
Dear Mrs. Frost Thank you for the patience you have shown with us regarding the settling of your claim. After the[1] storm on Saturday, July 14, that damaged your property, our representatives in your area have been[2] very busy.

One of our representatives will be calling you to make an appointment to discuss your claim within[3] the next few days. At the time that the representative does talk with you, please feel free to ask any questions[4] you may have. If all goes well, on that same day you should be able to receive a check to cover your damages.[5] Yours truly
Frank Jennings
Account Manager [108 words]

LESSON 13

13.1 Goal: 70 wam dictation speed

Dear Mrs. Sloan We appreciate your letter on behalf of Boyd Gates, our agent in your area. Customer[1] satisfaction is extremely important in a service industry such as the insurance business.[2] Mr. Gates has always been one of our best agents, and it is good to hear that he still maintains high standards.

Our[3] organization realizes that there is no substitute for service. Properly written insurance results[4] in prompt and satisfactory settlement of claims. More than 90 percent of our claims are settled within[5] 14 days.

You deserve the finest insurance service; we are pleased that Mr. Gates is delivering this[6] to you. Cordially yours [124 words]

13.2

1 Dear Mrs. Diaz As a young business professional
2 you are careful about what you do
3 you select a good bank
4 look into many options
5 has it occurred to you
6 before you make a decision
7 insurance on your property
8 careful planning can save you $5,000
9 insurance meets your special needs
10 take advantage of the service

13.3 Goal: 25 wam transcription rate

Dear Mrs. Diaz As a young business professional, you are careful about what you do with your money. When it is to be deposited, you select a good bank. When it is to be invested, you look into many options before you make a decision.

Has it occurred to you to be just as careful about the way you place insurance on your property? Careful planning can save you $5,000, $10,000, or even $20,000 over a period of years.

If you want to give your insurance the attention it deserves, call one of our agents. They are there to see that your insurance meets your special needs.

Take advantage of the service we are offering. By acting today, you may save money tomorrow. Sincerely yours

13.4 Time Limit: 15 minutes

August 20, 19--
Mr. George T. Charles
85201 State Street
Bridgeport, CT 06604
Dear Mr. Charles Your inquiry about your whole life insurance policy has been referred to me. The cash value[1] of the policy is $15,000. The value of this policy will increase considerably,[2] however, in the next three years it is in effect.

It will be a pleasure to have our agent, Joe Baker, call[3] you and discuss your current policy and other insurance offerings we have available. The programs[4] we offer are explained in the enclosed booklet. Perhaps you might wish to read this booklet and then ask Joe any[5] questions you may have when he calls.

If there is any other way in which we can serve you, please do not hesitate[6] to let us know. Sincerely yours
Frank Jennings
Account Manager [132 words]
Enclosure

LESSON 14

14.1 Goal: 70 wam speed dictation

Dear Mr. Benjamin Subject: Transfer of Account As you requested, the address on your policy has been[1] changed from 415 West Street, Hartford, Connecticut 06106, to 650 West Franklin Street, Pittsburgh,[2] Pennsylvania 15221.

Since most of the state of Pennsylvania is covered by our Harrisburg[3] office, your account is being transferred to that office. You will hear from the manager of that office just[4] as soon as the transfer has been completed.

If we can ever be of service to you at this office, do not[5] hesitate to contact us. Cordially yours [108 words]

14.2

1 it was a pleasure to receive your letter
2 service from our representative, Ms. Berg
3 Ms. Berg will look after your interests
4 you were wise to explain your needs
5 you were wise to ask for her recommendations
6 many business executives tell their agents
7 ask for the advice of your agent
8 the agent does not recommend the coverage
9 the kind of coverage the business needs
10 we will be here to meet your needs

14.3 Goal: 25 wam transcription rate

Dear Mr. Kane It was a pleasure to receive your letter telling us of the service that you received from our representative, Ms. Berg. Ms. Berg will continue to look after your interests to see that your insurance meets the changing needs of your business.

You were wise to explain your needs to Ms. Berg and to ask her for her recommendations. Many business executives tell their insurance agents what they want rather than ask for their advice. As a result, the agent often does not recommend the kind of coverage that the business needs.

As your business grows, we will be here to meet your growing insurance needs. Cordially yours

14.4 Time Limit: 15 minutes

August 21, 19--
Mr. Frank Katz
302 Howard Place
Springfield, MA 01105
Dear Mr. Katz Imagine buying a car and turning it in and getting your money back after driving it for[1] 15 years.

Imagine renting a house for 15 years and at the end of that time moving out and having all[2] the rent you have paid returned to you.

Imagine buying an airline ticket to Europe and after arriving[3] turning in your used ticket for your fare back home.

Imagine paying insurance premiums for 15 years and[4] at the end of that time getting back every dollar you ever paid in.

In one of these instances you do not have[5] to imagine. You can provide insurance protection for yourself for years and years and then receive back all the[6] money you paid in premiums. A number of examples proving this point are given in the enclosed booklet.[7]

Why not let us discuss your insurance program with you. Give us a call at your convenience. Sincerely yours
George[8] Sinclair
Insurance Agent [165 words]
Enclosure

LESSON 15

15.1 Goal: 70 wam speed dictation

Dear Miss Willis Have you recently increased the amount of insurance you carry on your property?[1] If you have not, you are probably underinsured. In case of loss you may find yourself carrying part of that loss[2] yourself.

During the last five years the cost of living in this country has increased by over 35 percent.[3] If your policies have not been reviewed or updated in the past few years, you should do something about it at[4] once.

Your Mutual Insurance agent will be glad to assist you in determining the right amount of[5] insurance you need to cover higher costs. Why not contact your local agent today. Yours sincerely [118 words]

15.2

1 Dear Mr. and Mrs. Hastings
2 in case a fire should break out
3 your children would come first
4 clothing, personal papers, or other valuables
5 insurance up to date with today's values
6 a $75,000 policy no longer covers
7 how much home and contents increased
8 convenient inventory booklet will quickly
9 how much your property is worth
10 let us give you one of these booklets

15.3 Goal: 25 wam transcription rate

Dear Mr. and Mrs. Hastings In case a fire should break out in your home, what would you save first? Your children, of course, would come first. What would come next? Would it be clothing, personal papers, or some other valuables?

All too often a fire brings out the fact that a $75,000 policy no longer covers your property and your belongings. Many of us do not realize how many valuables we have or how much our home and its contents have increased in recent years.

Is your insurance up to date with today's values? A convenient inventory booklet will quickly tell you how much your property is worth. Come in soon and let us give you one of these booklets. Cordially yours

15.4 Time Limit: 15 minutes

August 23, 19--
Miss Marilyn Travis
88 East State Street
Lynn, MA 01901
Dear Miss Travis We are enclosing your term life insurance policy in the amount of $10,000[1] and an accident and health insurance policy which has a monthly premium of $100.

You are[2] now covered for every accident and illness that might disable you up to 14 days. Your policy[3] takes care of all your medical bills. Should you be disabled for more than 14 days, please notify us so that[4] we may process the necessary papers to take care of your claim.

We hope you are satisfied with your insurance.[5] If you have any questions concerning your policies, please feel free to call us. Sincerely yours
Elizabeth[6] Barnes
Insurance Agent [125 words]
Enclosure

LESSON 16

16.1 Goal: 70 wam speed dictation

Dear Mr. Long As a forest fire fighter, you are in danger every day. Do you realize how tragic it would[1] be if you were to suffer a serious injury today?

It would mean that your income would be cut off[2] and that you would have to meet the heavy expenses that a serious injury brings with it. You would have to[3] pay all these expenses out of your savings. As you have allowed your policy to lapse, your insurance would pay[4] nothing.

Therefore, why not put your policy back into effect. You will never be sorry for the investment[5] you make by keeping your insurance policy paid up. Sincerely yours [113 words]

16.2

1 Dear Mr. Diaz
2 a disaster, such as a fire
3 your insurance is not adequate
4 your business could be temporarily shut down
5 one of our policies will protect you
6 provide you with many other benefits
7 your business is losing money
8 you cannot be without adequate protection
9 why not call one of our agents
10 explain how a policy can be adapted

16.3 Goal: 25 wam transcription rate

Dear Mr. Diaz It often takes a disaster, such as a fire, to make you aware that your insurance is not adequate. Either your business could be brought to a complete stop or it could be temporarily shut down.

One of our policies will protect you against a fire and provide you with many other benefits. One benefit is that we will pay you the amount of money you are losing while your business is shut down, either completely or partially.

Whatever your business may be, you cannot afford to be without adequate protection. Why not call one of our agents today and have them explain how a policy can be adapted to your needs. Cordially yours

16.4 Time Limit: 15 minutes

August 24, 19--
Ms. Carla Rossi
57 Garden Park Drive
Stamford, CT 06901
Dear Ms. Rossi Your mother's accident was indeed unfortunate, and we hope that by this time she is entirely[1] well.

You are correct in your understanding that your insurance policy covers this type of accident.[2] It is times like these that you are glad that you had the foresight to invest in this type of insurance.

Before we can[3] pay your claim for $370, however, it will be necessary for you to fill out[4] and sign the enclosed forms. As soon as we receive these forms, we will send you a check. Yours truly
George Sinclair
Insurance[5] Agent [101 words]
Enclosures

LESSON 17

17.1 Goal: 80 wam speed dictation

Dear Mr. and Mrs. Davis Yesterday Mr. Charles Wilson came into our real estate office to place his[1] home for sale. When he described the home and mentioned the location, I thought of you. This home appears to meet your[2] requirements better than any other home I have seen on the market.

The house is located in southern Phoenix,[3] has four bedrooms, a large family room, a dining room, and two baths.

The owners are asking $180,000,[4] but they will consider any reasonable offer. Call me immediately if you are interested.[5] Very truly yours

[104 words]

17.2

1 last week's classified section of the Daily Times
2 I saw your advertisement to sell your home
3 at 273 North Street
4 this is an outstanding location
5 I am sure there is a buyer
6 that buyer may not have seen your advertisement
7 your personal listing does not produce results
8 considered an exclusive listing
9 call the Franklin Real Estate Agency
10 you are under no obligation

17.3 Goal: 25 wam transcription rate

Dear Mr. Hughes In last week's classified section of the Daily Times, I saw your advertisement to sell your home at 273 North Street. Your home is in an outstanding location, and I am sure there is a buyer waiting to purchase it.

However, that buyer may not have seen your advertisement. If your personal listing does not produce results, I suggest you consider an exclusive listing with the Franklin Real Estate Agency.

When you call the Franklin Real Estate Agency, you are under no obligation unless you decide you want us to sell your home. Cordially yours

LESSON 18

18.1 Goal: 80 wam speed dictation

Dear Mrs. Turner You stated in our telephone conversation yesterday that you are looking for an[1] apartment. You wanted to be able to move in November 1.

A new building, a duplicate of the Lee[2] Building on Franklin Street, will be completed around the middle of October, and units are renting quickly.[3]

We can make an appointment to look at one of the two-bedroom units in the Lee Building to determine if the[4] unit meets your needs. Please give me a call if you are interested in doing so. Yours truly

[97 words]

18.2

1 a two-bedroom apartment
2 West Side development
3 unfortunately, there is a waiting list
4 interested in apartments
5 apartment that is now vacant
6 we would be glad to give you
7 one-year or two-year lease
8 the building superintendent, Miss Lopez
9 the rent is $620 a month
10 this includes utilities

18.3 Goal: 25 wam transcription rate

Dear Mr. Nelson Your request for a two-bedroom apartment in the West Side development has been forwarded to me. Unfortunately, there is a waiting list of ten families who are interested in apartments of this size.

However, there is a three-bedroom apartment that is now vacant and for which we would be glad to give you a one-year or two-year lease. If you are interested in this apartment, the building superintendent, Miss Lopez, will be glad to show it to you at your convenience. The rent is $620 a month, and this includes utilities.

If this apartment is too large for you and you would like to have us place you on the waiting list for two-bedroom apartments, please let us know. Sincerely yours

18.4 Time Limit: 15 minutes

September 12, 19--
Mr. Mark Baldwin
365 Oak Street
Scottsdale, AZ 85257
Dear Mr. Baldwin The manager of your building reported to us that you have asked to have your apartment[1] painted.

You will recall that you signed a one-year lease when you originally rented the apartment about[2] six months ago. As you were told then, one-year leases are not usually issued. You signed the lease on the[3] condition that you take the apartment as it was. This condition appears on page 2 of your lease.

Keeping in[4] accordance with your lease, we are not able to paint your apartment. If you were to lease the apartment for a[5] period of three years and at the same rent you are now paying, we would be glad to paint the apartment.

Let us know[6] your decision by September 20.
Sincerely
Sam Byrd
Sales Agent [133 words]

LESSON 19

19.1 Goal: 80 wam speed dictation

Dear Mrs. Murphy You asked that you be kept up to date of the success we have had in selling your house on Main[1] Street. In the past two weeks only one party has looked at it.

A young couple was considering purchasing your[2] house. In fact, they looked at the house on three occasions, but they finally decided against purchasing it.

The[3] real estate business is in a slump. With interest rates decreasing, however, the market should turn around in[4] about another month.

You will be informed, of course, when someone is interested in buying your house. Yours truly[5]

[100 words]

19.2

1 Dear Miss Ashley The renting situation in Phoenix
2 situation is no better in Tucson
3 apartments are scarce everywhere
4 you are being transferred to Phoenix
5 you would not be able to rent without a lease
6 currently there are no vacancies
7 no vacancies in the western part of Phoenix
8 sign at least a two-year lease
9 consider renting a furnished room
10 transfer to Phoenix will be permanent

19.3 Goal: 25 wam transcription rate

Dear Miss Ashley The renting situation in Phoenix is no better than it is in Tucson. Apartments are scarce and the rents are especially high in the western part of the city where you indicated you would like to live.

Currently, there are no vacancies in the western part of Phoenix. If an apartment were available, you would not be able to rent it without signing at least a two-year lease.

Since you are being transferred to Phoenix, you might consider renting a furnished room for a few months. By that time you may know whether your transfer to Phoenix will be permanent. Yours sincerely

19.4 Time Limit: 15 minutes

September 14, 19--
Mr. Bryan Palmer
45 Country Club Road
Scottsdale, AZ 85255
Dear Mr. Palmer Mrs. Joyce Davis, whose house you have purchased, just called. She tells me that the carpet in the living[1] room is one year old. The original cost of the carpeting was $800, but Mrs. Davis says[2] that she will be glad to sell you the carpet for $400. Please let Mrs. Davis know if you would be[3] interested in buying it at that price.

According to present plans, Mrs. Davis and her daughter will move[4] out of the house on the morning of September 18. A professional cleaning service will be cleaning the[5] house that day, and you will be able to move in on September 19 if you so desire. Cordially yours
Philip[6] Pierce
Sales Agent [123 words]

LESSON 20

20.1 Goal: 80 wam speed dictation

Dear Mr. Pierce I am submitting some information on property in Tucson for your review. From your[1] description this land is exactly what you have been looking for.

Although $75,000 is more[2] than you originally had in mind to pay for property, you may be willing to go that high for something[3] that really meets your needs. If flights can be arranged, you and your wife should visit the property next week.

If you decide[4] that the property is what you want, we will make the necessary arrangements for the purchase. Cordially yours[5] [100 words]

20.2

1 Dear Mr. Wong On September 15
2 moved out of the furnished house
3 a list of damages is enclosed
4 most of the damage is minor
5 one thing caused me great concern
6 top of the grand piano in the living room
7 there is a deep scratch
8 the damage amounts to about $750
9 get in touch with Mr. Davis and explain
10 I will be glad to explain to your client the situation

20.3 Goal: 25 wam transcription rate

Dear Mr. Wong On September 15 your client, Robert Davis, moved out of the furnished house he was renting from my client, George Franklin.

He did not leave the house in very good condition. A list of damages is enclosed. While most of the damage is minor, one thing caused me great concern. There is a deep scratch on the top of the new grand piano in the living room.

The rest of the damage amounts to about $750. Please get in touch with Mr. Davis and explain to him the situation. If you and your client wish me to do so, I will be glad to take you over to the house and point out the damages. Yours truly

20.4 Time Limit: 15 minutes

September 21, 19--
Ms. Diane Johnson
55 Columbus Street
Dallas, TX 75252
Dear Ms. Johnson Your offer of $160,000 for the Freeman house in Phoenix has been[1] rejected. Mr. Freeman contends that he cannot accept anything less than the $165,000[2] he is asking. There is little chance from his comments that he will lower the price.

Perhaps you should let me show you[3] some other houses that are available in your price range. There is another house listed at $162,000[4] that might interest you.

This house is a little smaller than the Freeman house, but it has an added attraction[5] — a swimming pool. The house will not stay on the market

long. If you would like to see it, call me to set up an[6] appointment. Sincerely
Carla Clark
Sales Agent [129 words]

LESSON 21

21.1 Goal: 80 wam speed dictation

Dear Mr. O'Bryan Your decision to move to Arizona after you retire is quite happy news. As you[1] requested, we will help you locate a home near Phoenix.

Enclosed are a number of booklets and folders that describe[2] what Phoenix has to offer for housing. Look over this material, and feel free to ask us any questions[3] you might have.

As you know, thousands of people turn to Arizona when they are looking for a place to retire.[4] You will make no mistake by following their example. Sincerely yours [93 words]

21.2

1 the lease expires on November 30
2 you can remain for another year
3 he must raise the rent
4 $500 a month to $650
5 taxes and maintenance have increased
6 remain at your current address
7 pay the higher rent
8 we will begin showing the house
9 people who might be interested
10 please call by 5 p.m.

21.3 Goal: 25 wam transcription rate

Dear Miss Young As you know, the lease on the furnished house you are now renting expires on November 30.

The owner of the house is willing to have you remain for another year. Since his taxes and maintenance costs have increased, he feels that he must raise the rent from $500 a month to $650, however.

If you would like to remain at your current address and pay the higher rent, please let us know and we will draw up a new lease for you. If not, we will begin showing the house to people who might be interested.

Please call by 5 p.m. on Friday to give us your decision. Cordially yours

21.4 Time Limit: 15 minutes

September 24, 19--
Mrs. Carol Simon
12 Third Street
Phoenix, AZ 85004
Dear Mrs. Simon You asked some very interesting questions during our meeting Wednesday regarding the housing[1] situation in Mesa. As a realtor, I think your insight was right on target. Here are a few more things[2] for you to consider before you put your house on the market.

The three new companies have brought many people[3] to the city. It is hoped that this will be a trend, but it is hard to tell at this point. Population experts[4] have estimated that there are 7,500 more people now than four months ago.

Why[5] not contact the personnel offices of each of the new companies and let them know that you have a house for[6] sale. One of their new employees may be looking for a home to buy.

If you decide that you would like to list your[7] house with a realtor, I would be more than happy to handle it. Cordially yours
Philip Franklin
President[8] [160 words]

LESSON 22

22.1 Goal: 80 wam speed dictation

Dear Mr. Brown Thank you for your letter requesting a copy of our booklet <u>Planning Parks for Cities</u>.[1] It is nice to know that you think this booklet may be able to help. However, the distribution of this booklet[2] is limited to members of the engineering departments of cities having a population of[3] 35,000 or more. Therefore, you can understand why we are unable to comply with your request.

Should[4] you have any specific questions concerning planning a park for a smaller city, I will gladly answer[5] them. Feel free to call or write me. Cordially yours [109 words]

22.2

1 we must take some action
2 planned expansion in the future
3 we will be overcrowded because of expansion
4 solution to the problem would be
5 try to rent additional space
6 option would give temporary relief
7 recommended building our own office building
8 board of directors meeting
9 free to attend the meeting
10 present the report you prepared

22.3 Goal: 25 wam transcription rate

Ms. Costa We must take some action about getting more office space. Because of the planned expansion in the future, we will be overcrowded.

As you have suggested, a solution to the problem would be to try to rent additional space in this building. However, that option would give only temporary relief. Our projected growth shows that in another year or two that space will not be adequate.

It has been more than a year since you recommended building our own office building. At the board of directors meeting in two weeks I will recommend this proposal. Are you free to attend the meeting and present the report you prepared for me last year? Frank

22.4 Time Limit: 15 minutes

September 26, 19--
Mr. Peter Blake
21 Grand Avenue
St. Louis, MO 63138
Dear Mr. Blake Thank you for your letter inquiring about business rentals. Franklin Real Estate handles only[1] apartment rentals. On rare occasions, however, we will help one of our regular clients who has an office[2] building for rent.

Your letter has been referred to a colleague who does handle business rentals. Her name is Paula[3] Taylor, and I am certain she will help you find something you will like. She has been in the real estate business[4] for over 15 years.

If you ever have the need for an apartment rental, please give me a call. Very truly yours[5]
Philip Pierce
Sales Agent [104 words]

LESSON 23

23.1 Goal: 80 wam speed dictation

Dear Ms. Howard You will recall that you visited our office last June and told us you were interested[1] in buying a house in Phoenix. You wanted an eight-room house with three bedrooms and two full baths. You were willing to[2] pay up to $185,000 for it. At that time, however, there were no such houses[3] available.

If you still have not found anything you like, you might be interested in a house on Jackson[4] Street that has been placed on the market. It meets your needs in every way, including the price. The owner is asking[5] $180,000 for it.

Please let me know as soon as possible whether or not you are[6] interested. If so, when are you available to see the property? Sincerely yours

[137 words]

23.2

1 Dear Dr. Reeves On August 10
2 the contractor completed the installation
3 installation of the new air-conditioning unit
4 you will be interested to know that the
5 we have not been able to cool the house
6 the past three weeks have been very warm
7 there are still warm weeks ahead
8 we have immediate assurance that our customer
9 our customer can be comfortable here
10 we may terminate their lease

23.3 Goal: 25 wam transcription rate

Dear Dr. Reeves On August 10 the contractor completed the installation of the new air-conditioning unit that you purchased for the house George Day is renting from you. You will be interested to know that the air-conditioning unit has been nothing but trouble for the three weeks it has been in operation.

We have not been able to cool the house properly. As you know, the past three weeks have been very warm. There are still some warm weeks ahead. Unless we have immediate assurance that our customer can be comfortable, we may have to take steps to terminate their lease. Sincerely yours

23.4 Time Limit: 15 minutes

September 27, 19--
Mr. Adam Stone
35 Hillside Avenue
Minneapolis, MN 55403
Dear Mr. Stone Now is the time to plan for your summer home for next year. If you plan to rent, why not purchase[1] one of the summer homes available at Brandon Lake instead. Your summer home could be a weekend[2] retreat throughout the year.

There are many nice homes available for less than $3,000 down and[3] small monthly payments. You could own a cottage instead of just renting one for about the same amount of money.[4]

Why not act now so that your family will have a pleasant summer next year and for many years to come. Let us[5] arrange a day on which we can drive you to Brandon Lake and show you the homes that are available.[6] Cordially yours
Philip Franklin
President [128 words]

LESSON 24

24.1 Goal: 80 wam speed dictation

Dear Mr. Ford Enclosed is your title to the land you purchased on Whitney Street. When you first looked at this lot, you[1] also expressed interest in the adjacent vacant lot. At that time another couple had already put[2] a down payment on it.

The couple contacted us yesterday to let us know that they have been transferred to[3] another city and no longer wish to retain this property. They are anxious to sell. If you would still like[4] to purchase this land, we will not list it in our real estate bulletin.

Please contact us as soon as possible[5] and give us your decision. We will be happy to help you finance this property along with your other lot.[6] Sincerely yours [123 words]

24.2

1 Dear Mr. and Mrs. Freeman
2 expressed an interest in purchasing an apartment
3 the building located at 718 West Street
4 all units are now rented
5 have been rented during the past four years
6 current owner has a waiting list
7 this building represents a wonderful value
8 looking for an income-producing property
9 are you available to view this building?
10 call me as soon as possible

24.3 Goal: 25 wam transcription rate

Dear Mr. and Mrs. Freeman Since you expressed interest in purchasing an apartment building, you will be glad to know that one has been listed with our office.

The building, located at 718 West Street, is four years old and is modern in every respect. All units are now rented and have been during the entire four years. The current owner has a waiting list of people wishing to get in.

The building represents a wonderful value for anyone looking for an income-producing property. I am anxious to show you this property. Is there some time that you can be available to view this building? Please call me as soon as possible. Sincerely yours

24.4 Time Limit: 15 minutes

Date: September 28, 19--
To: Sam Byrd
From: Philip Franklin
Subject: Property Auction
On Friday morning, October 26, the county will sell at auction several parcels of property[1] in the borough of Greensburg. These are vacant lots on which taxes have not been paid for the past five years.

I am[2] enclosing a list of the addresses of the lots that are to be sold. I hope you will spend some time looking at[3] each piece of property and then prepare a priority listing of those lots on which you think we should consider[4] making bids.

Please let me have your recommendations as soon as possible. [94 words]
Enclosure

24.5 Time Limit: 5 minutes

Property Listing
1. 385 East Main Street — one-acre lot
2. 4713 East Main Street — 200 x 385[1] lot
3. 35 Madison Avenue — 405 x 385 lot
4. 62 Whitney Street — 315[2] x 500 lot

[43 words]

LESSON 25

25.1 Goal: 80 wam speed dictation

Dear Ms. Rivera We appreciate receiving your letter which brought to my attention the correspondence regarding your outstanding[1] credit balance. You stated that we had received payment for the books that were shipped to you on August 3. In[2] reviewing the records, it is my understanding that you did indeed pay for those books on August 14.

Your[3] courteous handling of this matter is very much appreciated. We apologize for this error and hope[4] we may again serve you in the future. Very truly yours [92 words]

25.2

1 Dear Ms. Garcia You are a valued member
2 our sales records, however, indicate
3 many months have passed
4 have you not ordered any magazines
5 is there some dissatisfaction with our service?
6 some other aspect of our Club
7 we are anxious to know
8 where did we go wrong?
9 if you are dissatisfied in some way
10 your assistance would be greatly appreciated

25.3 Goal: 25 wam transcription rate

Dear Ms. Garcia You are a valued member of the Publishing Club. Our sales records, however, indicate that many months have passed since we have had a magazine order from you.

Have you not ordered any magazines because of some dissatisfaction with our service? Did you find some other aspect of our club not to your satisfaction? You are one of our best customers, and we are anxious to find out where we went wrong.

If you have been dissatisfied in some way, will you please call or write me and let me know? Your assistance in this matter will be greatly appreciated. Yours truly

LESSON 26

26.1 Goal: 80 wam speed dictation

Dear Mr. Bray On July 25 we received your order for 12 subscriptions to News Magazine. We[1] were to send the magazine to the persons listed on the enclosed sheet and to start the subscriptions with the September[2] issue.

Three of these subscriptions did not arrive at their destination because of errors in the addresses.[3] Will you please send us updated addresses for David Parks, Betty Michaels, and Peter Franklin. Sincerely[4] [80 words]

26.2

1 Dear Mrs. White Our representative in your area
2 Mr. Gray has suggested that your name be placed
3 people who receive complimentary copies
4 monthly magazine Financial Monthly
5 Financial Monthly has been serving the banking and investment field
6 its main purpose is providing helpful and practical information
7 we hope that you will find it interesting
8 it is our pleasure to do this
9 if you would let us know how you like the magazine
10 we welcome any suggestions

26.3 Goal: 25 wam transcription rate

Dear Mrs. White Our representative in your area, Mr. Gray, has suggested that your name be placed on our list of people who receive complimentary copies of our monthly magazine Financial Monthly. It is our pleasure to do this.

Financial Monthly has been serving the banking and investment field since 1902. Its main purpose is providing helpful and practical information to our friends.

We hope that you will find Financial Monthly interesting and helpful. We would appreciate it if you would let us know how you like the magazine, and we welcome any suggestions you might have. Yours truly

26.4 Time Limit: 15 minutes

October 9, 19--
Mrs. Agnes Samuels
102 First Avenue
Fort Wayne, IN 46206
Dear Mrs. Samuels When someone asked Lincoln how long a person's legs must be, he replied that "they should only be[1] long enough to reach the ground." This note is only long enough to remind you to send your check for your renewal[2] to News Magazine today.

Attach your check to the statement that is enclosed, and mail both the statement and the check[3] to us. That is all that is necessary to clear your account. Why not do it now.

If your check is already[4] in the mail, please disregard this note. Sincerely yours
Kenneth Lopez [92 words]
Enclosure

LESSON 27

27.1 Goal: 80 wam speed dictation

Dear Mr. Dale Thank you for your two-year subscription to News Magazine. We have received your check for $25,[1] and you will be getting the November issue of the magazine within two weeks.

You can be assured that you have[2] made a wise move in subscribing to this publication. Our unique format deals with the lighter side of the news.[3] It is pleasant reading for persons of all ages.

The value of this magazine increases with the years.[4] In effect, it becomes a record of another side of history. We hope, therefore, that you will make every[5] effort to hold on to your back issues. Yours truly [109 words]

27.2

1 Dear Mr. Moses It has been several weeks
2 I wrote you about a special offer
3 trial subscription to our magazine Sports Today
4 since you did not reply to the offer
5 the offer was good for only 15 days
6 let us know that you would like to receive
7 we will enter your one-year subscription
8 starting with next month's subscription
9 cents an issue rather than the $1.50 newsstand
10 fill out the order blank

27.3 Goal: 25 wam transcription rate

Dear Mr. Moses It has been several weeks since I wrote you about a special offer for a trial subscription to our magazine Sports Today. Since you did not reply, I was afraid that my letter may not have reached you. The letter stated that the offer was good for only 15 days. However, the offer has been extended for another week.

If you let us know that you would like to receive Sports Today, we will enter your one-year subscription for $28 starting with next month's issue. You will receive 52 issues for $28. That is only 54 cents an issue rather than the $1.50 newsstand price.

Why not take a few minutes now and fill out the order blank so next month you can be enjoying the excitement within the pages of Sports Today. Sincerely yours

27.4 Time Limit: 15 minutes

October 10, 19--
Mr. David Callahan
767 Hallmark Avenue
Cincinnati, OH 45225
Dear Mr. Callahan Have you wished for a way to end your Christmas shopping worries? Here is a simple way. Give[1] each of your friends a subscription to Sports Today. Every month your friends will enjoy the color photos and[2] captivating articles.

Make up a list now by writing the names and addresses on the enclosed order blank,[3] and mail it to us. We will do the rest. Your friends will receive a Christmas card telling them that they are receiving[4] a year's subscription to Sports Today as a gift from you.

If you use the enclosed order blank when you send in your[5] order, the rate for each subscription will be only $18. Cordially yours
Martin Tyler [118 words]
Enclosure

LESSON 28

28.1 Goal: 80 wam speed dictation

Dear Mr. Hoffmann Since you have been a regular contributor to our publication The Book Guide, we thought[1] it necessary to let you know of some changes.

Because of the difficulty in producing this[2] magazine under present conditions, the president thought it best to stop publication entirely. The[3] current issue will be the last until conditions improve. As soon as conditions improve, publication will[4] resume.

Thank you for the interest you have shown in our publication. You will be kept up to date on the status[5] of the magazine. Yours truly [105 words]

28.2

1 reviews of your manuscript have been returned
2 pleased to know that the reaction
3 your article "Time Management"
4 start at least three months ahead
5 it is ahead of its scheduled release
6 it will be a while before your article
7 your article will be published
8 published in the Executive Journal
9 we will keep you informed about its progress
10 we hope that you will not mind waiting

28.3 Goal: 25 wam transcription rate

Dear Mrs. Winters The reviews of your manuscript have all been returned. You will be pleased to know that the reaction to your article "Time Management" was favorable. We would like to publish it as soon as possible. However, we start to work on issues at least three months ahead of their scheduled release. Therefore, it will be a while before your article will fit into an issue.

Your article will be published in the Executive Journal, and we will keep you informed about its progress. We hope that you will not mind waiting. Cordially yours

28.4 Time Limit: 15 minutes

28315-07 Accounting Today $22.50

707831-30[1] Business Opportunities $35.25

715828-005 Office of[2] Tomorrow $28.25

473960-752 Reference Manual[3] $15.85

373821-786 English Essentials $18.20[4] [80 words]

LESSON 29

29.1 Goal: 80 wam speed dictation

Dear Ms. Barlow Your letter of October 5 informing us of a shortage in the shipment of books that we[1] mailed to you on September 20 has been referred to me. According to our shipping records, the order was[2] complete when it left our shipping room. As our own truck took the case of books to the air express company, we[3] believe that the shortage must have occurred after the books reached there.

We are sending you duplicate copies of the[4] books that are missing. We hope that this shortage has not caused you too much inconvenience. Cordially yours [98 words]

29.2

1 Dear Mr. Shepard Last July
2 error in computing your commission
3 company sold $25,000 worth of books
4 commission was to be divided
5 Ms. Morris was to get 25 percent
6 you were to get the remainder
7 we credited Ms. Morris' account
8 will you please tell us whether
9 have a check for $750 immediately
10 you would prefer us to add the amount to your next check

29.3 Goal: 25 wam transcription rate

Dear Mr. Shepard Last July we made an error in computing your commission. You will recall that the company sold $25,000 worth of books to the Klein Bookstore. The commission on that sale was to be divided between you and Ms. Morris. Ms. Morris was to get 25 percent of $1,000, and you were to get the remainder. However, we credited Ms. Morris' account with the entire $1,000.

Will you please tell us whether you would like to have a check for $750 immediately or whether you would prefer to have us add the amount to your next check. Sincerely yours

29.4 Time Limit: 15 minutes

October 15, 19--
Mrs. Rose Costa
135 Taylor Avenue
Rochester, MN 55403
Dear Mrs. Costa The October 31 date for payment of your Executive Club dues is rapidly[1] approaching. If you pay your dues by October 31, you will remain on the active member list and will[2] continue to receive all publications such as Financial Monthly, Executive Journal, the national[3] club newsletter, and the newsletter from your local club.

Will you please take a few minutes to write your check for[4] $65 for your Executive Club dues. Cordially yours
Kenneth Lopez [95 words]

LESSON 30

30.1 Goal: 80 wam speed dictation

Dear Mrs. Mendez We are sorry to hear that your night class in business English did not materialize and[1] that, therefore, you wish to return the 23 copies of our book Basic English that you ordered for the class.[2]

We will, of course, be glad to accept the books for full credit provided that they have not been marked in any way.[3] As you know, the books should be returned to our Denver office. We will reimburse you for postage.

When you return[4] the books, please use the enclosed packing list. Very truly yours [91 words]

30.2

1 lover of good books
2 you will be interested in the services
3 books that you wish to sell
4 we will be happy to receive a list
5 we will be glad to give a price quotation
6 tell you how much they are worth
7 enclosed is our latest catalog
8 receive each new edition of this catalog
9 whatever your book requirements may be
10 let our organization assist you

30.3 Goal: 25 wam transcription rate

Dear Mr. Hines As a lover of good books, you will be interested in the services that our organization offers.

If you have any books that you wish to sell, we will be happy to receive a list of them and tell you how much they are worth. If you need books on any subject, we will be glad to give you a price quotation.

Enclosed is our latest catalog of the books that we have available. If you would like to receive each new edition of this catalog, please let us know. Whatever your book requirements may be, let our organization assist you. Cordially yours

30.4 Time Limit: 15 minutes

October 16, 19--
Ms. Beatrice Dale
Phillips High School
241 Maxwell Avenue
Lexington, KY 40507
Dear Ms. Dale Thank you for your recent order of 20 copies of Introduction to Business. This is an[1] exciting new textbook that has eliminated the dry prose of most business texts. You will find that using[2] this book as a teaching aid will be most refreshing.

Perhaps you forgot or perhaps you were not aware that we[3] also offer an accompanying instructor's edition. Since you did order more than ten copies of the[4] textbook, you are entitled to receive the manual free. However, the manual will be only[5] sent upon request.

Your request must be submitted on your official purchase order form or on school letterhead.[6] As soon as we receive your request, your copy of the instructor's edition will be sent to you. Sincerely yours[7]
Martin Tyler [143 words]

LESSON 31

31.1 Goal: 80 wam speed dictation

Dear Mr. Walsh I am sorry you have been having difficulty in receiving our magazine Chemical[1] Engineer. Our computer shows that your correct address is on file. Therefore, you should have been receiving issues[2] regularly.

Sometimes confusion at the local post office causes this type of difficulty. Perhaps if you[3] go to your post office and explain that you are not receiving the magazines that are being sent to you, this[4] situation may get straightened out.

In the meantime, we are sending you the July, August, and September[5] issues that you have missed. Yours sincerely [106 words]

31.2

1 Dear Mrs. Wong
2 increased cost of production and paper
3 it will be necessary to advance the prices
4 the price changes are announced
5 other distributors are receiving this notice
6 you now have an opportunity
7 place your next order soon at the present low prices
8 enclosed folder gives a list
9 prices will go into effect on December 1
10 you will quickly see the worthwhile savings

31.3 Goal: 25 wam transcription rate

Dear Mrs. Wong Because of the increased cost of production and paper, it will be necessary for us to advance the prices of some of our magazines.

Before the price changes are announced, you and other distributors are receiving this advance notice. You now have an opportunity to place your next order at the present low prices.

The enclosed folder gives a list of our present prices and the prices that will go into effect on December 1. You will quickly see the worthwhile savings if you order now.

Send in your order soon. We will be waiting to hear from you. Cordially yours

31.4 Time Limit: 15 minutes

October 23, 19--
Miss Leslie Kramer
355 Madison Avenue
Pittsburgh, PA 15209
Dear Miss Kramer Several days ago our sales representative for the state of Colorado resigned, and we are[1] looking for a replacement. The job has a great future for a person who is interested in making a[2] career in publishing and marketing.

The position will pay $25,000 a year to start, and[3] there will be regular annual increases if the person shows interest and enthusiasm. In addition,[4] we pay all sales representatives a commission if they sell above their quota.

We want a person who has[5] a college education and who enjoys traveling. If you have a person listed in your files who you[6] think could handle this position, please let us know. Sincerely yours
Kenneth Lopez [134 words]

LESSON 32

32.1 Goal: 80 wam speed dictation

Dear Mr. Douglas Thank you for submitting your article to our publishing company for consideration.[1] As you know, it is our policy to send it out to a group of people who will read it, respond to it, and then[2] send their comments back to us. After we receive their appraisals, the editors will make the final decision[3] about publishing your article.

The readers' responses will be back in three weeks, and our editorial board will[4] meet on Friday, November 30. According to this time line, you will hear from us in six weeks.

You will be[5] interested to know that the initial reaction to your article was favorable. Your insight into the[6] many ways in which shorthand can increase productivity certainly proves that shorthand is indeed needed in the[7] office of today. Cordially yours [147 words]

32.2

1 share with me the results and observations
2 new textbook Communication Today
3 any difference in student achievement
4 achievement between this year and previous years
5 aptitude tests administered before the
6 after the course has been completed
7 accurate indicator of progress
8 above average in results
9 your taking the time
10 if we can be of assistance

32.3 Goal: 25 wam transcription rate

Dear Mrs. Barr Thank you for your letter of October 17 in which you share with me the results and observations concerning our new textbook Communication Today. From your letter it does appear that any difference in student achievement between this year and previous years can be attributed to the book.

The aptitude tests administered before the course begins and after the course has been completed seem to be an accurate indicator of progress. Your class is indeed above average in the results.

We appreciate your taking the time to share this information with us. Please let me know if we can be of any assistance in the future. Cordially yours

32.4 Time Limit: 15 minutes

397812-108 Principles of Accounting $25.60[1]

78218-765 Computers Today $36.20

27385-002 Secretaries'[2] Handbook $15.20

402866-158[3] Medical Assistant $35.50

37185-009 Introduction to Business[4] $38.50

[83 words]

LESSON 33

33.1 Goal: 90 wam speed dictation

Dear Mr. Knox If you do not already have a safe-deposit box at the First National Bank, take[1] advantage of our special offer to our regular depositors. For a limited time our regular[2] depositors can rent any box at half the advertised price.

All you have to do is stop in at the bank, sign[3] a short form, and take possession of the box.

Come in today to let us show you the best way to take care[4] of your company papers. Yours very truly [89 words]

33.2

1 planning your vacation for next spring
2 letter of introduction for you to use
3 banks in Europe and Asia
4 each individual bank
5 may not honor such letters
6 bank has a fine working relationship
7 numerous banks throughout the world
8 stop by the bank any weekday
9 between 9 a.m. and 4 p.m.
10 signed by one of our bank officers

33.3 Goal: 25 wam transcription rate

Dear Mrs. Torres We appreciate your thinking of the First National Bank when planning your vacation for next spring. We will be happy to write a letter of introduction for you to use at banks in Europe and Asia.

As you may know, each individual bank may or may not honor such letters. However, we are glad to tell you that our bank has a fine working relationship with numerous banks throughout the world.

Please stop by our bank any weekday between 9 a.m. and 4 p.m. We will be happy to have the letter signed by one of our bank officers. Sincerely yours

LESSON 34

34.1 Goal: 90 wam speed dictation

Dear Mr. Kelly Do not borrow money unless it is to your advantage. You may consider that unusual[1] advice coming from a company whose success depends on lending money.

There are times, however, when a[2] loan is the sensible answer to a financial problem. Sometimes borrowing is the only way to meet[3] necessary expenses no matter how thrifty a person may be.

If you need extra cash, we are ready[4] to make it available to you promptly. Sincerely [90 words]

34.2

1 you will be pleased to know
2 home improvement loan for $5,000
3 meet with one of our loan officers
4 you will be informed of the payment schedule
5 will be asked to sign the necessary papers
6 during the first part of next week
7 $5,000 loan has been approved
8 you will also receive a check
9 contact our office and set up an appointment
10 get your home improvement under way

34.3 Goal: 25 wam transcription rate

Dear Mr. Wade You will be pleased to know that your home improvement loan in the amount of $5,000 has been approved.

Is it possible for you to meet with one of our loan officers during the first part of next week? At that time you will be informed of the loan payment schedule and will be asked to sign the necessary papers. If all is in order, you will also receive a check.

Please contact our office and set up an appointment so that you will be able to get your home improvement under way. Cordially yours

34.4 Time Limit: 15 minutes

August 10, 19--
Miss Nancy Jennings
302 Atlanta Avenue
Nashville, TN 37202
Dear Miss Jennings You have probably been wondering why you have not heard from our office. We have just moved into[1] a new building, and it has taken a few days to get to the point where things are operating efficiently.[2]

The house in which you are interested is indeed in a good section of the city. One of our people has[3] inspected the house, and it is in excellent condition. You are right; the house is a good buy for[4] $100,000. We will be glad to arrange a mortgage for $70,000 on it.

If your offer[5] is acceptable, it will be necessary for you to fill out a number of forms before we can issue[6] the mortgage. This will take very little time. Sincerely yours
Elizabeth Adams [135 words]

LESSON 35

35.1 Goal: 90 wam speed dictation

Dear Ms. Costa Welcome to the city of Nashville. You will find Nashville to be a pleasant and friendly place[1] in which to live.

The property you looked at on Wilson Avenue has been examined by our staff, and we are[2] happy to report that it is in fine condition. If you can purchase the property for $85,000,[3] you will be getting a real bargain.

Both the president of your old bank in Chicago and the president[4] of your company give you the highest recommendation. As your new lending institution, we will,[5] therefore, be glad to give you a mortgage of $80,000 on the house. Very truly yours [117 words]

35.2

1 Dear Mr. Valdez If you are interested
2 look no further
3 wide range of services
4 interest is paid daily
5 requires no minimum balance
6 our Loan Department offers
7 payments are adjusted according
8 if you would like more information
9 please fill out the enclosed card
10 within five days you will receive

35.3 Goal: 25 wam transcription rate

Dear Mr. Valdez If you are interested in a full-service bank, look no further. First National Bank can offer you a wide range of services.

You can open a checking account that not only pays daily interest on your balance but also requires no minimum balance. Our Loan Department offers low-interest loans for many purposes. Payments are adjusted according to your income.

If you would like more information on any of the services mentioned here, please fill out and return the enclosed form to us. Within five days you will receive the information you requested. Yours truly

35.4 Time Limit: 15 minutes

August 14, 19--
Mr. Carlos Mendez
315 Parker Street
Nashville, TN 37202
Dear Mr. Mendez Thank you for your inquiry regarding a car loan from our bank. You may complete, of course, all[1] the paperwork by mail. However, it will be necessary for you to fill out the usual credit[2] application forms that are enclosed because you are not one of our regular depositors.

As soon as[3] we have been able to make a routine check, we will notify you. We are looking forward to doing business[4] with you. Cordially yours
Elizabeth Adams [88 words]
Enclosures
cc: Charles Hewitt

LESSON 36

36.1 Goal: 90 wam speed dictation

Dear Ms. Foreman Until recently you had to have a great deal of ready cash to buy a condominium[1] apartment. This was because the law required a down payment of at least 40 percent.

Now, thanks to a change in[2] state law, we can lend you up to 80 percent of the appraised value of any apartment you may wish to[3] purchase.

Call the First National Bank today for more information about an apartment loan. If you prefer,[4] stop in at any of our branches and let our officers explain how easy it is to obtain a loan.[5] Cordially yours [103 words]

36.2

1 Dear Mr. and Mrs. Joseph
2 our credit committee approved
3 loan application for $80,000
4 we know you are looking forward
5 getting your construction project under way
6 you will be pleased with the decision
7 my assistant, Ms. James
8 begin drawing up the necessary papers
9 they are ready for you to sign
10 you may expect her call

36.3 Goal: 25 wam transcription rate

Dear Mr. and Mrs. Joseph Yesterday our credit committee approved your loan application for $80,000 for the construction of your new home. We know that you are looking forward to getting your construction project under way and that you will be pleased with the decision of the committee.

My assistant, Ms. James, has already begun drawing up the necessary papers. She will call you when they are ready for you to sign. You may expect her call within a few days. Sincerely yours

36.4 Time Limit: 15 minutes

August 15, 19--
Mr. Carlos Mendez
315 Parker Street
Nashville, TN 37202
Dear Mr. Mendez We are sure that you will be happy to know that your credit has been approved up to a[1] limit of $12,000 for the purchase of a new car.

Now all you have to do is order the car you[2] want and then tell the automobile agency to contact us. Our well-trained staff will handle the necessary[3] paperwork.

We hope, Mr. Mendez, that you will enjoy your new car and that it will serve you for many years.[4]
Yours very truly
Elizabeth Adams [87 words]

LESSON 37

37.1 Goal: 90 wam speed dictation

Dear Mrs. Flynn We want to congratulate you on transferring your home office to Nashville. This decision is[1] a wise, forward-looking business move. Nashville has many advantages for you; you will not regret making this[2] move.

It is especially nice to hear that our bank has been recommended to you. It has always been our[3] policy to serve our customers in every way that we can, and you may be sure that you can expect the same[4] treatment.

When you arrive in Nashville, please get in touch with us so you can arrange to transfer your accounts to our[5] bank. Cordially yours [104 words]

37.2

1 chances with your valuable papers or family property
2 safe-deposit box in the First National Bank
3 it is needless to risk a loss
4 safe-deposit box can be rented easily
5 fire or theft can happen to anyone
6 before you leave on your vacation
7 safe-deposit box service
8 yearly rental rates begin at $25
9 $25 and go to $150
10 some personal items cannot be replaced

37.3 Goal: 25 wam transcription rate

Dear Mr. Rose Do not take any chances with your valuable papers or other family property. Place them in a safe-deposit box in the First National

Bank. It is needless to risk a loss when a safe-deposit box in our bank can be rented so easily.

A fire or theft can happen to anyone at any time. Before you leave on your vacation this summer, come in and talk to us about our safe-deposit box service. Our yearly rental rates begin at $25 and go to $150 for a larger box.

Please consider renting a safe-deposit box; some personal items just cannot be replaced. Cordially yours

37.4 Time Limit: 15 minutes

August 17, 19--
Miss Susan Kaplan
1221 Southern Avenue
Nashville, TN 37202

Dear Miss Kaplan Because credit cards are one of the major ways of paying for purchases, people sometimes tend[1] to get in over their heads. They often do not realize when they have gone over their credit limit.

Many people come[2] to our bank each day to obtain loans to pay their bills. Most debt consolidation loans are easy to obtain, and[3] the repayment arrangement is usually handled in convenient monthly payments.

You, too, can save time and[4] worry by letting our bank help you with your financial problems. If you ever have the need for a debt[5] consolidation loan, we are here to help you. Yours truly
Elizabeth Adams [116 words]

LESSON 38

38.1 Goal: 90 wam speed dictation

Dear Mr. Curtis You can never tell when you will need help in the form of either business advice or maybe[1] just a little extra cash. When you do, there is nothing like having a banker among your friends. People who do[2] business with us find that we operate like a small-town bank in a large city.

Why not come in and meet the[3] officers of the bank. You will get to know each other, and it will be easier to help you when the time[4] arrives. Cordially yours [84 words]

38.2

1 Dear Mr. Melrose You are invited
2 on September 15 we will celebrate 50 years
3 open house will be held at 2 p.m.
4 started with assets of $70,000
5 special event at our Nashville office
6 building their homes and businesses
7 assets exceed $150 million
8 we have a number of branches in different parts
9 directors and officers of your bank pledge
10 greater service in the future

38.3 Goal: 25 wam transcription rate

Dear Mr. Melrose You are invited to a very special event. On September 15 the First National Bank will celebrate 50 years of service to this county and its residents. An open house will be held at 2 p.m. at our Nashville branch.

Our bank started with assets slightly over $70,000. For 50 years it has provided a place for the savings of the people of this county. Thousands of people have received financial assistance from us when building their homes or businesses.

Today our assets exceed $150 million, and we have a number of branches in different parts of the state. The directors and officers of your bank pledge themselves to even greater service in the future. Cordially yours

38.4 Time Limit: 15 minutes

August 20, 19--
Ms. Barbara Mills
79 West Pine Nashville, TN 37202

Dear Ms. Mills It is smart to save money in an account for clothes, vacations, and other things. Also, this[1] type of account is welcome when you need funds quickly.

Opening such an account will add to your peace of mind. It[2] takes only $25 to open an account. Since interest is compounded daily, you will be amazed[3] at how quickly your account can grow.

If you stop in at our bank, you can open your account, or you can do your[4] banking by mail if you wish. In either case, why not open your account today. Sincerely yours
Elizabeth[5] Adams [101 words]

LESSON 39

39.1 Goal: 90 wam speed dictation

Dear Mr. Scott Although many people thought that they would never lose their money, it happened anyway.[1] If you want to be sure that you do not lose your money, here are three very simple things to remember:

1. Do not[2] carry large amounts of cash.
2. Never expose your money in public.
3. Pay your bills by check.

If you[3] follow these simple rules, the chances are that you will never experience the disappointment that comes from losing[4] money. Cordially yours [84 words]

39.2

1 you will worry less when you have money
2 money in your savings account
3 many worries are caused by financial difficulties
4 will help these worries disappear
5 making regular deposits is the secret
6 easier than you think to build a savings account
7 these deposits plus the interest earned
8 result in substantial growth
9 small initial deposit
10 save yourself from financial worries

39.3 Goal: 25 wam transcription rate

Dear Mr. Chase You will worry less when you have money in your savings account. Since many worries are caused by financial difficulties, money in your savings account will help these worries disappear.

Building up a savings account is easier than you think. The secret is, of course, making regular deposits. These deposits plus the interest that is earned on them can result in substantial growth of a small initial deposit.

Save yourself from financial worries. Open a savings account today. Yours truly

39.4 Time Limit: 15 minutes

August 21, 19--
Mrs. Frances Barr
135 North Pine Street
Albany, NY 12204
Dear Mrs. Barr Congratulations on your move to Albany. It has been a pleasure to take care of your[1] banking while you were here in Nashville.

As long as your business will be conducted from Albany, your[2] decision to transfer your banking business to that city is a wise one. There are a number of forms enclosed for you[3] to complete and return to us before we can close out your account and transfer your funds to your new bank.[4]

May you have the best of success in your new location. Sincerely yours
Elizabeth Adams[5] [100 words]
Enclosures

LESSON 40

40.1 Goal: 90 wam speed dictation

Dear Mrs. Wise When prices go up, what can you do to protect your money? Money that you simply set aside[1] may not buy so much in the future. However, money that you invest in good common stock is much more likely[2] to keep its purchasing power.

When prices of food and clothing and everything that you use go up, prices of[3] common stocks may also rise. Common stocks can be the best-known protection against inflation.

If you would[4] like to know more about how to protect your money against rising prices, please get in touch with the investment[5] department of our bank. Come in at any time, and talk to one of our investment officers. Cordially yours[6] [120 words]

40.2

1 you are not familiar with the operation
2 operation of the stock market
3 you will want to read our booklet
4 offered to our customers as a service of our bank
5 learn about every stock investment
6 bank is interested in the small investor
7 learn to buy stocks yourself
8 booklet answers questions anybody might
9 might have questions about the stock market
10 available free of charge; you can obtain a copy by simply

40.3 Goal: 25 wam transcription rate

Dear Mr. White If you have never purchased stocks before because you are not familiar with the operation of the stock market, you will want to read our booklet. It is offered to our customers as a service of our bank.

You will learn about every type of stock investment in this booklet. You will learn that our bank is interested in the small investor. You will learn to buy stocks yourself.

This booklet answers questions anybody might have about the stock market. It is available free of charge; you can obtain a copy by simply writing for it. Sincerely

40.4 Time Limit: 15 minutes

August 22, 19--
Mr. Robert Holden
George Manufacturing Company
35 Grove Lane
Little Rock, AR 72209

Dear Mr. Holden Satisfied customers are the key to any successful banking business. An investor[1] should know what the broker thinks about a particular security. As a banking service we give our[2] customers all the facts we have whether they are good or bad.

Many people have delayed investment and have put[3] their money either in government bonds or in the bank. Of course, this results in the loss of investments, but we[4] believe that is the only way to do business.

If you ever want information or assistance, you can count[5] on the investment department of the First National Bank. Sincerely yours
Elizabeth Adams [118 words]

LESSON 41

41.1 Goal: 90 wam speed dictation

Dear Ms. Palmer Thank you for the check for $3,785 to cover the cost of your[1] cruise to Nassau on January 26. You wrote that you would be sending the check. When we did not[2] receive it, we wondered if you had changed your mind.

Since you are definitely going, there are a couple of things[3] that you need to know. First, your airline tickets will be mailed directly to you. You have the seat assignment you[4] requested. You will fly to Miami on January 25. You have reservations for a hotel[5] room that evening. At 9 a.m. on January 26 a representative of the cruise line will pick[6] up you and other passengers at the hotel. The ship will leave Miami at approximately 10:30[7] a.m.

If you have any other questions, please call me. Sincerely yours [153 words]

41.2

1 we make lodging reservations and your friends
2 request has been referred to me
3 your last visit was quite enjoyable
4 cottage you had is not available
5 another three-bedroom cottage
6 the manager of the lodge said
7 is available from February 16 to February 23
8 have less than 100 yards
9 deposit has been charged to your credit card
10 airline tickets are enclosed in this letter

41.3 Goal: 30 wam transcription rate

Dear Mr. Nash Your letter requesting that we make lodging reservations for you and your three friends has been referred to me.

I am delighted that your last visit was quite enjoyable. The manager of the lodge said that the cottage you had last year is not available from February 16 to February 23. Instead, she is giving you another three-bedroom cottage that is less than 100 yards from the lake.

The reservations have been made in your name, and the deposit has been charged to your credit card. The airline tickets for you and your friends are also enclosed in this letter. Please call me if you have any questions. Sincerely

LESSON 42

42.1 Goal: 90 wam speed dictation

Dear Mr. Marsh Perhaps like other people you are not quite sure about your summer vacation plans. Why not[1] decide the matter right now. Make up your mind to treat yourself to a real vacation in Mexico. In Mexico[2] you will find genuine relaxation that will enable you to return to your job fully rested.

If you would[3] like complete information about what Mexico has to offer, fill out the business reply card and[4] we will send you a booklet within 24 hours of receipt of your card. Sincerely

[98 words]

42.2

1 one of our agents in Chicago sent us
2 you filled out a form giving information
3 necessary information about the unused portion
4 ticket has not been turned in after four months
5 ticket is like cash
6 unable to make any refund to you
7 a check for a portion of the trip from Chicago to New York
8 ticket not used in four months
9 you may be sure we will get in touch
10 as soon as we have any definite information

42.3 Goal: 30 wam transcription rate

Dear Ms. Adams One of our agents in Chicago sent us the form you filled out giving all the necessary information about the unused portion of the ticket you lost. Thus far the ticket has not been turned in.

As you know, your ticket is like cash, and anyone who finds it can use it. If someone does find it and uses it, we will be unable to make any refund to you. If the ticket is not used or turned in after four months, then you will receive a check for the portion of your trip from Chicago to New York.

You may be sure that we will get in touch with you as soon as we have any definite information on the matter. Cordially yours

42.4 Time Limit: 15 minutes

December 12, 19--
Mrs. Lorraine Lopez
767 West End Avenue
New York, NY 10045
Dear Mrs. Lopez You will be interested in a new service that is sponsored by our travel agency[1] and the Abbott chain of hotels.

Now when you purchase a round-trip ticket to any city through our agency,[2] you can also receive 50 percent off on up to three nights of lodging at the Abbott Hotel in that city.[3] You can take advantage of this in two ways. First, you can make your hotel reservation at the same time as your[4] airline reservation, and the hotel will reserve your room at the reduced rate. Or you can present the unused[5] portion of your ticket to the hotel reservation desk, and you will get a room at the discount rate.

This[6] service is being offered for a limited time. Please take advantage of it now. Cordially yours
Nancy Johnson[7]
Travel Agent [143 words]

LESSON 43

43.1 Goal: 90 wam speed dictation

Dear Mr. Harrington Your request for a room the week of February 11 has been received by our[1] reservation department. Thank you for thinking of us in your travel plans.

However, the reopening of the[2] Birmingham Hotel in Boston has been delayed. The reopening date was scheduled for February 1 but has[3] now been delayed until March 1.

You will be informed when we know the exact opening date. However, we would be[4] pleased to make another reservation for you in the Boston area. Please let us hear from you soon.[5] Cordially yours [103 words]

43.2

1 I was pleased to have the opportunity
2 vacation for you and your family
3 planning to spend your vacation in Europe
4 it will be a vacation you will remember
5 enclosed is all the printed material regarding Europe
6 enclosed are some possible flight routes
7 you live in southern Wisconsin
8 flights originate in Milwaukee and Chicago
9 work out some of the finite details
10 we will set up complete travel arrangements

43.3 Goal: 30 wam transcription rate

Dear Mr. Brandt I was pleased to have the opportunity to discuss the vacation you and your family are planning in Europe. I am sure that it will be a vacation you all will remember for a long time.

As you requested, enclosed is all the printed material we have regarding vacations in Europe.

Also enclosed are some possible flight routes. Since you live in southern Wisconsin, the proposed flights originate in Milwaukee and Chicago.

When you work out some of the more finite details of your trip, call me and we will set up complete travel arrangements. Cordially yours

43.4 Time Limit: 15 minutes

Itinerary of Thomas Owens
December 17-18, 19--
Monday, December 17[1]
10:30 a.m. Depart New York, Kennedy Airport, for San Francisco, American Flight 375[2]
12:45 p.m. Arrive San Francisco Airport; National rental car — return December 18 —[3]
Confirmation No. 786591 Overnight accommodations at Intercontinental Hotel,[4] 385 Powell Street
Tuesday, December 18
10:15 a.m. Depart San Francisco Airport for New York,[5] Kennedy Airport, American Flight 173
5:05 p.m. Arrive New York, Kennedy Airport[6]
[120 words]

LESSON 44

44.1 Goal: 90 wam speed dictation

Dear Miss Clark Thank you for contacting me regarding your plans for a trip in the summer. Before we can start[1] putting together a proposal, there are a few things that we need to know.

For instance, you mentioned that you wanted[2] to take your trip in the United States. You did not specify which type of transportation you preferred. Are you[3] planning on traveling alone, or are you interested in a group tour? Also, did you have a budget in[4] mind?

Once you have answers to these questions, it will be much easier to start planning. Write down a few ideas[5] you may have. Then give me a call and we can set up an appointment to meet here at the travel agency. Cordially yours[6] [120 words]

44.2

1 Dear Mr. and Mrs. George
2 tour of France and Italy
3 it has been almost six months
4 received many inquiries from members
5 tour group members are anxious
6 interest in the Scandinavian countries
7 drawn up four itineraries for a three-week trip
8 Norway, Sweden, Denmark, and Finland
9 decide your first choice and second
10 enclosed postage-paid envelope

44.3 Goal: 30 wam transcription rate

Dear Mr. and Mrs. George Last June you joined us on our tour of France and Italy. The group that went on that trip was delightful, and many of the members expressed an interest in going on another trip together.

It has been almost six months, and I have received many inquiries from tour group members who are anxious to start planning a trip. Many of you have expressed an interest in visiting the Scandinavian countries. I have drawn up four itineraries for a three-week trip to Norway, Sweden, Denmark, and Finland.

Please look at the proposed schedules and decide which would be your first choice. Write down your first choice and second choice. Return your responses in the enclosed postage-paid envelope. After all responses have been received, I will get in touch with you to let you know which itinerary was preferred. Cordially yours

44.4 Time Limit: 15 minutes

December 17, 19--
Ms. Alice Simpson
Lawrence Chemical Company
67 Lexington Avenue
New York, NY 10024
Dear Ms. Simpson Your dream vacation is not as out of reach as you may think. Many people believe that a[1] European vacation, an island vacation, a week-long cruise, and even an extensive tour of the[2] United States are out of their price range. You will be happy to know that all of these vacations can be very[3] affordable.

Experienced agents are able to find the lowest-priced, best-quality vacation.

Because[4] our travel agents are widely respected, airlines, cruise lines, railroads, car rental companies, hotels, motels, resorts,[5] and many other travel-related organizations work with us to get substantial discounts. Contact me[6] and ask for a price quote on a vacation. Yours truly
Nancy Johnson
Travel Agent
[135 words]

LESSON 45

45.1 Goal: 90 wam speed dictation

Dear Mrs. Crosby Your airline reservations for your trip to Salt Lake City have been confirmed, and your boarding[1] passes are enclosed.

On March 27 you will be leaving New York on Flight 173 at[2] 7 p.m. and arriving in Salt Lake City at 8:30 p.m. Your return flight on March 30 from[3] Salt Lake City is Flight 135. It departs at 9 a.m. and arrives in New York at[4] 12:45 p.m. The cost for the round trip is $350.

You have an aisle seat in the nonsmoking section on[5] both flights. If we can help you in any other way, please let us know. Yours truly [118 words]

45.2

1 a copy of a booklet on Canada
2 100 pages of information pertaining to vacations
3 this is a handy booklet
4 lists the larger cities of Canada
5 highlights the sites of each city
6 charming out-of-the-way places
7 make reservations well in advance
8 plan to fly to Canada
9 confirm reservations at least two months in advance
10 agents to make your reservations

45.3 Goal: 30 wam transcription rate

Dear Ms. Roberts As you requested, enclosed is a copy of a booklet on Canada. The booklet contains 100 pages of information pertaining to vacations in Canada.

Whether you are planning on staying a few days or a few weeks, this is a handy booklet. It lists the major cities of Canada and highlights the sites of each city. It also tells of charming out-of-the-way places.

If you plan on flying to Canada, you should make your reservations well in advance. We have special rates if you confirm your reservation at least two months before departure. Call one of our agents to make your reservations. Cordially yours

45.4 Time Limit: 15 minutes

Itinerary of Joyce Norris
December 19, 19--
Wednesday, December 19[1]
8:15 a.m. Depart Newark Airport for Washington International Airport, Eastern Flight 35[2]
9:10 a.m. Arrive Washington International Airport; limousine service to Capitol Hotel,[3] 273 Connecticut Avenue
11 a.m. Conference room at Capitol Hotel scheduled for[4] meeting
1 p.m. Luncheon scheduled in the State Room
4:10 p.m. Depart Washington International Airport[5] for Newark Airport, Eastern Flight 88
[107 words]

LESSON 46

46.1 Goal: 90 wam speed dictation

Dear Ms. Neal Whether you are planning to expand your business into Arizona or just contemplating a[1] vacation visit, you will enjoy reading Arizona Opportunities. It tells you about a state that[2] has great possibilities for growth and profit.

It contains 124 color photographs as well as much[3] information about the resources of Arizona. If you have any specific questions, contact the Arizona[4] State Travel and Development Bureau.

Send for a copy of Arizona Opportunities[5] today. All that you have to do is fill out and return the enclosed card. Yours sincerely [137 words]

46.2

1 offering our regular customers
2 new Airline Travel Guide
3 finest books of its type ever issued
4 it has a reference book section
5 especially pleased to see the travel guide
6 section on foreign flights
7 business has grown more than 30 percent
8 increase rapidly in the years ahead
9 section should be extremely helpful
10 will provide an important service

46.3 Goal: 30 wam transcription rate

Dear Mr. Cohen We are offering our regular customers a free copy of the new Airline Travel

Guide. It is one of the finest books of its type ever issued. It has a reference section that will aid you when speaking to our agents.

We are especially pleased to see the section on foreign flights. Our business in foreign flights among executives has grown more than 30 percent over the last three years and is expected to increase more rapidly in the years ahead. Consequently, this section should be extremely helpful to your executives.

We hope this reference guide will provide an important service to you. Please let us hear from you if we can assist you in any way. Sincerely yours

46.4 Time Limit: 15 minutes

December 20, 19--
Mr. Kevin Wiley
Kirkland Manufacturing Company
375 Broadway
New York, NY 10012
Dear Mr. Wiley Greetings of the season and thank you for the fine business you have given us this past year.

It is a[1] real source of satisfaction to know that our travel agency has been able to handle satisfactorily[2] all your frequent travel needs and to give you the kind of service that meets with your approval. The success of our[3] agency can be attributed to the friendship and goodwill of customers like you.

May your Christmas be a[4] very merry one and your New Year a profitable one. Cordially yours
Nancy Johnson
Travel Agent[5] [100 words]

LESSON 47

47.1 Goal: 90 wam speed dictation

Dear Ms. Katz Many executives find that a car is a great convenience once they reach their destination, but they[1] do not like to drive it to their destination.

For the convenience of this type of executive, we have worked out[2] a discount plan whereby you can fly to your destination and then rent a car for your business calls. If you[3] arrange to rent a car when you are making your flight arrangements, you will receive a discount of up to 50 percent[4] on the car rental.

With this plan you rent the car by the day, but you are not charged for mileage. When your business is[5] finished, just drive back to the airport, turn in the car, and board your plane for your home flight. If this sounds like something you would[6] like more information on, just complete the enclosed card and mail it to us. Cordially yours

[138 words]

47.2

1 Dear Ms. Kirby Our records indicate
2 have not been making travel arrangements
3 for the past four months
4 let us know if our service has not been satisfactory
5 a valued customer for over 15 years
6 we have enjoyed assisting your executives
7 enclosing a form regarding our service
8 would appreciate your completing the form
9 complete the form at your convenience
10 we are anxious to be of assistance to you

47.3 Goal: 30 wam transcription rate

Dear Ms. Kirby Our records indicate that your executives have not been making travel arrangements with us for the past four months. If our service has not been satisfactory, please let us know.

Your company has been a valued customer for over 15 years, and we have enjoyed assisting your executives with their travel plans. I am enclosing a form regarding our service and would appreciate your completing it at your convenience.

We are anxious to be of assistance to you in the near future. Sincerely

47.4 Time Limit: 15 minutes

Itinerary for Keith Jackson
January 2-3, 19--
Wednesday, January 2
11:15 a.m.[1] Depart New York, Kennedy Airport, for Boston Airport, Eastern Flight 718
1:20 p.m. Arrive[2] Boston Airport; limousine service to Premier Hotel, 145 Buckingham Street
3 p.m.[3] President's Room for board meeting and dinner. Overnight accommodations at University Hotel,[4] 275 Liberty Avenue

Thursday, January 3
10 a.m. Financial meeting at University[5] Hotel board room
1:10 p.m. Depart Boston Airport for New York, Kennedy Airport
3:05 p.m.[6] Arrive New York, Kennedy Airport
[127 words]

LESSON 48

48.1 Goal: 90 wam speed dictation

Dear Mr. Rich When you begin to plan your next vacation or business trip, let us have the privilege of helping[1] you with all the details. Our organization, the Morris Travel Agency, has been in the business of helping[2] executives plan their business and pleasure trips for more than ten years.

We have on our staff experts from every[3] continent in the world. Each of these people has many others on staff who can help you with everything from[4] purchasing your airline tickets to arranging visits to out-of-the-way places. Just call us for an appointment.[5] There is, of course, no fee for our services. Sincerely yours [111 words]

48.2

1 Dear Ms. Lawrence It was a pleasure
2 planning your recent vacation trip
3 found our services to be satisfactory
4 enclosing a questionnaire for you to fill out
5 return the questionnaire at your convenience
6 like to have your opinion of the services
7 airlines, hotels, and the other places visited
8 take only a few minutes of your time
9 help us serve you better in the future
10 let us have the opportunity to serve you again

48.3 Goal: 30 wam transcription rate

Dear Ms. Lawrence It was a pleasure planning your recent vacation trip for you. We hope you found our services to be helpful and satisfactory.

We are enclosing a questionnaire that I hope you will fill out and return to us at your convenience. We would like to have your opinion of the services provided by the airlines, the hotels, and the other places you visited. It will take only a few minutes of your time to fill out the form, and it will help us to serve you better in the future.

When you plan your next vacation, I hope you will let us have the opportunity to serve you again. Very sincerely yours

48.4 Time Limit: 15 minutes

Date: January 10, 19--
To: Charles Kennedy
From: Nancy Johnson
Subject: Note of Appreciation[1]
As you may remember, last year the Morris Travel Agency had another record-setting year. We made travel[2] plans for more than 5,000 people throughout the East. Needless to say, we are delighted with our record.

This was[3] the third consecutive year we have set new records, and the forecast for this year is very bright. If this forecast[4] is correct, we should be able to increase our business by as much as 10 percent. In order to do so,[5] however, we must continue to put forth that extra effort. Please express my appreciation to your staff.[6] [120 words]

LESSON 49

49.1 Goal: 100 wam speed dictation

Dear Mrs. Harrington You will be pleased to hear that Ms. Kathleen Barnes, formerly of the Dallas Clothing Company,[1] has joined our staff to take charge of our Women's Department.

For more than ten years Ms. Barnes has been keeping an eye[2] on fashion and looking after the clothing needs of the women of Dallas. We are happy to make her wonderful[3] experience available to our customers.

The next time you need some new clothing, either[4] for business or for fun, come in and let Ms. Barnes help you with your selections. Yours sincerely [97 words]

49.2

1 Dear Mr. Randall This week a new branch
2 Taylor Department Store on Powell Street
3 has been serving the needs of men and women
4 store in downtown Chicago
5 as an executive with an office uptown
6 make it much more convenient
7 will carry the same lines of clothing

8 also carry more designer sportswear
9 stop in our store and use the enclosed coupon
10 receive 25 percent discount on any purchase

49.3 Goal: 30 wam transcription rate

Dear Mr. Randall This week a new branch of the Taylor Department Store will open on Powell Street. Our store in downtown Chicago has been serving the clothing needs of the men and women in the city for 20 years. As an executive with an office uptown, this new branch will make it much more convenient for you to do your shopping.

The new store will carry the same lines of clothing as our main store. In addition, it will also carry more designer sportswear. Why not stop in at the new store, use the enclosed coupon, and receive a 25 percent discount on any purchase. Cordially yours

LESSON 50

50.1 Goal: 100 wam speed dictation

Dear Ms. Wallace As a valued customer, you should be kept informed about merchandise and market direction. This[1] has been our objective for as long as we have been in business.

You will be interested to know that now is the[2] time to buy your fall and winter clothes. You can still choose from a large selection and make your purchases at[3] reasonable prices. This situation is rapidly changing, and prices will be going up at the end[4] of the month.

Why not pay us a visit soon. It will be to your advantage. Cordially yours [96 words]

50.2

1 thank you for your letter explaining the problem
2 damage to the suit you ordered
3 unfortunate that the suit was damaged
4 we assume it was damaged in transit
5 every package is sealed at our facilities
6 seal on your package was broken
7 we did not incur the damage
8 understandable that you are disappointed
9 cannot wear the suit immediately
10 send a new suit in the shortest time possible

50.3 Goal: 30 wam transcription rate

Dear Mrs. Mendez Thank you for your letter explaining the problem with the suit you ordered from us. It is unfortunate that the suit was damaged when you received it.

The suit was in good condition when it left our shipping room on August 16. We assume, therefore, that it was damaged in transit. Every package is sealed before it leaves our facilities. Since the seal on your package was broken when you received it, we can safely say that we did not incur the damage.

If you will return the suit to us, we will send you a new suit and enter a claim against the express company.

It is understandable that you are disappointed that you cannot wear the suit immediately, but we will do our best to send you a new suit in the shortest time possible. Sincerely

50.4 Time Limit: 15 minutes

September 4, 19--
Miss Marilyn Russell
385 Market Street
Chicago, IL 60623
Dear Miss Russell I have been informed that you have just moved to Chicago from New York. No doubt the process of moving[1] was a busy one.

My family has lived in this city for many years, and we have found its residents friendly[2] and helpful. To continue this tradition, you are invited to visit our new store on Powell Street. We have been[3] providing clothes for both women and men in the Chicago area since 1950.

Stop into our store[4] soon and look around. You will find our prices very reasonable. As a new customer who has been referred[5] to us, you will receive a 15 percent discount on any purchase. Cordially yours
Philip Walters[6]
Marketing Manager [124 words]

LESSON 51

51.1 Goal: 100 wam speed dictation

Dear Mr. Feldman The week of September 10 is the final week of our annual shoe sale. You have just six days[1] remaining in which to get substantial savings on the shoes you need for the coming year.

Even at this late[2] date your choice of styles is unlimited. Remember, this is not a special clearance sale of old merchandise. Every[3] item of our regular stock is selling at a discount.

Why not drop in one day next week and save yourself some[4] money on quality footwear. Cordially yours [88 words]

51.2

1 thank you for your order for 25 printed football shirts
2 your order was shipped out today
3 merchandise should reach you by next week
4 this is your first order with us
5 welcome to our group of satisfied customers
6 beginning of a long and profitable relationship
7 designs are original and inexpensive
8 staff of experienced graphic artists
9 staff is available for consultation on designs
10 consultation on designs and printing

51.3 Goal: 30 wam transcription rate

Dear Mrs. Lee Thank you for your order for 25 printed football shirts that you gave our representative on August 28. Your order was shipped out today, and the merchandise should reach you by the early part of next week.

We hope you will find our designs to be original and inexpensive. Please feel free to use our staff of experienced graphic artists. They are available for consultation on designs and printing. There is no charge for their services.

As this is your first order with us, we welcome you to our large group of satisfied customers. It is hoped that this will be the beginning of a long and profitable relationship for both of us. Sincerely yours

51.4 Time Limit: 15 minutes

September 5, 19--
Mr. John Becker
Harrington Apartments
Apartment 21
Chicago, IL 60604
Dear Mr. Becker Thank you for your telephone order for five pairs of running shoes that were advertised in the[1] newspapers on Sunday, September 2. The response was so great that our entire supply of running shoes was gone[2] by 11 a.m. on Monday.

As you were told on the telephone, you can purchase the running shoes at the[3] same low price of $29.95 a pair by presenting the enclosed rain check to the salesclerk.[4]

A new shipment of running shoes should arrive within the next week. As soon as they do come in, you will be notified.[5] At that time you can come into our store, present your rain check, and purchase five pairs of running shoes. At this low price[6] you will agree that a week is not too long to wait.
Sincerely yours
Philip Walters
Marketing Manager[7] [140 words]

LESSON 52

52.1 Goal: 100 wam speed dictation

Dear Ms. Whitney Now is the time to select the clothes you need for your first job out of college. Where you buy your clothes[1] is, of course, a matter of personal choice, but do it now because stocks are complete and prices are reasonable.[2]

If you choose our store as your shopping place, you will enjoy three advantages over other stores.

1. You will[3] find the best materials. High-volume buying allows us to get first choice from the manufacturers.

2. You will[4] find the best quality. We own and operate America's largest tailoring plant.

3. You will find amazingly[5] low prices. Many selling expenses that add to the price of clothes are eliminated because we make[6] our own clothes.

Come in and see for yourself why more people wear our clothes than any other in the industry.[7]
Yours sincerely [144 words]

52.2

1 exhibit at the Dallas Hotel
2 unfortunately, I am going to San Francisco
3 exhibits of your designs are first-rate
4 my assistant is Kelly Peterson
5 your line was a considerable success
6 line should be comparable and a considerable success

7 your national advertisements on television are superb
8 should help sell your line
9 advertisements on television and in magazines
10 my assistant will view the designs

52.3 Goal: 30 wam transcription rate

Dear Mr. Cook Thank you for letting me know about your exhibit at the Dallas Hotel on September 26. The exhibits of your designs are always first-rate.

Unfortunately, I am going to San Francisco to see some new promotional designs. Therefore, I am sending my assistant, Kelly Peterson, to view your exhibit. When her report is complete, I will place an order.

Last year your line was a considerable success in all of our stores. If your new line is comparable, we should do even better next year.

By the way, your national advertisements both on television and in magazines are superb. They should help sell your line to a larger number of people. Yours truly

52.4 Time Limit: 15 minutes

September 6, 19--
Mrs. Arlene Robinson
302 Maple Avenue
Evanston, IL 60204
Dear Mrs. Robinson For years now you have come to us to take care of your clothing needs. The fact that you have come[1] back again and again indicates that you have been able to find the type of clothes you want.

You have always paid[2] cash or used your credit card when shopping at our store. Are you familiar, however, with our convenient[3] layaway plan? If you find something you would like to purchase but do not feel that you can afford it, you can put the[4] item on layaway.

For only 20 percent of the total purchase price, we can hold your item until[5] you can afford to pay the balance. This way you will not have to worry that this is the last available[6] item in your size. There is no interest charged, but you are required to pay a minimum amount each month until[7] the item is paid for.

If you are interested in this type of payment plan, inquire the next time you stop by the[8] store. Yours truly
Philip Walters
Marketing Manager [171 words]

LESSON 53

53.1 Goal: 100 wam speed dictation

Dear Mr. Sinclair We are pleased to announce the opening of our new department store in the Edison Shopping[1] Center in your neighborhood. Our new store is the largest, most complete department store in this part of the state.[2] You will find that our store has a wide range of clothing for men, women, and children; furniture for all rooms in your home;[3] major appliances; and numerous other items to meet your everyday needs.

Come to our convenient[4] new store for all your needs. We are open every day except Sunday from 10 a.m. to 9 p.m. Yours very truly[5] [100 words]

53.2

1 Taylor Department Store will have one of the biggest sales
2 there will be wonderful bargains available
3 you will be able to take advantage of low prices
4 low prices on sofas, chairs, and tables
5 save on coats, suits, and hats
6 clothing for men and women
7 great buys on single items
8 complete sets of dishes
9 make plans to be with us on September 24
10 biggest and best sale in our history

53.3 Goal: 30 wam transcription rate

Dear Mr. Thomas On Monday, September 24, the Taylor Department Store will have one of the biggest sales in its history. There will be wonderful bargains available in every department in the store.

In the furniture department you will be able to take advantage of low prices on sofas, chairs, and tables. In the clothing department you will be able to save on coats, suits, and hats for men and women. In the glass department you can take away great buys on single items or complete sets of dishes.

Make your plans to be with us September 24 for the biggest and best sale in our history. Sincerely yours

53.4 Time Limit: 15 minutes

Date: September 7, 19--
To: Building Maintenance, Dallas Office
From: Philip Walters, Marketing[1] Manager
Subject: News Tour
On the recommendation of Mr. Bradley, I have granted permission to the[2] Dallas Daily News to allow two of its reporters to make a tour of our Dallas plant. From a public relations[3] standpoint, we really have no choice. I think the reporters will be pleasantly surprised that our plant is a[4] showroom of modern, economical operations and maintains the best of all possible working conditions.[5]

Nevertheless, would you ensure that the plant have as clinical an appearance as possible during their visit.[6] The program of times and areas that the reporters will visit is attached. [134 words]

LESSON 54

54.1 Goal: 100 wam speed dictation

Dear Mr. Craig The Taylor Department Store is closing in the city of Los Angeles. It is[1] with regret that we make this announcement. Our lease has not been renewed, and we have not been able to find another[2] building in the area with ample space for our operation.

This means that customers can take advantage[3] of wonderful savings on all their purchases for the next few weeks. You will be able to save money on clothing,[4] furniture, appliances, and personal items. Come in any day during September and select the items[5] you need. You may never again be able to enjoy such great savings.

It has been a pleasure serving the people[6] of Los Angeles. Sincerely yours [127 words]

54.2

1 here is some good news
2 opened a leather goods department
3 stop in to find leather goods
4 find beautiful new leather jackets
5 pleased with our line of goods
6 pleased with our reasonable prices
7 offering new customers a discount
8 just bring this letter with you
9 show the letter to our salesperson
10 special discount on the regular prices

54.3 Goal: 30 wam transcription rate

Dear Ms. Brown Here is some good news for you. We have opened a leather goods department in our Chicago store. Stop in the next time you are in the market for leather goods. You will find beautiful new leather jackets, coats, and shoes. We are sure you will be pleased with our line of goods and with our reasonable prices.

We are offering new customers a special discount on their first leather purchase at the Taylor Department Store. Just bring this letter with you and show it to our salesperson when you make your first purchase. You will receive a special discount on the regular price.

We will be looking forward to seeing you in our store soon. Sincerely yours

54.4 Time Limit: 15 minutes

September 14, 19--
Mrs. Grace Washington
200 North Clinton Street
Chicago, IL 60606
Dear Mrs. Washington Our records show that you have not ordered from our company in over a year.[1] You have been a valued customer for over 15 years. If our service or merchandise has not been satisfactory,[2] please let us know.

Because of the high cost of mailing our catalogs, we can afford to send them only to[3] customers who place at least one order a year. If you order from the enclosed catalog, we will continue[4] to send it to you.

Please keep this good business relationship alive and place an order today. Very truly yours[5]
Philip Walters
Marketing Manager [108 words]
Enclosure

LESSON 55

55.1 Goal: 100 wam speed dictation

Dear Mr. Clayton For some time we have been hoping that we could give you a definite delivery date on the[1] walnut desk that you ordered from us. However, the supply situation has become worse rather than better;[2] we have no idea when we can fill your order.

In view of this situation, we find it necessary to[3] cancel your order at this time. If the situation does improve in the immediate future,[4] we will notify you and you may reinstate your order.

We are sorry that we have not been able to serve[5] you this time but hope that you will give us another chance when our manufacturing problems have been solved.[6] Cordially yours [121 words]

55.2

1 the desk that was shipped to your office
2 apparently, two orders were mixed up
3 appreciate the understanding tone of your letter
4 as you said, mistakes will happen in organizations
5 even the best-run organizations
6 your understanding was appreciated
7 our organization is no exception
8 you may be sure we will continue our efforts
9 prompt, efficient, and courteous service
10 you will derive many years of useful service from it

55.3 Goal: 30 wam transcription rate

Dear Miss Dolan You are correct; the desk that was shipped to your office was not the desk you ordered. Apparently, two orders were mixed up in the shipping room. Your desk was shipped to you this morning.

The understanding tone of your letter was appreciated. As you said, mistakes will happen in even the best-run organizations; we are no exception. You may be sure that we will continue our efforts to give you prompt, efficient, and courteous service.

Enjoy your new desk; you will derive many years of useful service from it. Yours truly

55.4 Time Limit: 15 minutes

Date: September 18, 19--
To: Paul Mason, Chief Copy Editor
From: Philip Walters
Subject: Promotional[1] Advertisement
Paul, will you please prepare a script for a one-minute television and radio spot to[2] promote the fall sale we will be having on coats for men and women. The enclosed sheet gives all the information[3] you will need to develop this script. Please stress the items I have underlined on page 2 of the data sheet.

Contact[4] me immediately if you have any questions or need additional resource information. [98 words]

Enclosure

LESSON 56

56.1 Goal: 100 wam speed dictation

Dear Mr. Burke Any business owner knows the importance of a good credit rating. You, then, fall into the[1] category of people who value a reputation of paying bills promptly. It would also be safe to[2] say that you would not want to do anything that might endanger your own credit rating. Yet our accounting records[3] show that your account in the amount of $161.48 is over 60[4] days past due.

Circumstances such as misplaced invoices, illness, or other factors do arise. We are positive[5] that something of this nature must have happened to you. Therefore, we are giving you ten days to get your payment[6] to us. If your payment is not received by then, we will be forced to take legal action. We are quite certain[7] that you would not want this to happen.

It is still possible to maintain your credit rating and to have continued[8] delivery from our store. All you have to do is send us a check for $161.48.[9] If for some reason you are unable to pay the entire amount immediately, you will find us willing[10] to discuss a definite arrangement with you to take care of the matter. Yours truly [216 words]

56.2

1 always recommend a qualified and experienced employee

2 started her career with World Wear Corporation as a salesperson
3 worked at the South Center location
4 was a full-time student
5 worked at least 20 hours a week
6 graduated with a degree in personnel management
7 after graduating she applied
8 her store has been our most profitable one
9 treats her employees with respect
10 they respect her and are extremely productive workers

56.3 Goal: 30 wam transcription rate

Dear Mr. Rubin It is always a pleasure to recommend a qualified and experienced employee. Betty Keller is that kind of person.

Betty started her career with the World Wear Corporation as a salesperson. She worked at our South Center location while attending college in Chicago. Although she was a full-time student, she still worked at least 20 hours a week.

In May 1986 Betty graduated with a degree in personnel management. Shortly after graduation she applied for and was offered a job as an assistant manager at our Chicago store. Within five months she was promoted to manager, and within two years her store has become our most profitable one in the Midwest.

She treats her employees with respect; in turn, they respect her and are extremely productive workers. Betty is a superb manager, and it seems only fitting that World Wear promote her to the position of district manager. Yours truly

56.4 Time Limit: 15 minutes

September 25, 19--
Ms. Wendy Monroe
495 Park Avenue
Chicago, IL 60623
Dear Ms. Monroe Many people believe that the clothes you wear make a statement that leaves a lasting impression. As[1] a professional in the business world, naturally you are concerned about your appearance. You want your clothes[2] to fit the position you currently hold. You also want to dress for the job you may hold tomorrow. At the[3] same time, however, you want the best value for your money.

Recently we opened a professional women's[4] department to meet the needs of women moving up the career ladder. Our well-trained staff will be able to help[5] you plan an extensive wardrobe and select all the purchases. We look forward to seeing you in this[6] new department in the near future. Very truly yours
Philip Walters
Marketing Manager [138 words]

LESSON 57

57.1 Goal: 100 wam speed dictation

Ladies and Gentlemen Re: Lease for Franklin Manufacturing I am enclosing three copies of a[1] 99-year lease for the factory site in Harrisburg, Pennsylvania, which we are negotiating with Franklin[2] Manufacturing on your behalf. Will you please have the lease signed by your company's legal representative.[3] Then return two copies so that we may retain one for our file and send a copy to Franklin Manufacturing.[4]

Since you will need to begin renovating the factory before the actual effective date of the lease[5] in order to maintain your production schedule, we have included these conditions in the terms of the lease.[6]

Please let me know if you have any questions or concerns. Sincerely yours [133 words]

57.2

1 Dear Mr. Spencer I have been studying
2 there are questions we may encounter
3 merger with Dempsey and Anderson
4 whenever a situation of this type
5 the merger has been allowed to stand
6 Martin case was a serious problem
7 we must be on firm ground
8 avoid similar trouble
9 call within the next week
10 set up a meeting

57.3 Goal: 35 wam transcription rate

Dear Mr. Spencer I have been studying the numerous questions we may encounter in the way of legal difficulties in going ahead with your proposed merger with Dempsey and Anderson.

Whenever a situation of this type has been tested

in the courts, the merger has been allowed to stand. However, the Martin case was a serious problem to the expansion of business in all forms. We must be on firm ground legally to avoid problems.

Please call my office within the next week to set up a meeting. Very truly yours

LESSON 58

58.1 Goal: 100 wam speed dictation

Dear Mr. Evans As you have requested, I have made some inquiries about the financial status of[1] Mr. Howell, the man who ran into your parked car on February 28.

Mr. Howell is married[2] and has two children. He is employed as a manager of a restaurant on Clark Avenue and has insurance[3] coverage with National Insurance Company. Therefore, you should have no difficulty in collecting any[4] judgment that you might get against him.

If you have any further questions regarding your case, do not hesitate[5] to get in contact with me. Cordially yours [108 words]

58.2

1 results of your physical examination
2 X-ray reports were negative
3 do not show any signs of injury
4 growth on the lower spine
5 probably the cause of your pain
6 this condition is normal
7 settlement will not exceed $3,000
8 happy to know you do not have a permanent injury
9 kept informed of the progress
10 kept informed of the progress by either me or my associates

58.3 Goal: 35 wam transcription rate

Dear Ms. Maddox Dr. Brown has forwarded the results of your physical examination to our office.

The X-ray reports were completely negative and do not show any signs of injury. The X ray shows a little growth on the lower spine, and that is probably the cause of your pain. The doctor says it could not have been caused by the accident; this condition is normal for a person of your age.

This means, therefore, that your settlement from the cab company probably will not exceed $3,000. While you may be disappointed with the amount we will be able to collect, I am sure you will be happy to know that you do not have a permanent injury.

You will be kept informed of the progress by either me or one of my associates. Cordially yours

58.4 Time Limit: 15 minutes

April 9, 19--
Mr. Charles Gray
375 Haymaker Boulevard
Monroeville, PA 15146
Dear Mr. Gray Re: Gray v. Montana Building Corporation Your case against the Montana Building[1] Corporation is scheduled for trial on June 14 at 10 o'clock. Consequently, it would be wise for you[2] to meet me at my office and review the entire case.

Would it be convenient for you to come to my office[3] on June 7? Be sure to bring all the correspondence and any other papers that you may have relating to the[4] case.

As you well know, I believe we have an excellent case and we should win without any difficulty.[5] Sincerely yours
George Frank, Esquire [106 words]

LESSON 59

59.1 Goal: 100 wam speed dictation

Dear Mr. Long Re: Charles David Deposition After your phone call yesterday, I realized that your perception[1] of Charles David's testimony was not clear.

Mr. David does not deny that he is partly responsible[2] for the collision between his car and the truck driven by your client, Mr. Harry Lee. He maintains, however, that Mr.[3] Lee was also negligent.

If this case should come to court, your client could not recover[4] more than the cost of his auto repairs. Rather than go to the expense and trouble of a trial, my client[5] is willing to settle by paying the sum of $1,200 for the repairs.

Please advise your client[6] of this offer to settle out of court. Yours sincerely [127 words]

59.2

1 your overdue account has been
2 $400 balance is more than four months past due
3 take whatever steps necessary
4 the billing department has sent six letters
5 Western Furniture Company did not reply
6 before any proceedings against you
7 legal proceedings can be expensive
8 you have until April 24
9 write us an explanation as to why
10 we will institute legal proceedings

59.3 Goal: 35 wam transcription rate

Dear Miss Peck Your overdue account at Western Furniture Company has been turned over to us. Your $400 balance is more than four months past due. Western Furniture Company has instructed us to take whatever steps necessary to collect your account.

The billing department at Western Furniture Company has sent you six letters asking for payment; you did not reply to any of the letters.

Before any proceedings against you are instituted, you will have one more opportunity to settle your account. As you know, legal proceedings can be very expensive.

You have until April 24 to either send us a check or write us an explanation as to why you have not paid your bill. If you do not respond by that time, we will institute legal proceedings against you. Please do not force us to do this. Sincerely yours

59.4 Time Limit: 15 minutes

DEPOSITION
Mary Parker, being duly sworn, deposes and says:

1. That she is over the age of[1] 21 and resides at 124 South Street in Miami, Florida.

2. That she is the holder[2] of a bond in the amount of $5,000, number 45202 issued on January 1,[3] 1988, by the National Bank of Florida.

3. That she is unable to locate said bond[4] among her personal papers and effects.

4. That she makes this affidavit in support of request for[5] replacement of this bond, number 45202.

IN WITNESS WHEREOF, I have hereunto set my hand and seal.[6]
Mary Parker [123 words]

LESSON 60

60.1 Goal: 100 wam speed dictation

Dear Mr. Ellis Thank you for inquiring about Mrs. Phillips' overdue account of $180.[1] We received a letter from Mrs. Phillips today.

The merchandise was charged to her account by her son. She had[2] instructed you not to let him use her account. After she received the first statement, she told you she would not pay the[3] account for the reason mentioned.

Will you please check to see whether the above information is accurate.[4] If it is, please check the exact date on which Mrs. Phillips gave you these instructions.

The way this case proceeds depends[5] on the information you give us. To dispose of this case quickly, please get in contact with me[6] as soon as possible. Yours truly [127 words]

60.2

1 Dear Mrs. Hodges Dr. Charles Franklin
2 retained me as his attorney
3 collect the $650 you owe him
4 work done on your teeth
5 to take whatever action is necessary
6 months of July and September
7 please do not make it necessary
8 legal proceedings are expensive
9 we will assume you are willing
10 Dr. Franklin sue you for the collection

60.3 Goal: 35 wam transcription rate

Dear Mrs. Hodges Dr. Charles Franklin has retained me as his attorney to collect the $650 you owe him for work done on your teeth during the months of July and September of last year. Dr. Franklin has instructed me to take whatever action is necessary, but it is only fair to give you one more chance to pay the $650.

Please do not make it necessary for me to take legal steps. As you know, legal proceedings are expensive.

No action will be taken for ten days. If you do not get in touch with me by the end of that time, we will assume that you are willing to have Dr.

Franklin sue you for the collection of your bill. Sincerely yours

60.4 Time Limit: 15 minutes

April 12, 19--
Ms. Elizabeth Nolan
360 College Avenue
Pittsburgh, PA 15260
Dear Ms. Nolan Your loan in the amount of $1,000 has been turned over to me for collection. Your[1] loan was due and payable on March 30. My client tells me that you have not made any payments on the[2] principal or interest of this loan since January.

If there is any reason why you have not found it possible[3] to take care of your obligation, please let us know. If there is no reason, your check should be sent to our office[4] within seven days. Cordially yours
George Frank, Esquire [90 words]

LESSON 61

61.1 Goal: 100 wam speed dictation

Dear Mr. Williams Your concern about your partner, Mr. Howell, is justified. We checked with the bank that issued[1] your company credit card, and their records show that your card was used many times. We believe that these were not[2] business-related purchases.

Since your partner has denied that he used your card and there is proof that he did,[3] you can take legal action against him. What you need to do is come to my office so that we can discuss your[4] options.

We will need the guidelines that you and Mr. Howell had drawn up for making credit-card purchases. With this[5] list we can determine the specific violations of the guidelines. Please let me know when is a convenient[6] time for you to meet with me. Cordially yours [128 words]

61.2

1 to help you recover $500 that rightfully belongs to you
2 store owner has been notified
3 sued for promising a prize of $1,000
4 realizes that you are serious about suing
5 wish to settle out of court
6 would not have a chance of winning the suit
7 would give the store some extremely bad press
8 wait for a response from the store
9 will you please prepare a complete account
10 what happened when you went to the store

61.3 Goal: 35 wam transcription rate

Dear Ms. Blair It is a pleasure for me to handle your case and to help you recover the $500 that rightfully belongs to you.

The store owner has been notified that he will be sued for promising a prize of $1,000 worth of clothes and then offering to give only $500 worth. As soon as he realizes that you are serious about suing, I am sure he will wish to settle out of court. He would not have a chance of winning, and the suit would give the store some extremely bad press.

While we wait for a response from the store owner, will you please prepare a complete account of what happened when you went to the store to collect your prize. This information is something which needs to be on file. Sincerely yours

61.4 Time Limit: 15 minutes

ASSIGNMENT
KNOW ALL MEN BY THESE PRESENTS, that for good and valuable consideration the undersigned, Frank T. Carlson of the[1] city of Washington, County of Washington, and Commonwealth of Pennsylvania, does hereby assign the[2] net proceeds that may be received by him from a particular lawsuit presently pending between Frank T.[3] Carlson and Donald S. Cohen and direct that to the extent of the unpaid balance on the note at the time the[4] proceeds of said case to be received that the same be applied and paid over and for the purposes of complete[5] and full satisfaction of the aforesaid note.

We do hereby instruct, authorize, and empower Robert B.[6] Davis, Attorney at Law, to so use and apply the foregoing proceeds.

IN WITNESS WHEREOF we have hereunto[7] set our respective hands this 16th day of April, 19--.
Frank T. Carlson
Donald S. Cohen [155 words]

LESSON 62

62.1 Goal: 100 wam speed dictation

Dear Mr. Brennan In my opinion, the Davis and Miller Company would be able to collect against[1] your company for late delivery of their order for ten computers.

The terms of your agreement specified[2] delivery to their client, Johnson Manufacturing, on or before January 31. Delivery,[3] which was made on February 8, was eight days late.

I think it would be worthwhile for you to go ahead with plans[4] to secure acceptance of the order if you can reach a reasonable settlement. You may be forced to take[5] a small loss on the transaction, but it would not be advisable to take legal action.

If you have any[6] additional questions or concerns, please contact me. Very truly yours

[133 words]

62.2

1 I have carefully examined the contract
2 building a new warehouse in Latrobe
3 the only clause that presents a problem
4 last sentence on the bottom of page 3
5 yield the contractor 13 percent
6 construction done on a cost-plus basis
7 does not protect against the inability
8 complete the work within the time
9 should have a clause added
10 assess them $500 a day

62.3 Goal: 35 wam transcription rate

Dear Ms. Mullen I have carefully examined the contract submitted to you by Martin Construction Company for building a new warehouse in Latrobe, Pennsylvania.

The only clause that seems to present a problem is the last sentence at the bottom of page 3. As agreed, construction is to be done on a cost-plus basis that will yield the contractor 13 percent of the costs. I think, however, that your section does not protect you against the possible inability of Martin Construction to complete the work within the time specified.

You should have a clause added that will assess them $500 a day for every day that the work extends beyond the contract completion date. Very truly yours

62.4 Time Limit: 15 minutes

CERTIFICATE OF INCORPORATION

In order to form a corporation for the purpose stated under[1] the provisions of the Pennsylvania Business Corporation Act, the undersigned does hereby certify as[2] follows:

1. The name of the corporation is Professional Women's Shop.
2. The office of the corporation[3] will be at 1030 South Street in Pittsburgh, Pennsylvania.
3. The purpose of the corporation is to[4] engage in any activity within the purposes for which a corporation may be organized under[5] the provisions of the Pennsylvania Business Corporation Act.
4. The number of directors of the[6] corporation will be fixed by and provided for in the bylaws of the corporation.

IN WITNESS[7] WHEREOF, I have hereunto set my hand and seal.

Christine Parker [151 words]

LESSON 63

63.1 Goal: 100 wam speed dictation

Dear Mr. Larson It was nice to hear that you have found a rental home to your liking. After living so many[1] years in an apartment, you should really enjoy having a whole house to yourself.

The lease you sent me is a[2] standard one used by many real estate companies. I have read it carefully, and there are no provisions that should[3] cause you any concern. You should probably keep your copy of the lease in your safe-deposit box. Would you like me[4] to keep a copy of the lease in my safe? Let me know what you would like me to do concerning the lease.

The[5] next time you are in Greensburg, stop in and see me. Perhaps you could arrange your schedule so we could have lunch.[6] Cordially yours

[122 words]

63.2

1 hold a series of preliminary hearings
2 case of Peterson v. Maxwell

3 six witnesses will be examined
4 the judge has informed me
5 court reporter has been in the hospital
6 arrange for a reporter to be present
7 the reporter will get paid for three days
8 case is finally coming together
9 has been pending for over three years
10 client is getting impatient to have the case settled

63.3 Goal: 35 wam transcription rate

Dear Mr. Jenkins As you know, we are planning to hold a series of preliminary hearings in Greensburg in the case of Peterson v. Maxwell. Six witnesses will be examined, and the hearings should last two or three days.

The judge has informed me that the court reporter who was supposed to cover the hearings has been in the hospital. Would you arrange for a reporter to be present on May 1 to May 3. If the hearings last only two days, the reporter will still get paid for three days.

It is good to know that this case is finally coming together. It has been pending for over three years, and my client is getting impatient to have it settled one way or another. Sincerely yours

63.4 Time Limit: 15 minutes

April 18, 19--
Ms. Martha Wise
315 Maple Avenue
Greensburg, PA 15601
Dear Ms. Wise Mr. Richard Miles, who was injured on March 20 by one of your people, has retained me as his[1] lawyer. As a result of his injuries, Mr. Miles has been unable to work for four weeks.

In addition,[2] he has incurred medical expenses that have already amounted to more than $4,500.[3] Furthermore, for another six or eight weeks he will have to continue physical therapy which will involve[4] additional expense.

From the police report it appears that your driver was, without question, at fault. Rather[5] than take this case to court, my client is willing to settle out of court for an amount that will cover both the[6] costs he has incurred and the estimated cost for further treatment.

If you care to discuss this matter with me,[7] please give me a call any weekday. Sincerely
George Frank, Esquire [152 words]

LESSON 64

64.1 Goal: 100 wam speed dictation

Dear Mr. Evans I have just returned from Washington where I examined Patent No. 43285[1] issued to Michael Adams on November 8, 1989. I compared that patent with Patent No.[2] 48612 held by your company.

After examining the description in the documents, I found[3] no basic resemblance to a patent that would justify your starting a suit against Mr. Adams.[4] Very truly yours [83 words]

64.2

1 Ladies and Gentlemen As attorney for
2 examined the records, briefs, and proceedings
3 in my judgment were necessary and appropriate
4 render Northern Products an opinion
5 are there any unsettled claims
6 could have an adverse impact
7 enforce the proposed agreement
8 issuance and delivery of 100,000 shares
9 cannot be examined from the registration requirements
10 Securities Act of 1933

64.3 Goal: 35 wam transcription rate

Ladies and Gentlemen As attorney for Hart Industries, I have examined the records, briefs, and proceedings that in my judgment were necessary and appropriate to render an opinion on the following areas of interest to your corporation:

1. There are not any unsettled claims against Northern Products as of January 1 that could have an adverse impact on the ability of Hart Industries to enforce the proposed agreement.

2. The issuance and delivery by Northern Products of 100,000 shares of its common stock included in the proposed agreement cannot be examined from the registration requirements of the Security Act of 1933.

If you have any other questions, please contact me immediately. Very truly yours

64.4 Time Limit: 15 minutes

DEPOSITION
Leon H. James, being duly sworn, deposes and says:

1. That he is over the age of[1] 21 and resides at 650 Pennsylvania Avenue, Greensburg, Pennsylvania 15601.[2]

2. That he is the holder of record of 50 shares of common stock of Northern Industries as represented[3] by Certificate Number 27602 issued on or before July 1, 1984.

3. That[4] he is unable to locate said certificate among his personal papers and effects and that he[5] assumes the certificate has been lost, stolen, or destroyed.

4. That attached hereto is a properly[6] implemented Lost Stock Agreement and Bond requested by the transfer department of Northern Industries.

5.[7] That he makes this affidavit in support of request for replacement of Certificate Number[8] 27602.

IN WITNESS WHEREOF, I have hereunto set my hand and seal.
Leon H. James [178 words]

LESSON 65

65.1 Goal: 110 wam speed dictation

Date: December 7, 19--
To: Staff
From: William Samuels
Subject: Globe Awards[1]
I am very pleased to announce that Robert White has won the prestigious Globe Award for his[2] five-part series last summer on technological advances in the last decade. Portions of this series were[3] picked up by the network broadcast on the national evening news program in November.

Robert will accept[4] this award at the national convention of the News Association in Boston on January 16.[5]

I know you will join me in extending warm congratulations to him. [115 words]

65.2

1 attached is holiday work schedule
2 apologize ahead of time
3 inconvenience of working on Christmas Day
4 Christmas Day and New Year's Day
5 no one will work both holidays
6 holidays fall on Tuesday
7 will have the advantage of a long weekend
8 this may be a small consideration
9 skeleton crew is required to ensure
10 smooth operations during the two holidays

65.3 Goal: 35 wam transcription rate

Date: December 7, 19--
To: Staff Members
From: A. H. Kirkpatrick, General Manager
Subject: Holiday Work Schedule
The attached list is the holiday work schedule. I apologize ahead of time for the inconvenience that working on Christmas Day or New Year's Day may cause, but no one will have to work both holidays. Furthermore, both holidays fall on Tuesday. Those working on Tuesday will have the advantage of a long weekend. This may be small consideration, but it is obvious that a skeleton crew is required to ensure smooth operations during the two holidays.

If you have any questions or concerns about the schedule, please see me immediately.

LESSON 66

66.1 Goal: 110 wam speed dictation

Dear Miss Graham Thank you very much for letting us know your feelings regarding sexism on television. Our[1] children's shows are screened for sexism by their producers in New York. Perhaps they have not done an adequate job of[2] monitoring this aspect of the show, or perhaps they are not aware of the guidelines set forth by special[3] interest groups.

I am writing the producers today about our concern that this and all other shows be free of[4] sexism. Thanks for alerting us to this problem. I will be in contact with you as to the steps we will be taking[5] in the future regarding this issue. Very sincerely yours [112 words]

66.2

1 Dear Mr. Benton When we purchased
2 the show the Children's Hour

3 assured that the show would picture males and females
4 there are a variety of roles
5 yet one of our viewers has complained
6 recent episodes have shown
7 males in traditional male roles
8 only females in traditional female roles
9 exactly what steps you have taken and will take
10 ensure it is free of all sexist bias

66.3 Goal: 35 wam transcription rate

Dear Mr. Benton When we purchased your show the Children's Hour, we were assured that the show would picture males and females in a variety of roles. Yet one of our viewers has complained to us that two recent episodes have shown males only in traditional male roles and females only in traditional female roles.

Would you tell us exactly what steps you have taken and will take to ensure that this show is free of all sexist bias. Sincerely yours

66.4 Time Limit: 15 minutes

Date: December 10, 19--
To: Annabelle Stevens
From: A. H. Kirkpatrick, General Manager[1]
Subject: Television Speech
I would appreciate your assisting me in pulling together all the information[2] in our files about Senator Loretta Lyons. We will be doing a 15-minute speech in two weeks on[3] her contributions to our city.

I am especially interested in the legislation she has[4] sponsored over the past five years. Please check the tape library to see what film clips and tapes we have available and[5] give them all to Michael Shaw, director of this speech. If you need any further information, please let me know.[6]

[120 words]

LESSON 67

67.1 Goal: 110 wam speed dictation

Ladies and Gentlemen I read in the October 10 issue of New York News that your company developed[1] some guidelines regarding equal treatment of the sexes which you were using to monitor the purchase of textbooks[2] for your university.

The article stated that these guidelines are available free of charge to the[3] general public. Would you please send us a copy of these guidelines for our use in monitoring programs for our[4] television station. In addition, we would appreciate any additional information or[5] resources you could provide.

Your publication of these guidelines is appreciated and is a valuable[6] service for the media industry. Yours truly [130 words]

67.2

1 our station is delighted
2 reply to Professor Irwin's commentary
3 commentary aired on December 7
4 comments generated much interest
5 we received over 200 letters
6 requests for equal time to reply
7 we ultimately selected you
8 your letter touched on relevant points
9 the information you need to prepare your rebuttal
10 we will tape your comments

67.3 Goal: 35 wam transcription rate

Dear Mr. Thompson Our station is delighted to provide you with the opportunity to reply to Professor Irwin's commentary which aired December 7.

Professor Irwin's comments generated much interest throughout the area. In fact, we received over 200 letters and 15 requests for equal time to reply. We ultimately selected you to present the opposing view because your letter touched on most of the relevant points of the topic.

The enclosed memorandum contains all the information you will need to prepare your rebuttal. If you concur, we will tape your comments on December 17 and will broadcast them sometime during the week of December 24. Sincerely yours

67.4 Time Limit: 15 minutes

December 11, 19--
Mr. Charles Thompson
57 Montgomery Street
San Antonio, TX 78205
Dear Mr. Thompson I was sorry to hear that you have had to change your plans to answer an edito-

rial which[1] appeared on our evening news on December 7. We try to broadcast any rebuttal to a commentary within[2] a week of the original newscast so that the commentary will still be fresh in our viewers' minds.

It is[3] unfortunate for both of us that previous commitments prevent you from presenting your views at this time.[4] However, I hope that you will again let us know if ever you wish equal time to reply to one of our[5] television editorials.

Thank you for showing an interest in our programming and in community affairs.[6] Sincerely yours
A. H. Kirkpatrick
General Manager [130 words]

LESSON 68

68.1 Goal: 110 wam speed dictation

To the Staff As the end of the year approaches, we should take care of several office details.

In November I[1] informed you that next year's goal statements would be due December 20. Because of the hectic schedule[2] that the holiday period always brings, I am changing the due date for these statements to January 10.[3] This should allow plenty of time to prepare the goal statements after the holiday rush. Please use the same format[4] you used last year.

Finally, on a personal note, my wife Diana and I will be having an open house[5] on December 22 from 7 to 11 p.m. If you do not already have plans, please stop by.[6] It has been a good year for all of us, and I would like the opportunity to thank you for your[7] contributions to the successful operation of our station. [149 words]

68.2

1 invited by the federal government
2 participate in the study of television news
3 news programming in European countries
4 delighted to take part in this project
5 invitation came from Mrs. Ann Andrews
6 chairperson of the Federal Communications Commission
7 exact mission of this study is vague
8 looking at both the quantity and quality
9 results will be published in a report
10 basis for segments on our nightly news

68.3 Goal: 35 wam transcription rate

Date: December 12, 19--
To: Leslie Wallace, News Department
From: A. H. Kirkpatrick, General Manager
Subject: Television Program in Europe
I have been invited by the federal government to participate in the study of television news programming in European countries. I am, of course, delighted to take part in this project. The invitation came from Mrs. Ann Andrews, chairperson of the Federal Communications Commission.

Although the exact mission of this study is still somewhat vague, I understand that one part of the study will consist of a trip to several countries to study news programming. We will be looking at both the quantity and quality of news programming. The results of our study will be published in a formal report to Mrs. Andrews.

It occurs to me that we should use this trip as the basis for several segments on our own nightly news program.

68.4 Time Limit: 15 minutes

Date: December 12, 19--
To: Gregory Fuller
From: A. H. Kirkpatrick, General Manager
Subject: Financial[1] Statements
I realize that fourth-quarter financial statements will not be audited until the middle of[2] January. In the meantime, however, I will need some preliminary figures to present to the board[3] of directors on January 7.

As soon as your staff has prepared the statements and you are satisfied with[4] their accuracy, please let me have ten copies of each. I am especially interested in the cash-flow[5] statement and the advertising revenue analysis because one of the decisions facing the board concerns[6] an ambitious expansion program that will tie up a lot of capital.
[134 words]

LESSON 69

69.1 Goal: 110 wam speed dictation

To the Staff I have decided to accept the recommendation of Anderson Associates, the management[1] consulting firm we hired last month, that we come up with new and innovative ways to assess management potential.[2] The tremendous growth that our station has experience over the past few years has created many new management[3] positions. Our policy of promoting from within makes it imperative that we develop some orderly[4] manner of identifying management talent.

Anderson Associates will develop materials[5] that we will use to assess our present employees' management potential. The candidates will receive detailed[6] feedback on all the areas measured. The participants and management will have a thorough picture of their strengths[7] and weaknesses at the conclusion of the assessment program.

Candidates chosen for the first round[8] of testing will be notified within the next few days.

[171 words]

69.2

1 Dear Mr. Demerest I was pleased
2 decided to answer an editorial
3 evening newscast on December 10
4 try to broadcast rebuttals
5 within a week of the original newscast
6 connection between the editorial and the rebuttal
7 invited Dr. Michael Edwards
8 views on caustic waste in our community
9 no idea the editorial would create such controversy
10 assure our viewers receive informed, perceptive insights into matters of interest

69.3 Goal: 35 wam transcription rate

Dear Mr. Demerest I was pleased to learn that you have decided to answer an editorial which appeared on our evening newscast on December 10. We try to make sure that we broadcast rebuttals to a commentary within a week of the original newscast. It is important that our viewers be able to make the connection between the editorial and the rebuttal.

When I invited Dr. Michael Edwards to present his views on caustic waste in our community, I had no idea the editorial would create such controversy.

I have attached a list of guidelines you should follow as you prepare your comments. By following these guidelines, you will assure that our viewers receive informed, perceptive insights into matters of interest to the community. Very truly yours

69.4 Time Limit: 15 minutes

Date: December 17, 19--
To: Steven Gilbert
From: A. H. Kirkpatrick, General Manager
Subject: Sexism in[1] Children's Programming
Steve, the attached letter from Elizabeth Graham concerns me. While such negative reactions[2] as those contained in this letter are bad for our reputation, I am more concerned with the emotional impact[3] of sexism on children.

Because the producers of our children's programs do not appear to be taking this[4] problem seriously enough, I would like to set up a local committee to screen our children's shows. Miss[5] Graham appears to have definite ideas about programming for children. Perhaps she would be willing to serve on[6] this committee. Would you please contact her to see if she is interested in working with us to improve television[7] programming for children.

[145 words]

LESSON 70

70.1 Goal: 110 wam speed dictation

Dear Mr. Williams Subject: Assessment Program I would like for you to develop a totally new series of[1] tasks to use in our assessment program. Although I would like these tasks to be related to the broadcast industry,[2] they should be sufficiently general so that no employee from any particular department will have[3] an advantage over others.

After you complete your own field testing of these tasks, I will ask the four people[4] who report directly to me to act as an internal review for the program. This will help assure that[5] we have a varied and effective assessment device. They will be able to review subsequent tasks because[6] they should know thoroughly what is involved.

Please let me know when I can expect to receive your first set of tasks for[7] review. Sincerely yours [144 words]

70.2

1 we met yesterday afternoon in my office
2 would be necessary to secure the reaction
3 renew our pledge to the Community Fund
4 present state of the economy
5 match the $10,000 we donated
6 corporate contribution of $7,500
7 pass along to our employees
8 make individual donations
9 urge them to make a serious attempt
10 quite sure this approach will help you

70.3 Goal: 35 wam transcription rate

Dear Mr. Carson When we met in my office yesterday afternoon, I told you that it would be necessary to secure the reaction of the executive committee before we could renew our pledge to the Community Fund.

The committee met this morning and decided that the present state of the economy will not allow us to match the $10,000 we donated last year. We have decided that we will make a corporate contribution of $7,500 and pass along to our employees a recommendation that they make individual donations. We will urge them to make a serious attempt to raise the remaining amount. I feel quite sure this approach will help you achieve the $10,000 goal. Cordially yours

70.4 Time Limit: 15 minutes

Date: December 19, 19--
To: Betty Anderson, Special Project Director
From: A. H.[1] Kirkpatrick, General Manager
Subject: Rapid Transit Interview
I have just returned from the screening room[2] where I saw the edited version of your 5-minute news segment on rapid transit. It was an excellent[3] piece of reporting, and I intend to use it as the lead-off segment on our new expanded newscast this spring.[4]

If I remember correctly, you had an interview with a representative from the Transportation[5] Department. Why don't you extract 5 minutes from this interview for a second segment on two consecutive[6] evenings. [121 words]

LESSON 71

71.1 Goal: 110 wam speed dictation

Dear Mrs. Summers I can well understand your annoyance at missing part of Children's Hour last week. Our production[1] director tells me that we did not experience any technical difficulties during the show. Perhaps[2] your reception problems were caused by adverse weather conditions or by interference from a citizen's[3] band radio.

I hope, at any rate, you have no further trouble in viewing your favorite program in the future.[4] Sincerely yours [82 words]

71.2

1 news show will be very similar
2 what we have had in the past
3 to make the segments longer
4 plan to add more segments
5 Edward Santos and Amy Baxter as co-anchors
6 Paul Hudson has left
7 William Hunter will remain as sportscaster
8 meteorologist with the federal government
9 looking for a new weather forecaster
10 adding seven or eight reporters to the news staff

71.3 Goal: 35 wam transcription rate

Date: December 20, 19--
To: Staff Members
From: A. H. Kirkpatrick, General Manager
Subject: Changes in News Show
Our new news show will be very similar to what we have had in the past. We are not going to make the segments longer but plan to add more segments to every show.

Edward Santos and Amy Baxter will remain as co-anchors, and William Hunter will remain as sportscaster. Because Paul Hudson has left to take a job as meteorologist with the federal government, we are looking for a new weather forecaster. We will also be adding seven or eight reporters to the news staff.

71.4 Time Limit: 15 minutes

December 20, 19--
Mr. Dennis Watson
Hartman Promotional Agency
1200 Madison Avenue
New York, NY 10016
Dear Dennis As you know, we were quite pleased with the audience profiles your firm made for three of our shows last year. These[1] profiles helped us in lining up sponsors and in determining when to air the shows.

We plan to produce four new[2] shows locally next season. Can you develop audience profiles for these shows? Also, is there some way to determine[3] probable audience reaction before these shows go on the air?

I will call you next week when I am in[4] New York to discuss this matter further. Sincerely yours
A. H. Kirkpatrick
General Manager [98 words]

LESSON 72

72.1 Goal: 110 wam speed dictation

Dear Mr. Cummings We are delighted that you will be taping a commentary for our news station. The[1] following guidelines have been developed to provide you with concise directions for making your commentary[2] as explicit and informative as possible. Please consult these guidelines as you prepare your remarks.

1. Please[3] confine your remarks to the issues involved and refrain from statements that cannot be proved.

2. Do not advocate[4] a particular point of view. A balanced presentation that introduces all sides of an issue will get best[5] results.

3. Submit your comments at least two days in advance of taping. This will allow our editorial[6] department time to review your remarks and will allow us enough time to prepare a script so that you will not have[7] to memorize your presentation. Please try to arrive at our studio at least one hour before taping so[8] that you can rehearse your talk.

4. You will be allowed 5 minutes to present your remarks. Please do not go over[9] the time limit.

If you follow these guidelines, you will be able to give our viewers informed, perceptive insights[10] into matters of current interest to the community. Very truly yours [216 words]

72.2

1 I am looking forward
2 study concerning news programming in European countries
3 news reporter to accompany us
4 allow Ms. Janet Klein
5 Ms. Kline's stories available free of charge
6 United States Information Agency for possible publication
7 Ms. Klein is fluent in French
8 can be of additional help to the delegation
9 session in Washington, DC, anytime in January
10 pleased to undertake this assignment

72.3 Goal: 35 wam transcription rate

Dear Mrs. Andrews I am looking forward to being part of the study you are planning concerning news programming in European countries.

I appreciate your agreeing to allow Ms. Janet Klein, our news reporter, to accompany us on this trip. I realize that this was an unusual request, and I am happy to make Ms. Kline's stories available free of charge to the United States Information Agency for possible publication. Ms. Klein is fluent in French and can be of additional help to the delegation.

I could meet for our first planning session in Washington, DC, anytime in January. I am pleased to undertake this assignment. Yours truly

72.4 Time Limit: 15 minutes

Date: December 21, 19--
To: Betty Anderson, Special Project Director
From: A. H.[1] Kirkpatrick, General Manager
Subject: Special Assignment
As you know, we intend to expand our[2] newscast to a full hour this spring. While your department is not directly involved with the news, I thought you might be able[3] to provide some support services to the news department.

You are already scheduled to produce six[4] documentaries next year. When each one is completed, I would like you to edit a 5-minute version[5] of the documentary to be used on the newscast. The format and content of the condensed version will[6] naturally be left up to you.

The contacts you have made throughout the area will be vitally important[7] in helping us to secure the services of these supporters, and I have promised the news department your[8] assistance. Please let me know if this conflicts in any way with your schedule. [175 words]

LESSON 73

73.1 Goal: 110 wam speed dictation

Dear Dr. Daniels Because of the type of injury sustained by Michael Adams while on the job at Keith[1] Manufacturing Company, I am referring him to you for further consultation.

Mr. Adams[2] injured his back on March 4 and was sent to Madison Hospital. The diagnosis revealed no apparent[3] permanent injury, and he was released. It has been three days, and Mr. Adams still complains about his back and has difficulty[4] remaining on the job without experiencing pain.

I am enclosing the medical history[5] of Mr. Adams on file in my office and the report we received from the hospital. After your diagnosis[6] I would appreciate a full report and recommendation for further treatment. Sincerely yours

[137 words]

73.2

1 disability of David Franklin
2 need for employment records
3 indefinite period of time
4 Mr. Franklin has sustained several injuries
5 the final report received from his physician
6 sustained substantial nerve damage
7 damage to upper right arm
8 inasmuch as his mobility is impaired
9 undergoing extensive treatment
10 granted disability status

73.3 Goal: 40 wam transcription rate

Date: March 8, 19--
To: Joyce Campbell
From: Dr. Doris Graham, Director
Medical Department
Subject: Disability of David Franklin

After reviewing the medical and employment records, I recommend that David Franklin be placed on disability for an indefinite period of time. Mr. Franklin has sustained several injuries throughout his employment at Keith Manufacturing. The final report received from his physician reveals substantial nerve damage to his upper right arm and upper left leg.

Inasmuch as his mobility is severely impaired and he will be undergoing extensive treatment, I recommend that he be granted disability status at this time. Verification of his medical condition is enclosed.

LESSON 74

74.1 Goal: 110 wam speed dictation

Dear Mr. Anderson After your visit to the Medical Department on Friday, I advised you to go[1] on vacation as planned and promised that I would send you the results of my examination. The weather[2] bothers many people and probably affected you too. On the other hand, you do seem to have a minor[3] chemical imbalance. The specialist who ran the tests believes that your chemical imbalance probably[4] can be controlled by diet.

I suggest that you see a private physician for more complete[5] information when you return from vacation. Sincerely yours [112 words]

74.2

1 Dear Dr. Stevens I am referring to you
2 Mr. Edward Michaels is an employee
3 complaining about a severe pain in his hip
4 medical record is enclosed
5 Mr. Michaels sustained a fracture
6 note in the patient's history
7 never caused work-related problems
8 I suspect arthritis developed
9 take the necessary X rays
10 Mr. Michaels carries group health insurance

74.3 Goal: 40 wam transcription rate

Dear Dr. Stevens I am referring to you Mr. Edward Michaels, an employee of Keith Manufacturing Company. Mr. Michaels has been complaining about a severe pain in his hip. A copy of his medical record at our company is enclosed.

As you will note in the patient's history, Mr. Michaels sustained a fracture of the hip when he was a child. This injury has never caused him any work- related problems, but I suspect arthritis may have developed.

Will you please take the necessary X rays and inform me of your findings. Mr. Michaels carries group health insurance; his policy will cover all medical costs. Sincerely yours

74.4 Time Limit: 15 minutes

Date: March 9, 19--
To: David Worth
From: Dr. Doris Graham, Director
Medical Department
Subject:[1] Early Retirement of Mark Diaz
After reviewing the medical and employment records of Mark Diaz,[2] I recommend that he be retired at the age of 62 because of medical disability.[3]

Mr. Diaz has a long history of arthritis. He visited this office regularly in connection[4] with this illness over the last five years. Last year I recommended that he contact an outside physician.[5]

Inasmuch as his mobility is severely impaired, I recommend Mr. Diaz be granted early[6] retirement. [122 words]

LESSON 75

75.1 Goal: 110 wam speed dictation

Dear Miss Stanley I am glad to report to you that every one of the X rays of your finger shows[1] only a simple break. The bone is not crushed as you originally feared, but the splint that I applied should be[2] kept on for about two more weeks.

Although you cannot type, you should be able to do most of your other tasks without[3] difficulty.

When you return to work next week, please come by this office so that I can check to see that your[4] finger is healing as expected. I will remove the splint just as soon as I am sure that the bone has healed[5] properly. Sincerely yours [105 words]

75.2

1 Dear Dr. Billings I am referring David Baxter
2 illness does not seem to be work-related
3 relating to Mr. Baxter's condition
4 Mr. Baxter had minor surgery
5 suffered a slight injury
6 result of an automobile accident
7 I would appreciate your diagnosis
8 there is routine medical attention
9 there is anything wrong that could affect
10 let me know what is needed

75.3 Goal: 40 wam transcription rate

Dear Dr. Billings I am referring David Baxter, one of our employees, to you for further examination because his illness does not seem to be work-related.

I am enclosing the medical records relating to Mr. Baxter's condition. As you can see, Mr. Baxter had minor surgery two years ago. In addition to this operation, he suffered a slight injury as a result of an automobile accident last year.

After your diagnosis, I would appreciate your letting me know if there is anything wrong that could affect his job performance. Also, if there is routine medical attention that Mr. Baxter needs while on the job, let me know what is needed. We will be glad to carry out your instructions. Sincerely yours

75.4 Time Limit: 15 minutes

Date: March 12, 19--
To: Donald Anderson, President
From: Dr. Doris Graham
Medical[1] Department
Subject: Physical Examinations
Our experience indicates that most of our executives[2]do not bother with yearly checkups. They go to a doctor's office only when something critical forces[3] them to do so. I would like to recommend that we require complete physical examinations every year[4] for all our company's division heads and other executives.

This office would make the appointments for the[5] examinations. Before each examination we would gather together all the medical data.[6] After the examination we would review the results and keep them on file.

I recommend that the directive[7] to initiate the program come from your office. [147 words]

LESSON 76

76.1 Goal: 110 wam speed dictation

Medical Report
Today most Americans enjoy a healthier and longer life span than ever before. This condition has been[1] attained primarily through the development of new medicines, research, better public health programs,[2] improved medical services, and health instruction.

Business and industry had a role in the[3] drive for health and safety in our lives. Business is concerned with the health and safety of its employees. In many[4] companies you will find a full-time or part-time medical office. The company doctor may give physical[5] examinations, treat diseases and injuries when required, and advise management in providing healthful and[6] safe surroundings.

[123 words]

76.2

1 Date: March 14, 19--
2 To: Mark Billings
3 From: Dr. Doris Graham
4 Subject: Injuries and Illness
5 employees injured are indemnified
6 doctors' bills are paid
7 whether or not injury was due to carelessness
8 doctors' fees and sick benefits are provided
9 employees who become ill
10 strive to protect employees

76.3 Goal: 40 wam transcription rate

Date: March 14, 19--
To: Mark Billings
From: Dr. Doris Graham
Subject: Injuries and Illness
I am pleased to have the opportunity to respond to the question about work-related injuries and illness.

All employees who are injured during the performance of their work are indemnified, and their doctors' bills are paid whether or not the injury was due to carelessness or to accident. If an employee becomes ill as a result of his or her occupation, doctors' fees and sick benefits are provided.

Employees who are injured or become ill during the workday should come to the medical center immediately.

You can be sure that we strive to protect employees from injuries, and we are committed to doing everything possible to insure the employees if injuries do occur.

76.4 Time Limit: 15 minutes

Date: March 14, 19--
To: Donald Anderson, President
From: Dr. Doris Graham
Medical[1] Department
Subject: Medical Examinations of Executives
I am pleased that you have accepted my[2] recommendation that we require yearly medical examinations of all executives. This attention to[3] health maintenance will be a good investment.

I will be glad to have a complete plan ready to present at the[4] monthly meeting of the executive committee on Tuesday, March 21. Prior to the meeting I will give you[5] my specific recommendations.

[106 words]

LESSON 77

77.1 Goal: 110 wam speed dictation

Ladies and Gentlemen I would like to contribute an article to Medical World on the subject of[1] industrial medicine. Many medical authorities are still not aware of the contributions[2] to the profession made by industrial health services.

My article would cover the following individual[3] points:

1. Preventive medicine and health maintenance.
2. Disability decisions and contractual[4] obligation.
3. Modification of the work environment for the physically disabled.

Would you be[5] interested in publishing such an article? Sincerely yours

[133 words]

77.2

1 Subject: Amy Kennedy
2 severe case of measles
3 condition is contagious at this stage
4 do everything possible to prevent an epidemic

5 observe carefully the employees
6 have been in contact with Mrs. Kennedy during the past two days
7 if anyone complains of a sore throat
8 send him or her to this office immediately
9 discourage employees who have a cold
10 manage with a reduced staff until this situation

77.3 Goal: 40 wam transcription rate

Date: March 16, 19--
To: Charles Williams
From: Dr. Doris Graham
Subject: Amy Kennedy
I examined Amy Kennedy this morning and sent her home with a severe case of measles. The condition is contagious at this stage, and I think that we should do everything possible to prevent an epidemic.

I suggest that you observe carefully the employees in your department who might have been in contact with Mrs. Kennedy during the past two days. If anyone complains of a sore throat, please send him or her to this office immediately. Also, discourage employees who have colds from coming to work. I hope you can manage with a reduced staff until this situation has been cleared up.

77.4 Time Limit: 15 minutes

Date: March 16, 19--
To: David Baxter, Personnel Director
From: Dr. Doris Graham,[1] Medical Director
Subject: Medical Absences
I regret that I am unable to provide you with[2] a list of illnesses that require absence from work or with a list showing the estimated number of days[3] absent to be expected from each type of common illness. Such lists would have only limited use because of the[4] highly individual nature of most illnesses and would be subject to possible abuse by the employees.[5]

I recommend that we continue our present policy of having an employee sent to this department.[6] We will then make the determination of whether the worker should go home or return to work. Employees who[7] are absent for more than three days must submit a doctor's statement. If an employee is absent for an[8] unreasonable period of time, my office will contact the physician for verification.

[179 words]

LESSON 78

78.1 Goal: 110 wam speed dictation

Dear Dr. Campbell I am referring to you Ms. Frances Gray, a secretary with Keith Manufacturing[1] Company. Ms. Gray has been complaining about a severe pain in her right wrist and cannot hold objects[2] without losing control. A copy of her medical record at our company is enclosed. As you will note[3] in the patient's history, Ms. Gray has never sustained any injuries on or off the job.

Will you please take the[4] necessary X rays and inform me of your findings and whether Ms. Gray should continue her secretarial[5] responsibilities. Ms. Gray carries group health insurance, and her policy will cover all medical costs.[6] Sincerely yours

[122 words]

78.2

1 Dear Dr. Ryan I have reviewed
2 medical records regarding Michael Davis
3 after studying the records very carefully
4 I am of the opinion that he can no longer be a truck driver
5 can no longer work in his capacity
6 provide employment in another department
7 train him if necessary for another department
8 Mr. Davis is experiencing severe pain
9 may be a hardship to work daily
10 I would appreciate discussing the condition in detail

78.3 Goal: 40 wam transcription rate

Dear Dr. Ryan I have reviewed the medical records you sent me regarding Michael Davis. After studying the records very carefully, I am of the opinion that Mr. Davis can no longer work in his capacity as a truck driver for our company. We would, of course, be willing to provide Mr. Davis with employment in another department and train him if necessary.

However, my concern is that Mr. Davis is experiencing severe pain, and it may be a hardship to come to work daily. I would appreciate an opportunity to meet with you to discuss the condition of Mr. Davis in detail. Please call me to set up an appointment at a time convenient to you. Very truly yours

78.4 Time Limit: 15 minutes

Date: March 19, 19--
To: Ann White, Supervisor
Records Management Department
From: Dr. Doris[1] Graham
Medical Department
Subject: Medical Records
I wonder if it would be possible for you to[2] work with Carol Harper, my secretary, to evaluate our files. We need to develop a better system of[3] handling our employees' medical records.

Perhaps if you review several of the current records, you would be able[4] to suggest a more functional form design. However, we do want to continue using visible files.[5]

Can you also give some criteria for determining how long to keep records after an employee leaves[6] the company? Which records can we destroy, and which ones should we send to the records storage unit?

I am asking[7] Miss Harper to work with you and to prepare a complete report based upon your recommendations. [158 words]

LESSON 79

79.1 Goal: 110 wam speed dictation

Date: March 21, 19--
To: All Employees
From: Dr. Doris Graham, Director
Medical[1] Department
Subject: CPR Course
Are you prepared to deal with life-threatening emergencies? If not, perhaps[2] you should consider taking a course in CPR.

Correct CPR techniques can be learned by every member[3] of our company through classes offered right here in our own recreation facilities. We will be offering[4] classes in CPR for those members of our staff who wish to be certified.

Each class will[5] consist of about ten people, and there will be approximately six hours of instruction. Enrollment is not[6] limited; we will offer as many classes as necessary to meet the needs of our employees.

If you or[7] any member of your family is interested in taking the course, please respond to the attached questionnaire. [159 words]

79.2

1 Mr. Evans needs physical therapy treatment
2 suffering from lower back pain on the right side
3 discomfort is a result of an injury
4 injury suffered while on the job
5 the X rays showed no bones were broken
6 must have been some muscle strain
7 still in pain at this time
8 hopefully physical therapy sessions will alleviate
9 Mr. Evans is experiencing pain
10 I would appreciate receiving from you a monthly progress report

79.3 Goal: 40 wam transcription rate

Dear Dr. Ellis I am referring to you Mr. Donald Evans for physical therapy treatment. He is suffering from lower back pain on the right side. This discomfort is a result of an injury Mr. Evans suffered while on the job at Keith Manufacturing Company.

The X rays showed that no bones were broken, but there must have been some muscle strain in order for him to still be in pain at this time.

Hopefully physical therapy sessions will alleviate the pain Mr. Evans is experiencing. I would appreciate receiving from you a monthly progress report concerning Mr. Evans. Cordially yours

79.4 Time Limit: 15 minutes

Date: March 21, 19--
To: All Company Employees
From: Dr. Doris Graham, Director[1]
Medical Department
Subject: Changes in Medical Benefits
Beginning immediately all employees[2] of Keith Manufacturing Company may submit claims for these four new medical services:

1. Preventive[3] dental services are provided for all employees and their dependents. Company coverage for all dental[4] services is 80 percent.

2. Prescription drugs are provided for all employees and their dependents.[5] Company coverage is 100 percent.

3. Eye examinations are provided for all employees[6] and their dependents. Company coverage is 100 percent.

4. Mental health and chemical dependency[7] outpatient benefits are provided for company employees. The extent of this benefit is a total[8] of $1,000 in a calendar year.

All other benefits remain the same. Please feel free to contact[9] our office if you have any questions. [187 words]

LESSON 80

80.1 Goal: 110 wam speed dictation

Date: March 23, 19--
To: Medical Department Staff
From: Dr. Doris Graham
Subject: Medical Update[1]
The enclosed pamphlet describes the dangers that may result from taking several medications simultaneously.[2] We just discovered a case in which one of our employees was given prescriptions for two different drugs[3] that are known to cause serious side effects in some people.

Page 2 of the pamphlet contains uniform guidelines to[4] follow when such cases are discovered. I will expect all medical personnel to conform strictly to these[5] guidelines. In addition, any occurrence of such cases should be reported to me immediately. [118 words]

80.2

1 skin problem he is experiencing
2 burning sensation may be caused by fabrics
3 caused by poor blood circulation
4 nerve disorder or some other illness
5 burning sensation caused by an allergic reaction
6 Mr. Baldwin has a burning sensation
7 material he handles daily
8 cannot permit employees to work
9 health is affected by the materials
10 you have completed your examination and medical report

80.3 Goal: 40 wam transcription rate

Dear Dr. Bradley Joseph Baldwin, an employee at Keith Manufacturing Company, has been referred to you because of the skin problem he is experiencing. The burning sensation may be caused by fabrics the company manufactures, but it may also be caused by poor blood circulation or a nerve disorder or some other illness.

It is also possible that Mr. Baldwin may find that the burning sensation is caused by an allergic reaction to the material he handles daily.

We cannot permit employees to work in the mill if their health is affected by the materials. Please send me a complete medical report after you have completed your examination. Sincerely yours

80.4 Time Limit: 15 minutes

Date: March 23, 19--
To: All Employees
From: Dr. Doris Graham, Director
Medical Department[1]
Subject: Preventive Care
Our department is trying to develop ways to make our employees aware of how[2] to prevent blindness. Glaucoma is the leading cause of blindness. This disease is marked by pressure in the eye caused[3] by small screenlike filters in the eyeball that thicken and prevent fluid in the eye from flowing from the eyeball.[4] If the pressure is too high, the eye is damaged and vision impaired.

This year we have introduced a device that[5] can be used to train people to detect glaucoma in its early stages before sight is destroyed. We will be[6] testing for glaucoma on April 4. If you are interested in having this test administered, please[7] call Extension 4713 to set up an appointment.

[151 words]